Revisiting Grooved Ware

Left: Alex and Jane Gibson at the British Academy, with his Grahame Clark medal; right: 'Cheers!' (Photos: British Academy, Jane Gibson)

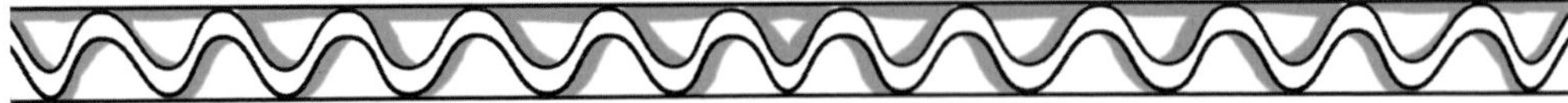

This volume, like the seminar that gave rise to it, is dedicated to Dr Alex Gibson, a long-standing member of the Neolithic Studies Group. Alex is a doyen of prehistoric ceramic studies and his *Prehistoric pottery for the archaeologist*, first published in 1990 (Gibson and Woods 1990), remains an essential textbook. Alex has reported on numerous Grooved Ware assemblages including those from Ringlemere, Kent (Gibson 2020), and King's Stanley, Gloucestershire (Gibson 2010). In October 2022, in recognition of his many contributions to prehistoric archaeology, Alex was awarded the British Academy's Grahame Clark medal. This volume is offered to Alex to thank him for helping to enhance our understanding of Grooved Ware.

Gibson, A. 2010. The pottery. In D. Evans, Two Neolithic pits at King's Stanley, Gloucestershire. *Transactions of the Bristol and Gloucestershire Archaeological Society* 128, 35–41.

Gibson, A. 2020. The Grooved Ware and Beaker pottery. In K. Parfitt and S. Needham, *Ceremonial living in the third millennium BC: excavations at Ringlemere Site M1, Kent, 2002–2006,* 201–44. London: British Museum Press.

Gibson, A. and Woods, A. 1990. *Prehistoric pottery for the archaeologist.* Leicester: Leicester University Press

Revisiting Grooved Ware: Understanding Ceramic Trajectories in Britain and Ireland, 3200–2400 cal BC

Essays in honour of Alex Gibson

Neolithic Studies Group Seminar Papers 20

Edited by

Mike Copper, Alasdair Whittle and Alison Sheridan

Oxford & Philadelphia

Published in the United Kingdom in 2024 by
OXBOW BOOKS
The Old Music Hall, 106-108 Cowley Road, Oxford, OX4 1JE

and in the United States by
OXBOW BOOKS
1950 Lawrence Road, Havertown, PA 19083

Paperback Edition: ISBN 979-8-88857-032-6
Digital Edition: ISBN 979-8-88857-033-3 (epub)

A CIP record for this book is available from the British Library

Library of Congress Control Number: 2023943535

Printed in Malta by Melita Press

Typeset in India by Lapiz Digital Services, Chennai.

For a complete list of Oxbow titles, please contact:

UNITED KINGDOM
Oxbow Books
Telephone (0)1226 734350
Email: oxbow@oxbowbooks.com
www.oxbowbooks.com

UNITED STATES OF AMERICA
Oxbow Books
Telephone (610) 853-9131, Fax (610) 853-9146
Email: queries@casemateacademic.com
www.casemateacademic.com/oxbow

Oxbow Books is part of the Casemate Group

Front cover: Image designed by Mike Copper
Back cover: Grooved Ware pot, Over, Cambridgeshire (copyright Cambridge Archaeological Unit).

Foreword

This book presents the proceedings of a hybrid in-person and on-line seminar held at the Bridewell Centre, London, in November 2022, organised by the Neolithic Studies Group (NSG). It forms part of an ongoing series of NSG Seminar Papers. Focusing on Late Neolithic Grooved Ware, and presented in honour of Alex Gibson, the papers here update an earlier volume on the same subject published in 1999.

The NSG is an informal organisation comprising archaeologists with an interest in Neolithic archaeology. It was established in 1984 and has a large membership based mainly in the UK and Ireland, but also including researchers and other interested people from the nations of the Atlantic seaboard. The annual programme includes two or three meetings spread throughout the year and includes seminars held in London and field meetings at various locations in north-west Europe.

Membership is open to anyone with an active interest in the Neolithic of Europe. The present membership includes academic staff and students, museums staff, archaeologists from government institutions, units, trusts, and amateur organisations. There is no membership procedure or application forms, and members are those on the current mailing list. Anyone can be added to the mailing list at any time, the only membership rule being that the names of those who do not attend any of four consecutive meetings are removed from the list (in the absence of apologies for absence or requests to remain on the list).

The Group relies on the enthusiasm of its members to organise its annual meetings and the two co-ordinators to maintain mailing lists and finances. Financial support for the group is drawn from a small fee payable for attendance of each meeting.

Anyone wishing to contact the Group and obtain information about forthcoming meetings should contact the co-ordinators at the following addresses:

TIMOTHY DARVILL
Department of Archaeology and Anthropology
Bournemouth University
Poole
Dorset BH12 5BB

KENNETH BROPHY
Department of Archaeology
University of Glasgow
Glasgow
G12 8QQ

Alternatively, visit the NSG website: http://www.neolithic.org.uk/

Neolithic Studies Group Seminar Papers

For a full list of titles please visit https://www.oxbowbooks.com

15. Neolithic Bodies
    edited by Penny Bickle and Emilie Sibbesson
16. Mining and Quarrying in Neolithic Europe
    edited by Anne Teather, Peter Topping and Jon Baczkowski
17. Houses of the Dead?
    edited by Alistair Barclay, David Field and Jim Leary
18. Marking Place: New Perspectives on Early Neolithic Enclosures
    edited by Jonathan Last
19. Ancient DNA and the European Neolithic: Relations and Descent
    edited by Alasdair Whittle, Joshua Pollard and Susan Greaney
20. Revisiting Grooved Ware: Understanding Ceramic Trajectories in Britain and Ireland, 3200–2400 cal BC
    edited by Mike Copper, Alasdair Whittle and Alison Sheridan

Contents

List of contributors

Alistair Barclay
Cotswold Archaeology
Stanley House
Walworth Road
Andover
Hampshire
SP10 5LH
UK

Sarah Botfield
Department of Archaeology
School of Arts, Languages and Cultures
The University of Manchester
Oxford Road
Manchester
M13 9PL
UK

Elina Brook
Wessex Archaeology
Portway House
Old Sarum Park
Salisbury
SP4 6EB
UK

David Clarke
Willow Cottage
243/1 Newhaven Road
Edinburgh
EH6 4LQ
UK

Rosamund M.J. Cleal
National Trust
Alexander Keiller Museum
High Street
Avebury
Marlborough
Wiltshire
SN8 1RF
UK

Mike Copper
School of Archaeological and Forensic Sciences
University of Bradford
Richmond Road
Bradford
BD7 1DP
UK

Christopher Evans
Director Emeritus
Cambridge Archaeological Unit
Dept. of Archaeology
Downing Street
Cambridge
CB3 0DT
UK

Richard P. Evershed
Organic Geochemistry Unit
School of Chemistry
University of Bristol
Cantock's Close
Bristol
BS8 1TS
UK

Paul Garwood
School of History and Cultures
University of Birmingham
Edgbaston
Birmingham
B15 2TT
UK

Eoin Grogan
Irish Cultural Heritage
School of Celtic Studies
Maynooth University
Maynooth
W23 F2H6
Ireland

GILL HEY
School of Archaeology
University of Oxford
1 South Parks Road
Oxford
OX1 3TG
UK

ANDY M. JONES
Cornwall Archaeological Unit
Pydar House
Pydar Street
Truro
Cornwall
TR1 1XU
UK

FRANCES LYNCH
Halfway House
Halfway Bridge
Bangor
Gwynedd
LL57 3DG

ANN MACSWEEN
Historic Environment Scotland
Longmore House
Salisbury Place
Edinburgh
EH9 1SH
UK

LILLY OLET
Organic Geochemistry Unit
School of Chemistry
University of Bristol
Cantock's Close
Bristol
BS8 1TS
UK

JOSHUA POLLARD
Department of Archaeology
University of Southampton
Avenue Campus
Highfield
Southampton
SO17 1BF
UK

HENRIETTA QUINNELL
39D Polsloe Road
Exeter
EX1 2DN
UK

HELEN ROCHE
Independent Consultant
62 Rockville Drive
Blackrock
Co. Dublin
A94 D344
Ireland

ALISON SHERIDAN
c/o Department of Scottish History and Archaeology
National Museums Scotland
Chambers Street
Edinburgh
EH1 1JF
UK

JESSICA SMYTH
School of Archaeology
University College Dublin
Newman Building
Belfield, Dublin 4
Ireland

JONATHAN TABOR
Cambridge Archaeological Unit
Dept. of Archaeology
Downing Street
Cambridge
CB3 0DT
UK

ALASDAIR WHITTLE
Department of Archaeology and Conservation
Cardiff University
John Percival Building
Colum Drive
Cardiff
CF10 3EU
UK

Chapter 1

Introduction: connected Grooved Ware worlds

Mike Copper and Alasdair Whittle

THE SIGNIFICANCE OF GROOVED WARE

For long centuries over much of Britain and Ireland, from the later 4th to well into the 3rd millennium cal BC, Grooved Ware pots were witness to both daily life and great events. Standing squarely on their flat bases, their bucket-shaped or otherwise straight-sided forms were often profusely decorated. The shifting array of geometric motifs and bounded panels could suggest complex worldviews for the people who made and used them. Some pots were very large; some in the famous houses at Skara Brae in Orkney were so big that they might have been regarded almost as permanent household members in their own right. At the other end of the spectrum, there were small cups, perhaps for individual consumption, and even miniature vessels. Some of the makers and users of this pottery lived in well-defined and occasionally spectacular settlements, such as Barnhouse and the Ness of Brodgar in Orkney or Durrington Walls near Stonehenge in Wiltshire, but others are often encountered in more modest settings, represented today only by pits, artefact scatters or traces of structures.

From perhaps the 32nd to the 25th century cal BC, down to and overlapping with the appearance of Beaker pottery around 2400 cal BC, certain of these people engaged in what now seem to us heroic enterprises, from probable long sea voyages between northern Britain and Ireland, to the construction of awe-inspiring stone circles and monumental earthworks, not infrequently built of materials brought from impressively afar, the best known but not the only examples being the bluestones and sarsens of Stonehenge. There are arguably many patterns in the development of this period, at one level a busy beginning, a gradual development in the middle and a final flourish, and at regional and local scales many other twists and turns which we have yet fully to pin down. Grooved Ware is an important key to unlocking this period, but its origins, the process of its spread, regional and local variation, and change through time still present major questions, as do the nature and density of settlement, levels of population, scales of connectivity, and the kinds of community and society involved. This volume addresses these many questions, principally through region-by-region coverage.

INSULAR WORLDS: 4TH- AND 3RD-MILLENNIUM QUESTIONS

Since the publication of the last major overview (Cleal and MacSween 1999), the evidence for this significant ceramic style has moved on considerably. Grooved Ware sites, numbering just 443 in 1999 (Longworth and Cleal 1999), are now so numerous that we have not included an overall gazetteer here; some chapters have regional ones. Excluding Orkney, recent work has raised the number of Grooved Ware sites in Scotland alone from the 47 identified in 1999 to over 120 today (Copper *et al.* 2021). In addition, Grooved Ware is now turning up more regularly in regions such as Aberdeenshire and south-west England where it was previously absent or rare, and its presence and distribution within Ireland have been consolidated (Carlin and Cooney 2017).

Our understanding of the appearance, spread and development of Grooved Ware has been significantly enhanced by recent large-scale dating projects. In Orkney, the European Research Council-funded *The Times of Their Lives* project has helped to clarify the dating of the earliest Grooved Ware currently known in Britain or Ireland. That drew particular attention to the significance of the west Mainland of Orkney, with its well known stone circles and settlements, including Barnhouse and the Ness of Brodgar, in the emergence, or even invention, of the style in the last couple of centuries of the 4th millennium cal BC (MacSween *et al.* 2015; Clarke *et al.* 2016; Richards *et al.* 2016; Bayliss *et al.* 2017; Card *et al.* 2018; 2020). The dating of Grooved Ware in mainland Scotland has been addressed by the Historic Environment Scotland-funded *Tracing the Lines* project (Copper *et al.* 2021). Grooved Ware and related practices in Britain and Ireland are also now within the remit of the Arts and Humanities Research Council-funded *Project TIME* (Griffiths *et al.* 2023); hundreds of new radiocarbon dates for contexts between 3500 and 1500 cal BC are anticipated (Seren Griffiths, pers. comm.). The dating of individual sites is also helping to clarify the timing of the adoption and development of Grooved Ware across Britain and Ireland. For example, the recent dating and modelling of Mount Pleasant, Dorset, have added further precision for a rapid succession of large-scale constructions in the generations around 2500 cal BC, as well as for the associated material culture (Greaney *et al.* 2020), while new, intriguingly early dates for Grooved Ware in Wessex are discussed, along with early dates from other individual projects, in several chapters in this volume.

For origins, it has been commonplace since renewed discussion in the 1970s (Wainwright and Longworth 1971) to treat Grooved Ware as a purely insular phenomenon, a development of the offshore islands which owed nothing to the adjacent European continent, perhaps involving a 'stratum of the population bound together by a common mode of pottery manufacture and a strong tradition of ritual practice' (Wainwright and Longworth 1971, 268). Stuart Piggott (1936, 197–201) had initially looked abroad for possible affinities, including in the material from the Baltic, and German and Dutch tombs, and by the 1950s had proposed that what he now termed *Rinyo-Clacton pottery* constituted one element of the Rinyo-Clacton culture, one of a series of 'Secondary Neolithic cultures' resulting from the Neolithisation of indigenous hunter-gatherer groups (Piggott 1954, 321–46).

The leading contender now for a specific point of origin, if such there was, is Orkney. As things stand, following extensive excavations, notably of Barnhouse (Richards and Jones 2016) and the Ness of Brodgar (Card *et al.* 2020) and the dating and modelling which have resulted, a plausible hypothesis is now widely followed that Grooved Ware emerged first in Orkney itself, arguably in or by the 32nd century cal BC (Carlin and Cooney 2017, 41; Cummings 2017, 168; Ray and Thomas 2018, 242; Bradley 2019, 116). It has been seen as the deliberate creation of difference by local aggrandisers (Sheridan 2014 and this volume), and one view of the speed with which it then appears to have spread is that people outside Orkney who were experiencing problems with climate, population and agricultural downturn sought to emulate the more successful communities of the north (Shennan 2018, 204–5), though other processes are possible (Copper *et al.* 2021, 100–8).

While origins in Orkney currently appear most plausible, it remains to be seen whether future research will throw up any comparably early dates elsewhere in Britain and Ireland. An alternative scenario could involve aspects of the wider connectivity which we have already mentioned. The very spread of Grooved Ware implies pre-existing networks of contact and communication (seen also in the movement of other raw materials around Scotland and the links between Orkney and eastern Ireland, and perhaps also further afield), and we wonder if Grooved Ware might have been an outcome of such linkage, perhaps catalysed initially within intercommunal gatherings in Orkney.

In Orkney, the occupation of Barnhouse probably ceased in the earlier 29th century cal BC, that of the Ness of Brodgar appears to decline after *c.* 2800 cal BC, and there is a hiatus in the sequence at Pool, Sanday, between *c.* 2800 and *c.* 2600 cal BC (MacSween *et al.* 2015; Richards *et al.* 2016; Card *et al.* 2018; 2020). After *c.* 2800 cal BC, settlement as a whole may have been largely beyond the west Mainland 'core' (Bayliss *et al.* 2017, fig. 7; cf. Bunting *et al.* 2022). Elsewhere, social change is reflected in the appearance of large ceremonial monuments such as Dunragit in Scotland (Thomas 2015) and Ballynahatty in Ireland (Hartwell 2002; Hartwell *et al.* 2023). Mortuary practices likely to date to this period on the basis of artefactual association include rare inhumations beneath barrows (e.g. Garton Slack 112 and Wharram Percy 65 (Mortimer 1905, 48 and 245–6; Folkton (Greenwell 1890, 14–15)), though cremation is the most visible form of funerary practice in the earlier 3rd millennium cal BC, including at Duggleby Howe (Gibson and Bayliss 2009, 64), albeit well dated at only a small number of sites, including Stonehenge (Marshall *et al.* 2012). Though not unchallenged (Bishop 2015), low levels of population in general have been mooted for the earlier 3rd millennium cal BC (Stevens and Fuller 2012; Shennan 2018, 205, and references). This is a claim to monitor closely in future research.

In southern Britain, a series of important monuments dates to the 26th and 25th centuries cal BC, including Stonehenge (the sarsen phase), Durrington Walls, Mount Pleasant and Silbury Hill; Marden and Avebury probably belong here too. (For references, see Ray and Thomas 2018; Greaney *et al.* 2020.) In the south, this late phase of elaborate and labour-consuming activity could be seen to start with the initiation of deep shafts at Grime's Graves, in the third quarter of the 27th century cal BC (Healy *et al.* 2018). The monumental character of the undertaking there and the nature of lithic production can be seen as both a reassertion of traditional ways of doing things but also perhaps one of the first signals of a rapidly changing world. Plenty of other significant, potentially late sites remain to be dated precisely.

At the end of Grooved Ware's currency, the question of how the tradition came to a close is closely linked to our understanding of its replacement, Beaker pottery. Recent projects, notably the *Beaker People Project* (Parker Pearson *et al.* 2019), have contributed significantly to clarifying the nature and timing of the arrival of Beaker pottery and Beaker-related practices in Britain and Ireland, while advances in the study of ancient DNA have allowed archaeologists to address the issue of migration, now recognised as one of the key reasons for this change (Cassidy *et al.* 2016; Olalde *et al.* 2018; see also Dulias *et al.* 2022). Whether, as has recently been suggested (Armit and Reich 2021; Booth *et al.* 2021), culturally isolated groups of primarily 'insular' ancestry, possibly continuing to produce Grooved Ware, persisted very long into the Chalcolithic is frustratingly hard to say given the impossibility of recovering genetic material from cremated remains (Bloxam and Parker Pearson 2022). It is likely that answering such questions will require a combination of techniques, both new and traditional. There is also scope yet again for the dating of individual late contexts, and for more precise dating of final events and depositions at major monuments, which ceased to be constructed after the arrival of Beakers.

New Grooved Ware discoveries have also helped to illuminate the regional and temporal characteristics of this style of pottery and its sub-styles (Table 1.1). Since 1999, it has become clear that what Isobel Smith (1956, 195–8) termed the 'Woodlands' sub-style represents the earliest type of Grooved Ware, though this sub-style is not without chronological variation itself, with vessels from early Grooved Ware sites outside Orkney, such as Balfarg Riding School in Fife, building on forms and decorative motifs that were in use slightly earlier at Barnhouse (Barclay and Russell-White 1993; Richards 2005; Richards *et al.* 2016; Copper *et al.* 2021). Later developments resulted in the distinctive regional stylistic trajectories in southern Britain, Orkney and Ireland that are discussed in the papers gathered here, as well as what Longworth termed the Durrington Walls sub-style which, to some extent, cross-cuts the distributions of the various regional styles. The degree of overlap between the earliest Grooved Ware and the latest Impressed Wares is touched on in several chapters. However, whether there was a correlation between specific Grooved Ware sub-styles and previous styles of Impressed Ware remains an open question. While flat-based Impressed Wares might be seen as a forerunner for flat-based Grooved Ware, these are almost entirely absent north-west of the Great Glen.

It is argued, in Chapters 4 and 15, that maintaining that Grooved Ware falls into unambiguous sub-styles may in fact impede understanding of its diachronic and geographical development. Key questions, touched upon in several of the chapters, include the extent to which the sub-styles may have been emic categories that were understood by their makers or etic categories employed by archaeologists; how much of the variation is chronological and how much regional or cultural; why multiple types of Grooved Ware were in use at the same time in the same region; and how we can account for Grooved Ware pots that combine features of more than one sub-style.

Piggott (1954, 340–1) suggested that decoration applied to a vessel from Woodlands represented 'a skeuomorph of knotted network', while Smith (1956, 197) felt that this idea could be extended, with this sub-style being characterised by skeuomorphic representations of organic containers. Though focused more on dating than meaning, Brindley (1999) considered the links between passage tomb ornamentation and Grooved Ware, and Cleal (1999) discussed the lattice as a possible Grooved Ware *leitmotif*. Though considering the possibility that it may have represented a net, she suggested that we were unlikely ever to know what it truly meant to the pots' makers and users. Is this unduly pessimistic? As we hinted at the start, there could be other ways of thinking about the overall grammar of the arrangement of Grooved Ware decoration.

Table 1.1. Key characteristics of Grooved Ware sub-styles as proposed by Ian Longworth (Wainwright and Longworth 1971, 236–43).

Sub-style	*Woodlands*	*Clacton*	*Durrington Walls*	*Rinyo*
Characteristic (though not exclusive) vessel forms	Small, open bowls and tubs often with thin walls	Vertical- to splay-sided, tub-shaped pots	A range of forms, but notably deep bucket-shaped vessels often with closed mouths	Flat-bottomed, trunconic and tub-shaped vessels of various sizes
Definitive features	Plain and slashed horizontal or converging cordons applied to, or pinched up from, the external surface. Ladder patterns on the external surface. Groups or strips of clay applied across the rim. Incised herringbone motif on rim. Applied or grooved 'knots' at intersections of converging cordons.	Simple, rounded rims with horizontally grooved internal decoration. Complex plastic decoration on internal rim bevel. Dot-filled grooved or incised triangles, lozenges and rectangles. Multiple grooved or incised chevrons, often opposed. Staggered or evenly arranged oval impressions.	Internally concave or 'vertically bevelled' rims. Internal incised decoration below rim. Grooved spirals or concentric circles. Vertical cordons or multiple or single incised lines dividing the vessel surface into panels. Incised or grooved filled triangles. Twisted or whipped cord impressions.	Rims with internal step bevels. Continuous scalloped rims. Applied roundels and pellets. Applied complex patterns. Grooved cordons other than horizontal or vertical. Cordons other than horizontal or vertical with round impressions.

Twenty-five years ago, differences in the types of fats present in Impressed Ware and Grooved Ware pots from Upper Ninepence drew attention to potential changes in animal exploitation or dietary preferences during the Neolithic (Dudd *et al.* 1999), and Ros Cleal (1999, 7) expressed the hope that residue analysis and the dating of carbonised residues on Grooved Ware would, in particular, help to refine our understanding of the tradition. The study of lipids from Grooved Ware at Durrington Walls has suggested that vessels of different sizes at the site were differentially associated with porcine and dairy fats (Craig *et al.* 2015), though the unusual nature of this site needs to be borne in mind, as does the fact that the distinction is not absolutely clear-cut (Fernandes *et al.* 2018) or uncontested (Shillito 2019). Chapter 7 gives a sample of recent work in this field.

Finally, there are questions of the scale and nature of connectivity. The justification for thinking that different regions of Britain and Ireland were more strongly connected at this time than earlier in the Neolithic rests in the widespread, if not universal, adoption of Grooved Ware itself, timber and stone circles, new types of flintwork, henge monuments and other characteristic features of the British and Irish Middle and Late Neolithic. Thus, early pots from Barnhouse can be paralleled in contexts far to the south (in the so-called Woodlands sub-style); it can make sense to compare the character of the Ring of Brodgar, whatever its precise date, with great monuments in the south such as Avebury; and isotopic analyses suggest the potentially long-range movement of animals to southern monumental centres, even if there is plenty of scope for debate about precise points of departure (Madgwick *et al.* 2019). That is not necessarily to claim that everything, everywhere, was identical or that earlier practices were entirely abandoned; while early Grooved Ware is found in passage tombs and alongside polished stone maceheads and carved stone balls, and later Grooved Ware occurs at palisaded enclosures, Grooved Ware sherds were also placed in pits in ways closely resembling practices associated with the deposition of earlier styles of pottery. The significance of Grooved Ware may therefore have varied, and its meaning may not have been the same in formal and informal contexts.

Opinion has fluctuated, from unifiers, some in the tradition of archaeological culture and others seeking broader social and political processes (e.g. Piggott 1954; Thomas 2010; Parker Pearson 2012; Parker Pearson *et al.* 2020), to splitters (Barclay and Brophy 2021). It seems to us that this was a more rather than less connected world, arguably in ways not necessarily confined to Britain and Ireland themselves (a perspective we raise briefly below), but the means by which linkage may have been effected probably varied across space and through time. It is for the reader to decide, on reading the chapters of this volume, where the balance lies at any one time or place, and it is for future research to go on establishing the detailed narratives from region to region which may enable the eventual resolution of such problems.

THE WIDER WORLD

At first sight, the archaeologies of Britain and Ireland and of the adjacent continent in the later 4th and 3rd millennia cal BC down to the advent of Beakers seem to have very little in common. There are no continental parallels for henges, for example, or probably for stone or timber circles, and, conversely, no sign in Britain or Ireland of anything resembling the *allées sépulcrales* and *hypogées* used so abundantly for collective burial in northern France at that time. For those sorts of reason, after the days of Childe and Piggott, the later parts of the Neolithic in Britain and Ireland have generally been seen as purely insular phenomena.

This inward-looking perspective can be questioned. At the very least, looking at continental developments in this period offers many case studies which are good to think with in relation to Britain and Ireland, reinforcing possibilities of interpretation and posing fresh questions. Are there relevant parallel processes and responses to the changing circumstances of the wider world at work on the other side of the Channel, from which researchers in Britain and Ireland could learn? Might there even be grounds for thinking again about possible pre-Beaker connections with the continent?

The wider world of continental Europe at this time seems to have been very connected, a useful perspective for thinking about potential linkage within Britain and Ireland. At its most extreme, it has been suggested recently that movement westwards from the steppes, on the Yamnaya–Corded Ware trajectory (Heyd 2017; 2021), now documented by aDNA analysis (Allentoft *et al.* 2015; Haak *et al.* 2015), was one effect of expansion by aggressive, newly formed city states in the Near East (Furholt 2021). And although Corded Ware practices (Furholt 2017) are not normally found west of the Rhine or south of the Alpine foreland, it has also been mooted that one notable early 3rd millennium burial as far away as Valencina de la Concepción in south-west Spain was influenced by Corded Ware mortuary ritual (Heyd 2017). Hostile interaction, migration at varying and disputed scales, long-range effects and contacts are all thus on the agenda. Just one specific example in this maelstrom of movement and change should make us think carefully about potential relations among communities in Britain and Ireland. At Koszyce in south-east Poland in the 29th or 28th centuries cal BC, the massacre of a small population of mobile cattle herders of the Globular Amphorae culture, with predominantly Neolithic farmer genetic ancestry and lacking any steppe input, could have been the outcome of local conflict with expanding Corded Ware communities (Schroeder *et al.* 2019). By comparison, how did change play out in Orkney, in the period of evident overlap between round-based pottery and Grooved Ware (Bayliss *et al.* 2017, fig. 5)? What was the relationship between Grooved Ware users at Barnhouse and the Ness of Brodgar and contemporaneous communities using round-based bowls who buried their dead at Isbister, where extensive evidence for interpersonal violence has been found (Lawrence 2012, 521–5; Bayliss *et al.* 2017)? Indeed, do the darkly glamorous maceheads and axes from the Ness of Brodgar represent a valorisation of violence at this time?

On the adjacent continent during the timespan of Grooved Ware, there are further major themes of continuing shifts in the kaleidoscope of cultures, probable population pressures and the spread of disease, and processes of social definition and differentiation. In northern France, in the *Néolithique récent* from about 3500 cal BC (Salanova *et al.* 2011), the abundant collective tombs in the form of *allées sépulcrales*, such as at Bury, Oise (Salanova *et al.* 2017) and chalk-cut *hypogées*, as at Les Mournouards II, Marne (Chambon *et al.* 2018), seem to speak to issues of community definition and concerns for land and resources: in the 34th and 33rd centuries cal BC in the case of Les Mournouards (Chambon *et al.* 2018, 134). Continuing use of *allées sépulcrales* in the *Néolithique final* of the earlier 3rd millennium suggests the existence of more tightly-defined social groupings, and to this period belong also large, often enclosed, houses, which may have the same social connotations (Bradley 2021, 117–27, and references). In northern Germany, a pattern of 'boom and bust' has been suggested and concerns with community definition and population can again be mooted; tens of thousands of often quite small megaliths constructed through the phases of the developed TRB may be one symptom of crowded and disputed landscapes (Müller 2019). Disease is also now a factor. So far, evidence for the plague bacterium *Yersinia pestis*, shown by aDNA analysis (Rasmussen *et al.* 2015), is not dated in the west of its sampled distribution earlier than a Corded Ware grave in Estonia in the mid-3rd millennium cal BC, but it has been suggested as relevant to late 4th-millennium change and potential turmoil further west (Kristiansen *et al.* 2017, 335).

Although the weight of evidence is clearly on the side of offshore insularity, could there be some connections after all between the Continent and Britain and Ireland at this time, in both directions, creating a conscious link or alignment with communities further afield, to draw on the power of the distant (cf. Helms 1988)? Might the big, enclosed houses of northern France owe anything to the renown of places such as the Ness of Brodgar and Barnhouse? Could the widespread flat-based forms of the *Néolithique récent* of northern France and the Horgen culture of the Alpine foreland, and indeed of the later TRB in the Netherlands, have anything to do with the inspiration for Grooved Ware pottery itself? That need not exclude Orkney as a specific point of initial adoption and there remains the intriguing and tantalising evidence of the possible introduction of the Orkney vole from somewhere in north-west Europe in the later 4th millennium cal BC (Martínková *et al.* 2013; Bayliss *et al.* 2017, fig. 4, *start Orkney voles*). The issue is complex (for a different view of possible directionality, see Sheridan and Pétrequin 2014), and relict populations in the pre-insulation North Sea can also be considered (Keith Dobney, pers. comm.), but the chance that Orkney voles came with people in the later 4th millennium, speculatively to escape problems with over-population and disease as noted above, may deserve consideration. There is as yet, however, no clue to any such movement in the Bronze Age aDNA evidence from Orkney (Dulias *et al.* 2022; Martin Richards, pers. comm.). But we would do well to keep looking.

THIS VOLUME

The papers in this volume variously deal with or touch on many of these issues. The majority offer coverage of regions, running from north to south, highlighting especially new finds, dating evidence, aspects of style and varying settlement presence and density. Lilly Olet and colleagues back up the paper by Frances Lynch on Wales with a review of existing and new lipid analyses, while David Clarke reflects critically on the overall validity of a concept of a unified Grooved Ware style, an important question also raised in the chapter on mainland Scotland by Mike Copper. Finally, Alison Sheridan weaves together many of the threads laid out in this introduction and discussed through the papers listed above, to give her personal view not only of the trajectory of Grooved Ware ceramic development but also of its many wider implications.

ACKNOWLEDGEMENTS

We are grateful to: Julie Gardiner and Jessica Hawxwell at Oxbow Books for guidance and support; Tim Darvill and Kenny Brophy for advice and organisation of the online NSG seminar; Keith Dobney, Seren Griffiths, Chris Scarre and Martin Richards for information; Susan Greaney and our co-editor Alison Sheridan for constructive critique of earlier drafts; and Sarah Botfield, Seren Griffiths and Neil Carlin, Roy Loveday, and especially our honorand, Alex Gibson, for presentations on the day, which will find publication elsewhere.

REFERENCES

Allentoft, M.E., Sikora, M., Sjögren, K.-G., Rasmussen, S., Rasmussen, M., Stenderup, J. *et al.* 2015. Population genomics of Bronze Age Eurasia. *Nature* 522, 167–72.

Armit, I. and Reich, D. 2021. The return of the Beaker folk? Rethinking migration and population change in British prehistory. *Antiquity* 95, 1464–77.

Barclay, G.J. and Brophy, K. 2021. 'A veritable chauvinism of prehistory': nationalist prehistories and the 'British' late Neolithic mythos. *Archaeological Journal* 178, 330–60.

Barclay, G. and Russell-White, C. 1993. Excavations in the ceremonial complex of the fourth to second millennium at Balfarg/Balbirnie, Glenrothes, Fife. *Proceedings of the Society of Antiquaries of Scotland* 123, 43–210.

Bayliss, A., Marshall, P., Richards, C. and Whittle, A. 2017. Islands of history: the Late Neolithic timescape of Orkney. *Antiquity* 91, 1171–88.

Bishop, R. 2015. Did Late Neolithic farming fail or flourish? A Scottish perspective on the evidence for Late Neolithic arable cultivation in the British Isles. *World Archaeology* 47, 834–55.

Bloxam, A. and Parker Pearson, M. 2022. Beaker diversity and cultural continuity: the British Beaker phenomenon beyond the stereotype. *Proceedings of the Prehistoric Society* 88, 261–84.

Booth, T., Brück, J., Brace, S. and Barnes, I. 2021. Tales from the supplementary information: ancestry change in Chalcolithic–Early Bronze Age Britain was gradual with varied kinship organization. *Cambridge Archaeological Journal* 31, 379–400.

Bradley, R. 2019. *The prehistory of Britain and Ireland* (2nd edition). Cambridge: Cambridge University Press.

Bradley, R. 2021. *Temporary palaces: the Great House in European prehistory*. Oxford: Oxbow Books.

Brindley, A. 1999. Sequence and dating in the Grooved Ware tradition. In R. Cleal and A. MacSween (eds) 1999, 133–44.

Bunting, M.J., Farrell, M., Dunbar, E., Reimer, P., Bayliss, A., Marshall, P. *et al.* 2022. Landscapes for Neolithic people in Mainland, Orkney. *Journal of World Prehistory* 35, 87–107.

Card, N., Edmonds, M. and Mitchell, A. (eds) 2020. *The Ness of Brodgar: as it stands*. Kirkwall: Kirkwall Press.

Card, N., Mainland, I., Timpany, S., Towers, R., Batt, C., Bronk Ramsey, C. *et al.* 2018. To cut a long story short: formal chronological modelling for the Late Neolithic site of Ness of Brodgar, Orkney. *European Journal of Archaeology* 21 (2), 217–63.

Carlin, N. and Cooney, G. 2017. Transforming our understanding of Neolithic and Chalcolithic society (4000–2200 BC) in Ireland. In M. Stanley, R. Swan and A. O'Sullivan (eds), *Stories of Ireland's past: knowledge gained from NRA roads archaeology*, 23–56. Dublin: Transport Infrastructure Ireland.

Cassidy, L., Martiniano, R., Murphy, E., Teasdale, M., Mallory, J., Hartwell, B. *et al.* 2016. Neolithic and Bronze Age migration to Ireland and establishment of the insular Atlantic genome. *Proceedings of the National Academy of Sciences of the United States of America* 113 (2), 368–73.

Chambon, P., Blin, A., Bronk Ramsey, C., Kromer, B., Bayliss, A., Beavan, N. *et al.* 2018. Collecting the dead: temporality and disposal in the Neolithic *hypogée* of Les Mournouards II (Marne, France). *Germania* 95, 93–143.

Clarke, D.V., Sheridan, J.A., Shepherd, A., Sharples, N., Armour-Chelu, M., Hamlet, L., Bronk Ramsey, C., Dunbar, E., Reimer, P.J., Marshall, P. and Whittle, A. 2016. The end of the world, or just 'goodbye to all that'? Contextualising the red deer from Links of Noltland, Westray, within late 3rd-millennium cal BC Orkney. *Proceedings of the Society of Antiquaries of Scotland* 146, 57–89.

Cleal, R. 1999. Introduction: the what, where, when and why of Grooved Ware. In R. Cleal and A. MacSween (eds) 1999, 1–8.

Cleal, R. and MacSween, A. (eds) 1999. *Grooved Ware in Britain and Ireland.* Oxford: Oxbow Books.

Copper, M., Hamilton, D. and Gibson, A. 2021. Tracing the lines: Scottish Grooved Ware trajectories beyond Orkney. *Proceedings of the Society of Antiquaries of Scotland* 150, 81–117.

Craig, O., Shillito, L.-M., Albarella, U., Viner-Daniels, S., Chan, B., Cleal, R. *et al.* 2015. Feeding Stonehenge: cuisine and consumption at the Late Neolithic site of Durrington Walls. *Antiquity* 89, 1096–1109.

Cummings, V. 2017. *The Neolithic of Britain and Ireland.* Abingdon: Routledge.

Dudd, S., Evershed, R. and Gibson, A. 1999. Evidence for varying patterns of exploitation of animal products in different prehistoric pottery traditions based on lipids preserved in surface and absorbed residues. *Journal of Archaeological Science* 26, 1473–82.

Dulias, K., Foody, M.G.B., Justeau, P., Silva, M., Martiniano, R., Oteo-Garcia, G. *et al.* 2022. Ancient DNA at the edge of the world: continental immigration and the persistence of Neolithic male lineages in Bronze Age Orkney. *Proceedings of the National Academy of Sciences of the United States of America* 119 (8). https://doi.org/10.1073/pnas.2108001119.

Fernandes, R., Eley, Y., Brabec, M., Lucquin, A., Millard, A. and Craig, O. 2018. Reconstruction of prehistoric pottery use from fatty acid carbon isotope signatures using Bayesian inference. *Organic Geochemistry* 117, 31–42.

Furholt, M. 2017. Massive migrations? The impact of recent aDNA studies on our view of third millennium Europe. *European Journal of Archaeology* 21, 159–91.

Furholt, M. 2021. Mobility and social change: understanding the European Neolithic period after the archaeogenetic revolution. *Journal of Archaeological Research* 29, 481–535.

Gibson, A. and Bayliss, A. 2009. Recent research at Duggleby Howe, North Yorkshire. *Archaeological Journal* 166, 39–78.

Greaney, S., Hazell, Z., Barclay, A., Bronk Ramsey, C., Dunbar, E., Hajdas, I. *et al.* 2020. Tempo of a mega-henge: a new chronology for Mount Pleasant, Dorchester, Dorset. *Proceedings of the Prehistoric Society* 86, 199–236.

Greenwell, W. 1890. Recent researches in barrows in Yorkshire, Wiltshire, Berkshire etc. *Archaeologia* 52, 1–72.

Griffiths, S., Carlin, N., Edwards, B., Overton, N., Johnston, P. and Thomas, J. 2023. Events, narrative and data: why new chronologies or ethically Bayesian approaches should change how we write archaeology. *Journal of Social Archaeology*, Online First, https://doi.org/10.1177/14696053231153499.

Haak, W., Lazaridis, I., Patterson, N., Rohland, N., Mallick, S., Llamas, B. *et al.* 2015. Massive migration from the steppe was a source for Indo-European languages in Europe. *Nature* 522, 207–11.

Hartwell, B. 2002. A Neolithic ceremonial timber complex at Ballynahatty, Co. Down. *Antiquity* 76, 526–32.

Hartwell, B., Gormley, S., Brogan, C. and Malone, C. (eds) 2023. *Ballynahatty: excavations in a Neolithic monumental landscape.* Oxford: Oxbow Books.

Healy, F., Marshall, P., Bayliss, A., Cook, G., Bronk Ramsey, C., van der Plicht, J. *et al.* 2018. When and why? The chronology and context of the flint mining at Grime's Graves, Norfolk, England. *Proceedings of the Prehistoric Society* 84, 277–301.

Helms, M.W. 1988. *Ulysses' sail: an ethnographic odyssey of power, knowledge, and geographical distance.* Princeton: Princeton University Press.

Heyd, V. 2017. Kossinna's smile. *Antiquity* 91, 348–59.

Heyd, V. 2021. Yamnaya, Corded Wares, and Bell Beakers on the move. In V. Heyd, G. Kulcsár and B. Preda-Bălănică (eds), *Yamnaya interactions: Proceedings of the International Workshop held in Helsinki, 25–26 April 2019*, 383–414. Budapest: Archaeolingua.

Kristiansen, K., Allentoft, M.E., Frei, K.M., Iversen, R., Johannsen, N.N., Kroonen, G. *et al.* 2017. Re-theorising mobility and the formation of culture and language among the Corded Ware culture in Europe. *Antiquity* 91, 334–47.

Lawrence, D.M. 2012. *Orkney's first farmers: reconstructing biographies from osteological analysis to gain insights into life and society in a Neolithic community on the edge of Atlantic Europe.* Unpublished PhD thesis, University of Bradford.

Longworth, I.H. and Cleal, R. 1999. Grooved Ware gazetteer. In R. Cleal and A. MacSween (eds) 1999, 177–206.

MacSween, A., Hunter, J., Sheridan, J.A., Bond, J., Bronk Ramsey, C., Reimer, P. *et al.* 2015. Refining the chronology of the Neolithic settlement at Pool, Sanday, Orkney: implications for the emergence and development of Grooved Ware. *Proceedings of the Prehistoric Society* 81, 283–310.

Madgwick, R., Lamb, A., Sloane, H., Nederbragt, A.J., Alberella, U., Parker Pearson, M. *et al.* 2019. Multi-isotope analysis reveals that feasts in the Stonehenge environs and across Wessex drew people and animals from throughout Britain. *Science Advances* 5(3), eaau6078. https://doi.org/10.1126/sciadv.aau6078.

Marshall, P., Darvill, T., Parker Pearson, M. and Wainwright, G. 2012. *Stonehenge, Amesbury, Wiltshire: chronological modelling.* Portsmouth: English Heritage.

Martínková, N., Barnett, R., Cucchi, T., Struchen, R., Pascal, M., Pascal, M. *et al.* 2013. Divergent evolutionary processes associated with colonization of offshore islands. *Molecular Ecology* 22, 5205–20.

Mortimer, J.R. 1905. *Forty years' researches in British and Saxon burial mounds of East Yorkshire.* London: A. Brown.

Müller, J. 2019. Boom and bust, hierarchy and balance: from landscape to social meaning –megaliths and societies in northern central Europe. In J. Müller, M. Hinz and M. Wunderlich (eds), *Megaliths – societies – landscapes: early monumentality and social differentiation in Neolithic Europe*, Volume 1, Proceedings of the International Conference «Megaliths – Societies – Landscapes. Early Monumentality and Social Differentiation in Neolithic Europe» (16th–20th June 2015 in Kiel), 31–77. Bonn: Habelt.

Olalde, I., Brace, S. Allentoft, M. Armit, I. Kristiansen, K. Rohland *et al.* 2018. The Beaker phenomenon and the genomic transformation of northwest Europe. *Nature* 555, 190–6.

Parker Pearson, M. 2012. *Stonehenge: exploring the greatest Stone Age mystery.* London: Simon and Schuster.

Parker Pearson, M., Jay, M., Chamberlain, A., Richards, M. and Evans, J. (eds) 2019. *The Beaker People: isotopes, mobility and diet in prehistoric Britain.* Oxford: Prehistoric Society Research Papers 7.

Parker Pearson, M., Pollard, J., Richards, C., Thomas, J., Tilley, C. and Welham, K. 2020. *Stonehenge for the ancestors: Part 1, Landscape and monuments.* Leiden: Sidestone Press.

Piggott, S. 1936. Grooved Ware. In S.H. Warren, S., Piggott, J.G.D., Clark, M. Burkitt, H. Godwin and M.E. Godwin, Archaeology of the submerged land-surface of the Essex coast, 191–201. *Proceedings of the Prehistoric Society* 2, 178–210.

Piggott, S. 1954. *The Neolithic cultures of the British Isles.* Cambridge: Cambridge University Press.

Ray, K. and Thomas, J. 2018. *Neolithic Britain: the transformation of social worlds.* Oxford: Oxford University Press.

Rasmussen, S., Allentoft, M.K., Nielsen, K., Orlando, L., Sikora, M., Sjogren, K.-G. *et al.* 2015. Early divergent strains of *Yersinia pestis* in Eurasia 5,000 years ago. *Cell* 163, 571–82.

Richards, C. (ed.) 2005. *Dwelling among the monuments: the Neolithic village of Barnhouse, Maeshowe passage grave and surrounding monuments at Stenness, Orkney.* Cambridge: McDonald Institute for Archaeological Research.

Richards, C. and Jones, R. (eds) 2016. *The development of Neolithic house societies in Orkney: investigations in the Bay of Firth, Mainland, Orkney (1994–2014).* Oxford: Windgather Press.

Richards, C., Jones, A.M., MacSween, A., Sheridan, J. A., Dunbar, E., Reimer, P. *et al.* 2016. Settlement duration and materiality: formal chronological models for the development of Barnhouse, a Grooved Ware settlement in Orkney. *Proceedings of the Prehistoric Society* 82, 193–225.

Salanova, L., Brunet, P., Cottiaux, R., Hamon, T., Langry-François, F., Martineau, R. *et al.* 2011. Du Néolithique récent à l'Âge du Bronze dans le centre-nord de la France: les étapes de l'évolution chrono-culturelle. In F. Bostyn, E. Martial and I. Praud (eds), *Le Néolithique du Nord de la France dans son contexte européen: habitat et économie aux 4e et 3e millénaires avant notre ère. Revue Archéologique de Picardie*, 1/2, 77–101.

Salanova, L., Chambon, P., Pariat, J.-G., Marçais A.-S. and Valentin, F. 2017. From one ritual to another: the long-term sequence from the Bury gallery grave (northern France, 4th–2nd millennia BC). *Antiquity* 91, 57–73.

Schroeder, H., Margaryan, A., Szmyt, M., Theulot, B., Włodarczak, P., Rasmussen, S. *et al.* 2019. Unraveling ancestry, kinship and violence in a Late Neolithic mass grave. *Proceedings of the National Academy of Sciences of the United States of America* 116 (22), 10705–10.

Shennan, S. 2018. *The first farmers of Europe: an evolutionary perspective.* Cambridge: Cambridge University Press.

Sheridan, J.A. 2014. Little and large: the miniature 'carved stone ball' beads from the eastern tomb at Knowth, Ireland, and their broader significance. In R.-M. Arbogast and A. Greffier-Richard (eds), *Entre archéologie et écologie, une préhistoire de tous les milieux. Mélanges offerts à Pierre Pétrequin*, 303–14. Besançon: Presses universitaires de Franche-Comté.

Sheridan, J.A. and Pétrequin, P. 2014. Constructing a narrative for the Neolithic of Britain and Ireland: the use of 'hard science' and archaeological reasoning. In P. Bickle and A. Whittle (eds), *Early farmers: the view from archaeology and science*, 369–90. Oxford: Oxford University Press.

Shillito, L.-M. 2019. Building Stonehenge? An alternative interpretation of lipid residues in Neolithic Grooved Ware from Durrington Walls. *Antiquity* 93, 1052–60.

Smith, I. 1956. *The decorative art of Neolithic ceramics of south-eastern England and its relations.* Unpublished PhD thesis, University of London.

Stevens, C. and Fuller, D. 2012. Did Neolithic farming fail? The case for a Bronze Age agricultural revolution in the British Isles. *Antiquity* 86, 707–22.

Thomas, J. 2010. The return of the Rinyo-Clacton folk? The cultural significance of the Grooved Ware complex in later Neolithic Britain. *Cambridge Archaeological Journal* 20, 1–15.

Thomas, J. 2015. *A Neolithic ceremonial complex in Galloway: excavations at Dunragit and Droughduil, 1999–2002.* Oxford: Oxbow Books.

Wainwright, G.J. and Longworth, I. 1971. *Durrington Walls: excavations 1966–1968.* London: Society of Antiquaries.

Chapter 2

Grooved Ware in Orkney

Alison Sheridan

There is no evidence to suggest that this grooved ware had either a long or very important life... ***At the most we can consider the grooved-ware episode as a minor cultural individuality.*** *(Piggott 1936, 197; my emphasis)*

While the pottery from 'cooking holes' at Lion Point, Clacton, in Essex was the first assemblage to be named as 'Grooved ware' by Stuart Piggott in his influential 1936 publication that launched the idea of this type of pottery (Piggott 1936, 191), it is actually at the other end of the British landmass, in Orkney, where the story of this ceramic tradition begins. The transformation in our understanding of Grooved Ware in the 87 years since Piggott produced this first attempt at a synthesis of finds of this pottery type, and indeed in the 69 years since he developed his model of a fully blown 'Rinyo-Clacton Culture' (Piggott 1954), has been complete. Arguably the biggest change in perception has been the realisation that Orkney, and not southern England, is where Grooved Ware first appeared. Equally significant has been the revelation that, far from being a short-lived episode or a 'minor cultural individuality' dating to the Early Bronze Age, the period of Grooved Ware use lasted several centuries and was marked by extensive and profound changes in the social dynamics of Late Neolithic Britain and Ireland – topics that feature in other chapters in this volume.

Our current state of knowledge of Grooved Ware in Orkney, as elsewhere, owes much to developments since the last attempt at a synthesis of this pottery type was published, 24 years ago (Cleal and MacSween 1999). In common with elsewhere in Britain and Ireland (but to a greater extent), Orkney has witnessed a significant increase in the amount of Grooved Ware that has been found and many more radiocarbon dates are now available. In contrast with these other areas, however, this increase in Orkney has come about not because of developer-funded archaeology – there has been relatively little infrastructural or building work in Orkney – but thanks to research-based fieldwork and dedicated radiocarbon-dating programmes, including Alasdair Whittle and Alex Bayliss's invaluable *The Times of Their Lives* (ToTL) project (Bayliss *et al.* 2017; Sheridan *et al.* in prep.). Moreover, the enormous increase in the amount of Grooved Ware pottery comes largely from just three sites: the Ness of Brodgar and Barnhouse-Barnhouse Odin, in west Mainland, and Links of Noltland, on Westray. Excavations by Nick Card at the

Ness of Brodgar since 2003 have produced an estimated 100,000+ sherds, while those by Colin Richards at Barnhouse and the adjacent site of Barnhouse Odin (probably part of the same settlement) produced 6000 sherds. Those by EASE Archaeology on behalf of Historic Environment Scotland at Links of Noltland from 2000 to the early 2020s have, according to ephemeral posts on the excavation's Facebook account, added tens of thousands of sherds to the 10,000+ sherds from David Clarke's 1978–81 excavations at that site that were reported on by the present author (Sheridan 1999).

The post-excavation processing of the pottery from the Ness of Brodgar is at an early stage and, to the author's knowledge, there has been no post-excavation work on the EASE pottery finds from Links of Noltland since her own rapid assessment of the finds from the 2007–10 excavation seasons (Sheridan 2011). For this reason and others – including the fact that much of the pottery from these sites comes from secondary contexts such as rubbish dumps – it is not yet possible to provide a definitive, fine-grained typochronology of Orcadian Grooved Ware. There is certainly scope for refinement through radiocarbon dating absorbed lipids in sherds – something already underway for Jessica Smyth's *Passage Tomb People* project (cf. Chapter 7, Olet *et al.*, for Welsh results). Nevertheless, sufficient information exists to offer the provisional statement that follows. Further details on the Skara Brae assemblage, and on the relationship between Orcadian Grooved Ware and that found elsewhere in Scotland, are presented in Chapters 3 and 4, and detailed expositions on the dating of Grooved Ware at Pool, Barnhouse, Links of Noltland (Clarke excavations) and the Ness of Brodgar can be found in a suite of ToTL publications (MacSween *et al.* 2015; Clarke *et al.* 2016; Richards *et al.* 2016b; Card *et al.* 2018).

ORCADIAN GROOVED WARE: GENERAL INTRODUCTION

To the author's knowledge, definite and possible examples of Grooved Ware have been found at 22 findspots in the Orkney archipelago (counting Barnhouse and Barnhouse Odin as a single site, as it probably was: Fig. 2.1, Table 2.1). The findspots are not evenly distributed: there are marked concentrations on the west part of Mainland on and around the isthmus between the Lochs of Stenness and Harray, and around the Bay of Firth, and smaller clusters on the Westray–Papa Westray–Holm of Papa Westray archipelago and on Sanday. Other findspots are scattered around Mainland, and on Rousay and Eday; several islands (including those in the southernmost part of the archipelago) have no recorded finds of this pottery type.

Grooved Ware occurs in a narrow range of contexts: settlements, including the nucleated settlements at Skara Brae (described in Chapter 3 and discussed in Shepherd 2016), Links of Noltland and Barnhouse; the site at Ness of Brodgar which can, as argued below, be regarded as a special-purpose kind of settlement; Maeshowe-type passage tombs (at Quanterness, Quoyness and Pierowall); and the stone circle set within a henge at the Stones of Stenness. The few other finds include those at the stalled cairn of Holm of Papa Westray North (Henshall 2009), where the few sherds were clearly deposited long after the monument was built; and those discovered as stray surface finds at Evie, and others found during excavations of the Iron Age Broch of Deerness at Dingieshowe, where they were clearly residual (Stevenson 1946). The absence of Grooved Ware from chamber tombs of types other than Maeshowe-type passage tombs (except for the aforementioned secondary

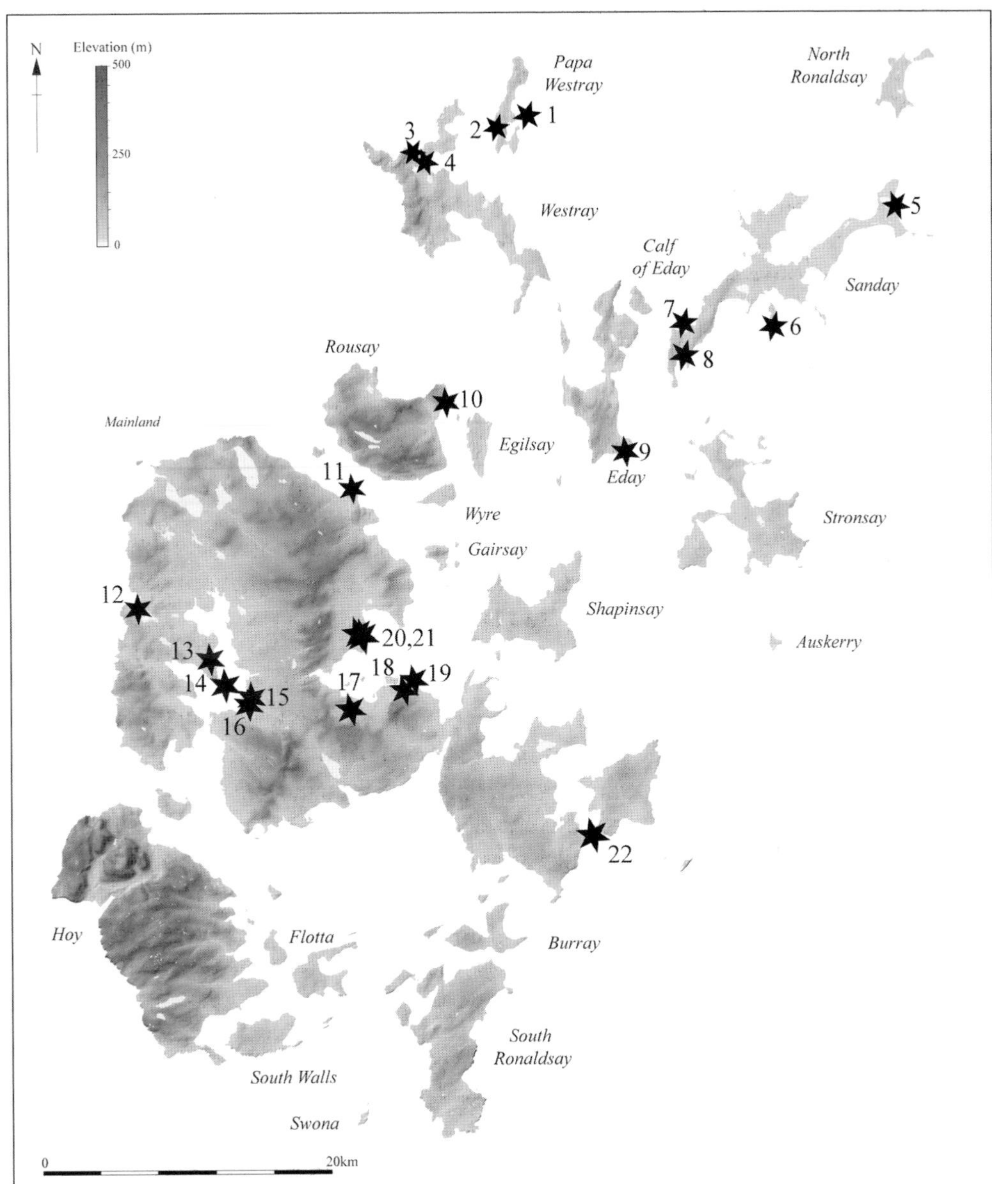

Figure 2.1. Distribution of findspots of Grooved Ware in Orkney. The numbers correspond to those given in Table 2.1 (base map courtesy of Ness of Brodgar Trust).

deposits at Holm of Papa Westray North) has long been recognised and commented upon (e.g. Davidson and Henshall 1989, 64–84).

The findspot of Grooved Ware at Brae of Muckquoy, at the north-western corner of the Bay of Firth, is potentially highly significant because it appears, from fieldwalking, geophysical survey and small-scale excavation, to be a large settlement. (Whether it had

Table 2.1. Findspots of Grooved Ware in Orkney.

	Location	*Site type*	*References*
1	Holm of Papa Westray North	Stalled cairn	Henshall 2009
2	Knap of Howar, Papa Westray	Settlement (house)	Henshall 1983
3	Links of Noltland, Westray	Settlement	Sheridan 1999; 2011
4	Pierowall Quarry	Maeshowe-type passage tomb	Yarrington 1984
5	Tofts Ness, Sanday	Settlement	Dockrill 2007
6	Quoyness, Sanday	Maeshowe-type passage tomb	Childe 1952
7	Pool, Sanday	Settlement	Hunter 2007; MacSween *et al.* 2015
8	Stove Bay (Bay of Stove), Sanday	Settlement	Bond *et al.* 1995
9	Green, Eday	Settlement	Coles and Miles 2013; see also Canmore ID 108272 entry
10	Rinyo, Rousay	Settlement	Childe and Grant 1939; 1947
11	Evie, Mainland	Surface find	Stevenson 1946
12	Skara Brae, Mainland	Settlement	This volume, Chapter 3 (with further references)
13	Buckan, Sandwick, Mainland	Surface find	Christopher Gee, pers. comm.
14	Ness of Brodgar, Mainland	Special purpose settlement	Card *et al.* 2020
15	Barnhouse and Barnhouse Odin, Mainland	Settlement	Richards 2005; Richards *et al.* 2016b
16	Stones of Stenness, Mainland	Stone circle & henge	Henshall and Savory 1976
17	Stonehall Farm, Mainland	Settlement	Richards and Jones 2016
18	Quanterness, Mainland	Maeshowe-type passage tomb	Renfrew 1979
19	Crossiecrown, Mainland	Settlement	Richards and Jones 2016
20	Braes of Muckquoy, Mainland	Settlement	Richards and Jones 2016
21	Redland, Mainland	Settlement	Christopher Gee, pers. comm.
22	Dingieshowe, Broch of Deerness, Mainland	Residual in Iron Age broch	Stevenson 1946

been 'a massive settlement mound of greater proportions than either Skara Brae or Ness of Brodgar', according to claims by Colin Richards *et al.* (2016a, 250), remains to be seen, however.) Weathered Grooved Ware sherds found at Redland, just *c.* 500 m away (Christopher Gee, pers. comm.), could conceivably belong to the same site. Of note is the fact that a sandstone slab with a pecked spiral design had been found, reused, in the Iron Age broch at Redland during the 19th century (NMS X.IA 4, Simpson 1866, 40 and pl. xix, fig. 6; Thomas 2016, 46). This may well attest to the former presence of a Maeshowe-type passage tomb in the vicinity. This under-researched area would undoubtedly repay further investigation as a focus of activity by Grooved Ware users.

As for the pottery from the paired houses at Knap of Howar on Papa Westray, Audrey Henshall noted the presence, in an assemblage comprising round- and slightly pointed-based and saggy-based vessels, of a few sherds with Grooved Ware-type features (principally broad applied cordons: Henshall 1983, 72, figs 7.35–6).

Pottery from three other Orcadian sites has been claimed to be Grooved Ware, but this can be refuted. The two sherds with incised decoration (one in a herringbone design) found in secondary contexts at the horned stalled cairn at Point of Cott, Westray, were tentatively described as being 'possibly from incised Grooved Ware vessels' (MacSween 1997), but the curvature of the herringbone-decorated sherd suggests that it is more likely to belong to the Orcadian Beaker tradition, and the other incised sherd is also more likely to be Beaker than Grooved Ware. Also belonging to Orkney's small assemblage of Beaker pottery are the two vessels with incised geometric decoration from the 'red house' (house 1) at Crossiecrown, published by Andrew Meirion Jones as Grooved Ware (Jones *et al.* 2016, fig. 11.3.5); one of these (SF 150) is from a context (003) radiocarbon-dated to 1980–1740 cal BC (Griffiths 2016, 262). Finally, a vessel with incised herringbone decoration found at the Braes of Ha'Breck settlement on Wyre and published as Grooved Ware (Thomas 2010, and featured on the back cover of that publication) clearly belongs to the Orcadian domestic Beaker repertoire – minimal though that repertoire may be – and is associated with a date of 2300–2050 cal BC (SUERC-37960: Griffiths 2016, 263). It is important to highlight these mis-identifications as they have already entered debates about the currency of Grooved Ware in Orkney (e.g. Griffiths 2016, 280–1).

EARLY USE (TO *c.* 2900 CAL BC), GENESIS, AND RELATIONSHIP TO THE ROUND- (AND POINTED/SAGGY-) BASED POTTERY THAT PRECEDED, AND PARTLY OVERLAPPED WITH IT

The earliest Grooved Ware in Orkney

One of the major contributions of the radiocarbon-dating project, *The Times of their Lives*, to Neolithic Orkney has been the demonstration that Grooved Ware was in use as early as the late 32nd century BC at Barnhouse, on Mainland (Richards *et al.* 2016b), and that at Pool, on Sanday, the transition to the use of flat-based Grooved Ware with complex incised decoration had occurred by *3210–2935 cal BC (95% probability*: MacSween *et al.* 2015, 300). These constitute the earliest dates for Grooved Ware pottery throughout its distribution in Britain and Ireland, even though an increasing number of dates indicate its use by or around 3000 cal BC outside of Orkney – and hence, this author would contend, a very rapid southwards adoption from Orkney (as discussed, for example, in Chapter 4 and Copper *et al.* 2021).

Briefly – because the matter is also discussed elsewhere (principally Chapters 3, 4, MacSween *et al.* 2015 and Richards *et al.* 2016b) – the assemblages from Pool and Barnhouse offer an intriguing picture of Orkney's earliest Grooved Ware. At Pool, as Ann MacSween has pointed out, it is possible to discern a process of gradual transition from the undecorated, deep-bellied pottery with rounded, slightly pointed or saggy bases (Phases 1.2 and 2.1) that was a characteristic element of the ceramic repertoire of the Orkney archipelago during the late 4th millennium (as seen, for example, at Knap of Howar: Henshall 1983; see also Sheridan 2016, 198–9) to the use of flat-based pots with incised geometric decoration including nested lozenges, some with impressed infill (Phase 2.3: Chapter 3, fig. 3.10). An intermediate stage in this process (Phase 2.2) is marked by pots with mostly narrow flat bases, some of which have occasional diagonal or curving lines (MacSween *et al.* 2015, fig. 6). Technological continuity is indicated in the predominance of shell as a filler. While the tempo and duration of this stylistic transformation cannot be gauged owing to the absence of dates for Phases 1 and 2.1 (MacSween *et al.* 2015, 293), it is clear, as noted above, that the Phase 2.3 Grooved Ware was in use by *3210–2935 cal BC (95% probability)*. A gap of several centuries then ensued before a later phase of Grooved Ware use is attested, featuring larger vessels with mostly applied decoration and mostly stone as a filler and dating to between *2680–2515 cal BC (95% probability)* and *2460–2280 cal BC (95% probability)* (MacSween *et al.* 2015, 297, fig. 9).

At Barnhouse, by contrast, the Grooved Ware appeared as a fully-fledged ceramic tradition, consistent with the establishment of this settlement, apparently *de novo*, as a planned nucleated settlement of several houses in the later 32nd century cal BC (Richards *et al.* 2016b). A process of *in situ* evolution of the repertoire can be traced over the estimated ten generations of the settlement's use, with the appearance, from *3025–2975 cal BC (95% probability)* of large, coarseware vessels with uneven surfaces and thick applied cordons, and of the use of applied, dimpled pellets ('doughnuts'). This development seems to have coincided with the construction of a large, monumental, communal structure (Structure 8) in which, it is safe to surmise, feasting occurred; the large pots will have been deployed in the preparation of food (and drink?) consumed on such occasions.

The earliest, pre-Structure 8, Barnhouse pottery (Fig. 2.2) features relatively small dishes (e.g. SF 1890: estimated rim diameter *c.* 170 mm, estimated height just under 80 mm) and larger, tub- and bucket-shaped vessels, some with gently curving walls, others straight-walled. The dish SF 1980 had been placed on a twined organic mat to dry, acquiring an impression of the matting on its base (Fig. 2.3). Decoration is overwhelmingly by incision, often featuring horizontal lines interspersed with wavy or diagonal lines; sometimes the lines are accentuated by the use of impressions to create a false-relief wavy line (e.g. in SF 1905) or to create a fringe (e.g. SF 1655). Triangles, filled with jab impressions, occur (as on SF 1085). Impression was also used to create 'rosette' motifs (e.g. SF 4261, 5940 and 5116xii). Among the pottery from the houses dating to *3075–3025 cal BC* (houses 6 and 10, Fig. 2.4) is a vessel that probably had an incised lozenge (SF 448ii) and a large dish with thin applied cordons, arranged in a design featuring zig-zags interspersed with horizontal lines (SF 3720). A larger vessel, also with thin applied cordons and with paired projections on its rim (SF 3502–3492–3508–3487), could be broadly contemporary. Examples of the larger, coarseware vessels with broader applied cordons (e.g. SF 6016) and of a vessel with applied 'doughnuts' (SF 5010), are shown in the lower part of Figure 2.4, along with a tiny pot (SF 6025); these are from Structure 8 and similarly 'late' structures. Interestingly, the decoration on the Barnhouse pottery does not closely match the designs incised into stone at the site (Richards 2005, fig. 4.29).

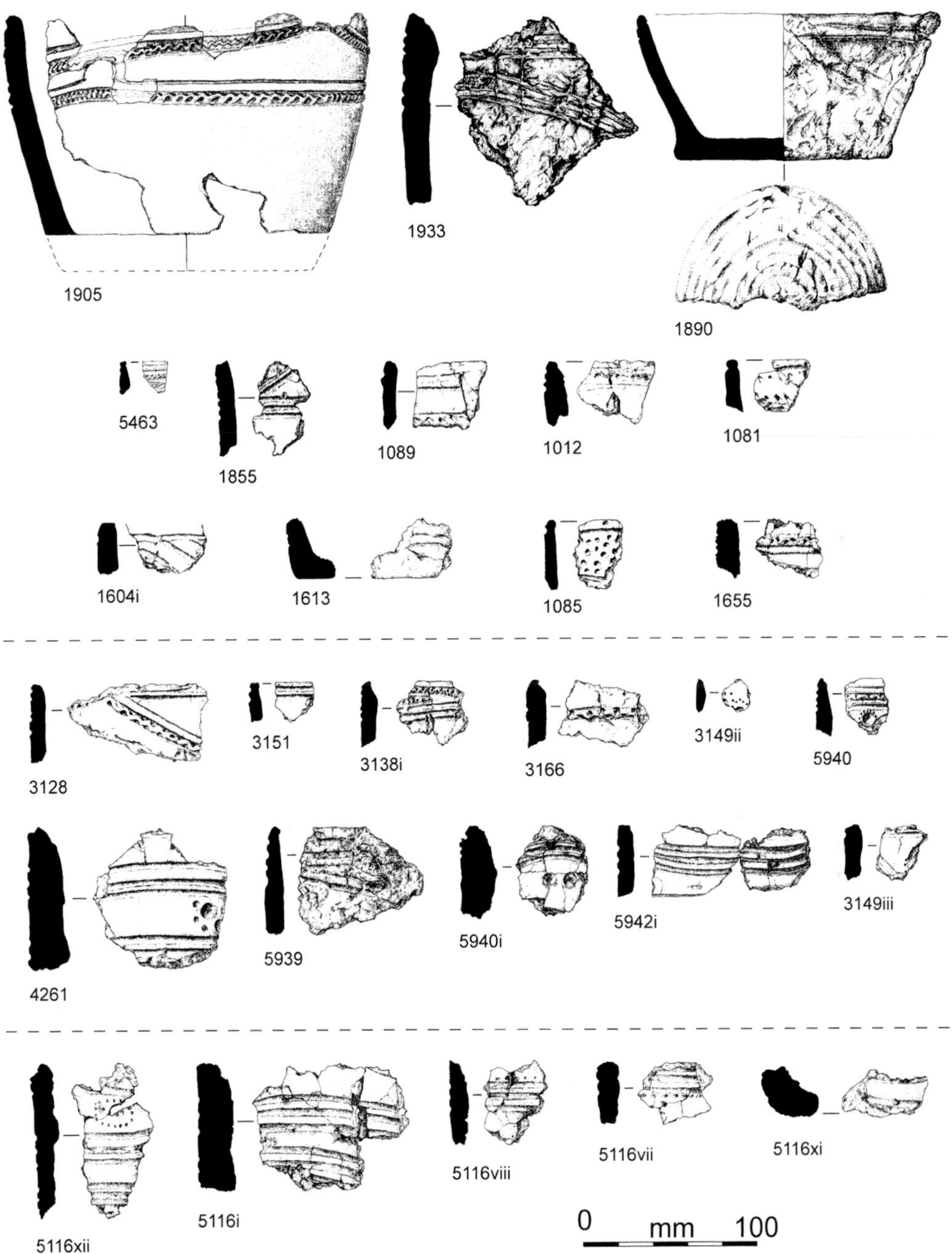

Figure 2.2. Examples of the earliest, pre-Structure 8 pottery at Barnhouse. Top: Houses 2, 3 and 9; middle: House 5a/5b, occupation material pre-dating structure 8 and early occupation activity; bottom: House 12a and early occupation/refuse spread beneath House 12b (after Richards et al. *2016b).*

Figure 2.3. Impression of matting on the base of a Grooved Ware pot (also shown in Fig. 2.2) from Barnhouse (photo: Lynda Aiano).

This pottery differs in several respects from the Pool Grooved Ware, not least in its predominant use of stone as a filler, although the use of shell is also attested, and the pottery from Barnhouse Odin is exclusively shell-tempered (Jones 2005, 280). Nevertheless, the two assemblages are united in the emphasis on incision as the dominant decorative technique (at least for the early phase at Barnhouse) and in the use of zig-zag lines and lozenge motifs.

Grooved Ware pottery that definitely or probably dates to before 2900 cal BC is known from several other sites in Orkney (Fig. 2.5). It echoes the Barnhouse repertoire in its emphasis on incised (and occasionally impressed) designs, often featuring zig-zag or serpentine lines interspersed with horizontal lines. That found in the Maeshowe-type passage tomb at Quanterness and at the Stones of Stenness shares lithic inclusions with the Barnhouse pottery and it has been suggested that three of the pots deposited in Quanterness had been made at Barnhouse, just over 11 km away (reported in Jones 2005, 280–1). The dating of the Quanterness tomb has most recently been discussed by Sheridan and Schulting (2020), while the dating of the construction and use of the Stones of Stenness to around the 30th century cal BC is discussed in Bayliss *et al.* (2017).

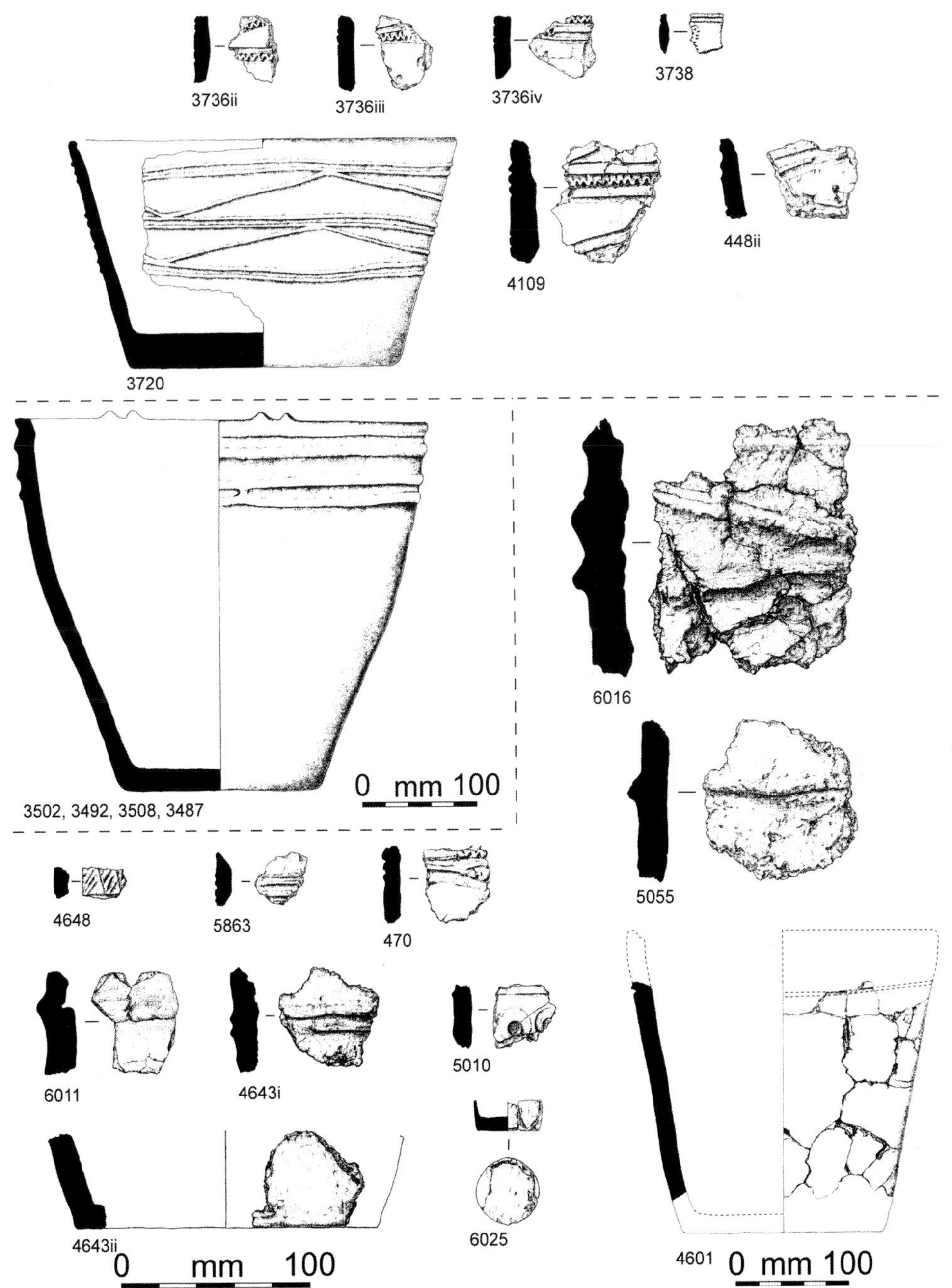

Figure 2.4. Examples of Grooved Ware from the middle and later occupation phases at Barnhouse. Top: Houses 6 and 10; Middle, left: old land surface predating House 4; rest: Structure 8 and Houses 1 and 12b. Note 5010, with applied 'doughnuts', and 6025, miniature pot (after Richards et al. *2016b).*

Figure 2.5. Other Grooved Ware that probably or definitely dates to before 2900 cal BC in Orkney. Top four images: Ness of Brodgar – top row shows dish from Structure 14, being held by Roy Towers and on its own (photos by Woody Musgrove and ORCA; cf. sketchfab 3D model https://skfb.ly/K68K); bottom left: Quanterness (after Davidson and Henshall 1989); bottom right: Stones of Stenness (after Henshall and Savory 1976).

The presence of similar pottery at the Ness of Brodgar is consistent with the chronology of this site, whose use overlapped with that of Barnhouse (Card *et al.* 2018). It is also attested at the settlement at Rinyo on Rousay, with vessels including those with impressed dot infill of lines and of a probable lozenge being associated with Gordon Childe's 'Phase I' of occupation (Childe and Grant 1939, pl. XXII, 1–7).

It is this early type of Grooved Ware which spread widely over Britain and Ireland, usually being given Ian Longworth's label 'Woodlands' sub-style; examples can be seen elsewhere in this volume (e.g. Chapters 4, 6, 8, 12).

Origin

Much ink has been expended on speculation about the origin of Grooved Ware, with Stuart Piggott casting his net wide to seek *comparanda* from many parts of Europe, shifting his focus from the far north and the Netherlands (Piggott 1936) to France and Iberia, describing the Rinyo I pottery as a 'coarse provincial variant' (Piggott 1954, 344–5). Such claims simply do not stand up to close inspection, however. Similarly, the idea that its appearance may have been associated with the arrival of new settlers from the Continent, more specifically Belgium, who brought the Orkney Vole with them (Martínovká *et al.* 2013) – an hypothesis alluded to by Alasdair Whittle in Chapter 1 – does not withstand close scrutiny. Sheridan and Pétrequin (2014, 377–80) have pointed out that not only is there no evidence for the influx of new settlers during the late 4th millennium but also, the 'Belgian homeland' hypothesis is based on the fact that the closest genetic match for the Orkney Vole comes from a medieval nunnery in Belgium! Moreover, the potential Continental *comparanda* flagged by Alasdair Whittle in Chapter 1 are unconvincing.

The possibility that Grooved Ware may have originated elsewhere in Britain other than Orkney can similarly be dismissed since, even though the number of pre-3000 cal BC dates is growing, no clear chronological primacy or clear trajectory of genesis in any of these areas can be demonstrated (and the radiocarbon calibration plateau towards the end of the 4th millennium does not help). The stylistic attribution as Grooved Ware of the pot from Milton of Leys, Highland, that has produced a radiocarbon date from encrusted organic material of 3331–3106 cal BC (SUERC-84856, 4448±24 BP) has been convincingly challenged by Mike Copper (Copper *et al.* 2021 and this volume). Rather than being an exceptionally early example of the so-called 'Durrington Walls sub-style' (Connolly and MacSween 2003), this vessel is more plausibly to be understood as an example of Impressed Ware.

Colin Renfrew's suggestion (1979) that Grooved Ware is the outcome of an organic process of evolution of the pre-existing style of Neolithic pottery in Orkney – a style widely, but problematically, referred to as 'Unstan Ware' (Sheridan 2016) – appears *prima facie* to be borne out by the evidence from Pool although, as Mike Copper astutely points out in Chapter 4, it could be that that assemblage reflects an adoption of Grooved Ware features from elsewhere on Orkney.

It is the current author's belief that Orcadian Grooved Ware is that rarest of phenomena, an invented tradition. This makes sense in terms of the social dynamics and power play of later 4th millennium Orkney, as discussed elsewhere (e.g. this volume, Chapter 16; Sheridan 2014; Sheridan and Schulting 2020; cf. Bayliss *et al.* 2017). Essentially, there appears to have been competition for power and authority between prosperous groups of farmers in Orkney, from at least as early as *c.* 3500 cal BC, played out in the construction of bigger and more ostentatious monuments for the dead (Sheridan and Schulting 2020 and see also Chapter 16). During the 32nd century cal BC the stakes in this strategy of competitive conspicuous consumption were raised when one group – based in the west Mainland – indulged in what could be described as 'cosmological acquisition' (cf. Helms 1988). Using knowledge obtained through pre-existing, extensive networks of contacts along the Atlantic façade of Britain, they travelled to the Boyne Valley to witness the wonders of the massive passage tombs of Newgrange, Knowth and Dowth and the seasonal (especially midwinter) ceremonies that occurred there, and brought back big ideas, building Maeshowe as an Orcadian version of Newgrange (Sheridan and Schulting 2020). It also appears that they travelled yet further, to the Continent (probably north-west France or western Iberia), bringing back the Orkney Vole as a handy source of food on the journey; the aforementioned genetic data for this rodent indicate that it was first released on Mainland Orkney.

These ambitious and innovative Orcadians set out to create a new world order, featuring themselves on top. In addition to inventing Grooved Ware as a distinctively new pottery tradition, over subsequent generations they also invented the stone circle within a henge (and arguably also the timber circle, though none has yet been found in Orkney) as a wholly novel monument type. Other innovations include nucleated settlements (such as Barnhouse and Skara Brae), ostentatious jewellery and dress accessories, and unusually shaped carved stone objects which were used both as weapons and as weapons of social exclusion (see Clarke *et al.* 1985 and Card *et al.* 2020 for examples). As people from far and wide came to witness the magnificent monuments and participate in the midwinter solstice ceremonies, just as they had previously done in the Boyne Valley, the Ness of Brodgar site arguably developed as a place where numerous important 'pilgrims' could be accommodated and fed – hence its huge piered buildings.

In their invention of Grooved Ware, this powerful and influential group deliberately appropriated and, importantly, adapted the sacred symbols that they had seen on the Irish passage tombs – in particular, the zig-zag and meandering lines and the nested lozenges (cf., for example, Eogan and Shee Twohig 2022). This *bricolage* approach to cultural appropriation can also be seen in the designs pecked into some Maeshowe-type passage tombs, with the distinctive 'horned spiral', as seen at Eday Manse and Pierowall, constituting an Orcadian 'twist' on the Boyne Valley spiral motif (Clarke *et al.* 1985, figs 3.14, 7.21). It is also apparent on a slab from Pool, decorated with rows of nested zig-zag lines with dots along the bottom (Hunter 2007, illus. 3.18). It may reasonably be assumed that these symbols possessed specific meanings, deployed in the new ideology and the new practices that were being forged by this dominant group in Orkney.

Relationship between Grooved Ware and the round- (and pointed- and saggy-) based pottery in Orkney

The question of the chronological relationship between Grooved Ware and what has traditionally been termed 'Unstan Ware' – specifically, whether there was a neat succession – has been much debated (e.g. Clarke 1983). The evidence from Pool demonstrates the existence of an overlap, in its fusion of design elements of the two traditions. (Elements of

Grooved Ware design also appear on the Knap of Howar pottery, as discussed by Audrey Henshall in 1983.) Moreover, the growing number of radiocarbon dates are making it increasingly clear that the appearance of Grooved Ware did not herald an immediate end to the manufacture of non-Grooved Ware pottery in Orkney (Bayliss *et al.* 2017; Sheridan and Schulting 2020, fig. 18.7). While some dates fall within the late 4th millennium calibration plateau, others have calibrated ranges extending into the beginning of the 3rd. Once again, the direct dating of absorbed lipids will be a useful tool in clarifying the extent of this chronological overlap.

SUBSEQUENT DEVELOPMENT OF ORCADIAN GROOVED WARE, *c.* 2900–*c.* 2500 CAL BC

In their description of the Grooved Ware from Skara Brae (Chapter 3), Ann MacSween and David Clarke set out the trajectory of development at that settlement, with its initial phase of Grooved Ware use dating to *2900–2825 cal BC* and its second phase dating to *2740–2500 cal BC*. As at Pool Phase 3 (which appears roughly contemporary with Skara Brae Phase 2), and at Links of Noltland (Sheridan 1999), where decoration is present, it is dominated by the use of applied motifs, especially cordons (either plain or embellished with slashes, incised lines or impressions), pellets and 'doughnuts', deployed in a variety of designs, and on vessels of various sizes and with variously-shaped rims (including undulating 'pie-crust' rims and others with projecting pellets).

While rare, the use of incision as the sole decorative technique did not altogether disappear, as the iconic 'lozenge with spiral' sherd from Skara Brae makes clear (Chapter 3, fig. 3.9). This is the sherd whose motif adorned the cover of Piggott's *Neolithic cultures of the British Isles* (1954) and, notwithstanding MacSween and Clarke's reasoned critique of the way the motif has been extrapolated in the past, its resemblance to the design on the kerbstone at the back of the main passage tomb at Newgrange, opposite the entrance with its midwinter solstice alignment, is hard to deny (Fig. 2.6). This, and other representations of spirals on Orcadian Grooved Ware pottery (Fig. 2.6), suggest (to this author, at least) that visitations from Orkney to the Boyne Valley did not just take place during the 32nd or 31st centuries cal BC, but continued into the 29th century cal BC. By the same token, visitations to Orkney from far afield were not restricted to the period of the earliest use of Grooved Ware in Orkney, as is clear from the pottery from Pit 3196 at Barrow Hills, Radley, Oxfordshire (Barclay and Halpin 1999, figs. 4.32, 4.33). This includes a vessel with a relief 'network' design akin to that seen at Links of Noltland (Sheridan 1999, illus. 12.6, 5). The Radley assemblage could theoretically date to *c.* 2900 cal BC (as opposed to the 2600–2000 cal BC date (BM-2706) previously obtained; the pit contents need to be re-dated).

As the burgeoning amounts of Grooved Ware from the Ness of Brodgar make clear, there was variability, on a site-by-site basis, in the evolution of Orcadian Grooved Ware over the first half of the 3rd millennium, even though elements of a shared overall design 'vocabulary' can be discerned. It was at the Ness of Brodgar that the use of red-, white- and black-painted pottery was recognised, by Roy Towers (Fig. 2.7 and back cover; Jones *et al.* 2019; Card *et al.* 2020, fig. 20.9). This appears to be a feature specific to the Ness.

Figure 2.6. Top: the Skara Brae 'spiral and lozenge' sherd with its design comparandum *at Newgrange passage tomb, Co. Meath, kerbstone 67 (images: National Museums Scotland and Anthony Murphy/www.mythicalireland.com). Bottom: sherd with spiral decoration from Links of Noltland (reproduced by permission of Historic Environment Scotland (HES) Licence no. IMSL-R-205195).*

Also idiosyncratic at the Ness is a pot that may be a skeuomorph of a sewn animal skin container (Fig. 2.7); and a specific manufacturing technique, featuring the use of a recessed groove for keying in applied cordons, has also been identified by Roy Towers in that assemblage (Towers and Card 2015). Interestingly, neither at Ness of Brodgar nor at Skara Brae does the pottery bear the kind of decoration (Thomas 2016) seen pecked or incised into structural and other stone at these sites.

It remains to be seen, when comparative post-excavation analysis of the massive Ness of Brodgar and Links of Noltland assemblages takes place, whether the near-complete vessel at the latter site (Fig. 2.8) constitutes a peculiarity there. There are, however, other elements of the Links of Noltland assemblage that are held in common with other Orcadian assemblages, and these include elaborately decorated vessels, of a type that could be dubbed 'statement pots' (Fig. 2.9). Often large, and including the very large vessel from a Phase 1 context at

Figure 2.7. Distinctive features of Ness of Brodgar Grooved Ware: 1. Use of colour: the cordon has been painted red; 2. Groove for keying in an applied cordon; 3. Unique pot resembling a sewn animal skin container (height c. *150 mm) (photos: Roy Towers, drawing: Alette Blom; images reproduced courtesy of Ness of Brodgar Trust/ORCA).*

Figure 2.8. Near-complete pot from Links of Noltland (reproduced by permission of HES).

Skara Brae shown in Chapter 3, Figure 3.6, these feature all-over decoration, usually by applied motifs, including cordons, pellets and 'doughnuts'. These must have been possessions for ostentatious display, probably used for feasting and for prominent storage inside houses; the very large example from Skara Brae has encrusted organic residues, demonstrating its use for cooking food. As Figure 2.9 demonstrates, there was clearly scope for creative licence in their decoration. The example from Crossiecrown, *c.* 420 mm high and with a rim diameter of 430 mm, comes from a layer of midden dated to 3270–2910 cal BC (SUERC-4858) and 3020–2880 cal BC (SUERC-4857) (Griffiths 2016, 262; Jones *et al.* 2016, 352–3, fig. 11.3.10).

What is notable by its absence, however, is the kind of Grooved Ware that is usually referred to as belonging to the 'Durrington Walls sub-style'. While vertical cordons are indeed present on some Orcadian Grooved Ware (including the large Skara Brae pot), they are not deployed in the basketry-skeuomorphic way of these other pots, of which the most northerly example is in Inverness (Copper, Chapter 4). Furthermore, with the aforementioned exception of the Radley pot, Grooved Ware south of Orkney does not echo the 'developed' kinds of Orcadian Grooved Ware; clearly regionalised trajectories of change were occurring (despite the widespread distribution of 'Durrington Walls sub-style' pots).

THE END OF THE GROOVED WARE TRADITION IN ORKNEY AND THE APPEARANCE OF BEAKER POTTERY

Much still needs to be discovered about the latest use of Grooved Ware in Orkney (cf. Chapter 4), and information about its latest use at the Ness of Brodgar and Links of Noltland will have to await further work. It should be noted, however, that the inflationary 'bubble' of construction at the Ness appears to have 'burst' by around 2800 cal BC and there was a considerable gap between then and the next episode of activity at that site, namely the deposition of huge numbers of cattle remains among the ruins of the large communal Structure 10 (Card *et al.* 2018). That episode's date has been modelled as occurring either in the mid-25th century cal BC or the late 24th/23rd century cal BC. Significantly, it was not Grooved Ware but Beaker pottery that was associated with that feasting episode; judging from what is known about Beaker dating more generally, it seems most likely that the episode occurred at the latter date. How much earlier than that Grooved Ware use ceased at the Ness remains to be seen; but at Skara Brae and Pool, the latest dates for its use are *c.* 2500 cal BC. As discussed elsewhere (Clarke *et al.* 2016), and despite recent

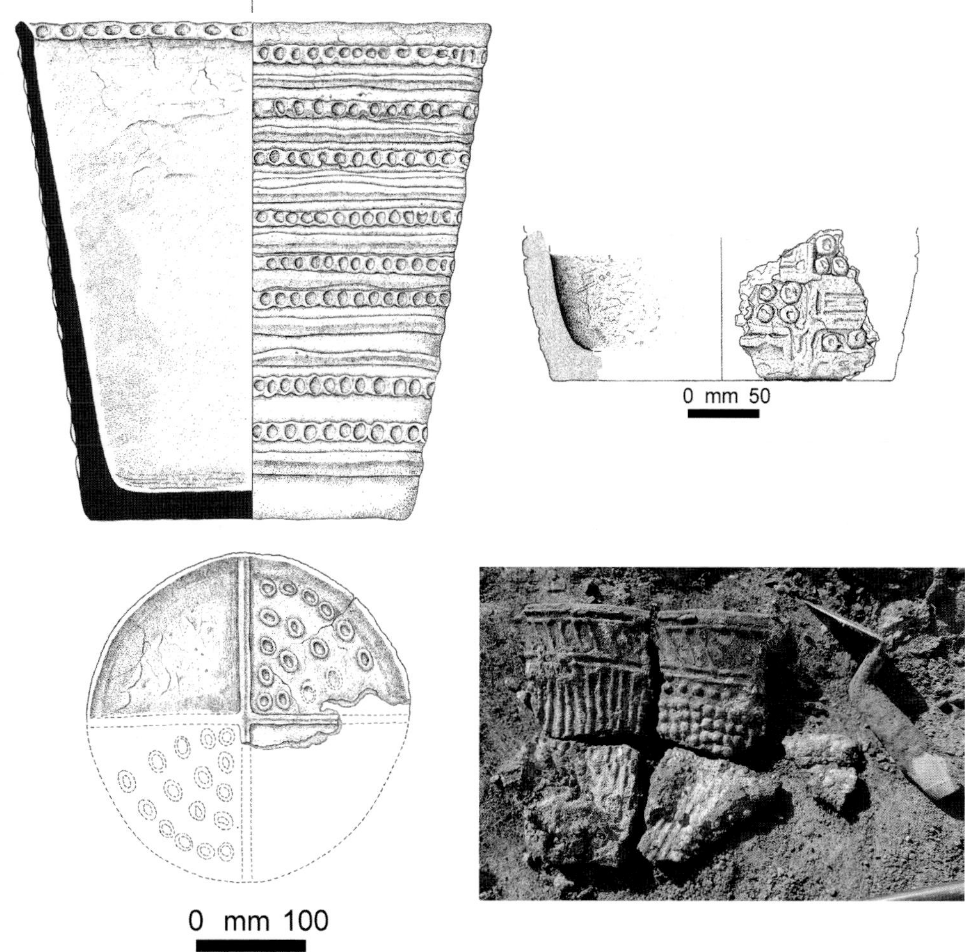

Figure 2.9. Three examples of 'statement pots': Left: Crossiecrown (from Jones et al. *2016); right: Links of Noltland (drawing from Sheridan 2011, photo: Roland Spencer-Jones, reproduced with permission of HES). See also Chapter 3, Figures 3.6 and 3.8, for further examples.*

claims to the contrary (Dulias *et al.* 2022), we are not dealing with any significant influx of 'Beaker People' in Orkney (even though people with steppe ancestry certainly did arrive, though not directly from the Continent). There is no example of the earliest, Continental-style Beaker in the archipelago; and there is currently no evidence that the appearance of Beaker pottery heralded any significant social (or other) changes. Whenever it occurred, the demise of the use of Grooved Ware is most likely to relate to internal social changes, i.e. the collapse of the early 3rd millennium social system (as discussed, for example, in Clarke *et al.* 2016 and Bunting *et al.* 2022).

CONCLUSIONS

While our understanding of Orcadian Grooved Ware and its significance has been transformed, even since 1999, clearly there is still much work to do, especially in clarifying the end-point of Grooved Ware use and what happened thereafter. We await the results of outstanding post-excavation projects with interest.

ACKNOWLEDGEMENTS

Roy Towers and Ann MacSween are thanked for sharing their expertise, and the following are thanked for allowing me to reproduce their images: Lynda Aiano, Nick Card, Anthony Murphy, Woody Musgrove, Colin Richards, Anna Ritchie, Roland Spencer-Jones, Richard Strachan and Roy Towers. My co-editors are thanked for their comments on a previous draft.

REFERENCES

Barclay, A. and Halpin, C. 1999. *Excavations at Barrow Hills, Radley, Oxfordshire. Volume 1: the Neolithic and Bronze Age monument complex.* Oxford: Oxford Archaeological Unit.

Bayliss, A., Marshall, P., Richards, C. and Whittle, A. 2017. Islands of history: the Late Neolithic timescape of Orkney. *Antiquity* 91, 1171–88.

Bond, J.M., Braby, A., Dockrill, S.J., Downes, J.M. and Richards, C. 1995. Stove Bay: a new Orcadian grooved ware settlement. *Scottish Archaeological Review* 9/10, 125–30.

Bunting, M.J., Farrell, M., Dunbar, E., Reimer, P., Bayliss, A., Marshall, P. *et al.* 2022. Landscapes for Neolithic people in Mainland, Orkney. *Journal of World Prehistory* 35, 87–107.

Card, N., Edmonds, M. and Mitchell, A. (eds) 2020. *The Ness of Brodgar: as it stands.* Kirkwall: The Orcadian.

Card, N., Mainland, I., Timpany, S., Batt, C., Bronk Ramsey, C., Dunbar, E., Reimer, P.J., Bayliss, A., Marshall, P. and Whittle, A. 2018. To cut a long story short: formal chronological modelling for the late Neolithic site of Ness of Brodgar, Orkney. *European Journal of Archaeology* 21(2), 217–63.

Childe, V.G. 1952. Re-excavation of the chambered cairn of Quoyness, Sanday, on behalf of the Ministry of Works in 1951–2. *Proceedings of the Society of Antiquaries of Scotland* 86 (1951–52), 121–39.

Childe, V.G. and Grant, W.G. 1939. A Stone Age settlement at the Braes of Rinyo, Rousay, Orkney (first report). *Proceedings of the Society of Antiquaries of Scotland* 73 (1938–39), 6–31.

Childe, V.G. and Grant, W.G. 1947. A Stone Age settlement at the Braes of Rinyo, Rousay, Orkney (second report). *Proceedings of the Society of Antiquaries of Scotland* 81 (1946–47), 16–42.

Clarke, D.V. 1983. Rinyo and the Orcadian Neolithic. In A. O'Connor and D.V. Clarke (eds), *From the Stone Age to the 'Forty-five*, 45–56. Edinburgh: John Donald.

Clarke, D.V., Cowie, T.G. and Foxon, A. 1985. *Symbols of power at the time of Stonehenge.* Edinburgh: Her Majesty's Stationery Office.

Clarke, D.V., Sheridan, J.A., Shepherd, A., Sharples, N., Armour-Chelu, M., Hamlet, L., Bronk Ramsey, C., Dunbar, E., Reimer, P.J., Marshall, P. and Whittle, A. 2016. The end of the world, or just 'goodbye to all that'? Contextualising the red deer from Links of Noltland, Westray, within late 3rd-millennium cal BC Orkney. *Proceedings of the Society of Antiquaries of Scotland* 146, 57–89.

Cleal, R. and MacSween, A (eds) 1999. *Grooved Ware in Great Britain and Ireland.* Oxford: Oxbow Books.

Coles, D. and Miles, M. 2013. The Neolithic settlement at Green Farm. *Orkney Archaeology Society Newsletter* 9, 3–8.

Connolly, R. and MacSween, A. 2003. A possible Neolithic settlemewnt at Milton of Leys, Inverness. *Proceedings of the Society of Antiquaries of Scotland* 113, 35–45.

Copper, M., Hamilton, D. and Gibson, A. 2021. Tracing the lines: Scottish Grooved Ware trajectories beyond Orkney. *Proceedings of the Society of Antiquaries of Scotland* 150, 81–117.

Davidson, J.L. and Henshall, A.S. 1989. *The chambered cairns of Orkney*. Edinburgh: Edinburgh University Press.

Dockrill, S.J. 2007. *Investigations in Sanday, Orkney Vol 2: Tofts Ness, Sanday, an island landscape through 3000 years of prehistory*. Kirkwall: The Orcadian.

Dulias, K., Foody, M.G.B., Justeau, P., Silva, M., Martiniano, R., Oteo-García, G. *et al.* 2022. Ancient DNA at the edge of the world: Continental immigration and the persistence of male lineages in Bronze Age Orkney. *Proceedings of the National Academy of Sciences of the United States* 119(8) e2108001119. https://doi.org/10.1073/pnas.2108001119.

Eogan, G. and Shee Twohig, E. 2022. *The megalithic art of the passage tombs at Knowth, Co. Meath*. Dublin: Royal Irish Academy.

Griffiths, S. 2016. Beside the ocean of time: a chronology of Neolithic burial monuments and houses in Orkney. In C. Richards and R. Jones (eds) 2016, 254–302.

Helms, M. 1988. *Ulysses' sail: an ethnographic odyssey of power, knowledge, and geographical distance*. Princeton: Princeton University Press.

Henshall, A.S. 1983. Pottery: catalogue and discussion. In A. Ritchie, Excavation of a Neolithic farmstead at Knap of Howar, Papa Westray, Orkney, 59–74. *Proceedings of the Society of Antiquaries of Scotland* 113, 40–121.

Henshall, A.S. 2009. The pottery. In A. Ritchie, *On the fringe of Neolithic Europe: excavation of a chambered cairn on the Holm of Papa Westray, Orkney*, 35–8. Edinburgh: Society of Antiquaries of Scotland.

Henshall, A.S. and Savory, L. 1976. Small finds from the 1973–4 excavations. In J.N.G. Ritchie, The Stones of Stenness, Orkney, 22–5. *Proceedings of the Society of Antiquaries of Scotland* 107 (1975–76), 1–60.

Hunter, J. 2007. *Investigations in Sanday, Orkney. Vol 1: excavations at Pool, Sanday, a multi-period settlement from Neolithic to Late Norse times*. Kirkwall: The Orcadian.

Hunter, F. and Sheridan, J.A. (eds) 2016. *Ancient lives: object, people and place in early Scotland. Essays for David V Clarke on his 70th birthday*, 213–32. Leiden: Sidestone Press.

Jones, A.M. 2005. The Grooved Ware from Barnhouse. In C. Richards (ed.) 2005, 261–82.

Jones, A.M., Jones, R., Tully, G., Maritan, L., Mukherjee, A., Evershed, R. *et al.* 2016. Prehistoric pottery from sites within the Bay of Firth: Stonehall, Crossiecrown, Wideford Hill, Brae of Smerquoy, Muckquoy, Ramberry and Knowes of Trotty. In C. Richards and R. Jones (eds) 2016, 303–412.

Jones, R., Towers, R., Card, N. and Odling, N. 2019. Analysis of coloured Grooved Ware sherds from the Ness of Brodgar, Orkney. *Journal of Archaeological Science: Reports* 28 (1),10204. DOI: 10.1016/j.jasrep.2019.102014.

MacSween, A. 1997. The pottery. In J. Barber, *The excavation of a stalled cairn at the Point of Cott, Westray, Orkney*, 27–9. Edinburgh: Scottish Trust for Archaeological Research.

MacSween, A., Hunter, J., Sheridan, J.A., Bond, J., Bronk Ramsey, C., Reimer, P.J., Bayliss, A., Griffiths, S. and Whittle, A. 2015. Refining the chronology of the Neolithic settlement at Pool, Sanday, Orkney. *Proceedings of the Prehistoric Society* 81, 283–310.

Martínovká, N., Barnett, R., Cucchi, T., Struchen, R., Pascal, M., Pascal, M. et al. 2013. Divergent evolutionary processes associated with colonization of offshore islands. *Molecular Ecology* 22, 5205–20.

Piggott, S. 1936. The pottery from the submerged surface. In S.H. Warren, S. Piggott, J.G.D. Clark, M.C. Burkitt and H. and M.E. Godwin, Archaeology of the submerged land surface of the Essex coast, 186–201. *Proceedings of the Prehistoric Society* 2, 178–210.

Piggott, S. 1954. *The Neolithic cultures of the British Isles.* Cambridge: Cambridge University Press.
Renfrew, A.C. 1979. *Investigations in Orkney.* London: Society of Antiquaries of London.
Richards, C. (ed.) 2005. *Dwelling among the monuments: the Neolithic village of Barnhouse, Maeshowe passage grave and surrounding monuments at Stenness, Orkney.* Cambridge: McDonald Institute for Archaeological Research.
Richards, C. and Jones, R. (eds) 2016. *The development of Neolithic house societies in Orkney: investigations in the Bay of Firth, Mainland, Orkney (1994–2014)*, 332–57. Oxford: Oxbow Books.
Richards, C., Downes, J., Gee, C. and Carter, S. 2016a. Materializing house societies in Orkney. In C. Richards and R. Jones (eds) 2016, 224–53.
Richards, C., Jones, A.M., MacSween, A., Sheridan, J.A., Dunbar, E., Reimer, P., Bayliss, A., Griffiths, S. and Whittle, A. 2016b. Settlement duration and materiality: formal chronological models for the development of Barnhouse, a Grooved Ware Settlement in Orkney. *Proceedings of the Prehistoric Society* 81, 283–310.
Shepherd, A. 2016. Skara Brae life studies: overlaying the embedded images. In F. Hunter and J.A. Sheridan (eds) 2016, 213–32.
Sheridan, J.A. 1999. Grooved Ware from the Links of Noltland, Westray, Orkney. In R. Cleal and A. MacSween (eds) 1999, 112–24.
Sheridan, J.A. 2011. The pottery. In H. Moore and G. Wilson, *Shifting sands. Links of Noltland, Westray: interim report on Neolithic and Bronze Age excavations, 2007–09*, 92–5. Edinburgh: Historic Scotland.
Sheridan, J.A. 2014. Little and large: the miniature 'carved stone ball' beads from the eastern tomb at Knowth, Ireland, and their broader significance. In R.-M. Arbogast and A. Greffier-Richard (eds), *Entre archéologie et écologie, une préhistoire de tous les milieux. Mélanges offerts à Pierre Pétrequin*, 303–14. Besançon: Presses universitaires de Franche-Comté.
Sheridan, J.A. 2016. Scottish Neolithic pottery in 2016: the big picture and some details of the narrative. In F. Hunter and J.A. Sheridan (eds) 2016, 189–212.
Sheridan, J.A. and Pétrequin, P. 2014. Constructing a narrative for the Neolithic of Britain and Ireland: the use of 'hard science' and archaeological reasoning. In A. Whittle and P. Bickle (eds), *Early farmers: the view from archaeology and science*, 369–390. Oxford: Oxford University Press/the British Academy.
Sheridan, J.A. and Schulting, R.J. 2020 Making sense of Scottish Neolithic funerary monuments: tracing trajectories and understanding their rationale. In A.-B. Gebauer, L. Sørensen, A. Teather and A.C. Valera (eds), *Monumentalising Life in the Neolithic: narratives of change and continuity*, 195–215. Oxford: Oxbow Books.
Simpson, J.Y. 1866. Appendix: on ancient sculpturings of cups and concentric rings, & c. *Proceedings of the Society of Antiquaries of Scotland* 6 (1864–66).
Stevenson, R.B.K. 1946. Notes (3): jottings on ancient pottery. *Proceedings of the Society of Antiquaries of Scotland* 80 (1945–46), 141–3.
Thomas, A. 2010. The Braes of Ha'breck, Wyre. Excavation. *Discovery and Excavation in Scotland* 11, 121–3.
Thomas, A. 2016. *Art and architecture in Neolithic Orkney: process, temporality and context.* Oxford: Archaeopress.
Towers, R. and Card, N. 2015. Technological adaptation in Grooved Ware pottery from the Ness of Brodgar, Orkney, or how to make your cordons stick. *Scottish Archaeological Journal* 36–37, 51–63.
Yarrington, C. 1984. Pottery. In N.M. Sharples, Excavations at Pierowall Quarry, Westray, Orkney, 93–5. *Proceedings of the Society of Antiquaries of Scotland* 114, 75–125.

Chapter 3

Skara Brae: the significance of the Grooved Ware assemblages

Ann MacSween and David Clarke

Skara Brae in Orkney is one of Scotland's most instantly recognisable sites. Its preservation beneath a blanket of sand left walls standing and furniture in place, allowing for its current presentation and use as a popular visitor site managed by Historic Environment Scotland (Fig. 3.1). Skara Brae, the Maeshowe passage tomb, the Ring of Brodgar and the Stones of Stenness, along with some unexcavated sites, form *The Heart of Neolithic Orkney* World Heritage Site (https://whc.unesco.org/en/list/514/). Yet in spite of its high profile, most visitors to Skara Brae are unaware of the extent of the research that has been carried out over the past 50 years, investigations that will allow us to refine our understanding of Skara Brae's place in the Neolithic of Orkney.

One element of that research is to report on the 5000 sherds of pottery recovered during investigations and excavations on the site. This paper sets out the significance of the pottery assemblages recovered during Professor Vere Gordon Childe's excavations at Skara Brae in 1927–30 (Childe 1930; 1931), and during David Clarke's excavations in 1972–3, and explains how their study has contributed to our understanding of the use of the site.

The pottery also has significance for understanding not only Skara Brae's place in Neolithic Orcadian society and the interpretation of the later Neolithic in Orkney (see Sheridan this volume, Chapter 2), but also for the history of Grooved Ware studies. We will introduce the site and the excavations, then go on to describe the assemblages, before linking the pottery into wider questions of chronology.

EXCAVATIONS AT SKARA BRAE

Childe's work at Skara Brae was excavation in the loosest sense. He was there to observe and record as best he could the archaeological aspects of a clearing-out exercise intended to turn Skara Brae into a viable visitor experience. Exposed by a major storm around 1850, the site saw desultory digging during the rest of that century and the start of the 20th century. After Skara Brae was placed in Guardianship in 1924, a sea wall was built to prevent further storm damage. There then followed four seasons of work at the site to prepare it for visitors (Fig. 3.2).

Childe was only present during the last three seasons and work continued when he was absent. His supervision of the works began in 1928 and in his volume describing the excavations (Childe 1931, 5–6) he noted that:

> *When I reached the site that year, Skara Brae appeared as a grass-grown sand-dune from the seaward side of which protruded the ruinous walls of five huts and some sections of a connecting passage. A little excavation, however, revealed that the sand was only superficial. On removing a couple of feet of it, we would come upon a very tough clay-like soil, full of broken bones, shells, pottery and implements ….*

The primary concern was to identify and stabilise walls and to clear out the houses, with the collection of archaeological data of secondary importance. Consequently, most of the material culture recovered during this period was from the final phase of occupation and there is virtually no detailed contextual information.

David Clarke's excavations in 1972 and 1973 were designed to recover data that would illuminate three key aspects of the site: its chronology; the economic activities associated with the site; and its contemporary environment. As was the case with Childe's work, there was no possibility of demolishing any existing structures. The work was restricted to two areas. The main area, Trench I, was in the centre of the settlement bounded by passages A, B and F, and by House 7 (Fig. 3.2). The other, Trench II, was at the edge of the settlement where Childe had encountered waterlogged material in one of 12 test pits he dug to investigate the feasibility of roofing the entire site. These new excavations established a threefold occupation of the site (Fig. 3.3). Phase 0, dated to *3360–3160 cal BC* (Shepherd 2016, fig. 5), was represented by only a small amount of apparently pre-Grooved Ware occupation. This was followed by two phases of Grooved Ware occupation with a short but significant break between the two (relating to inundation by sand), Phase I dating to *2900–2825 cal BC* and Phase 2 to *2740–2500 cal BC* (date estimates after Bayliss *et al.* 2017, fig. 5).

Clarke's excavations collected considerable data which helped satisfy the project's key research aims – in particular the site's chronology and its ecofactual basis. The areas available for excavation restricted the definitive conclusions that could be drawn on major developments or changes within the three phases of occupation. The recovered finds assemblages, although substantial, were only in a few instances of sufficient size to enable distinct variability through time to be discerned, but one such instance of material ample enough to support such judgements is the pottery (Clarke 1976).

Figure 3.1. Looking across the site of Skara Brae, Orkney Mainland (photo: Ann MacSween).

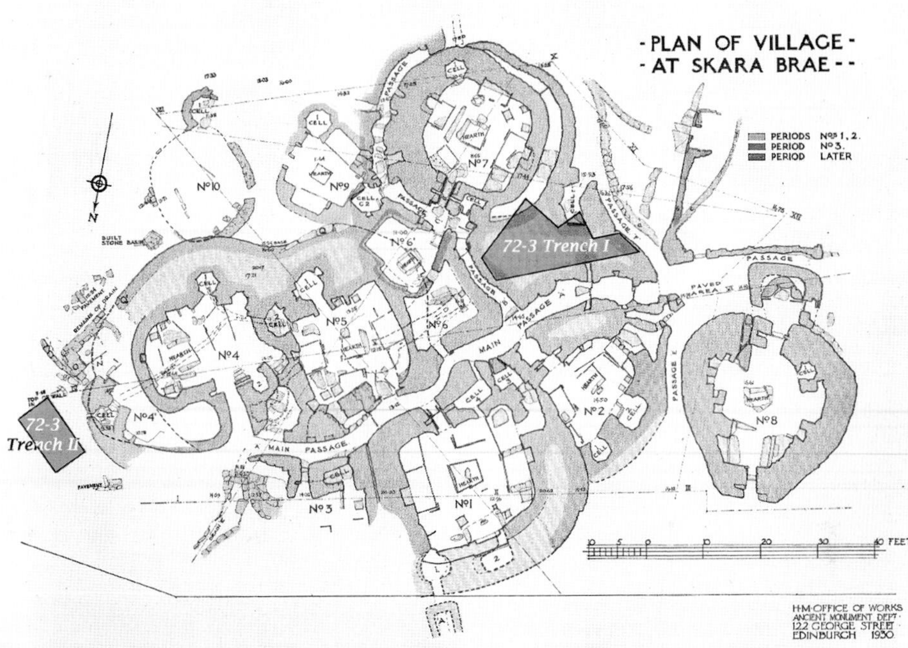

Figure 3.2. Childe's plan of Skara Brae (1931, pl. LX) with location of Clarke's 1972–3 trenches indicated (illustration: Alexandra Shepherd).

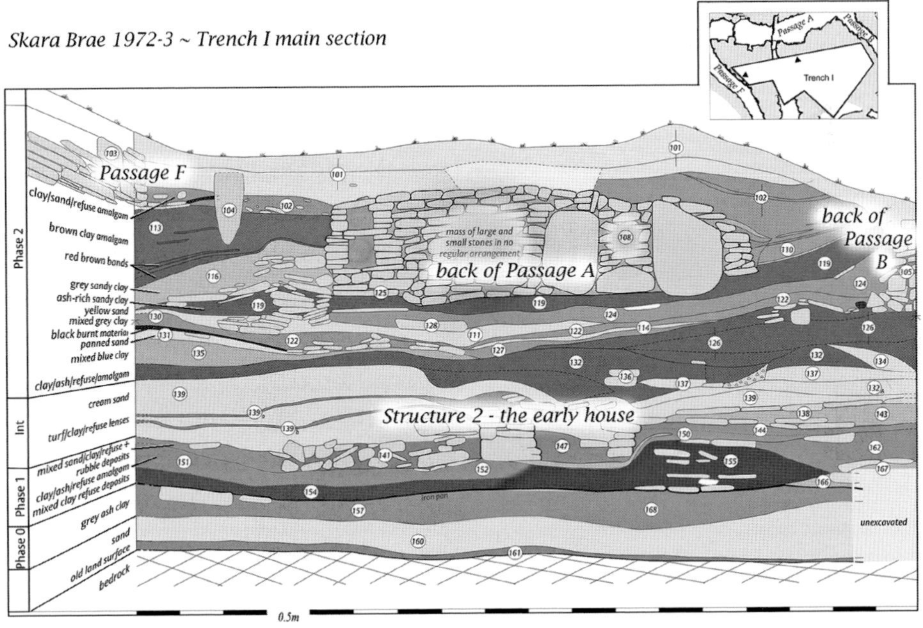

Figure 3.3. Skara Brae 1972–3: Trench 1 main section (illustration: Alexandra Shepherd).

SUMMARY OF THE CLARKE AND CHILDE ASSEMBLAGES

Classic illustrative reconstructions of the interior of the Skara Brae houses, including one from the 1989 site guide (Fig. 3.4; Clarke and Maguire 1989), show large vessels in place on the shelves of dressers but the reality of the pottery assemblages as excavated is very different. Clarke's excavations produced just under 5000 sherds of pottery, many of them tiny and abraded. Vessels were often represented by only one or two sherds. For example, in context 110 (occupation deposits preceding the site's final construction stage), 286 sherds were recovered. Detailed examination and recording, and comparison of fabric, colour, surface finish and decoration, concluded that, in that context, 208 vessels were represented, with rim sherds included for 18 of these. Of these 208 vessels, 156 were represented by one sherd, 36 vessels by two sherds, nine by three sherds, five by four sherds, one by five sherds, and one vessel by six sherds. This is typical of the nature of the pottery assemblages from the occupation deposits and is discussed further below.

In analysing the assemblages from Skara Brae, the finds were recorded and the sequence for Clarke's excavations was established, and then that understanding was applied to re-evaluating the finds from Childe's excavations (Fig. 3.5). Despite the considerable deposits removed during Childe's investigations, only 368 sherds are present in the assemblage held in the National Museums Scotland collections, with an additional 200 sherds distributed at the behest of the landowner between the British Museum and museums in Orkney. A high proportion of the vessels (83%) are represented by rim, basal and decorated sherds. In contrast, of the full assemblage recovered by Clarke's excavations, only 29% of vessels are represented by rim, basal and decorated sherds. A bias in collection strategies during Childe's work, with the jettisoning of undiagnostic wall sherds, is indicated by this comparison.

Of Clarke's assemblage, a very small amount of pottery was recovered from the Trench I Phase 0 deposits dating to *3360–3160 cal BC* and representing the earliest human activity on the site. The rim sherds are typical of those found on round-based vessels, and the assemblage includes 'corky' sherds with flat voids, indicating the addition of shell to the fabric mix. This type of pottery is not found in the Grooved Ware phases at Skara Brae. Similar shell-tempered pottery has been found on other Orcadian sites, including chambered cairns such as Point

Figure 3.4. Detail of House 7 interior reconstruction from Historic Scotland Skara Brae guidebook (Clarke and Maguire 1989, 17; illustration: Bil Fulton; reproduced by kind permission of Historic Environment Scotland).

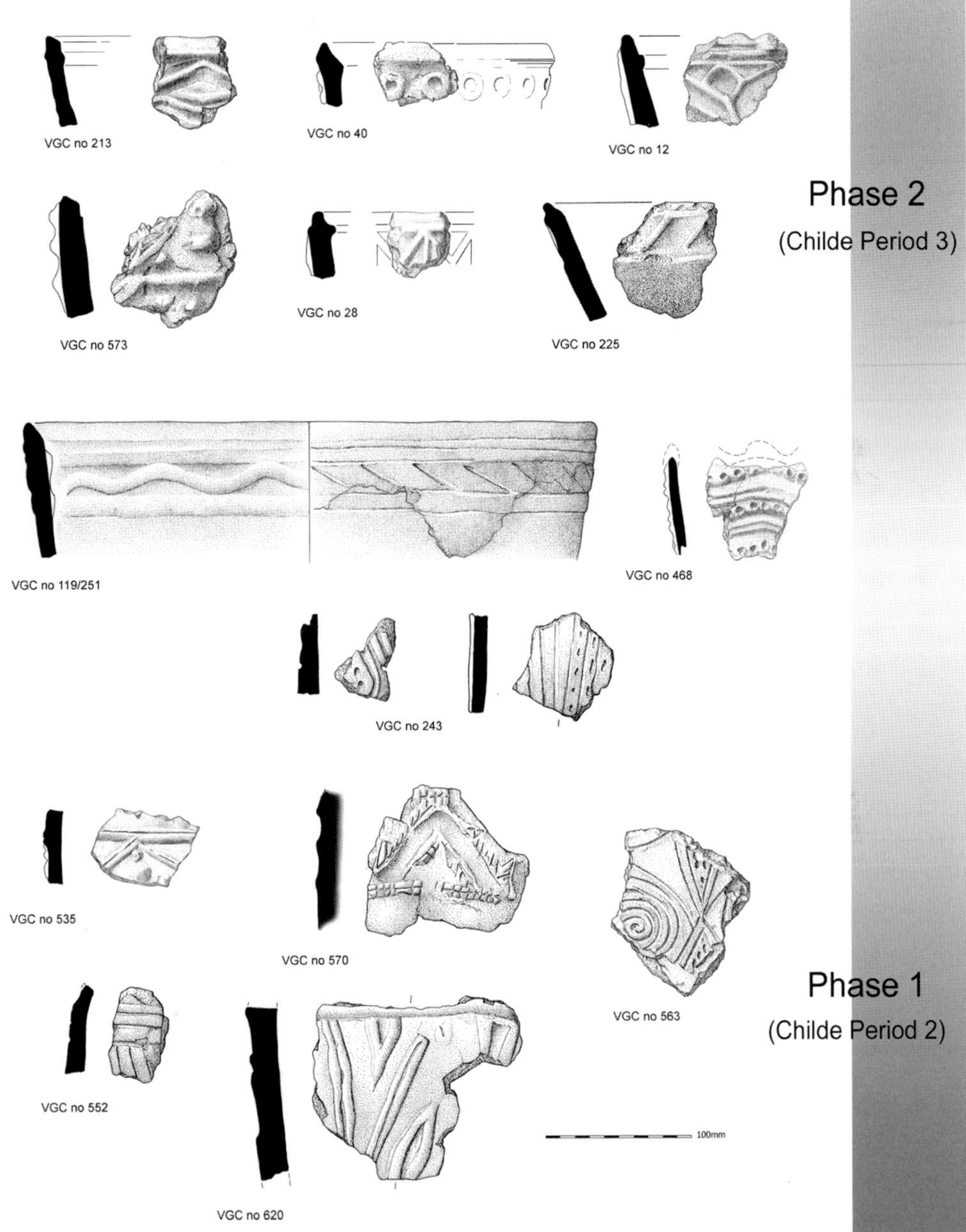

Figure 3.5. The only decorated sherds from Childe's assemblage with precise contextual information (illustration: Alexandra Shepherd). Note: 'VGC' stands for 'Vere Gordon Childe'.

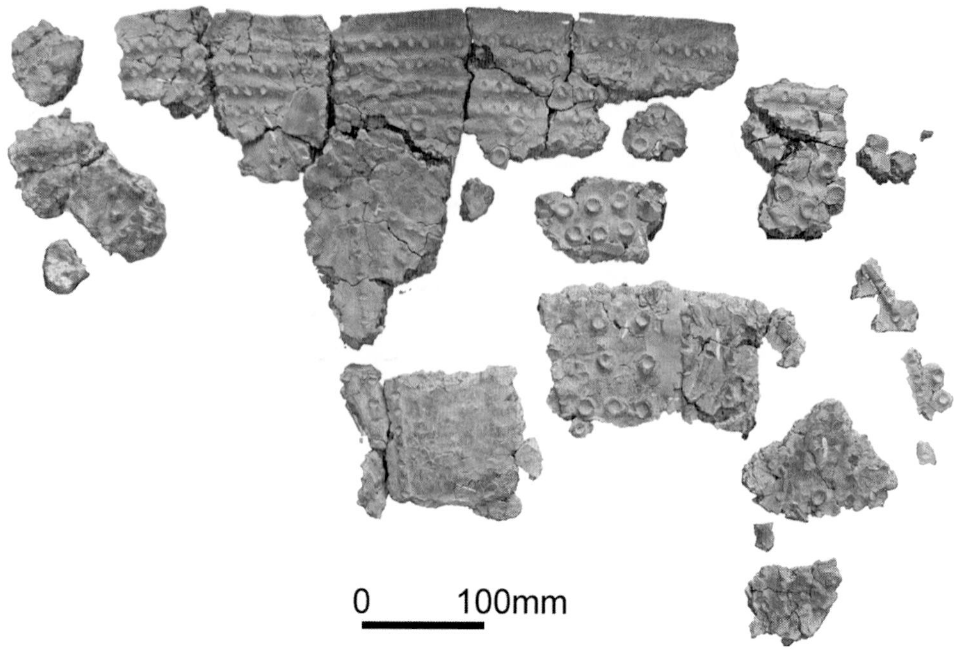

Figure 3.6. Large, squashed vessel, V3405 (NMS X.HA 2877) from accumulated waste material on the periphery of the settlement, Trench II. The estimated rim and body diameter of this tub-shaped pot is c. *450 mm (photo: Alison Sheridan).*

of Cott (MacSween 1997), and in the pre-Grooved Ware contexts of domestic sites including Rinyo (Childe and Grant 1947, 36–7), Pool (MacSween 2007) and the Ness of Brodgar (Towers and MacSween 2020, 257).

The typical vessel shapes throughout the two Grooved Ware phases at Skara Brae, suggested by reconstructions from remnant bases and the very few almost intact vessels from the later levels, are buckets, flowerpots and vertical-walled tubs, in a wide range of sizes from thumb pots to vessels the size of a small saucepan, to much larger pots, with rim diameters in excess of 400 mm (Fig. 3.6). Many of the vessels have large angular rock fragments forming part of the fabric and Childe commented on the coarse nature of the pottery. From analysis of the ceramic thin sections of some of the Skara Brae sherds that were prepared by David Williams, the fragments were most commonly dyke rock (mainly camptonite, available locally to the site). Because of the amount of rock present by volume – often over 50% – and the fact that it is mainly angular, it has been assumed that these fragments are likely to have been deliberate additions of crushed stone (as a filler) rather than natural inclusions in the clay.

That said, experience of a modern potter using clay gathered in the vicinity of Skara Brae was that, to get a viable fabric, the challenge lay in *removing* stone fragments that adhered to the clay on collection, rather than adding more, so this may have depended on the nature of the clay source being used (Alexandra Shepherd, pers. comm.). We know that there were plentiful deposits of clay near to the site. Shepherd (2016, 224) notes

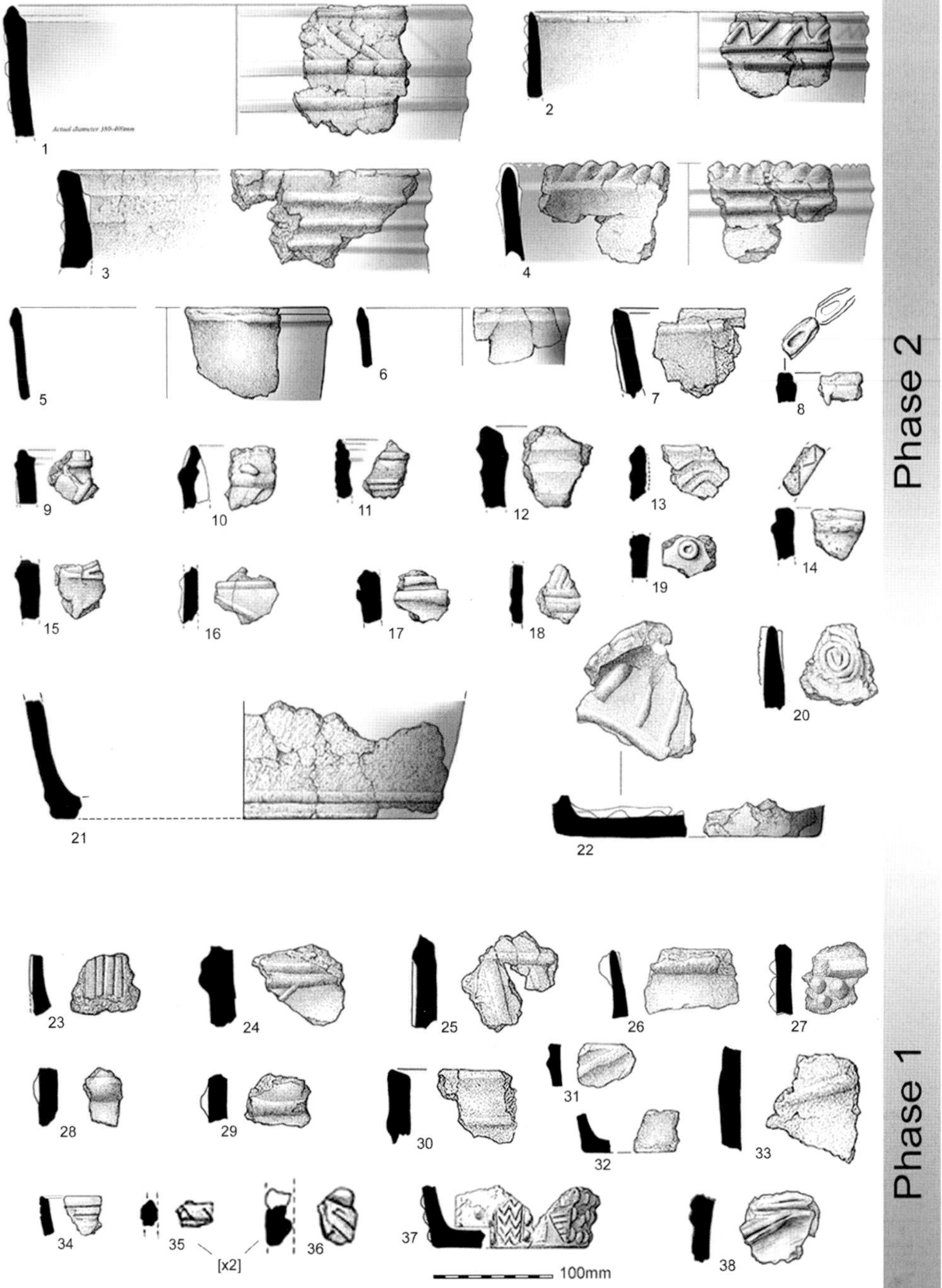

Figure 3.7. A selection of principal decorated sherds from the 1972–3 excavations by phase (illustration: Alexandra Shepherd).

that 'characteristic blue-grey deposits outcrop between bedrock and the turf cover', and that this is the likely source of the clay at Skara Brae used in building foundations, wall cladding, and much else. This familiarity with working clay suggests that whatever recipe the potters chose for a vessel would have been carefully considered, depending on its intended use and appearance.

The decoration in the first Grooved Ware phase at Skara Brae was principally by applied cordons or by parallel horizontal or vertical grooves. The amount of rock inclusions in the fabric mix required a layer of finer clay to be applied to many of the vessels so that grooves and incisions could be made, and cordons attached, to a fairly smooth surface. For the majority of vessels in the early phase there is seldom enough of the vessel remaining to be sure of the overall design, but from what we can determine, many vessels had fairly simple schemes featuring parallel horizontal or vertical grooves (Fig. 3.7, 23), or a horizontal cordon just below the lip of the vessel on the exterior (Fig. 3.7, 30). Branching and vertical cordons hint at more complex schemes (Fig. 3.7, 24). Some cordons were decorated with an incision along their length, but there are also examples of cordons decorated with incisions forming triangle-based designs or decorated with oblique lines (Fig. 3.5, Childe no. 570).

One unparalleled vessel (V1787, Fig. 3.8) recovered from the early Phase I house (Structure 2) combines a number of unique decorative features. These comprise vertical panels infilled with different decoration: incised lattice, applied oval bosses, two sets of parallel lines with incised zig-zags/triangle-based decoration between, a narrower panel of

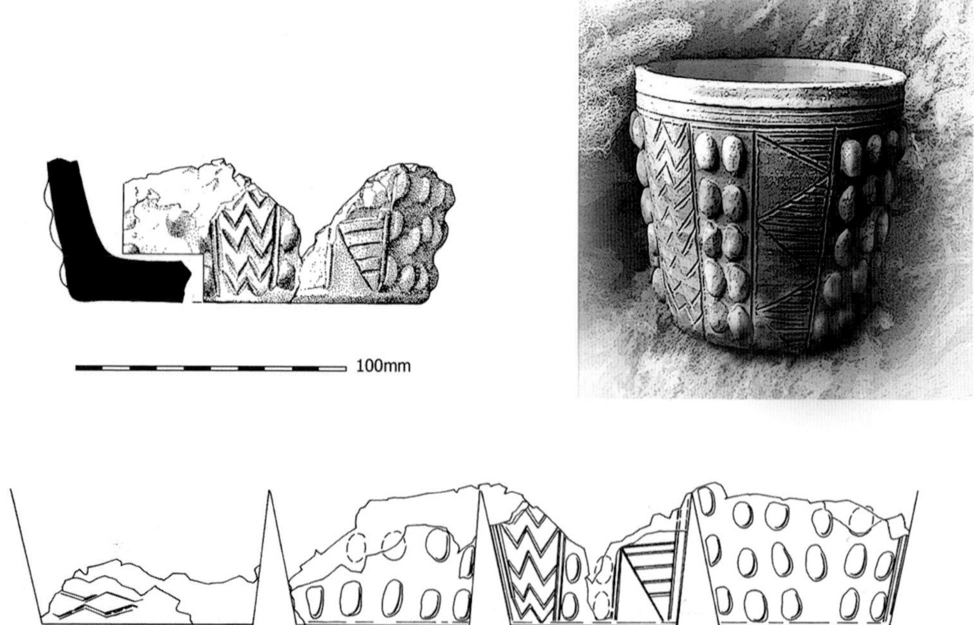

Figure 3.8. Base of panelled vessel from the early house, 1972–3 Structure 2, with motifs indicated and suggested reconstruction (illustration: Alexandra Shepherd).

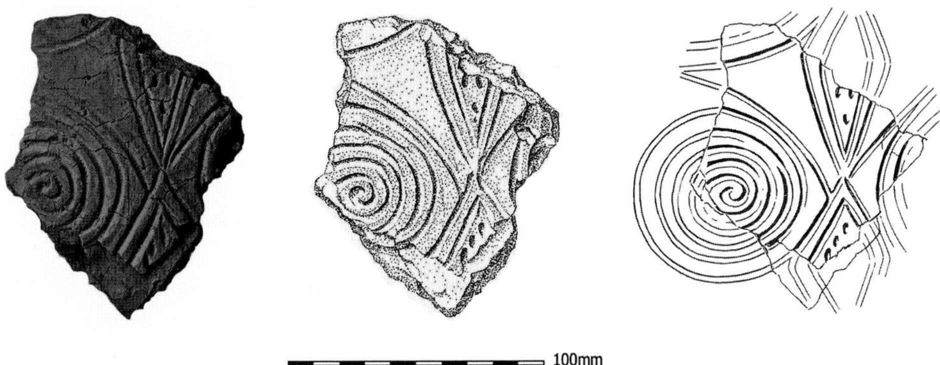

Figure 3.9. Spiral-decorated sherd from Childe's excavations, part of a larger decorative scheme (Childe 1931, 68, fig. 27; drawing and motif reconstruction: Alexandra Shepherd).

oval bosses, two sets of parallel lines with triangle-based decoration (an incised diagonal line splits the lower part of the panel; the triangle below the line is undecorated, the triangle above is infilled with horizontal lines), and a further panel of oval dots, wider than the previous panel.

Only a very few sherds from the Childe operations – just 15 – have contextual information (extracted from his notebook records; Fig. 3.5, above) that allows them to be ascribed to the earlier or later Grooved Ware phases. One of those from Phase 1 is the now iconic 'spiral and lozenge' sherd (Fig. 3.9), the only spiral recovered from this early phase and likely to have been part of a larger scheme as the incipient spirals indicate. The exterior of the sherd, from the body of the vessel, is coated with a thick slip into which have been incised thick grooves forming a complex pattern comprising most of a spiral and possibly part of a second one beside it, between which are two elongated triangular shapes (traditionally interpreted as the parts of two lozenges) made up of double grooves and infilled with short incisions/stabs. Two remnant curved lines at the edge of the sherd (the outer very fragmentary and lost since its initial publication), may indicate a third spiral.

In the later contexts, rim forms become more plastic, including scalloped and chain forms (Fig. 3.7, 4 and 8). Many vessels have a 'step' in the interior (Fig. 3.7, 1), possibly similar to the 'lid-sitter' rims in medieval pottery, and many stone discs of appropriate diameters for lids were recovered. Applied decoration is the most common form, often a plain cordon just below the rim (Fig. 3.7, 5), sometimes a band of decoration around the upper part of the vessel, for example double or triple cordons just below the rim (Fig. 3.7, 3), or horizontal cordons with chevron or trellis decoration between (Fig. 3.7, 2). Again, there are some instances where the whole of the vessel appears to have been decorated (Fig. 3.6). Applied decoration was occasionally noted on base interiors. One vessel (Fig. 3.7, 22) has a branching cordon and two bosses formed from a thick slip in the interior. Decorated cordons are not common in the later contexts. Nor is incised decoration, although there are examples of simple horizontal incisions, either single or multiple, giving a corrugated effect (Fig. 3.7, 11). There are also two cases of spirals incised into a thick slip (Fig. 3.7, 20).

The use of bosses may have been more common than in the earlier contexts. It is worth noting that the most elaborate designs are 'one-offs' within the assemblage, although also worth noting that the excavated area is a very small part of the settlement, so it is possible that there may be similarly decorated vessels in other parts of the site.

Analysis of the material from the 1970s excavations confirmed some of Childe's observations about the pottery, including that applied decoration formed of strips or pellets was found throughout the sequence. His observation that decorated cordons were found early in the sequence was also confirmed, as was his observation that applied decoration is most commonly restricted to a band of parallel cordons around the upper part of the vessel, with bands of more complex decoration being less common. Overall, however, only minor differences were observed between the pottery from the earlier and later contexts. The impression is that while the emphasis on decoration moved towards a higher percentage of applied decoration in the later contexts, we are dealing with one tradition of pottery manufacture, defined latterly by its highly plastic design and the high degree of creative expression. The break in occupation between Phase 1 and Phase 2 does not presage a change in the way that pottery was made when occupation was re-established.

The analysis of the Skara Brae assemblage carried out so far allows us to draw some conclusions about the use of the pottery on the site. First, the amount of pottery recovered from what is a relatively small area of the site gives a glimpse of the intensity of occupation over the years, something that it is easy to forget when looking at the cleaned-out floors of the houses as presented today. Interestingly, there seems to be no difference in the disposal of pottery with decoration compared with pottery without decoration; it all ends up in the settlement deposits together. Similarly, both decorated and undecorated pottery appear, from the sooting residues, to have been used on the hearth.

As discussed above, the occupation deposits have a high proportion of vessels represented by single sherds. This is not reflective of the pattern that would be expected from periodic cleaning out of the rubbish from a house. If broken pots had been put out with the ash from the hearth, food remains and discarded items, we would expect to see more sherds from the same vessel in the same area of deposits. The high percentage of vessels represented by single sherds is perhaps more indicative of broken vessels being retained somewhere and used as needed, perhaps being shovelled into a deposit to firm up its composition, or to create a surface.

THE SKARA BRAE ASSEMBLAGE IN THE HISTORY OF GROOVED WARE STUDIES

Alison Sheridan (2016, 204–5) defines the appearance of Grooved Ware in Scotland as a 'significant change' in the story of Scottish Neolithic pottery not only because Grooved Ware seems to result from an intention to create a new style of pottery, but also because its adoption disrupted the development of established regional pottery styles. The origins and progress of this disruption are less clear.

Grooved Ware was first defined as a distinct style by Stuart Piggott in the 1930s (Piggott 1936). He later favoured a change of name to Rinyo-Clacton Ware to mark its extensive geographic spread (Piggott 1954), Rinyo being Childe's other excavated site with Grooved Ware in Orkney (Childe and Grant 1939; 1947).

In 1971, in the publication of the Durrington Walls excavations, Ian Longworth redefined Grooved Ware as four sub-styles to characterise the main differences from Orkney to the south of England (Wainwright and Longworth 1971). The use of 'Rinyo' for the Orcadian pottery was retained and the pottery was characterised as having flat-bottomed, trunconic and tub-shaped vessels of different sizes, rims with internal step bevels, continuous scalloped rims, applied roundels and pellets, applied complex patterns, grooved cordons other than horizontal or vertical in orientation and cordons other than horizontal and vertical with round impressions. For years, the Skara Brae and Rinyo pottery represented Grooved Ware in Orkney, and beyond, with sherds from Childe's excavations becoming the face of Grooved Ware in Scotland.

Eight sites in total are listed for Longworth's Rinyo sub-style. The other six are on mainland Scotland. Seven decorative features were picked out as defining the Rinyo sub-style. Of the Orkney sites, Skara Brae had all seven features and Rinyo had six, while the mainland Scottish sites shared one decorative feature each with the Orkney sites. In the report, Skara Brae is also included under the Durrington Walls and Clacton sub-styles and Rinyo under the Clacton and Woodlands sub-styles. The sub-styles, which at that point had no chronological definition, did little to clarify the relationship between Orcadian Grooved Ware and that from Mainland Scotland (Cowie and MacSween 1999; Sheridan 1999; and see Copper, this volume).

Work carried out since the 1980s has shown that Orcadian Grooved Ware is not part of one northern British Grooved Ware style. In 1991 Hunter and MacSween published a short note in *Antiquity*, 'A sequence for the Orcadian Neolithic?', which summarised the pottery sequence from the excavations at the settlement site of Pool on the Orkney island of Sanday in the 1980s. The sequence indicated that at Pool the earliest Grooved Ware had either shell temper or no temper in the fabric mix and was mainly decorated with incised designs (Fig. 3.10), whereas the later pottery had applied decoration and a high percentage of crushed rock in the fabric mix. Importantly, in the early phases of Grooved Ware use at Pool we can see an earlier tradition of potting with shell temper continuing as new vessel styles and incised grooved decoration are incorporated (MacSween 2007, 325).

While the Pool sequence provided an indication of temporal differences, defined by the exceptional stratigraphy on the site, the dating available did not allow for a detailed chronology to be established. Establishing links between Grooved Ware assemblages from different sites was restricted to comparisons of decorative features (MacSween 1992; 1995).

At the Neolithic Studies Group Grooved Ware Conference in 1994, Ros Cleal (1999, 2) noted that when the sub-styles were defined, they 'appear[ed] to reflect some real differences within the material, that is, differences which were deliberately intended by the makers and recognised by the users', but that new excavation and analysis had caused a reassessment of the applicability of the scheme to Scotland.

Shortly after the conference, the publication of the excavations at Pool (Hunter with Bond and Smith 2007) and Barnhouse (Richards 2005) provided details of the results of the analysis of two large assemblages (10,000 Neolithic sherds from Pool and 6000 from

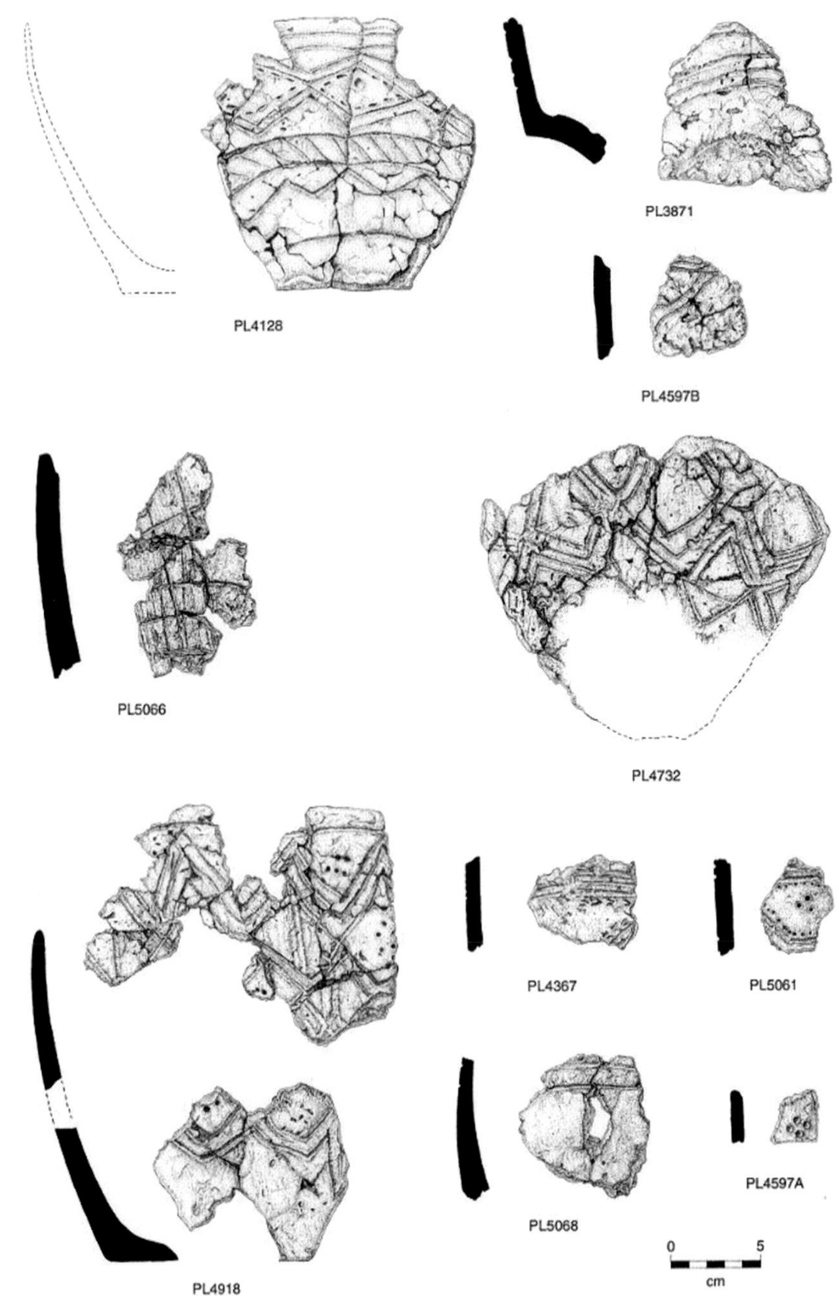

Figure 3.10. Incised Grooved Ware from Pool (Phase 2.3) on Sanday, Orkney (Hunter with Bond and Jones 2007, 300, illus. 8.1.9; reproduced by kind permission of The Orcadian Ltd).

Barnhouse) but the chronological links between the two assemblages remained elusive. The amount of pottery being analysed and published was now providing the data that would allow for a detailed regional study, a need highlighted by Sheridan and Sharples (1992).

While a chronological framework for the Neolithic for Orkney was beginning to emerge when Colin Renfrew presented his paper at the 1998 conference, *Neolithic Orkney in its European context* (Renfrew 2000), it was not until the Orkney-focused work within *The Times of Their Lives* project, led by Alasdair Whittle and Alex Bayliss, that a chronology was established (Bayliss *et al.* 2017). The modelling of the new radiocarbon dates, many from residues adhering to the pottery, suggested that the early phase of Grooved Ware use in Orkney was represented by sites including Pool Phase 2, the Stones of Stenness and Quanterness, with the earliest dates for the Barnhouse early phases falling within the later 32nd century cal BC (MacSween *et al.* 2015; Richards *et al.* 2016). The parallels between this pottery and other assemblages across Britain and Ireland are discussed elsewhere in this volume.

As dates were added to the Orkney framework, we adjusted our view of the significance of the Skara Brae assemblage as a northern sub-style, to understanding it as one of several Orcadian assemblages that represent the last 400 or so years of Orcadian Grooved Ware. While the early phase of Grooved Ware use in Orkney is characterised by the frequent use of incised decoration and is part of a distribution across much of Britain and Ireland, reflecting the distribution of stone circles, the later phase of Grooved Ware in Orkney is characterised by the plasticity of its decoration, the creativity of the decorative schemes and the fact that, unlike the earlier phase, it has qualities specific to Orkney. Recent work on the Ness of Brodgar pottery has also demonstrated the use of colour on some of the later Grooved Ware, adding another dimension (Jones *et al.* 2019). It is possible that by this time the focus of the communities at those sites had moved from shared expression across wide areas to greater expressions of regional identity.

Longworth's definition, in 1971, of a northern Grooved Ware sub-style based on the Skara Brae and Rinyo assemblages was, then, correct, but the difference was both chronological and geographical rather than simply geographical. The earliest Grooved Ware assemblages from Orkney that would have tied in with the Woodlands sub-style in Scotland and beyond, such as those from the earlier phases of the settlement at Barnhouse (Richards 2005; Jones 2005), the Stones of Stenness (Henshall and Savory 1976; Ritchie 1976) and the tomb at Quanterness (Henshall 1979; Renfrew 1979), had yet to be discovered.

One of the characteristics of the later Grooved Ware in Orkney is its varied design but within the confines of a tradition that can still be recognised as Grooved Ware. As well as at Skara Brae and Rinyo, it is seen at sites including the late phases at Pool (MacSween 2007), the later phases at the Ness of Brodgar (Towers and MacSween 2020), the later phases at Links of Noltland (Sheridan 1999), the pottery associated with monumental Structure 8 and Area 2 at Barnhouse (Jones 2005, 271), Stonehall (R. Jones 2016) and Crossiecrown (A.M. Jones 2016). It is because of the amount of excavation of Neolithic Grooved Ware sites in Orkney that has been carried out since Childe's excavations at Rinyo, and the subsequent dating of this change at sites including Links of Noltland (Clarke *et al.* 2016), the Ness of Brodgar (Card *et al.* 2018) and Skara Brae (David Clarke, pers. comm.), that we are now able to look at regional development in some detail. Sheridan (2016, 205) reminds us to see these changes in the ceramics of Orkney in the context of innovative changes in ceremonial practice in the islands.

The impression from the later (post-2900 cal BC) Grooved Ware in Orkney is that broader creativity was being exercised within Grooved Ware norms, with expression taking place within the limits of the language of the design. By the time of the latest Grooved Ware in Orkney, the Neolithic makers and users of Grooved Ware were perhaps not so constrained in their choices. When the potters saw a new motif or arrangement of motifs, they could choose to ignore it, adopt or modify it (MacSween 2018). From the variety of designs represented on the pottery of the latest phases of Grooved Ware in Orkney, including the Skara Brae assemblage, it is likely that decorating pots with innovative combinations of motives was accepted, expected and encouraged.

It seems, looking at other aspects of the site, that Skara Brae is showing us a later phase of Grooved Ware in Orkney where the developments are essentially Orcadian in character. Almost nothing in the Skara Brae assemblages seems to have come from outside Orkney, and in the site's 4 m of stratigraphy we can see one of the clearest examples we have of Grooved Ware as an evolving phenomenon at the end of its use, an aspect little discussed anywhere hitherto. That the pottery is reflecting this situation is particularly important because it is pottery that gives unity to the wider pan-British Grooved Ware complex.

CONCLUSION

Since Childe's excavations at Skara Brae, we have seen a change in how the pottery assemblages from the site have moved from being, with Rinyo, the face of the northern Grooved Ware sub-style, to being understood as an assemblage that was part of a second iteration of Grooved Ware in Orkney and late in the story of the Neolithic of these islands. Skara Brae is a good example of the way that the sites that we choose to excavate, present and interpret gain their own status and momentum which can be useful but also challenging. While it will always be an iconic site, and an important part of 100 years of research of the Grooved Ware of Orkney, Skara Brae is now viewed as a key site in understanding the changes that took place in Orkney society in the first half of the 3rd millennium cal BC. Understanding the design, use and disposal of the pottery during that time is an important part of that continuing research.

ACKNOWLEDGEMENTS

The considerable input from Lekky Shepherd, both in producing most of the illustrations and for many useful discussions about the site, is acknowledged and appreciated. Historic Environment Scotland is thanked for permission to reproduce Bil Fulton's illustration from the 1989 Skara Brae Guidebook, Alison Sheridan for allowing us to publish her photograph of a large vessel from Skara Brae, and John Hunter and The Orcadian Ltd for permission to include the illustration of the incised decorated sherds from Pool. Thanks to the many colleagues who have discussed the Neolithic of Orkney with us over the years, including the contributors to this volume.

REFERENCES

Bayliss, A., Marshall, P., Richards, C. and Whittle, A. 2017. Islands of history: the Late Neolithic timescape of Orkney. *Antiquity* 91, 1171–88.

Card, N., Mainland, I., Timpany, S., Batt, C., Bronk Ramsey, C., Dunbar, E., Reimer, P.J., Bayliss, A., Marshall, P. and Whittle, A. 2018. To cut a long story short: formal chronological modelling for the late Neolithic site of Ness of Brodgar, Orkney. *European Journal of Archaeology* 21(2), 217–63.

Childe, V.G. 1930. Operations at Skara Brae during 1929. *Proceedings of the Society of Antiquaries of Scotland* 64 (1929–30), 158–91.

Childe, V.G. 1931. *Skara Brae: a Pictish village in Orkney*. London: Kegan Paul, Trench, Trubner and Co.

Childe, V.G. and Grant, W.G. 1939. A Stone Age settlement at the Braes of Rinyo, Rousay, Orkney (first report). *Proceedings of the Society of Antiquaries of Scotland* 73 (1938–39), 6–31.

Childe, V.G. and Grant, W.G. 1947. A Stone Age settlement at the Braes of Rinyo, Rousay, Orkney (second report). *Proceedings of the Society of Antiquaries of Scotland* 81 (1946–47), 16–42.

Clarke, D.V. 1976. *The Neolithic village at Skara Brae, Orkney: 1972–1973 excavations*. Edinburgh: HMSO.

Clarke, D. and Maguire, P. 1989. *Skara Brae: northern Europe's best preserved prehistoric village*. Historic Scotland Guidebook: Historic Scotland – Historic Buildings and Monuments, Scotland.

Clarke, D.V., Sheridan, J.A., Shepherd, A., Sharples, N., Armour-Chelu, M., Hamlet, L., Bronk Ramsey, C., Dunbar, E., Reimer, P.J., Marshall, P. and Whittle, A. 2016. The end of the world, or just 'goodbye to all that'? Contextualising the red deer from Links of Noltland, Westray, within late 3rd-millennium cal BC Orkney. *Proceedings of the Society of Antiquaries of Scotland* 146, 57–89.

Cleal, R. 1999. Introduction: the what, where, when and why of Grooved Ware. In R. Cleal and A. MacSween (eds) 1999, 1–8.

Cleal, R. and MacSween, A (eds) 1999. *Grooved Ware in Britain and Ireland*. Oxford: Oxbow Books.

Cowie, T. and MacSween, A. 1999. Grooved Ware from Scotland: a review. In R. Cleal and A. MacSween (eds) 1999, 48–56.

Henshall, A.S. 1979. Artefacts from the Quanterness cairn: pottery. In C. Renfrew, *Investigations in Orkney*, 75–9. London: Society of Antiquaries.

Henshall, A.S. and Savory, L. 1976. Small finds from the 1973–4 excavations. In J.N.G. Ritchie 1976, 22–5.

Hunter, J. with Bond, J.M. and Smith, A.S. 2007. *Investigations in Sanday, Orkney. Vol. 1: excavations at Pool, Sanday. A multi-period settlement from Neolithic to Late Norse times*. Kirkwall: The Orcadian in association with Historic Scotland.

Hunter, J.R. and MacSween, A. 1991. A sequence for the Orcadian Neolithic? *Antiquity* 65, 911–14.

Hunter, F. and Sheridan, J.A. (eds) 2016. *Ancient lives: object, people and place in early Scotland. Essays for David V Clarke on his 70th birthday*, 213–32. Leiden: Sidestone Press.

Jones, A.M. 2005. The Grooved Ware from Barnhouse. In C. Richards (ed.) 2005, 261–82.

Jones, A.M. 2016. Prehistoric pottery: Crossiecrown. In C. Richards and R. Jones (eds) 2016, 332–57.

Jones, R. 2016. Prehistoric pottery: Stonehall. In C. Richards and R. Jones (eds) 2016, 305–32.

Jones, R., Towers, R., Card, N. and Odling, N. 2019. Analysis of coloured Grooved Ware sherds from the Ness of Brodgar, Orkney. *Journal of Archaeological Science: Reports* 28, 102014. https://www.sciencedirect.com/science/article/pii/S2352409X19303219

MacSween, A. 1992. Orcadian Grooved Ware. In N. Sharples and J.A. Sheridan (eds) 1992, 257–71.

MacSween, A. 1995. Grooved Ware from Scotland: aspects of decoration. In I. Kinnes and G. Varndell (eds), *'Unbaked urns of rudely shape': essays on British and Irish pottery for Ian Longworth*, 41–8. Oxford: Oxbow Books.

MacSween, A. 1997. The pottery. In J. Barber, *The excavation of a stalled cairn at the Point of Cott, Westray, Orkney*, 27–9. Edinburgh: Scottish Trust for Archaeological Research.

MacSween, A. 2007. The pottery. In J. Hunter with J.M. Bond and A.S. Smith 2007, 287–353.

MacSween, A. 2018. Regional and local identities in the later Neolithic of Scotland as reflected in the ceramic record. In L. Campbell, D. Wright and N. Hall (eds), *Roots of nationhood: the archaeology and history of Scotland*, 55–73. Oxford: Archaeopress.

MacSween, A., Hunter, J., Sheridan, J.A., Bond, J., Bronk Ramsey, C., Reimer, P.J., Bayliss, A., Griffiths, S. and Whittle, A. 2015. Refining the chronology of the Neolithic settlement at Pool, Sanday, Orkney. *Proceedings of the Prehistoric Society* 81, 283–310.

Piggott, S. 1936. The pottery from the submerged surface. In S.H. Warren, S. Piggott, J.G.D. Clark, M.C. Burkitt, H. Godwin and M.E. Godwin, Archaeology of the submerged land surface of the Essex coast, 186–201. *Proceedings of the Prehistoric Society* 2, 178–210.

Piggott, S. 1954. *The Neolithic cultures of the British Isles.* Cambridge: Cambridge University Press.

Renfrew, C. 1979. *Investigations in Orkney.* London: Society of Antiquaries.

Renfrew, C. 2000. Introduction: The Auld Hoose speaks: society and life in Stone Age Orkney. In A. Ritchie (ed.) 2000, 1–20.

Richards, C. (ed.) 2005. *Dwelling among the monuments: the Neolithic village of Barnhouse, Maeshowe passage grave and surrounding monuments at Stenness, Orkney.* Cambridge: McDonald Institute for Archaeological Research.

Richards, C. and Jones, R. (eds) 2016. *The development of Neolithic house societies in Orkney: investigations in the Bay of Firth, Mainland, Orkney (1994–2014).* Oxford: Windgather Press

Richards, C., Jones, A.M., MacSween, A., Sheridan, J.A., Dunbar, E., Reimer, P., Bayliss, A., Griffiths, S. and Whittle, A. 2016. Settlement duration and materiality: formal chronological models for the development of Barnhouse, a Grooved Ware settlement in Orkney. *Proceedings of the Prehistoric Society* 81, 283–310.

Ritchie, A. (ed.) 2000. *Neolithic Orkney in its European context.* Cambridge: McDonald Institute for Archaeological Research.

Ritchie, J.N.G. 1976. The Stones of Stenness, Orkney. *Proceedings of the Society of Antiquaries of Scotland* 107 (1975–76), 1–60.

Sharples, N. and Sheridan, J.A. (eds) 1992. *Vessels for the ancestors: essays on the Neolithic of Britain and Ireland in honour of Audrey Henshall.* Edinburgh: Edinburgh University Press.

Shepherd, A. 2016. Skara Brae life studies: overlaying the embedded images. In F. Hunter and J.A. Sheridan (eds) 2016, 213–32.

Shepherd, A.N. 2000. Skara Brae: expressing identity in a Neolithic community. In A. Ritchie (ed.) 2000, 139–58.

Sheridan, J.A. 1999. Grooved Ware from the Links of Noltland, Westray, Orkney. In R. Cleal and A. MacSween (eds) 1999, 112–24.

Sheridan, J.A. 2016. Scottish Neolithic pottery in 2016: the big picture and some details of the narrative. In F. Hunter and J.A. Sheridan (eds) 2016, 189–212.

Sheridan, J.A. and Sharples, N. 1992. Introduction: the state of Neolithic studies in Scotland. In N. Sharples and J.A. Sheridan (eds) 1992, 1–10.

Towers, R. and MacSween, A. 2020 The age of clay: pottery by another name. In N. Card, M. Edmonds and A. Mitchell (eds), *The Ness of Brodgar: as it stands*, 254–65. Kirkwall: The Orcadian.

Wainwright, G.J. and Longworth, I.H. 1971. The Rinyo-Clacton Culture reconsidered. In G.J. Wainwright and I.H. Longworth, *Durrington Walls: excavations 1966–1968*, 235–306. London: Society of Antiquaries.

Chapter 4

Scottish Grooved Ware beyond Orkney

Mike Copper

This chapter will discuss how recent work contributes to our understanding of how, when and why Grooved Ware was adopted in northern Britain beyond Orkney and the ways in which it subsequently developed. In the light of this discussion, the latter part of the paper will address the relevance today of the concept of sub-styles and will propose an alternative way to think about Grooved Ware variation.

THE EARLIEST GROOVED WARE BEYOND ORKNEY

Currently, the earliest dated Grooved Ware from anywhere in Britain and Ireland comes from the small settlement at Barnhouse, part of a complex of monuments and settlements centred on the Brodgar peninsula in Orkney, where it was in use from the site's earliest phase dating to the 32nd century cal BC (Jones 2005; Richards *et al.* 2016). Interestingly, there is as yet no evidence that Grooved Ware developed organically from earlier pottery styles; its seemingly gradual emergence at Pool on Sanday post-dates the fully-fledged Barnhouse Grooved Ware (MacSween *et al.* 2015) and is best explained as the piecemeal adoption of Grooved Ware characteristics by an outlying community. The presence in Orkney of exotic materials (Anderson-Whymark 2020, 213), Atlantic rock art and monuments such as the arguably Irish-style passage tomb of Maeshowe, make it clear that at least a sub-set of the Orcadian population had connections with regions as distant as the Boyne Valley during the 4th millennium cal BC. It is in this context that the significance of the monumental settlement at the Ness of Brodgar, lying just 500 m north-west of Barnhouse, must be understood, and it may be proposed that Grooved Ware was one aspect of a new set of material and behavioural characteristics that emerged within intercommunity gatherings at this and other nearby sites, including Barnhouse, towards the end of the millennium.

So similar is the Barnhouse pottery to that from the important ceremonial centre at Balfarg Riding School in Fife (Fig. 4.2, cf. Figs 2.2 and 2.4; Barclay and Russell-White 1993) that it is reasonable to suggest that potters were travelling between these sites at around 3000 cal BC. The dates for Grooved Ware-related activity at Balfarg Riding School overlap with those of Barnhouse (Copper *et al.* 2021, 86–90), and it is of note that the nearby stone circle at Balbirnie possibly pre-dates the henge around the Stones of Stenness in Orkney, if not the Stenness stone circle itself (Gibson 2010; Schulting *et al.* 2010, 35–6).

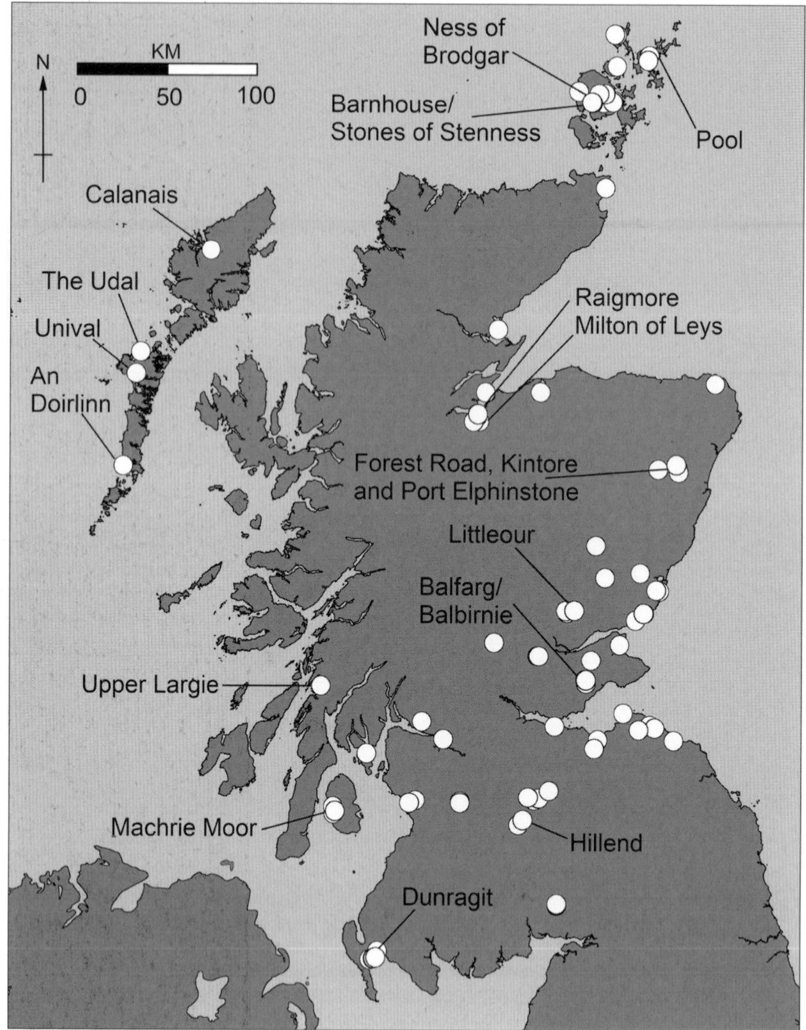

Figure 4.1. Grooved Ware findspots in Scotland with key sites mentioned in text indicated.

The Balfarg Riding School Grooved Ware exhibits the same range of vessel forms, alongside decorative elements recognised at Barnhouse that include applied and incised net-like motifs, horizontally and diagonally incised parallel lines, false-relief wavy lines and rim pellets. Significantly, however, there are also differences – including elongated lozenges and motifs composed entirely of horizontal and vertical elements – suggestive of stylistic drift.

Further long-distance connections are evidenced at what is presently the earliest dated Grooved Ware assemblage outside Orkney – and also Britain and Ireland's earliest known square-within-circle timber circle – at Machrie Moor Site 1 on Arran (Fig. 4.3), which was probably in use from shortly before 3000 cal BC (Haggarty 1991; Copper *et al.* 2021, 96).

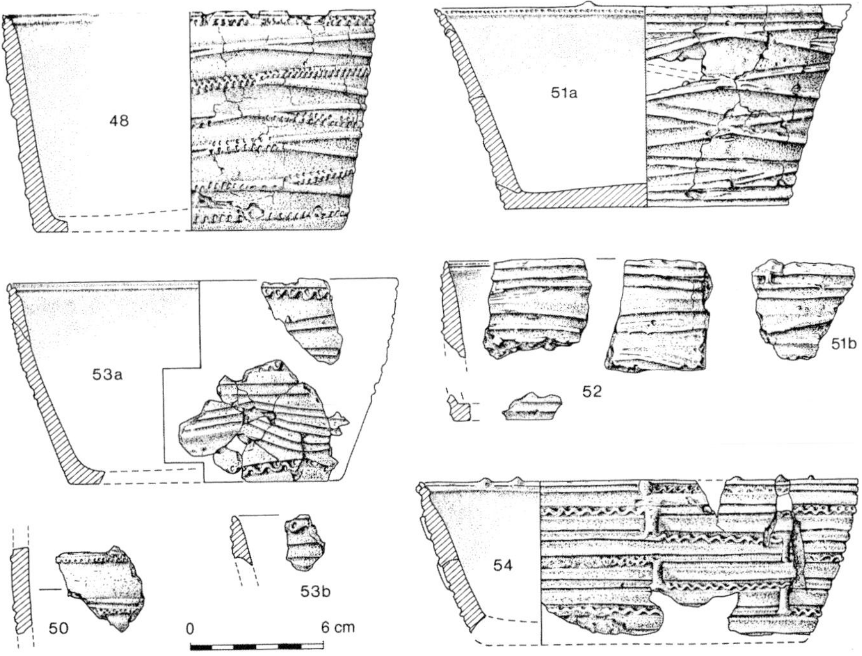

Figure 4.2. Grooved Ware from Balfarg Riding School (after Barclay and Russell-White 1993, illus. 28; image courtesy of the Society of Antiquaries of Scotland).

If so, then this would pre-date the style's first appearance in southern England by around just 50 years (Wessex Archaeology 2020; Brook this volume). Once again, features noted at Barnhouse are apparent on flat-based, tub-shaped vessels at a probable regionally significant centre of ceremonial activity. Other Barnhouse-style Grooved Ware occurs at ceremonial monuments including Calanais on the Isle of Lewis (Sheridan *et al.* 2016), the Tormore chambered cairn on Arran (Henshall 1972, 305, 371–2) and Kilmartin Glen in Argyll (Sheridan 2012). As this author has previously noted (Copper *et al.* 2021, 105), rather than a wave of advance, the process of adoption of Orcadian-style pottery at widely spaced ceremonial sites resembles a stone skimming across the surface of a pond. It is important to note, however, that Grooved Ware exhibits temporal and regional variation from its earliest phase, with stylistic drift occurring between the pre- and post-3000 cal BC pottery at Barnhouse itself as well as between Barnhouse and Balfarg Riding School.

RIPPLES ON THE SURFACE

The latest dates for Scottish Impressed Ware pottery are on organic residue from a Fengate-style vessel from Mountcastle Quarry in Fife dating to 3010–2883 cal BC (Copper *et al.* 2021 supplementary materials, 25). This suggests limited overlap in the use

Figure 4.3. Grooved Ware Vessel 17a from Machrie Moor Site 1, Arran. Scale: 5 cm (image: author, courtesy of National Museums Scotland).

Figure 4.4. Vessel 5 (ABDUA: 104526) from Forest Road, Kintore, Aberdeenshire (image: author, courtesy of University of Aberdeen).

of Grooved Ware and Impressed Ware in Scotland, as also appears to have been the case further south (Marshall *et al.* 2009, 68–81). Soon, however, Grooved Ware appears to have been taken up by all pottery-making communities in Scotland – a process that can perhaps be compared to ripples spreading outwards from the sites where the Grooved Ware 'stone' touched the water while skimming southwards. This process may have been mediated by intercommunity meetings at key gathering places.

This new Grooved Ware varied little from that noted at Balfarg Riding School. At Forest Road, Kintore, Aberdeenshire (Fig. 4.4), sherds were deposited in pits, in continuity of Middle Neolithic practices at the site. Here, motifs noted at Balfarg Riding School recur alongside new patterns including 'slashed' cordons and 'ladder' motifs (probably variations on the wavy line motif). At both Forest Road and nearby Port Elphinstone (Murray and Murray 2013), applied rosettes or 'knots' appear to tie together converging incised lines, strongly suggesting that certain early Grooved Ware motifs were skeuomorphs of cordage. Grooved Ware from a midden at Upper Largie in the Kilmartin Valley (Ellis 2017), resembling that from Balfarg Riding School and Barnhouse, may represent the remains of a feasting event (Alison Sheridan, pers. comm.), again suggesting significant commensal gatherings.

A DRIFT IN STYLE

At some point between the mid-29th and early 27th centuries cal BC, an assemblage of Grooved Ware was deposited at a monumental timber circle constructed a short distance to the west of Balfarg Riding School, probably as a single event (Mercer *et al.* 1981, 81, 96–7; Copper *et al.* 2018). There are significant differences between the Grooved Ware from Balfarg Riding School and the timber circle. Only one sherd from the timber circle bore a false-relief wavy line and there were no ladder motifs or rim pellets. In comparison with the Riding School, decoration is reserved, occasionally being confined to simple incised lines. Notably, multiple grooves occur

Figure 4.5. Grooved Ware sherds from An Doirlinn, North Uist (above) and from Pit F2 (Area 3) at Melbourne Farm, Biggar, South Lanarkshire. Scale: 5 cm (images: author, Biggar sherd courtesy of Biggar and Upper Clydesdale Museum).

internally below the rim on Vessels P1 and P18 and roughly executed multiple-line chevrons and dot infill are also present. While maintaining certain features noted at the Riding School, the timber circle pottery therefore appears to represent further development of the earliest style of Grooved Ware. Significantly, dot infill, internal grooving and multiple-line-defined chevrons are features of what Smith (1956, 192–6) and Longworth (Wainwright and Longworth 1971, 236–8) termed the 'Clacton' sub-style of Grooved Ware. It may be proposed that the Balfarg timber circle Grooved Ware therefore represents a process of stylistic drift from about 2900 cal BC in which 'Clacton'-style characteristics take on more and more prominence at the expense of earlier Orcadian (traditionally 'Woodlands' sub-style) features. Interestingly, Gibson (1982, 180) observed that a Grooved Ware vessel dating to 3080–2920 cal BC from Tomb 6 at Knowth (below, Fig 8.2A; Eogan 1984, 312–3, fig. 116; Schulting *et al.* 2017, 353) 'is virtually 'classic' Grooved Ware in the Clacton style', hinting at interaction with the Boyne Valley in this process, though the Clacton sub-style is primarily a southern British phenomenon.

At the coastal settlement of An Doirlinn in the Outer Hebrides, an assemblage of Grooved Ware in some respects analogous to that from the Balfarg timber circle was dated to between 2830–2600 and 2480–2330 cal BC (Fig. 4.5) (Garrow and Sturt 2017). Dot infilling and multiple-line-defined lozenges occur here and elsewhere in the Western Isles, including at the Udal and the Unival passage tomb on North Uist (Scott 1948, 26 and pl. vii; Squair and Ballin Smith 2018, 183–97). At An Doirlinn, however, notched rims and decorated internal bevels also recall Grooved Ware from Orcadian assemblages post-dating that at Barnhouse (Links of Noltland: Sheridan 1999; Pool: MacSween 2007, 304; Stonehall Farm: Jones *et al.* 2016, 319, fig. 11.2.12). In Scotland, aside from Balfarg, Clacton sub-style characteristics are currently known only from the Western Isles and the Borders, suggestive of stylistic development amongst interconnected potting communities.

REGIONAL DEVELOPMENTS IN ORKNEY AND ECLECTICISM AT RAIGMORE

Post-3000 cal BC developments in Orcadian Grooved Ware are dealt with in more detail in Chapter 2 of this volume. It is pertinent to mention here, however, that the so-called Rinyo sub-style of Grooved Ware (Wainwright and Longworth 1971, 242–3), characterised by extensive use of applied ornamentation, 'scalloped' rims and internal modelling (including on vessel bases), does not represent a clearly-bounded entity but emerged through a dynamic process of continual stylistic development; that is, pots were being made in an increasingly insular fashion as time progressed and not in imitation of a standardised Orcadian template.

To the south, the assemblage from Stoneyfield, Raigmore in Inverness (Simpson 1996), indicates how Grooved Ware elements may be shared between regions. Here, sherds from Pit 20, which has produced a date of 3090–2907 cal BC (though dates from this site need to be treated with caution and some material may have been curated or redeposited: Copper *et al.* 2018, 93), exhibit features such as rows of circular impressions and an internal rim bevel decorated with a herringbone motif that would not look out of place at Machrie Moor Site 1 or Balfarg Riding School. Vessel P4 from this feature bears vertical cordons suggestive of Longworth's Durrington Walls sub-style. Paired fingernail impressions on vessel P6 recall decoration on the Durrington Walls sub-style Pot 3 from Littleour (Barclay and Maxwell 1998, 63, illus. 51). Pit 49, less reliably dated to between the 29th and 26th centuries by charcoal of unidentified species (Simpson 1996, 82), contained a sherd bearing a motif of incised horizontal lines flanking a row of dots that resembles motifs from later sites such as An Doirlinn (though on a much smaller vessel at the latter site: Fig. 4.5). A redeposited sherd from Pit 50 (P40) is part of a scalloped rim, a form well represented in Orkney. As such, the Raigmore assemblage exhibits an eclectic mixture of features that link it with Grooved Ware from a range of sites of differing ages from across Scotland at a location lying at the intersection of potential routeways through the Great Glen and along the east coast.

A NEW WAVE?

Bayesian modelling of Durrington Walls sub-style Grooved Ware suggests that this type of pottery first appeared in Scotland in the *3025–2760 cal BC (95% probability)* timeframe, and probably *2910–2825 cal BC (68% probability)* (Copper *et al.* 2021). Durrington Walls-style Grooved Ware is characterised in particular by deep, bucket-shaped vessel bodies divided into panels by vertical cordons or incised lines descending from a horizontal cordon located on the upper body, the spaces between the vertical divisions usually being filled with opposed diagonal lines or filled triangles (Fig. 4.6; Wainwright and Longworth 1971, 240–2). Novel rim forms and combed or twisted cord decoration (notably pre-dating the earliest Beaker pottery: Copper *et al.* 2021) also occur on this sub-style, as well as plain vessels (Jorge 2014, 5–6) and complex panelling (Curle 1908, 313). The sub-style therefore contrasts strongly with other forms of Grooved Ware, raising questions of how it arose and its place within the Grooved Ware tradition.

Claims have been made for a potentially pre-3000 cal BC date for Durrington Walls-style Grooved Ware from Milton of Leys, Inverness (Fig. 4.7; Conolly and MacSween

2003, 38–9; Copper *et al.* 2019). Such an early date outside Orkney would be of significance for our understanding of the development of Grooved Ware both within and beyond Scotland. I suggest, however, that this vessel has more in common with north-east Scottish Middle Neolithic pottery, as exemplified by vessels from Kinbeachie on the Black Isle and Forest Road, Kintore (Barclay *et al.* 2001; MacSween 2008, 180–1), where cordons were also employed. Like the Kinbeachie and Forest Road pots, but unlike most Grooved Ware from this area, the cordons on the Milton of Leys vessel were crudely pinched-up rather than applied and do not descend from a horizontal cordon. Furthermore, there is no decoration between the cordons, a common – though not universal – feature of the sub-style, exemplified in Scotland at sites such as Hillend (Armit

Figure 4.6. Grooved Ware sherd from Powmyre Quarry, Angus. Scale: 5 cm (image: author, courtesy of Angus Museums).

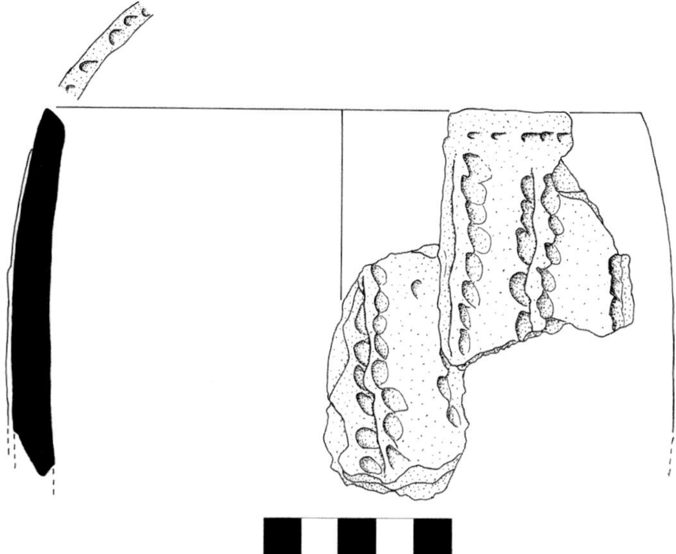

Figure 4.7. Vessel 1 from Milton of Leys, Inverness. Scale: 5cm (after Copper et al. *2021: illus. 9 and Conolly and MacSween 2003, illus. 4).*

et al. 1994, 118–22), a site now known to post-date 2900 cal BC (Copper *et al.* 2021, 98). The vessel's impressed rim decoration is unknown on Grooved Ware elsewhere in Scotland. Finally, it is uncertain whether this pot had a round or a flat base. Though I propose that the Milton of Leys vessel is not a Grooved Ware pot, whether it is implicated in the later development of the Durrington Walls sub-style remains an intriguingly open question.

In the absence of vessels resembling the Milton of Leys pot, there is currently no evidence that Durrington Walls sub-style Grooved Ware developed from earlier Orcadian-style Grooved Ware by the same process of stylistic drift noted at Balfarg. It is of interest, however, that it occurs not only in similar contexts to earlier Neolithic pottery (for example, deposited with varying degrees of formality in pits) but also at a new type of site: large, palisaded enclosures such as Dunragit (Thomas 2015) and Leadketty (Brophy *et al.* n.d.). Also of interest is that with the current exceptions of Orkney, the far south and the Western Isles, this is the only sub-style of Grooved Ware currently known to have been in use in Scotland after the 29th century cal BC.

GROOVED WARE AND BEAKERS

Dating the end of the Grooved Ware tradition is important for understanding significant cultural changes of the second half of the 3rd millennium cal BC. This is especially important in the light of recent aDNA evidence indicating substantial genetic change at this time alongside the possibility that a genetically distinct population descended from the Neolithic inhabitants of Britain and Ireland, possibly still using Grooved Ware, may have existed alongside Beaker-using immigrants and their descendants (Booth *et al.* 2021; Bloxam and Parker Pearson 2022; Brace and Booth 2023). Unfortunately, it is difficult to say how long Grooved Ware continued in use in Scotland after the arrival of Beakers, with recent Bayesian modelling of Scottish Grooved Ware dates suggesting an overlap between the latest Grooved Ware and the earliest Beakers of between 1 and 145 years at 95% probability or 1 and 60 years at 68% (for details see Copper *et al.* 2021, 102). It is also highly probable that there was significant regional variation in the timing of the abandonment of Grooved Ware manufacture across Scotland.

BEYOND 'SUB-STYLES'?

I have discussed the dynamic and evolving character of Scottish Grooved Ware, from its early adoption beyond Orkney at key locales such as Balfarg Riding School to its mutation into the southern Clacton and northern Rinyo 'sub-styles'. In addition, I have noted eclectic assemblages in the Western Isles and Inverness, the appearance of a parallel but related ceramic style (the Durrington Walls sub-style) after 2900 cal BC and the cut-off in Grooved Ware development – if not manufacture – after *c.* 2500 cal BC. This picture contrasts strongly with the idea of fixed, monothetically defined sub-styles with rare and aberrant 'hybrids' that has been in use since the mid-20th century (Smith 1956). Can we then re-characterise Grooved Ware in a way that recognises its dynamic and constantly changing nature?

One alternative is to reconsider Grooved Ware in terms of two distinct *trajectories* – here termed Trajectories 1 and 2. In contrast to closed and atemporal Grooved Ware sub-styles, these represent *constantly evolving stylistic and technological traditions.* The earliest Trajectory 1 Grooved Ware, represented at sites including Barnhouse and Balfarg Riding School, is here grouped under the term Trajectory 1(a). A process of stylistic drift then led to distinctive regional trajectories, here termed Trajectory 1(b) in southern Britain, 1(c) in Orkney and 1(d) in Ireland (the latter not discussed here, but see Grogan and Roche this volume), with the Balfarg timber circle assemblage representing a mid-point in the emergence of Trajectory 1(b), and with sharing of otherwise regionally distinct features visible in the Western Isles and at Raigmore. Trajectory 2 represents a parallel tradition, conventionally understood, in a monothetic sense, as the Durrington Walls sub-style, exhibiting less variation through time and whose origin is currently uncertain.

GROOVED WARE TRAJECTORIES IN SCOTLAND

With the benefit of many more assemblages and high-quality radiocarbon dates than were available to previous researchers, it is now possible to move beyond the four exclusive Grooved Ware sub-styles proposed by Longworth and to consider Grooved Ware stylistic *progression.* This development is summarised in Figure 4.8.

Trajectory 1 Grooved Ware appears to have developed (or, more likely, been *invented*) in the West Mainland of Orkney, centred on the Brodgar peninsula, by 3100 cal BC. The earliest variants, grouped as Trajectory 1(a), are well represented by the Barnhouse assemblage. It is likely that the Ness of Brodgar played a key role in this process, possibly relating to the forging and subsequent materialisation of a new sense of identity amongst visitors from politically significant centres across Britain and Ireland catalysed within commensal gatherings. Differences between the pre- and post-3000 cal BC pottery from Barnhouse illustrate, however, that even at this early stage Grooved Ware was an evolving tradition.

Drawing on decorative motifs and vessel forms seen across Orkney, as well as on motifs that may have been adopted from a broader repertoire reflected in Irish passage tomb art, the appearance of Grooved Ware at sites such as Machrie Moor Site 1 on Arran shortly before 3000 BC and Balfarg Riding School in the first century of the 3rd millennium cal BC indicates that the style held a particular significance amongst increasingly interconnected groups at this time, though initially these need not have constituted more than a sub-set of the wider Neolithic population. Both the Machrie Moor and Balfarg Riding School Grooved Ware assemblages exhibit characteristics that differ from Barnhouse while also maintaining a high degree of 'family resemblance' that included distinctive features such as the false-relief wavy line motif, indicative of the gradual, albeit constrained, development of Trajectory 1(a).

The Balfarg timber circle Grooved Ware of the 29th or 28th century BC reflects the mutation of Trajectory 1(a) to a degree sufficient for us to begin using a new term: Trajectory 1(b). This trajectory is well represented south of the border but is rare in Scotland outside the Western Isles and the Borders.

So far in Scotland, only An Doirlinn on South Uist has produced reliable dates for a variant of Trajectory 1(b) Grooved Ware after the 27th century cal BC, and outside Orkney only

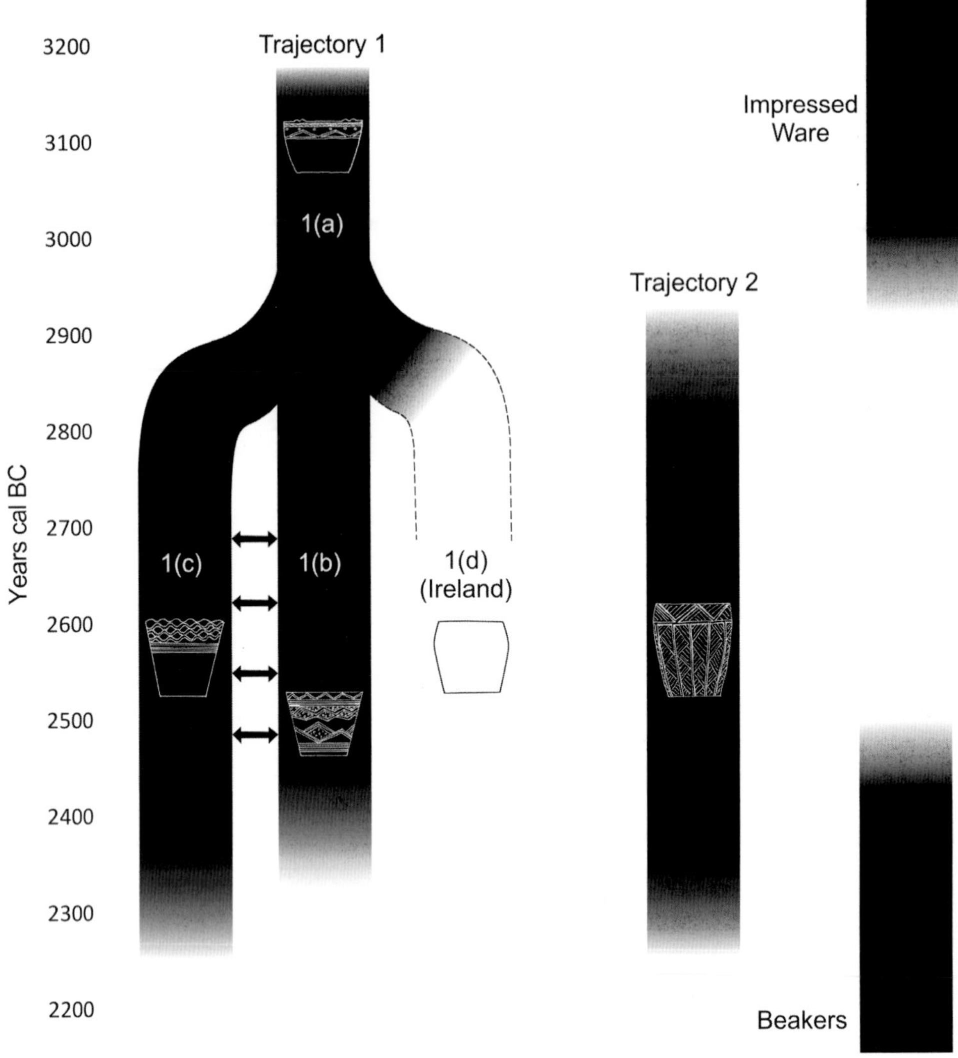

Figure 4.8. Grooved Ware stylistic development in Scotland (dating based on Copper et al. *2021).*

Trajectory 2 Grooved Ware appears (potentially) to have continued in use after 2400 cal BC. As Trajectory 1(a) Grooved Ware was transforming into Trajectory 1(b) in southern mainland Scotland and the Hebrides – a process that most likely accounts for MacSween's observation of overlapping stylistic features in some Scottish assemblages (MacSween 1995) – Orcadian pottery was developing along its own stylistic trajectory, here termed Trajectory 1(c), possibly as a result of increasing cultural isolation (Bayliss *et al.* 2017). The presence of 'Orcadian' features at Raigmore and An Doirlinn demonstrates, however, that pottery traditions in Orkney, the Western Isles and on the mainland continued to cross-fertilise and highlights the problems inherent in trying to place pottery into monothetic categories. The development of Trajectory 2 Grooved Ware – traditionally termed the Durrington Walls sub-style – over much of Britain, including southern and eastern Scotland, could well reflect changing, or parallel social alignments following the early spread of Grooved Ware. Only this latter trajectory seems to have persisted after the first appearance of Beaker pottery, though there is no unambiguous evidence of stylistic cross-fertilisation with Beakers.

It is also worth considering whether Grooved Ware constituted a unitary phenomenon, especially given that Trajectories 1(b) and 2 were produced and used contemporaneously in some regions. While Longworth, unlike Clarke (1970, 269), felt that Grooved Ware did indeed form a single tradition (Wainwright and Longworth 1971, 243–4), it should be borne in mind that Neolithic potters were not trying to fit their work into modern categories but were drawing upon their knowledge to create vessels that were both functionally and socially useful. Thus, what we are dealing with is *British and Irish Late Neolithic Pottery* that, within limits, may be lumped or split to the extent that one wishes to understand similarity or difference. Emic categories remain conjectural.

CONCLUSION: GROOVED WARE TRAJECTORIES IN SCOTLAND

I have argued that Longworth's four Grooved Ware sub-styles are not in fact fixed, essential categories into which Grooved Ware naturally falls but abstractions derived from dynamic stylistic *trajectories* with regional variants (though questions remain about the significance of Trajectory 2). In this regard, it is of interest that subtle regional variations within broader trajectories are discussed elsewhere in the volume by Frances Lynch and Josh Pollard and Ros Cleal. As such, and in contrast to Longworth's emphasis on recurrent features defining fixed styles, the model proposed above draws on a polythetic understanding of ceramic categorisation in which traditions blend, divide and change in character, while 'prototype effects' (the tendency for membership of a category to be a case of 'more or less' rather than 'all or nothing': Lakoff 1987, 40–6) mean that ceramic traditions, while exhibiting family resemblance, were never completely unconstrained. In some respects, a very loose analogy with modern-day fashions in clothing and music would in many respects be fitting to the extent that more-or-less bounded styles may be recognised in both Grooved Ware and contemporary clothing and music, perhaps reflecting similar processes of 'identity signalling' (Gal 2015), even while their dynamic and constantly evolving natures are acknowledged.

While the argument has focused exclusively on Scotland and has not discussed regional trajectories elsewhere that will exhibit their own idiosyncrasies, it has nonetheless been possible to draw out a number of salient points relating to Grooved Ware more generally. These may be summarised as follows:

1. Grooved Ware currently appears to have developed in Orkney – probably on the West Mainland – before 3100 cal BC. There is presently no evidence that it emerged by a process of stylistic drift from the earlier ceramic traditions, and it therefore remains possible that it resulted from a conscious attempt to create a new style of pottery, perhaps in the context of ritualised commensal practices at sites such as the Ness of Brodgar.

2. The earliest Grooved Ware variants – Trajectory 1(a) – were almost certainly being made outside Orkney by 3000 cal BC, as reflected in its presence at the very early timber circle at Machrie Moor Site 1, though stylistic innovation is already visible even at this early stage, indicating that this was a dynamic and changing tradition from its very start.
3. Stylistic drift within Trajectory 1(a) (already noted from 3000 cal BC at Barnhouse) means that it is useful to refer to later iterations of Trajectory 1 as Trajectories 1(b), 1(c) and 1(d). In Scotland, Trajectory 1(b) appears in the south, the west and the Hebrides and Trajectory 1(c) emerged in Orkney, with their distributions possibly reflecting what Olivier Gosselain (2010) termed 'social spaces'. Intermediate (but not 'hybrid') assemblages include that from the Balfarg timber circle. Longworth's Clacton sub-style is derived from Trajectory 1(b), though regional developments visible in Scotland demonstrate that this was not a closed category (that is, a *sub-style*) but, once again, part of a dynamic and malleable tradition. Importantly, this sequence is an inversion of that suggested by Garwood (1999) for Woodlands and Clacton Grooved Ware in southern England.
4. Trajectory 2 Grooved Ware probably developed by a different process from Trajectories 1(b), 1(c) and 1(d), though where this occurred is currently unknown. In Scotland, Trajectory 2 Grooved Ware, which exhibits less stylistic development than Trajectory 1, is presently known only from the south and east of the country as far north as the Moray Firth. The fact that twisted cord and comb impression were employed at Littleour before the arrival of Beakers suggests that (*contra* Pollard and Cleal, this volume) these techniques were not influenced by the latter style.
5. Current dating suggests that only Grooved Ware Trajectory 2 continued after the introduction of Beaker pottery, though there is almost no evidence for a Grooved Ware influence on Beaker or Early Bronze Age pottery (Copper *et al.* 2021, 102). Current dating suggests that while the overlap between the two styles in Scotland could have lasted for seven or eight generations, it is more likely to have been a matter of at most two or three generations, and it is not beyond the bounds of possibility that Grooved Ware was abandoned in any one area as soon as Beaker pottery was introduced.

The Grooved Ware trajectories proposed above represent dynamic stylistic traditions that exhibit both temporal and regional variations while having no fixed boundaries. In the case of Trajectories 1(a), 1(b), 1(c) and 1(d), these also reflect differences between the starting point and end points of Grooved Ware development. In keeping with a strictly polythetic approach, no attempt has therefore been made to define necessary or sufficient conditions for any of the trajectories, although characteristic features, some shared by vessels belonging to different trajectories, certainly exist. Likewise, regional trajectories beyond Scotland have not been discussed in any detail. As a result of our expanding range of assemblages and dates it is becoming increasingly clear that Grooved Ware was a dynamic phenomenon that cannot be contained within a rigid framework of fixed sub-types, as useful as these may have been in the past. It is therefore necessary to endeavour to understand the style within its temporal, geographical, social and political contexts, however challenging that may be. After all, Grooved Ware pots were not made to illustrate Platonic forms, but to play their various roles within the ceaselessly unfolding world of Late Neolithic Britain and Ireland.

ACKNOWLEDGEMENTS

This article arises from the Historic Environment Scotland-funded project *Tracing the Lines: Uncovering Grooved Ware Trajectories in Neolithic Scotland.* The author would like to thank everyone involved with that project, especially Dr Alex Gibson and Professor Derek Hamilton. Thanks also to Dr Alison Sheridan, Professor Alasdair Whittle and Claire Copper for their feedback on earlier drafts of this chapter.

REFERENCES

Anderson-Whymark, H. 2020. Ness of Brodgar flaked stone assemblage: 2004–2018. In N. Card, M. Edmonds and A. Mitchell (eds), *The Ness of Brodgar: as it stands*, 208–23. Kirkwall: The Orcadian.

Armit, I., Cowie, T. and Ralston, I. 1994. Excavation of pits containing Grooved Ware at Hillend, Clydesdale District, Strathclyde Region. *Proceedings of the Society of Antiquaries of Scotland* 124, 113–27.

Barclay, G. and Maxwell, G. 1998. *The Cleaven Dyke and Littleour: monuments in the Neolithic of Tayside.* Edinburgh: Society of Antiquaries of Scotland.

Barclay, G. and Russell-White, C. 1993. Excavations in the ceremonial complex of the fourth to second millennium at Balfarg/Balbirnie, Glenrothes, Fife. *Proceedings of the Society of Antiquaries of Scotland* 123, 43–210.

Barclay, G., Carter, S., Daland, M., Hastie, M., Holden, T., MacSween, A. and Wickham-Jones, C. 2001. A possible Neolithic settlement at Kinbeachie, Black Isle, Highland. *Proceedings of the Society of Antiquaries of Scotland* 131, 57–85.

Bayliss, A., Marshall, P., Richards, C. and Whittle, A. 2017. Islands of history: the Late Neolithic timescape of Orkney. *Antiquity* 91, 1171–88.

Bloxam, A. and Parker Pearson, M. 2022. Beaker diversity and cultural continuity: the British Beaker phenomenon beyond the stereotype. *Proceedings of the Prehistoric Society* 88, 261–84.

Booth, T., Brück, J., Brace, S. and Barnes, I. 2021. Tales from the Supplementary Information: ancestry change in Chalcolithic–Early Bronze Age Britain was gradual with varied kinship organization. *Cambridge Archaeological Journal* 31(3), 379–400.

Brace, S. and Booth, T. 2023. The genetics of the inhabitants of Britain: a review. In A. Whittle, J. Pollard and S. Greaney (eds), *Ancient DNA and the European Neolithic: relations and descent*, 123–46. Oxford: Neolithic Studies Group Seminar Papers 19.

Brophy, K., Gould, A., Noble, G., Wright, D. and Younger, R. n.. *Leadketty excavations 2012. Unpublished Data Structure Report: Strathearn Environs Royal Forteviot Project (SERF).* Available from https://www.gla.ac.uk/media/Media_296371_smxx.pdf (accessed 29/06/2019).

Clarke, D.L. 1970. *Beaker pottery of Great Britain and Ireland. Vol. 1.* Cambridge: Cambridge University Press.

Cleal, R. and MacSween, A. (eds) 1999. *Grooved Ware in Britain and Ireland.* Oxford: Oxbow Books.

Conolly, R. and MacSween, A. 2003. A possible Neolithic settlement at Milton of Leys, Inverness. *Proceedings of the Society of Antiquaries of Scotland* 133, 35–45.

Copper, M., Hamilton, D. and Gibson, A. 2021. Tracing the lines: Scottish Grooved Ware trajectories beyond Orkney. *Proceedings of the Society of Antiquaries of Scotland* 150, 81–117.

Copper, M., Sheridan, J.A., Gibson, A., Tripney, B., Hamilton, D. and Cook, G. 2018. Radiocarbon dates for Grooved Ware pottery from mainland Scotland arising from the project Tracing the Lines: Uncovering Grooved Ware Trajectories in Neolithic Scotland. *Discovery and Excavation in Scotland* 19, 214–7.

Copper, M., Sheridan, J.A., Gibson, A., Tripney, B., Hamilton, D. and Cook, G. 2019. Further radiocarbon dates for Grooved Ware pottery from mainland Scotland arising from the project

Tracing the Lines: Uncovering Grooved Ware Trajectories in Neolithic Scotland. *Discovery and Excavation in Scotland* 21, 232–4.

Curle, A.O. 1908. Notice of the examination of prehistoric kitchen middens on the Archerfield estate, near Gullane, Haddingtonshire, in November 1907. *Proceedings of the Society of Antiquaries of Scotland* 42, 308–25.

Ellis, C. 2017. Upper Largie Quarry. Watching brief and excavation. *Discovery and Excavation in Scotland* 18, 56.

Eogan, G. 1984. *Excavations at Knowth 1: smaller passage tombs, Neolithic occupation and Beaker activity.* Dublin: Royal Irish Academy.

Gal, D. 2015. Identity-signaling behavior. In M. Norton, D. Rucker, and C. Lamberton (eds), *The Cambridge Handbook of Consumer Psychology*, 257–81. Cambridge: Cambridge University Press.

Garrow, D. and Sturt, F. 2017. *Neolithic stepping stones: excavation and survey within the western seaways of Britain, 2008–2014.* Oxford: Oxbow Books.

Garwood, P. 1999. Grooved Ware in southern Britain: chronology and interpretation. In R. Cleal and A. MacSween (eds) 1999, 145–76.

Gibson, A. 1982. *Beaker domestic sites: a study of the domestic pottery of the late third and early second millennia B.C. in the British Isles.* Oxford: British Archaeological Report 107.

Gibson, A. 2010. Dating Balbirnie: recent radiocarbon dates from the stone circle and cairn at Balbirnie, Fife, and a review of its place in the overall Balfarg/Balbirnie site sequence. *Proceedings of the Society of Antiquaries of Scotland* 140, 51–77.

Gosselain, O. 2010. De l'art d'accommoder les pâtes et de s'accomoder d'autrui au sud du Niger: espaces et échelles d'analyse. In C. Manen, F. Convertini, D. Binder and I. Sénepart (eds), *Premières sociétés paysannes de la Méditerranée orientale. Structures des productions céramiques*, 249–63. Paris: Société Préhistorique Française.

Haggarty, A. 1991. Machrie Moor, Arran: recent excavations at two stone circles. *Proceedings of the Society of Antiquaries of Scotland* 121, 51–94.

Henshall, A. 1972. *The chambered tombs of Scotland. Vol. 2.* Edinburgh: Edinburgh University Press.

Jones, A. 2005. The Grooved Ware from Barnhouse. In C. Richards (ed.), *Dwelling among the monuments: the Neolithic village of Barnhouse, Maeshowe passage grave and surrounding monuments at Stenness, Orkney*, 261–82. Cambridge: McDonald Institute for Archaeological Research.

Jones, A.M., Jones, R., Tully, G., Maritan, L., Mukherjee, A., Evershed, R., MacSween, A., Richards, C. and Towers, R. 2016. Prehistoric pottery from sites within the Bay of Firth: Stonehall, Crossiecrown, Wideford Hill, Brae of Smerquoy, Muckquoy, Ramberry and Knowes of Trotty. In C. Richards and R. Jones (eds), *The development of Neolithic house societies in Orkney: investigations in the Bay of Firth, Mainland, Orkney (1994–2014)*, 303–412. Oxford: Windgather Press.

Jorge, A. 2014. *Monktonhall, East Lothian: prehistoric pottery report.* Unpublished specialist report. Available from https://www.academia.edu/36134276/Monktonhall_East_Lothian_Prehistoric_pottery_report (Accessed 29/06/2019).

Lakoff, G. 1987. *Women, fire and dangerous things: what categories reveal about the mind.* Chicago: University of Chicago Press.

MacSween, A. 1995. Grooved Ware from Scotland: aspects of decoration. In I. Kinnes and G. Varndell (eds), *Unbaked urns of rudely shape: essays on British and Irish pottery for Ian Longworth*, 41–8. Oxford: Oxbow Books.

MacSween, A. 2007. The pottery. In J. Hunter with J. Bond and A. N. Smith. 2007. *Investigations in Sanday Orkney. Volume 1: excavations at Pool, Sanday. A multi-period site from Neolithic to Late Norse times,* 287–353. Kirkwall: The Orcadian.

MacSween, A. 2008. The prehistoric pottery. In M. Cook and L. Dunbar (eds), *Rituals, roundhouses and Romans: excavations at Kintore, Aberdeenshire, 2000–2006. Volume 1. Forest*, 173–89. Edinburgh: Scottish Trust for Archaeological Research.

MacSween, A., Hunter, J., Sheridan, J.A., Bond, J., Bronk Ramsey, C., Reimer, P., Bayliss, A., Griffiths, S. and Whittle, A. 2015. Refining the chronology of the Neolithic settlement at Pool, Sanday, Orkney: implications for the emergence and development of Grooved Ware. *Proceedings of the Prehistoric Society* 81, 283–310.

Marshall, P., Hamilton, W.D., van der Plicht, J., Bronk Ramsey, C., Cook, G. and Goslar, T. 2009. Scientific dating. In M.G. Beamish, Island visits: Neolithic and Bronze Age activity on the Trent valley floor. Excavations at Eggington and Willington, Derbyshire, 1998–1999, 62–81. *Derbyshire Archaeological Journal* 129, 17–172.

Mercer, R., Wickham-Jones, C., Henshall, A., Whittington, G., Harman, M., Lunt, D., Brock, J., Williams, D., Dickson, C., Stenhouse, M., Pare, C. and Nebelsick, L. 1981. The excavation of a Late Neolithic henge-type enclosure at Balfarg, Markinch, Fife, Scotland, 1977–78. *Proceedings of the Society of Antiquaries of Scotland* 111, 63–171.

Murray, H. and Murray, J. 2013. *Site west of International Paper, Port Elphinstone, Inverurie, Aberdeenshire. Report Number MAS 2012–15.* Unpublished Excavation Report: Murray Archaeological Services. *http://archaeologydataservice.ac.uk/archives/view/greylit/details.cfm?id=23291*

Richards, C., Jones, A.M., MacSween, A., Sheridan, J.A., Dunbar, E., Reimer, P., Bayliss, A., Griffiths, S. and Whittle, A. 2016. Settlement duration and materiality: formal chronological models for the development of Barnhouse, a Grooved Ware settlement in Orkney. *Proceedings of the Prehistoric Society* 82, 193–225.

Schulting, R., Sheridan, J.A., Crozier, R. and Murphy, E. 2010. Revisiting Quanterness: new AMS dates and stable isotope data from an Orcadian tomb. *Proceedings of the Society of Antiquaries of Scotland* 140, 1–50.

Schulting, R., Bronk Ramsey, C., Reimer, P., Eogan, G., Cleary, K., Cooney, G. and Sheridan, J.A. 2017. Dating the Neolithic human remains at Knowth. In G. Eogan and K. Cleary (eds), *Excavations at Knowth 6: the passage tomb archaeology of the Great Mound at Knowth.* Dublin: Royal Irish Academy. 331–85.

Scott, W.L. 1948. The chamber tomb of Unival, North Uist. *Proceedings of the Society of Antiquaries of Scotland* 82, 1–49.

Sheridan, J.A. 1999. Grooved Ware from the Links of Noltland, Westray, Orkney. In R. Cleal and A. MacSween (eds) 1999, 112–24.

Sheridan, J.A. 2012. Contextualising Kilmartin: building a narrative for developments in western Scotland and beyond, from the Early Neolithic to the Late Bronze Age. In A.M. Jones, J. Pollard, M.J. Allen and J. Gardiner (eds), *Image, memory and monumentality: archaeological engagements with the material world*, 163–83. Oxford: Prehistoric Society Research Papers 5.

Sheridan, J.A., Henshall, A., Johnson, M. and Ashmore, P. 2016. The pottery assemblage. In P. Ashmore (ed.), *Calanais: survey and excavation 1979–88*, 573–803. Edinburgh: Historic Environment Scotland.

Simpson, D. 1996. Excavation of a kerbed funerary monument at Stoneyfield, Raigmore, Inverness, Highland, 1972–3. *Proceedings of the Society of Antiquaries of Scotland* 126, 53–86.

Smith, I. 1956. *The decorative art of Neolithic ceramics of south-eastern England and its relations.* Unpublished PhD thesis, University of London.

Squair, R. and Ballin Smith, B. 2018. The prehistoric pottery. In B. Ballin Smith (ed.), *Life on the edge: the Neolithic and Bronze Age of Iain Crawford's Udal, North Uist*, 183–97. Oxford: Archaeopress.

Thomas, J. 2015. *A Neolithic ceremonial complex in Galloway: excavations at Dunragit and Droughduil, 1999–2002.* Oxford: Oxbow Books.

Wainwright, G.J. and Longworth, I.H. 1971. *Durrington Walls: excavations 1966–1968.* London: Society of Antiquaries.

Wessex Archaeology 2020. *Bulford Service Family Accommodation, Bulford, Wiltshire: post-excavation assessment.* Salisbury: Wessex Archaeology, unpublished report (Ref. 200770.1).

Chapter 5

Grooved Ware in northern England since 2000

Sarah Jayne Botfield and Gill Hey

When Terry Manby wrote his contribution to the 1999 *Grooved Ware in Britain and Ireland* volume, the distribution of Grooved Ware in northern England was focused firmly on the east side of the Pennines and in Derbyshire (Manby 1999, illus. 6.1), and this remains the case today. Twenty-four new findspots have joined the list in this eastern region since that time, including the first known instance of Grooved Ware in south Yorkshire (Roberts and Weston 2016; Fig. 5.1). Additionally, a small number of sherds, including some not previously assigned to a sub-style, have been assessed and, where relevant, added to or removed from the *corpus* (Figs 5.1–5.2, Table 5.1). (Note: those removed include a sherd found in 1951 in an Early Bronze Age cemetery at Eddisbury, Cheshire (Manby 1999, 69), which is now considered to be an Encrusted Urn (Mike Copper, pers. comm.)). Although the number of findspots of Grooved Ware in northern England may not have increased dramatically from the 62 listed by Manby in 1999, our knowledge and understanding of the temporal and distributional aspects of this pottery tradition, and of its form, function and decoration, have been enhanced.

Manby was only able to identify two isolated sites in North West England: Walney Island on the north side of Morecambe Bay and Eddisbury in Cheshire, in addition to a scatter of sherds from fieldwalking on the Westmorland Fells (Cherry and Cherry 1987) and possible discoveries from limestone caves on the west side of the Pennine watershed. A barrel-shaped bowl or jar from an old excavation at Rathmell near Settle in Upper Ribblesdale also belongs with this group from the Pennines limestone (Manby 1999, illus. 6.3.10). Manby updated his synthesis in a volume on North West England dedicated to the memory of Clare Fell, which enabled him to illustrate more of this material (Manby 2007, fig. 4.7), and to note an additional Grooved Ware sherd from Lesser Kelcoe Cave which had previously been recorded amongst the Victoria Cave finds (Manby 2007, 91; Gilks 2005). He also discussed the previously accepted attribution of the Walney Island material as Clacton sub-style Grooved Ware. Otherwise, he was not able to identify any further discoveries, though he did highlight the potential for future finds from projects in advance of development and for subsequent radiocarbon dating and residue analysis. Opportunities have increased in the intervening years, but the absolute quantity of Grooved Ware from North West England has remained stubbornly small, with only seven new sites added to the corpus. For four of these the attribution is not certain, so small are the assemblages.

On the southern fringes of this region, in Leicestershire and Staffordshire, Manby was able to cite just one findspot of Grooved Ware in Leicestershire – a gravel pit at Thurmaston on the north edge of Leicester, where a Clacton sub-style rimsherd was found – and two in Staffordshire, both associated with burial contexts. Since that time there have been important new discoveries (nine sites in total), all in the course of development work.

DISTRIBUTION OF NEW SITES

The distribution of post-2000 Grooved Ware findspots in northern England is shown in Figure 5.1 and listed in Table 5.1.

Developer-led archaeology has provided the majority of new Grooved Ware discoveries in North East England, from eight residential developments and nine mineral extraction schemes. These include three quarry sites in the Milfield Basin, Northumberland, at Lanton Quarry and Cheviot Quarry (Johnson and Waddington 2008; ARS 2010) and at Wooperton on the Cheviot Fringe to the south of Wooler, where a single residual Grooved Ware sherd was found (Ansell 2004). A discovery at Morpeth in the south of the county lies in a transitional area between the Northumberland Hills and the coastal plain where Grooved Ware had previously been absent (Lotherington 2016).

Further south, a large assemblage of Grooved Ware was recorded during residential development at White House Farm, Stokesley, North Yorkshire (ASDU unpublished client report, 2015), on the broad, open plain of the Tees Valley. Discoveries were also made on the gravel terraces of the River Swale in the Vale of Mowbray at Hollow Banks Quarry, Scorton, and along the line of the A1 Dishforth to Barton upgrade. The A1 work (Speed 2021) and the A66 upgrade from Greta Bridge to Scotch Corner (Zant and Howard-Davis 2013) both provided opportunities to examine a variety of topographies rich in Neolithic and Bronze Age monuments along the Vale of Mowbray. Only one new find has been recorded on the North York Moors since 1999 and none has come from the Vale of Pickering.

Sites previously identified by Manby as lying within the Vale of Mowbray (Manby 1999, 73) are located further to the south in the Vale of York and on the Southern Magnesian Limestone (Natural England 2013; 2014) but, even so, the number of Grooved Ware discoveries within eastern Yorkshire since 2000 has numbered just seven. The post-2000 discoveries are fairly widely scattered and include several within the Vale of York and on the Yorkshire Wolds as well as one at North Ferriby on the River Humber (Evans 2018). The first instance of Grooved Ware from south Yorkshire lay a little further west on the edge of the Humberhead Levels (Roberts and Weston 2016).

Discoveries of Grooved Ware have marginally increased in West Yorkshire since those on Ilkley Moor (Manby 1999, 73), following excavations within the Metropolitan Boroughs of Kirklees and Dewsbury, but they are still absent between this part of West Yorkshire and Buxton, Derbyshire, with the exception of one pre-2000 findspot in the Dark Peak to the west of Sheffield. Further discoveries have been made within the White Peak, the lower Derwent Valley and the Trent Valley Washlands; previous discoveries had mainly been located in the White Peak.

Only two new Grooved Ware sites have been recorded in Lincolnshire and there has been nothing to supplement the single pre-2000 Grooved Ware discovery in Nottinghamshire. Leicestershire, on the other hand, has seen a rise in new sites. Mostly situated near to

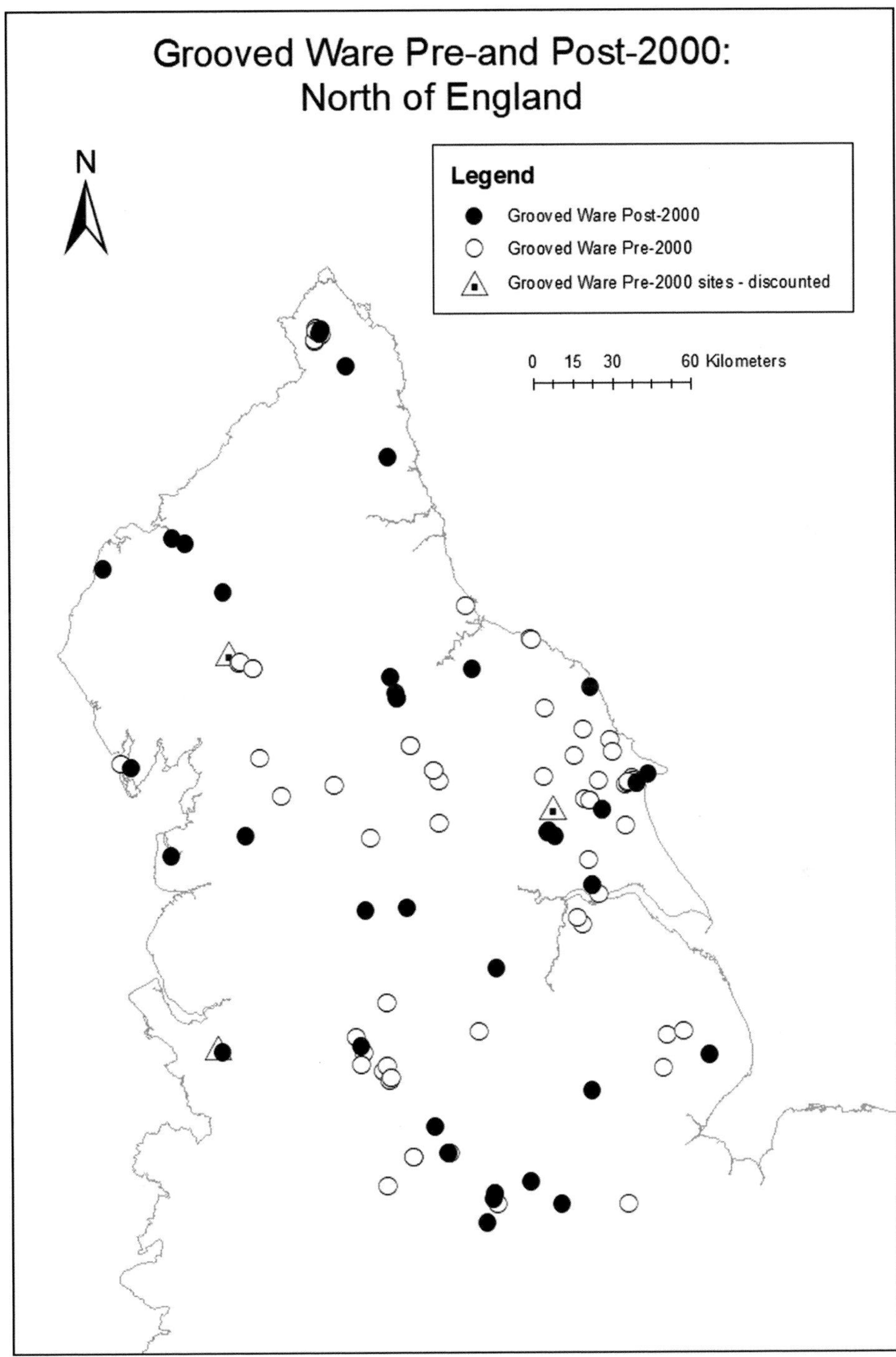

Figure 5.1. Distribution of known Grooved Ware sites in northern England.

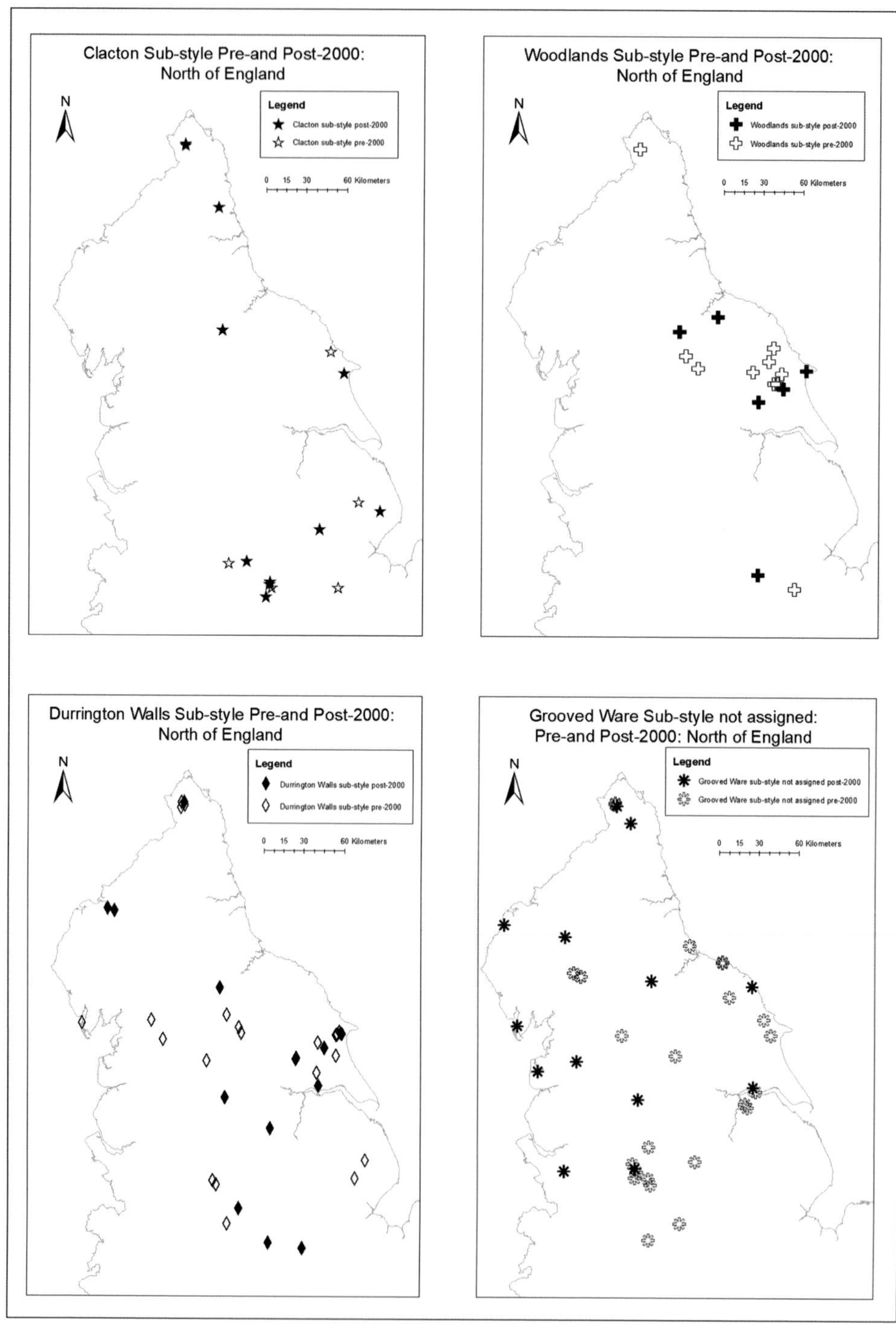

Figure 5.2. Distribution of Grooved Ware sub-styles in northern England. a) Clacton sub-style b) Woodlands sub-style c) Durrington Walls sub-style d) style uncertain (not all of these are definitely Grooved Ware).

Table 5.1. Gazetteer of post-2000 finds of Grooved Ware (GW) northern England

Site	*Grid ref*	*Find circumstances and context*	*Description*	*GW sub-style*	*Reference*
		Cheshire			
Eddisbury	SJ 5660 6699	Training excavation. Redeposited with Collared Urn in 2 pits found below early Bronze Age barrow. Note: site is just over 1 km SSE of findspot of alleged GW at Eddisbury discovered 1851 (Manby 1999, 69)	6 sherds with horizontal & slanting grooves, of which 5 from 1 vessel	U	Garner 2021; Vyner 2021
		Cumbria			
Breast Mill Beck Road, Barrow-in-Furness	SD 2150 7240	Scatter of features on housing scheme	1 sherd	Poss. GW or Food Vessel	NAA 2020
Durranhill, Carlisle	NY 42897 55261	Housing. Pits, including in pairs & small clusters. 17 certainly Late Neolithic pits amongst 32 others	>100 sherds with parts of at least 6 tub-like vessels with applied plastic decoration in 1 pit, & a ceramic ball	U	Jackson 2016; Vyner 2016
Long Meg and her Daughters, Penrith	NY 57110 37210	Research excavation	1 small base sherd with incised decoration	U	Young in ASDU 2016
New Cowper Quarry, Abbeytown Ridge	NY 1161 4590	Sand quarry	1 sherd from straight-sided vessel with simple flattened rim & 3 parallel grooves	U but more likely to be Beaker than GW	Jackson and Churchill 2017; Young 2017
Stainton West, Carlisle	NY 37594 57137	Road bridge. Deposits within palaeochannel & features inc. burnt mounds on adjacent bank	Large part of 1 large flat-bottomed bucket-shaped vessel & 3 sherds from another pot nearby. Horizontal & diagonal incised lines	U	Brown *et al.* in press
		Derbyshire			
Aston Hall Hospital, Aston-on-Trent	SK 41692 29248	Housing/health care. Pits	7 sherds from highly decorated vessel	C	Flintoft 2015

(Continued)

Table 5.1. Gazetteer of post-2000 finds of Grooved Ware (GW) northern England (Continued)

Site	*Grid ref*	*Find circumstances and context*	*Description*	*GW sub-style*	*Reference*
Brierlow Quarry, Buxton	SK 08935 69011	Mineral extraction. Pits, poss.tree-throw holes	23 sherds from 2–4 vessels. Bowls, rounded rims	U	Whittaker and Burpoe 2016
Land at Breadsall Hilltop, Mansfield Road, Derby	SK 36774 38911	Housing. Pits	52 sherds from 4 vessels, bevelled rim, upright rim	DW	Huxley 2018
		Lancashire			
Fairy Hole Caves, Whitewell	SD 6553 4678	Sieving spoil from 19thC excavations in cave in limestone cliffs	1 small sherd, possibly GW	U	Peterson 2013
Windy Harbour, Poulton-le-Fylde	SD 368 395	Road scheme, in area of intensive Mesolithic–Bronze Age activity. On bank above Lytham-Skippool Valley	Many small sherds from 1 vessel decorated with incised lines & applied cordons	U	Brown *et al.* in prep.
		Leicestershire			
De Verdon Road, Lutterworth	SP 5328 8423	Housing. On glacial sands & gravel near River Swift & headwaters of Soar	Partial remains of 8 vessels, at least 3 of which are of DW sub-style. Incised horizontal, vertical & oblique & curving grooves & striations. Applied vertical rib	DW	Cooper 2019; Flavell 2019
Elmsthorpe Rise, Braunstone	SK 5640 0350	Housing on higher ground overlooking River Soar. Hollow containing dense deposit inc. pot, flintwork & stone, animal bone & charred plant remains. Also 1 pit & a posthole	112 sherds from at least 16 vessels with horizontal & diagonal grooves, some infilled with impressed or fingernail designs	C	Albone 2001; Allen 2001c
Eye Kettleby, Melton Mowbray	SK 7318 1796	New premises for the Melton Foods & Kettleby Foods companies. Pit with posthole.	40 sherds from 1 vessel. Most of a cup decorated with slashed/notched cordons & 'knots' or pellets of clay on the rim	W	Finn 2011; Gibson 2011

(Continued)

Table 5.1 (Continued)

Site	*Grid ref*	*Find circumstances and context*	*Description*	*GW sub-style*	*Reference*
Hinckley Island Hotel, Burbage	SP 4439 9052	Storage & distribution facility. Tree-throw pit	8 base & body sherds of single tub-shaped vessel, 1 of which has grooved decoration suggesting Clacton sub-style	Poss. C	Percival 2022; Walton *et al.* 2022
Rearsby Lodge Farm, Rearsby	SK 6508 1345	A607 Rearsby Bypass Road Scheme. Pit	Fragments of GW	?	Beamish and Clarke 2008
Rothley Lodge Farm, Rothley	SK 592 140	Industrial units. Large hollow & small pits & postholes	762 sherds (3.9 kg) from tubs, small & medium jars & small bowls, with open profiles & flat bottoms. Fine fabrics. Internal grooves on rim, incised lines & chevrons externally. Some whipped maggots. 2 fired clay balls	Some W, C	Clay and Hunt 2016; Cooper 2016
Temple Grange Farm, Rothley	SK 58817 12357	Housing. 3 separate groups of postholes & pits, inc 1 definite circular structure & 2 other possibles	102 sherds (338g), inc. rims, from at least 4 vessels. Fine fabric, mainly shell temper. Abraded. Internal grooves & external horizontal & diagonal lines with fingernail impressions	C	Cooper 2015; Speed 2015
Weatherby Close, Queniborough	SK 640 126	Housing. 3 pits, 7 postholes & tree-throw pits. 1 pit with GW.	No report	?	Hall 2003
		Lincolnshire			
Land to south of High Farm, Halton Holegate	TF 41310 656	Geological research – drill site. 1 GW pit, 4 fills, GW within each fill	11 sherds from 4 vessels, inc. 1 thin-walled vessel	C	Pre-Construct Archaeology 2001
Leadenham, Welbourn	SK 96300 52500	Mineral extraction. GW deposited within 2 pits in a pit alignment	27 sherds from 4 vessels. Straight-sided vessels, rounded rims	C	WYAS 2001

(Continued)

Table 5.1. Gazetteer of post-2000 finds of Grooved Ware (GW) northern England (Continued)

Site	*Grid ref*	*Find circumstances and context*	*Description*	*GW sub-style*	*Reference*
		Northumberland			
Cheviot Quarry, Milfield Basin	NT 9485 326	Mineral extraction. Pits	37 sherds from at least 13 vessels. Bucket & tub-shaped, open dish, vertical rims, flattened rim, rim with internal bevel	W, C	Johnson and Waddington 2008
Lanton Quarry, Milfield Basin	NT 95338 31281	Mineral extraction. Pits containing midden. Vessel 1 had collapsed *in situ*	40 sherds from 4 vessels. Splayed sides, open jar, rounded rim, internally bevelled rim	DW, C	ARS 2010
St George's Hospital, Morpeth	NZ 20378 86868	Housing. Pit & residual in wall construction trench of Middle Iron Age roundhouse	6 sherds from 3 vessels. Tub- & bucket-shaped	C	Lotherington 2016
Wooperton Quarry, Wooler	NU 049 204	Mineral extraction. Residual sherd in Roman context	1 sherd	U	Ansell 2004
		Rutland			
Barleythorpe, Oakham	SK4892 1024	Housing. Small group of pits & gully	3 or 4 sherds, inc. 2 from flat bases, 1 with horizontal band of fingernail impressions & 1 with random nail impressions	U	Cooper 2013 Hyam 2013
		Yorkshire			
		East Yorkshire			
Auchinleck Close, Driffield	TA 0095 5595	Housing. Pits.	604 sherds, crumbs & flakes. Open bowls. Barrel-shaped jars, pointed rims, internally bevelled rims	W, DW	Walsh *et al.* 2012
Burnby Lane, Hayton	SE 8255 4650	Research Project. Pits. Cross-links between 2 GW pits	29 sherds from at least 6 vessels. Convex-sided bowl, splayed walls, simple rim, rounded rim, expanded rim with overhanging bevel	W	Halkon *et al.* 2010

(Continued)

Table 5.1 (Continued)

Site	*Grid ref*	*Find circumstances and context*	*Description*	*GW sub-style*	*Reference*
Burnby Lane, The Mile, Pocklington	SE 801 486	Housing. Pits	Sherds	DW	Stephens 2023, 65
Canal Lane, Pocklington	SE 7976 4785	Water utilities. Pits	129 sherds. Internally expanded rim, pointed rim	DW	Tabor 2009
East Coast Pipeline, Fields 4, 6, 7, 10, 12	TA 14 66	Water pipeline. Pits, posthole, tree-throw hole	1483 sherds, Open bowls, bucket- & barrel-shaped splayed bowls, flattened rim, internally bevelled rim, internally expanded rim, rounded rim, pointed rim, in-turned rim, protruding moulded foot	DW, C	Manby unpublished client report, 2016; Gavin Robinson pers. comm.
Melton Quarry, North Ferriby.	SE 96760 28400	Mineral extraction. Pits. Multiple stake setting, Exploitation of clay.	130 sherds. Cylindrical, tub-shaped, poss. internal bevel.	DW	Evans 2018
Sewerby Cottage Farm, Sewerby	TA 185 692	Housing. Farmyard dump assemblages (midden)	63 sherds from 11 vessels	W	Fenton-Thomas 2009
		North Yorkshire			
A1 Dishforth to Barton motorway upgrade, Fields 160, 162, 163N, 164, 164S	SE 23100 97600	Highways. Pits	119 sherds from at least 5 vessels, inc. barrel-shaped jar, tub-shaped, simple rim	C, W	Gibson 2018
A66 Greta Bridge to Scotch Corner (SCA13)	NZ 2071 0551	Highways, Pit	28 sherds. Barrel-shaped jar, bevelled rim	GW? Has DW features	Zant and Howard-Davis 2013
Brow Moor, Fylingdales Moor	NZ 962 017	Research project. Land surface 4 m from earthfast rock with rock art	4 sherds, jar	U	Vyner 2017

(Continued)

Table 5.1. Gazetteer of post-2000 finds of Grooved Ware (GW) northern England (Continued)

Site	*Grid ref*	*Find circumstances and context*	*Description*	*GW sub-style*	*Reference*
Hollow Banks Quarry, Scorton	SE 228 998	Mineral extraction. Pit	30 sherds from 3–4 vessels	DW	NAA 2002
White House Farm, Stokesley	NZ 51582 08325	Housing. Pits. Context suggests non-utilitarian function	29 sherds from *c.* 20 vessels. Tubs, open jars	W	ASDU unpublished client report, 2015
		South Yorkshire			
Rossington Grange Farm, Rossington	SK 605 975	Mineral extraction & restoration scheme. Pit	16 sherds	DW	Roberts and Weston 2016
		West Yorkshire			
Lindley-cum-Quarby, Huddersfield	SE 1106 1917	Housing. Pit	3 sherds	U	Vyner 2008, 7
Mitchell Laithes, Ossett	SE 2650 1990	Water utilities. Pit	53 sherds, 1 flake, 99 crumbs, from 9 vessels. Large splayed-wall vessel, open bowl, rounded rim	DW	Speed 2007

Key to Grooved Ware sub-styles: W – Woodlands, C – Clacton, DW – Durrington Walls, U – unattributed the River Soar, these sites were discovered as a result of development around the city of Leicester and include important assemblages from Elmsthorpe Rise, Braunstone (Albone 2001), and two sites around Rothley (Speed 2015; Clay and Hunt 2016). Eye Kettleby (Finn 2011) lies to the north-east, on the River Wreake, a tributary of the Soar, as do single features producing finds at Wetherby Close, Queniborough (Hall 2003), and Rearsby Lodge Farm (Beamish and Clarke 2008), and small assemblages have also been uncovered at the headwaters of the Soar at Burbage and Lutterworth (Flavell 2019; Walton *et al.* 2022). Barleythorpe, Oakham (Hyam 2013), lies on the claylands of the Vale of Catmose. Geographically, this is a restricted distribution.

In North West England there has been one further possible discovery on the Furness Peninsula near the Walney Island site, from a housing development in Barrow-in-Furness (Gibson 2020; NAA 2020), and six redeposited sherds were uncovered during a training excavation at the Seven Lows Barrows in Cheshire, only *c.* 2 km away from the earlier (and now rejected) Eddisbury find (Garner 2021; Vyner 2021). The distribution of sites has expanded, however, with the main discoveries having been made in the Carlisle/Solway Plain area, in particular from a housing scheme at Durranhill, Carlisle (Jackson 2016), and at Stainton West on a road scheme just north-west of Carlisle (Brown *et al.* in press). One possible rimsherd was also recovered from excavations at New Cowper Quarry (Young 2017, 72) on the Abbeytown Ridge to the west (although its tentative identification as Grooved Ware has been challenged; it could be Beaker: Claire Copper, pers. comm.), and upstream on the Eden, the Altogether Archaeology community group recovered a possible Grooved Ware base sherd in the recut of an Early Neolithic enclosure at Long Meg, Penrith, where the ditch intersected with the stone circle (ASDU 2016, 8, fig. 5a; Frodsham 2021, 162).

Very recently, Grooved Ware has been identified from a pit on a site at Windy Harbour near the north Lancashire coast, north of Blackpool (Rick Peterson, pers. comm.), and further material may emerge from the ongoing analysis of the assemblages from this extensive site (Brown *et al.* in prep.). No further discoveries have been reported from the limestone uplands on the west side of the Pennines, however, with the exception of one possible Grooved Ware sherd retrieved from sieving material from earlier excavations at Fairy Holes Cave, Whitewell, Lancashire (Peterson 2013).

Low-lying situations on or near river estuaries typify the landscape locations of the great majority of these northern sites, but this distribution, and the absence of discoveries in areas such as the Dark Peak, parts of the Pennines and the Border Moors, might reflect the areas of most intense modern development as much as, or rather than, the pattern of prehistoric deposition.

CONTEXTS OF DEPOSITION

The majority of the Grooved Ware from northern England was recovered from pits, in common with the pattern across Britain. Recent exceptions include a midden at Sewerby Cottage Farm, Bridlington (Fenton-Thomas 2009), and amorphous hollows at Elmsthorpe Rise, Braunstone, and Rothley Lodge Farm, Rothley (Albone 2001; Speed 2015). Two sherds also came from the old land surface at Brow Moor on the North York Moors, 4 m from an earthfast rock with rock art (Vyner 2017).

At Temple Grange Farm in Leicestershire, the pottery was associated with a circular, post-built structure and two other possible structures lay nearby; environmental sampling provided evidence of the small-scale generation of cereal waste from food preparation and the gathering of wild foods (Clay and Hunt 2016). As elsewhere, however, most pits were found singly, in pairs or small clusters along with postholes, and these probably represent the remains of short-lived occupation sites. Examples in North East England stretch from Lanton Quarry, Northumberland (ARS 2010), to Aston Hall Hospital, Aston-on-Trent, Derbyshire (Flintoft and Stein 2016). In North West England, the most extensive spread of pits was at Durranhill, Carlisle, where 17 definitely late Neolithic features were found (Table 5.2, below) along with 32 others which were undated (Jackson 2016). Single pits were the source of Grooved Ware at other sites such as Windy Harbour, Lancashire (Brown *et al.* in prep.). Occasional tree-throw pits with Grooved Ware have also been excavated which could represent clearances adjacent to settlements, such as the tree-throw pit and posthole from Fields 4 and 10, Low Caythorpe, East Yorkshire (Pole, unpublished client report for Yorkshire Water, 2010, 7; Manby unpublished client report, 2016). The original contexts of deposition of the Grooved Ware from Seven Lows Barrows, Eddisbury, Cheshire (Garner 2021), and the possible Grooved Ware from Long Meg and Fairy Holes Caves, are unknown.

The pot found at Stainton West, Carlisle, seems to have been deliberately placed within a pit or scoop dug into the peaty deposits of a palaeochannel; two burnt mounds on the bank appear to be contemporary. A ceremonial or ritual purpose also seemed to lie behind the substantial deposits found within the shallow, amorphous hollows on the sites of both Elmsthorpe Rise, Braunstone, and Rothley Lodge Farm (Albone 2001; Speed 2015). The density of material from these features is striking and includes large assemblages of lithics (including transverse arrowheads) and charred material, including cereal grains, as well as Grooved Ware. Other examples of possible special deposits were thought to be represented by the contents of two pits at Leadenham Quarry, Lincolnshire, which formed part of a pit alignment (WYAS 2001); by the Grooved Ware in pits at Mitchell Laithes, West Yorkshire, which were found within an occupation setting (Speed 2007, 26); and by the pottery and cremated human bone in the tree-throw pit in Field 4, Carnaby, East Yorkshire (Pole, unpublished client report for Yorkshire Water, 2010, 7). It is also noteworthy that the Grooved Ware pot from Eye Kettleby was found in a posthole (Finn 2011). Perhaps the best examples of ritual deposition came from Rothley Lodge Farm, Leicestershire, where an engraved sandstone plaque was found within one pit and, within another, a thin rectangular stone rubber had been suggestively placed between two fired clay balls, a possible fertility symbol (Clay and Hunt 2016, figs 10, 18 and 19).

Associations between Grooved Ware pits and Neolithic monuments may be evidenced at Aston Hall Hospital, Aston, Derbyshire, where the pit had been placed within 200 m of the Aston Cursus (Flintoft and Stein 2016) and at Hollow Banks Quarry, North Yorkshire, where a pit had been placed close to a hengiform monument and the Scorton Cursus (NAA 2002). The proximity of Grooved Ware sherds to a panel of rock art on Brow Moore, Fylingdales (Vyner 2017), is intriguing but geographical proximity (4 m) does not imply contemporaneity or association. These deposition patterns seem to follow those recorded by Manby in 1999, the majority being associated with occupation and with some clearer examples of ritual/formal activity (Manby 1999, 58–9).

STYLES, FORM, FABRICS AND DECORATION

The various sub-styles will be discussed in the order in which Manby discussed them in his 1999 publication.

Clacton sub-style

Clacton sub-style pottery was identified on six of the new Grooved Ware sites in North East England and three in the north Midlands (although a Woodlands element was noted in the Rothley Lodge Farm assemblage; Cooper 2016), but none has been found in North West England (Fig. 5.2a). These new discoveries alter the spatial patterning presented in the 1999 review, with the Clacton sub-style now also represented in North and East Yorkshire and Leicestershire as well as in Lincolnshire, Derbyshire and Northumberland. Complete profiles are still lacking in Lincolnshire, however (Manby 1999, 60). Many of these assemblages are small, but large quantities were recovered from the only Clacton-associated post pit in East Coast Pipeline Field 12 between High Caythorpe and Boynton, East Yorkshire (505 sherds; 5151 g), although many of the sherds are small (Manby unpublished client report, 2016, 30; Gavin Robinson, pers. comm.). Similarly, only one Clacton-associated pit was identified from the mid-20th century Caythorpe Pipeline excavations, compared to the several Durrington Walls and Woodlands contexts recorded (cf. Manby 1974, 64–70; 2016, 16). Elements of both Clacton and Durrington Walls sub-styles have been found on sherds from different Grooved Ware vessels from Cheviot Quarry, Northumberland (Johnson and Waddington 2008, 215). The characteristically splay-sided vessels of this sub-style were recorded from most of these sites. In contrast, the vessels from Leadenham, Lincolnshire, were described as straight-sided although the characteristic simple rim described by Longworth (1971, 237) was present (Allen 2001a).

Shell was dominant as a tempering agent within the small assemblage at Leadenham Quarry, Lincolnshire, and was a common source of inclusions within this area during the Neolithic (Allen 2001a), as elsewhere in northern England for the Clacton/Woodlands sub-style, regardless of whether it was available locally (Barclay 1999, 12). The burnt flint and quartz opening agents used at Halton Holegate, however, may indicate that the vessels were produced elsewhere and brought to be deposited within the pit alignment (Allen 2001b). Grog was used as a tempering agent at Aston Hall Hospital, Derbyshire, the East Yorkshire excavations and the A1 Barton to Dishforth route, although only Aston Hall Hospital had grog as the sole inclusion. Crushed stone was used in the fabric of three Clacton sub-style vessels from Cheviot Quarry, St George's Hospital, Morpeth, and the A1 Dishforth to Barton upgrade.

Horizontal grooves and fingernail decoration, as found at Halton Holegate, Lincolnshire, are a common decorative feature in both Lincolnshire and Derbyshire (Manby 1999, 60), whilst the zoned decoration covering upper, middle and lower parts of the vessel from Leadenham has parallels at the Clacton type-site of Lion Point, Essex (Fig. 5.3b; cf. Piggott 1936, 190, fig. 4.5). Maggot impressions on one Clacton vessel from the East Yorkshire Pipeline work (Manby unpublished client report, 2016, 30) are similar to those employed on two Clacton vessels from Rothley Lodge Farm, Leicestershire (Clay and Hunt 2016, 45, fig. 29.4.8). The triangular infilled panel decoration from Aston Hall Hospital, Derbyshire, is characteristic of this sub-style, as is the zoned decoration found on pottery from Field 12, between Low Caythorpe and Boynton, East Yorkshire (Manby unpublished client report, 2016, 30), and at Cheviot Quarry. Zoned decoration is also found at St George's Hospital, Morpeth, where the design features bird-bone impressions, horizontal parallel grooves and grooved chevrons with bird bone-impressed infill (Lotherington 2016).

The three sites near Leicester all produced quantities of Grooved Ware in the Clacton sub-style (Allen 2001c; Cooper 2015; 2016). They comprise open, flat-bottomed, splaying-walled vessels with horizontal grooves internally, and external horizontal and diagonal lines, including chevrons, with fingernail decoration, for example at Braunstone (Fig. 5.3a); whipped maggot decoration is present at Rothley Lodge Farm. The fabrics are fine and mainly shell-tempered. A tub-shaped vessel from the Hinckley Island Hotel site is also suggested to be in the Clacton sub-style (Percival 2022).

Woodlands sub-style

The Woodlands sub-style was identified on three of the recently discovered Grooved Ware sites in East Yorkshire, two in North Yorkshire and one in Northumberland, an area from where it had previously been absent (Fig. 5.2b). The assemblages range in size from 173 sherds, fragments and crumbs (229 g) at Auchinleck Close, Driffield, to 79 sherds, fragments and crumbs (184 g) at Burnby Lane, Hayton. Grooved Ware from sites that had not previously been attributed to a sub-style but are in fact Woodlands are Burythorpe, Whitegrounds; Cowlam, Willy Howe (Manby 1988); Sawndon Moor Barrow 2 (Manby 1995, 43–4, 172, fig. 71.9); and Nosterfield, North Yorkshire (Copp and Toop 2005, Dvi).

The vessels from East and North Yorkshire are open bowls with internally bevelled and simple rims (Longworth 1971, 239); the expanded rim with overhanging bevel from Burnby

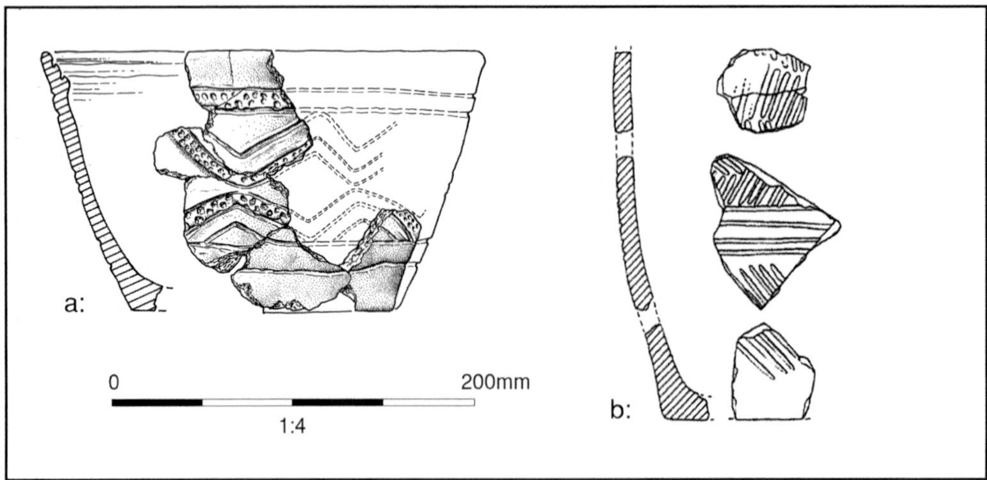

Figure 5.3. Examples of Clacton sub-style Grooved Ware in the north. a) Elmsthorpe Rise, Braunstone, Leicestershire (© David Hopkins, Archaeological Project Services); b) Leadenham Quarry, Lincolnshire (© ASWYAS).

Lane, Hayton, East Yorkshire, may have parallels to a rim from Yeavering (Manby 1999, 64). Grog was well represented as a tempering agent in Woodlands fabrics at Auchinleck Close, Driffield, and was also present at Burnby Lane, Hayton, the A1 Dishforth to Barton route and White House Farm, Stokesley, but a variety of opening agents are present, for example, at Nosterfield, where fabrics contained chert, gypsum, mudstone, shale and quartz (Copp and Toop 2005, Dvi).

Classic Woodlands decoration was present on a vessel from Auchinleck Close, including a rim with incised herringbone, moulded grooved ridges with notched decoration, an applied lug with vertical fluting and a moulded ridge manipulated to create a wavy line or relief (cf. Manby 1999, 61, table 6.2; 2012). Several vessels from Burnby Lane, Hayton, have decoration just within their interior and exterior of converging bands of closely spaced lines embellished with maggot impressions between each band (Manby 2010, fig. 5; Fig. 5.4b). Other decorative elements from Hayton are seen at Auchinleck Close and sites along the A1 Dishforth to Barton Road Scheme. A large, bucket-shaped vessel with the typical widely spaced pellets over the rim came from Sewerby Farm Cottage, Bridlington. The cup identified at Eye Kettleby, Leicestershire, was decorated with slashed/notched cordons and also had 'knots' or pellets of clay on the rim (Gibson 2011; Fig. 5.4a).

Durrington Walls sub-style

Durrington Walls is the most common sub-style amongst the new Grooved Ware discoveries in all areas other than Leicestershire (Fig. 5.2c). Its presence with other sub-styles has already been noted, including at Nosterfield where the material had not previously been assigned to a sub-style. The classic Durrington Walls forms – deep, bucket-or barrel-shaped vessels with simple, internally bevelled and internally moulded rims, open bowls and splayed walls – were present, for example at Breadsall Hilltop, Derby; Mitchell Laithes Farm, West Yorkshire; Melton Quarry, East Yorkshire; and Cheviot and Langton Quarries, Northumberland.

Grog and stone were previously identified as the most common opening agents for Durrington Walls fabrics (Manby 1999, 66) and this mixture continues to be present. Grog was used almost exclusively for pots at Breadsall Hilltop (Cooper 2018) and is found in the material from Windy Harbour, Lancashire (Rick Peterson, pers. comm.). Quartz (and grog) appears to have been the temper of choice at a number of sites such as Mitchell Laithes, West Yorkshire; Canal Lane, Pocklington, East Yorkshire; and Cheviot and Lanton Quarries, Northumberland. Sites around Carlisle produced fabrics utilising temper selected from local glacial till sources, in keeping with earlier local production (Vyner 2016; Young 2017, 72; Sheridan in Brown *et al.* in press), and the pottery from Seven Lows Barrows, Cheshire, was also made from locally sourced material (Vyner 2021, 36, illus. 10.26.10 and 10.26.17).

Panelled decoration at Mitchell Laithes, West Yorkshire, included D-shaped impressions, incised diagonal lines or rows of fingernail impressions between vertical cordons, and incised diagonal lines between vertical lines. Panelled decoration was also present at Auchinleck Close, East Yorkshire, here with dot- and line-infilled triangles (Fig. 5.5b), and six tub-like vessels in a pit at Durranhill, Carlisle, had applied plastic decoration, including vertical and horizontal bands and, on one vessel, a row of horseshoes below the rim (Vyner 2016, 161, fig. 8). A clay ball from this feature was made from the same fabric and can be compared with the two balls from the pit at Rothley Lodge Farm, Leicestershire

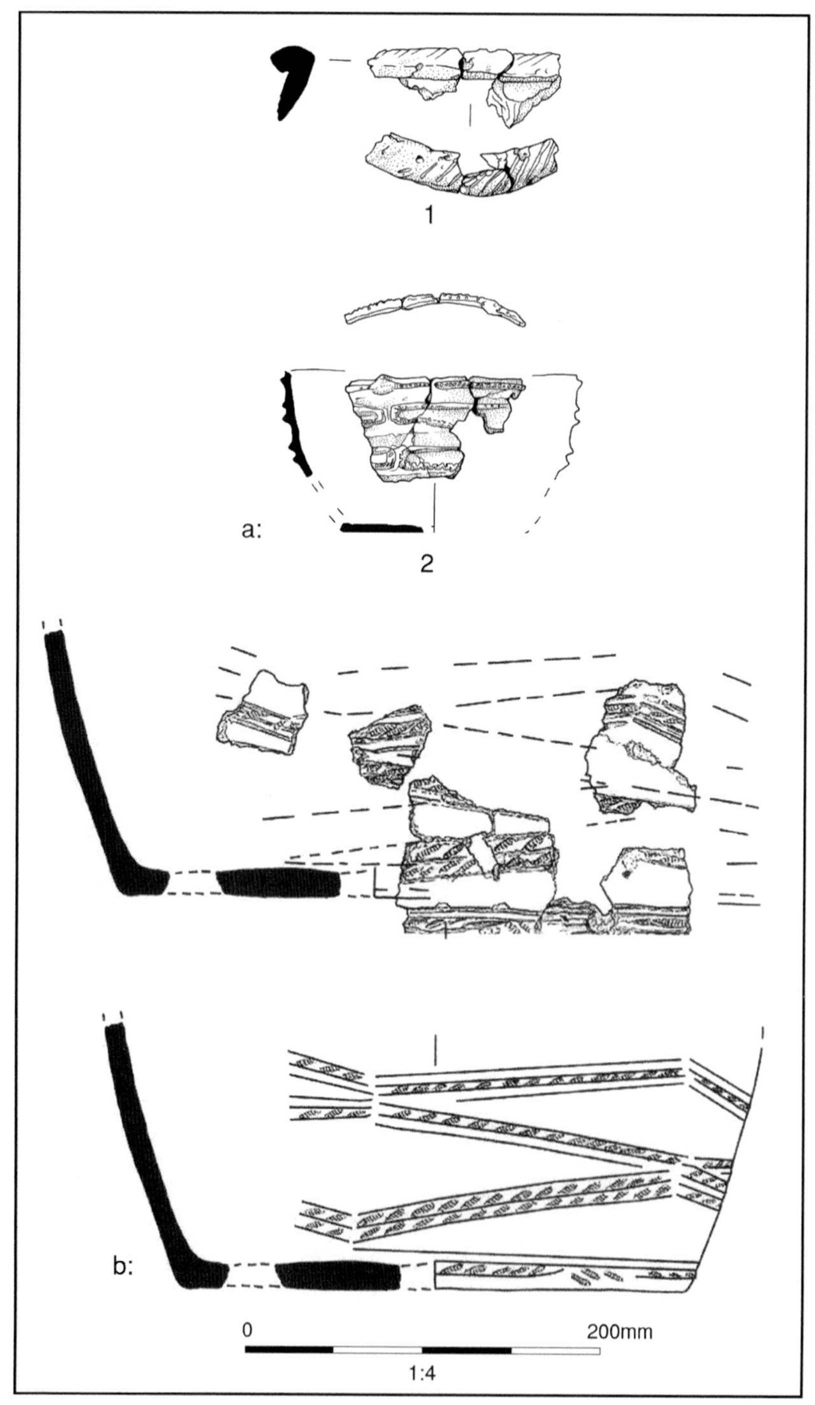

Figure 5.4. Examples of Woodlands sub-style Grooved Ware in the north: a) Eye Kettleby, Leicestershire (© University of Leicester Archaeological Services); b) Hayton, East Yorkshire (with permission of the Yorkshire Archaeological & Historical Society).

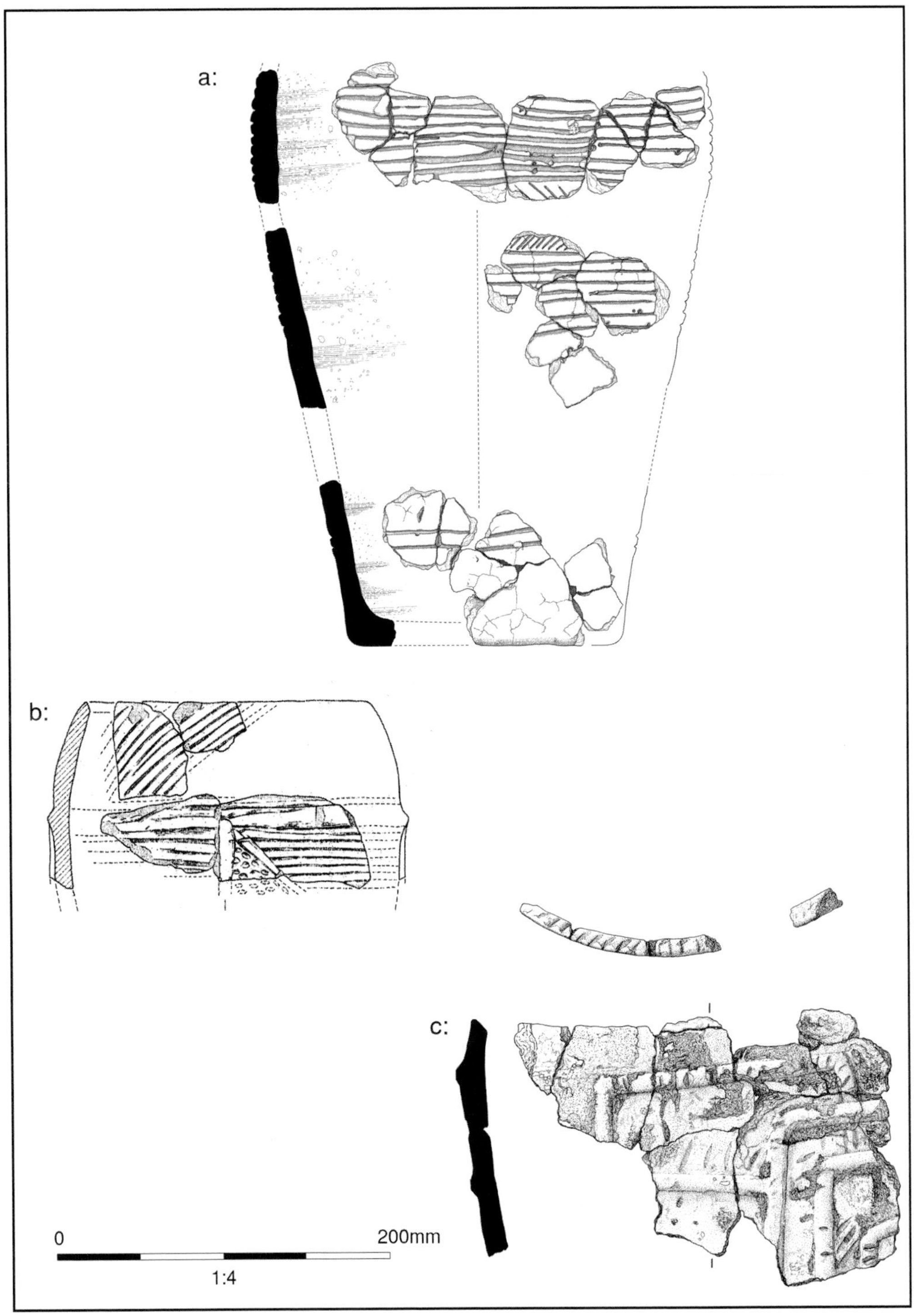

Figure 5.5. Examples of Durrington Walls sub-style Grooved Ware in the north. a) Stainton West, Carlisle (© Oxford Archaeology); b) Auchinleck Close, East Yorkshire (©ASWYAS and with permission of the Yorkshire Archaeological & Historical Society); c) A66, Scotch Corner, North Yorkshire (© Oxford Archaeology).

(Cooper 2016; see above). It is unclear whether the vessel from the A66 Greta Bridge to Scotch Corner excavation is definitely Grooved Ware; its decoration has Durrington Walls characteristics (Fig. 5.5c) although there are late 3rd millennium radiocarbon dates, including from residue on the vessel interior (Zant and Howard-Davis 2013, 29–30, 116).

Grooved Ware of Durrington Walls or Clacton sub-style from Cheviot Quarry was decorated with fingernail impressions and nested lozenge motifs, in keeping with other vessels in the Milfield basin (Johnson and Waddington 2008, 215). Fingernail impressions are also present at Breadsall Hilltop, Derbyshire. Three of the eight vessels from De Verdon Road, Lutterworth, had infilled zones of parallel grooves abutting obliquely, vertical striations and ribs, and parallel curving grooves (Cooper 2019), and the flat-based, bucket-shaped vessel from Stainton West had roughly horizontal, irregularly spaced, incised lines and a band of what may have been a herringbone design around part of the upper body (Fig. 5.5a; Howard-Davis *et al.* in press).

In his 1999 article, Manby assigned the material from Walney Island to the Clacton sub-style, following Wainwright and Longworth (1971, 279, fig. 97) but in 2007 he revised his view, comparing its decoration to northern Rinyo and southern Durrington Walls sub-styles and drawing parallels with the designs found on Irish passage tombs (Manby 2007, 81–2, fig. 4.7, 2–4). The nested lozenge design on one of the Walney Island pots indeed echoes Irish passage tomb art motifs (Sheridan 2021) and there are other indications in Cumbria that people there were aware of Irish passage tomb art (Bradley and Watson 2021), although it appears that the idea of making Grooved Ware (complete with its Irish-inspired designs) was adopted not from Ireland but from Orkney (Sheridan 2021 and this volume, Chapters 2 and 16). Walney Island's inhabitants could have had extensive and varied long-distance contacts; Bradley has suggested that it could have been a 'maritime haven' during the Neolithic (Bradley 2022).

DATING

In 1999, Terry Manby was able to cite only 13 radiocarbon dates from five sites in northern England (Manby 1999, table 6.4), none of which was in North West England. Since that time, to the authors' knowledge, some 35 new Grooved Ware-associated dates have been obtained, including 14 from residues on the walls of vessels. In addition, their precision has improved. These post-Manby 1999 dates are presented in Table 5.2 and plotted in Figure 5.6, together with those cited by Manby.

Currently, the earliest Grooved Ware-associated date from northern England comes from a pit containing Clacton sub-style sherds at St George's Hospital, Morpeth, where charred hazel charcoal produced a date of 3365–3106 cal BC at 95.4% probability (or 3239–3106 cal BC at 63.1%: Lotherington 2016, appendix IV). If correct, this would mean that this small assemblage would be the earliest known Grooved Ware outside Orkney, inverting the now widely accepted Woodlands–Clacton sequence. It could reflect the rapid adoption of this ceramic tradition outside of Orkney, but the possibility that the dated material was redeposited in the shallow (0.21 m) pit must also be considered.

Residues from Clacton/Woodlands sub-style vessels at Rothley Lodge Farm provided two later dates (2880–2630 cal BC and 2870–2500 cal BC) and hazelnut shells from three

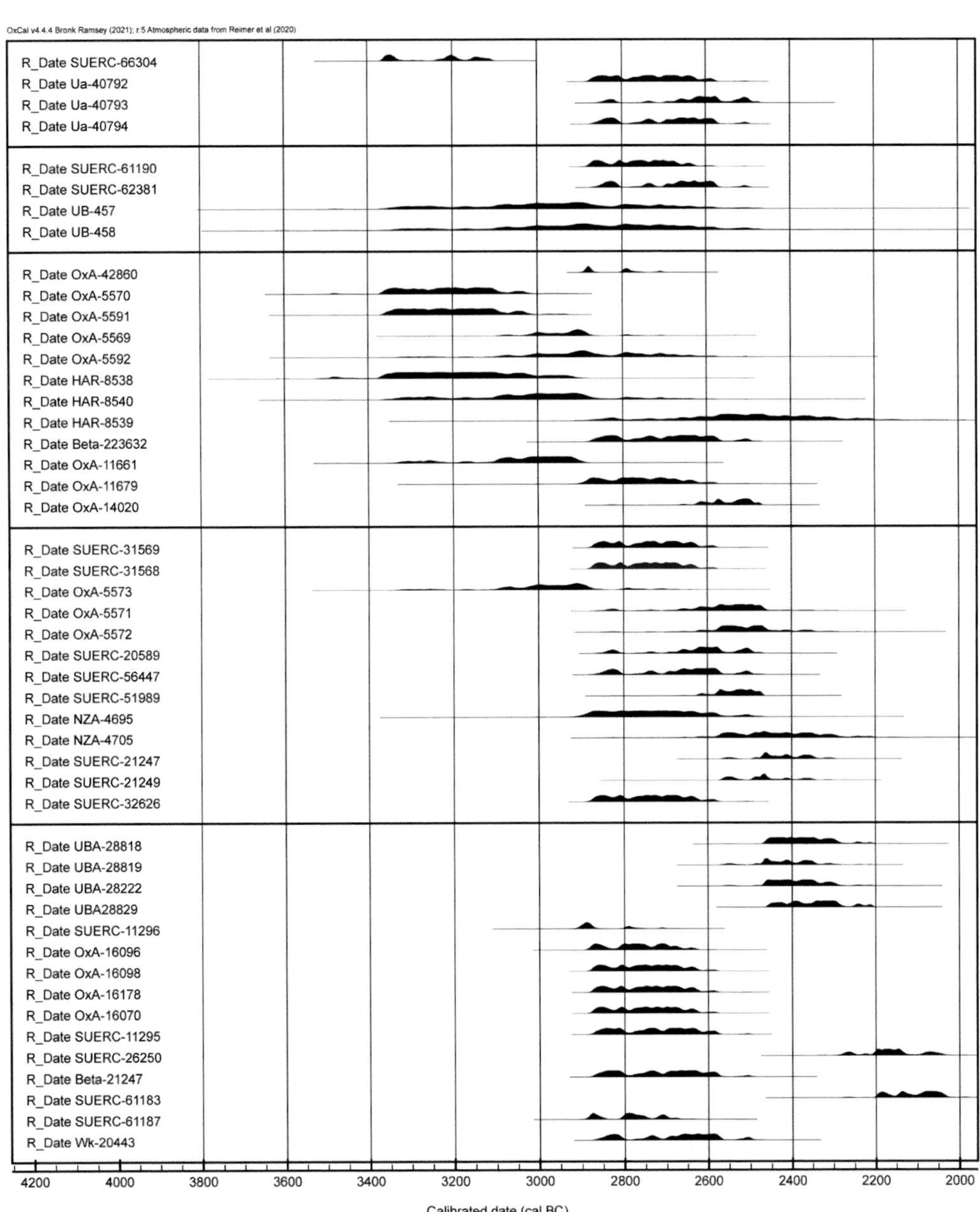

Figure 5.6. Plot of calibrated radiocarbon dates.

Table 5.2. Radiocarbon dates associated with Grooved Ware from northern England, including those previously cited by Manby (1999, table 6.4).

Site	*Context*	*Dated material*	*Lab ref*	*Age BP*	*Calibrated date range cal BC*	*Reference*
			Clacton sub-style			
St George's Hospital, Morpeth, Northumberland	Pit	Charred wood: hazel	SUERC-66304	4542±25	3370–3100	Lotherington 2016
Temple Grange, Rothley, Leicestershire	Posthole 190	Charred hazelnut shell	Ua-40792	4137±37	2880–2580	Speed 2015
	Posthole	Charred hazelnut shell	Ua-40793	4069±36	2860–2470	
	Posthole	Charred hazelnut shell	Ua-40794	4106±35	2870–2500	
			Clacton/Woodlands sub-style			
Rothley Lodge Farm, Leicestershire	Hollow	Residue on pot	SUERC-61190	4159±30	2880–2630	Clay and Hunt 2016
	Hollow	Residue on pot	SUERC-62381	4100±30	2870–2500	
Barholm, Lincolnshire	Pits	Charcoal (species not stated in original site report cited by Manby)	UB-457	4305±130	3350–2680	Manby 1999
		Charcoal (species not stated in original site report cited by Manby)	UB-458	4255±135	3340–2490	
			Woodlands sub-style			
Yeavering, Northumberland	Pit	Charred hazelnut shell	OxA-42860	Date withheld pending publication of full report	2900–2750	Seren Griffiths, pers. comm.
Marton-le-Moor, North Yorkshire	Pit	Charred hazelnut shell	OxA-5570	4515±55	3370–3020	Abramson 2003
		Charred hazelnut shell	OxA-5591	4495±50	3370–3020	
		Charred hazelnut shell	OxA-5569	4305±55	3100–2700	
		Charred hazelnut shell	OxA-5592	4270±90	3320–2570	

(Continued)

Table 5.2 (Continued)

Site	*Context*	*Dated material*	*Lab ref*	*Age BP*	*Calibrated date range cal BC*	*Reference*
Wetwang Slack, East Yorkshire	Pits (3)	Charcoal, mixed species	HAR-8538	4490±90	3500–2910	Manby 1999 (where the wrong HAR-numbers are given for HAR-8538 and -8540); Bayliss *et al.* 2012
		Charcoal, mixed species	HAR-8540	4340±100	3360–2670	
		Charcoal, mixed species (no pottery in this pit)	HAR-8539	3980±100	2870–2200	
Burnby Lane, Hayton, East Yorkshire	Pit	Hazelnut shell	Beta-223632	4110±50	2880–2490	Halkon *et al.* 2010
Sewerby Cottage Farm, Bridlington, East Yorkshire	Midden	Residue on pot	OxA-11661	4380±60	3330–2890	Fenton-Thomas 2009
	Midden	Residue on pot	OxA-11679	4180±55	2900–2580	
	Midden	Residue on pot	OxA-14020	4042±27	2670–2470	
Durrington Walls sub-style						
Lanton Quarry, Northumberland	Pit	Residue on pot	SUERC-31569	4140±30	2880–2580	ARS 2010
	Pit	Residue on pot	SUERC-31568	4150±30	2880–2620	ARS 2010
Marton-le-Moor, North Yorkshire	Pit	Charred hazelnut shell	OxA-5573	4320±75	3330–2690	Abramson 2003
		Charred hazelnut shell	OxA-5571	4025±55	2860–2350	
		Charred hazelnut shell	OxA-5572	3990±55	2840–2300	
Auchinleck Close, Driffield, East Yorkshire	Pit	Residue on pot	SUERC-20589	4070±35	2860–2470	Walsh *et al.* 2012
East Coast Pipeline, Carnaby Field 4, East Yorkshire	Pit	Charred grain	SUERC-56447	4090±38	2870–2490	Manby unpublished client report, 2016
	Pit	Animal bone	SUERC-51989	4026±30	2630–2460	
Burton Agnes, East Yorkshire	Pit	Hazelnut shell	NZA-4695	4160±80	2910–2490	Manby 1999 (which includes reference to site report)
		Animal bone	NZA-4705	3950±70	2670–2200	

(Continued)

Table 5.2. Radiocarbon dates associated with Grooved Ware from northern England, including those previously cited by Manby (1999, table 6.4). (Continued)

Site	*Context*	*Dated material*	*Lab ref*	*Age BP*	*Calibrated date range cal BC*	*Reference*
Mitchell Laithes, Ossett, West Yorkshire	Pit	Residue on pot	SUERC-21247	3935±30	2570–2300	Speed 2010
	Pit	Residue on pot	SUERC-21249	3955±30	2580–2340	
Stainton West, Carlisle, Cumbria	Scoop in palaeochannel	Residue on pot	SUERC-32626	4145±35	*2880–2610 (modelled)*	Brown *et al.* in press
			Sub-style unassigned			
Durranhill, Carlisle, Cumbria	Pit F8	'charred ceramic residue'	UBA-28818	3890±34	2470–2210	Jackson 2016
	Linear F7	'charred ceramic residue'	UBA-28819	3932±30	2570–2300	
	Pit F6	Hazelnut shell	UBA-28222	3908±35	2480–2230	
	Pit F4	Hazelnut shell	UBA28829	3866±26	2460–2200	
Cheviot Quarry, Northumberland	Pit F2168	Hazelnut	SUERC-11296	4250±35	2920–2700	Johnson and Waddington 2008
	Pit F2168	Hazelnut	OxA-16096	4177±33	2890–2630	
	Pit F219	Residue on pot	OxA-16098	4155±33	2880–2620	
	Pit F219	Residue on pot	OxA-16178	4148±32	2880–2620	
	Pit F2133	Hazelnut	OxA-16070	4152±31	2880–2620	
	Pit F2133	Hazelnut	SUERC-11295	4130±35	2880–2580	
A66 Greta Bridge to Scotch Corner, North Yorkshire (SCA13)	Pit	Residue on pot	SUERC-26250	3755±30	2290–2030	Zant and Howard-Davis 2013
Melton Quarry, North Ferriby, East Yorkshire	Pit	Silty clay with frequent charcoal	Beta-21247	4120±40	2880–2570	Evans 2018
Brierlow Quarry, Buxton, Derbyshire	Pit	Charred hazelnut shell	SUERC-61183 (GU-37593	3721±29	2210– 2030	Whittaker and Burpoe 2016
	Pit	Charred wood	SUERC-61187 (GU-37954)	4199±29	2900–2670	
Rearsby Lodge Farm, Leicestershire		Hazelnut shell	Wk-20443	4098±39	2870–2490	Beamish and Clarke 2008

Note: dates calibrated using OxCal v.4.4.4 and cited at 95.4% probability, rounded out to the nearest decade.

pits on the Temple Grange, Rothley site also had dates in the first half of the 3rd millennium cal BC (Table 5.2, Fig. 5.6; Speed 2015, table 2). Four of the six radiocarbon dates from Cheviot Quarry were from residues on vessels with both Clacton and Durrington Walls characteristics and these spanned 2880–2580 cal BC, with hazelnuts providing four dates lying between 2920 and 2570 cal BC (Table 5.2; Johnson and Waddington 2008). Two dates for 'Clacton and Woodlands' pottery from pits at Barholm, Lincolnshire, cited by Manby (1999, table 6.4), have such large standard deviations (±135 and ±130) as to render them of little help.

There are 12 dates for Woodlands sub-style pottery in northern England (Table 5.2), although the three dates for Wetwang Slack, cited by Manby (1999, table 6.4) have standard deviations of ±140 and cannot be used, while one from Marton-le-Moor (3710–3140 cal BC, OxA-5592) appears unfeasibly early. The other three dates from this site calibrate to between 3370–3020 cal BC and 3100–2700 cal BC. A date of 2900–2750 cal BC was recently obtained from charred hazelnut shell from the assemblage from the 'Ritual pit' at Yeavering, Northumberland (Manby 1999, illus. 6.2, 1–2), by Seren Griffiths for her *Project TIME* initiative. The other dates are from Burnby Lane, Hayton, and Sewerby Cottage Farm, Bridlington, East Yorkshire, and fall within the first half of the 3rd millennium (Table 5.2, Fig. 5.6).

A dozen dates have recently been obtained relating to the Durrington Walls sub-style (Table 5.2), and these join the four cited by Manby (1999, table 6.4). Some of these, such as the dates from organic residue from Stainton West and Lanton Quarry, fall within the first half of the 3rd millennium; others, such as the Auchinleck Close organic residue date, fall within the second quarter of that millennium; while the two from organic residue from pots from Mitchell Laithes extend into the third quarter, both calibrating to 2570–2340 cal BC.

As regards dates for Grooved Ware not assigned to a sub-style (Table 5.2), the remarkably late date of 2290–2030 cal BC for organic residue on a vessel from the A66 Greta Bridge to Scotch Corner upgrade has already been commented upon, and re-dating is recommended, if possible. One of two dates from Brierlow Quarry, Derbyshire, is similarly late (although the dated burnt hazelnut shell could well be intrusive in the pit in question) while another lies in the first half of the 3rd millennium. The dates for Durranhill lie in the third quarter of that millennium.

SOME CONCLUDING THOUGHTS

Developer-led archaeology has provided the opportunity to examine 41 new Grooved Ware sites in northern England. Radiocarbon dating has enabled a better understanding of the chronological range of this pottery style and the relationship of the different sub-styles. It also raises the question of the relationship between Grooved Ware and the other pottery traditions (including Beaker) that appear to have been in contemporary use over part of its currency.

The distribution of known sites has widened considerably and includes areas where Grooved Ware was previously unknown, such as south Yorkshire and Lancashire. This has reinforced the link between late Neolithic activity and communication routes along the coast, up rivers and across the Pennines. Manby had noted the importance of river systems such as the Trent, of which the River Soar in Leicestershire, with its cluster of new sites, is a tributary. He also pointed to the relationship of Grooved Ware with monuments such as henges, and sites such as Scorton reinforce this link. The continuing paucity of Grooved Ware from North West England is surprising, however, given the amount of evidence for other activity at that time, including the construction of henges, stone circles large and small, and the carving of passage tomb-inspired art on Long Meg and at Copt Howe in the Langdale Valley (Bradley and Watson 2021; Frodsham 2021). Fieldwalking collections, particularly from the Pennine valleys, include plentiful evidence of later Neolithic activity (Evans *et al.* 2021) and demonstrate the enduring importance of east–west links at this time, while palaeoenvironmental sequences evidence the maintenance and creation of clearings in the wider landscape (Walker 2001) and some small-scale cultivation (Brown *et al.* in press). The character of settlement may have been more mobile than during the Early Neolithic. The apparently local manufacture of pottery and its variety suggest a pottery industry that was much healthier than the quantities of Grooved Ware and its widespread distribution imply. These discoveries must be the tip of the iceberg of late Neolithic pottery production in this region.

ACKNOWLEDGEMENTS

The authors owe a debt of gratitude to the officers and staff of the following HER and local government offices (in no particular order): Matt Allcock (North Lincs), Louise Jennings (NE Lincs), David Littlewood (Nottinghamshire), Scott Lomax (Nottinghamshire City), Dr Dana Campbell (Derbyshire), Zac Nellist (Sheffield), Rhona Finlayson (West Yorkshire), Georgina Richardson (Humber), Victoria Bowns (East Riding of Yorkshire), Claire MacRae (York), Leonora Goldsmith (North Yorks), Ellie Leary (North York Moors), Luke Barker (Yorkshire Dales), Jessica Bell (Middlesborough), Janice Adams (Hartlepool), David Marsay (Redcar-Cleveland), Nick Boldrini (Durham), Rachel Grahame (Newcastle), Liz Williams (Northumberland), Moya Watson (Cheshire Archaeology Planning Advisory Services), Mark Brennand (Cumbria County Council), Eleanor Kingston (Lake District National Park), Ben Croxford (Merseyside), Joanne Smith (Lancashire), Lesley Dunkley (Greater Manchester), Grahame Appleby (Leicester City), Helen Wells (Leicestershire and Rutland). We would also like to express considerable thanks to Blaise Vyner; Alex Gibson; Andy Crowson, Gavin Robinson and Greg Speed (ECUS Ltd.); Nicholas Cooper (University of Leicester Archaeological Services); Zoe Horn (ASWYAS); Ian Roberts (Yorkshire Archaeological and Historical Society); Sue Unsworth (APS); Peter Halkon; Peter Carne (Archaeological Services Durham University); Rick Peterson (UCLan); and to Fraser Brown, Antony Dickson and Adam Tinsley (Oxford Archaeology). Seren Griffiths very kindly recalibrated the radiocarbon dates and provided the calibration plot. She is also thanked for permission to cite the Yeavering radiocarbon date. Anne Stewardson undertook the illustrations and we are grateful to Oxford Archaeology North for providing this facility.

REFERENCES

Abramson, P. 2003 Appendix 1: Marton-le-Moor radiocarbon dates. In T.G. Manby, S. Moorhouse and P. Ottaway (eds), *The archaeology of Yorkshire: an assessment at the beginning of the 21st century*, 114–16. Huddersfield: Charlesworth.

Albone, J. 2001. *Archaeological watching brief and excavation at Elmsthorpe Rise, Braunstone, Leicester.* Sleaford: Archaeological Project Services, Report 082/01.

Allen, C. 2001a. The pottery. In West Yorkshire Archaeological Services 2001, 5.17–5.29.

Allen, C. 2001b. Report on prehistoric pottery. In J. Rylatt, *Archaeological evaluation report: land to the south of High Farm, Halton Holegate, Lincolnshire*, appendix 13.2. Unpublished client report by Pre-Construct Archaeology for Cirque Energy. https://doi.org/10.5284/1014327 [accessed 23/03/23].

Allen, C. 2001c. The prehistoric pottery. In J. Albone 2001, appendix 4.

Ansell, J. 2004. *Wooperton Quarry: Phase 2, second strip, assessment report.* Unpublished client report by Headland Archaeology Ltd for Northern Aggregates Ltd. https://doi.org/10.5284/1030307 [accessed 28/03/23].

Archaeological Research Services Ltd (ARS) 2010. *Lanton Quarry, Northumberland phase 3 archaeological excavation.* Unpublished client report No. 2010/69 by ARS for Tarmac Ltd. https://www.archaeologicalresearchservices.com/wp-content/uploads/2018/01/Lanton-Report-2010_2.pdf [accessed 25/05/23].

Archaeological Services Durham University (ASDU) 2016. *Long Meg and her Daughters, Little Salkeld, Cumbria. Altogether Archaeology excavations. Post-excavation full analysis.* Unpublished client report No. 4043 by ASDU for North Pennines AONB Partnership. https://altogetherarchaeology.org/reports.php [accessed 25/05/23].

Barclay, A. 1999. Grooved Ware from the Upper Thames region. In R. Cleal and A. MacSween (eds) 1999, 10–22.

Bayliss, A., Hedges, R.E.M., Otlet, R., Switsur, R. and Walker, J. 2012. *Radiocarbon dates from samples funded by English Heritage between 1981 and 1988.* Swindon: English Heritage.

Beamish, M. and Clarke, S. 2008. Rearsby Bypass Road Scheme. *Transactions of the Leicestershire Archaeological and Historical Society* 82, 286–7.

Bradley, R. 2022. *Maritime archaeology on dry land: special sites along the coasts of Britain and Ireland from the first farmers to the Atlantic Bronze Age.* Oxford: Oxbow Books.

Bradley, R. and Watson, A. 2021. Langdale and the northern Neolithic. In G. Hey and P. Frodsham (eds) 2021, 7–16.

Brown, F., Clark, P., Dickson, A., Gregory R.A. and Zant, J. in press. *From an ancient Eden to a new frontier: an archaeological journey along the Carlisle Northern Development Route.* Lancaster: Lancaster Imprints 31.

Cherry, J., and Cherry, P. J. 1987. *Prehistoric habitation sites on the limestone uplands of Eastern Cumbria.* Kendal: Cumberland and Westmorland Antiquarian and Archaeological Society.

Clay, P. and Hunt, L. 2016. Late Neolithic art and symbolism at Rothley Lodge Farm, Leicester Road, Rothley (SK 592 140). *Transactions of the Leicestershire Archaeological and Historical Society* 90, 13–66.

Cleal, R. and MacSween, A. (eds) 1999. *Grooved Ware in Britain and Ireland.* Oxford: Oxbow Books.

Cooper, N.J. 2013. Late Neolithic or Beaker pottery. In A. Hyam 2013. 24-6.

Cooper, N. J. 2015. The late Neolithic Grooved Ware pottery. In G. Speed 2015, 25–7.

Cooper, N.J. 2016. The Peterborough Ware and Grooved Ware pottery. In P. Clay and L. Hunt 2016, 37–51.

Cooper. N.J. 2018. Late Neolithic, Early Iron Age and Roman pottery. In R. Huxley 2018, 54–7.

Cooper, N.J. 2019. The late Neolithic Grooved Ware pottery. In N. Flavell 2019, 59–61.

Copp, A. and Toop, N. 2005. *Watching brief Nosterfield Quarry, North Yorkshire interim report.* Unpublished client report by Field Archaeology Specialists Ltd for Tarmac Northern Ltd. https://doi.org/10.5284/1029294 [accessed 25/05/23].

Evans, H. 2018. *Melton Quarry Extension, North Ferriby, East Riding of Yorkshire. Archaeological post-excavation analysis final report.* Unpublished client report No. 2017-18/1880 by Oxford Archaeology North for CgMs Consulting Ltd and OMYA. https://eprints.oxfordarchaeology.com/5782/1/L10480PXanalysis_all.pdf [accessed 23/03/23].

Evans, H., Dickson, A. and Druce, D. 2021. Recent work on the Neolithic landscape of Cumbria and North Lancashire. In G. Hey and P. Frodsham (eds) 2021, 111–24.

Fenton-Thomas, C. 2009. *A place by the sea: excavations at Sewerby Cottage Farm, Bridlington.* York: On-Site Archaeology Monograph 1.

Finn, N. 2011. *Bronze Age ceremonial enclosures and cremation cemetery at Eye Kettleby, Leicestershire.* Leicester: University of Leicester School of Archaeology and Ancient History.

Flavell, N. 2019. *An archaeological evaluation on land at De Verdon Road, Lutterworth, Leicestershire.* Unpublished client report No. 2019-146 by University of Leicester Archaeological Services for ECUS/Willmott Dixon. https://doi.org/10.5284/1090101 [accessed 14/04/23].

Flintoft, P. 2015. *Final report an archaeological strip, plan and record excavation at Aston hall Hospital, Aston-on-Trent, Derbyshire.* Trent and Peak Archaeology unpublished client report no. 025/2015 for CGMS Ltd. https://doi.org/10.5284/1053621 [accessed 28/03/23]

Flintoft, P. and Stein, S. 2016. A multiphase prehistoric site in a middle Trent valley landscape: excavations at Aston Hall Hospital, Aston-on-Trent, Derbyshire. *Derbyshire Archaeological Journal* 136, 35–45.

Frodsham, P. 2021. 'A most notable work', at the heart of Neolithic Britain: some thoughts on the Long Meg complex in the light of recent fieldwork. In G. Hey and P. Frodsham (eds) 2021, 147–75.

Garner, D. 2021. The Seven Lows prehistoric barrow cemetery, Fishpool Lane, Delamere, Cheshire: a reassessment. *Journal of the Chester Archaeological Society* 91, 9–87.

Gibson, A. 2011. The prehistoric pottery. In N. Finn 2011, 18–20.

Gibson, A. 2018. *The Neolithic and Early Bronze Age pottery from the Barton to Leeming Bar A1 road improvements, North Yorkshire.* Unpublished client report no.138 for Northern Archaeological Associates/Highways England.

Gibson, A. 2020. Prehistoric pottery assessment. In NAA 2020, appendix J, 54–5. Unpublished client report No. NAA 20-90 by NAA for Oakmere Homes North West. https://doi.org/10.5284/1092283 [accessed 25.05.23].

Gilks, J.A. 2005. A sherd of later Neolithic Grooved Ware from Lesser Kelcoe Cave, Giggleswick, North Yorkshire, with a note on other finds of Grooved Ware from caves in the north of England. *Transactions of the Hunter Archaeological Society* 22, 15–22.

Halkon, P, Manby, T.G. Millett, M. and Woodhouse, H. 2010. Neolithic settlement evidence from Hayton, East Yorkshire. *Yorkshire Archaeological Journal* 82, 31–58.

Hall, R. 2003. Queniborough, Wetherby Close. *Transactions of the Leicestershire Archaeological and Historical Society* 77, 145.

Hey, G. and Frodsham, P. (eds) 2021. *New light on the Neolithic of northern England.* Oxford: Oxbow Books.

Howard-Davis, C., Tinsley, A. and Sheridan, J.A. in press. Appendix 13. Ceramics. In F. Brown *et al.* in press.

Huxley, R. 2018. *An archaeological evaluation and strip, map and sample excavation of land at Breadsall Hilltop, Mansfield Road, Derby, Derbyshire.* Unpublished client report by University of Leicester Archaeological Services for Redrow Homes Ltd. https://doi.org/10.5284/1055127 [accessed 23/03/23].

Hyam, A. 2013. *An archaeological trial trench evaluation on land off Main Road, Barleythorpe, Parcels 3, 7 and 8, Oakham, Rutland.* Unpublished client report No. 2013-039V2 by University of Leicester Archaeological Services for CgMs Consulting Ltd. https://doi.org/10.5284/1030980 [accessed 25/05/03].

Jackson, D. 2016. Neolithic to Romano-British occupation at Durranhill, Carlisle: archaeological investigations 1997–8 and 2011. *Transactions of the Cumberland and Westmorland Antiquarian and Archaeological Society* (3) 16, 145–76.

Jackson, D. and Churchill, D. 2017. *Life, death and landscape on the Abbeytown Ridge in the 2nd and 3rd millennium BC: excavations at Overby Quarry and New Cowper Quarry.* Bowness on Windermere: Cumberland and Westmorland Antiquarian and Archaeological Society.

Johnson, B. and Waddington, C. 2008. Prehistoric and Dark Age settlement remains from Cheviot Quarry, Milfield Basin, Northumberland. *Archaeological Journal* 165, 107–264.

Lotherington, R. 2016. *An archaeological excavation at St. George's Hospital, Morpeth, Northumberland.* Unpublished client report No. 2016/70 by Archaeological Research Services Ltd for Linden Homes Ltd. https://doi.org/10.5284/1042651[accessed 06/11/22].

Longworth, I. 1971. The Neolithic pottery. In G.J. Wainwright and I.H. Longworth 1971, 48–155.

Manby, T.G. 1974. *Grooved Ware sites in the north of England.* Oxford: British Archaeological Report 9.

Manby, T.G. 1988. The Neolithic period in East Yorkshire. In T.G. Manby (ed.), *Archaeology in eastern Yorkshire: essays in honour of T.C.M. Brewster*, 35–88. Sheffield: Department of Archaeology and Prehistory, University of Sheffield.

Manby, T.G. 1995. Neolithic and Bronze Age pottery – implications. In T.C.M. Brewster and A.E. Finney. *The excavations of seven Bronze Age barrows in the moorlands of North-East Yorkshire*, 41–51. Leeds: Yorkshire Archaeological Society: Prehistory Research Section.

Manby, T.G. 1999. Grooved Ware sites in Yorkshire and northern England. In R. Cleal and A. MacSween (eds) 1999, 57–75.

Manby, T.G. 2007. Ehenside Tarn and the Neolithic pottery of north-western England. In P. Cherry (ed.), *Studies in northern prehistory: essays in memory of Clare Fell*, 61–97. Kendal: The Cumberland and Westmorland Antiquarian and Archaeological Society.

Manby, T.G. 2010. The Grooved Ware pottery. In P. Halkon *et al.* 2010, 36–44.

Manby, T.G. 2012. Early prehistoric pottery. In A. Walsh *et al.* 2012, 7–13.

Natural England 2013. *National character area profile: 12: Mid Northumberland.* York: Natural England. https://publications.naturalengland.org.uk/publication/4839052410880000 [accessed 25/05/23].

Natural England 2014. *National character area profile: 28. Vale of York.* York: Natural England. https://publications.naturalengland.org.uk/publication/3488888 [accessed 02/04/23].

Northern Archaeological Associates (NAA) 2002. *Hollow Banks Quarry, Scorton, North Yorkshire. Archaeological post-excavation assessment.* Unpublished client report No. 02/121 by NAA for Tarmac Northern. https://doi.org/10.5284/1029286 [accessed 6/1/23].

Northern Archaeological Associates (NAA) 2020. *Archaeological evaluation and monitoring assessment report, Breast Mill Beck Road, Barrow-in-Furness.* Unpublished client report No. NAA 20-90 by NAA for Oakmere Homes North West. https://doi.org/10.5284/1092283 [accessed 25.05.23].

Percival, S. 2022. Prehistoric pottery. In P. Walton *et al.* 2022, appendix B.

Peterson, R. 2013. *Excavations at Fairy Holes Caves, Whitewell, Lancashire, 2013.* Unpublished draft interim report, University of Central Lancashire. https://shelteringmemory.files.wordpress.com/2012/08/fh13-interim-report2.pdf [accessed 1/8/23]

Piggott, S. 1936. The pottery from the submerged surface. In S.H. Warren, S. Piggott, J.G.D. Clark, M.C. Burkett and H. and M.E. Godwin, Archaeology of the submerged land-surface of the Essex coast, 186–201. *Proceedings of the Prehistoric Society* 2, 178–210.

Pre-construct Archaeology 2001. Archaeological evaluation report: Land to the south of High Farm, Halton Holegate, Lincolnshire. Unpublished client report for Cirque Energy (UK) Ltd. https://doi.org/10.5284/1014327 [accessed 06.08.2023].

Roberts, I. and Weston, P. 2016. Excavations at Rossington Grange Farm, South Yorkshire, *Yorkshire Archaeological Journal* 88(1), 1–37.

Sheridan, J.A. 2021. A view from north of the border. In G. Hey and P. Frodsham (eds) 2021, 177–88.

Speed, G. 2010. *Mitchell Laithes Farm, Ossett, West Yorkshire.* Unpublished client report No. NAA 09/42 by Northern Archaeological Associates (NAA) for Arup/Yorkshire Water Services Ltd. https://doi.org/10.5284/1029397 [accessed 26/03/23].

Speed, G. 2015. Neolithic settlement and special deposits at Temple Grange, Rothley, Leicestershire. *Transactions of the Leicestershire Archaeological and Historical Society* 89, 1–36.

Speed, G.P. 2021. *Living between the monuments: the prehistory of the Dishforth to Barton A1 motorway improvement.* Barnard Castle: Northern Archaeological Associates https://doi.org/10.5284/1086870 [accessed 01/11/22].

Stephens, M. 2023. The early prehistoric landscape. In Stephens. M (ed.), *Chariots Swords and Spears: Iron Age burials at the foot of the East Yorkshire Wolds*, 65-71. Oxford: Oxbow Books.

Tabor, J.L. 2009. Excavations at Canal Lane, Pocklington. In D.H. Evans (ed.), *East Riding archaeologist: an East Riding miscellany*, 127–66. Hull: The East Riding Archaeological Society.

Vyner, B. 2008. West Yorkshire Archaeology Advisory Service. Research Agenda: The Neolithic, Bronze Age and Iron Age in West Yorkshire. https://www.wyjs.org.uk/media/1270/later-prehistoric.pdf. [accessed 20/10/2022].

Vyner, B. 2017. Wildfire and archaeological research on Fylingdales Moor. *Prehistoric Yorkshire* 55, 38-46.

Vyner, B. 2016. Neolithic ceramics. In D. Jackson 2016, 158–62.

Vyner, B. 2021. Prehistoric pottery. In D. Garner 2021, 36–42.

Wainwright, G.J. and Longworth, I.H. 1971. *Durrington Walls: excavations 1966–1968.* London: Society of Antiquaries.

Walker, D. 2001. The dates of human impacts on the environment at Ehenside Tarn, Cumbria. *Transactions of the Cumberland and Westmorland Antiquarian and Archaeological Society* 3(1), 1–20.

Walsh, A., Manby, T. and Roberts, I. 2012. Prehistoric pits at Auchinleck Close, Driffield, East Yorkshire. *Yorkshire Archaeological Journal* 84(1), 3–21.

Walton, P., Barker, J. and Brindle, T. 2022 *Land east of Hinckley Island Hotel, Watling Street, Burbage, Leicestershire: archaeological excavation.* Cotswold Archaeology Unpublished client report No. MK0318_1 by Cotswold Archaeology for The Environmental Dimension Partnership. https://reports.cotswoldarchaeology.co.uk/content/uploads/2022/12/MK0318-J1-M69-Hinckley-TS-Report1.30.pdf [accessed 14/04/23].

West Yorkshire Archaeological Services (WYAS) 2001. *Leadenham Quarry, Welbourn, Lincolnshire: archaeological excavation volume 1.* Unpublished client report No. 901 by WYAS for Waste Recycling Group plc. https://doi.org/10.5284/1014730 [accessed 24/03/23].

Whittaker, P. and Burpoe, M. 2016. *An archaeological watching brief at Brierlow Quarry Buxton, Derbyshire.* Unpublished client report No. 2016/31 by Archaeological Research Services Ltd for Lhoist UK Ltd. https://doi.org/10.5284/1012016 [accessed 23/03/23].

Young, R. 2017. Prehistoric ceramic. In D. Jackson and D. Churchill 2017, 69–80.

Zant, J. and Howard-Davis, C. 2013. *Scots Dyke to turnpike: the archaeology of the A66, Greta Bridge to Scotch Corner.* Lancaster: Lancaster Imprints 18.

Chapter 6

Grooved Ware in Wales

Frances Lynch

In the 24 years since *Grooved Ware in Britain and Ireland* was published, the situation in Wales has changed a great deal. In that book only four sherds were illustrated and only eight sites were mentioned in the gazetteer, of which only one, Trelystan, produced more than one or two sherds (Longworth and Cleal 1999, 203–4, 206). A general textbook on Welsh prehistory published in the following year (Lynch *et al.* 2000) added little more but did show a selection of the material from Upper Ninepence in the Walton Basin (Gibson 1999).

Today, there is vastly more material from the north – including ten assemblages from Anglesey alone – though there are still only small collections from the south, where the situation has changed little since 1999 (Figs 6.1–6.7). Much of the material from the north (Figs 6.1–6.5) derives from several extensive excavations which have stripped large areas, revealing groups of shallow pits often containing substantial quantities of pottery, lithics, burnt stone and charcoal. A lot of effort has been spent on trying to understand why these pits were dug in the first place, and whether the broken pottery, stone tools and hearth debris with which they were eventually filled held some magical significance or was simply rubbish. Whatever the answer to that question, these pits have greatly increased our knowledge of the development and distribution of Middle and Late Neolithic pottery styles and there is little difference in the ways that these various styles of pottery were used in what may be judged to be domestic contexts, even though evidence for associated structures generally remains elusive. The aura of exceptionalism which has hung over Grooved Ware should be dispelled by these mundane discoveries. Though the context may be mundane, some of the material from north Anglesey is stunning pottery, made and decorated with exceptional skill.

CONTEXT AND DISTRIBUTION

North-west Wales

Three major assemblages of Grooved Ware have come to light as a result of recent developer-funded excavation, at Parc Bryn Cegin, Parc Cybi and Llanfaethlu (Kenney 2008; 2021; Rees and Jones 2016). In each case there are significant Neolithic monuments nearby and the excavations have revealed several phases of occupation activity (mostly represented by clusters of pits) running from the Early Neolithic to the Early Bronze Age, and beyond in the case of the two largest sites.

Parc Bryn Cegin, near Bangor, is a large and long-occupied settlement area between the Cegin and Ogwen rivers (Fig. 6.2, Table 6.1). There are two Early Neolithic rectangular buildings on this ridge and, in the later Neolithic, two massive henges were established, with Bronze Age barrows following (Lynch and Musson 2001; Kenney 2008). Both of the Early Neolithic houses were short-lived, and the Middle Neolithic is represented by clusters of pits containing pottery, flint and stone implements and burnt material. Each cluster is typologically distinct and the majority contain Fengate Ware, but there is one cluster with Mortlake Ware and two have Grooved Ware.

Parc Cybi, a new business park outside Holyhead on Anglesey, close to a megalithic tomb, was excavated by Gwynedd Archaeological Trust between 2006 and 2010 (Kenney 2021). In the Early Neolithic, a large wooden house or hall, with Irish Sea Ware, was built and soon demolished. The Middle and Late Neolithic evidence is less spectacular: pit clusters filled with burnt material, stone and flint tools and broken pottery. One cluster contained Mortlake Ware and four contained Fengate Ware. All these Impressed Ware pits are in the vicinity of the tomb and hall (Area J). One Grooved Ware cluster is there too, but the other is some 500 m away to the west (Area D) where pottery was found in a pit close to a Trelystan-style hearth (Fig. 6.1, Table 6.1; Kenney 2021, 60–75).

The excavations at Llanfaethlu, Anglesey, by CR Archaeology in 2016–18 were prompted by a decision to build a new school close to the ancient church. By chance, one of the many exploratory trenches found Neolithic structures and pits. Eventually, four rectangular houses with Early Neolithic pottery, a densely clustered group of Middle Neolithic pits with Mortlake pottery, and three groups of more widely dispersed pits with Grooved Ware were discovered (Rees and Jones 2016; 2017; in prep.). A rough estimate of the number of Mortlake bowls is 17 and of Grooved Ware vessels 59, the largest assemblage in north Wales (Fig. 6.3, Table 6.1). No Fengate Ware was found. The Mortlake pits occupy the same valley-bottom location as the Early Neolithic houses. The distribution of sherds from individual pots suggests that these pits were filled from a midden built up during the currency of Mortlake Ware, but two pits (6008 and 6013) contain both Mortlake sherds and a few pieces of Grooved Ware, one of which is undoubtedly from a jar belonging to the Durrington Walls sub-style (Fig. 6.3).

The general pattern at these three sites, then, is that there are rather few Early Neolithic pits; the majority are Middle and Late Neolithic, but some ceramic styles may be missing. For instance, Parc Cybi (Fig. 6.1) and Parc Bryn Cegin (Fig. 6.2) have some Early Neolithic pottery, and quite a lot of Mortlake, Fengate and Grooved Ware; Llanfaethlu has Early Neolithic pottery in association with houses, Mortlake and Grooved Ware in pits (Fig. 6.3), but no obvious Fengate Ware. Beaker pottery is in use at Parc Cybi, where it is found as a scatter within soil layers and as a grave good, but not in pits.

In addition to Parc Cybi and Llanfaethlu, eight other sites on Anglesey have produced Grooved Ware. A field in Tregele (Evaluation area 9), just over 7 km north-east of Llanfaethlu, was excavated in advance of the proposed Wylfa Newydd power station and its pylon route. Field 14 contained nine pits, some postholes and a shallow ditch. Six pits contained pottery, mostly Grooved Ware, very close in style and technique to that from Llanfaethlu (Fig. 6.4).

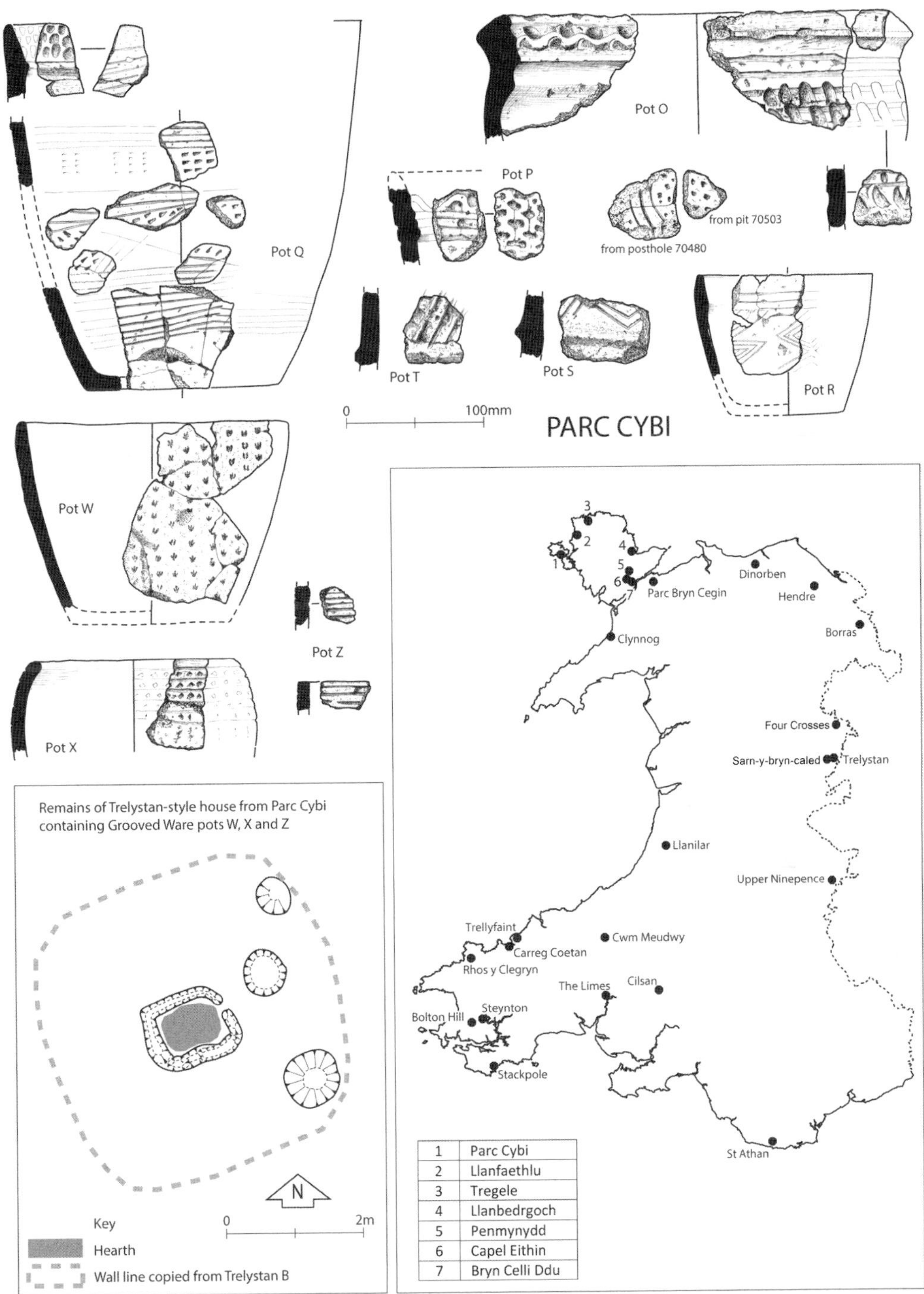

Figure 6.1. Distribution of Grooved Ware in Wales 2023; Grooved Ware and remains of Trelystan-style house, Parc Cybi, Holyhead.

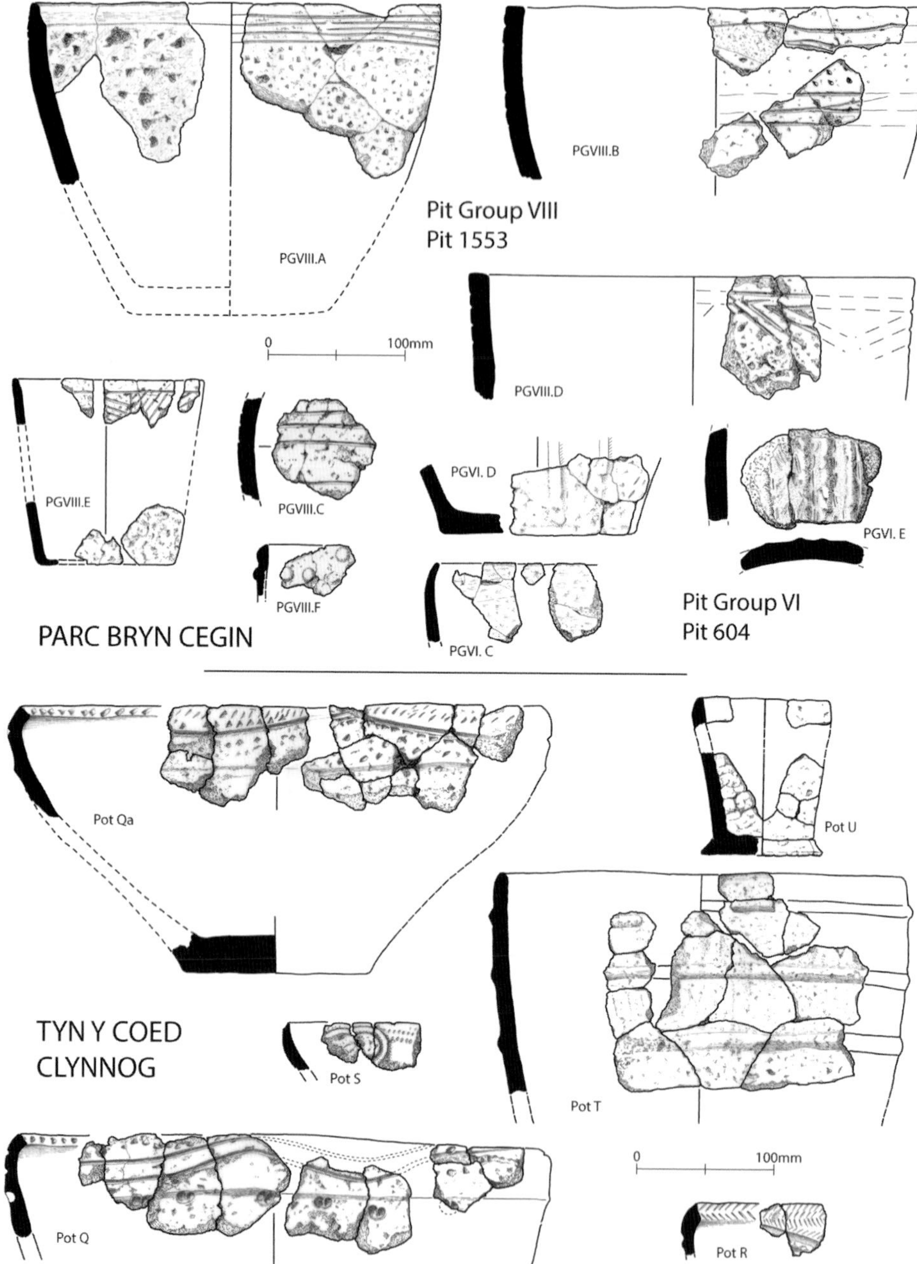

Figure 6.2. Grooved Ware from Parc Bryn Cegin and Clynnog, Gwynedd.

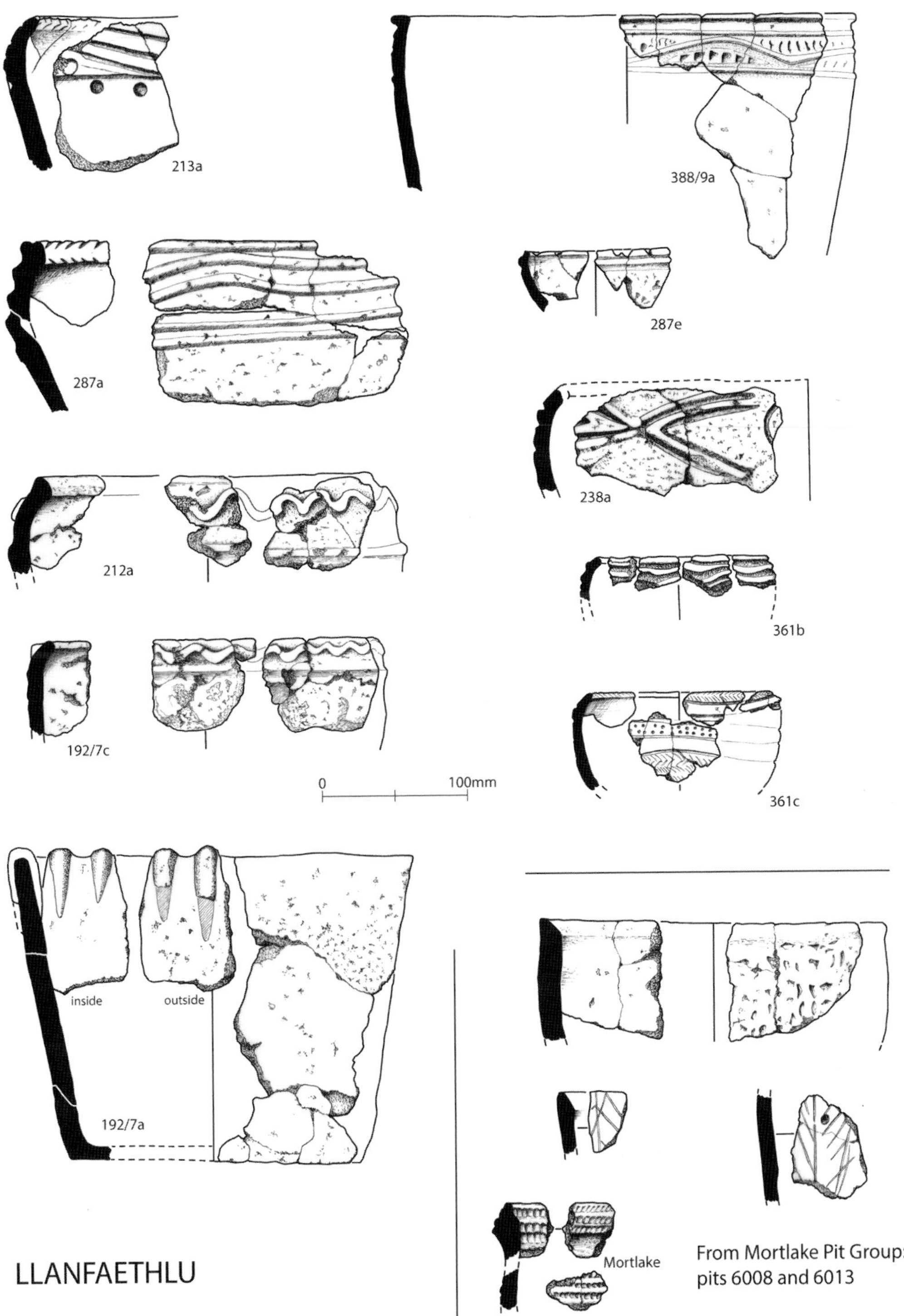

Figure 6.3. Grooved Ware from Llanfaethlu, north Anglesey.

A series of pits near a natural spring at Glyn, Llanbedrgoch – a site better known for its post-Roman history – contained Ebbsfleet Ware and some Grooved Ware (Fig. 6.5), but not in the same pits. At Capel Eithin, a hilltop site with a long history (White and Smith 1999), some of the small amount of Grooved Ware was found in one of the large postholes of a tower-like structure; other sherds were found in a pit 20 m to the west (Fig. 6.5). Subsequent funerary activity is attested from the Early Bronze Age and the 1st millennium AD. This is perhaps the best example of Grooved Ware in Wales associated in some way with a ceremonial site of lasting significance.

There are three sites, megalithic tombs at Trefignath, Lligwy and Bryn Celli Ddu, which might also be thought to be ceremonial; but in fact the Grooved Ware is not in a primary or significant relationship to the monuments. The same is true in south Wales, at Trellyffaint and Carreg Coetan Arthur. The 'Grooved Ware' from Trefignath consisted of a single sherd of non-local pottery, with an incised diagonal line (Pot K) on the floor of the central chamber which had been disturbed in the 19th century (Smith and Lynch 1987, 65, 73–9). Little can be said about this context but it is not far away from the eastern Grooved Ware pit group at Parc Cybi. Three sherds from the same pot are amongst mixed pottery from the chamber at Lligwy (Baynes 1909, 224–5; Lynch 1991, fig. 21.6–8). They were listed as 'possibly Grooved Ware' by Longworth and Cleal (1999, 206) but are not very convincing candidates. The name Bryn Celli Ddu may suggest a connection with the famous passage tomb but the Grooved Ware has no association with it. The pottery (Fig. 6.5) was found in three pits, part of a tight cluster of five on a ridge some 75 m beyond the Bronze Age barrow behind the passage tomb, located through geophysical work by Manchester Metropolitan University (Edwards *et al.* in prep.).

The material from Penmynydd (Fig. 6.4, Table 6.1) comes from a site dug by Gwynedd Archaeological Trust in 2009 during work to upgrade the water main (Davidson *et al.* 2010). The site consisted of nine pits (six with pottery and seven with flintwork), four postholes (one containing a polished stone axehead) and three stakeholes but no convincing building plan. One pit, 0098, contained most of the pottery and flint. Four sherds of soft, grog-tempered Grooved Ware (not illustrated) are reported from another group of pits south of Llangefni. The decoration is said to be akin to that at Parc Bryn Cegin (Saunders 2021, 16).

Elsewhere in north-west Wales, roadwork excavations by Gwynedd Archaeological Trust north of Clynnog, Gwynedd, produced a scatter of some 50 pits close to Ty'n Coed Farm containing pottery ranging from Early Neolithic to Early Bronze Age in date (Roberts 2007). Two undecorated Grooved Ware jars came from one pit, and three vases came from another, some 18 m away (Fig. 6.2, Table 6.1).

North-east Wales

Three findspots are known from this part of Wales, at Borras Quarry near Wrexham, at Hendre, and at Dinorben. Borras Quarry – a very extensive site on a low gravel ridge, with continuing excavations by Clwyd-Powys Archaeological Trust – had a long period of perhaps intermittent Neolithic to Early Bronze Age occupation without convincing structures but with numerous groups of chronologically distinct pits, hearths and ovens, the pits clustering around a number of natural kettle holes (Grant 2014). Grooved Ware comes from Pit Groups N and O (Fig. 6.5) and does

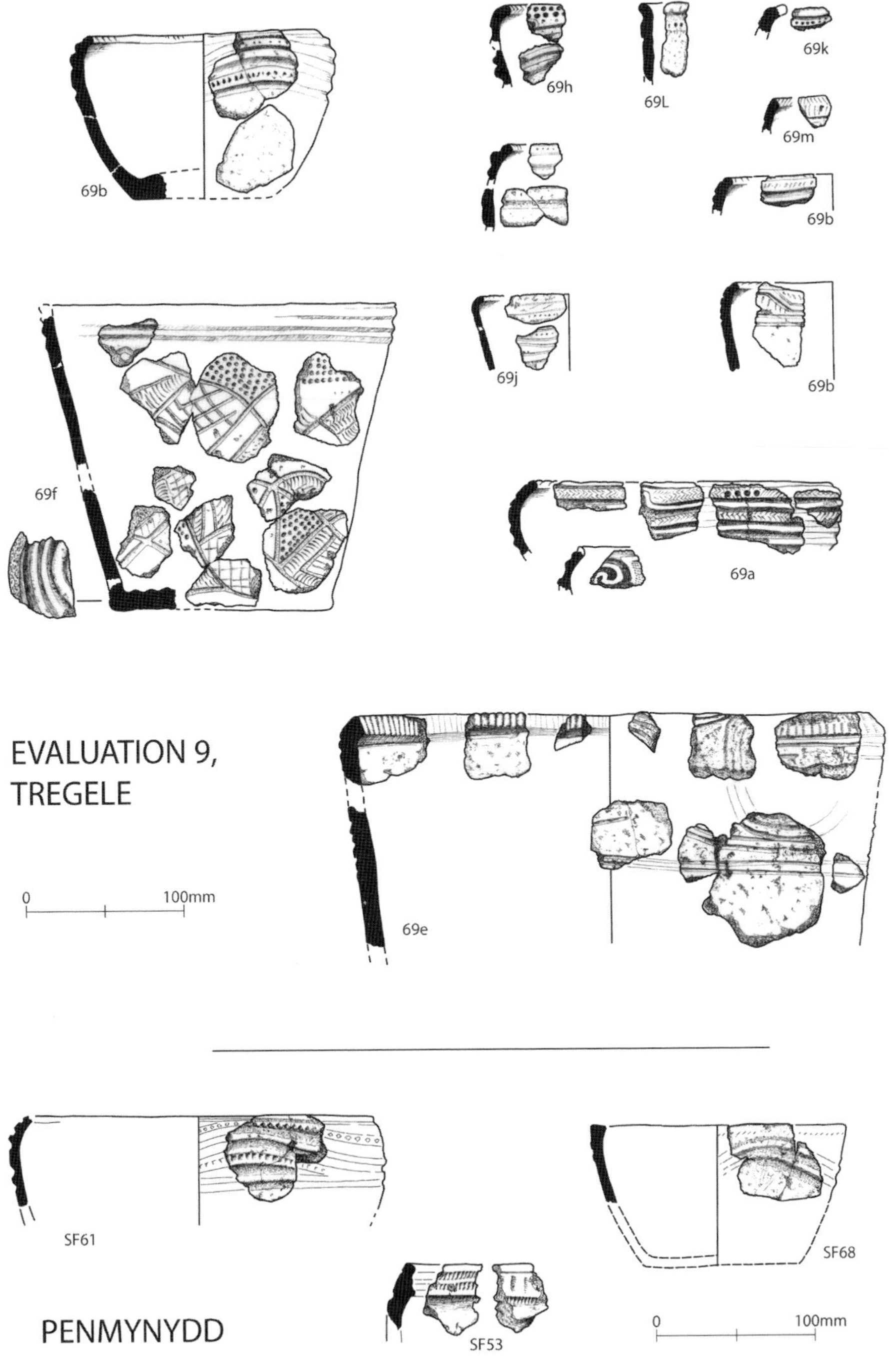

Figure 6.4. Grooved Ware from Tregele, north Anglesey, and Penmyndd, east Anglesey.

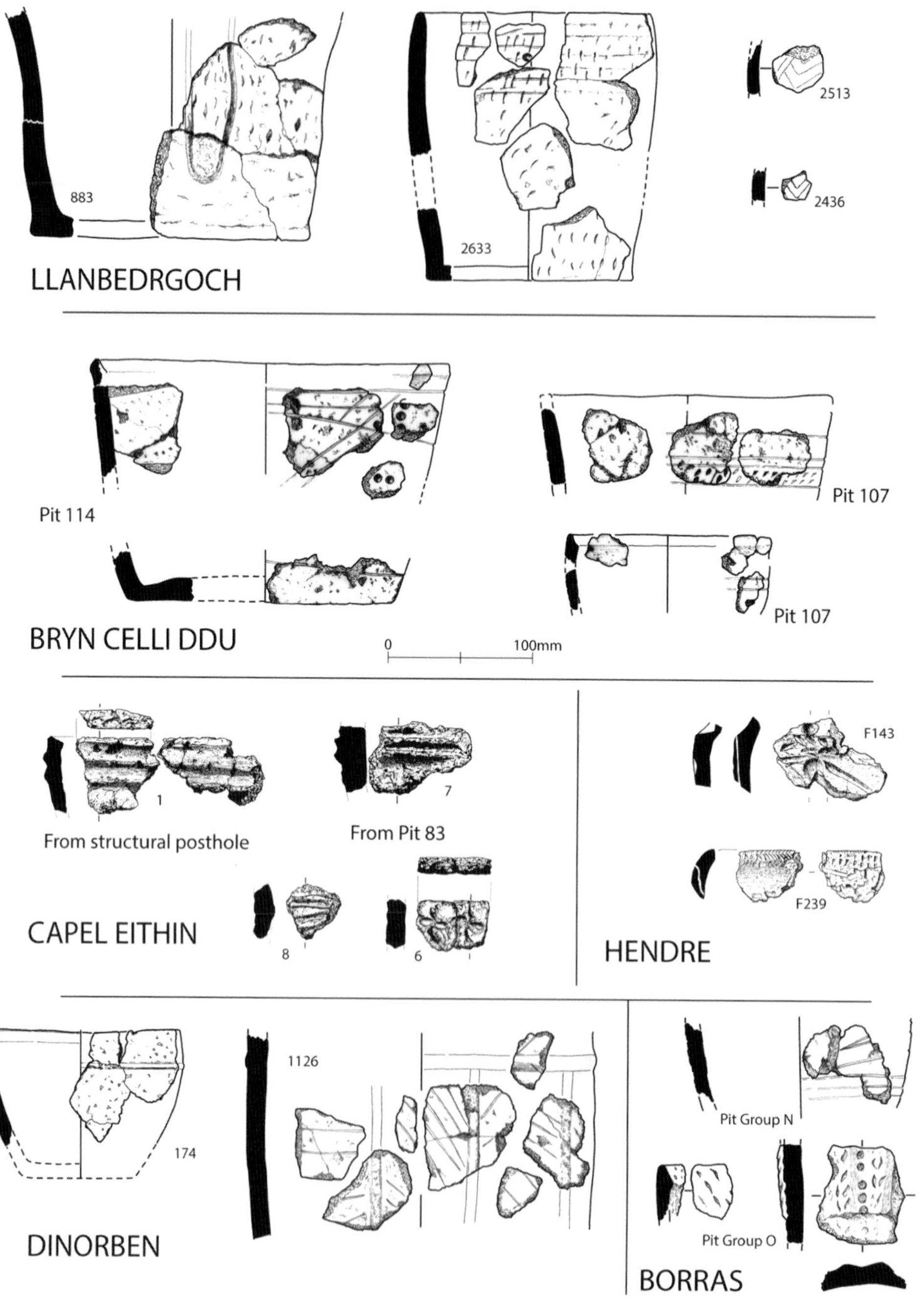

Figure 6.5. Grooved Ware from Llanbedrgoch, Bryn Celli Ddu and Capel Eithin, all east Anglesey; Hendre (after Brassil and Gibson 1999); Dinorben, Denbighshire, and Borras, Wrexham.

not amount to much; elsewhere on the site, Ebbsfleet Ware, some Mortlake Ware, a lot of domestic Beaker, and perhaps some Food Vessel pottery have been found. The pit group at Hendre in which Grooved Ware (Fig. 6.5; Table 6.1) was found has been fully published (Brassil and Gibson 1999).

At Dinorben, Grooved Ware (Fig. 6.5) was found in a series of pits on the high plateau south of Dinorben hillfort/quarry (Wood 2009). Northern Archaeology's excavations in 2005 found some Early Neolithic material, a little Fengate Ware and, in Pit 1126, several sherds from a typical vertically cordoned Grooved Ware jar together with the rim of a plain bowl. In 2008 a smaller undecorated bowl with an encircling cordon was found in another quite distant pit.

Mid-Wales

There are five findspots of Grooved Ware in this part of Wales. At Trelystan (Fig. 6.6; Table 6.1) and at Upper Ninepence (Fig. 6.7; Table 6.1), the Grooved Ware is associated with domestic structures: at Trelystan (as at Parc Cybi) with small squarish huts, each containing a large hearth, and at Upper Ninepence with similar small huts and also larger round houses. Since these discoveries, similar small houses with large central hearths have been discovered at Durrington Walls (Larsson and Parker Pearson 2007). There, the compacted chalk floors reveal a surrounding zone for beds and dressers, as in the famous stone houses of Skara Brae which are much the same size (Parker Pearson *et al.* 2015, 56–7, though see Clarke, this volume).

The area of the Severn Valley near Welshpool has some notable earthworks and timber circles (Gibson 1994) and also small quantities of Impressed Wares and Grooved Ware in pits, but the association with the ceremonial monuments does not appear to be more than accidental. At Sarn-y-bryn-caled, the Peterborough Ware and the meagre Grooved Ware (Fig. 6.6) are from pits and surfaces some distance from the timber circle (Gibson 1994; Blockley and Tavener 2002).

A single large Grooved Ware pot (28 sherds) was found in an isolated pit at Four Crosses, Powys (Fig. 6.6; McSloy 2016). The site at Llanilar near Aberystwyth consisted of pits and hearths, close to Early Bronze Age barrows (Briggs 1997). The 'Group A' pits contained a few Mortlake and Grooved Ware sherds and small deposits of human cremated bone (Fig. 6.7).

South Wales

Looking at South Wales, the situation has not changed much since 1999. The excavations have not been as extensive as in the north and many are incompletely published. The quantity of pottery, especially the Grooved Ware, is also low. The only significant quantities of sherds, about 30 in each case, have come from under a Middle Bronze Age barrow at The Limes, Carmarthen (Poucher 2012); from a pit near Trellyffaint in Pembrokeshire (Nash *et al.* 2021); and from St Athan (Sheridan 2020; Thomson 2020). Settlement contexts are perhaps more common than pit groups, though these do exist, but the pottery is meagre and seldom illustrated (Pannett 2012). The fully published material suggests a comparison with Trelystan; and some material, of which

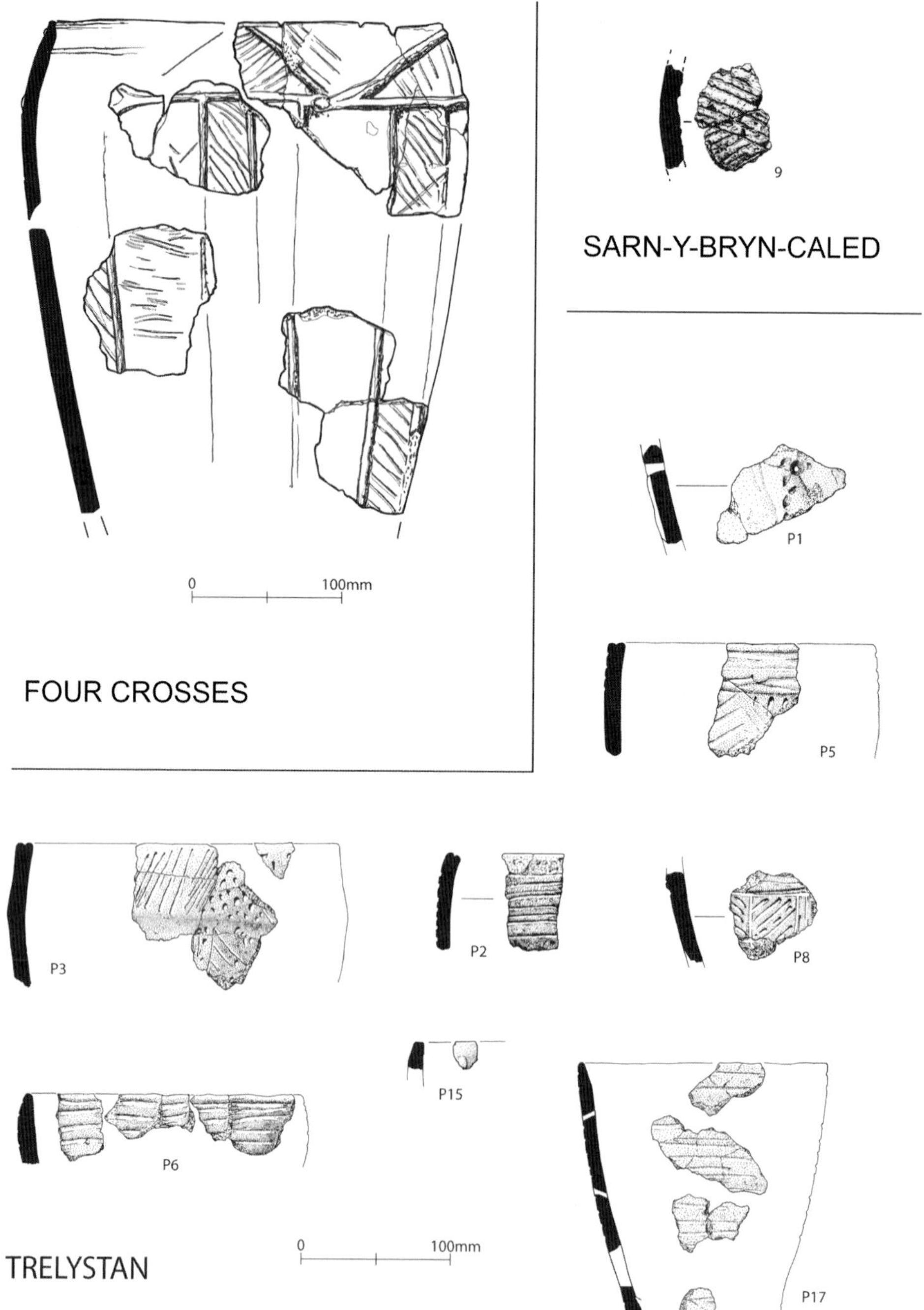

Figure 6.6. Grooved Ware from Four Crosses (after McSloy 2016); Sarn-y-bryn-caled (after Blockley and Tavener 2002); and Trelystan (after Britnell 1982), all Powys.

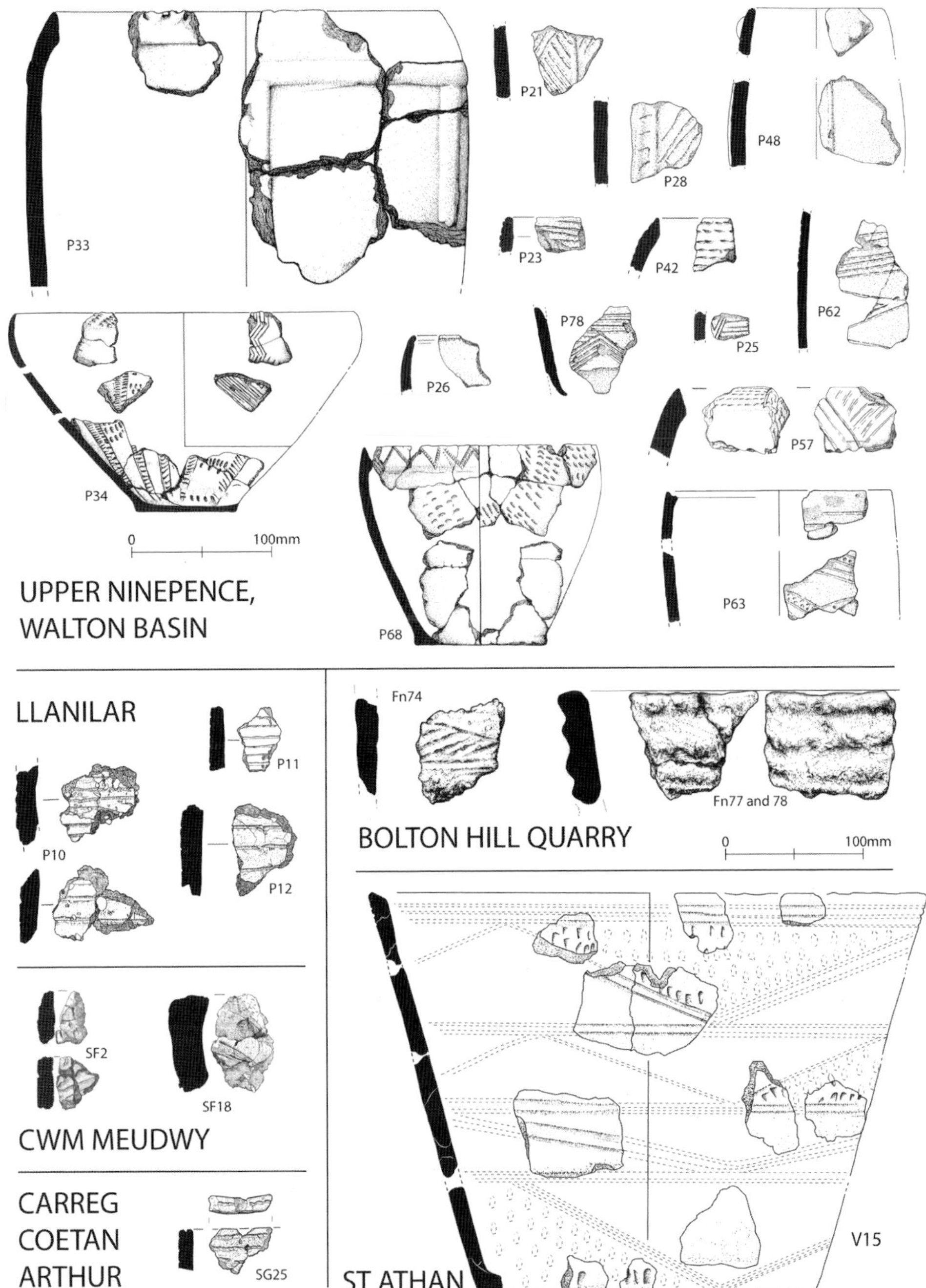

Figure 6.7. Grooved Ware from south Wales: Upper Ninepence (after Gibson 1999); Llanilar (after Briggs 1997); Cwm Meudwy (after Murphy and Evans 2006); Carreg Coetan Arthur (after Rees 2012); Bolton Hill Quarry (after Johnson and Tinsley 2010); and St Athan (after Sheridan 2020; Thomson 2020).

only photographs have been available, indicates that raised cordons, like those at Capel Eithin, are present, together with the soft pitted fabric.

At Cwm Meudwy (Murphy and Evans 2006) on higher ground with later enclosure, there are several pits with Early Neolithic pots and two with pottery judged to be Grooved Ware (Fig. 6.7). At Bolton Hill Quarry near Milford Haven (Johnson and Tinsley 2010, 97–102) there were pits ranging in date from Neolithic to Later Bronze Age, suggesting a domestic context. Grooved Ware sherds from two or three pots have incised triangles and raised cordons at the rim (Fig. 6.7 and Table 6.1). This site is near Milford Haven, as is Stackpole Warren Site B (Benson *et al.* 1990, 200–202 and 210), where two Grooved Ware sherds are recorded from a settlement context, with Beaker and Early Bronze Age pottery. Sherd B94 is a rim with a Trelystan-style encircling groove.

A group of pits near Steynton (Hart *et al.* 2014, Table 6.1; Darvill *et al.* 2020, 92) included two with Grooved Ware (Gibson 2014, 33–5). Three vessels with incised geometric decoration including triangles (on Pot 2) and lozenges (on Pot 3) are represented; all are grog-tempered and two are badly pitted. Pot 1 had been a large tub with a complex rim and with horizontal incised lines and diagonal lines on the exterior. Fourteen scattered pits were found at Cilsan near Llandeilo (Pannett 2012, 130–4; Hart *et al.* 2013; Table 6.1). Two had Early Neolithic pottery, but Pits 7 and 5, 3, and 36 produced dated Grooved Ware. Little remained of the eight pots, but all were grog-tempered and most rather soft and light in colour. Decoration, where present, was mostly of incised lines, arranged on one pot into chevrons or lozenges. One pot had a tub-like profile (Gibson 2013, 17–19).

Two Pembrokeshire tombs – Trellyffaint and Carreg Coetan Arthur – have, like the Anglesey tombs, an insignificant association with Grooved Ware. At Carreg Coetan Arthur there are two sherds from the badly disturbed chamber (Fig. 6.7; Rees 2012, 89, 95) and at Trellyffaint (Nash *et al.* 2021) there are 34 sherds from a pit some 10 m away from the chamber, associated perhaps with some later occupation. The date (3085–2900 cal BC (BRAMS 3041, 4353±35 BP), from encrusted organic residue on one of the sherds, is appropriate for Grooved Ware.

At Rhos y Clegyrn, always a puzzling site, sherds 65/9.1 might be Grooved Ware rather than Food Vessel (Lewis 1974, 21 and 36; Savory 1980, 158 and 204: fig. 56).

Two sites further east have produced Grooved Ware from probable settlement contexts. Excavations beside the Towy at The Limes, Carmarthen, revealed three eroded barrows, one overlying a scatter of Grooved Ware sherds in a tree-throw in Trench 10 of the preliminary excavation (Poucher 2012). Photographs of some of the pottery show that most is pale, perhaps soft, and with cordons as the main decorative feature. One sherd shows two close-set triangular cordons probably near a lost rim, which is reminiscent of rims at Capel Eithin in Anglesey. There is also harder, redder pottery with incised lines. At St Athan, Glamorgan, about a quarter of one very large tub (Sheridan 2020) with classic Clacton sub-style decoration comes from what may be a posthole of a small approximately square building (2 x 2.5 m) in the centre of a ditched enclosure *c.* 7 m across (Group 4003) (Thomson 2020, 24). Another pot from the same pit may also be Grooved Ware, found with a good deal of flint, fired clay, burnt bone and hazelnut shell. While this is not a very close parallel, it can be compared to the Trelystan enclosed hearths or small houses (Fig. 6.7, Table 6.1).

TYPOLOGY

Every attempt to generalise in archaeology is bedevilled by the fact that we have no control over sampling. The small assemblages from Four Crosses (Fig. 6.6), Borras (Fig. 6.5), Dinorben (Fig. 6.5), Bryn Celli Ddu (Fig. 6.5), Llanbedrgoch (Fig. 6.5) and even Parc Bryn Cegin (which has masses of Fengate Ware, but less Grooved Ware: Fig. 6.2) have produced tubs with incised horizontal bands with triangular motifs between, together with the occasional large vertically-cordoned jar, that share features of Longworth's Clacton and Durrington Walls sub-styles (Wainwright and Longworth 1971). These tubs and large jars are also present in the larger assemblages from north Anglesey (Parc Cybi, Llanfaethlu and Tregele: Figs 6.1, 6.3, 6.4) but these assemblages include a wider range of shapes, sizes and decorative techniques, constituting a more flamboyant local variant of Grooved Ware that might be named 'Anglesey sub-style'. The small collection from Penmynydd consists exclusively of this kind of pottery (Fig. 6.4) yet has the earliest date (Table 6.1). The implications of this are discussed below. The collection from Clynnog, part of a continuum of pottery from Early Neolithic to Early Bronze Age, contains one pit where the collared vessels in this 'Anglesey sub-style' might, with equal justification, be described as Fengate Ware (Fig. 6.2); the relationship between Fengate Ware and Grooved Ware is also discussed below.

In north-east Wales the pottery mostly belongs to the Durrington Walls and Clacton sub-styles. At Dinorben (Fig. 6.5) a large jar, with vertical applied cordons, was found in a pit together with the rim of a plain bowl. In 2008, a smaller undecorated bowl with an encircling cordon was found in another, quite distant pit. At least one pot that could be described as belonging to the Durrington Walls sub-style was found at Borras Quarry near Wrexham (Fig. 6.5). Further south, the tall jar from Four Crosses in mid-Wales (Fig. 6.6; McSloy 2016) is a classic example of the Durrington Walls sub-style, with widespread *comparanda* in Britain.

The only Anglesey site to have produced exclusively Clacton sub-style pottery is Bryn Celli Ddu, where the Grooved Ware found in three pits comprised tubs and a smaller bowl (Fig. 6.5). The largest collection of these grooved tubs is from Parc Bryn Cegin near Bangor (Fig. 6.2). Sherds from six pots came from Pit 1553 in Pit Group VIII. Five of them are tub-like pots of varying size. The fabric of PGVIIIA, and of several other Grooved Ware pots in north Wales and some in the south, is unusually lightweight and soft, often a pale yellow colour. It is vulnerable to erosion and pitting and often contains grog. A fragment of rim, Pot VIIIF, is noteworthy for having applied rounded pellets just below the rim, a feature that appears to be relatively uncommon in England but is found in Ireland (albeit on Grooved Ware of a different design: Brindley 1999, 24). Grooved Ware also came from Pit Group VI (a loose grouping) 400 m away from VIII. Pit 6041 contained fine flint tools and sherds from three Grooved Ware pots. Two were lower body sherds from substantial jars with vertical cordons.

One of the other findspots to have produced Grooved Ware in the soft yellow fabric as seen at Parc Bryn Cegin is Glyn, Llanbedrgoch (Fig. 6.5), where two pots – a large jar with a broad, flat cordon and a smaller jar with random fingernail marks, comparable to material from Llanfaethlu – were found. This fabric also seems to be present further south in Wales.

Parc Cybi (Fig. 6.1) has produced two groups of pottery which each combine tubs of the Clacton sub-style with somewhat globular pots with complex three-dimensional decoration and the raised wavy line 'pie crust' cordons which are a feature of the very large Grooved Ware collection from Llanfaethlu. The western group has a tub (W) with unusual vertical lines of impressed decoration, alongside the top of a rounded pot (X) with close-set grooves and ridges encrusted with sharp triangular impressions. The eastern group is larger but includes a rather similar mixture. There are two tubs, both with the characteristic sharply cut banded grooves and upright rims with an internal slope, as has P, with the addition of the undulating 'pie crust' cordon. This cordon is also seen on O, a pot with a heavily rusticated body which might be mistaken for Mortlake-style Peterborough Ware. Pots T and S suggest large, cordoned jars belonging to the Durrington Walls sub-style.

As noted above, the assemblage from Llanfaethlu (Fig. 6.3) is Wales's largest Grooved Ware find, with the remains of some 59 pots present, of which enough survives in 34 cases to reconstruct their shapes. The pottery was found in two different areas, and it differs between those areas. Pits 6008 and 6013 produced a few sherds that are attributable to (or at least comparable with) the Durrington Walls sub-style. In contrast, pits on the eastern slopes of the site produced distinctly different pottery. Over 50 pots are represented and virtually all are richly decorated, with deep rounded grooves and thin triangular cordons in undulating patterns with frequent smaller wavy line 'pie crust' decoration immediately below the rim, as seen at Parc Cybi on rim interiors. Among the 34 reconstructable pots there are five vases of varying diameter with incurving rims, such as 238a. I have deemed these to be Grooved Ware but there are sufficient Fengate-style traits in some (e.g. 213a, with its inturned 'collar' and body that narrows markedly below this) to occasion debate about their classification, as discussed below. The seven cordon-banded pots form another group, which most would consider more typical of Grooved Ware. One, 287a, has a body that narrows markedly below its convex 'neck', linking it with the previous group; the others are smaller and more straight-sided. Both cordoned groups are made in the distinctive lightweight fabric used for other Grooved Ware pots in north Wales. There are two straight-sided tubs (including 328/9a) which are notably thin-walled and well fired with a narrow band of decoration below the rim. Six other pots (212a, 192/197c) have wavy line 'pie crust' cordons below the rim, more tightly waved and standing well proud of the surface. Finally, there are small bowls and cups.

Cordon-decorated pots are in the majority at Llanfaethlu, but the cordons are produced in several different ways. Some are thin clay fillets pressed into a slight groove, some are pinched out and others are created by gouging grooves to either side (false relief). Most seem to restrict the decoration to the upper part of the body, but variety is achieved by use of horizontal and wavy cordons, and some are obviously made with a finger and thumb as in a modern pie crust. Some cordons are gently lipped to create a slightly undulating appearance, as on 361b where the cordon was pulled out over a rounded stick to create a richly carved effect. Flatter cordons may be decorated with dots or neat hatching (361c). Body sherds are relatively rare and what there are suggest that the lower part of the pot was normally undecorated.

One vessel (192/7a) appears unique within a Welsh Grooved Ware context. It is undecorated except for two applied strips over the rim. It is made of a thick, rather soft clay without obvious stone grit and has flared sides and a plain upright rim. The tub shape and the applied strips over the rim are readily paralleled in northern Britain, for example at Yeavering, Northumberland, and Sawdon Moor, North Yorkshire (Manby 1999), and at Sewerby Cottage Farm, Bridlington, East Riding of Yorkshire (Manby 2009, 161).

The kind of dense, rich decoration seen on most of the Llanfaethlu pottery appears again at Tregele (in Evaluation area 9a), not far from Llanfaethlu (Fig. 6.4), and at Penmynydd in eastern Anglesey (Fig. 6.4). On the mainland, it occurs less elegantly at Clynnog (Fig. 6.2) on vases akin to those from Upper Ninepence in the Walton Basin (Fig. 6.7), but this rich density of grooving, incision and dotting seen in north-west Wales is not currently recognisable in other areas of Wales.

At Tregele, 20 individual pots, from six pits, can be recognised, albeit some only by a single rimsherd. Among the pots are two large, straight-sided vessels and six smaller cordoned bowls (Fig. 6.4). Vessel 69b has gently curved cordons with impressions like those from Penmynydd (Fig. 6.4). Its full profile and base are useful for establishing the varying size of containers made. Another feature of this assemblage is the thin, straight walls on small vases (69c and d). Pot 69f from Tregele is so eccentric that it has few close parallels, but the shape, the technique of decoration and the rare internal grooving of the base can be found in Grooved Ware in a wider area, notably Scotland (e.g. at Links of Noltland, for internal base decoration: Sheridan 1999, illus. 12.7). Pot 69e, assembled from sherds from Pits 52, 69 and 70, is difficult to reconstruct confidently except to say that it has a straight profile and a sharply in-turned rim like some at Upper Ninepence (Fig. 6.7). The decoration combines grooving and impressed whipped cord, which is not common in Anglesey but does appear at Penmynydd. The scheme, which appears to involve some kind of near-circular motif, occurs as a broad band of decoration around the upper part of the pot, bounded by a double groove.

Pit 72 at Tregele contained part of a large, urn-like jar, virtually undecorated except for herringbone fingernail marks on the inner edge of the rim and deep pits under the collar. This is something which would be judged to be a Fengate Ware jar, but also in the same pit were two small rims, which could be Grooved Ware. This association is something that will be discussed below.

At Penmynydd (Fig. 6.4), where most of the pottery came from one pit (Pit 0098), the assemblage is not very large (parts of eight pots) but much is of high quality, though thin and fragile. The thinness of the walls suggests that these are mostly small bowls, but SF 53 may represent a larger, straight-sided jar. This pot is decorated with whipped cord impressions, as is another very fragile smaller bowl. The cordoned bowl (SF 61) is the finest piece and the one that is most characteristic of the 'Anglesey sub-style' of rich, dense decoration seen at Llanfaethlu (Fig. 6.3) and Tregele (Fig. 6.4).

The rim sherd from Capel Eithin with close-set triangular-sectioned cordons (Fig. 6.5) has similarities to Llanfaethlu 287a. The lightweight, soft yellow fabric is also comparable. The body sherds from Capel Eithin, assigned to the Woodlands sub-style in 1999 (White and Smith 1999, 76, 88), reflect the density and complexity of decoration, which is also to be seen in the sherd from Hendre, Denbighshire (Fig. 6.5; Brassil and Gibson 1999). The incurved rim from Hendre can also be paralleled at Parc Cybi and, very closely, at Clynnog.

Table 6.1. Radiocarbon dates from features with Grooved Ware pottery in Wales. Compiled by Jane Kenney.

Site	*Material*	*Date BP*	*Cal BC (95%)*	*Lab no.*	*Reference*
Bolton Hill Quarry, Pembs	Hazelnut shell	3715 ± 40	2280–1970	SUERC–30138	Johnson and Tinsley 2010, 23
	Hazelnut shell	3810 ± 40	2460–2130	SUERC–30139	
Capel Eithin, Gaerwen, Anglesey	Charcoal	3950 ± 75	2840–2200	CAR–446	White and Smith 1999, 34–8
	Charcoal	3580 ± 70	2140–1740	CAR–447	
	Charcoal	4740 ± 80	3660–3360	CAR–481	
Cilsan (site 21.02) Carms.	Charcoal (alder)	4224 ± 40	2910–2670	SUERC–56040	Hart *et al.* 2013, 6, 7, 20, 23
	Charcoal (hazel)	4289 ± 40	3020–2770	SUERC–56039	
	Hazelnut shell	4158 ± 29	2880–2630	SUERC–54690	
	Hazelnut shell	4160 ± 29	2880–2630	SUERC–54689	
	Hazelnut shell	4143 ± 29	2880–2620	SUERC–54688	
	Hazelnut shell	4136 ± 29	2880–2610	SUERC–54684	
Clynnog, Gwynedd	Charcoal (hazel)	3956 ± 15	2550–2460	NZA–34257	Roberts in prep.
	Charcoal (hazel)	3665 ± 15	2565–2460	NZA–34256	
Hendre, Flintshire	Charcoal (alder)	3870 ± 70	2570–2130	CAR–1279	Brassil and Gibson 1999, 91
Llanfaethlu, Anglesey	Barley grain	4354 ± 25	3074–2903	BRAMS–4136	Rees and Jones in prep.
	Hazelnut shell	4367 ± 25	3082–2908	BRAMS–4137	
	Wheat grain	4367 ± 25	3082–2908	BRAMS–4138	
	Hazelnut shell	4376 ± 26	3089–2911	BRAMS–4139	
	Hazelnut shell	4368 ± 25	3082–2909	BRAMS–4140	
	Hazelnut shell	4381 ± 27	3092–2912	BRAMS–4145	
	Hazelnut shell	4119 ± 26	2866–2578	BRAMS–4150	
	Hazelnut shell	4345 ± 26	3023–2899	BRAMS–4151	
	Hazelnut shell	4358 ± 26	3076–2905	BRAMS–4152	

(Continued)

Table 6.1 (Continued)

Site	*Material*	*Date BP*	*Cal BC (95%)*	*Lab no.*	*Reference*
Penmynydd, Anglesey	Charcoal (hazel)	4380 ± 40	3100–2900	Beta–280900	Davidson *et al.* 2010, 14–15
	Charcoal (hazel)	4390 ± 40	3260–2910	Beta–280901	
	Lipids	4322 ± 25	3011–2892	BRAMS–6051	Olet *et al.* in prep.
Parc Bryn Cegin, Llandygai, Gwynedd	Hazelnut shell	3976 ± 30	2580–2460	NZA–26681	Kenney 2008, 124–5
	Hazelnut shell	4201 ± 30	2900–2670	NZA–26693	
	Hazelnut shell	4192 ± 30	2890–2670	NZA–26694	
Parc Cybi, Holyhead, Anglesey	Hazelnut shell	4133 ±23	2880–2600	SUERC–81333	Kenney 2021, 209
	Hazelnut shell	4195 ±29	2900–2670	SUERC–83266	
	Hazelnut shell	4175 ±23	2890–2670	SUERC–81337	
	Hazelnut shell	4172 ±29	2890–2630	SUERC–83267	
	Hazelnut shell	4105 ±24	2860–2570	SUERC–81357	
	Hazelnut shell	4110 ±29	2870–2570	SUERC–83286	
	Hazelnut shell	4050 ±20	2840–2480	SUERC–85151	
St Athan, Glam.	Hazelnut shell	4172 ± 30	2890–2630	SUERC–82556	Thomson 2020, 10; Sheridan 2020
Steynton (site 513), Pembs	Charcoal (hazel)	4120 ± 29	2870–2570	SUERC–54660	Hart *et al.* 2014, 9, 76
	Charcoal (hazel)	4138 ± 29	2880–2610	SUERC–54659	
	Charcoal (hazel)	3966 ± 29	2580–2340	SUERC–54662	
	Hazelnut shell	4185 ± 29	2890–2660	SUERC–54661	
Trelystan, Powys	Charcoal (hazel)	4260 ± 70	3090–2620	CAR–272	Britnell 1982, 191
	Charcoal (hazel)	4135 ± 65	2890–2500	CAR–273	
	Hazelnut shells	3985 ± 70	2860–2280	CAR–274	
Upper Ninepence, Powys	Charcoal	4240 ± 70	3040–2610	SWAN–24	Gibson 1999, 43, 82–3
	Charcoal (hazel)	4060 ± 40	2870–2490	BM–3069	
	Charcoal (mixed short lived)	4050 ± 35	2870–2490	BM–2969	
	Charcoal (mixed short lived)	4160 ± 35	2890–2610	BM–2968	

The assemblage from near Ty'n Coed Farm, Clynnog, comprised two undecorated Grooved Ware jars from one pit, and several vases another, some 18 m away (Fig. 6.2). The cordoned jar (Pot T) and the smaller vessel with a flared base (Pot U) are uncontroversial Grooved Ware. The vases, like the urn from Tregele and Pots 213a and 287a from Llanfaethlu, have a number of Fengate traits, such as a clear collar, pits under the collar and a very narrow base. They are comparable to the vases first recognised at Upper Ninepence (Fig. 6.7) but the collar and heavier rim are a noticeable difference, though the smaller pot S has the pointed rim as seen at Upper Ninepence.

The two influential assemblages of Grooved Ware from the Welsh Marches, Trelystan near Welshpool and Upper Ninepence in the Walton Basin, have both been well illustrated and fully published (Britnell 1982; Gibson 1999). I present a selection of drawings here, for comparison (Figs 6.6, 6.7) but will not discuss them in detail. Upper Ninepence is the larger collection, with some 61 pots, as against nine at Trelystan, and it has a greater variety, with examples of vases and internal decoration. Both have been compared to Clacton and Durrington Walls sub-style Grooved Ware, and Upper Ninepence shows hints of the Fengate curved collar but not the richness of decoration seen in Anglesey. Trelystan's rim-tops are often grooved (P2, 3, 5) a feature repeated in south Wales but not in the north. Both have good settlement contexts, preserved, as so often, beneath barrows. In south Wales there is so little Grooved Ware that the much-used phrase 'probably belonging to the Clacton and Durrington Walls sub-styles' covers it all at present (Fig. 6.7). The Orcadian *comparanda* for a large pot from St Athan (Thomson 2020) have been discussed in the unpublished specialist report for this site (Sheridan 2020).

DATING AND DISCUSSION

Previously, Garwood (1999) had only two moderately reliably dated assemblages to discuss from Wales: Trelystan and Hendre. Very soon, dates from Upper Ninepence were available from a hearth and three pits, all associated with Grooved Ware contexts (Gibson 1999, 41–4). At 95.4% confidence, these mostly gave dates spanning the period *c.* 2930–2500 cal BC, a range which corresponded to that of Trelystan and was earlier than that of Hendre. The subsequent discovery of so much more Grooved Ware in Wales has produced a further 40 dates from ten findspots (Table 6.1), with a further date (for a putative Grooved Ware pot from Trellyffaint) having been determined recently.

Much of the Grooved Ware from Wales now has associated radiocarbon dates. In 2019 the dates available at the time were collected, along with dates for Peterborough Ware, and were subjected to Bayesian analysis (Kenney and Hamilton 2020). This excludes Llanfaethlu and other more recent sites, but it provides a preliminary indication of the date of use of Grooved Ware in Wales. Only dates with a close association to pottery were included in the model, which was created using OxCal following a simple bounded phase model (Kenney and Hamilton 2020, 775–7). The model estimates that Grooved Ware began being used in Wales in *3125–2910 cal BC* (*95% probability*), probably in *3025–2930 cal BC* (*68% probability*). Grooved Ware went out of use in either *2480–2370 cal BC* (*11% probability*) or *2130–1895 cal BC* (*84% probability*), probably in *2110–1985 cal BC* (*68% probability*).

This suggests the possibility of Grooved Ware in Wales by the 30th century cal BC. This interpretation relies heavily on the two dates from Penmynydd, but a recent date on lipids from one of the sherds backs this up (Olet *et al.* in prep.). Dates from Llanfaethlu are also around the 30th century cal BC. The date modelled for Fengate Ware (Kenney and Hamilton 2020) showed an overlap in use with Grooved Ware, but on individual sites where both styles have been dated, such as Parc Bryn Cegin (Kenney 2008) and Parc Cybi (Kenney and Hamilton 2020), there is no significant overlap between the dates, creating a sense of chronological separation between these types.

The question of whether there is a chronological separation between the incised tubs and the richly cordoned styles must await more dates. The dates from Penmynydd and Llanfaethlu, where the incised tubs are not present, are early. Where the two styles are associated in the same pits, as at Parc Cybi, the dates are a little later, as they are also at Parc Bryn Cegin, where there are no richly cordoned pots.

Of the various questions that remain about Grooved Ware in Wales, that of its relationship to Fengate Ware – a style of pottery that developed from the earlier Ebbsfleet and Mortlake styles of Peterborough (Impressed) Ware – seems the most pressing, given the existence of vessels that appear to share elements of both ceramic traditions. While it had formerly been thought that Fengate Ware ceased to be used before Grooved Ware appeared, the dating evidence cited above now suggests some general chronological overlap in their use, although not necessarily at the level of individual findspots where both traditions are present. It may be that the appearance of Grooved Ware – thanks to its adoption from Orkney as strongly suggested, for example, by the Orcadian-like St Athan pot (Sheridan 2020) – influenced the design of Fengate Ware, leading to the combining of Orcadian Grooved Ware motifs (such as wavy or zig-zag lines) with the vase-like shape of some Fengate Ware vessels, as seen for example at Clynnog. Wales is not the only place where Fengate-like vessel shapes are associated with designs that can be paralleled on (or evoke) Grooved Ware. One such example is known from Tregurra Valley in Cornwall, found in a pit with indubitably Grooved Ware pottery and made in the same fabric (Vessel P16: Quinnell with Taylor 2022, fig. 4.3; see also Jones and Quinnell, this volume). The boundary between the two traditions can be vague, with for example Pot 69e from Tregele being described as Grooved Ware in this chapter, while a very similar-looking pot from Sewerby Cottage Farm, Bridlington, East Riding of Yorkshire, was described by Manby as Fengate Ware (2009, fig. 124, Pot D24). Similarly, the ascription of some pots from the Walton Basin seems fluid (Gibson 1999). So, it is likely that, if the dates begin to merge and Fengate Ware can be shown to still exist at the beginning of the 3rd millennium cal BC, the stylistic affinities will be recognised more widely.

ACKNOWLEDGEMENTS

Very sincere thanks are due to Jane Kenney, the excavator of Parc Bryn Cegin and Parc Cybi, collector of dates and scanner and organiser of my illustrations, and also to Cat Rees, excavator of Llanfaethlu and willing research assistant. I must also thank all the other excavators who have allowed publication of published and not yet published material, and those who sent photographs of recent finds.

REFERENCES

Baynes, E. Neil 1909. The excavation of the Lligwy cromlech in the Island of Anglesey. *Archaeologia Cambrensis* 6th series 8, 217–31.

Benson, D.G., Evans, J.G. and Williams, G.H. 1990. Excavations at Stackpole Warren, Dyfed. *Proceedings of the Prehistoric Society* 56, 179–245.

Blockley, K. and Tavener, N. 2002. Excavations at Sarn-y-bryn-caled, Welshpool, Powys in 1998–99. *Montgomeryshire Collections* 90, 41–68.

Brassil, K. and Gibson, A.M. 1999. A Grooved Ware pit group and Bronze Age multiple inhumation at Hendre, Rhydymwyn, Flintshire. In R. Cleal and A. MacSween (eds) 1999, 89–97.

Briggs, C.S. (ed.) 1997. A Neolithic and Early Bronze Age settlement and burial complex at Llanilar, Ceredigion. *Archaeologia Cambrensis* 146, 13–59.

Brindley, A. 1999. Irish Grooved Ware. In R. Cleal and A. MacSween (eds) 1999, 23–35.

Britnell, W. 1982. The excavation of two round barrows at Trelystan, Powys. *Proceedings of the Prehistoric Society* 48, 133–201.

Cleal, R. and MacSween, A. (eds) 1999. *Grooved Ware in Britain and Ireland.* Oxford: Oxbow Books.

Darvill, T., David, A., Griffiths, S., Hart, J., James, H., Murphy, K. and Rackham, J. 2020. *Timeline: the archaeology of the South Wales Gas Pipeline.* Cirencester: Cotswold Archaeology.

Davidson, A., Jones, M., Kenney, J., Rees, C. and Roberts, J. 2010. *Gwalchmai Booster to Bodffordd link water main and Llangefni to Penmynydd replacement main: Archaeological Mitigation Report.* Bangor: Gwynedd Archaeological Trust, unpublished client report 885.

Garwood, P. 1999. Grooved Ware in southern Britain: chronology and interpretation. In R. Cleal and A. MacSween (eds) 1999, 145–76.

Gibson A.M. 1994. Excavations at Sarn-y-bryn-caled cursus complex, Welshpool, Powys, and the timber circles of Great Britain and Ireland. *Proceedings of the Prehistoric Society* 60, 143–223.

Gibson, A.M. 1999. *The Walton Basin Project: excavation and survey in a prehistoric landscape 1993–7.* York: Council for British Archaeology Research Report 118.

Gibson, A.M. 2013. Prehistoric pottery. In J. Hart, D. Sausins and D. Brannlund 2013, 17–19.

Gibson, A.M. 2014. Prehistoric pottery. In J. Hart, A. Barber and C. Leonard 2014, 32–54.

Grant, I. 2014. *Borras Quarry, Wrexham: Archaeological Watching Brief and Excavation 2014.* Welshpool: Clwyd-Powys Archaeological Trust, unpublished client report 1295.

Hart, J, Sausins, D. and Brannlund, D. 2013. *South Wales Gas Pipeline Project Sites OEA11 and 21.02. Land east of Cilsan, Llangathen, Carmarthenshire.* Cirencester: Cotswold Archaeology, unpublished client report for National Grid. https://reports. cotswoldarchaeology.co.uk/content/uploads/2016/10/9150-Sites-OEA-11-and-21.02-Land-East-of-Cilsan-report-13338.pdf [accessed 28/05/23].

Hart, J., Barber, A. and Leonard, C. 2014. *South Wales Gas Pipeline Project Site 513: Land north- west of Steynton, Milford Haven, Pembrokeshire, archaeological excavation.* Cirencester: Cotswold Archaeology, unpublished client report for National Grid. https:// reports. cotswoldarchaeology.co.uk/content/uploads/2016/10/9150-Site-513-Land-North-West-of-Steynton-report-13261.pdf [accessed 28/05/23].

Johnson, B. and Tinsley, A.S. 2010. *Archaeological excavations at Bolton Hill Quarry, Pembrokeshire.* Bakewell: Archaeological Research Services Ltd, unpublished client report for F.H. Gilman and Co, 2010/50.

Kenney, J. 2008. Recent excavations at Parc Bryn Cegin, Llandygai, near Bangor, north Wales. *Archaeologia Cambrensis* 157, 9–142.

Kenney, J. 2021. *A Welsh landscape through time: excavations at Parc Cybi, Holy Island, Anglesey.* Oxford: Oxbow Books.

Kenney, J. and Hamilton D. 2020. Radiocarbon dating. In J. Kenney, N. McGuinness, R. Cooke, C. Rees and A. Davidson 2020. *Parc Cybi, Holyhead: Final Report on excavations*, 747–74. Bangor: Gwynedd Archaeological Trust, unpublished client report for the Welsh Government, 1512. http://www.heneb.co.uk/parccybi/reports/GAT_Report_1512_vol%20I.pdf [accessed 29/05/23].

Larsson, M. and Parker Pearson, M. (eds) 2007. *From Stonehenge to the Baltic: cultural diversity in the third millennium BC*. Oxford: British Archaeological Report S1692.

Lewis, J.M. 1974. Excavations at Rhos-y-Clegryn prehistoric site, St. Nicholas, Pembrokeshire. *Archaeologia Cambrensis* 123, 13–42.

Longworth, I.H. and Cleal, R. 1999. Grooved Ware gazetteer. In R. Cleal and A. MacSween (eds) 1999, 177–206.

Lynch, F. 1991. *Prehistoric Anglesey* (second edition). Llangefni: Anglesey Antiquarian Society.

Lynch, F. and Musson, C. 2001. A prehistoric and early medieval complex at Llandegai, near Bangor, North Wales. *Archaeologia Cambrensis* 150, 17–142.

Lynch, F., Aldhouse Green, S. and Davies J.L. 2000. *Prehistoric Wales*. Stroud: Sutton.

McSloy, E. 2016. The pottery. In T. Havard, T. Darvill and M. Alexander, A Bronze Age round barrow cemetery, Iron Age burials, Iron Age copper working, and later activity at Four Crosses, Llandysilio, Powys, 21–3. *Archaeological Journal* 174, 1–67.

Manby, T. 1999. Grooved Ware sites in Yorkshire and northern England 1974–1994. In R. Cleal and A. MacSween (eds) 1999, 57–76.

Manby, T. 2009. Neolithic pottery. In C. Fenton-Thomas, *A place by the sea: excavations at Sewerby Cottage Farm, Bridlington*, 151–85. York: On-Site Archaeology.

Murphy, K. and Evans, R.T.J. 2006. Excavation of Neolithic pits, three ring-ditches and a palisaded enclosure at Cwm Meudwy, Llandysul, Ceredigion, 2003. *Archaeologia Cambrensis* 155, 23–48.

Nash, G., James, C., Wellicome, T. with Dunne, J. and Casanova, E. 2021. How excavating a Pembrokeshire portal dolmen illuminated Neolithic dairy farming in Wales. *Current Archaeology* 380, 20–5.

Pannett, A. 2012. Pits, pots and plant remains: trends in Neolithic deposition in Carmarthenshire, South Wales. In H. Anderson-Whymark and J. Thomas (eds), *Regional perspectives on Neolithic pit deposition: beyond the mundane*, 126–43. Oxford: Neolithic Studies Group Seminar Papers 12.

Parker Pearson, M., Pollard, J., Richards, C., Thomas, J. and Welham, K. 2015. *Stonehenge: making sense of a prehistoric mystery*. York: Council for British Archaeology.

Poucher, P. 2012. *The Limes, Carmarthen: archaeological evaluation*. Llandeilo: Dyfed Archaeological Trust, unpublished client report for Persimmon Homes.

Quinnell, H. with Taylor, R. 2022. The ceramics. In S.R. Taylor, *Down the bright stream: the prehistory of Woodcock Corner and the Tregurra Valley, Cornwall*, 107–26. Oxford: Archaeopress.

Rees, S. 2012. Excavations at Carreg Coetan Arthur chambered tomb, Pembrokeshire. *Archaeologia Cambrensis* 161, 51–163.

Rees, C. and Jones, M. 2016. Excavations at Llanfaethlu, Anglesey 2014–2015. *Transactions of the Anglesey Antiquarian Society* for 2015–16, 46–58.

Rees, C. and Jones, M. 2017. Neolithic Life at Llanfaethlu. *Current Archaeology* 323, 12

Roberts, J.A. 2007. Clynnog Fawr: A497 improvement scheme. *Archaeology in Wales* 47, 128–9.

Saunders, B. 2021. Neolithic and Romano-British lowland farming practices in north-west Wales: archaeological investigations along Section 3 of the Llangefni Link Road, Ynys Môn. *Archaeology in Wales* 61, 7–40

Savory, H.N. 1980. *Guide catalogue of the Bronze Age collections*. Cardiff: National Museum of Wales.

Sheridan, J.A. 1999. Grooved Ware from the Links of Noltland, Westray, Orkney. In R. Cleal and A. MacSween (eds) 1999, 112–24.

Sheridan, J.A. 2020. *Report on the pottery from St John's Well, St Athan, Glamorgan*. Unpublished client report for Headland Archaeology. https://www.academia.edu/105426549/Report_on_the_pottery_from_St_Johns_Well_St_Athan_Glamorgan

Smith, C.A. and Lynch, F.M. 1987. *Trefignath and Din Dryfol: the excavation of two megalithic tombs in Anglesey*. Cardiff: Cambrian Archaeological Monograph 3.

Thomson, S. 2020. Circles of life and death: lines of renewal and remembrance. Excavation of a prehistoric site in St. Athan, Glamorgan. *Archaeology in Wales* 60, 7–28.

Wainwright, G.J. and Longworth, I.H. 1971. *Durrington Walls: excavations 1966–1968*. London: Society of Antiquaries.

White, S.I. and Smith, G. 1999. A funerary and ceremonial centre at Capel Eithin, Gaerwen, Anglesey. *Transactions of the Anglesey Antiquarian Society* for 1999, 17–166.

Wood, P. 2009. St George Quarry, Dinorben, near Abergele, Conwy (SH 9695 7515). *Archaeology in Wales* 49, 59–60.

Chapter 7

Land of milk and honey? Grooved Ware use in Neolithic Wales

Lilly Olet, Richard Evershed and Jessica Smyth

INTRODUCTION

Organic residue analysis is concerned with characterising the molecular and isotopic composition of ancient remnant fats. Frequently, pottery is the analysed substrate, owing to the ubiquity of potsherds in the archaeological record from later prehistory onwards and the often excellent state of lipid preservation within the ceramic matrix. The porous micro-structure of pottery provides a protective environment for lipids absorbed during food processing/storage. While other classes of biomolecules can also be targeted, lipids are most commonly preserved because of their hydrophobic properties (Evershed 1993, 76–7). Questions can thereby be addressed concerning past diet, vessel use and technological features. This is possible because the structures of some lipids, termed *biomarkers*, are indicative of a specific biological origin (Evershed 2008), and because the stable carbon isotope values ($\delta^{13}C$) of the major fatty acids that survive from animal fats preserve dietary and metabolic differences between the source animals (Evershed *et al.* 1997).

Topics addressed through organic residue analysis include the introduction and use of secondary products (e.g. Copley *et al.* 2005; Cramp *et al.* 2014), the exploitation of aquatic resources (e.g. Copley *et al.* 2004; Bondetti *et al.* 2021) and changes in dietary practices (e.g. Mukherjee *et al.* 2007). Research can focus on the connection and/or the discrepancy between vessel use and overall past diet (e.g. Lucquin *et al.* 2016; Dunne *et al.* 2019) or specific uses of vessels (e.g. Salque *et al.* 2013). Technological aspects can also be considered, such as the use of organic materials in the manufacturing process, for example as sealants (Roffet-Salque *et al.* 2017). A degree of caution is necessary when interpreting the results of organic residue analysis to infer past diet and subsistence practices due to preservation biases and the potential for some staple foods to have been processed without using pottery vessels (Whelton *et al.* 2021). Additionally, foods containing high abundances of lipids may constitute only part of a society's diet. Furthermore, differences in the structures of lipids result in highly variable resistance to degradation during food processing and burial. However, within these limits, organic residue analysis has proved to be invaluable for investigating prehistoric and historic vessel use. It can also be used to provide integrated interpretations of past diet and subsistence if the results are linked with other strands of evidence, such as faunal assemblages, dietary stable-isotope analyses and archaeobotanical evidence.

This chapter presents the results of the organic residue analysis of Grooved Ware and other Neolithic pottery from four sites in north Wales that was undertaken for Jessica Smyth's *Passage Tomb People* project and sets these within the context of previous organic residue analysis of Grooved Ware from Britain and Ireland.

LIPID RESIDUES IN GROOVED WARE FROM BRITAIN AND IRELAND

In over three decades of organic residue analysis of pottery, a large dataset from Neolithic vessels from Britain and Ireland has been produced. Most Neolithic pottery types from this part of north-west Europe were used for cooking lipid-rich animal products, which is indicated by lipid profiles with high concentrations of degraded animal fat. The advances in organic residue analysis in the late 1990s, in particular the compound-specific stable isotope analysis of palmitic and stearic acid (Mottram *et al.* 1999), were crucial to studying trends in processing dairy, ruminant or non-ruminant carcass products. Earlier studies of Grooved Ware by Bonfield (1997) on the assemblage from Pool (Orkney), and by Jones (Jones *et al.* 2005) on Grooved Ware from Barnhouse (Orkney), relied on molecular identification alone, showing that these assemblages were predominantly used for cooking purposes. Jones' claimed identification of barley lipids at Barnhouse, based on the distribution of saturated fatty acids, is now known to be erroneous, although thanks to recent advances, evidence for cereal processing in pottery can now be detected, based on cereal-specific lipid biomarkers (Colonese *et al.* 2017; Hammann and Cramp 2018). The success of this technique has been demonstrated with Neolithic pottery from the Outer Hebrides (Hammann *et al.* 2022).

One of the earliest case studies that determined compound-specific stable isotope ratios of fatty acids from pottery in order to distinguish between different animal fats was one that compared Impressed Ware with Grooved Ware (Dudd *et al.* 1999). Impressed Ware (also known as Peterborough Ware) comprises several sub-styles, including Mortlake and Fengate, which constituted the dominant pottery traditions in the Middle Neolithic in large parts of Britain and Ireland *c.* 3500–2900 cal BC (Alison Sheridan pers. comm.; see also Ard and Darvill 2015), while Grooved Ware appeared later (*3160–3045 cal BC, 95% probability; start Barnhouse:* Richards *et al.* 2016), then spread from Orkney to the rest of Britain and Ireland, remaining in use in Scotland until *2455–2290 cal BC (95% probability; Last: Durrington Walls*: Copper *et al.* 2021). The results from a small set of pottery (five Impressed Ware vessels, 12 Grooved Ware vessels) from Upper Ninepence, Powys, in mid-Wales revealed a difference in use between the two styles. Absorbed residues from the Impressed Ware showed fatty acid $\delta^{13}C$ values characteristic of dairy and ruminant carcass fats, while the fatty acids from two Grooved Ware vessels showed the processing of non-ruminant meat. Charred encrusted material showed that dairy products also were heated in Grooved Ware vessels.

In a follow-up, large-scale study comparing Grooved Ware with other Neolithic and later prehistoric pottery across Britain, pig processing was found to coincide with Grooved Ware use (Mukherjee *et al.* 2007). The Grooved Ware sites studied were in southern Britain (Cranborne Chase, Durrington Walls, West Kennet palisade enclosures, Betchworth, Yarnton Floodplain), mainland Scotland (Melbourne, Balfarg Riding School) and Orkney (Stonehall, Crossiecrown, Skara Brae, Links of Noltland). Overall, 16% of Grooved Ware vessels were used predominantly for processing porcine products (>75% porcine contribution calculated using a mixing model), compared to 7% among other Neolithic pottery styles, 5% among Bronze Age vessels and 0% among Iron Age vessels. While this could be the result of restricted or specialised vessel use, for example relating to specific food taboos or traditions, there was good agreement with the proportion of pig remains in faunal assemblages, despite varying recording techniques. Thus, at West Kennet for example, an NISP (number of identified specimens) total of 73% for pig bones corresponds to a total of 67% of the vessels with predominantly non-ruminant lipids while at Skara Brae, where pig bones formed a minority element in the faunal assemblage (0.4% by minimum number of individuals), this is reflected in the low (4%) incidence of predominantly porcine lipids in the sampled pottery.

Mukherjee's study also highlighted, for the first time, the marked geographic differences in Grooved Ware use (Mukherjee *et al.* 2008). There was a significant difference between sites in the north and in the south. The Grooved Ware assemblages from Scotland were mainly used for dairy products (65%) and only rarely for other products (5% porcine), contrasting with 30% porcine fats in southern Britain. Additional analyses, including sherds from the Ness of Brodgar, Pool, Quanterness and Links of Noltland (Cramp *et al.* 2014) and the A9 Dualling excavation (McLaren *et al.* 2022) have supported this observation (Fig. 7.1). Lipid residues from 106 sherds representing 99 Irish Grooved Ware vessels were analysed and published in Smyth and Evershed (2015). The sites studied are Ballynahatty, Lowpark, Balregan, Longstone and Ballynacarriga, the selection representing both settlement sites and non-domestic sites. All vessels at Lowpark and Ballynahatty were used predominantly for dairy processing, while those from the settlement site of Ballynacarriga showed some contribution from ruminant and non-ruminant carcass fat. Overall, Grooved Ware use in Ireland (comparable to Late Neolithic pottery use on the Isle of Man: Cramp *et al.* 2014) shows similarity to Grooved Ware use in Scotland but with stronger specialisation of vessel use. The predominant commodity processed in Neolithic vessels is milk or dairy products; this remains unchanged throughout the Neolithic (Fig. 7.1).

A similar split in the lipid residues was found between non-domestic and domestic assemblages. The Grooved Ware from non-domestic sites (henges and palisade enclosures) was more strongly associated with pork products than that from domestic sites. Because there is an inherent bias in the available Grooved Ware assemblages – most large Grooved Ware assemblages in Orkney are found within domestic sites while non-domestic sites (such as passage tombs) have only produced relatively few pots by comparison – it is difficult to assess whether geography, site type or a combination of both was the driving factor. Predominantly non-domestic sites could be linked with feasting activities, and evidence from several sites in southern Britain with large faunal assemblages, most notably Durrington Walls, suggests that pigs were important animals for feasting purposes there (Madgwick *et al.* 2019).

Further evidence for varying patterns of vessel use according to site type came from a study by Craig *et al.* (2015). Currently, the largest organic residue dataset from one single Grooved Ware site, 317 sherds from Durrington Walls, was analysed to investigate intra-site variation of vessel use by comparing pottery from a timber circle within the enclosure

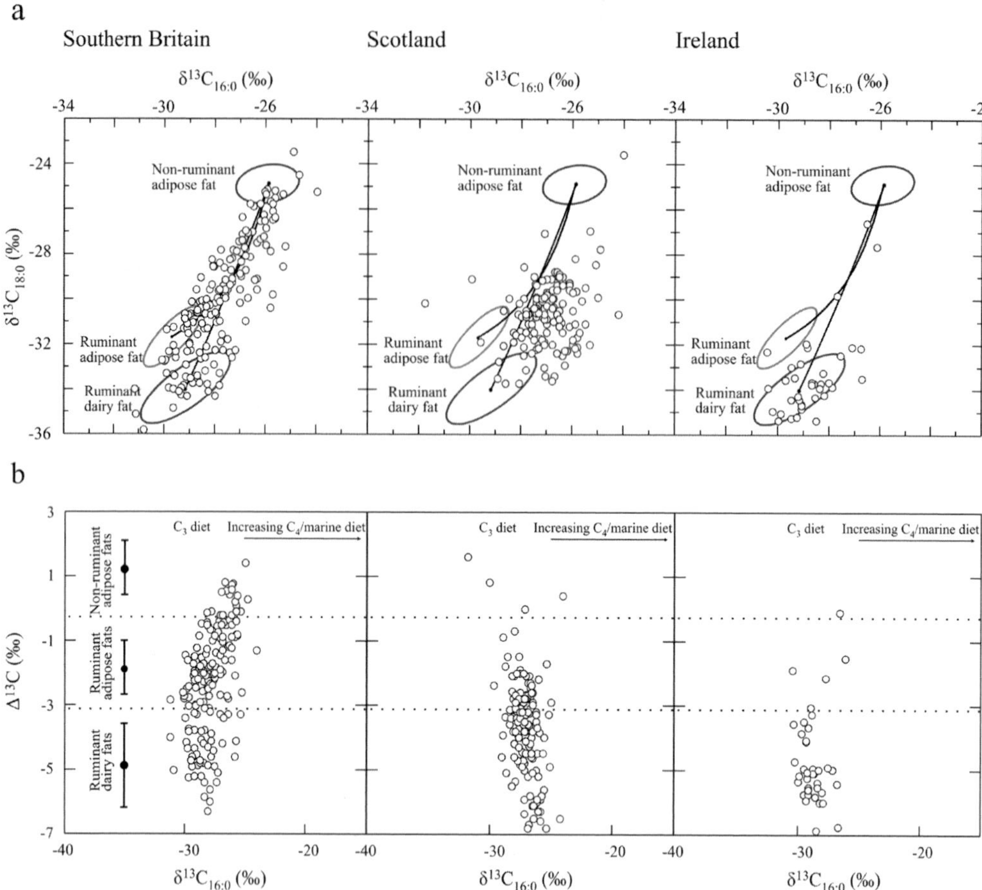

Figure 7.1. (a) Collated $\delta^{13}C$ values for the $C_{16:0}$ and $C_{18:0}$ fatty acids from Grooved Ware in Britain and Ireland; data from Mukherjee et al. *(2008), Cramp* et al. *(2014), Craig* et al. *(2015) and Smyth and Evershed (2015). The ellipses represent the P=0.684 confidence ranges for animals raised on a C_3 plant diet in Britain (Copley* et al. *2003). (b) $\Delta^{13}C$ values, which represent the differences between the individual fatty acids ($\Delta^{13}C=\delta^{13}C_{18:0}-\delta^{13}C_{16:0}$). The bars represent the mean $\pm 1\sigma$ of the $\Delta^{13}C$ values from a database reported in Dunne* et al. *2012, including global modern animal fats (Dunne* et al. *2012; Copley* et al. *2003; Outram* et al. *2009; Spangenberg* et al. *2006; Gregg* et al. *2009; Pitter 2013). The $\delta^{13}C$ values of modern reference fats were corrected for the Suess-effect by adding 1.2‰ (Friedli* et al. *1986).*

with that from pits and middens associated with houses. The analysis confirmed that the proportion of porcine fats (27%) is comparable to other southern Grooved Ware sites but does not reflect the predominance of pig remains in the faunal assemblage (63%, MNI: Harcourt 1971). Burning patterns at the articular ends of pig limb bones indicate that roasting joints of meat was a common practice on the site, and one that did not involve the use of pots (Albarella and Serjeantson 2002). Interestingly, vessels from the pits show a stronger porcine signal than the ones from the midden context, while pottery from the timber circle was predominantly used for dairy products (55%). While organic residue analyses showed an overall correlation between non-domestic feasting-related sites and increasing pig consumption in southern Britain, intra-site comparison at Durrington Walls yielded the opposite result: a majority of porcine fats associated with the houses, with dairy fats more prevalent at the timber circle, which is more likely to be a public and ceremonial site. While this is surprising, it should be considered that Durrington Walls is arguably a specialised site with short-term habitation and all areas of the site can be understood within the context of feasting, with intra-site differences representing a spatial division of feasting preparations and practices.

As the body of data on Grooved Ware pottery from Britain and Ireland has grown, the early work on Grooved Ware from Wales is now somewhat limited by comparison. To increase our understanding of Grooved Ware use, four sites in north Wales were selected for lipid analysis. North Wales is a region that has not been studied previously and one that shows strong connections with other regions along and across the Irish Sea during this period.

MATERIALS AND METHODS

The pottery

Grooved Ware sherds from four Neolithic sites in north Wales (Fig. 7.2) were subjected to organic residue analysis, along with sherds of Impressed Ware in three cases. The pottery selection comprised 45 Mortlake and Grooved Ware sherds from Llanfaethlu (Rees and Jones unpublished client report, Grooved Ware: n=24); 30 Mortlake, Fengate and Grooved Ware sherds from Parc Bryn Cegin (Kenney 2008, Grooved Ware: n=8); 23 Mortlake, Fengate and Grooved Ware sherds from Parc Cybi (Kenney 2021, Grooved Ware: n=11); and four Grooved Ware sherds from Penmynydd (Davidson *et al.* unpublished client report). Charred surface residues were sampled from one Grooved Ware sherd from Parc Bryn Cegin and two from Llanfaethlu. Further detail of these sites and their pottery assemblages is given by Frances Lynch (this volume, Chapter 6). Briefly, the studied sites are all located on the island of Anglesey or on the adjacent Welsh mainland (Parc Bryn Cegin). At all the sites, the Grooved Ware was recovered from pits, in isolated pit clusters or associated with structural features such as hearths (e.g. Parc Cybi, Area D3 or western area; Kenney 2021). Parc Cybi, Parc Bryn Cegin and Llanfaethlu are multi-phase sites with Middle and Late Neolithic pits following Early Neolithic timber buildings; in some cases there is also Mesolithic activity and continued use of the area in the Bronze Age. Pottery from a fifth site – Clynnog – was also part of the study but the sampled pottery (Chapter 6, Fig. 6.4) was not unambiguously identified as Grooved Ware because of several Fengate Ware features. Pottery analysis by Frances Lynch suggested that the assemblages from Penmynydd and Llanfaethlu represent early Grooved Ware, while dates from Parc Bryn Cegin and Parc Cybi suggest that some of the pottery (including shallow Clacton sub-style pots) may be later than the Penmynydd and Llanfaethlu assemblages, an argument supported by compound-specific radiocarbon dates (in a forthcoming study by Olet *et al.*).

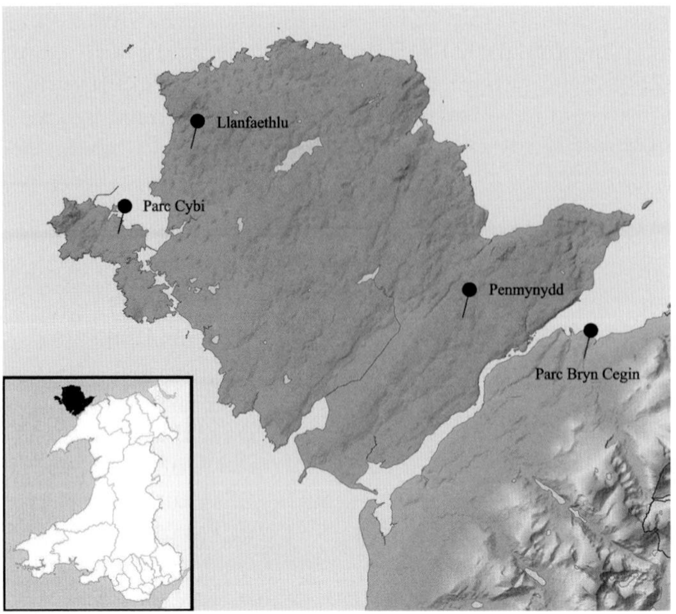

Figure 7.2. Map of Anglesey and surroundings showing the location of the sites (adapted from Ordnance Survey OpenData map).

Extraction

Absorbed lipids were extracted from the pottery using acidified methanol, as described in Correa-Ascencio and Evershed (2014). About 1 g of each potsherd was cleaned using a modelling drill and ground with a solvent-cleaned mortar and pestle. Surface residues were removed with a solvent-cleaned scalpel and extracted alongside the pottery (16–77 mg). An internal standard (*n*-tetratriacontane, 20–40 μg) was added for the purpose of quantification. H_2SO_4/MeOH (4% *v:v*, 5 mL, 70°C, 1 h) was used for one-step methylation (producing fatty acid methyl esters, FAME) as well as for quicker and higher recovery of lipids. *n*-Hexane (10 ml) was used to extract the lipids from the residual clay and from the H_2SO_4/MeOH extract in four steps. Excess *n*-hexane was evaporated under a stream of N_2. An aliquot for instrument analysis was derivatised using 20 μL of *N,O*-Bis[trimethylsilyl]trifluoroacetamide (BSTFA, Sigma Aldrich; 20–30 μL, 70°C, 1 h). Samples which yielded compounds associated with beeswax or plant waxes were further extracted with organic solvents to identify wax esters and other complex lipids. The protocol (Evershed *et al.* 1990) consists of two extraction steps with $CHCl_3$:MeOH (2:1 *v:v*, 2 × 10 mL, ultra-sonicated for 20 min, centrifuged at 2500 rpm). Excess solvent was evaporated under a stream of N_2. Aliquots of the extracts were filtered through activated-silica columns. The analytes were derivatised with 40 μL BSTFA (Sigma Aldrich; 20–40 μL, 70°C, 1 h) prior to GC analysis. An internal standard (20 μg *n*-tetratriacontane) was used for quantification.

Gas chromatography (GC-FID)

The diluted samples were auto-injected (1 μL) on to a non-polar capillary column (HP-1, 50 m × 0.32 mm × 0.17 μm, stationary phase: 100% dimethylpolysiloxane) on an Agilent 7820A GC, with helium as the carrier gas (flow: 2 mL.min^{-1}) and a flame ionisation detector (FID). The temperature setup started with 2 min at 50°C followed by an increase to 300°C (10°C.min^{-1}) and a 15 min isothermal (Correa-Ascencio and Evershed 2014).

Solvent extracts were analysed with a HT-GC. The instrument (Agilent 7890A) was fitted with a high-temperature column (DB1-HT, 15 m × 0.32 mm × 0.1 µm, 100% dimethylpolysiloxane), with helium as the carrier gas (flow: 4 mL.min^{-1}) and an FID. After a 2 min isothermal at 50°C, the temperature was increased to 350°C at 10°C.min^{-1} followed by a 10 min isothermal (modified from Evershed *et al.* 1990).

Gas chromatography-mass spectrometry (GC-MS)

The extracts were initially analysed with a Thermo Trace 1300 GC coupled to an ISQ single-quadrupole MS and fitted with a non-polar column (Rtx-1, 50 m × 0.32 mm × 0.17 µm, 100% dimethylpolysiloxane). The GC was programmed to a 1 min isothermal at 50°C, followed by an increase to 300°C at 10°C.min^{-1} and an 8 min isothermal. The MS (transfer line at 300°C, EI mode at 70eV) acquired *m/z* 50–650 at 2 scans/s. Selected ion monitoring mode (SIM) was used to detect dihydroxy-FAMEs (*m/z* 215, 243, 259, 443, 459, 471, 487, 499, 515) (Cramp and Evershed 2014, 331–2). For the detection of other aquatic biomarkers, pottery extracts were analysed with a polar column on the same instrument (2 min isothermal at 50°C, 10°C.min^{-1} ramp to 100°C and then 4°C.min^{-1} to 240°C followed by a 15 min isothermal), for a better separation of the target compounds. A SIM mode set to *m/z* 105, 262, 290, 318, 346 was used to detect ω-(*o*-alkylphenyl)alkanoic acids (APAAs) (Cramp and Evershed 2014, 328–31). Transfer line and ion source temperature were at 260°C and 240°C. Solvent extracts were analysed using the same instrument fitted with a high-temperature column (Rxi-1HT; film thickness 0.1 µm) and a temperature program starting with a 2 min isothermal at 50°C, followed by a ramp to 380°C. The transfer line was heated to 380°C; the ion source to 340°C. Two scans/s between *m/z* 50–950 were acquired and SIM mode was set to *m/z* 268 to screen for *Triticum* sp. cereal biomarkers (Hammann and Cramp 2018).

GC-C-IRMS

The samples that yielded sufficient $C_{16:0}$ and $C_{18:0}$-FAME were analysed by GC-C-IRMS to determine compound-specific $\delta^{13}C$ values. The GC instrument was an Agilent 7890A GC (HP-1 column, 50 m × 0.32 mm × 0.17 µm, stationary phase: 100% dimethylpolysiloxane, 2 min isothermal at 40°C, ramp to 300°C at 10°C min^{-1}, 10 min isothermal), coupled to an Isoprime 100 MS via an Isoprime combustion interface (850°C). The MS used EI (70 eV), faraday cup collection was programmed for *m/z* 44, 45, 46 (Mottram *et al.* 1999).

RESULTS: GROOVED WARE USE IN NORTH WALES

Lipid preservation

The preservation of lipids was generally good, with 85% of absorbed residues from Grooved Ware yielding appreciable amounts of lipids that could be analysed further for their stable carbon isotopic compositions. The lipid concentrations were high overall but varied between sites and periods. At several multi-phase sites elsewhere (Upper Ninepence:

Dudd *et al.* 1999; or at Orcadian and Irish sites, unpublished data), a decrease in lipid concentration in the Grooved Ware phase is visible; this was not observed in the data from north Wales. At Parc Bryn Cegin, Mortlake sherds show the highest lipid concentration; at Parc Cybi, the highest lipid concentration is found among Fengate sherds; while at Llanfaethlu, the Grooved Ware shows the most saturated lipid signals.

While the average lipid concentration in Grooved Ware sherds is similar between sites (Llanfaethlu: 993 $\mu g.g^{-1}$, Parc Cybi: 1091 $\mu g.g^{-1}$, Parc Bryn Cegin: 730 $\mu g.g^{-1}$, Penmynydd: 1443 $\mu g.g^{-1}$), there is a distinct difference between the Grooved Ware from Area D3 at Parc Cybi, where the pits are associated with a hearth (n=3; 3694 $mg.g^{-1}$), and the Grooved Ware from the pit cluster in Area J at Parc Cybi (n=8; 116 $\mu g.g^{-1}$), potentially indicating spatial differentiation or different phases of the site.

Overall, most vessels seem to have been used for cooking. This is not only suggested by the high lipid concentration but also by the presence of long-chain ketones in many samples throughout all phases (n=22; 20%), albeit lower in the Grooved Ware phase (n=6; 13%). These compounds tend to form at temperatures higher than 270°C, so their absence does not necessarily mean that vessels were used for purposes other than cooking, but could be caused by different cooking practices, such as avoiding placing the vessel directly into the fire.

At all sites, degraded animal fats were the most commonly detected lipids. The remaining vessels usually exhibited lipid profiles identified as post-depositional or modern contamination. It is possible that these vessels were used for storing or processing commodities with low lipid contents. Three extracts that yielded small amounts of plant-derived compounds, including *n*-alkanes and *n*-alkanols, were investigated for traces of plant waxes and *Triticum* sp. biomarkers (using solvent extraction). Only one sample, from Parc Bryn Cegin, contained wax esters.

Grooved Ware and pork

Owing to the high lipid recovery rate, the majority of extracts were submitted to compound-specific stable carbon isotope analysis. The analysed Grooved Ware vessels were shown to have been used for processing a variety of animal fats. Most samples plot within the dairy range and either in the ruminant-adipose fat range or along mixing lines (Fig. 7.3). The Grooved Ware from Llanfaethlu includes several samples that plot along the mixing lines, but *c.* 70% yield a predominantly dairy lipid signal; the same proportion was observed among the Mortlake sherds from this site. At Parc Bryn Cegin, four residues each plot in the dairy range and ruminant-carcass range, while one sample plots along the mixing lines. At Parc Cybi, all seven extracts yielded predominantly dairy fats, indicating specialised vessel use in the Grooved Ware phase at the site. This is also interesting in that the other assemblage likely to be of later Grooved Ware, Parc Bryn Cegin, shows indications that vessels were frequently used for processing the same kind of food. The clustering of extracts within the reference ellipses, and the trough between samples in the dairy range and in the ruminant-carcass fat range in their $\Delta^{13}C$-values (compare Craig *et al.* 2015), indicate that we are not dealing with the regular mixing of dairy and ruminant carcass products. This characteristic is not observed at the Mortlake and Fengate phases of these sites (Fig. 7.4) nor is it visible in the Grooved Ware data from the earlier site, Llanfaethlu.

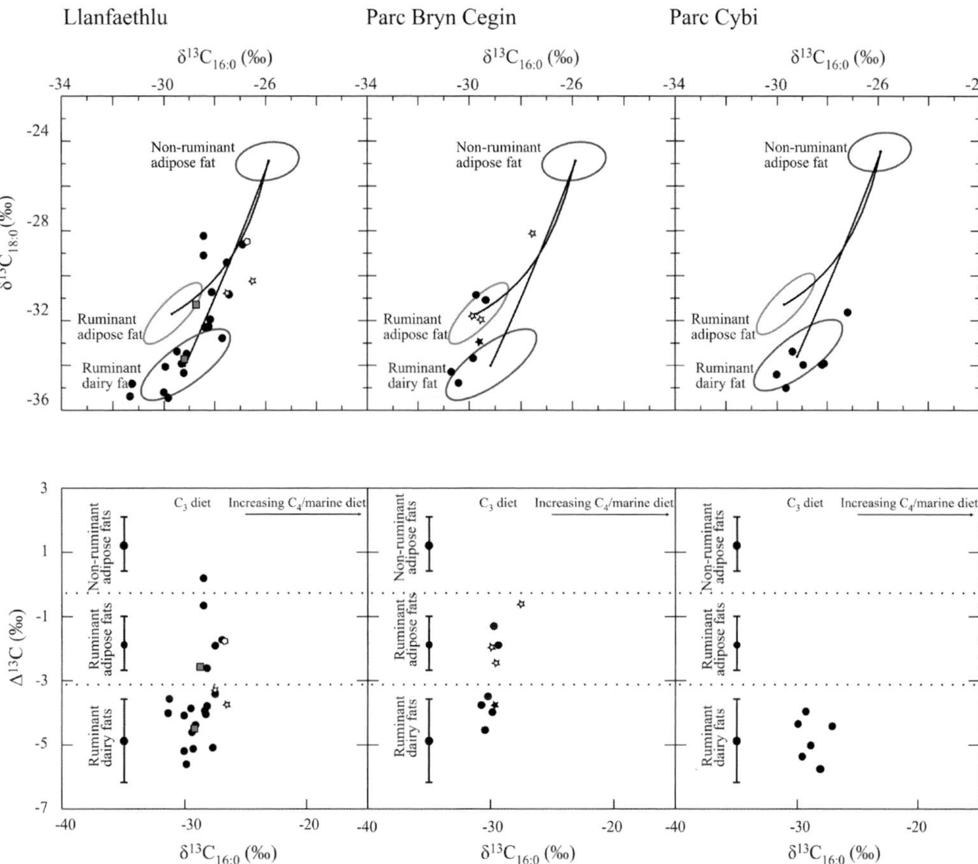

Figure 7.3. Scatter plot showing $\delta^{13}C$ values of individual fatty acids from Grooved Ware, plotted by site. As there are only three datapoints from Penmynydd, these are not plotted here. Circles represent absorbed lipid residues and squares are charred surface residues. Asterisks represent samples where possible aquatic biomarkers are present (filled icons for surface residues); the hexagon stands for the sample containing beeswax. The archaeological samples are plotted against modern reference fats from a global database. For detailed description of the parameters and references see Figure 7.1.

While each site yielded different patterns of vessel use, the overall trend when comparing Mortlake, Fengate and Grooved Ware is shown in Figure 7.4. There is no statistical correlation between pottery style and reliance on dairy produce. Only the assemblage from Parc Bryn Cegin shows a trend away from dairy fats. The $\Delta^{13}C$ values of the Grooved Ware sub-sample are statistically different from those of the combined Mortlake and Fengate samples (one-tailed homoscedastic t-tests with two samples, $p=0.011$), as well as from the Fengate subsample (one-tailed homoscedastic t-tests with two samples, $p=0.020$). However, there is no clear evidence for pig processing in this case; most extracts plotting outside the dairy range indicate the processing of ruminant adipose products. The only

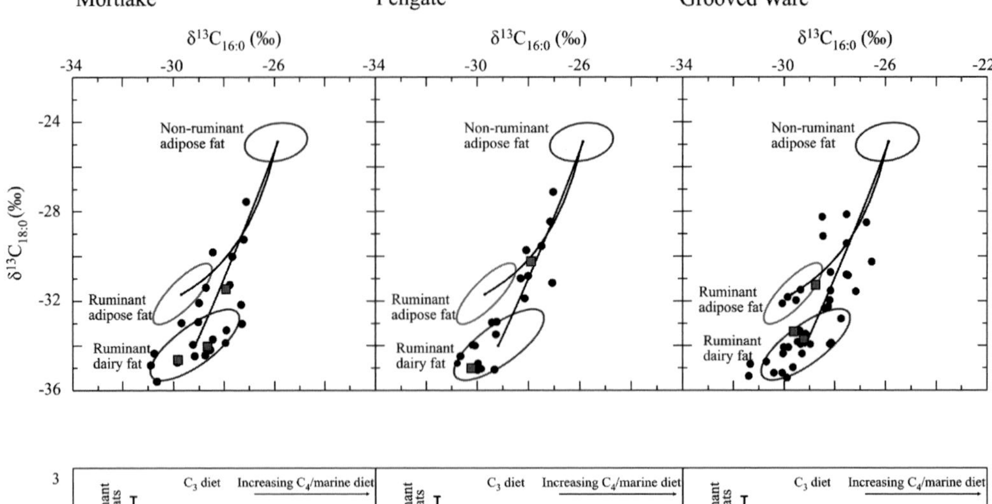

Figure 7.4. Scatter plot showing $\delta^{13}C$ values for palmitic and stearic acids from all sites combined and all pottery styles. Circles represent absorbed lipid residues and squares represent charred surface residues. The archaeological samples are plotted against modern reference fats from a global database. For detailed description of the parameters and references, see Figure 7.1.

extract plotting close to non-ruminant reference fats contained (albeit weak) indication of aquatic fat contribution (as discussed below) and could therefore be linked to marine rather than porcine fat consumption.

Marine resources

The strong shift away from a diet heavily reliant upon marine resources in the Mesolithic in Britain and Ireland towards a mainly terrestrial diet with only ephemeral traces of fish, seafood or marine mammal consumption in the Neolithic has been extensively discussed based on studies of bone collagen stable isotopes as well as lipid residues in pottery and faunal remains (Richards *et al.* 2003; Milner *et al.* 2004; Schulting 2013; Cramp *et al.* 2014).

While up to 20% of marine resource consumption could remain undetectable in dietary stable isotopes of bone collagen, lipid residue analysis indicates that marine oils are virtually absent in Neolithic pottery vessels. While few sites in Wales have been investigated previously, it could be assumed that the same is true for this region in the Neolithic, despite the sites' proximity to the coast.

Nevertheless, several extracts from the sites analysed here contained APAAs, which form from polyunsaturated fatty acids (PUFA) at high temperatures and, in contrast to PUFAs, can survive archaeological timespans. The Grooved Ware from Llanfaethlu and Parc Bryn Cegin yielded five samples (two and three, respectively) that contained at least C_{18}- and C_{20}-APAA homologues. However, as PUFAs are present not only in aquatic organisms but also in nuts and seed oils, only a distribution >C_{20} or a combination of C_{20} APAAs and other biomarkers, such as the chlorophyll-derived trimethyltetradecanoic acid (TMTD), can be strongly linked to aquatic resources (Evershed *et al.* 2008; Bondetti *et al.* 2021). This is the case for one extract only, the charred surface residue from LLA35/VI.C from Parc Bryn Cegin (Fig. 7.5). Even in this case, we argue that the marine contribution was small, as can be seen in the low peak height of APAAs >C_{18} compared to C_{18} in the first chromatogram. Stronger evidence for marine resource exploitation can be found in the pottery from

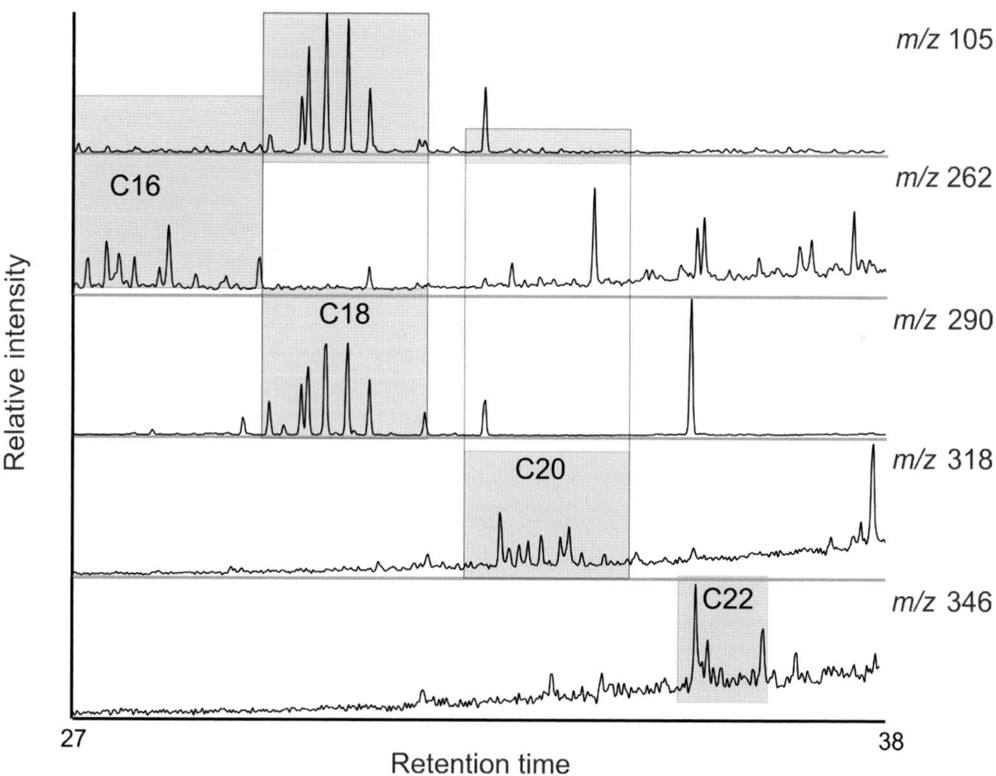

Figure 7.5. Partial selected ion monitoring chromatograms of lipid extracts containing APAAs, which indicate aquatic fats: Sample LLA35 (Parc Bryn Cegin, Pot VI.C) with C_{16}-C_{22} APAAs present.

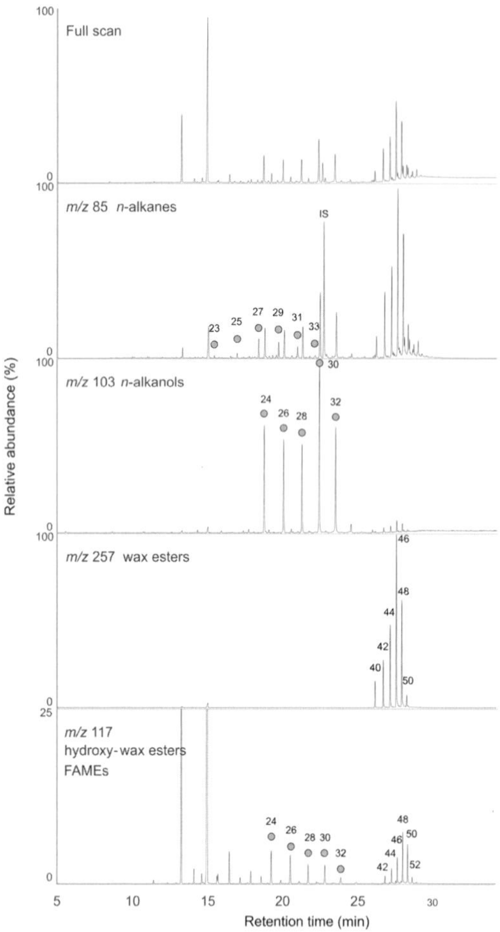

Figure 7.6. Partial GC/MS mass chromatogram of LFT086 (Llanfaethlu, Pot 192/7c) with the chemical fingerprint of beeswax. At the top is the total ion current, while the lower chromatograms are selected by diagnostic fragment ions. The characteristic compounds are labelled with their carbon chain length.

Clynnog. For the remaining Grooved Ware extracts with only a narrow APAA distribution and a very low abundance of the C_{20} homologues, it can only tentatively be assumed that this is linked with aquatic resource acquisition activities in Neolithic north Wales. The possibility remains that this is linked to nut oils, as hazelnut shells were commonly found on all studied sites and at other sites in Wales (Treasure *et al.* 2019). However, this would not explain the absence of these biomarkers from earlier phases and from many other Neolithic assemblages, and there is only rare evidence for the processing of hazelnuts in pottery (Saul *et al.* 2012). The low abundance of these biomarkers might suggest that marine products played a minor part in the community's diet, although such low abundances could be linked to marine species that do not contain high amounts of $>C_{20}$ PUFAs, such as limpets (Fernandes *et al.* 2019). Unfortunately, bone preservation at the sites is poor due to unfavourable soil properties. It is therefore difficult to compare lipid data with faunal remains.

Beeswax

The solvent extract of one Grooved Ware sherd (LFT86/197c; Fig. 7.6) yielded a characteristic chemical fingerprint of degraded beeswax. Beeswax consists of a mixture of lipid compounds, many of which are resistant to degradation. The sum of these compounds forms a diagnostic chemical fingerprint that can be used to identify ancient use of honey or beeswax (Regert *et al.* 2001). In the vessel from Llanfaethlu, the beeswax lipids seem to be mixed with degraded animal fat, indicated by the high abundance of stearic acid, usually absent from beeswax. The extract is plotted in Figure 7.3, but it should be noted that beeswax contributes to the isotopic composition of the palmitic acid. No further examples of beeswax were detected from the sites in north Wales. Beeswax residues can be the result of using honey as a sweetener or beeswax as sealant. While the isolated find in one vessel does not suggest a systematic use for waterproofing vessels, such a use cannot firmly be ruled out.

CONCLUSION

Studying lipid residues has shown that the introduction of Grooved Ware in Britain and Ireland coincided with an increase in processing animal carcass products in pots in several regions. The importance of porcine products is especially obvious in southern Britain, in contrast to Scotland where there is a tendency towards more ruminant carcass processing or food mixing. The lipid residues in pottery from Ireland suggest a more dairy-focused use of Grooved Ware. In Neolithic north Wales, there seems to be more variety in vessel use compared to Ireland, a trend that probably originated in the Middle Neolithic and is mirrored in the greater variety of vessel types, including Fengate Ware, which has no parallels in Ireland. The Grooved Ware from Parc Cybi is exceptional for north Wales in its specialised vessel use with a focus on dairy products. A trend away from dairy products is only statistically significant at one of the sites (Parc Bryn Cegin), but biomarkers suggest that the use of beeswax and, potentially, marine animal consumption only occurred during the currencies of Fengate Ware and Grooved Ware. The association between pork and Grooved Ware that is so characteristic in southern Britain is not visible in north Wales. Only 7% of extracts have $\Delta^{13}C>-1$, and while higher values indicate predominantly non-ruminant fat, the presence of potential marine lipids would also explain enriched $\delta^{13}C$ values. Human dietary isotope data from southern Wales (Schulting and Richards 2002) indicate a mainly terrestrial-based protein intake even at coastal sites, but a minor marine contribution could be evident in some cases. Archaeobotanical data from Neolithic Wales (Treasure *et al.* 2019) provide evidence for extensive cereal farming in the Early Neolithic followed by a decline in later phases, with a component of wild plant exploitation (hazelnuts) throughout the Neolithic. Together with the results from pottery and lipid analysis, this suggests a society that relied on a model of pastoralism and extensive agriculture but which included wild resources in its diet.

ACKNOWLEDGEMENTS

This research was undertaken as part of the *Passage Tomb People* project (PI: JS; Irish Research Council Consolidator Laureate Award IRCLA/2017/206). We thank the Natural Environment Research Council for partially funding the National Environmental Isotope Facility and for funding GC-MS and GC-IRMS capabilities (contract no. NE/V003917/1) together with the European Research Council (ERC) under the EU Seventh Framework Programme (FP/2007-2013) and ERC Grant Agreement number 340923 for GC-MS and the University of Bristol for GC-IRMS capabilities. We also wish to thank Frances Lynch, Jane Kenney and Cat Rees for their advice regarding the pottery assemblages and Emmanuelle Casanova for providing laboratory training.

REFERENCES

Albarella, U. and Serjeantson, D. 2002. A passion for pork: meat consumption at the British Late Neolithic site of Durrington Walls. In N. Milner and P. Miracle (eds), *Consuming passions and patterns of consumption*, 33–49. Cambridge: MacDonald Institute for Archaeological Research.

Ard, V. and Darvill, T. 2015. Revisiting old friends: the production, distribution and use of Peterborough Ware in Britain. *Oxford Journal of Archaeology* 34, 1–31.

Bondetti, M., Scott, E., Courel, B., Lucquin, A., Shoda, S., Lundy, J. *et al.* 2021. Investigating the formation and diagnostic value of ω-(o-alkylphenyl) alkanoic acids in ancient pottery. *Archaeometry* 63, 594–608.

Bonfield, K. 1997. *The analysis and interpretation of lipid residues associated with prehistoric pottery: pitfalls and potential.* Unpublished PhD thesis, Bradford University.

Colonese, A., Hendy, J., Lucquin, A., Speller, C., Collins, M., Carrer, F. *et al.* 2017. New criteria for the molecular identification of cereal grains associated with archaeological artefacts. *Scientific Reports* 7(1), 6633. https://doi.org/10.1038/s41598-017-06390-x.

Copley, M., Hansel, F., Sadr, K. and Evershed, R. 2004. Organic residue evidence for the processing of marine animal products in pottery vessels from the pre-colonial archaeological site of Kasteelberg D east, South Africa. *South African Journal of Science* 100, 279–83.

Copley, M., Berstan, R., Dudd, S., Aillaud, S., Mukherjee, A., Straker, V. *et al.* 2005. Processing of milk products in pottery vessels through British prehistory. *Antiquity* 79, 895–908.

Copley, M., Berstan, R., Dudd, S., Docherty, G., Mukherjee, A., Straker, V. *et al.* 2003. Direct chemical evidence for widespread dairying in prehistoric Britain. *Proceedings of the National Academy of Sciences of the United States of America* 100, 1524–9.

Copper, M., Hamilton, D. and Gibson, A. 2021. Tracing the lines: Scottish Grooved Ware trajectories beyond Orkney. *Proceedings of the Society of Antiquaries of Scotland* 150, 81–117.

Correa-Ascencio, M. and Evershed, R. 2014. High throughput screening of organic residues in archaeological potsherds using direct acidified methanol extraction. *Analytical Methods* 6, 1330–40.

Craig, O., Shillito, L.-M., Albarella, U., Viner-Daniels, S., Chan, B., Cleal, R. *et al.* 2015. Feeding Stonehenge: cuisine and consumption at the Late Neolithic site of Durrington Walls. *Antiquity* 89, 1096–1109.

Cramp, L. and Evershed, R. 2014. Reconstructing aquatic resource exploitation in human prehistory using lipid biomarkers and stable isotopes. In H. Holland and K. Turekian (eds), *Treatise on geochemistry* (2nd edition), 319–39. Amsterdam: Elsevier.

Cramp, L., Jones, J., Sheridan, J.A., Smyth, J., Whelton, H., Mulville, J. *et al.* 2014. Immediate replacement of fishing with dairying by the earliest farmers of the northeast Atlantic archipelagos. *Proceedings of the Royal Society B-Biological Sciences* 281, 20132372. https://doi.org/10.1098/rspb.2013.2372.

Dudd, S., Evershed, R. and Gibson, A. 1999. Evidence for varying patterns of exploitation of animal products in different prehistoric pottery traditions based on lipids preserved in surface and absorbed residues. *Journal of Archaeological Science* 26, 1473–82.

Dunne, J., Grillo, K.M., Casanova, E., Whelton, H. and Evershed, R. 2019. Pastoralist foodways recorded in organic residues from pottery vessels of modern communities in Samburu, Kenya. *Journal of Archaeological Method and Theory* 26, 619–42.

Dunne, J., Evershed, R., Salque, M., Cramp, L., Bruni, S., Ryan, K. *et al.* 2012. First dairying in green Saharan Africa in the fifth millennium BC. *Nature* 486, 390–4.

Evershed, R. 1993. Biomolecular archaeology and lipids. *World Archaeology* 25, 74–93.

Evershed, R. 2008. Organic residue analysis in archaeology: the archaeological biomarker revolution. *Archaeometry* 50, 895–924.

Evershed, R., Heron, C. and Goad, L. 1990. Analysis of organic residues of archaeological origin by high-temperature gas chromatography and gas chromatography-mass spectrometry. *Analyst* 115, 1339–42.

Evershed, R., Mottram, H., Dudd, S., Charters, S., Stott, A., Lawrence, G. *et al.* 1997. New criteria for the identification of animal fats preserved in archaeological pottery. *Naturwissenschaften* 84, 402–6.

Evershed, R., Copley, M., Dickson, L. and Hansel, F. 2008. Experimental evidence for the processing of marine animal products and other commodities containing polyunsaturated fatty acids in pottery vessels. *Archaeometry* 50, 101–13.

Fernandes, I., Fernandes, T. and Cordeiro, N. 2019. Nutritional value and fatty acid profile of two wild edible limpets from the Madeira Archipelago. *European Food Research and Technology* 245, 895–905.

Friedli, H., Lötscher, H., Oeschger, H., Siegenthaler, U. and Stauffer, B. 1986. Ice core record of the $^{13}C/^{12}C$ ratio of atmospheric CO_2 in the past two centuries. *Nature* 324, 237–8.

Gregg, M., Banning, E., Gibbs, K. and Slater, G. 2009. Subsistence practices and pottery use in Neolithic Jordan: molecular and isotopic evidence. *Journal of Archaeological Science* 36, 937–46.

Hammann, S. and Cramp, L. 2018. Towards the detection of dietary cereal processing through absorbed lipid biomarkers in archaeological pottery. *Journal of Archaeological Science* 93, 74–81.

Hammann, S., Bishop, R.R., Copper, M., Garrow, D., Greenwood, C., Hewson, L., Sheridan, J.A., Sturt, F., Whelton, H.L. and Cramp, L.J.E. 2022. Neolithic culinary traditions revealed by cereal, milk and meat lipids in pottery from Scottish crannogs. *Nature Communications* 13, 5045. https://doi.org/10.1038/s41467-022-32286-0

Harcourt, R., 1971. The animal bones. In G. Wainwright and I. Longworth, *Durrington Walls: excavations 1966–1968,* 338–50. London: Society of Antiquaries.

Jones, A., Cole, W. and Jones, R. 2005. Organic residue analysis of Grooved Ware from Barnhouse. In C. Richards (ed.), *Dwelling among the monuments: the Neolithic village of Barnhouse, Maeshowe passage grave and surrounding monuments at Stenness, Orkney*, 283–91. Cambridge: MacDonald Institute for Archaeological Research.

Kenney, J. 2008. Recent excavations at Parc Bryn Cegin, Llandygai, near Bangor, north Wales. *Archaeologia Cambrensis* 157, 9–142.

Kenney, J. 2021. *A Welsh landscape through time: excavations at Parc Cybi, Holy Island, Anglesey.* Oxford: Oxbow Books.

Lucquin, A., Gibbs, K., Uchiyama, J., Saul, H. Ajimoto, M., *et al.* 2016. Ancient lipids document continuity in the use of early hunter–gatherer pottery through 9,000 years of Japanese prehistory. *Proceedings of the National Academy of Sciences of the United States of America* 113, 3991–6.

McLaren, D., Dunne, J., Gillard, T., Evershed, R., Hamilton, D., Engl, R. *et al.* 2022. Expanding current understanding of the function, style and chronology of Grooved Ware from the A9 Dualling. *Proceedings of the Society of Antiquaries of Scotland* 151, 31–73.

Madgwick, R., Lamb, A., Sloane, H., Nederbragt, A., Albarella, U., Parker Pearson, M. and Evans, J. 2019. Multi-isotope analysis reveals that feasts in the Stonehenge environs and across Wessex drew people and animals from throughout Britain. *Science Advances* 5(3), eaau6078. Doi: 10.1126/sciadv.aau6078.

Milner, N., Craig, O., Bailey, G., Pedersen, K. and Andersen, S. 2004. Something fishy in the Neolithic? A re-evaluation of stable isotope analysis of Mesolithic and Neolithic coastal populations. *Antiquity* 78, 9–22.

Mottram, H., Dudd, S., Lawrence, G., Stott, A. and Evershed, R. 1999. New chromatographic, mass spectrometric and stable isotope approaches to the classification of degraded animal fats preserved in archaeological pottery. *Journal of Chromatography A* 833, 209–21.

Mukherjee, A., Berstan, R., Copley, M., Gibson, A. and Evershed, R. 2007. Compound-specific stable carbon isotopic detection of pig product processing in British Late Neolithic pottery. *Antiquity* 81, 743–54.

Mukherjee, A., Gibson, A. and Evershed, R. 2008. Trends in pig product processing at British Neolithic Grooved Ware sites traced through organic residues in potsherds. *Journal of Archaeological Science* 35, 2059–73.

Outram, A., Stear, N., Bendrey, R., Olsen, S., Kasparov, A. and Zaibert, V. *et al.* 2009. The earliest horse harnessing and milking. *Science* 323, 1332–5.

Pitter, S. 2013. *Molecular and stable isotopic analyses of the fatty acyl components of the pottery of Çatalhöyük, Turkey.* Unpublished PhD thesis, Stanford University.

Regert, M., Colinart, S., Degrand, L. and Decavallas, O. 2001. Chemical alteration and use of beeswax through time: accelerated ageing tests and analysis of archaeological samples from various environmental contexts. *Archaeometry* 43, 549–69.

Richards, C., Jones, A. M., MacSween, A., Sheridan, J. A., Dunbar, E., Reimer, P., Bayliss, A., Griffiths, S. and Whittle, A. 2016. Settlement duration and materiality: formal chronological models for the development of Barnhouse, a Grooved Ware settlement in Orkney. *Proceedings of the Prehistoric Society* 82, 193–225.

Richards, M., Schulting, R. and Hedges, R. 2003. Sharp shift in diet at onset of Neolithic. *Nature* 425, 366.

Roffet-Salque, M., Dunne, J., Altoft, D., Casanova, E., Cramp, L., Smyth, J. *et al.* 2017. From the inside out: upscaling organic residue analyses of archaeological ceramics. *Journal of Archaeological Science: Reports* 16, 627–40.

Salque, M., Bogucki, P., Pyzel, J., Sobkowiak-Tabaka, I., Grygiel, R., Szmyt, M. and Evershed, R. 2013. Earliest evidence for cheese making in the sixth millennium BC in northern Europe. *Nature* 493, 522–5.

Saul, H., Wilson, J., Heron, C., Glykou, A., Hartz, S. and Craig, O. 2012. A systematic approach to the recovery and identification of starches from carbonised deposits on ceramic vessels. *Journal of Archaeological Science* 39, 3483–92.

Schulting, R. 2013. On the northwestern fringes: Earlier Neolithic subsistence in Britain and Ireland as seen through faunal remains and stable isotopes. In S. Colledge, J. Conolly, K. Dobney, K. Manning and S. Shennan (eds), *The origins and spread of domestic animals in southwest Asia and Europe*, 313–38. Walnut Creek: Left Coast Press.

Schulting, R. and Richards, M. 2002. Finding the coastal Mesolithic in southwest Britain: AMS dates and stable isotope results on human remains from Caldey Island, South Wales. *Antiquity* 76, 1011–25.

Smyth, J. and Evershed, R. 2015. The molecules of meals: new insight into Neolithic foodways. *Proceedings of the Royal Irish Academy, Section C: Archaeology, Celtic Studies, History, Linguistics and Literature* 115, 27–46.

Spangenberg, J., Jacomet, S. and Schibler, J. 2006. Chemical analyses of organic residues in archaeological pottery from Arbon Bleiche 3, Switzerland–evidence for dairying in the late Neolithic. *Journal of Archaeological Science* 33, 1–13.

Treasure, E., Gröcke, D., Caseldine, A. and Church, M. 2019. Neolithic farming and wild plant exploitation in western Britain: archaeobotanical and crop stable isotope evidence from Wales (*c.* 4000–2200 cal BC). *Proceedings of the Prehistoric Society* 85, 193–222.

Whelton, H., Hammann, S., Cramp, L., Dunne, J., Roffet-Salque, M. and Evershed, R. 2021. A call for caution in the analysis of lipids and other small biomolecules from archaeological contexts. *Journal of Archaeological Science* 132, 105397. https://doi.org/10.1016/j.jas.2021.105397.

Chapter 8

Grooved Ware in Ireland

Eoin Grogan and Helen Roche

EARLIER IDENTIFICATIONS AND RESEARCH

Since the publication of *Grooved Ware in Britain and Ireland* (Cleal and MacSween 1999), the number of findspots of Grooved Ware in Ireland has more than quadrupled, thanks to developer-funded archaeology. This chapter presents the current state of knowledge, in the light of this greatly expanded evidence base. In addition, the discoveries of the Grooved Ware- and timber circle-associated complexes at Ballynahatty, Co. Down, and Knowth, Co. Meath, in the 1990s sparked reinvigorated interest and study that resulted in significant reviews, including assessment of several older assemblages (Roche 1995; Brindley 1999a; Eogan and Roche 1997; 1999; Sheridan 2004). In 1999 Brindley was able to identify 13 Irish sites with Grooved Ware. The discovery of many new sites greatly expanded the known distribution of Grooved Ware, especially in the west (Lowpark and Cloonbaul/Kilbride), mid-west (Whitewell) and south-west (Ballynacarriga) of the island. Nevertheless, these discoveries also tended to confirm pre-existing clusters, especially in the wider landscape of the Boyne Valley in North Leinster (Fig. 8.1). Currently at least 58 sites have been identified.

During the past 25 years there has also been a dramatic increase in the number of Grooved Ware-associated radiocarbon dates. These have confirmed the general Late Neolithic (*c.* 2900–2400 cal BC) timeframe for the use of this pottery. Dates from the burial with an elaborate vessel (Fig. 8.2, A) in Tomb 6 at Knowth (see below) of *c.* 3090–2910 cal BC (Schulting *et al.* 2017) suggest a slightly earlier beginning. A more clear-cut overlap with the use of passage tombs is also affirmed by the dating of deposits, including human skulls, in the Mound of the Hostages at Tara, Co. Meath, to *c.* 2895–2835 cal BC (Cooney *et al.* 2011, 640). While precise dating is not always available, it appears that elaborately decorated Grooved Ware belongs to the earlier part of the period but was quickly replaced by pottery with simple grooved ornament around the rim and, especially, by entirely plain vessels. The end of this period is more clearly demarcated to *c.* 2400 BC and there is currently no evidence for any overlap in the use of Grooved Ware and Beaker pottery (Carlin 2017, fig. 15).

Several reviews of individual assemblages and their contexts form an important backdrop to the present discussion (Grogan and Roche 2010a; Roche unpublished client report for National Monuments Service; Carlin 2016; 2017; Cleary 2017). More recently, there has been

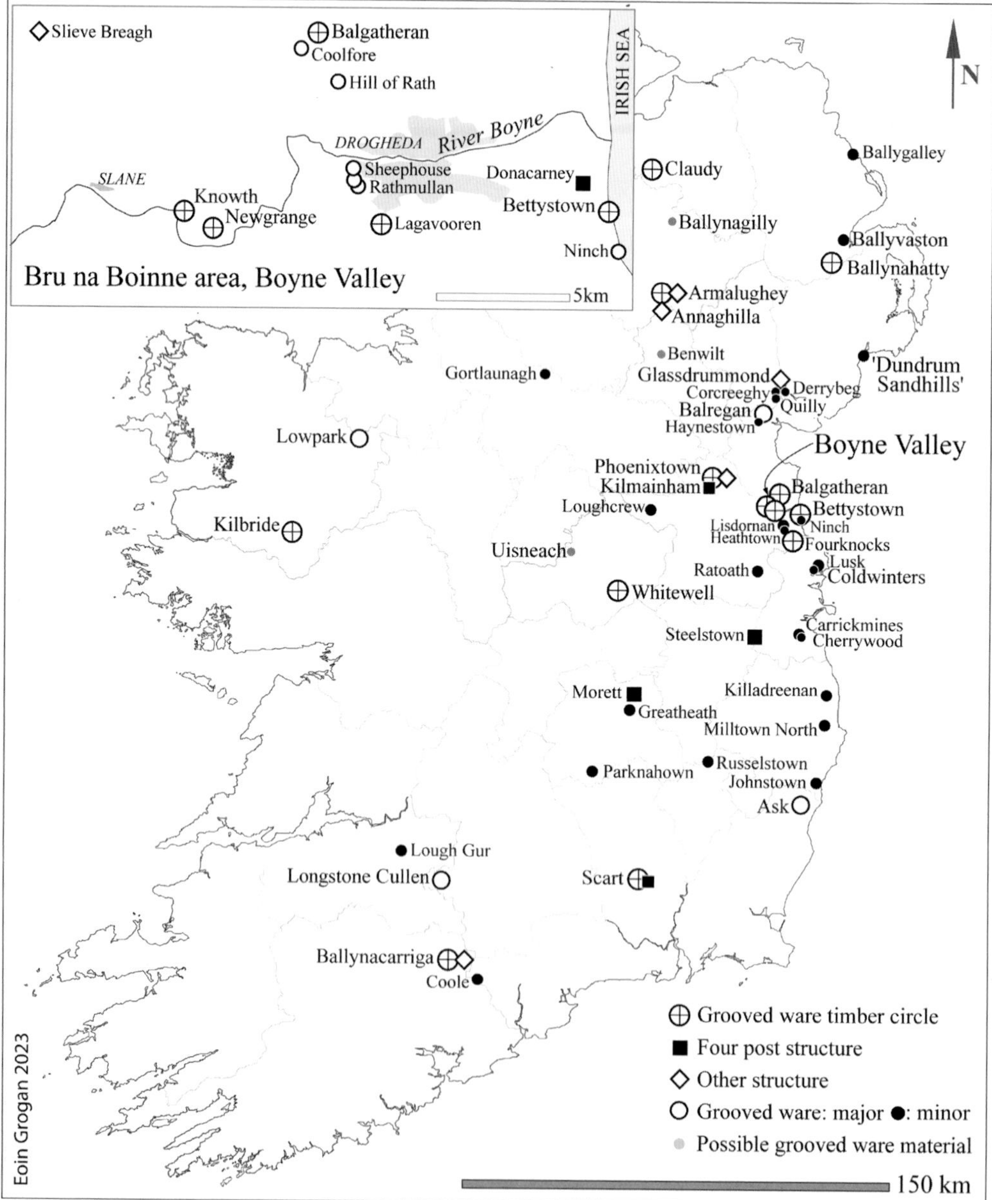

Figure 8.1. Distribution of Grooved Ware and related sites in Ireland.

extensive reconsideration of Irish Grooved Ware contexts; much of this has focused on relationships with Britain and especially Orkney (Carlin 2017; Carlin and Cooney 2017; 2020).

Recent reviews of older discoveries have served to remove some finds from the Grooved Ware corpus. The material from 'Concentrations A and C' at Knowth (Eogan and Roche 1997, 196–211, figs 44–5) has been found to be of Middle Bronze Age date, while the sherd from Burial 4 at Kiltierney Deerpark, Co. Fermanagh, which has lurked on the edge of the publication record for some years, has been shown to be of Early Bronze Age date (Foley and Warner 2022). Ó Ríordáin, in his 1951 publication of the Grange Stone Circle, Lough Gur, Co. Limerick, made the first reference to 'Grooved ware' (his quotation marks) in Ireland. Some of this material clearly represents other traditions, such as domestic Beaker of 'Rockbarton type' (Ó Ríordáin 1951, 62–3, fig. 8, 1–6) or Middle Bronze Age domestic pottery (Ó Ríordáin 1951, fig. 8, 21–2, 24, 27). Nevertheless, he correctly referenced a very small quantity of Grooved Ware from under the surrounding bank (Ó Ríordáin 1951, fig. 9:17; Roche 2004). Very small quantities also came from Geroid Island, Co. Limerick (Liversage 1958; Brindley 1999a; Roche 1995). However, despite frequent suggestions, there is no Grooved Ware at any of the sites on the Knockadoon peninsula at Lough Gur.

IRISH GROOVED WARE: OVERVIEW OF ITS MAIN CHARACTERISTICS

The essential form and production techniques have been described in several of the papers referenced above so a simple outline suffices here.

Shape and size

The pots are bucket- to slightly barrel-shaped in profile with flat bases. Rims are generally simple, flat or slightly round-topped but there are also rounded, slightly in-turned and occasionally bevelled examples. Bases are universally flat, but a domed form with a slightly concave underside also occurs. Wall-base junctions are generally simple, even sharply defined, but there are some slightly footed forms. The vessel can be almost straight-sided, but gently curved or even more barrel-shaped profiles are the most common part of the repertoire (Fig. 8.2).

Most vessels can be described as medium-sized, generally 220–280 mm in rim diameter and height and 140–160 mm wide at the base. However, there are some substantially larger pots such as that with a rim diameter of *c.* 320 mm identified at Fourknocks, Co. Meath (Brindley 1999b, 190). Smaller pots, in the 150–200 mm range, are also common, in the Knowth assemblages for example. Small tubs (where the height ($\leq$ 150 mm) is generally greater than the rim diameter) have been identified at a number of sites in the Brú na Bóinne area and may represent a particular function, such as food or beverage consumption.

Fabric and finish, colour and fineness

Where identifiable, the Irish vessels are universally of locally sourced clays with a body thickness range of 5–9 mm. They contain modest quantities of stone inclusions, usually

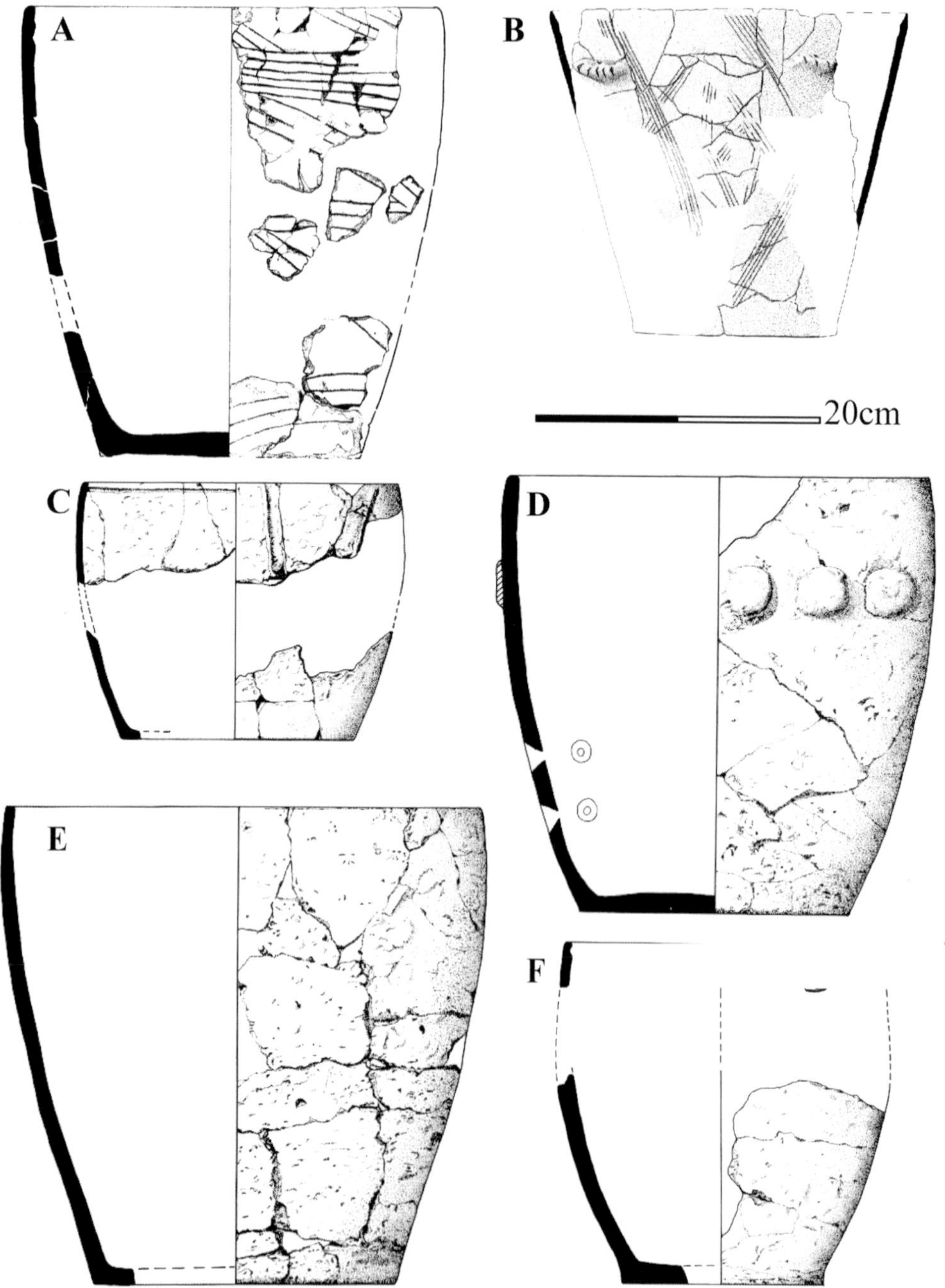

Figure 8.2. Reconstruction drawings of Irish Grooved Ware. A: Tomb 6, Knowth, Co. Meath (Eogan and Roche 1997, fig. 47); B: Coole, Co. Cork (Cleary 2015, fig. 3.4); Lowpark, Co. Mayo, Vessels C: 1 (600), D: 1 (628), E: 8 (600) F: 1 (660), (Cleary 2017, figs 7, 8 5, 2).

less than 3 mm in size, but larger pieces up to 7 mm also occur. Volcanic material was generally preferred, with diorite and dolerite being the most common, while quartzite is also frequently present; this suggests a perceived 'proper' recipe even in areas where these materials were not readily accessible. The vessels are coil-built, with compact to hard fabric, well and evenly made, with N- or U-shaped coil joints. Frequently, the base is made of a separate disc with its edge pulled up to connect with the lowermost coil of the body. In a very few examples the lower pot wall was folded around the basal disc, such as at Gortlaunaght, Co. Cavan (Chapple 2010). Various finishes have been observed including scraping the surfaces to produce thinner walls or, more frequently, smoothing the surfaces with the hand or fingers. Residual tooling marks and striations are occasionally preserved. Further finishes, such as applied slip or burnishing, have not been identified. The wide colour range of prehistoric pottery also occurs but with a significant concentration of darker, brown to grey-brown or dark grey; however, buff to red-buff and even red are also recorded. The cores generally remain grey to dark grey suggesting rapid firing, but slower, more controlled efforts with full oxidisation have been noted occasionally.

Despite the generally accomplished production, there are two broad categories of ceramic quality. The most common consists of fine, thin-walled, evenly finished and well fired vessels (Roche 1995; Eogan and Roche 1999, 98–103, 'Knowth Style I'; Brindley 1999a, 'sub-style Dundrum-Longstone/Knowth types'). These dominate many assemblages – Ballynahatty (Hartwell 1998; 2002; Hartwell *et al.* 2023), Ballynacarriga 3, Co. Cork (Roche and Grogan 2010a; Lehane *et al.* 2019), Longstone Cullen, Co. Tipperary (Roche 1995; unpublished client report for National Monuments Service), Dundrum Sandhills, Co. Down (Collins 1952; 1959), Slieve Breagh, Co. Meath (de Paor and Ó h-Eochaidhe 1956; Carlin 2017, 163), Scart, Co. Kilkenny (Laidlaw 2009; 2010; Monteith 2011) and most of the Knowth pottery – and these sites produced some impressive, elegant, vessels.

There is also a thicker, coarser variant that has been referred to as Knowth Style II (Roche 1995; Brindley 1999a, 30: 'Donegore-Duntryleague group'); this occurs both separately and in assemblages with the finer material. At Lagavooren 7, Co. Meath, for example, five of the 18 vessels are of much coarser ware with thicker walls, especially in the lower body, and heavy thick bases – probably intended to provide stability (Grogan and Roche 2012). The 110 mm diameter base of vessel 17 was 19.2 mm thick and the pot walls were 11.6 mm thick. This type came from possible timber circles at Fourknocks (King 1999) and Bettystown (Eogan 1999), Co. Meath, and Cloonbaul/Kilbride, Co. Mayo (Cotter 2008), while a coarse fabric, although finer than the Lagavooren material, was also found, in limited quantities, from the Knowth timber circle (Eogan and Roche 1997, 155–61, fig. 31). Some of these pots can be deceptive, with coarse bases and lower bodies blending into handsome, finer, upper fabric as at Glassdrummond 7, Co. Armagh (Grogan and Roche unpublished client report for ADS Ltd), and Scart (Roche and Grogan 2010b; Grogan and Roche 2011a). Brindley (1999b, 190–1) noted more careful finish on rims and upper bodies at Fourknocks, where a 16 mm-thick base sherd (H) had an attached lower body only 8 mm thick.

Use

Areas of sooting occur frequently and, while this is occasionally derived from firing, most examples represent use. Burnt accretions on the inner surface, usually in the lower part of the pots, indicate more definite evidence for cooking. These residues are common, including on material from postholes in timber circles and four-poster structures. Some of the material, as at Lowpark, Co. Mayo (Gillespie 2017), is clearly derived from domestic contexts, possibly from middens, but at Knowth, for example, some vessels at least appear to have been broken immediately prior to deposition. These were used in associated ritual or celebratory feasting, as was much of the very large assemblage from Longstone Cullen (Roche unpublished client report for National Monuments Service).

Decoration

While simple decoration is a widespread feature of Irish Grooved Ware (Fig. 8.2), the tradition is dominated by entirely plain pots (Fig. 8.2, E). These, both very fine and more often coarser examples, occur in most assemblages. The most common ornament consists of typical 'grooves', usually comparatively deep and sharp-edged, that occur on the outer, but more frequently on the inner, surface of the rim. The similarity of the grooves suggests the widespread adoption of a specific tool type, although no examples of such a tool have yet been found. However, less well-defined simple scores, including examples of thumbnail impressed lines, also occur as at Glassdrummond and Rathmullan 7, Co. Meath. Amongst these vessels, the majority have a single groove on the internal surface. Two, or very occasionally three, lines are also recorded. However, the early vessel from Tomb 6 at Knowth (see above) has an elaborate, all-over, arrangement of grooved lines forming loosely arranged bands of horizontal lines alternating with groups of diagonal lines (Fig. 8.2, A).

One, or sometimes two, lines of impressed twisted cord are present on the inside of rims at several sites including Ask, Co. Wexford (Grogan and Roche 2011b); Glassdrummond 7 (Grogan and Roche unpublished client report for ADS Ltd); Knowth and Rathmullan 7 (Eogan and Roche 1997, 150–1, nos 2–3, figs 28–9; Grogan and Roche 2011c); and Lowpark vessel 4/5 (Cleary 2017, 284, fig. 3). Twisted cord is sometimes combined with other decorative features, such as fine, raised flanking cordons on Lowpark vessel 7 (C660, Cleary 2017, 286, fig. 4).

Applied ('plastic') ornament is a very rare occurrence in Ireland, although a coarse vessel from Newgrange, Co. Meath has a heavy applied cordon at about midpoint on the body (Cleary 1983, 102: group 66g, fig. 49). There are narrow fillets or cordons on pots from, for example, Scart (no. 16) and Lowpark (no. 1, C600). A small bowl from Lowpark, with an internal line of twisted cord, also has long, converging, applied cordons (Fig 8.2, C; Cleary 2017, no. 1 (C600), 289–90).

Other applied elements, such as pellets, lugs or bosses, are also rare but occur on pots from Longstone Cullen, Newgrange, Coole, Co. Cork – where an irregular lattice pattern formed by groups of twisted cord is combined with applied lunate lugs or handles – and Lowpark, (Fig. 8.2, B, D) (Cleary 1983, 91: group 35a. fig. 37; no. 1 (C629); 2015; 2017, 293; Roche 1995; unpublished client report for National Monuments Service). Vessel 1, from the timber circle at Knowth, combined groups of grooves (three) on the outer and two on the inner side of the rim with an applied external pellet (Eogan and Roche 1997, 150, no. 1, fig. 28).

At Knowth, in addition to the previously mentioned decorated vessel from Tomb 6, lines of twisted cord, a pair on the rim interior and a single circumferential example on the inner face of the base, occurred on a pot from the timber circle; another pot from the same context had internal rim grooves and twisted cord lines around the external edge of the base (Eogan and Roche 1997, 150–2, nos 2, 8, fig. 28). Decoration on the underside of bases is an occasional feature of the Irish material, such as at Longstone Cullen (circumferential and radial lines); Greatheath, Co. Laois (Roche 1995); and Gortlaunaght, Co. Cavan (Chapple 2010).

Not a decorative feature, but nevertheless of note, are the perforations, drilled either before firing (as with those in the upper body of vessel 24, Glassdrummond 7, possibly to aid ventilation in this large storage vessel: Grogan and Roche unpublished client report for ADS Ltd) or after firing, on the lower body of Lowpark Vessels 1 (C629, Fig. 8.2, D) and 7 (C660; Cleary 2017, 293, fig. 4, 285–6) where they were interpreted as repair features.

CONTEXTS AND ASSOCIATIONS

Timber circles

Small circles of free-standing posts represent the most common site type associated with Irish Grooved Ware. Examples include Ballynahatty (Hartwell *et al.* 2023); Bettystown (Eogan 1999); Knowth (Eogan and Roche 1997); Lagavooren 7 (Grogan and Roche 2012) and Newgrange (Brindley 1999a, 33, fig. 3.6); Cloonbaul/Kilbride, Co. Mayo (Cotter 2008, 26); Whitewell, Co. Westmeath (Phelan 2007); and Scart (Monteith 2011, 111–14). Typically, these are 8–11 m in diameter and have a well-defined, monumental, even porch-like, entrance and internal square setting formed by four large posts. The entrances generally face south-eastwards. More unusual examples include four-post arrangements at Kilmainham, Co. Meath, Sites 1c (Structure 6) and 3 (no. 2) that appear to be enclosed by double post circles (Walsh 2021, 81–93, illus. 5.2, 5.4). Other sites with enclosing features include Ballynahatty, Claudy (Clagan townland), Co. Derry (Nicol 2016a); and Armalughey (Ballygawley), Co. Tyrone (Dunlop 2016, 33–47). For Armalughey, Carlin (2016) has discussed the sequence of elaboration of the monument and this will be an important area for research on other complex structures.

Four-post structures

The square arrangement of four posts, a prominent feature of most timber circles, also occurs as separate, free-standing monuments. As at Scart and Morett, Co. Laois (Cotter 2003), these consist of simple squares, measuring 3–3.5 m and 2.5 × 2.5 m respectively. Three very similar structures occurred at Scart where, unusually, foundation trenches on two opposing sides of nos 2 and 3 (Monteith 2011, figs 13–14) suggest plank walls or shuttering possibly mimicking the porches in the timber circles. Other more rectangular four-post arrangements, as at Donacarney Great, Co. Meath (5 × 4 m; Giacometti 2010, 3), and Kilmainham 1C (Walsh 2011), have post-defined access – at the former, a porch-like arrangement – on the south-east sides. At Balgatheran, Co. Louth, and Steelstown, Co. Kildare, the postholes of four-post structures contained structured deposits of pottery (Ó Drisceoil 2003; Grogan and Roche 2010b).

Ritual or domestic

There are a few sites where the activity appears to be domestic. The most frequently referenced is that at Slieve Breagh (de Paor and Ó h-Eochaidhe 1956; Brindley 2008), where three circular houses with central rectangular hearth settings have basic plans similar to the timber circles. Less well-defined structures, but several with comparable hearths, at Newgrange (Cooney and Grogan 1999, 80; Carlin 2017, 169), are less easily dated as the mixed, apparently associated ceramic assemblage included Middle Neolithic Impressed Ware as well as Beaker ('Beaker layers', O'Kelly *et al.* 1983, 27–9, fig. 9).

Two houses at Armalughey, and two further oval structures at Annaghilla (Site 4), Co. Tyrone, were dated to the Late Neolithic although none produced pottery (Dunlop and Barclay 2016, 26–9). A poorly defined structure at Phoenixtown 5, Co. Meath, produced sherds from three Grooved Ware vessels (Walsh 2021, 80, illus. 5.1). Very similar, narrow oblong structures at Kilmainham 3 (no. 3, with sherds from a flanking pit) and Glassdrummond (nos 1–2, sherds from a posthole in the former, Grogan and Roche unpublished client report for ADS Ltd), measuring *c.* 5 × 3 m, have pronounced porch-like entrances (Dunlop 2016, 41–2; Walsh 2021, 88).

Other apparently domestic sites are represented at Dundrum Sandhills Site 1, Co. Down (Collins 1952, 10–12, fig. 6: 27–31; 1959, 5–7, fig. 2:1); Corcreeghy and Glassdrummond 7, Co. Armagh (Dunlop 2016, 41–3, fig. p. 42); Ballyvaston, Co. Antrim (Nicol 2016b); The Heath (Greatheath), Co. Laois (Keeley 1994); Parknahown, Co. Laois (Grogan and Roche 2009); and Heathtown, Co. Meath (Campbell 2008).

The difficulties in differentiating ritual from purely domestic activities are well represented by the changing interpretation of some complexes. At Balgatheran, Co. Louth, the original interpretation of the structure as a timber circle was revised to suggest a domestic function (Ó Drisceoil 2009). Conversely, at Ballynacarriga – with one of Ireland's largest Grooved Ware assemblages (Roche and Grogan 2010a) – the initial suggestion that the site served a purely domestic function (Lehane and Leigh 2010) has been revisited and altered in favour of a mainly ritual function, including three timber circles (Lehane *et al.* 2019, Structures 1, 3 and 7, illus. 2.8.2). The site produced evidence for several other structures and buildings apparently located within a rectangular ditched enclosure.

Debris and deposition

Whether sites or individual features are identified as domestic or ritual in function – or indeed both – it is clear that the users of Grooved Ware engaged in the careful disposal of broken ceramics. This is most evident in relation to the formal contexts such as the timber circles and four-posters where the pottery, along with flint artefacts and occasionally stone axeheads (both often deliberately broken), was placed into the post pits as part of the construction phase. However, the wear and use history of this pottery vary. At Knowth, for example, the pots appear in many cases to have been deliberately broken immediately prior to deposition although much of the assemblage had been used for cooking. This was possibly associated with on-site feasting that formed part of the ceremonial construction of the monument. Some contrast is presented at Lowpark, where the similarly careful deposition in the post pits was of much-worn material possibly derived from domestic middens. At this site, a large pit 10 m to the north of the circle was filled with pottery (over 1700 sherds plus 4618 smaller fragments and crumbs, total weight: 8.63 kg) from at least nine vessels (Cleary 2017, C660, 282–8, pl. 5). Despite the fragmentary nature of much of the material, the identifiable pots consisted of large, refitting sherds suggesting that some breakage, at least, occurred soon before deposition.

Similar contexts were identified at Scart North (Laidlaw 2009; 2010, 39–41, fig. 3, pit A), where a single pit produced around 1000 sherds from at least seven vessels (nos 4–10; Roche and Grogan 2010b). Within a complex depositional arrangement, the pottery from separate vessels appears to have been placed sequentially, and in some cases in discrete locations. The condition of the pottery suggests deliberate breakage but at some time before deposition and may have been recovered from domestic contexts. A second pit (Laidlaw 2010, 41–3, pit B) produced 242 sherds representing seven appreciably finer pots.

At least seven pots, one of them (no. 1) almost complete, came from a single pit at Rathmullan 7 (Bolger 2011; Grogan and Roche 2011c). The context of the material, the presence of 200 lithics including four convex end scrapers (Sternke 2010), and the occurrence of cremated bone indicate a votive deposit, albeit at least partly made up of material previously used in a domestic context. A stone-lined pit at Armalughey, sealed by a capstone, contained an intact pottery vessel (Dunlop and Barclay 2016, 28), while the base of a pot, damaged but originally a carefully deposited upright vessel set in a natural hollow, came from Kilmainham 1c (no. 56, Grogan and Roche 2011d, cclxvi; Walsh 2021, 81, illus. 5.3).

Burial

Very limited evidence for burials of this period has been identified. However, a pit at Quilly, Co. Armagh – partly encircled by four postholes – produced two deposits of cremated remains, one an infant associated with sherds from three pots (Dunlop 2016, 44). There was no pottery with the cremated remains (two adults, one a female) behind orthostat 5 in Tomb 1C West at Knowth dated to this period (Eogan and Cleary 2017, 247–9). Also at Knowth, Tomb 6, the cremated remains of an adult and a sub-adult, with an unburnt adult bone, may have been associated with the early, elaborately decorated pot discussed above (Eogan and Cleary 2017, 353; Eogan and Roche 1997, 211). Tomb 18 also produced a pot possibly with an unburnt human skull fragment (Eogan and Cleary 2017, 42; Eogan and Roche 1997, 211–13). At the complex site of Armalughey, a pit contained the cremated remains of an adult, mixed with animal bone, that appears to have been buried within an inverted Grooved Ware vessel; this is associated with a date of 2854–2571 cal BC (UBA-14523) (Dunlop and Barclay 2016, 35).

Complexes

A few complex and extensive sites have been excavated. That at Ballynacarriga has already been mentioned, as have the Armalughey, Kilmainham/Phoenixtown and Ballynahatty Late Neolithic landscapes, all published recently (Dunlop 2016; Lehane *et al.* 2019; Walsh 2021; Hartwell *et al.* 2023). These have been interpreted as predominantly, if not exclusively, ceremonial centres and, given the extensive areas investigated (Kilmainham 1c alone covered *c.* 21,330 m²), these appear to be plausible suggestions. Another large site at Scart contained what the (separate) directors assessed as ritual (Scart: Monteith 2011) or domestic features (Scart North: Laidlaw 2010), although the substantial deposits of pottery in two pits at the latter site (see above) argue against that conclusion. Overall, it appears, separate spaces were maintained for mundane and sacred activities, although structured deposits at ritual sites indicate conscious melding of both.

CONCLUSIONS

It is clear that while closely influenced by developments, especially in the Orkney Islands, Irish Grooved Ware quickly developed along more insular lines, including both plain pots and those with simple grooved ornament on the rims. Similarly, the wider British monumental repertoire, including stone circles and, to a perhaps lesser extent, large earthen enclosures, gained limited traction in Ireland. Following observations by Eogan and Roche (1999, 106), Carlin (2016, 204) has aptly noted, 'many of the more recently excavated timber circles in Ireland suggest that a shared architectural vocabulary was in existence in the Late Neolithic with various interchangeable components that could be arranged and re-arranged and there may even have been a prescribed sequence to the addition of these different elements'.

A number of basic points emerge from this brief review. It is clear that grooved or less well-defined scored lines, mainly on the inner but often on the outer rim surface, are the dominant decorative treatment on Irish vessels. A single line is most common but two or even three lines are also represented. While very similar treatment is occasionally recorded in Britain (Wainwright and Longworth 1971), a marked preference for plainer, or entirely plain, pots appears to have emerged early in the Irish sequence and represents an insular tradition present in almost every assemblage. The more complex design of grooves on the pot from a cremation burial in Tomb 6, Knowth, is comparable to examples from the Balfarg timber circle, Barnhouse and the Quanterness passage tomb (Eogan and Roche 1997, 211, fig. 47; Copper *et al.* 2021, 88–90, illus. 5: 2–3; Copper, this volume). Interestingly, Carlin (2017, 163) has drawn parallels between this vessel, and examples from Coole, and passage tomb art. The Knowth vessel is one of the earliest dated Irish examples (*c.* 3000–2900 cal BC; Schulting *et al.* 2017, 353). Indeed, the similarity of the pottery and the closely comparable dating for the Knowth pot and the Balfarg timber circle further underline the close connections between Scotland and Ireland at this early stage.

Applied ('plastic') ornament, in the form of cordons and bosses, is a very significant, indeed even dominant, feature of Grooved Ware in Britain (Wainwright and Longworth 1971; Copper *et al.* 2021). As noted, it is a rare element in Ireland. The occasional presence of pellets, bosses, lugs and applied cordons certainly indicates British influence but, with rare exceptions, such as the Coole pots, it appears that the Irish tradition developed largely along its own, insular trajectory. While MacSween (1995, 43) noted that on the Scottish material the decoration follows general patterns but is not closely similar on any two vessels, the Irish pottery is reasonably homogeneous and, where decorated, has simple grooved lines largely confined to the rim.

Given the scarcity of more complex designs, and early dates for many of them, it is probable that highly decorated Grooved Ware stands at the beginning of the Irish sequence and this is probably underscored by the rapid emergence and dominance of simpler and entirely plain forms. As Carlin and Cooney noted (2020, 331, their italics) '*we should expect things to emerge differently in different regions*'.

One emerging pattern, although not absolutely clear-cut, is the limited occurrence of pottery in apparently domestic contexts; this contrasts with the more frequent, and structured, deposits in, for example, timber circles. If the evidence from the Scart and Lowpark pits is indicative, it may be that domestic debris was deposited in designated locations; on occasion, material, including pottery and lithics, was subsequently collected and finally, and perhaps reverently, disposed of within sacred settings. This fits in with what appears to be the very definitely structured deposits of pottery, lithics and occasionally other artefacts, that had previously seen mundane use in cooking and food preparation, in postholes in timber circles or four-posters. In some cases, as at Knowth and Ballynahatty, this may have been associated with dedicatory feasting but in others, such as at Lowpark, it derived from curated material in domestic middens.

Many questions remain about Irish Grooved Ware, not least whether its use was contemporary or associated with the use of a particular monument type, the embanked enclosure ('henge') – a very specifically ritual or ceremonial arena. Limited excavation has not clearly demonstrated that these monuments date to the Late Neolithic in Ireland; so far, only one example, at Balregan, Co. Louth (Ó Donnchadha and Grogan 2010), can unequivocally be ascribed to this period, and no Grooved Ware has yet been found in any other Irish henge. Nevertheless, contemporaneity with the currency of Grooved Ware remains a possibility. It also remains to be seen, through excavation, whether Grooved Ware was used in any of the sites in the remarkable complex of previously known and new large circular timber and/or earthen monuments on the Boyne floodplain below Newgrange (Condit and Keegan 2018; Carlin and Cooney 2020, fig. 26.8). Of these sites, only one – the extraordinary rectangular post structure or avenue at Newgrange Farm – is dated, to the Late Neolithic (Leigh *et al.* 2018). This area undoubtedly has the potential to enrich our understanding of the Grooved Ware ceramic tradition.

REFERENCES

(Key to abbreviations: NRA – National Roads Authority; TII – Transport Infrastructure Ireland)

Bolger, T. 2011. *Archaeological excavation report, 01E0295 Rathmullan 7, Co. Meath.* M1 Northern Motorway. Bray: Irish Archaeological Consultancy Ltd, unpublished client report for Meath County Council and the NRA. https://doi.org/10.7486/DRI.dv14c7977.

Brindley, A.L. 1999a. Irish Grooved Ware. In R. Cleal and A. MacSween (eds) 1999, 23–35.

Brindley, A.L. 1999b. Appendix II. The pottery. In H.A. King 1999, 190–2.

Campbell, K. 2008. 2005:1181 – Heathtown, Meath, pit with Grooved Ware. In I. Bennett (ed.), *Excavations 2005*, 292. Wordwell: Bray.

Carlin, N. 2016. Discussion of the timber circle at Armalughey (Sites 18 and 20). In C. Dunlop and J. Barkley, *Road to the west. A road to the past, Volume 2*, 194–210. Belfast: Northern Archaeological Consultancy Ltd.

Carlin, N. 2017. Getting into the groove: exploring the relationship between Grooved Ware and developed passage tombs in Ireland *c.* 3000–2700 cal. BC. *Proceedings of the Prehistoric Society* 83, 155–88.

Carlin, N. and Cooney, G. 2017. Transforming our understanding of Neolithic and Chalcolithic society (4000–2200 cal. BC) in Ireland. In M. Stanley (ed.), *Stories of Ireland's past*, 23–56. Dublin: NRA.

Carlin, N. and Cooney, G. 2020. On the sea roads: the ebb and flow of links with a wider world. In N. Card, M. Edmonds and A. Mitchell (eds), *The Ness of Brodgar: as it stands*, 320–32. Kirkwall: The Orcadian.

Chapple, R.M. 2010. One point through time: archaeological continuity at Gortlaunaght, Swanlinbar, Co. Cavan. *Archaeology Ireland* 91, 35–9.

Cleal, R. and MacSween, A. (eds) 1999. *Grooved Ware in Britain and Ireland.* Oxford: Oxbow Books.

Cleary, R.M. 1983. The ceramic assemblage. In M.J. O'Kelly, R.M. Cleary and D. Lehane (eds), *Newgrange, Co. Meath, Ireland: the Late Neolithic/Beaker Period settlement*, 58–117. Oxford: British Archaeological Report S190.

Cleary, R.M. 2015. Ballynora to Lehenaghamore – prehistoric pottery. In K. Cleary, *Archaeological networks: excavations on six gas pipelines in County Cork*, 346–48. Cork: Collins Press.

Cleary, R.M. 2017. Appendix II (a) – Pottery from the N5 Charlestown Bypass. In R. Gillespie, *Lowpark, Co. Mayo. A multi period archaeological complex*, 269–309. Dublin: TII.

Collins, A.E.P. 1952. Excavations in the Sandhills at Dundrum, Co. Down, 1950–51. *Ulster Journal of Archaeology* 15, 2–26.

Collins, A.E.P. 1959. Further investigations in the Dundrum Sandhills. *Ulster Journal of Archaeology* 22, 5–20.

Condit, T. and Keegan, M. 2018. *Aerial investigation and mapping of the Newgrange landscape, Brú na Bóinne, Co. Meath.* Dublin: Department of Culture, Heritage and the Gaeltacht.

Cooney, G. and Grogan, E. 1999. *Irish prehistory: a social perspective.* 2nd ed. Dublin: Wordwell.

Cooney, G., Bayliss, A., Healy, F., Whittle, A., Danaher, E., Cagney, L., Mallory, J., Smyth, J., Kador, T. and O'Sullivan, M. 2011. Ireland. In A. Whittle, F. Healy and A. Bayliss, *Gathering time: dating the Early Neolithic enclosures of southern Britain and Ireland*, 562–669. Oxford: Oxbow Books.

Copper, M., Hamilton, D. and Gibson, A. 2021. Tracing the lines: Scottish Grooved Ware trajectories beyond Orkney. *Proceedings of the Society of Antiquaries of Scotland* 150, 81–117.

Cotter, E. 2003. *03E0461 Site D, Morett Townland, Co. Laois. N7 Heath-Mayfield Motorway Scheme.* Kilkenny: Valerie J. Keeley Ltd, unpublished client report for Laois County Council.

Cotter, E. 2008. *Final excavation report Cloonbaul/Kilbride.* Dublin: Department of the Environment, Heritage and Local Government.

de Paor, L. and Ó h-Eochaidhe, M. 1956. Unusual group of earthworks at Slieve Breagh, Co. Meath. *Journal of the Royal Society of Antiquaries of Ireland* 86, 97–101.

Dunlop, C. 2016. *Road to the west. A road to the past, Volume 1.* Belfast: Northern Archaeological Consultancy Ltd.

Dunlop, C. and Barkley, J. 2016. *Road to the west. A road to the past, Volume 2.* Belfast: Northern Archaeological Consultancy Ltd.

Eogan, G. and Cleary, K. (eds) 2017. *Excavations at Knowth 6: the passage tomb archaeology of the Great Mound at Knowth.* Dublin: Royal Irish Academy.

Eogan, G. and Roche, H. 1997. *Excavations at Knowth 2.* Dublin: Royal Irish Academy.

Eogan, G. and Roche, H. 1999. Grooved Ware from Brugh na Bóinne and its wider context. In R. Cleal and A. MacSween (eds) 1999, 98–111.

Eogan, J. 1999. Recent excavations at Bettystown, Co. Meath. *Irish Association of Professional Archaeologists Newsletter* 30, 9.

Foley, C. and Warner, R. 2022. Excavation of Iron Age burials at Kiltierney, County Fermanagh, 1969 and 1983–44, *Ulster Journal of Archaeology* 77, 1–20.

Giacometti, A. 2010. *A prehistoric ritual landscape at Donacarney Great, Bettystown, Co. Meath*. Dublin: Arch Plan Ltd.

Gillespie, R. 2017. *Lowpark, Co. Mayo. A multi period archaeological complex*. Dublin: TII.

Grogan, E. and Roche, H. 2009. Appendix 7. Prehistoric pottery analysis. In T. O'Neill, *M7 Portlaoise–Castletown/ M8 Portlaoise–Cullahill Motorway Scheme. Contract 1 Gortnaclea–Oldtown. Phase 2 – excavation. Report on the archaeological excavation of Parknahown 5, Co. Laois, Volume 2*, 260–4. Dublin: Archaeological Consultancy Services Ltd, for Laois County Council and the NRA. https://repository.dri.ie/catalog/cf95xs255, accessed 26 July 2023.

Grogan, E. and Roche, H. 2010a. Appendix A. The prehistoric pottery from Balregan 1, Co. Louth (03E0157). In B. Ó Donnchadha and E. Grogan 2010, i–xx.

Grogan, E. and Roche, H. 2010b. Appendix 2.2: The prehistoric pottery from Steelstown, Co. Kildare (04E0858). In C. Duffy and T. Coughlan, *Steelstown 1. N7 Naas Road-Widening and Interchanges Scheme, Co. Dublin*, xxx-xxxvii. Kilcoole: Irish Archaeological Consultancy Ltd for Louth County Council and the NRA. https://repository.dri.ie/catalog/hq388965f, accessed 26 July 2023.

Grogan, E. and Roche, H. 2011a. 4.2 Prehistoric pottery report. In J. Monteith 2011, 87–104.

Grogan, E. and Roche, H. 2011b. The prehistoric pottery. In P. Stevens, *N11 Gorey to Arklow Link: Site 42–44, Ask Townland, Co. Wexford (A003/020, E3502)*, 155–78. Kilkenny: Valerie J. Keeley Ltd, unpublished client report for Wexford County Council.

Grogan, E. and Roche, H. 2011c. Appendix 2.1: The prehistoric pottery assemblage from Rathmullan 7, Co. Meath (01E0295). In T. Bolger 2011, xxxi–xl.

Grogan, E. and Roche, H. 2011d. Appendix 2.1. The prehistoric pottery assemblage from Kilmainham 1C (E3140). In F. Walsh, *M3 Clonee–north of Kells Motorway scheme. Archaeological services Contract 4. Navan to Kells and Kells Bypass. E3140: Kilmainham 1C. Ministerial Direction Ref. No.: A029/. NGR:275700/274100. Final report. Volume 2: Appendices*, 263–300. Kilcoole: Irish Archaeological Consultancy Ltd for Meath County Council and the NRA. https://repository.dri.ie/catalog/mp495t552, accessed 22 May 2023.

Grogan, E. and Roche, H. 2012. The prehistoric pottery assemblage from Lagavooren 7, Co. Meath (00E0914). In E. Stafford, *Archaeological excavation report, 01E0914 Lagavooren 7, Co. Meath. M1 Northern Motorway*, cxiii–cxxxv. Kilcoole: Irish Archaeological Consultancy Ltd, for Meath County Council and the NRA, https://repository.dri.ie/catalog/1j92vp21j, accessed 26 July 2023.

Hartwell, B. 1998. The Ballynahatty complex. In A. Gibson and D. Simpson (eds), *Prehistoric ritual and religion*, 32–44. Stroud: Sutton.

Hartwell, B. 2002. A Neolithic ceremonial timber complex at Ballynahatty, Co. Down. *Antiquity* 76, 526–32.

Hartwell, B., Gormley, S., Brogan, C. and Malone, C. (eds) 2023. *Ballynahatty: excavations in a Neolithic monumental landscape*. Oxford: Oxbow Books.

Keeley, V.J. 1994. The Heath, Heath. Excavations – miscellaneous. In I. Bennett (ed.), *Excavations 1993*, 50. Bray: Wordwell.

King, H.A. 1999. Excavation on the Fourknocks Ridge, Co. Meath, *Proceedings of the Royal Irish Academy* 99C, 157–98.

Laidlaw, G. 2009. Breaking pots – the grooved ware assemblage from Scart, Tory Hill, Mullinavat, Co Kilkenny. *Old Kilkenny Review* 61, 37–46.

Laidlaw, G. 2010. *Scart (North), Co. Kilkenny E3021 Final Report*. N9/N10 Kilcullen to Waterford Scheme. Dublin: V.J. Keeley Ltd for Kilkenny County Council and the NRA. https://repository.dri.ie/catalog/f475fz83x, accessed 26 July 2023.

Lehane, J. and Leigh, D. 2010. *Archaeological excavation report, E2412 Ballynacarriga 3, County Cork*. Dublin: Eachtra Archaeological Projects for Cork County Council and TII. https://doi.org/10.7486/DRI.bk12nr78m

Lehane, J., Johnson, P. and Leigh, D. 2019. 2.8 Ballynacarriga 3–Multi-period prehistoric ceremonial site. In P. Johnson and J. Kiely, *Hidden voices – the archaeology of the M8 Fermoy–Mitchelstown motorway*, 40–51. Dublin: TII Heritage 7.

Leigh, J., Stout, G. and Stout, M. 2018. A pathway to the cosmos at Newgrange Farm. *Archaeology Ireland* 32(4), 25–9.

Liversage, D. 1958. An island site at Lough Gur. *Journal of the Royal Society of Antiquaries of Ireland* 88, 67–81.

MacSween, A. 1995. Grooved Ware from Scotland: aspects of decoration. In I. Kinnes and G. Varndell (eds), *'Unbaked urns of rudely shape': essays on British and Irish pottery for Ian Longworth*, 41–8. Oxford: Oxbow Books.

Monteith, J. 2011. *Scart, Co. Kilkenny E3001 Final Report. N9/N10 Kilcullen to Waterford Scheme.* Kilkenny: Valerie J. Keeley Ltd, unpublished client report by for Kilkenny County Council and the NRA.

Nicol, S. 2016a. 2016:380 – Glenshane Road Quarry, Claudy (Clagan td.), Derry. In I. Bennett (ed.), *Excavations 2016*. Dublin: Wordwell. https://excavations.ie/report/2016/Derry/0025536/.

Nicol, S. 2016b. 2016:293 – Upper Hightown Road (Ballyvaston td.), Newtownabbey, Antrim. In I. Bennett (ed.), *Excavations 2016*. Dublin: Wordwell. https://excavations.ie/report/2016/Antrim/0025407/

Ó Donnchadha, B. and Grogan, E. 2010. *Balregan 1 and 2 (03E0157), Site 116*: M1 Dundalk Western Bypass. Kilcoole: Irish Archaeological Consultancy Ltd, unpublished client report for Louth County Council and the NRA. https://repository.dri.ie/objects/tm711893r/files/tq582577w/download?type=surrogate, accessed 22 May 2023.

Ó Drisceoil, C. 2009. Archaeological excavations of a Late Neolithic Grooved Ware site at Balgatheran, County Louth. *Journal of the County Louth Archaeological and Historical Society* 27(1), 77–102.

O'Kelly, M.J., Cleary, R.M. and Lehane, D. (eds) 1983. *Newgrange, Co. Meath, Ireland: the Late Neolithic/Beaker Period settlement*. Oxford: British Archaeological Report S190.

Ó Ríordáin, S.P. 1951. Lough Gur excavations: The Great Stone Circle (B) in Grange townland. *Proceedings of the Royal Irish Academy* 54C, 37–74.

Phelan, S. 2007. 1903. Whitewell. Grooved Ware timber circle. In E. Grogan, L. O'Donnell and P. Johnson, *The Bronze Age landscapes of the Pipeline to the West*, 349–50. Bray: Bord Gais/ Wordwell.

Roche, H. 1995. *Style and context for Grooved Ware in Ireland with special reference to the assemblage at Knowth, Co. Meath.* Unpublished MA thesis, National University of Ireland.

Roche, H. 2004. The dating of the embanked stone circle at Grange, Co. Limerick. In H. Roche *et al.* 2004, 109–16.

Roche, H. and Grogan, E. 2010a. Appendix 7. Late Neolithic and Beaker pottery. In J. Lehane and D. Leigh, Archaeological excavation report, E2412 Ballynacarriga 3, County Cork, 245–65. Clashmore: Eachtra Archaeological Projects for Cork County Council and the NRA, Dublin. https://repository.dri.ie/catalog/bk12nr78m, accessed 26 July 2023.

Roche, H. and Grogan, E. 2010b. 4.3 Prehistoric pottery report. In G. Laidlaw 2010, 52–9.

Roche, H., Grogan, E., Bradley, J., Coles, J. and Raftery, B. (eds) 2004. *From megaliths to metals: essays in honour of George Eogan*. Oxford: Oxbow Books.

Schulting, R.J., Bronk Ramsey, C., Reimer, P.J., Eogan, G., Cleary, K., Cooney, G. and Sheridan, J.A. 2017. Dating the human remains from Knowth. In G. Eogan and K. Cleary (eds) 2017, 319–67.

Sheridan, J.A. 2004 Going round in circles? Understanding the Irish Grooved Ware 'complex' in its wider context. In H. Roche *et al.* 2004, 26–37.

Sternke, F. 2010. Appendix 2.3: The lithics, Rathmullan 7 (01E0295), Co. Meath. In T. Bolger 2010, xliii–lviii.

Wainwright, G.J. and Longworth, I.H. 1971. *Durrington Walls: excavations 1966–68*. London: Society of Antiquaries.

Walsh, F. 2011. E3140: Kilmainham 1C. M3 Navan–Kells & Kells Bypass. In F. Walsh, *M3 Clonee–north of Kells Motorway scheme. Archaeological services Contract 4. Navan to Kells and Kells Bypass. E3140: Kilmainham 1C. Ministerial Direction Ref. No.: A029/. NGR:275700/274100. Final report. Volume 2: Appendices*, 263–300. Kilcoole: Irish Archaeological Consultancy Ltd for Meath County Council and the NRA. https://repository.dri.ie/catalog/mp495t552, accessed 26 July 2023.

Walsh, F. 2021. *The road to Kells*. Dublin: TII Heritage 12.

Chapter 9

Niche bunching and the Inland Sea: Grooved Ware settlement at Over, Cambridgeshire, and River Great Ouse distributions

Christopher Evans, Joshua Pollard and Jonathan Tabor

The implications of the Fenland Region's 'Inland Sea' – the 3rd and earlier 2nd millennium cal BC marine inundations – upon its prehistoric communities are not widely appreciated (Evans 2015a; see, also, Sturt 2006).[1] Drowning vast tracts of its lowlands, this would have severely impacted upon vegetation and pushed human and animal populations inland. The resulting bunching of both in the tidal limits of river valleys is a theme explored here in the context of the Barleycroft/Over excavations in Cambridgeshire and their many period 'occupations'. The issues raised resonate with the origins of Grooved Ware and the submerged landscape studies of the 'Essex Coast Sub-Committee of the Fenland Research Committee' (Hazzledine Warren *et al.* 1936; Wilson *et al.* 1971).

Developing from out of the 1980s Haddenham Project, occurring just south of the Old West River and the Upper Delphs great causewayed enclosure (Evans and Hodder 2006), over nearly 30 years Over's ongoing fieldwork programme has progressed across Hanson's Needingworth Quarry lands (Fig. 9.1). It has extended across the mid-stream islands and both terrace-sides of the River Great Ouse where it debouches into the fen marshlands. Its over-arching research directive has been the changing status of a major river in prehistory – when primarily a communications corridor and when a socio-territory divide? – with how the mid-stream islands were utilised, as opposed to the riverside terraces, also a priority.[2] Of the Grooved Ware sites discussed here, those on the northern island-ridges – *The Narrows* – featured in the project's first volume, *Twice-crossed river* (Evans *et al.* 2016; hereafter *TCR*), with the southern islands appearing in the next, *A book of sites* (completed, it will be issued shortly).

OVER'S OCCUPATIONS

Generally omitting the period's single, isolated pit occurrences, of the 17 designated Grooved Ware sites (Fig. 9.2; Table 9.1), all but four thus far have been located on the islands. Reflecting a marked low riverine preference, even the western and eastern terrace-side outliers have been identified within 150–250 m of its then-active palaeochannels. While expressing a distinct locational preference, this does not amount to a 'rule' and, as the quarry-led exposures extend further back from the eastern riverside, other contemporary

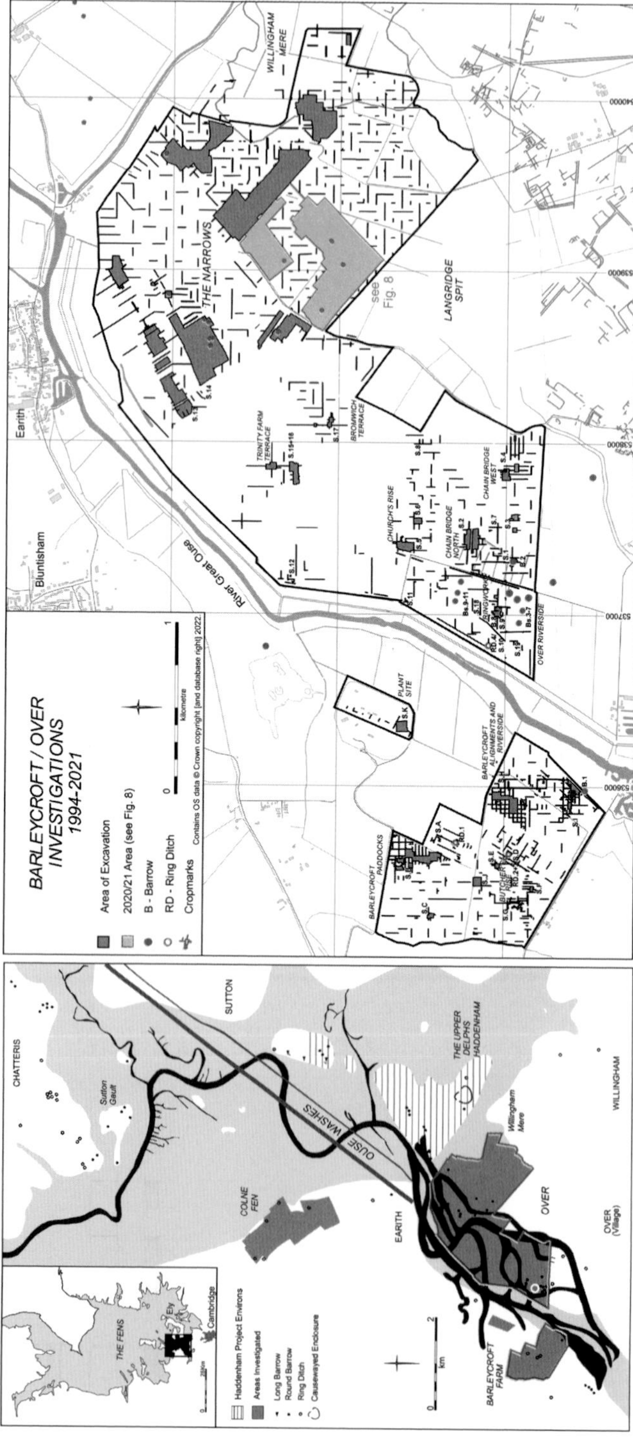

Figure 9.1. Barleycroft Farm/Over, location map left (with project-area islands and palaeochannels shown); right, evaluation trenching and areas of excavation.

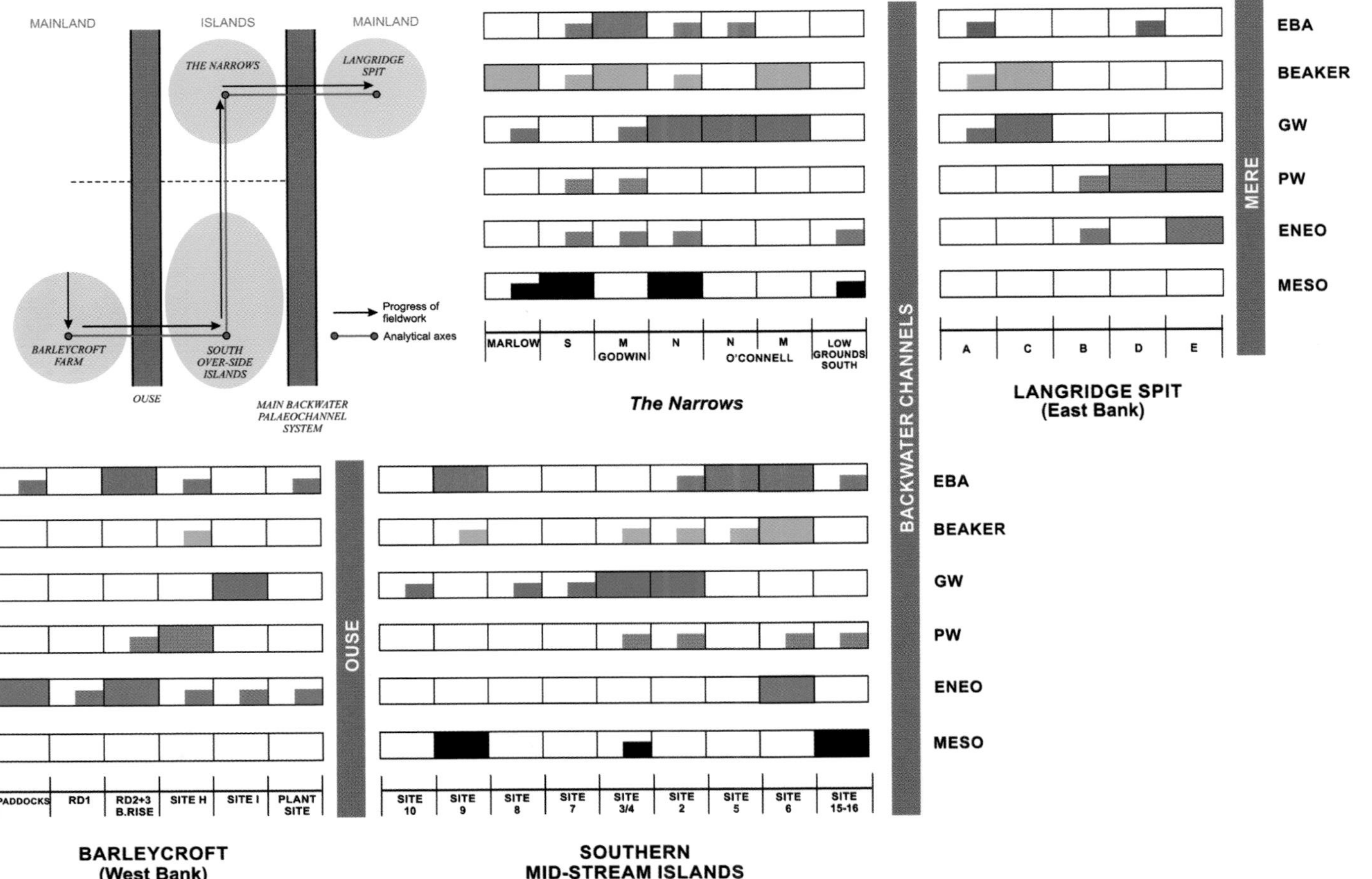

Figure 9.2. Analytical frameworks and sequence-phasing matrix, with horizontal axes showing site areas relative to the river and its main backwater channels. As rendered, the vertical sequence axes only extend until the Early Bronze Age (GW = Grooved Ware), omitting Middle–Late Bronze Age, Iron Age and Roman (full period box highlighting indicates major occupation; quarter-size, minor).

Table 9.1. The Barleycroft/Over investigations, Grooved Ware occupation designations (to 2019), including pottery sub-styles by site: CL, Clacton; DW, Durrington Walls.

Location	*Pits with pottery*	*Sherds*	*Weight (g)*	*Sub-style*
Barleycroft-side				
Site I/GW1	8	89	822	DW
Islands				
The Narrows				
Godwin				
GW1**	1	4	*c.* 25	DW
GW2	3	17	335	DW
GW3	3	7	1183	DW
Marlow				
GW4	2	45	212	DW
O'Connell				
GW5	4	34	483	CL & DW
GW6	9	75	339	CL
S. Islands				
Site 2	30	520	4940	CL
Site 3B	16	225	838	CL
Site 4C & D	21	309	6794	DW
Site 4E	1	9	100	CL
Site 7*	1	14	59	CL
Site 8*	1	2	54	DW
Site 10*	1	96	*c.* 1300	?CL
Langridge-side				
Site XII/House	1	6	30	CL
Site XII/Cluster	2	42	248	CL & DW
Site IX	11	357	2711	CL & DW
Total	115	1851	20,473	

* *indicates evaluation-trench exposure only;* ** *designation based on material in tree-throw and minor associated surface spread.*

occupations will surely eventually occur. Nevertheless, their distribution is distinctly different from those of the Early Neolithic, which have almost all been 'inland' and well back from the riversides and is more comparable to those of the Mesolithic. Of the bracketing periods, both the Middle Neolithic and Beaker have a wide – but then largely only 'light' – island register.

With some 1850 sherds of Grooved Ware recovered and 115 pottery-attributed pits (as of 2019), as will become apparent, this clearly amounts to a major period 'bunching'. At the beginning of the 3rd millennium cal BC, the locale would have lain some 15 km

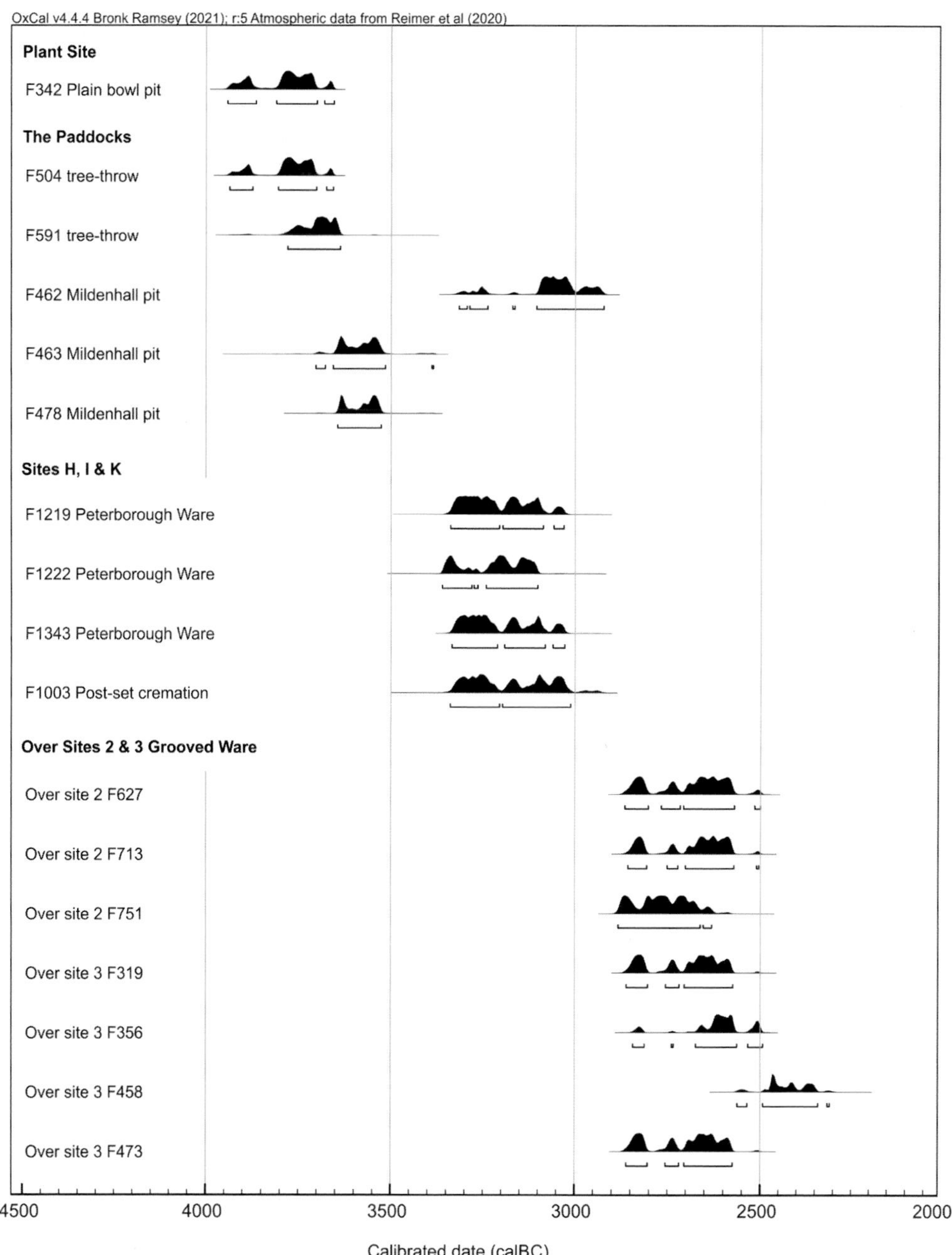

Figure 9.3. Calibration plot of the Barleycroft-side and southern mid-stream islands' Neolithic radiocarbon dates (see also TCR, *197, 287–93, 508 for Grooved Ware radiocarbon dates achieved from* The Narrows' *excavations).*

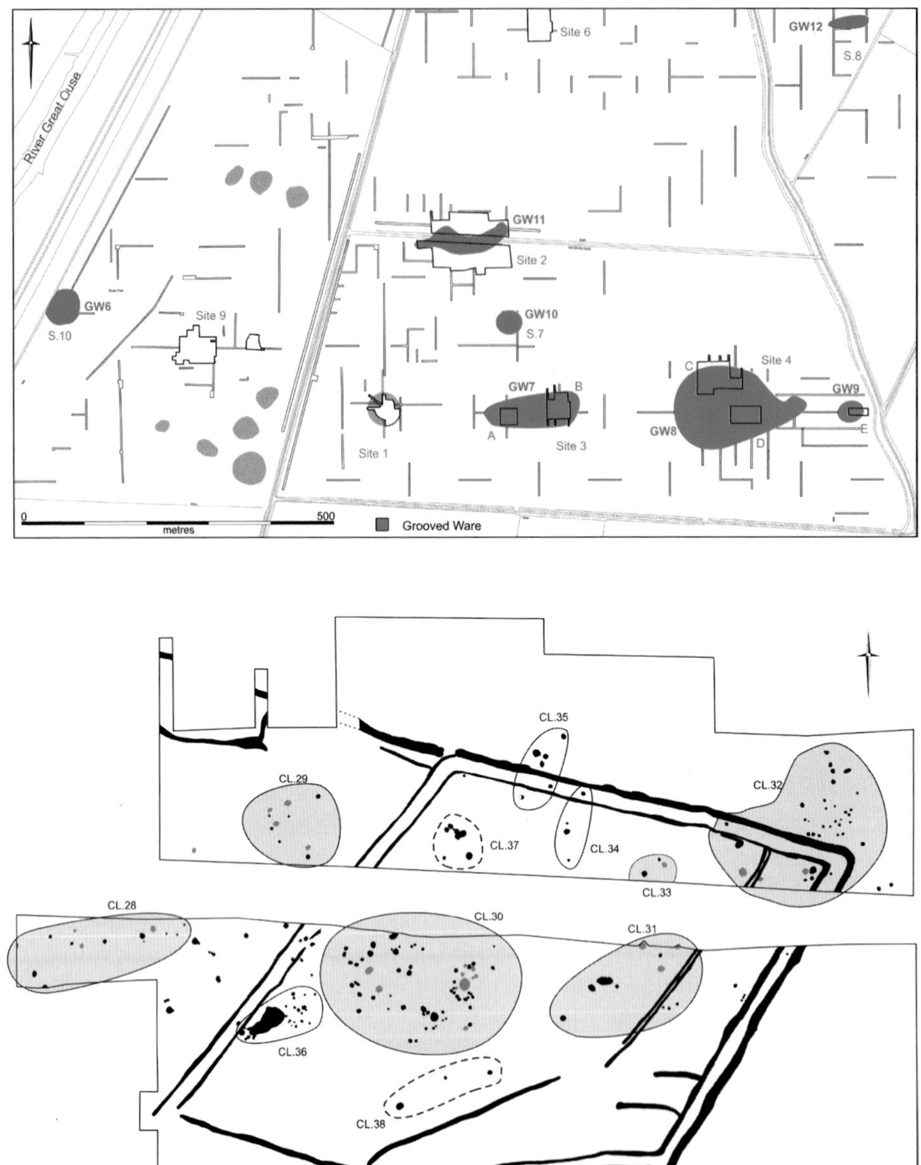

Figure 9.4. Southern mid-stream islands' Grooved Ware distributions (top; see TCR, *fig. 7.3; Evans* et al. *2014, fig. 3 for* The Narrows*); below, Site 2 base-plan, with pit clusters and Middle Bronze Age field system shown.*

back from the sea (see Fig. 9.7; Sturt 2006, figs 3–4).[3] Over the next thousand years its front pushed further inland, with the waters' tidal limits (i.e. 'halo') extending further still. Deep, laminated marine silt deposits occur within the project-area's main palaeochannel (No. I; *TCR*, 56–9, figs 1.10, 2.17; Evans 2022, fig. 8.1), whose onset at this point would date to the end of the 3rd millennium cal BC. A connection with the sea is nonetheless evident within the period's pottery, with 'fresh' marine shells used as temper in Clacton sub-style vessels (*TCR*, 278–81).

While Over's Grooved Ware presence has extended down to a maximum depth of *c.* 1.00 m OD, upon the 'low' islands the occupation sites largely lay on the highest immediate locales. As indicated in Table 9.1, they show considerable variability. Many just consist of a few pits and have few finds, while others involve multi-pit clusters and substantial assemblages. There are also distinct differences in the pit cluster sites' surface densities. Some show 'tidying up' of the occupation traces, with others having a finds-dense surface footprint (see Fig. 9.5); in some cases, the latter suggest separate lithics-only reuse. Clearly, there is no scope here for their detailing and just two will be discussed – Sites 2 and 3/4 – with the latter's Area B featuring as a case-study in Garrow's 2006 volume (93–117).

As depicted in Figure 9.2's matrices, both sites shared similar sequences, this largely being realised by the metre-square sampling of their overlying buried soils and the forthcoming traces of their bracketing surface occupations. Reflective of the establishment of their clearances, both were initiated with Middle Neolithic tree-throw utilisation and, following their Grooved Ware occupations, saw Beaker usage; Site 2 not only had a burnt lithic spread of that date but – reflecting its more elevated locale – also Collared Urn pits and the corner of the area's Middle Bronze Age field system (Fig. 9.4).

Excavated in 1997, due to the day's limited resourcing, both Sites 3 and 4 could only be sample-investigated. Dug two years later, Site 2's excavation was much more extensive. Having 91 later Neolithic-assigned pits, with Grooved Ware present in 20, these fell within nine pit cluster groupings, with three not having any ceramics and, arguably, representing 'lithics-only' episodes of activity (Table 9.2). Of the more than 70 (78%) of the period's aceramic pits, many had no other, or only negligible, finds. This is common to all the project's pit cluster configurations. It is this negative evidence – plus the recent recovery of an upright pot in one pit, and some of the features' multiple fill sequences – that indicates the pits had a function other than just the eventual receipt of occupation debris, with storage of foodstuffs and water being likely in most cases.

The period's economic evidence attests to a wide resource base. The 'wild' is widely documented – particularly deer but also some aurochs – with a number of the pit clusters' faunal remains being pig-dominated. Yet, while seeing a variety of wild plant and fruit species, albeit in low numbers, there have also been cereal remains, such as have now been recovered on several other sites in the region (*pace* Stevens and Fuller 2012). More telling in Over's case is that, throughout the Neolithic, arable has registered in the project's many pollen cores and there is no doubt that cultivation was practised in the Late Neolithic.

The ceramic assemblages from Sites 2 and 3 are dominated by Clacton sub-style Grooved Ware: over 500 sherds (nearly 5 kg) from the former and *c.* 250 sherds (*c.* 1 kg) from the latter. Diagnostic traits include straight-sided, tub-shaped, open forms, simple rims, and the employment of horizontal grooved and incised lines covering large areas of the external

Table 9.2. Summary of the Site 2 pit clusters and associated pottery, flint and animal bone finds.

Cluster	Area (m^2)	Feats	Pits	Mean diam. (pits) (m)	Mean depth (pits) (m)	No finds	Pottery Present	Pottery Total	Pottery ≥5	Max. feature	
28	242	14	8	0.65	0.37	7	4	107	2	F.618	61
						50.00%	28.57%	1509g	14.28%		410g
29	267	10	9	0.55	0.22	1	4	23	3	F.806	10
						10.00%	40.00%	71g	30.00%		11g
30	535	46	24	0.63	0.21	18	5	99	3	F.631	76
						39.13%	10.87%	1398g	6.52%		1294g
31	260	13	12	0.81	0.28	6	5	40	3	F.752	17
						46.15%	38.46%	279g	23.08%		126g
32	407	37	18	0.58	0.22	21	5	109	3	F.825	64
						56.76%	13.51%	583g	8.11%		387g
33	39	3	3	0.73	0.31	1	1	18	1	F.799	18
						33.33%	33.33%	27g	33.33%		27g
34	65	4	4	0.53	0.61	3	–	–	–	–	
						75.00%	–	–	–		
35	77	6	6	0.7	0.19	3	–	–	–	–	
						50.00%	–	–	–		
36	102	22	6	0.7	0.13	19	1	1	–	F.696	1
						86.36%	4.55%	3g	–		3g
37	75	8	6	0.86	0.48	4	2	8	–	F.770	4
						50.00%	25.00%	55g	–		42g
38	105	3	3	0.69	0.3	–	2	4	–	F.754	2
						–	66.67%	30g	–		24g
Str.21		23	1	2.2	0.32	6	8	50	3	F.713	17
						26.09%	34.78%	302g	13.04%		21g

(Continued)

Table 9.2. (Continued)

Cluster	*Flint*					*Animal bone*				
	Present	*Total*	*≥5*	*Max. feature*		*Present*	*Total*	*≥5*	*Max. feature*	
28	7	202	6	F.616	79	5	359	5	F.613	127
	50.00%	2038g	14.85%		659g	35.71%	5790g	35.71%		3369g
29	7	74	4	F.814	33	8	76	3	F.814	41
	70.00%	667g	40.00%		147g	80.00%	987g	30.00%		170g
30	20	99	5	F.629	16	15	307	11	F.630	97
	43.48%	1190g	10.87%		227g	32.61%	2623g	23.91%		767g
31	7	360	6	F.751	233	6	509	6	F.752	280
	53.85%	1453g	46.15%		450g	46.15%	3622g	46.15%		1048g
32	13	222	6	F.821	58	6	287	5	F.825	110
	35.14%	1938g	16.22%		301g	16.22%	3856g	13.51%		1403g
33	2	6	0	F.799	4	1	45	1	F.799	45
	66.67%	33g	0.00%		32g	33.33%	285g	33.33%		285g
34	–	–	–	–		–	–	–	–	
	–	–	–	–		–	–			
35	3	5	–	F.782	2	1	14	1	F.786	14
	50.00%	36g	–		15g	16.67%	23g	16.67%		23g
36	2	10	1	F.696	8	–	–	–	–	
	9.09%	69g	4.55%		67g	–	–	–		
37	3	5	0	F.772	3	4	41	3	F.772	27
	37.50%	39g	0.00%		12g	50.00%	325g	37.50%		18g
38	3	33	2	F.753	23	2	18	1	F.753	16
	100.00%	258g	66.67%		217g	66.67%	49g	33.33%		46g
Str.21	15	123	8	F.719	23	15	186	10	F.713	33
	65.22%	1136g	34.78%		153g	65.22%	2221g	43.48%		393g

Present = number of features (and proportion of cluster) containing find type; Total = total number and weight of find type per cluster; ≥5 = number of features (and proportion of cluster) containing 5 or more of that find type. For Max. feature, the pit with largest number of pottery sherds/flint pieces/bone fragments has been selected.

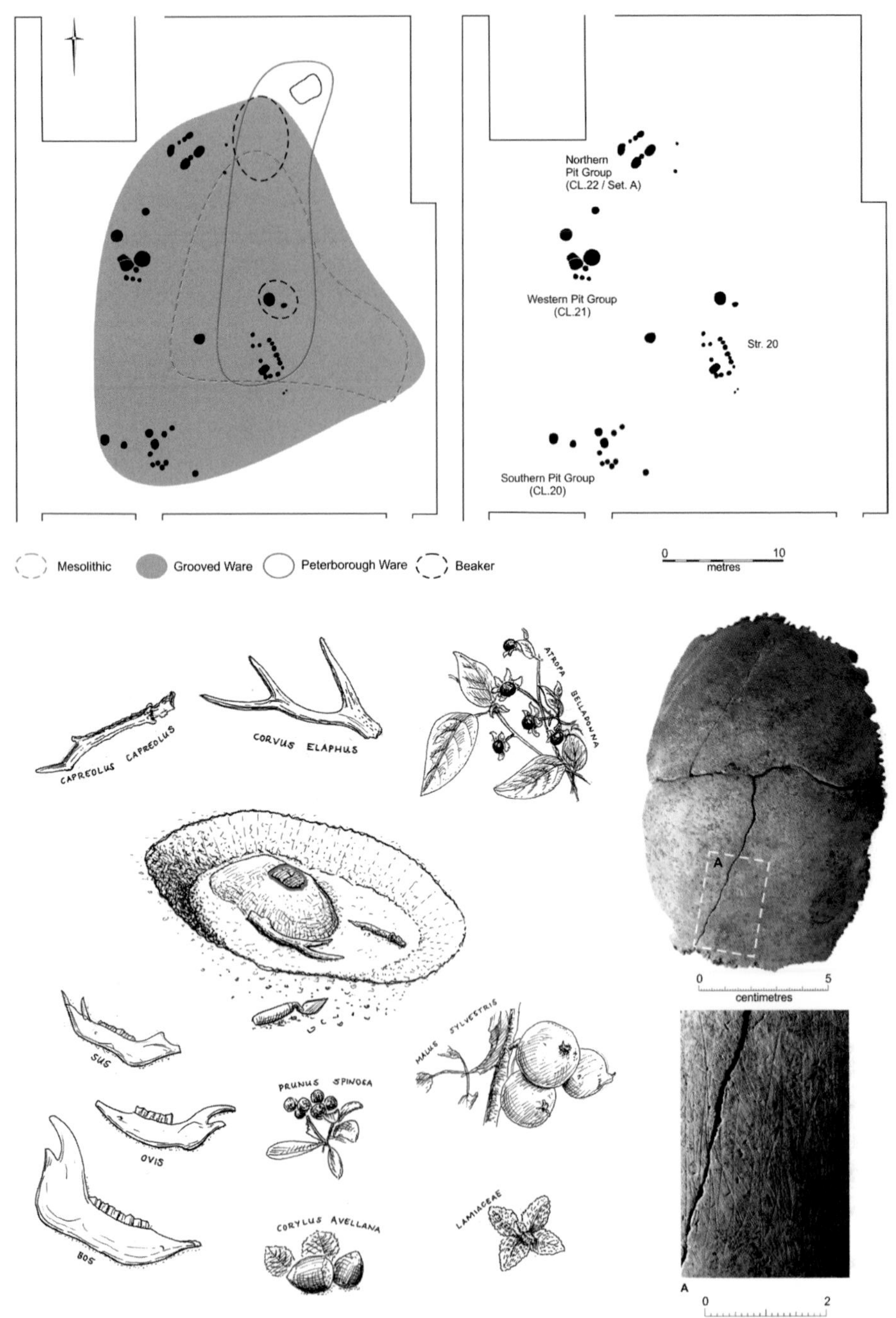

Figure 9.5. Site 3B: top, base-plans, with surface-spread occupations and total Grooved Ware 'footprint' indicated; below, Pollard's reconstruction of the F.473 pit deposit and its components (with skull fragment red-highlighted; left) and, right, the mound-top skull fragment with detail below of its scratches.

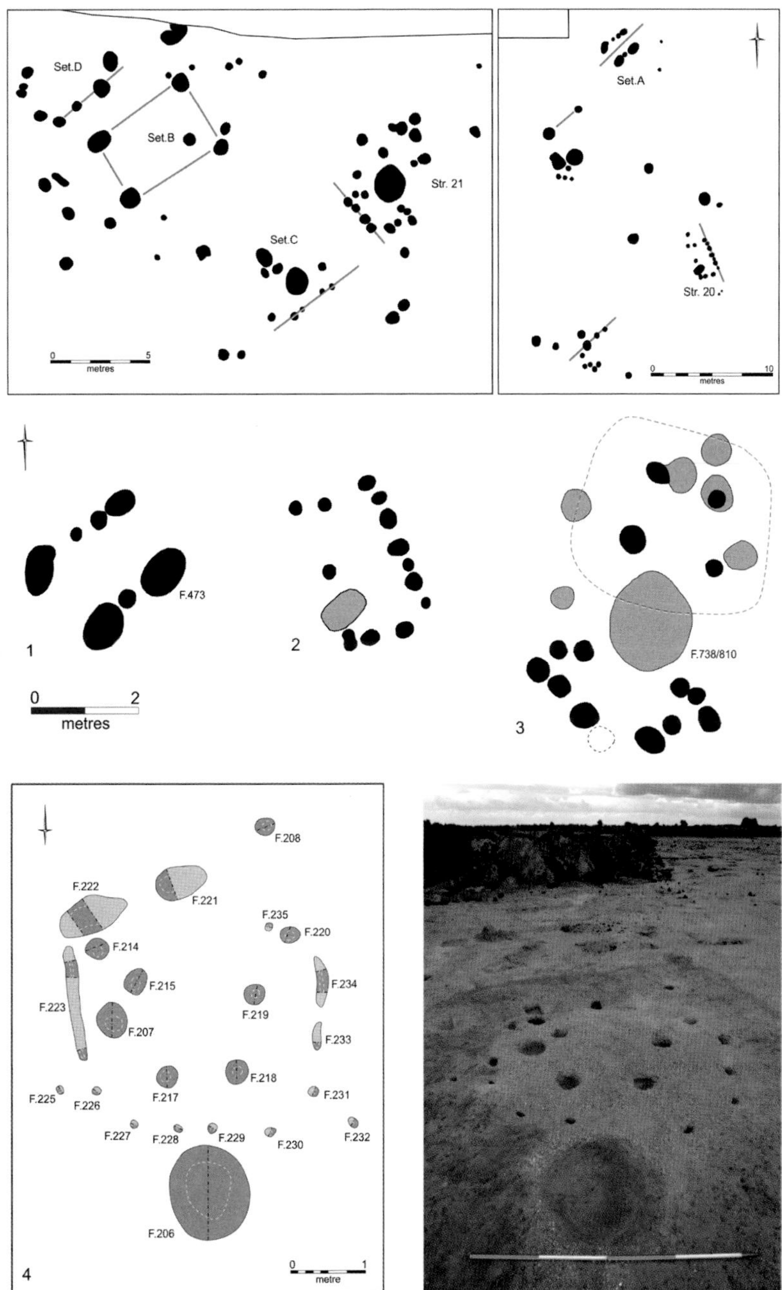

Figure 9.6. Over's Grooved Ware alignments and structures: top, core swathe of Site 2's Cluster 30 (right; see Fig. 9.3) and, right, Site 3B; 1) Setting A, Site 3B; 2) Structure 20, Site 3B; 3) Structure 21, Site 2, with an outline of Over 2015's Durrington Walls-type house imposed in red; 4) plan and photograph of Over 15's Durrington Walls-type house.

surface. Triangles, lozenges and chevrons are not a feature of Site 3's assemblage, with decoration largely limited to multiple grooved lines and fingernail impressions, while vessels from Site 2 framed lozenge-shaped panels infilled with small blunt stab-marks and 'panels' of finger-tip rustication. These contrast with Site 4's assemblage, dominated by Durrington sub-style vessels, comprising plain or lightly decorated neutral and open bowls, and larger jars, heavily potted with internally bevelled rims and having complex and applied decoration.

With a high percentage of implements and utilised pieces, and a broad range of implement types, the lithic assemblages from both sites are typical of contemporary occupation contexts in East Anglia (e.g. the material from the Grooved Ware pits at Storey's Bar Road, Fengate; Pryor 1978, 124–7). Scrapers, serrated flakes, knives, along with chisel and oblique arrowheads, and discoidal cores from which arrowhead blanks were probably struck, feature strongly.

Moulded clay pieces are amongst Sites 3/4's more intriguing finds. There are a number of kneaded small lumps, with some having distinct finger impressions, possibly relating to pottery production. There is also part of a moulded clay ring, with a flattened base. Its interior carries the impression of a basket and its form suggests that the ring was intended to support an upright basket. Accordingly, both such clay items are suggestive of sustained occupation.

Amongst Over's now many Neolithic/Early Bronze Age pit sites, with few exceptions, the Late Neolithic is the one period where 'arranged' deposition was widespread. Variously seeing the placing of antler picks in the central bases of pits, selected large pottery sherds and even a 'stack' (?bagged) of flint implements (Garrow 2006, fig. 6.10), there are also more 'formal' settings; one, a large rectangular four-pit arrangement at Site 2, involved axehead fragments, wild animal remains and quantities of pottery (Setting B; see Fig. 9.6).

An unassailable instance of pit 'placement' occurred at Site 3B's northern end. Dating to 2862–2572 cal BC (SUERC-103725, 4110±24 BP), this was part of a larger feature setting (A; 2.3 × 2.6 m) consisting of a rectangular arrangement of four corner pits, a scoop and three postholes. The pit within its north-eastern corner proved extraordinary (F.473). Dumped within it, with its top 'sculpted', had probably been a basket-load of domestic refuse (including Grooved Ware sherds) that then had a large human skull fragment set upon its crown, with the rise ringed with deer antlers. The skull fragment's inner and exterior faces have fine scratch marks. Scanning indicates that, rather than defleshing cuts, these were probably the result of abrasion, possibly arising from its use as a digging implement. As portrayed on Pollard's illustration (Fig. 9.5), an array of plant/fruit species occurred within the pit's fills, most notably deadly nightshade (*Atropa belladonna*): the witch's flying drug of choice. As an assemblage, the deposit was certainly 'special' and, arguably speaking of magic, quickly became referred to as 'the shaman's pit'.

At one point it was observed that the setting's south-west–north-east orientation would match that of the winter solstice and, hence, Stonehenge's main axis (and that of other key latest 4th millennium cal BC monuments, including Maeshowe, Newgrange and Bryn Celli Ddu). This was initially dismissed as far-fetched on the basis that no close orientation could ever be established from such a short-length setting. Yet, opinions changed in the course of preparing the sites' publication, with the recognition that the area's Neolithic oval barrows and five 'long' mortuary-type enclosures (one possibly the end of a cursus) recently excavated on the river's eastern terrace-side also broadly followed this orientation (see Fig. 9.8). This led to a reappraisal of the Grooved Ware sites' various post-setting lengths and structures, and the acknowledgement that they, too, were so aligned. This is not for a moment to suggest any kind of direct connection with Stonehenge's landscape or that they attest to an exact celestial geometry. Rather, a dominant Middle–Late Neolithic orientation is apparent and that, at least in the case of Over's Sites 2 and 3, is reflected in their settlement architecture, suggesting more highly organised settlement spaces than the period's occupations are usually credited with.

Of the period's structures that have been recovered, at Site 3B – of comparable size to its Setting A/F.473 arrangement – was a post-built rectangle (1.8 × 3.2 m; Str. 20; Fig. 9.6), whose deep postholes were unequivocal. That said, its function was ambiguous. Perhaps a shed for cached goods; at a pinch, a small (close) family could, however, cram in to sleep there, with some manner of shrine another possibility.

Amid Site 2's various fragmentary post-line lengths and many pits, was an equally ambiguous post-built structure (no. 21; Fig. 9.6); again, its constituent parts were robust and definite. With a few accompanying pits, in this case it involved two parts: a four-'square'/trapezoidal setting and, in its southern end, a chevron-like posthole arrangement. From the larger pit, bridging the two and dated to 2857–2511 cal BC (SUERC-103717, 4100±24 BP), there were 41 sherds (many large and refitting). Obviously not making a great deal of structural sense, some manner of shrine again seemed plausible, with the chevron-setting perhaps a screen/porch of sorts.

These settings remained in an interpretative limbo until, in 2015, when excavating the first site on the river's eastern terrace-side, a 'proper' square Durrington Walls-type house was exposed (3.5 × 4 m; Fig. 9.6; see e.g. Parker Pearson 2007). Lacking any surface strata and having only very few accompanying pits, only its four central posts were substantial, with its stakeholes and wall-line traces shallow. There were few associated finds apart from in the one larger pit on its northern backside: six sherds and a large Group III (Cornish rock) ground stone axehead piece, plus part of a cow's tooth. The latter refitted with a tooth splinter in one of the building's interior features and, when dated, gave a result of 2896–2678 cal BC (SUERC-66982, 4202±31 BP).

Had that building been heavily machine-stripped, all that would remain would be its central four-post arrangement (1.4 and 1.7 × 1.4 m). Acknowledging this and, having at last found a definite house, it then provided a datum to reconsider the earlier recovered structures. The four-post portion of Site 2's structure would then seem to represent another such 'standard plan' house, with the 'chevron' before it then remaining as an elaborate screen, cache-shed or shrine. The latter two are still possibilities for Site 3B's Structure 20, with a shrine seeming the more likely given its proximity and similarity to that site's F.473's setting.

COMMUNITY BUNCHINGS

Appreciation of the Ouse's fen/river valley interface settlement 'bunching' requires awareness of 'negatives', and that huge tracts have now been investigated either without any, or with only negligible, evidence of Grooved Ware occupation. This is apparent both along the river's upper/middle reaches and the fen-edge. Of the 'edge', extending over more than 2 km north of Earith, at for example Colne Fen (see Fig. 9.1), just one such

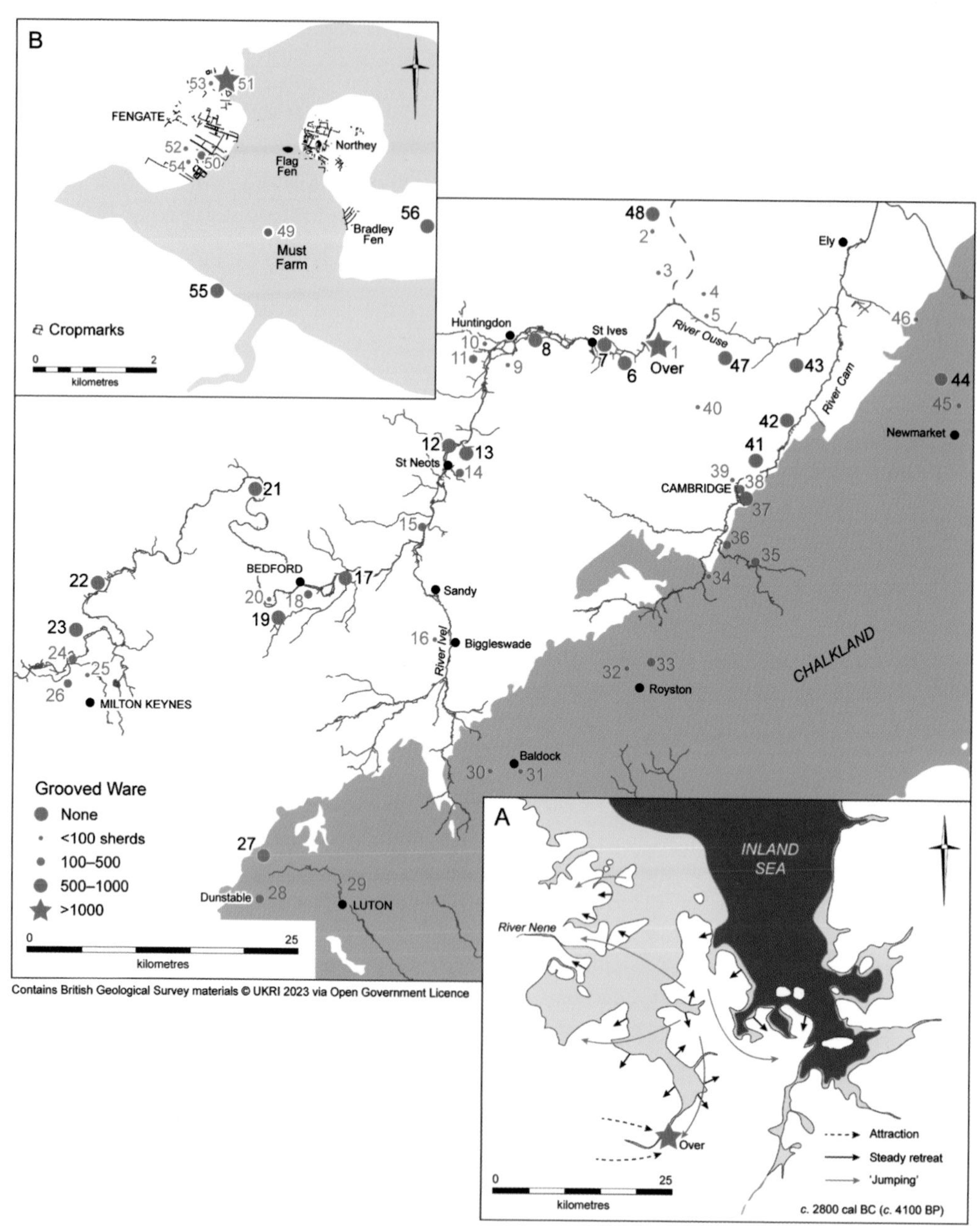
B
53
51
FENGATE
52
54
50
Flag Fen
Northey
Bradley Fen
56
49
Must Farm
55
Cropmarks
0
2
kilometres
48
2
3
4
5
Ely
46
River Ouse
Huntingdon
St Ives
10
11
9
8
7
6
1
Over
47
43
River Cam
44
45
40
42
Newmarket
41
12
13
St Neots
14
39
38
CAMBRIDGE
37
21
15
36
35
34
22
BEDFORD
17
20
18
19
Sandy
16
Biggleswade
River Ivel
23
24
25
26
MILTON KEYNES
32
33
Royston
CHALKLAND
Baldock
30
31
Grooved Ware
None
<100 sherds
100–500
500–1000
>1000
27
Dunstable
28
29
LUTON
0
25
kilometres
A
INLAND SEA
River Nene
Over
Attraction
Steady retreat
'Jumping'
0
25
kilometres
c. 2800 cal BC (c. 4100 BP)

*Figure 9.7. River Great Ouse Grooved Ware settlement distributions, with population landscape-retreat/-'jumping' model (A) and Flag Fen embayment plot (B) inset: 1) Barleycroft/Over; 2) Sutton Gault/North Fen and Stocking Drove Farm, Chatteris; 3) Colne Fen; 4) Haddenham, Foulmire Fen; 5) Haddenham, Upper Delphs; 6) Fen Drayton; 7) Meadow Lane, St Ives; 8) Rectory Farm, Godmanchester; 9) Bearscroft; 10) Huntingdon Racecourse/Stukeleys; 11) A14 (Brampton West to Ouse-crossing length); 12) Little Paxton Quarry; 13) Love's Farm and Wintringham; 14) Eynesbury; 15) Black Cat Quarry; 16) Broom Quarry; 17) Willington (*et al.*); 18) Bunyan Centre, Bedford; 19) Marsh Leys; 20) Biddenham Loop; 21) Radwell; 22) Ravenstone; 23) Gayhurst Quarry; 24) Manor Farm, Milton Keynes; 25) Stacey Bushes; 26) Passenham Quarry; 27) Houghton Regis; 28) Dunstable-area (Maiden Bower, Five Knolls, Puddlehill and Totternhoe); 29) Waulud's Bank; 30) Letchworth area; 31) Baldock Bypass; 32) Littlington; 33) Melbourn; 34) Hinxton Genome Campus; 35) Linton; 36) Babraham Institute; 37) Babraham Road Park-&-Ride; 38) Cambridge-area (Cherry Hinton, Wort's Causeway & Hills Road); 39) North West Cambridge; 40) Northstowe/Longstanton; 41) Milton Landfill and Rowing Lake; 42) Waterbeach; 43) Mitchell's Hill; 44) Fordham Bypass; 45) Chippenham Barrow; 46) Isleham; 47) Cottenham; 48) Somersham Quarry; 49) Must Farm and Flag Fen Basin; 50) Storey's Bar Road, Fengate; 51) Edgerley Drain Road, Fengate; 52) Wyman Abbott's Fengate finds; 53) Fengate, Perkins Engines South; 54) TK Packaging Site; 55) Stanground; 56) Whittlesey. (On the grounds of map intelligibility, a number of other major negative-result project-areas are not included: e.g. on the Isle of Ely or the Greater Addenbrooke's environs; see Evans* et al. *forthcoming for other major inland 'negatives'.)*

attributed pit, with some 60 sherds from three vessels, was recovered (Evans *et al.* 2013, 66, figs 3.4, 3.6). Similarly, at Thorney, east of Peterborough (and Fengate), a *c.* 2.5 km length of the fen-edge terraces (and its immediate Eye-area hinterland) has now been continuously excavated (Richmond *et al.* 2022). Whereas Early Bronze Age monuments and an ensuing 'Middle' field system extend across that tract, no Grooved Ware has been forthcoming. Indeed, exposures such as these could lead us to question whether the resource advantages of the fen-edge generally, at least prior to the Bronze Age, may have been over-estimated and that much of the region's 'abundant' intense-use caricature has actually been based on its conjoining river valleys.

In respects comparable to Over's, Grooved Ware 'bunching' also seems apparent at Fengate and Flag Fen's embayment (Fig. 9.7). There, involving 34 pits (with some only attributed on the basis of their flintwork), along the length of the Edgerley Drain Road Site, these were widely dispersed within four broad 'swathes' (two having tighter clustered arrangements). Together, 1066 sherds of Durrington Walls sub-style Grooved Ware were recovered (11.8 kg), with a minimum of 56 vessels represented (Evans *et al.* 2009, 124–31, 151–4, 157–60; see also Brudenell *et al.* 2020).

The other major Fengate site is that at Storey's Bar Road (Pryor 1978). Having quantities of both Clacton and Durrington Walls sub-style Grooved Ware from across a range of features (estimated *c.* 200 sherds), its occupation was originally held to include, not just pits/hollows, but also a circular ditched 'settlement enclosure' (i.e. ring-ditch) and the area's renowned field system. The sequence, however, was subsequently revised; its non-pit components were assigned to the Bronze Age, they simply had quantities of residual material within them (Evans and Pollard 2001, 25–6). Stripped of these later elements, the site's scattering of Grooved Ware-attributed pits – with localised clusters and some post-settings (Evans *et al.* 2009, 89, fig. 3.20) – are then much more akin to both the Edgerley Site's and Over's evidence. Its faunal assemblage included both numbers of *Bos primigenius* elements (aurochs: 18) and, possibly, wild pig (four; Pryor 1978, 177–80). The frequency of 'Late-type' arrowheads within its flintwork assemblage – 26 (Pryor 1978, 138–41) – could prompt speculation that, at least at times, this primarily served as a hunting camp. This interpretation would be furthered by the nearby occurrence at the Eliot Site of a pit, dated to 2880–2610 cal BC (OxA-2182, 4150±37 BP), having wild pig and aurochs; and from the TK Packaging Site was reported another such feature having an aurochs' skull deposited with a complete 'Grooved Ware type' pot (see Evans *et al.* 2009, 75).

Quantities of Grooved Ware and aurochs remains have also been recovered along the River Welland's fenland interface. This is not just a matter of the Etton landscape (Pryor 1998; French and Pryor 2005; see also Simpson 1993), but more recent fieldwork both at Maxey and West Deeping (Northamptonshire Archaeology/Museum of London Archaeology (MOLA) and Cambridge Archaeological Unit respectively).

In reference to Waller's Fenland sequence maps (1994, figs 5.15–18; see also Sturt 2006, fig. 4; Evans 2015a, fig. 2), through the 3rd and earlier 2nd millennium cal BC marine inundations, in excess of 800 km^2 of (freshwater) marshland would have been lost across the region south-east of the Welland Valley (Fig. 9.7). This is not just a matter of its blanket drowning (i.e. Fen Clay) but also its more extensive mudflat and tidal 'halo' affecting soil quality and vegetation cover. This surely would have had an enormous impact on both human and animal communities, resulting in major displacements of both. Strictly on a basis of here providing 'ballpark' estimates, van Vuure's aurochs population densities (2005, table 14) cite a figure of 0.2 per km^2 for Poland's Jaktorow forest. This is qualified, however, as Polish forest densities are probably low and the figure for Canada's sedge marsh bison of one per km^2 is thought more plausible. This would then imply the displacement of at least some 800 aurochsen. Similarly preferring the enhanced biomass of wetlands, the carrying capacity of the area's other main species – deer and wild pig – would have been considerably higher and, therefore, we should envisage their displacement as amounting to thousands (Evans 2015b).

We do not know the manner of the species' retreat. Would they, for example, have bunched along the encroaching 'edge' and/or upon immediate higher grounds – leading to browsing stress/competition and, potentially, lower reproduction rates – or, instead, did their displacement front extend deeply inland? This means that there would be little point attempting to detail this further. Nevertheless, it is likely that the incoming sea would have resulted in the movement of animals inland along preferred-habitat river corridors, this having correlation with aurochs' isotopic register (Lynch *et al.* 2008). Accordingly, what were already niche (human) environments would have become that much more bountiful.

Figure 9.7 demonstrates just how much of the Ouse Valley and its tributaries has now been excavated as a result of gravel quarries and house building. The Grooved Ware distribution is clearly riverine and the figure omits the now vast 'interior' areas of the north-of-Cambridge claylands, between the fen-edge and the Ivel, that have been investigated (Evans *et al.* forthcoming).[4] That said, great swathes of the riversides have been excavated with little or no Grooved Ware forthcoming. Their distribution seems patchy and one cannot talk of any regular 'settlement fabric' densities in the way that is apparent for later prehistoric and Roman-era sites. Such exposures include, for example, a 3.7 km length of the western terrace bankside of its River Ivel tributary at Broom. There, with over 60 ha continuously strip-exposed, just three Grooved Ware pits, yielding 19 sherds,

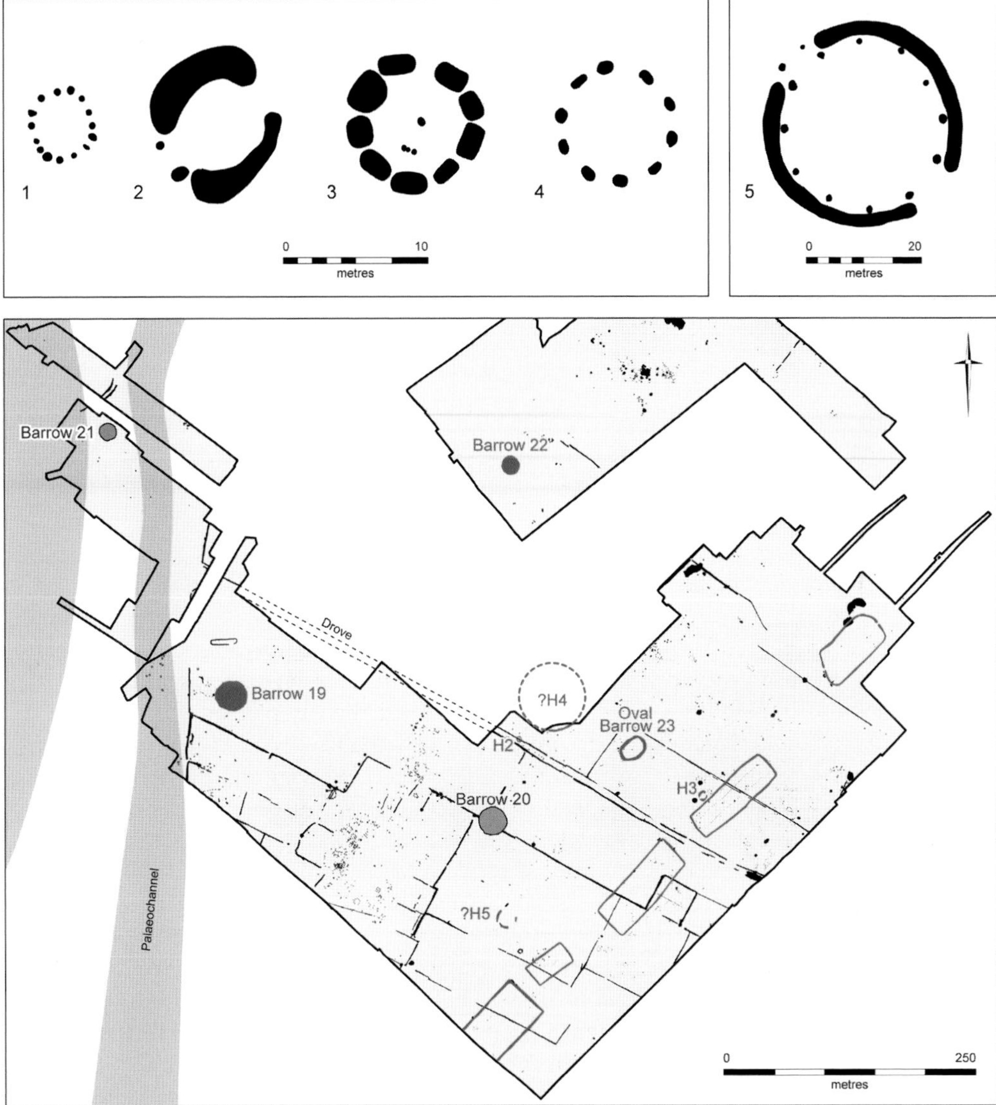

Figure 9.8. Over's 2020/21 eastern terrace-side exposure (see Fig. 9.1), with Neolithic monuments red-highlighted against the area's Middle Bronze Age field system; above, henge-plans: 1 & 2) Over Henges 2 and 3; 3) Manor Farm, Milton Keynes; 4) Maxey Pit Circle IIIB; 5) King's Dyke, Whittlesey (see Luke 2016, 37–50, fig. 3.9 for the Biddenham Loop's two c. *24 diameter probable henges, with a* c. *22m diameter Class II henge also recovered north of Alconbury in the recent A14 programme: MOLA Headland Infrastructure 2019).*

have been recovered. Equally, the west side of the Cam, between its junction with the Ouse and south to Cambridge, has seen extensive excavations but with no Grooved Ware whatsoever forthcoming. Largely providing negative evidence, are also the many Bedford-area investigations. Foremost are those at Biddenham Loop, with its many Neolithic and

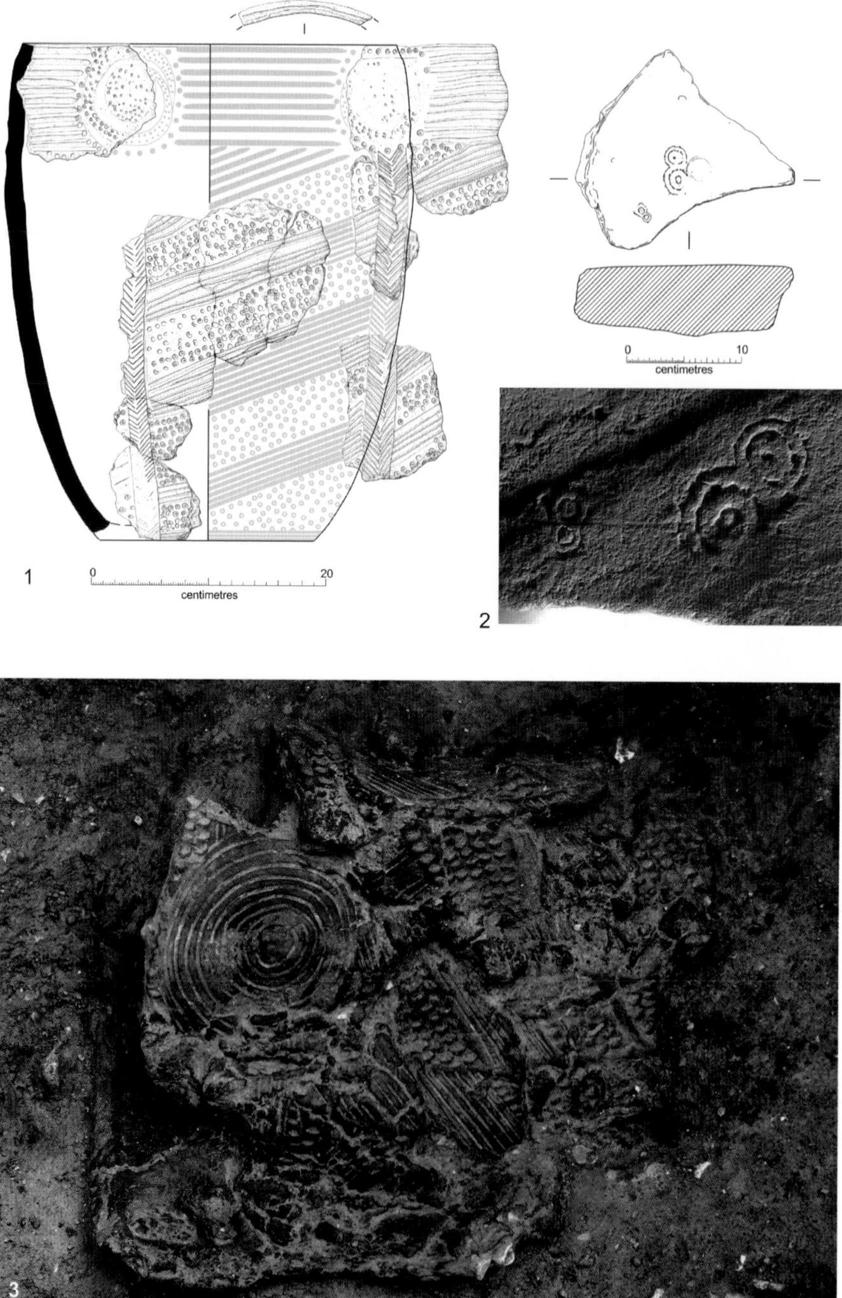

Figure 9.9. Concentricities: 1) barrel-shaped vessel from Edgerley Drain Road, Fengate (with 'flower-on-stem' circles; see Evans et al. *2009, 126–7); 2) Over's rock slab, with detail of its pecked circles below (*TCR*, 68–70; see also Clay and Hunt 2016); 3) crushed Grooved Ware pot in Over's ongoing excavations (2023).*

Bronze Age monuments, and Middle Bronze field system and settlements. Despite having later Neolithic flint scatters, it yielded little Grooved Ware: *c.* 40 sherds from four pits (Luke 2016). Indeed, in the area Grooved Ware has only occurred in substantial numbers at the Bunyan Centre Site (Steadman 1999).

Despite the vast scale of its exposures, the recent A14 Improvement fieldwork – most of it admittedly on 'inland' clays – along the almost continuously excavated *c.* 4 km of its length across gravel terraces west of Brampton and where, in the south, it arced eastward to cross the Ouse, produced just two Grooved Ware pits (*c.* 250 sherds/2.5 kg recovered in total; MOLA Headland Infrastructure 2019). With no Grooved Ware forthcoming adjacent to Rectory Farm, Godmanchester's great cursus (Lyons 2019) and just one such pit by Eynesbury's monuments (Ellis 2004),[5] there would be little point in further reiterating the period's many Ouse Valley 'negatives'. Yet, one other site warrants notice. Extending over *c.* 50 ha along the western Ouse-side south of Roxton, Black Cat Quarry showed significant occupation, with three pit groups yielding some 320 sherds (Dyson 2021). As at Over, it was a floodplain exposure proper, when most of the 'negatives' cited here have been along terraces above and immediately 'behind' the river's deep-cover floodplains. Some of the period's lower settlements may then still go undetected; however, viewed as a whole, their sporadic recovery does nonetheless suggest low population levels.

Other 'bunching' concentrations are, however, evident (and see below for Milton Keynes). With only relatively minor assemblages recovered through a number of small-scale exposures there are, of course, the earlier findings from the Dunstable/Luton area (e.g. Matthews 1976) – including the Waulud's Bank enclosure – adjacent to the headwaters of the River Lea, and Baldock's occurrences are probably similarly situated in relationship to the Ivel's headwaters. The most marked southern chalkland site grouping is along the upper reaches of the River Cam south of Cambridge. In part reflecting the intensity of that area's recent development and ensuing fieldwork, nevertheless a greater availability of 'quality' flint would certainly have been a major attraction. Yet, another factor would have been its water resources from the many springs issuing from the lower downlands. The most significant of these sites has been at the Babraham Road Park-&-Ride (Hinman 2001). On Cambridge's southern margins, it lay adjacent to the Nine Wells springs, an early source of the city's main water supply. Such locales would not just have drawn (human) communities but also animals (Evans 2015b). Indeed, 'the wild' was well documented at the Babraham Road site and accompanying almost 800 sherds of Grooved Ware were quantities of aurochs remains.

The combined attraction of chalk flint and water sources would not have just been restricted to the river valley and some frequency of such sites can be anticipated to extend along the foot of the region's downs, especially north-eastward where they border with the fens.[6] That said, the Cam Valley's immediate chalkland flanks seem to have been 'special', and a critical interface, one now known to be marked by four Early Neolithic causewayed enclosures (Evans *et al.* 2018, 401–4).

DISTANT CONNECTIONS AND SUSTAINED OCCUPATIONS

Malim's 2000 paper reviewed the monument complexes along the Ouse's middle and lower reaches. As this was based largely on aerial photography, since then some of its entries have had to be omitted (e.g. Biddenham Loop's would-be cursus; Luke 2016), with others added (e.g. Biggleswade's cursus; Abrams 2010). Beyond that study's reach, directly relevant to this chapter's concerns – plus contributing to another 'bunching' with their correspondence with earlier Grooved Ware findings (Kidd 2010) – has been the series of monuments subsequently revealed within the vicinity of Milton Keynes (Fig. 9.7). There, along with ten pits, a small, Grooved Ware-associated, cremation-related ring-ditch/hengiform and two larger ring-ditches have recently been excavated at Passenham Quarry (Atkins 2021). Nearby, at Manor Farm at the Ouse's confluence with the River Tove, aside from a few pits, a pit-circle henge was sited within the axes of its multiple-part cursus monument (Fig. 9.8, 4; Hogan 2013). Also associated with cremated remains, and having a central post setting, some 270 sherds of Grooved Ware were recovered from the henge's features. Its plan morphology shares attributes with both Dorchester's and Maxey's pit-circle henges (Fig. 9.8, 4; Atkinson *et al.* 1951; Simpson 1985; see also French and Pryor 2005, 23–38). Differing in its form (though also involving a pit-circle), on its southern Whittlesey-side, Flag Fen's embayment now also has a henge (Fig. 9.8, 5; Knight and Brudenell 2020, 55–60).

Until recently, Over's later Neolithic monuments appeared sparse. The western, Barleycroft, side saw none, with only one sited on the mid-stream islands: a small hengiform, just 4.30 m across, having a pit in its reduced internal-ring 'platform' where a complete Durrington Walls sub-style pottery base had been set (*TCR*, 19, fig. 1.8). Understanding of the character of the wider area's Neolithic radically changed when the project's fieldwork progressed to the river's eastern terrace south of Willingham Mere and the Haddenham Project's lands. Indeed, the results are such that it now calls for a radical reappraisal of that earlier project's simple tripartite Neolithic model featuring on its first volume's cover: causewayed enclosure plus long barrows plus settlement. There, apart from four Neolithic barrows – both round and oval (one subsequently transformed into a Class II henge) – and the alignment of mortuary-type enclosures, were two definite and two possible henges. Of the first, one was a somewhat ovoid, small pit-/timber-circle (*c.* 4 × 4.5 m; H2; Fig. 9.8, 1), with the other a 'diminutive Class II type', consisting of two opposed crescent-plan ditches (*c.* 7 m diam.; H3; Fig. 9.8, 2) opening north-east–south-west, with two postholes set within the latter. Of the two candidates, one – possibly a small ploughed-out barrow – was a 'C'-shaped ring of wide-interval ditch segments with a diameter of *c.* 17.5 m (H5); the other was probably a large, *c.* 55 m diameter henge (H4), that within the area's agreed limits could unfortunately only be partially dug. Regardless of the status of the latter two, there can be no doubt that a major Neolithic ritual landscape has now been exposed across Over's east side terrace.

With their post-excavation still in progress, there is no opportunity to add further detail to these recent findings. What is crucial is simply the occurrence of later Neolithic monuments at each of the fenland river valley interfaces discussed: the Ouse, Nene and Welland. Equally important are the affinities of the pit-circle henges at Manor Farm, Milton Keynes, Maxey and Dorchester, as it tells of the connectivity of Grooved Ware communities. This also extends to Grooved Ware's decorative repertoire and, especially, its employment of concentric circle motifs. Not only do they occur within the Upper Thames Valley (Barclay 1999)[7] – that river's headwaters only lying some 7 km east of the Ouse's – but now at Fengate and Over, with the latter also having a rock art slab having such circle motifs (Fig. 9.9).

Given the interconnectivity of the period's monument forms and ceramic styles, in the knowledge of what seems its low settlement density, this indicates that there must have been considerable distant inter-community communication and, arguably, 'movement'. How then is 'permanent settlement' to be gauged in the light of Over's evidence? Should Site 3B and, at least, the core of Site 2, Cluster 30 be considered long-duration, year-round 'base' settlements, arguably lasting for decades (i.e. a generation or more) and where portions of the immediate community remained while others 'went out'? Other such 'traversing' groups may, in fact, have also come into the Over area's landscape from further afield in the course of their procurement rounds/expeditions. This might, for example, be what the area's Late Neolithic flint scatters attest.

The duration of 'occupations' is clearly crucial for understanding of the period. In this regard, what the occurrence of single pit 'stays' even evinces, with some having three/four vessels represented, remains to be discerned. It is likely that many pots would not have been broken wantonly (if they were not deposited with ritual intention), and such sparse remains may well attest to stays lasting, at least, weeks. What is singularly important arising from Over's findings is the 'betwixt' status of some of its occupations. With their robust shrine settings and now, Durrington Walls-type houses, they can be seen as bridging the period's usual pit cluster-only register and that of the latter's more developed type-site settlement evidence.

Although suspecting that otherwise surface-eradicated, four-central-post square buildings of the period may have gone unnoticed on some sites, this is not to claim such robust settlement configurations as some kind of 'universal' (e.g. Speed 2015, fig. 20 for the variety of the period's accredited structures). It instead seems attributable first to the attractions of Over's niche situation, and then the subsequent bunching of humans and animals in the wake of the region's marine inundations. Far from amounting to a last word here, the impact of the 'inland sea' on the Fenland's later Neolithic and earlier Bronze Age communities is now surely an issue demanding far greater problematisation and study.

ACKNOWLEDGEMENTS

We are variously grateful for discussions with, and information provided by, Rob Atkins, Emma Beadsmoore, Lawrence Billington, Marcus Brittain, Matt Brudenell, Charly French, Duncan Garrow, Kasia Gdaniec, Dave Gibson, Mark Haughton, Mark Hinman, Robin Holgate, Roy Loveday, Mike Luke, Mark Knight, Steve Macaulay, Eduardo Machicado, Nick Overton, Mike Parker Pearson, Sarah Percival, Francis Pryor, Vida Rajkovača, Alex Smith and Simon Timberlake. The contribution's graphics reflect the skills of Andrew Hall and Ellie Winter, with its photography by Dave Webb.

NOTES

1 For comparative environmental change and social response studies see, for example, Lane and Trimble (2010), Bell (2013) and Jones and Allen (2023).

2 The project's second volume, *A book of sites,* includes comparison with the sequences of Britain's other major riverine island projects: Raunds, Eton, and Yarnton.

3 Lying some 6 km north of the Over Project-area, respectively on a small island and, adjacent, on the flanks of Chatteris Island, the North Fen, Sutton (Webley and Hiller 2009) and Stocking Drove Farm, Chatteris (see Crowson *et al.* 2000, 36–8) investigations are amongst the furthest known 'in-fen' occurrences of Grooved Ware (the former lying at just 0.50 m OD; Fig. 9.7, 2). Both, however, proved insubstantial, with just a handful of sherds accompanying their lithic scatters.

4 Of what few inland occurrences of Grooved Ware there have been on the 'heavy' lands between the fen-edge and the Ivel, across the *c.* 1490 ha investigated at both Northstowe/Longstanton (three pits) and North West Cambridge (one pit; Fig. 9.7, 39 and 40), they lay adjunct to springheads upon the 'inland' gravel terraces that run as a diagonal from Cambridge north-west towards Over.

5 See Ellis 2004 (7–13) for Eynesbury's Early Neolithic hengiform ring-ditch. It had been hoped to include a review of the Grooved Ware-attributed 'enclosure', with 40–60 such sherds recovered, that apparently preceded an Early Bronze Age ring-ditch complex in the south of the Eynesbury lands. Excavated by Andrew Herne in the 1980s and never fully written up, unfortunately, due to an ongoing move of the British Museum stores where the site's archives reside, this proved impossible.

6 Substantial portions of that swathe were subject to 19th- and early 20th-century coprolite quarrying. Occurring at a time prior to the recognition of Grooved Ware as a pottery type, any such findings then arising went unregistered.

7 In addition to those in South Wiltshire and Dorset (see Cleal 1991, 141–4).

REFERENCES

Abrams, J. 2010. Aspects of a prehistoric landscape in the Ivel Valley, north of Biggleswade. *Bedfordshire Archaeology* 26, 41–54.

Atkins, R. 2021. Two Late Neolithic ring ditches and a hengiform monument, a Middle to Late Iron Age farmstead and Roman Stones Mausoleum at Areas 7, 8 & 9, Passenham Quarry, Calverton, Milton Keynes. *Records of Buckinghamshire* 61, 1–47.

Atkinson, R.J.C., Piggott, C.M. and Sanders, N.K. 1951. *Excavations at Dorchester, Oxon*. Oxford: Ashmolean Museum.

Barclay, A. 1999. Grooved Ware from the Upper Thames Region. In R. Cleal and A. MacSween (eds), *Grooved Ware in Britain and Ireland,* 9–22. Oxford: Oxbow Books.

Bell, M. 2013. *The Bronze Age in the Severn Estuary*. York: Council for British Archaeology Research Report 172.

Brudenell, M., Billington, L. and Mason, N. 2020. Above the Fen Edge: prehistoric activity on land west of Newark Road, Fengate, Peterborough. *Proceedings of the Cambridge Antiquarian Society* 109, 25–40.

Clay, P. and Hunt, L. 2016. Late Neolithic art and symbolism at Rothley Lodge Farm, Leicester Road, Rothley. *Transactions of the Leicestershire Archaeological and Historical Society* 90, 13–66.

Cleal, R. 1991. Cranborne Chase – the earlier prehistoric pottery. In J. Barrett, R. Bradley and M. Hall (eds), *Papers on the prehistoric archaeology of Cranborne Chase*, 134–200. Oxford: Oxbow Books.

Crowson, A., Lane, T. and Reeve, J. (eds) 2000. *Fenland Management Project Excavations 1991–1995*. Sleaford: Heritage Trust of Lincolnshire.

Dyson, B. 2021. *Archaeological excavations at Black Cat Quarry (North & South)*. Bakewell: Archaeological Research Services Ltd, unpublished client reports nos 2018/134 and 2020/57for Hope Construction Materials.

Ellis, C.J. 2004. *A prehistoric ritual complex at Eynesbury, Cambridgeshire: excavation of a multi-period site in the Great Ouse Valley, 2000–2001*. Salisbury: East Anglian Archaeology Occasional Paper 17

Evans, C. 2015a. Wearing environment and making islands: Britain's Bronze Age inland North Sea. *Antiquity* 89, 1110–24.

Evans, C. 2015b. Disappearance beyond recall: a social context for Bronze Age aurochs extinction in Britain? *Proceedings of the Prehistoric Society* 81, 107–23.

Evans, C. 2022. Modelling, mimicking and fighting waters: Lower River Great Ouse and Ouse Washlands investigations. In F. Sulas, H. Lewis and M. Arroyo-Kalin (eds), *Inspired geographies: past landscapes and social change,* 129–43. Cambridge: McDonald Institute for Archaeological Research.

Evans, C. and Hodder, I. 2006. *A woodland archaeology: Neolithic sites at Haddenham*. Cambridge: The Haddenham Project Vol. I.

Evans, C. and Pollard, J. 2001. The dating of the Storey's Bar Road fields reconsidered. In F. Pryor, *The Flag Fen Basin: archaeology and environment of a fenland landscape,* 25–6. London: English Heritage.

Evans, C., Aldred, O. and Cooper, A. forthcoming. Landscape after Fox's *Cambridge Region* (1923): appraising settlement densities. *Antiquity*.

Evans, C., Lucy, S. and Patten, R. 2018. *RIVERSIDES: Neolithic barrows, a Beaker grave, Iron Age and Anglo-Saxon burials and settlement at Trumpington, Cambridge*. Cambridge: McDonald Institute for Archaeological Research.

Evans, C., Tabor, J. and Vander Linden, M. 2014. Making time work: sampling floodplain artefact frequencies and populations. *Antiquity* 88, 241–58.

Evans, C., with J. Tabor and M. Vander Linden 2016. *Twice-crossed river. Prehistoric and palaeoenvironmental investigations at Barleycroft Farm/Over, Cambridgeshire*. Cambridge: McDonald Institute for Archaeological Research.

Evans, C., with Beadsmoore, E., Brudenell, M. and Lucas, G. 2009. *Fengate revisited: further fen-edge excavations, Bronze Age fieldsystems and the Wyman Abbott/Leeds archives*. Cambridge: Cambridge Archaeological Unit.

Evans, C., with Brudenell, M., Patten, R. and Regan, R. 2013. *Process and history: prehistoric fen-edge communities at Colne Fen, Earith*. Cambridge: McDonald Institute for Archaeological Research.

French, C. and Pryor, F. 2005. *Archaeology and environment of the Etton landscape*. Peterborough: Fenland Archaeological Trust.

Garrow, D. 2006. *Pits, settlement and deposition during the Neolithic and Early Bronze Age in East Anglia*. Oxford: British Archaeological Report 414.

Hazzledine Warren, S., Piggott, S., Clark, J.G.D., Burkitt, M.C. and Godwin, H. and M.E. 1936. Archaeology of the submerged land-surface of the Essex Coast. *Proceedings of the Prehistoric Society* 9, 178–210.

Hinman, M. 2001. Ritual activity at the foot of the Gog Magog Hills, Cambridge. In J. Brück (ed.), *Bronze Age landscapes: tradition and transformation*, 33–40. Oxford: Oxbow Books.

Hogan, S. 2013. Manor Farm cursus complex: floodplain investigations of the River Great Ouse, Milton Keynes. *Past* 73, 2–4.

Jones, A.M. and Allen, M.J. 2023. *The drowning of a Cornish prehistoric landscape: tradition, deposition and social responses to sea level rise*. Oxford: Prehistoric Society Research Papers 14.

Kidd, S. 2010. Prehistoric farmers. In M. Farley (ed.), *An Illustrated History of Early Buckinghamshire*, 27–74. Aylesbury: Buckinghamshire Archaeological Society'

Knight, M. and Brudenell, M. 2020. *Pattern and process: landscape prehistories from Whittlesey brick pits: the King's Dyke and Bradley Fen excavations 1998–2004*. Cambridge: McDonald Institute for Archaeological Research.

Lane, T. and Trimble, D. 2010. *Fluid landscape and human adaption: excavations on prehistoric sites on the Lincolnshire fen edge 1991–1994*. Sleaford: Heritage Trust of Lincolnshire.

Luke, M. 2016. *Close to the loop: landscape and settlement evolution beside the Biddenham Loop, west of Bedford.* Bedford: Albion Archaeology.

Lynch, A.H., Hamilton, J. and Hedges, R.E.M. 2008. Where the wild things are: aurochs and cattle in England. *Antiquity* 82, 1025–39.

Lyons, A. 2019. *Rectory Farm, Godmanchester, Cambridgeshire: excavations 1988–95, Neolithic monument to Roman villa farm.* Bar Hill: East Anglian Archaeology 170.

Malim, T. 2000. The ritual landscape of the Neolithic and Bronze Age along the middle and lower Ouse Valley. In M. Dawson (ed.), *Prehistoric, Roman and Post-Roman landscapes of the Great Ouse Valley,* 57–88. York: Council for British Archaeology Research Report 119.

Matthews, C.L. 1976. *Occupation sites on a Chiltern ridge: excavations at Puddlehill and sites near Dunstable, Bedfordshire.* Oxford: British Archaeological Report 29.

MOLA/Headland Infrastructure 2019. *A14 Cambridge to Huntingdon Improvement Scheme, Cambridgeshire archaeological investigations, Volume 1: Post-Excavation Assessment.* London: MOLA/Headland Infrastructure, unpublished client report for Highways England. https://doi.org/10.5284/1081261.

Parker Pearson, M. 2007. The Stonehenge Riverside Project: excavations at the east entrance of Durrington Walls. In M. Larsson and M. Parker Pearson (eds), *From Stonehenge to the Baltic,* 125–44. Oxford: British Archaeological Report S1692.

Pryor, F. 1978. *Excavation at Fengate, Peterborough, England: the second report.* Toronto: Royal Ontario Museum.

Pryor, F. 1998. *Etton: excavations of the Neolithic causewayed enclosure near Maxey, Cambridgeshire, 1982–7.* London: English Heritage.

Richmond, A., Francis, K. and Coates, G. 2022. *Waterlands: prehistoric life at Bar Pasture, Pode Hole Quarry, Peterborough.* Oxford: Archaeopress/Phoenix Consulting Archaeology Ltd.

Simpson, W.G. 1985. Excavations at Maxey, Bardyke Field, 1962–63. In F. Pryor and C.A.I. French, *The Fenland Project, No. 1: archaeology and environment in the Lower Welland Valle,* 245–64. Cambridge: East Anglian Archaeology 27.

Simpson, W.G. 1993. The excavation of a Late Neolithic settlement at Barholm, Lincolnshire. In W.G. Simpson, D.A Gurney, J. Neve and F. Pryor, *The Fenland Project Number 7: excavations in Peterborough and the Lower Welland Valley 1960–1969,* 7–28. Peterborough: East Anglian Archaeology 61.

Speed, G. 2015. Neolithic settlement and special deposits at Temple Grange, Rothley, Leicestershire. *Transactions of the Leicestershire Archaeological and Historical Society* 89, 1–36.

Steadman, S. 1999. A later Neolithic and Bronze Age mortuary complex and Iron Age settlement at the Bunyan Centre, Bedford. *Bedfordshire Archaeology Journal* 23, 2–31.

Stevens, C.J. and Fuller, D.Q. 2012. Did Neolithic farming fail? The case for a Bronze Age agricultural revolution in the British Isles. *Antiquity* 86, 707–22.

Sturt, F. 2006. Local knowledge is required: a rhythmanalytical approach to the late Mesolithic and early Neolithic of the East Anglian Fenland, UK. *Journal of Maritime Archaeology* 1, 119–39.

van Vuure, C. 2005. *Retracing the aurochs: history, morphology and ecology of an extinct wild ox.* Sofia: Pensoft.

Waller, M., 1994. *Flandrian environmental change in Fenland.* Cambridge: Fenland Project Committee and Cambridgeshire Archaeological Committee.

Webley, L. and Hiller, J. 2009. A fen island in the Neolithic and Bronze Age: excavations at North Fen, Sutton, Cambridgeshire. *Proceedings of the Cambridge Antiquarian Society* 98, 11–36.

Wilson, K.E., Longworth, I.H. and Wainwright, G.J. 1971. The Grooved Ware Site at Lion Point, Clacton. *British Museum Quarterly* 35, 93–124.

Chapter 10

The only way isn't Essex, but it may be one of them …: Grooved Ware, Beakers and long-distance connections in southern Britain

Rosamund Cleal and Joshua Pollard

This paper offers a contribution to matters of long-distance connectivity during the Late Neolithic through a study of selected Grooved Ware assemblages and other elements of material culture from sites in southern Britain. A specific focus is placed on that intriguing period towards the end of the Grooved Ware tradition and in which early Beakers appear, principally the 25th and 24th centuries cal BC, and begins with two Wiltshire sites with Grooved Ware assemblages which show evidence for long-distance connections. These two sites – Durrington Walls and West Kennet palisade enclosures – are the starting point for our arguments. In both cases, the contexts containing the Grooved Ware are relatively well dated by multiple radiocarbon dates, placing their ceramics late in the period of Grooved Ware use.

DURRINGTON WALLS

The large Grooved Ware assemblage (5861 sherds) from the 1966–68 excavations at Durrington Walls (DW) henge, 3 km north-east of Stonehenge (Fig. 10.1), has been in print for over 50 years (Wainwright and Longworth 1971). In the 21st century, an even larger assemblage from the same site has been excavated in the *Stonehenge Riverside Project* (SRP) and is close to publication. As would be expected, the majority of the ceramics from the more recent excavations are classifiable as Durrington Walls sub-style. The sub-style was defined by Ian Longworth (Wainwright and Longworth 1971, 241–2), whose criteria include several diagnostic features which were found to be rare at the time and, even after 50 years, have remained infrequent. Whipped- and twisted-cord impressions remain very rare (as discussed below), while internal decoration and spirals/concentric circles have been found more frequently but remain uncommon. Conversely, there are techniques and motifs which occurred in the DW 1966–68 assemblage but were not included in the diagnostic features for the Durrington Walls sub-style, which excavation over the succeeding half-century has shown do appear in association with the diagnostic features. Included in this category are comb or comb-like impressions, while impressions of various forms including those made by fingernails and fingertips have been found frequently on vessels showing the Durrington Walls diagnostic features. It is some of these rarer techniques and motifs that will be focused on here.

Although whipped- and twisted-cord impressions are listed as diagnostic features of the Durrington Walls sub-style in Longworth's 1971 definition (Wainwright and Longworth 1971, 240–2), only one sherd of the former and 71 of the latter occurred in that assemblage (Wainwright and Longworth 1971, 59, 67 and table vii), probably representing one whipped cord-decorated vessel and several vessels with twisted-cord impressions. The SRP assemblage also contains only a small number of cord-impressed sherds, representing very few vessels. Only one vessel, represented by multiple sherds, has whipped cord 'maggot' impressions (Fig. 10.2, 1) and several vessels, represented by 48 sherds, carry twisted-cord impressions. One unillustrated sherd with a circular or spiral motif almost certainly belongs to the same vessel as Figure 10.2, 1. Looking for parallels for this very distinctive vessel, we observed that there was a strikingly similar example at a site in north-eastern Essex – Tye Field, Lawford – close to the Stour Estuary (Fig. 10.1). This was excavated over four episodes between 1959 and 1971 and comprised a rich, midden-like deposit surrounded by a ditch which probably post-dated the midden (Shennan *et al.* 1985, 212). While the use of whipped cord in Grooved Ware certainly occurs elsewhere – see below and Table 10.1 – the combination of vertical cordons and whipped cord impression on the same vessel is very rare. In her report on the assemblage from Lawford, Isobel Smith commented on the features which placed the assemblage firmly within the Durrington Walls sub-style (Smith 1985, 175–7), and this is mirrored in Ian Longworth's report on the Durrington Walls pottery (Wainwright and Longworth 1971, 241, fig. 91). Smith also noted a particularly striking parallel with Durrington Walls: 'Attention may also be drawn to the remarkable similarities in appearance between P99 [at Lawford], with its finely executed incised decoration and lug set on a girth-cordon, and two vessels from the type-site (Wainwright and Longworth 1971, P219–20)' (Smith 1985, 175, fig. 11; P99 from the 1985 report is redrawn from one of the author's (RC) notes as Fig. 10.2, 3 here). To this parallel another can now be added from SRP (Fig. 10.2, 4). On first sight, perhaps, the SRP vessel might not seem to justify the extension of the description 'remarkable similarity' in connection with the Lawford vessel, but judged against the Durrington Walls sub-style as a whole, the use of a square-sectioned, decorated lug set on a cordon and on a vessel with finely executed, complex and unusual incised decoration, the rarity of the decorative traits and their combination is indeed striking.

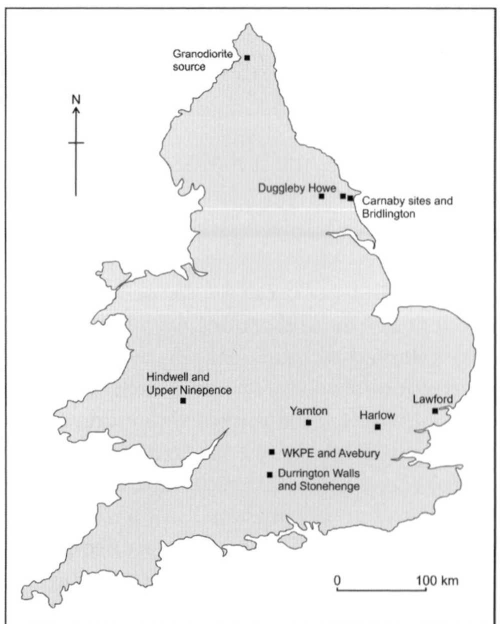

Figure 10.1. Map showing key sites mentioned in the text.

Lawford and Durrington Walls also both feature internally decorated bowls, which occur more widely than impressions of whipped cord or twisted cord, but even with this type of vessel both sites share

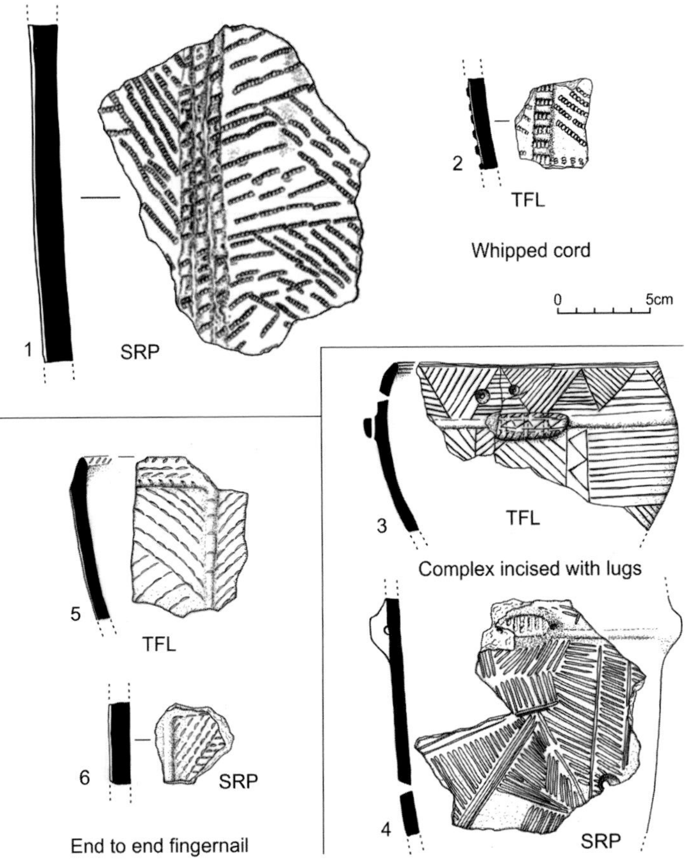

Figure 10.2. Grooved Ware from Wiltshire and Essex.

an uncommon feature. Typically, bowls with internal decoration carry little or no exterior decoration, often only showing multiple horizontal lines on the exterior below the rim (e.g. Grime's Graves (Longworth *et al.* 1988) and Wyke Down, Dorset (Cleal 1991)). In the DW 1966–68 assemblage there are several internally decorated bowls, two of which, although small, seem to carry complex decoration both internally and externally (Wainwright and Longworth 1971 fig. 58, P455, P460 and P461), and this is also the case in the SRP and Lawford assemblages. At SRP, a single small sherd from the Western Enclosures shows some decoration on both surfaces, and that on the exterior appears complex, while at Lawford (Smith 1985, fig. 11), vessels P87, P88, P89, P91 and P93 have complex decoration both internally and externally. Although only a limited literature search has been conducted, Table 10.1 shows that while internally decorated bowls occur widely, complexity of external decoration is a much rarer feature (a notable occurrence, in deep bowls, being from Upper Ninepence in Powys, a site where whipped cord impressions were also used (Gibson 1999, 89, fig. 54: P34 and P68)).

Turning to features of both the Lawford and Durrington Walls assemblages that are not included in the diagnostic features for the Durrington Walls sub-style, most notable is impression in various forms, including that made by comb, fingernail and fingertip. (Comb impression, which occurs at both sites, is discussed below.) Unusual techniques shared between Durrington Walls and Lawford include: cuneiform-like impressions (triangular with 'keel-like' rather than flat bases, also noted as 'wedge' shaped: Smith 1985, 170, P60 and P77)) which occur in the SRP Durrington Walls assemblage, and end-to-end, non-plastic single fingernail impression (ETEFN). The latter is noted by Smith as being used to create linear motifs at Lawford (Smith 1985, 168, fig. P44, P50, P56 and P58) and this

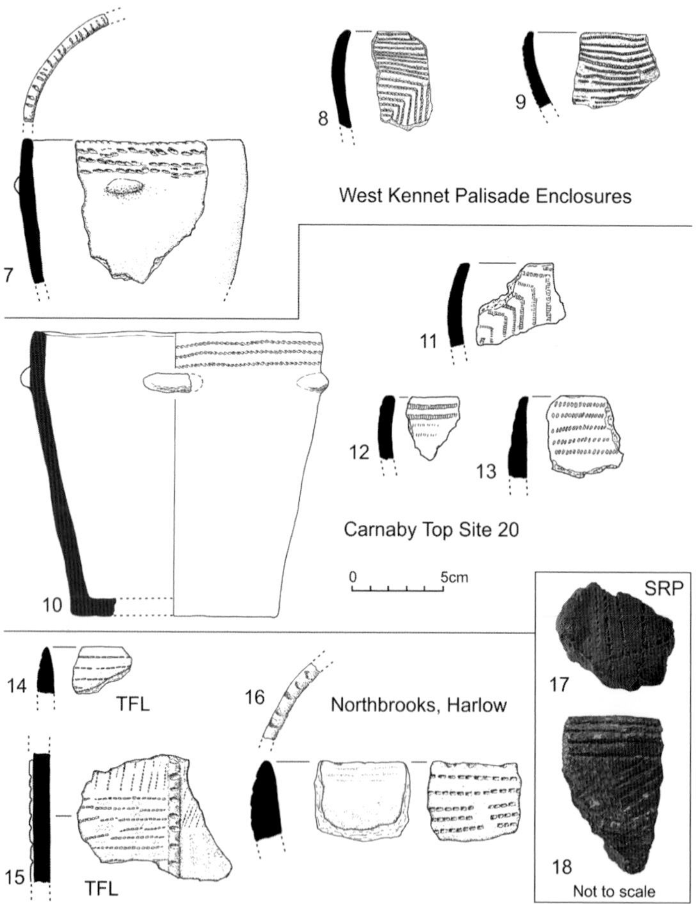

Figure 10.3. Types of impressed decoration on Grooved Ware from Wiltshire (top and bottom right), East Yorkshire (centre) and Essex (bottom left): twisted cord (nos 7, 8, 10); whipped cord (nos 9, 12); comb (nos 11, 13–18). TFL: Tye Field, Lawford, Essex. (East Yorkshire sherds from Manby 1974, fig. 11: 1, 6, 3 and 5, with kind permission of T.G. Manby. WKPE redrawn from Alexander Keiller Museum (AKM). TFL, SRP and Harlow from author's records).

is also true at SRP (Fig. 10.2, 6, which also illustrates Lawford P44 as Fig. 10.2, 5). The occurrence of these techniques is shown in Table 10.1.

This consideration of the similarities between Durrington Walls and Lawford would only suggest contact if the features identified as unusual were not widespread or frequent. Table 10.1 is clearly only an overview of the features discussed here for Lawford and Durrington but it gives some indication of their frequency. In particular, it shows very strikingly that the number of unusual features shared by Lawford and Durrington Walls is high and that those features are infrequent elsewhere and, in some cases, rare. This is all the more striking because the Lawford assemblage is much smaller than the combined Durrington Walls assemblages. At the very least, it seems reasonable to infer that there was contact between south Wiltshire and north-east Essex, and it is also reasonable, then, to look for other cases of where this might be true. For this, north Wiltshire offers some compelling evidence.

WEST KENNET PALISADE ENCLOSURES

The West Kennet palisade enclosures (WKPE) lie on the floor of the Kennet Valley *c.* 1.5 km to the south-east of the Avebury henge. Excavations directed by Alasdair Whittle between 1987 and 1992 produced large assemblages of animal bone, generated through episodes of feasting, along with Grooved Ware and worked flint (Whittle 1997). Further work on the palisades was undertaken in 2019 and 2021 as part of the AHRC-funded *Living with Monuments* project (https://livingwithmonuments.org/). This established that the key components of the complex were constructed in short order, though an outlying component (Structure 5) has a more complex and longer history, beginning as a massive, rectilinear timber structure, subsequently enclosed by a short-lived henge and then a palisade which is connected to Enclosure 2 by a radial fence line.

Although recent dates on charcoal from the post-pipes of the palisades place their construction in the 34th–33rd centuries cal BC (Bayliss *et al.* 2017), these are inconsistent with the material associations (e.g. the Grooved Ware), and the main enclosures are better dated by results on antler and bone from primary contexts in Enclosures 1 and 2 and Structure 3 which cluster in the third quarter of the 3rd millennium cal BC.

The Grooved Ware assemblage from WKPE is distinctive and differs considerably from that at Durrington Walls. Michael Hamilton, in his report on the Grooved Ware from the 1987–1992 excavations, notes of the assemblage that there is 'quite a divergence from the type site' (i.e. of the Durrington Walls sub-style) and that the WKPE assemblage varies most notably from the DW assemblage in the 'absence of grooved/incised decoration' (Hamilton 1997, 116). Hamilton was also one of the first commentators to note that there was an apparent change in Wessex Grooved Ware which seemed to be chronological, noting that there was mainly horizontal decoration from around 2900–2600 cal BC, and vertical decoration, with occasional rustication, cord and comb impression in later Grooved Ware, from around 2650–2300/2200 cal BC. Hamilton's consideration of Wiltshire Grooved Ware is detailed and insightful, but few parallels are noted further afield. Excavations at WKPE in 2019 and 2021, however, produced unexpected and intriguing evidence for contact in a direction which had not previously been considered.

Table 10.1. Selected decorative features. Grooved Ware is Durrington Walls sub-style unless specified otherwise. See Key at end for sites.

Table 10.1a	*Durrington Walls*					*TFL*	*WKPE*	*CT20*	*NCT*
	66–8	*SRP*	*1971*	*1954*	*DWA*				
Circles & spirals	P	P	–	–	P	P	–	–	–
Internally decorated bowls	P	P	–	–	–	P	P	–	–
Twisted cord	P	P	–	P	–	P	P	P	P
Whipped cord	P	P	–	–	–	P	P	P	–
Cordon & comb	P	P	P	–	–	P	–	–	–
Beaker-like comb	P	P	–	–	–	P	–	–	–
Other comb	P	P	P	?P	–	P	–	P	–
Semi-denticulated	–	P	?P	–	–	P	–	–	–
Cuneiform	–	P	–	–	–	P	–	–	–
ETEFN	–	P	–	–	–	P	–	–	–
Complex incised with dec. lugs	P	P	–	–	–	P	–	–	–
Twisted cord/plain	P	–	–	–	–	–	P(L)	P(L)	P(L)
Rectilinear	–	–	–	–	–	–	P	P	–
Fine whipped cord	–	–	–	–	–	–	P	–	–
Multiple plain vertical cordons	P	–	–	?P	–	–	P	P	P

66–8: Durrington Walls, Wiltshire (Wainwright and Longworth 1971); SRP: Stonehenge Riverside Project; 1971: Durrington Walls, Larkhill Married Quarters (Longworth in Wainwright 1971), P25 description appears to be semi-denticulated; 1954: Stone *et al.* (1954), Comb appears to be present but not described as such (e.g. fig. 8: 21, 22), multiple vertical cordons may be present but illustrated as horizontal (e.g. fig. 7: 11, 14, 16); DWA: Packway site, Ditch A north of henge (Wainwright and Longworth 1971, 317–18); TFL: Tye Field, Lawford, Essex (Smith 1985); WKPE: West Kennet palisade enclosures, Wiltshire (Hamilton 1997); CT20 and NCT: Carnaby Top Site 20 and North Carnaby Temple sites, East Yorkshire (Manby 1974).

Table 10.1b	*SNC*	*WDH*	*FIG*	*SHD*	*MtP*	*WD*	*MAR*	*HUN (W/C)*
Circles & spirals	–	P	–	–	–	P	?P	–
Internally decorated bowls	P	–	–	–	–	P	–	–
Twisted cord	–	–	–	–	P	P	P	–
Whipped cord	–	–	–	–	P	–	P	P
Cordon & comb	–	–	–	–	–	–	–	–
Beaker-like comb	–	–	–	–	–	–	–	–
Other comb	–	–	–	P	–	–	(P)	–

(Continued)

Table 10.1. Selected decorative features. Grooved Ware is Durrington Walls sub-style unless specified otherwise. See Key at end for sites. (Continued)

Table 10.1b	*SNC*	*WDH*	*FIG*	*SHD*	*MtP*	*WD*	*MAR*	*HUN (W/C)*
Semi-denticulated	–	–	–	–	–	–	–	–
Cuneiform	–	–	–	–	–	P	–	–
ETEFN	–	P	P	–	–	–	?P	–
Complex incised with dec. lugs	–	–	–	–	–	–	–	–
Twisted cord/plain	–	–	–	–	–	–	P	–
Rectilinear	–	–	–	–	–	P	P	–
Fine whipped cord	–	–	–	–	–	–	–	–
Multiple plain vertical cordons	–	–	–	–	P	P	–	–

SNC: The Sanctuary, Avebury, Wiltshire (Cunnington 1930); WDH: Woodhenge (Cunnington 1929); FIG: Figsbury Rings, Firsdown, Wiltshire (Guido and Smith 1981); SHD: Stonehenge Down, Wiltshire (Cleal with Raymond 1990); MtP: Mount Pleasant, Dorset (Longworth 1979); WD: Wyke Down 1 and 2, Sixpenny Handley, Dorset: (Cleal 1991; 2007); MAR: Marden (Longworth 1971); HUN: Hunstanton, Norfolk, Woodlands/Clacton (Cleal 1993).

Table 10.1c	*YRN*	*MUCK*	*IPS*	*FSBR*	*GG*	*PDD*	*GRO*	*ERL*	*Up9p*
Circles & spirals	–	–	P	–	–	–	–	–	–
Internally decorated bowls	?P(E)	–	–	–	P	P	–	–	P(E)
Twisted cord	–	P	–	–	P	P	–	–	P
Whipped cord	–	–	–	P	–	–	–	–	P
Cordon & comb	–	–	–	–	–	–	–	–	–
Beaker-like comb	–	–	–	P	–	–	–	–	–
Other comb	P	–	–	P	–	–	–	–	–
Semi-denticulated	–	–	–	–	–	–	–	–	–
Cuneiform	–	–	–	–	–	–	–	P	–
ETEFN	?P	–	–	–	–	–	–	–	P
Complex incised with dec. lugs	–	–	–	–	–	–	–	–	–
Twisted cord/plain	P	P	–	–	–	–	–	–	–
Rectilinear	–	–	–	P	–	–	–	–	–
Fine whipped cord	–	–	–	–	–	–	–	–	P
Multiple plain vertical cordons	–	P	–	–	–	P	P	–	–

YRN: Yarnton, Oxfordshire (Barclay and Edwards 2016), fig. 12.36 P236c may be complex externally; MUCK: Mucking, Essex (Birley 2016); IPS: Dales Road Brickfield, Ipswich, Suffolk (unpublished); FSBR: Storey's Bar Road, Fengate (Pryor 1978); GG: Grime's Graves, Norfolk (Longworth 1981; Longworth *et al.* 1988), including a variant with internal lines of twisted cord; PDD: Puddlehill, Bedfordshire (Matthews 1976); GRO: Godwin Ridge, Over, Cambridgeshire (Evans *et al.* 2016); ERL: Eton Rowing Lake, Buckinghamshire (Barclay 2013); Up9p: Upper Ninepence, Powys (Gibson 1999).
Key: P = Present; (E) = includes complex external decoration; (L) = lug in addition; (W/C) = Woodlands/Clacton sub-styles; 'Twisted cord/plain' = largely plain vessels with twisted cord below rim.

An unusual non-ceramic discovery within Structure 5 was a quantity of weathered granodiorite, or 'grus'. Over 70 pieces were recovered, weighing *c.* 22 kg, predominantly from pits cut into the tops of the erstwhile postholes of the timber structure and from a Beaker-period double grave. The rock probably arrived on site in the third quarter of the 3rd millennium cal BC. Petrological and geochemical analyses led by Rob Ixer and Richard Bevins point to a geological source around Threestoneburn, on the eastern edge of the Cheviot massif, Northumberland, 450 km north of Avebury. In its weathered and rounded state, there is a likelihood the granodiorite came not from its geological source but was collected from deposits of glacial till on the east coast of England, the coastal zone around Bridlington/Flamborough Head perhaps affording the best match based on size and weathering of the blocks. No similar occurrences of 'grus' are known from other Wessex sites and the specific association with Structure 5 at West Kennet is striking. Without a 'trail' of granodiorite across Late Neolithic sites from source to the Avebury region, direct transportation rather than down-the-line exchange offers the most parsimonious explanation for the mechanisms of movement and, with it, proxy evidence of human travel between these areas.

Other proxy evidence of long-distance human movement linked to extended gatherings connected to construction and feasting events derives from isotopic signatures in cattle and pig bone, which show wide catchments for the animals consumed at the site, including source locations on Palaeozoic geology in England and Wales (Evans *et al.* 2019; Madgwick *et al.* 2019). Isotopic analyses are much less able to detect movement from regions of similar chalk or Mesozoic geologies to the east and north-east of southern Britain, yet it is to the till deposits of the east coast that the finds of granodiorite point. Other lithic finds from the palisades reinforce these connections. Of especial note is an exceptionally large fan-shaped flint core (16 kg) of Late Neolithic date recovered by Wessex Archaeology during surface collection across the central part of the complex in 2009 (Harding and Lord 2017). It belongs to a small group of expertly worked massive cores from locations in the Breckland region of East Anglia, *c.* 220 km east-north-east, Grime's Graves being one possible source. Harding and Lord (2017, 60) suggest that the exceptional quality of the core marks it out as an object of ceremonial function, perhaps intended to be displayed, rather than used as a core *per se*, though flakes from similar cores were found during excavations in 2019 and 2021, strongly suggesting the presence of additional examples which were reduced.

Among the range of flint implements from the 1987–1992 excavations at the palisades are two ripple-flaked oblique arrowheads (Whittle 1997, 92) (Fig. 10.4). The form has an overall distribution extending from Scotland to Wessex, with a particular concentration in East Yorkshire and north Lincolnshire (Manby 1974, 84–6). Regionally, the type is represented at Durrington Walls (Wainwright and Longworth 1971, fig. 74), Woodhenge (Cunnington 1929), Marden (Bishop *et al.* 2011) and near Silbury Hill and Avebury Down. It has been suggested that the highly invasive 'ripple' pressure flaking on this form was perhaps achieved using copper awls (Ben Chan, pers. comm.; Whittaker 1994, 175). While the majority of Wessex examples are likely to have been of local manufacture, those recovered from the West Kennet palisades stand out as possible 'imports'; their broad, as opposed to narrow, form has an exact match with examples from the Bridlington region, including the artefact-rich lithic scatter at North Dale (Evans 1897, fig. 336; Manby 1974, fig. 34; Durden 1995) (Fig. 10.4), while the creamy-grey flint on which they are made (and which is not a product of patination) is best matched by 'northern' sources (Jim Rylatt, pers. comm.). Ethnographic

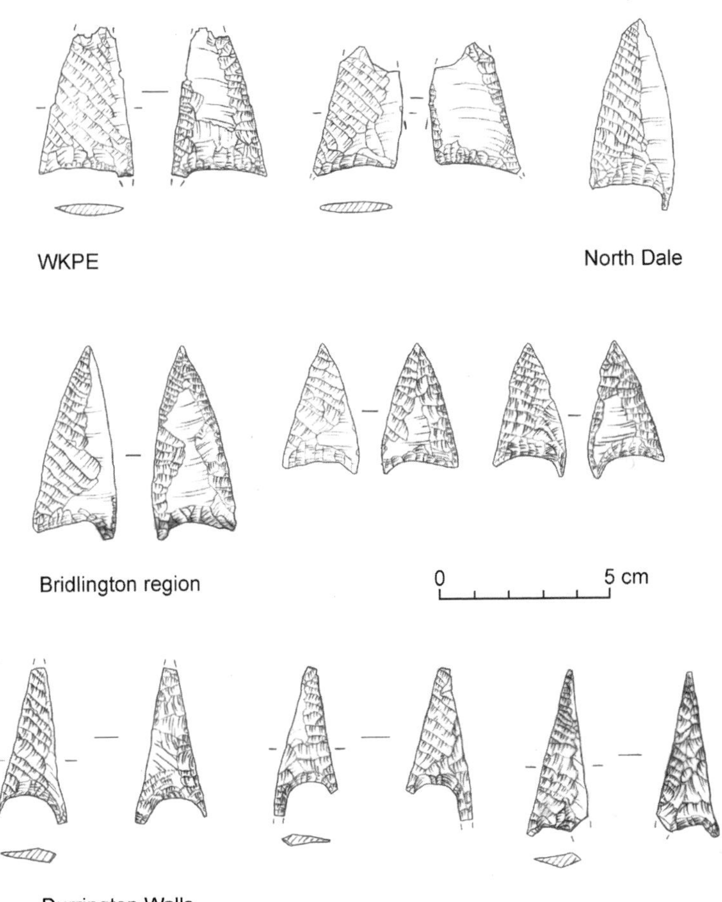

Figure 10.4. Ripple-flaked oblique arrowheads from WKPE (redrawn from AKM), North Dale (after Evans 1897, fig. 336), North Dale and Wilsthorpe (after Manby 1974, fig. 34), and Durrington Walls (after Wainwright and Longworth 1971, fig. 74). Note the broad form and diminutive tangs of the northern examples, and the markedly concave bases of the Durrington arrowheads.

instance recurrently highlights the personalised and inalienable character of arrows and arrow-making within 'traditional' societies (e.g. Blackwood 1950; González-Ruibal *et al.* 2011), and it would follow that rather than operating as exchange items, and if genuinely of northern manufacture, the WKPE ripple-flaked obliques provide further proxy evidence for human movement between north-eastern England and the Avebury region.

The form of the arrowheads from the earlier excavations at WKPE had drawn the authors' attention to Yorkshire even before the discovery and later identification of granodiorite from the 2019 excavations, and a striking similarity was noted between Grooved Ware published by Manby (1974) and some vessels from WKPE published by Hamilton (1997). Three vessels from WKPE are of particular interest here (Fig. 10.3, 7–9). Vessels such as that shown in Figure 10.3, 7, with limited horizontal cord-impressed decoration on an otherwise plain body, are not common anywhere in the Grooved Ware tradition but are represented west of Bridlington, particularly at Carnaby Top and North Carnaby Temple Fields (Fig. 10.3, 10) (Manby 1974). At both the East Yorkshire sites and at WKPE there are very rare rectilinear motifs, at Carnaby Top Site 20 executed in a 'faint comb impressed pattern' (Fig. 10.3, 11; Manby 1974, 35, fig. 11, 6) and at WKPE in very fine twisted cord impressions (Fig. 10.3, 8). In addition, at WKPE very fine whipped cord-impressed decoration occurs below the rim of a vessel discovered in a watching brief in the 1970s (by Faith Vatcher, first published by Hamilton 1997), as parallel horizontal lines (Fig. 10.3, 9), and whipped cord-impressed decoration appears in a similar position at Carnaby Top (Manby 1974, fig. 11, 3) (Fig. 10.3, 12). Multiple closely-spaced vertical cordons on plain vessels also emerge as a shared technique between WKPE and the Yorkshire sites (e.g. Hamilton 1997, fig. 68, 81a and Manby 1974, figs 11, 12, 18, 18) although this occurs more widely (Table 10.1).

A final, and intriguing, observation concerns two sherds from Ducks Meadow, Marlborough, 8 km east of WKPE, which were found in a possible post-setting (Harrison 2001, 220). Both are small rim sherds, one with twisted cord-impressed decoration below the rim and similar to a rim from WKPE (Timby 2001, vessel 1; Hamilton 1997, fig. 61, 17) and the other, a small plain rim of a form which would not be out of place at either WKPE or the Yorkshire sites. The latter sherd contained at least one fragment of decomposing granite (Timby 2001); it is worth noting that decomposing granite would not be distinguishable from decomposing granodiorite in such small fragments without petrological analysis.

THE INTRIGUING CASE OF COMB-IMPRESSED DECORATION

Another type of distinctive decoration which occurs at both Durrington Walls and Lawford (and elsewhere), and which raises wider questions, is comb-impressed decoration. This was noted by both Isobel Smith at Lawford and Ian Longworth at Durrington Walls, and at both sites there were variations within this type (e.g. Wainwright and Longworth 1971, 69–70; Smith 1985, 170). At Lawford these included two sherds which Smith noted as having impressions with clear separation between the teeth (Smith 1985, P34, with an applied rib, and P38; here Fig. 10.3, 15 and 14 respectively). P34, with its Durrington Walls-style cordon-defined panel, is highly unusual and is paralleled in the SRP assemblage (Fig. 10.3, 17). The incidence of comb, therefore, adds more evidence to the case for connection between Essex and south Wiltshire, a connection which other occurrences may also support, including a comb-impressed Grooved Ware sherd from Northbrooks, Harlow, Essex (Fig. 10.3, 16).

There may also be a chronological dimension identifiable in relation to some of these traits, including comb impression. Where comb occurs on Grooved Ware of identifiable sub-style, this is the Durrington Walls sub-style; other occurrences are isolated, but the comb-impressed sherds at the type-site are dated to late in the tradition (Table 10.2). Of the rare types of decoration discussed here, however, whipped cord impression is one which certainly occurs, rarely, in earlier material. Manby has pointed out for Hayton, Yorkshire, that whipped-cord 'maggots' in an extremely fine cord occur on a typically Woodlands-style vessel (Manby 2010, 41, fig. 5, GW3). Manby also points out their occurrence at Hunstanton, Norfolk (Cleal 1993, 42, fig. 39, P6), and similarly at Barholm,

Lincolnshire (Simpson 1993, fig. 11, P34). At Barholm the vessel is clearly Woodlands sub-style, at Hunstanton Woodlands/Clacton. By contrast, there are no occurrences of Beaker-type comb occurring on Woodlands or Clacton sub-style vessels known to the authors, nor any occurrences that are well dated, by association with radiocarbon dates, to earlier Grooved Ware contexts.[1] An unavoidable observation is that while there is not an identifiable history to Beaker-type comb impression on early British ceramics, whipped cord has very a long history of widespread use in the Middle Neolithic, extending over perhaps half a millennium in the Peterborough tradition; this would seem to support the inference that comb impression, and particularly, but not exclusively, Beaker-type comb, appeared because Grooved Ware users came into contact with Beaker vessels. Because of this, it seems relevant to examine the degree of potential overlap between Grooved Ware and Beaker use, and relevant narratives and dates are given in Table 10.2.

DISCUSSION

Grooved Ware connections

Through a consideration of distinctive Grooved Ware decorative traits, we have sought to highlight long-distance connections within southern, central and eastern Britain as well as further afield during the second and third quarters of the 3rd millennium cal BC. Such connections are further affirmed by the shared occurrence of other forms of material culture and the occasional movement of materials (notably the granodiorite recovered from the WKPE).

That a sustained degree of connectedness existed among communities using Grooved Ware is well established, being implicit in Piggott's 1954 'Rinyo-Clacton Culture' label (Piggott 1954, 321–46). House styles, decorative motifs and monumental architecture – henges, four-post timber structures, timber and stone circles, palisades and monumental mounds – are among other shared traits whose form is sufficiently idiosyncratic to indicate the direct transmission of ideas and practices within a 'Grooved Ware world' (Bradley 2019, 115–43). Important proxy evidence comes from isotopic analyses of mid-3rd millennium cal BC faunal assemblages excavated from ceremonial centres such as Durrington Walls and the WKPE (Craig *et al.* 2015; Evans *et al.* 2019; Madgwick *et al.* 2019). Questions remain, however, about the frequency, character and context of long-distance interactions. These have been modelled as fluid and intermittently responsive to larger-scale events (e.g. resource gathering around the building of larger monuments), sustained within a framework of shared practices and material performances that constituted an 'imagined community' (Thomas 2010, after Anderson 1983). In other scenarios, sporadic connections, sometimes with long-reaching consequences, are posited through elite travel and exchange (e.g. Sheridan's model of Irish–British connections, a kind of peer polity interaction model: 2004, 16–17), and through patterns of pilgrimage that took in major ceremonial complexes such as the Thornborough henges, Yorkshire (e.g. Harding 2013).

The observations presented here originate from work on two Wiltshire sites, but they contribute more generally to these debates on long-distance contacts in two ways. First, they fill in some of the 'gaps' left by combined strontium and oxygen isotopic analyses,

Table 10.2. Selected radiocarbon dates for the Avebury and Stonehenge areas and Grime's Graves

Description	*Range (italics indicate modelled, as given in the source)*	*Source*
	Avebury area	
'Grooved Ware occupation at West Kennet began'	'*2575–2405 cal BC (95% probability)* … probably in *2520–2440 cal BC (68% probability)*'	Bayliss *et al.* 2017, 263 & fig. 17.6
'The [WKPE Grooved Ware] occupation ended in'	'*2115–1865 cal BC (95% probability)* … probably in *2100–2080 cal BC (5% probability)* or *2015–1905 cal BC (63% probability)*'	Bayliss *et al.* 2017, 263 & fig. 17.6
'[*Sk*] *177* [*Beaker People Project* ref. no.] West Kennet Avenue (grave by stone 25b, smaller mandible fragment of adolescent)'	SUERC-26158 3855±30 BP *Posterior Density Estimate (95% confidence; cal BC) 2370–2200*	Jay *et al.* 2019, table 2.4b, 71
'[*Sk*] *307* [The] Sanctuary, West Overton'	SUERC-26186 3875±30 BP *Posterior Density Estimate (95% confidence; cal BC) 2390–2270 (81%)* or *2260–2205 (14%)*	Jay *et al.* 2019, table 2.4b, 71
Silbury Hill, Model B (preferred by authors) 'completion of Lower Organic Mound/Mini-mound'	'*2460–2395 cal BC (95% probability: Lower Organic Mound_constructed* … [fig. ref. omitted] or *2450–2410 cal BC (68% probability)*'	Marshall *et al.* 2013, 104
Silbury Hill, Model B 'completion of mound'	'estimated to have taken place in *2335–2270 cal BC 95% probability:end Silbury Hill* [fig. ref. omitted] and probably *2335–2285 cal BC (68% probability)*'	Marshall *et al.* 2013, 104
	Stonehenge area	
'Stonehenge, Wiltshire burial 4028' Beaker period burial in ditch with barbed-and-tanged arrowheads; five dates combined.	'Calibrated date BC (95%) confidence)' 'combined 2440–2140'	Jay *et al.* 2011, 179, table 30
Durrington Walls Grooved Ware settlement (SRP)	'the settlement began in the period: 2525–2470 cal BC'	Parker Pearson 2012, 110
Durrington Walls end of Grooved Ware settlement (SRP)	'ended in 2480–2440 cal BC'	Parker Pearson 2012, 110
Durrington Walls henge ditch and bank constructed	'the ditch around the henge, with its four openings, was dug out sometime in the years 2480–2460 BC'	Parker Pearson 2012, 112
A303/Wilsford G1, Wiltshire, grave 1502 Wessex/Middle Rhine Beaker	Calibrated date BC (95% confidence). NZA-29534 3878±20 2465–2285	Barclay *et al.* 2011, table 30, 179

(Continued)

Table 10.2 (Continued)

Description	*Range (italics indicate modelled, as given in the source)*	*Source*
Amesbury Archer & Beaker Bowmen activity: 'the models show that the burials of the Boscombe Bowmen, the Amesbury Archer, and the "Companion" belong to an early phase of Beaker activity that starts between':	*'2480 and 2340 cal BC (at 68% probability)* (Amesbury Archer) and *2510 and 2300 cal BC (at 68% probability)* (Boscombe Bowmen)'	Barclay *et al.* 2011, 175
'NZA-32510 Cremation burial associated, with Late Neolithic pit/post alignment'	'Calibrated date BC (95% confidence 3934±30 BP 2560–2310'	Barclay *et al.* 2011, table 28, 172
	Grime's Graves	
Beginning of deep shafts Deep shaft working associated with 600 sherds of Grooved Ware (Healy *et al.* 2018, 291)	'start galleried shafts' *'Highest posterior density interval (95%) cal BC 2665–2605' & '(68%) cal BC 2650–2620'*	Healy *et al.* 2018, 287, table 1
End of deep shafts	*'end galleried shafts' 'Highest posterior density interval (95%) cal BC 2435–2360'* & *'(68%) cal BC 2420–2385'*	Healy *et al.* 2018, table 1
Beginning of pits in West Field. West Field working associated with 4 sherds of Grooved Ware, probably redeposited (Healy *et al.* 2018, 291–2)	*'start simple pits on West Field' 'Highest posterior density interval (95%) cal BC 2670–2500'* & *'(68%) 2615–2520'*	Healy *et al.* 2018, table 1
End of pits in West Field	*'end simple pits on West Field' 'Highest posterior density interval (95%) cal BC' '2185–1995'* & *'(68%) 2155–2050'*	Healy *et al.* 2018, table 1

which currently only reliably identify movements off older, and therefore western and northern, Palaeozoic geologies on to the chalk. Taking into account the distinctive features of the Durrington Walls and WKPE Grooved Ware described here, which are sufficiently striking to negate the likelihood of independent or convergent 'evolution', alongside the lithic record in the case of the WKPE, allows other networks to be identified that emphasise connections to the east and north-east, too, from southern East Anglia to the Yorkshire coast and perhaps beyond. Certain regions stand out, notably Essex and, in the context of the WKPE, that part of East Yorkshire which includes the Great Wold Valley and Flamborough Head. Direct movement may have occurred between these regions and Wessex. Alex Gibson has drawn attention to a striking series of similarities between the great mound and surrounding enclosure at Duggleby Howe and the Wessex sites discussed here. The Duggleby Howe enclosure is comparable in overall dimensions to the Avebury and Durrington Walls earthworks; there are parallels to be drawn in the staged construction of both Duggleby and the Avebury henge; while the construction of the enclosure, and probably also the massive mound enlargement at Duggleby, fall within the same third quarter of the 3rd millennium cal BC horizon as the creation of Silbury Hill (Gibson *et al.* 2011, 33–4). One can note, too, the setting of Duggleby Howe in proximity to the source of the Gypsey Race 'winterbourne', very much akin to that of Silbury and the source of the Kennet (Leary *et al.* 2013). The Gypsey Race is an even more erratic intermittent stream than those of the Wiltshire chalk and, as recently as the early 20th century, it was associated with considerable folklore, including being known as a 'woe water' ('Y.H.' 1912); a comment in the same article also seems pertinent: 'in these out-of-the-way wolds people are still to be found whom it is difficult to dissuade that the running of a stream fed by an intermittent spring is not in some way associated with the supernatural'.

The close similarity between the WKPE and Rudston Grooved Ware assemblages and the likely northern origin of the ripple-flaked oblique arrowheads from the WKPE reinforce a sense of very real and direct connection between the Avebury region and that of the Bridlington-Rudston-Great Wold Valley area.

Silbury may be intimately linked to the massive enlargement of Duggleby Howe, but as other research by Alex Gibson has highlighted, the WKPE find a 'remarkable comparison' with the two palisade enclosures at Hindwell, on the border between Powys and Herefordshire (Jones and Gibson 2017, 74). The networks that drew in people to gather and engage in construction at Avebury and Stonehenge clearly possessed different centres of gravity, though were not too geographically exclusive, with connections and catchments being more like Venn diagrams, with overlap, as seen, for example, with the Durrington and WKPE links to Lawford. While, in the context of this paper, we are 'looking out' from Wessex, it would be wrong to give primacy to any one of these regions; we are certainly not dealing with a case of core–periphery relations. The contemporary significance of Duggleby Howe and those interred under its primary mound may have equalled or surpassed that of the Avebury henge, while the WKPE are dwarfed by the truly massive scale of the Hindwell complex.

Implicit are varied geographic connections sustained by movement, knowledge sharing, material practice and kinship. The Grooved Ware evidence outlined here itself speaks of direct contact across distant regions, copying, shared practices of making, and even perhaps common authorship of vessels widely separated in their place of deposition. It may well have been the same groups of people, coming together to form notional larger communities of builders, that constructed both Silbury Hill and the enlarged Duggleby Howe, and the WKPE and Hindwell complexes. The regularity of long-distance contact within more routine circumstances is hinted at in other, contemporary, contexts, notably the transportation of Yorkshire flint to sites in the Scottish Borders and Lowlands (Ballin 2011; McLaren 2022), on a scale that seems greater than would have resulted through episodic exchange (e.g. comprising *c.* 50% of the raw material for the Overhowden and Airhouse assemblages: Ballin 2011).

Matters of mobility and demography come into play in terms of their being variables that facilitated or constrained levels of long-distance interaction. An apparent move from mixed farming to pastoralism post-3400 cal BC within southern Britain at least (Stevens and Fuller 2012) is seemingly connected to greater levels of residential mobility, and a significant reduction in population levels (cf. Shennan 2018, 195–8; Armit and Reich 2021, 1471–2). The latter is registered too in much reduced artefact numbers in Middle and Late Neolithic contexts versus Early Neolithic contexts (e.g. East Anglian pit sites in Garrow 2006, tables 4.4, 5.4, 6.4). Changes of this kind could have created conditions in which sustained long-distance relations between Grooved Ware groups were both possible and necessary. With less densely settled landscapes came greater capacity for routine movement – fewer tenurial and boundary issues, for instance – and perhaps reduced potential for inter-personal conflict. The 'social glue' for these links might be found in shared lineage histories, marriage networks (and with this, the movement of people taking potting skills and traditions with them), exchanges, and of course regular movements and meetings. Clan systems and moieties provide other models in which values might be shared over much longer distances, facilitating travel and welcome even among groups without regular contact (Graeber and Wengrow 2021, 456–63).

Grooved Ware and Beakers

In the areas we have considered in both north and south Wiltshire there is early Beaker-associated activity. Table 10.2 summarises some of this activity and shows that people using the West Kennet palisade enclosures were sharing their familiar landscape with early Beaker users. This includes a sub-adult male who had spent time in an area with Palaeozoic geology buried beside one of the standing stones at The Sanctuary, and other individuals, including one associated with a radiocarbon date, buried beside the stones of the West Kennet Avenue (Table 10.2). The associated Beakers include a Cord-Zoned Maritime vessel, a type recognised as early, and vessels of forms more usual in the east and north. (Note, however, that the Beaker from The Sanctuary, classified by Clarke (Clarke 1970, 323, fig. 347) as Barbed Wire (BW), does not carry the 'barbed wire' decoration of Clarke's type. It is, nevertheless, of a form shared by both Clarke's BW and East Anglian types.) In addition, another grave on the West Kennet Avenue includes a vessel which Smith considered to show traits of both Grooved Ware and Beakers (Smith 1965, 229, 231, P352).

In southern Wiltshire there are radiocarbon dates associated with early Beakers which span the late 25th/early 24th century cal BC around Amesbury, 4.5 km south-east of Stonehenge, principally those for the Amesbury Archer and Boscombe Bowmen (Fitzpatrick 2011). In the volume discussing those individuals, the question of the overlap between the start of Beaker use and the end of Grooved Ware use is addressed, with the conclusion that 'any overlap between the final use of Grooved Ware and the first use of Beaker pottery was relatively short', with an illustration showing this as occurring most probably in the early 24th century cal BC (Barclay *et al.* 2011, fig. 62 and caption, 176). Subsequently The *Beaker People Project* modelled the first Beaker use in a funerary context in Britain at '*2460–2330 cal BC (95% confidence),* probably *2415–2345 cal BC (68% confidence)*' (Parker Pearson *et al.* 2019, 426). Dating of activity associated with Grooved Ware and with Beakers in these areas indicates that there is neither demonstrably 'clear water' between 'late' Grooved Ware and early Beakers in southern Britain, nor is there currently a well-defined overlap. It does seem, however, that the dates for late Grooved Ware and early Beakers are perilously close for there to be any confidence in the argument that there is no meaningful overlap. Here note should be taken of modelled date ranges from sites in eastern Scotland that show the latest Grooved Ware to be contemporary with the earliest Beakers (McLaren 2022, 65–6; cf. Copper *et al.* 2021, and Chapter 4, this volume). As early dates for Beakers are funerary-related, it might be assumed that the people buried had lived some years in Britain, except where there is good evidence to the contrary (which of course there is for some individuals, e.g. Parker Pearson *et al.* 2019). In many cases the ages of the people concerned extend the period of Beaker use back by some years from the burial date, periods in which transmission of potting practice might well occur. That such transmission occurred would imply close interaction between immigrant Beaker groups and local Late Neolithic populations, even if the genetic evidence does not show significant inter-marriage (Olalde *et al.* 2018), and so a degree of consciously maintained ethnic separation. It remains striking that the distribution of early Beaker presence as defined by dated burials is notably coincident with significant areas of late Grooved Ware settlement and gathering, including regions such as Wessex, East Yorkshire and Eastern Scotland (Bloxam and Parker Pearson 2022, fig. 2). Events at major monument centres could have provided attraction to these locations; and as Armit and Reich note, resident populations even in key regions were perhaps 'sufficiently small and/or sparsely distributed that large groups of [Beaker] incomers could be accommodated without substantial conflict over resources' (Armit and Reich 2021, 1471).

Interactions between these different communities were negotiated at a local scale, with early Beaker presence seemingly accommodated in the goings-on at major monuments (e.g. Cleal and Pollard 2012). As we have seen, within the Avebury area early Beaker burials occurred in the heart of the Late Neolithic monument complex, against stones on the West Kennet Avenue, at the Longstones and The Sanctuary (Cleal and Pollard 2012, 322–5), though Beaker pottery was not apparently part of the repertoire of feasting 'kit' at the WKPE (Whittle 1997; late Beaker was present in the fills of a large water cistern within Enclosure 1 excavated in 2019).

There is the issue of how movement into, and settlement within, what would have been unfamiliar landscapes (cf. Rockman and Steele 2003) was achieved by earliest Beaker groups and how knowledge of key locations of gathering and monument building (e.g. major monument complexes) was transmitted. For Beaker groups to relocate to such areas, often well inland, implies geographic knowledge which we believe was probably shared through 'Grooved Ware' networks and the support and acceptance of Late Neolithic populations. Perhaps telling here is the occasional blurring of 'authorship' of pots and practices, as we have highlighted. Rather than positing separation and tension between culturally Late Neolithic and Beaker groups, we suggest models of cooperation, engagement and knowledge sharing in the two or three centuries after 2500 cal BC.

ACKNOWLEDGEMENTS

This paper would have been impossible to write without the important and substantial work of the 1970s and 1980s, carried out by, in particular, Ian Longworth, Terry Manby and Isobel Smith, when the understanding of Grooved Ware was still in its early stages and which they did so much to develop. This paper also draws upon the work of Rob Ixer and Richard Bevins (on the WKPE granodiorite), the AHRC-funded *Living with Monuments* project team, and the AHRC-funded *Stonehenge Riverside Project* and *Feeding Stonehenge Project.* Thanks, too, are offered to Alex Gibson for his inspirational work on Duggleby Howe and the Hindwell-Walton complex, which has provided invaluable insight into the connections outlined here. The pottery figures were prepared by Abby George.

NOTE

1 There is a Grooved Ware vessel from Littleour, Perth and Kinross, with extensive comb-impressed decoration (Sheridan 1998, 62, illus. 49.1) which has been dated from organic residue from the pot to 2872–2631 cal BC (95.4% probability) (SUERC-77487, 4144±24 BP; Copper et al. 2021, supplementary material 5–6, 45–6, table S1, illus. S1). Organic residues on this and other vessels from the same homogeneous fill of this single pit were also dated and the results modelled. The start of Grooved Ware use is modelled as 2970–2610 cal BC (95% probability) and its end as 2470–2295 cal BC (95% probability) (Copper et al. 2021, supplementary material 5–6, 45–6, table S1, illus. 1). These dates include two from organic residue on a single pot which seem inconsistent (table S1, illus. S1, pot 6, OxA-8993: 3845±75 BP and SUERC-77493: 4079±23 BP). The Littleour vessel is an interesting occurrence of comb impression on Grooved Ware and authors are grateful to Michael Copper and Alison Sheridan for drawing this vessel to their attention.

REFERENCES

Anderson, B. 1983. *Imagined communities: reflections on the origin and spread of nationalism.* London: Verso.

Armit, I. and Reich, D. 2021. The return of the Beaker folk? Rethinking migration and population change in British prehistory. *Antiquity* 95, 1464–77.

Ballin, T.B. 2011. *Overhowden and Airhouse, Scottish Borders: characterization and interpretation of two spectacular lithic assemblages from sites near the Overhowden henge.* Oxford: British Archaeological Report 539.

Barclay, A. 2013. Late Neolithic pottery from Area 16. In T. Allen, A. Barclay, A.M. Cromarty, H. Anderson-Whymark, A. Parker, M. Robinson and G. Jones, *Opening the wood, making the land. The archaeology of the Middle Thames landscape: the Eton College Rowing Course Project and the Maidenhead, Windsor and Eton Flood Alleviation Scheme. Volume 1: Mesolithic to early Bronze Age*, 398–401. Oxford: Oxford Archaeology.

Barclay, A. and Edwards, E. 2016. Chapters 10 and 12 Pottery. In G. Hey, C. Bell, C. Dennis and M. Robinson, *Yarnton: Neolithic and Bronze Age settlement and landscape,* 354–5, 357–60, 399–402, 476–7, 504–10, 513–15. Oxford: Oxford Archaeology.

Barclay, A. and Marshall, P. with Higham, T.F.G. 2011. Chronology and the radiocarbon dating programme. In A. Fitzpatrick 2011, 167–84.

Bayliss, A., Cartwright, C., Cook, G., Griffiths, S., Madgwick, R., Marshall, P. and Reimer, P. 2017. Rings of fire and Grooved Ware settlement at West Kennet, Wiltshire. In P. Bickle, V. Cummings, D. Hofmann and J. Pollard (eds), *The Neolithic of Europe,* 249–78. Oxford: Oxbow Books.

Birley, M. 2016. Pottery. In C. Evans, G. Appleby, S. Lucy. with J. Appleby and M. Brudenell, *Lives in land. Mucking excavations by Margaret and Tom Jones, 1965–1978*, 70–7. Oxford: Oxbow Books.

Bishop, B., Leary, J. and Robins, P. 2011. Introducing the 'Long Tailed Oblique' arrowhead: examples from Marden Henge, Wiltshire, and Santon Warren, Norfolk. *PAST* 68, 1–2.

Blackwood, B. 1950. *The technology of a modern Stone Age people in New Guinea.* Oxford: Pitt Rivers Museum.

Bloxam, A. and Parker Pearson, M. 2022. Funerary diversity and cultural continuity: the British Beaker phenomenon beyond the stereotype. *Proceedings of the Prehistoric Society* 88, 261–84.

Bradley, R. 2019. *The prehistory of Britain and Ireland* (2nd edition). Cambridge: Cambridge University Press.

Clarke, D.L. 1970. *Beaker pottery of Great Britain and Ireland.* Cambridge: University Press.

Cleal, R. 1991. Cranborne Chase – the earlier prehistoric pottery. In J. Barrett, R. Bradley and M. Hall (eds), *Papers on the prehistoric archaeology of Cranborne Chase,* 134–200. Oxford: Oxbow Books.

Cleal, R. 1993. Pottery and fired clay. In R. Bradley, P. Chowne, R.M.J. Cleal, F. Healy and I. Kinnes, *Excavations on Redgate Hill, Hunstanton, Norfolk, and at Tattershall Thorpe, Lincolnshire,* 40–60. Norwich: East Anglian Archaeology Report 57.

Cleal, R. 2007. Pottery of Wyke Down 2 henge, and The pottery [structures and associated features]. In C. French, H. Lewis, M.J. Allen, M. Green, R. Scaife and J. Gardiner, *Prehistoric landscape development and human impact in the upper Allen valley, Cranborne Chase, Dorset,* 313–19, 321–32. Cambridge: McDonald Institute.

Cleal, R. and Pollard, J. 2012. The revenge of the native: monuments, material culture, burial and other practices in the third quarter of the 3rd millennium BC in Wessex. In M.J. Allen, J. Gardiner and A. Sheridan (eds), *Is there a British Chalcolithic? People, place and polity in the late 3rd millennium BC,* 317–32. Oxford: Prehistoric Society Research Papers 4.

Cleal, R. with Raymond, F. 1990. Prehistoric ceramics from surface collection. In J. Richards, *The Stonehenge Environs Project*, 30–9. London: English Heritage.

Copper, M., Hamilton, D. and Gibson, A. 2021. Tracing the lines: Scottish Grooved Ware trajectories beyond Orkney. *Proceedings of the Society of Antiquaries of Scotland* 150, 81–117.

Craig, O.E., Shillito, L-M., Albarella, U., Viner-Daniels, S., Chan, B., Cleal, R. *et al.* 2015. Feeding Stonehenge: cuisine and consumption at the Late Neolithic site of Durrington Walls. *Antiquity* 89, 1096–1109.

Cunnington, M.E. 1929. *Woodhenge.* Devizes: Simpson.

Cunnington, M.E. 1930. The 'Sanctuary' on Overton Hill, near Avebury. *Wiltshire Archaeological and Natural History Magazine* 45, 300–55.

Durden, T. 1995. The production of specialised flintwork in the later Neolithic: a case study from the Yorkshire Wolds. *Proceedings of the Prehistoric Society* 61, 409–32.

Evans, C. with Tabor, J. and Vander Linden, M. 2016. *Twice-crossed river. Prehistoric and palaeoenvironmental investigations at Barleycroft Farm/Over, Cambridgeshire.* Cambridge: McDonald Institute for Archaeological Research.

Evans, J.A., Parker Pearson, M., Madgwick, R., Sloane, H. and Albarella, U. 2019. Strontium and oxygen isotope evidence for the origin and movement of cattle at Late Neolithic Durrington Walls, UK. *Archaeological and Anthropological Sciences* 11, 5181–97.

Evans, J. 1897. *The ancient stone implements, weapons and ornaments of Great Britain* (2nd edition). London: Longman.

Fitzpatrick, A. 2011. *The Amesbury Archer and the Boscombe Bowmen.* Salisbury: Wessex Archaeology Report 27.

Garrow, D. 2006. *Pits, settlement and deposition during the Neolithic and Early Bronze Age in East Anglia.* Oxford: British Archaeological Report 414.

Gibson, A. 1999. *The Walton Basin Project: excavation and survey in a prehistoric landscape 1993–7.* York: Council for British Archaeology Research Report 118.

Gibson, A., Allen, M., Bradley, P., Carruthers, W., Challinor, D., French, C. *et al.* 2011. Report on the excavation at the Duggleby Howe causewayed enclosure, North Yorkshire, May–July 2009. *Archaeological Journal* 168, 1–63.

González-Ruibal, A., Hernando, A. and Politis, G. 2011. Ontology of the self and material culture: arrow-making among the Awá hunter-gatherers (Brazil). *Journal of Anthropological Archaeology* 30(1), 1–16.

Graeber, D. and Wengrow, D. 2021. *The dawn of everything: a new history of humanity.* London: Allen Lane.

Guido, M. and Smith, I.F. 1981. Figsbury Rings: a reconsideration of the inner enclosure. *Wiltshire Archaeological and Natural History Magazine* 76, 21–6.

Hamilton, M.A. 1997. Pottery. In A. Whittle 1997, 93–117.

Harding, J. 2013. *Cult, religion and pilgrimage: archaeological investigations at the Neolithic and Bronze Age monument complex of Thornborough, North Yorkshire.* York: Council for British Archaeology Research Report 170.

Harding, P. and Lord, J. 2017. Thoughts on massive flint cores from Wiltshire and East Anglia, the movement of flint and its role in Late Neolithic Britain. *Antiquaries Journal* 97, 49–63.

Harrison, E. 2001. Neolithic activity in Ducks Meadow, Marlborough. *Wiltshire Archaeological and Natural History Magazine* 94, 218–23.

Healy, F., Marshall, P., Cook, G., Bronk Ramsey, C., Van der Plicht, J. and Dunbar, E. 2018. When and why? The chronology and context of flint mining at Grime's Graves, Norfolk, England. *Proceedings of the Prehistoric Society* 84, 277–301.

Jay, M., Richards, M.P. and Marshall, P. 2019. Radiocarbon dates and their Bayesian modelling. In M. Parker Pearson *et al.* 2019, 43–80.

Jones, N.W. and Gibson, A.M. 2017. Neolithic palisaded enclosures of Radnorshire's Walton Basin. *Archaeologia Cambrensis* 166, 33–88.

Leary, J., Field, D. and Campbell, G. (eds) 2013. *Silbury Hill: the largest prehistoric mound in Europe.* Swindon: English Heritage.

Longworth, I.H. 1971. The pottery. In G.J. Wainwright with J.G. Evans and I.H. Longworth, The excavation of a Late Neolithic enclosure at Marden, Wiltshire. *Antiquaries Journal* 51, 197–215.

Longworth, I.H. 1979. The Neolithic and Bronze Age pottery. In G.J. Wainwright, *Mount Pleasant, Dorset 1970–1971,* 75–124. London: Society of Antiquaries.

Longworth, I.H. 1981. Neolithic and Bronze Age Pottery. In R.J. Mercer, *Grimes Graves, Norfolk: excavations 1971–72. Volume 1,* 39–59. London: Her Majesty's Stationery Office.

Longworth, I.H., Ellison, A. and Rigby, V. 1988. *Excavations at Grimes Graves, Norfolk, 1972–1976.* London: British Museum Publications.

McLaren, D. 2022. Expanding current understanding of the function, style and chronology of Grooved Ware from the A9 Dualling: Luncarty to Pass of Birnam. *Proceedings of the Society of Antiquaries of Scotland* 151, 31–73.

Madgwick, R., Lamb, A., Sloane, H., Nederbraat, A., Albarella, U., Parker Pearson, M. and Evans, J. 2019. Multi-isotope analysis reveals that feasts in the Stonehenge environs and across Wessex drew people and animals from throughout Britain. *Science Advances* 5(3). eaau6078. doi: 10.1126/sciadv.aau6078.

Manby, T.G. 1974. *Grooved Ware Sites in Yorkshire and the north of England.* Oxford: British Archaeological Report 9.

Manby, T.G. 2010. The Grooved Ware pottery. In P. Halkon, T.G. Manby, M. Millett and H. Woodhouse, Neolithic settlement evidence from Hayton, East Yorks. *Yorkshire Archaeological Journal* 82, 36–44.

Marshall, P.D., Bayliss, A., Leary, J., Campbell, G., Worley, F., Bronk Ramsey, C. and Cook, G. 2013. The Silbury chronology. In J. Leary *et al.* (eds) 2013, 97–116.

Matthews, C.L. 1976. *Occupation sites on a Chiltern ridge.* Oxford: British Archaeological Report 29.

Olalde, I., Brace, S., Allentoft, M.E., Armit, I., Kristiansen, K., Rohland, N. *et al.* 2018. The Beaker phenomenon and the genomic transformation of northwest Europe. *Nature* 555, 190–6.

Parker Pearson, M. 2012. *Stonehenge.* London: Simon and Schuster.

Parker Pearson, M., Sheridan, J.A., Jay, M., Chamberlain, A., Richards, M.P. and Evans, J. (eds) 2019. *The Beaker people: isotopes, mobility and diet in prehistoric Britain.* Oxford: Prehistoric Society Research Papers 7.

Piggott, S. 1954. *Neolithic cultures of the British Isles.* Cambridge: Cambridge University Press.

Pryor, F. 1978. *Excavation at Fengate, Peterborough, England: the second report.* Toronto: Royal Ontario Museum.

Rockman, M. and Steele, J. (eds) 2003. *The colonization of unfamiliar landscapes: the archaeology of adaptation.* London: Routledge.

Shennan, S.J. 2018. *The first farmers of Europe: an evolutionary perspective.* Cambridge: Cambridge University Press.

Shennan, S.J., Healy, F. and Smith, I.F. 1985. The excavation of a ring-ditch at Tye Field, Lawford, Essex. *Archaeological Journal* 142, 150–215.

Sheridan, J.A. 1998. The pottery from Littleour. In G. Barclay and G. Maxwell, *The Cleaven Dyke and Littleour: monuments in the Neolithic of Tayside,* 62–8. Edinburgh: Society of Antiquaries of Scotland.

Sheridan, J.A. 2004. Going round in circles? Understanding the Irish Grooved Ware 'complex' in its wider context. In H. Roche, E. Grogan, J. Bradley, J. Coles and B. Raftery (eds), *From megaliths to metals: essays in honour of George Eogan,* 26–37. Oxford: Oxbow Books.

Simpson, W.G. 1993. The Excavation of a Late Neolithic settlement site at Barholm, Lincolnshire. In W.G. Simpson, D.A. Gurney, J. Neve and F.M.M. Pryor, *The Fenland Project No. 7. Excavations in Peterborough and the Lower Welland Valley 1960–1969,* 7–28. Peterborough: East Anglian Archaeology 61.

Smith, I.F. 1965. *Windmill Hill and Avebury. Excavations by Alexander Keiller 1925–1939.* Oxford: Clarendon Press.

Smith, I.F. 1985. The pottery. In S. Shennan *et al.* 1985, 165–77.

Stevens, C. and Fuller, D. 2012. Did Neolithic farming fail? The case for a Bronze Age agricultural revolution in the British Isles. *Antiquity* 86, 707–22.

Stone, J.F.S., Piggott, S. and Booth, A. St J. 1954. Durrington Walls, Wiltshire: recent excavations at a ceremonial site of the early second millennium B.C. *Archaeological Journal* 34, 155–77.

Thomas, J. 2010. The return of the Rinyo-Clacton folk? The cultural significance of the Grooved Ware Complex in Later Neolithic Britain. *Cambridge Archaeological Journal* 20(1), 1–15.

Timby, J. 2001. The finds. In E. Harrison 2001, 221–2.

Wainwright, G.J. 1971. The excavation of prehistoric and Romano-British settlements near Durrington Walls, Wiltshire. *Wiltshire Archaeological and Natural History Magazine* 66, 76–128.

Wainwright, G.J. and Longworth, I.H. 1971. *Durrington Walls: excavations 1966–1968.* London: Society of Antiquaries.

Whittaker, J.C. 1994. *Flintknapping: making and understanding stone tools.* Austin: University of Texas Press.

Whittle, A. 1997. *Sacred mound, holy rings. Silbury Hill and the West Kennet palisade enclosures: a later Neolithic complex in north Wiltshire.* Oxford: Oxbow Books.

'Y.H.' 1912. A mysterious East Riding stream. Woe waters of the Wold. In Mrs Gutch, *Examples of printed folklore concerning the East Riding of Yorkshire,* 11–12. London: The Folklore Society.

Chapter 11

Between Essex and Wessex: a review of Grooved Ware from the Upper and Middle Thames Valley

Alistair J. Barclay

It is nearly 25 years since the last comprehensive review of Grooved Ware (Cleal and MacSween 1999), one of a series of reviews that have been undertaken almost every generation since Stuart Piggott's first attempt in the 1930s (Piggott 1936). Between the '30s and the '90s, Piggott (1954) reaffirmed the connections between pottery from the Essex coast (the Thames estuary) and Orkney that he had noted in 1936 and, in the late 1960s, the recovery of several key assemblages of Durrington Walls sub-style Grooved Ware by Wainwright and Longworth during their excavations of major Wessex henges led to Longworth's re-analysis of the Grooved Ware sub-styles (Wainwright and Longworth 1971). However, over recent years, the four defined British sub-styles – leaving aside the Grooved Ware found in Ireland – have been brought into question as being rather simplistic and concealing a complex picture of ceramic development over 600 years or longer (Cleal 1999). Even the label 'Grooved Ware' seems a misnomer at times, given the occurrence of plain vessels and assemblages with the wide variety of impressed decoration that occurs. Viewed from southern England, pottery undergoes a rapid transformation shortly after 3000 cal BC with the introduction of a new Orcadian-derived style of flat-based pottery in which near-identical details and copies occur. This process suggests a period of dynamic, expansive and rapid cultural transformation throughout much of Britain and Ireland (Bradley 2007).

Since the 1990s, and the publication of *Grooved Ware in Britain and Ireland* (Cleal and MacSween 1999), the opportunities provided not only by commercial archaeology, but also by various research projects, have greatly enhanced our knowledge, the distribution of sites and our dataset overall (Fig. 11.1). One significant factor in the last 24 years has been a more critically applied radiocarbon methodology to create improved datelists and the use of Bayesian modelling to refine results and measure temporality better (Fig. 11.2). This has revealed the inter-regional spread of Grooved Ware pottery along with its wider and long-distance connections and trajectories. It is long accepted that Grooved Ware has its beginnings in Orkney in the closing centuries of the 4th millennium cal BC, but less certain is the tempo of any cultural drift: the *how, why, where* and *when.* New radiocarbon dates hint that some of the uptake could have been quite rapid, at least at the beginning of this cultural process, and certainly by the 30th century cal BC. Less well understood are the beginnings of what is currently labelled as the Durrington Walls sub-style, although earlier origins in northern Britain are likely but not proven (see Copper *et al.* 2021, 108).

The demise of Grooved Ware within the Thames Valley is not currently clear and is obscured by the need to re-evaluate critically an old and imprecise radiocarbon dataset.

The Thames Valley in the early 3rd millennium is a region that connects the Neolithic of the Wessex Chalklands with that of Britain's south-east coast. It is one of contrasting monumental histories despite a similar material culture. Unlike the complexity of Wessex Grooved Ware sites, most Thames Valley sites consist of pit clusters and pit scatters; monuments directly associated with pottery rarely feature.

Despite the issues noted above, the Grooved Ware sub-styles are retained here as a convenient shorthand. Throughout the regions that make up the Thames Valley, their spatial distribution is far from uniform. Of the three recognised sub-styles in southern England, two (Clacton and Woodlands) can be closely matched with vessels in Orkney and mainland Scotland as well as other areas of Britain. The Clacton and Woodlands sub-styles have relatively few findspots in the Upper and Middle Thames, whilst the Clacton sub-style is more abundantly represented around the Thames estuary and the coastal areas of East Anglia and Kent (as discussed in Chapter 13). Certain sites stand out, such as the henge-circle at Tye Field, Lawford, Essex, with its large Durrington Walls sub-style assemblage (Shennan *et al.* 1985). This assemblage, along with others from the Thames Valley, has elements that can all be matched further west, although one notable feature

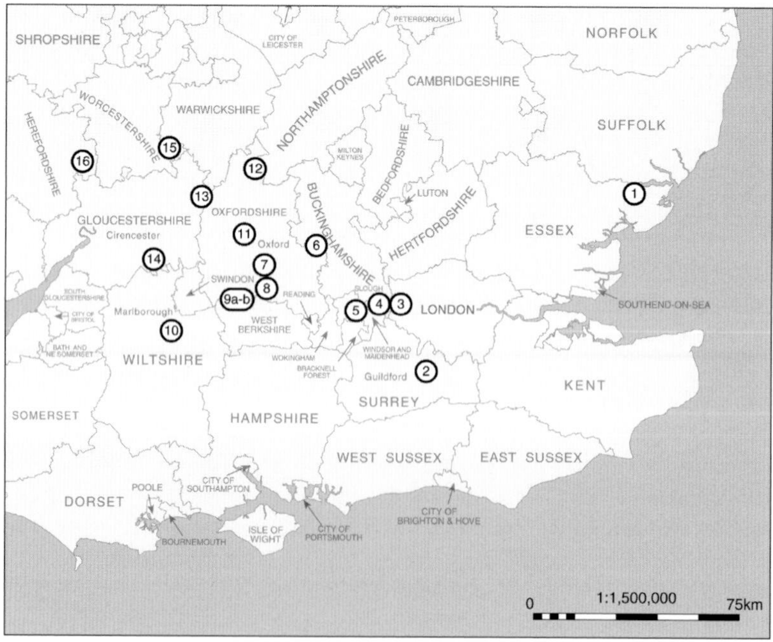

Figure 11.1. Selected sites mentioned in the text. 1. Tye Farm: 2. Betchworth; 3. Heathrow and Imperial College Sports Ground; 4. Kingsmead Quarry, Horton; 5. Eton Rowing Course; 6. Church Farm, Thame; 7. Barrow Hills, Radley; 8. Halls Close, Drayton Cursus and Corporation Farm; 9a. Slade Farm, Wallingford; 9b. Childrey Warren; 10. Avebury; 11. Yarnton; 12. Southam Road, Banbury; 13. Bourton-on-the-Water; 14. Siddington Road, Cirencester; 15. Arrow Valley; 16. Clifton Quarry.

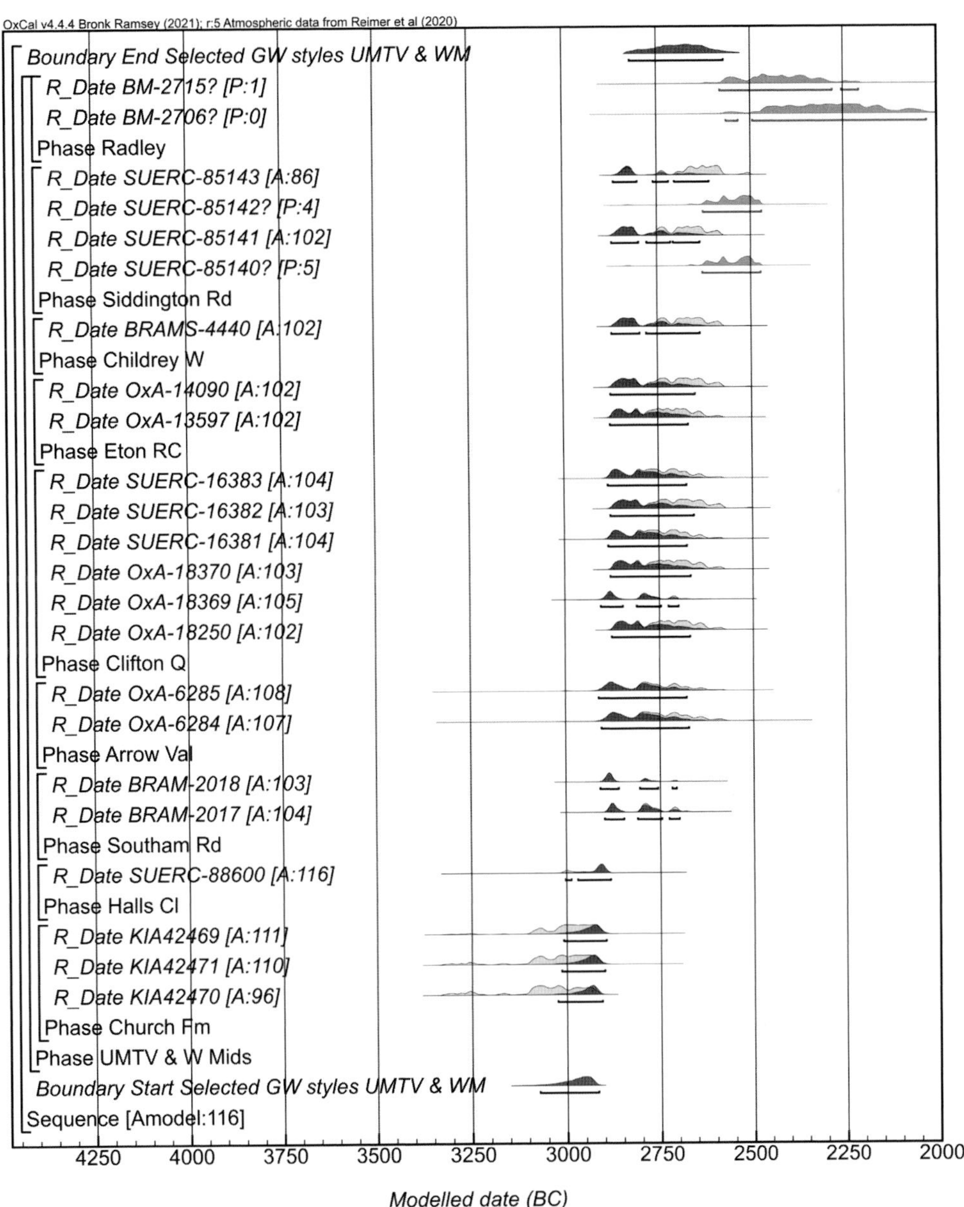

Figure 11.2. Selected radiocarbon dates from various Grooved Ware pit sites in the Upper and Middle Thames and the adjacent area of the West Midlands.

could be a greater use of cord and other impressions; this could derive from, or hark back to, the Peterborough (Impressed) Wares that were still current during the initial spread of Grooved Ware. Whilst much is made of long-distance similarities in the various Grooved Ware sub-styles, there is also much variation within each sub-style and it is perhaps the more subtle differences that are worth highlighting here.

Currently less well understood is the temporality of the various strands or trajectories, although the application of critically focused Bayesian-based chronologies is beginning to produce more nuanced histories (Whittle 2018). Within the context of Grooved Ware, we now understand more of its origins within the settlement sites of Orkney (summarised in Whittle 2018, 97–8 and fig 4.6, and see Chapters 2, 3, 4 and 16 in this volume) and we have a glimpse of when and where it may have first appeared in southern England. The great henges and other related sites within Wessex experienced intense activity during the 26th century cal BC (Greaney *et al.* 2020) and a decline in activity during the 25th century prior to the introduction of (initially ephemeral) Beaker-associated activity by 2400 cal BC. The possible relationship between the final Grooved Ware-using Neolithic and the appearance of Beaker activity is touched on below within the context of the Thames Valley.

Since the 1990s (Barclay 1999), in both the Upper and Middle Thames regions, new discoveries are filling in some areas where little research or excavation had previously taken place (e.g. North Oxfordshire, the Thame Valley and the Vale of the White Horse; Bourton-on-the-Water/Cotswolds). Mineral extraction on the gravel terraces and infrastructural projects, especially in more rural areas, continue to add significant new evidence – such as that from the Childrey Warren pipeline in the Vale of the White Horse (Guarino and Barclay 2023). However, there are also linear schemes and large-scale developments that have produced very little or no Late Neolithic evidence.

We know very little about the tempo of activity at pit sites. Some could have developed over many lifetimes with the persistent use of a place or location, whilst others could simply reflect short bursts of activity. There is both intensity and an indifference, as well as pattern and randomness, in the practices associated with Late Neolithic pit digging, from the deliberate selection and careful placement of large fragments of unusually decorated pottery to the more casual discard of a handful of sherds as well as the burying of mostly used and broken objects, and of similar and conjoining material in adjacent and, more rarely, between pit groups.

THE EMERGENCE OF GROOVED WARE: THE CLACTON AND WOODLANDS SUB-STYLES OR THE ORCADIAN-DERIVED POTTERY

The chronology put forward for southern Britain in my previous regional review (Barclay 1999) and by Garwood (1999) was based on a very limited number of radiocarbon dates, totalling just seven for the Upper Thames Region, and entirely produced by Harwell and the British Museum using beta counting methods prior to the introduction of Accelerator Mass Spectrometry (AMS). Targeting small samples (charred food residues on pots) and short-lived (charred) plant material, the latter has resulted in much smaller errors of less than 30 years (Fig. 11.2). As AMS dating was in its infancy in the early 1990s, projects such as Yarnton (discussed below) were not subjected to the routine intensive radiocarbon dating that would be considered *de rigueur* today (Gill Hey, pers. comm.).

While most of the sites discussed below have radiocarbon dates, individual features often have only single dates (Fig. 11.2). The better practice of obtaining multiple dates per feature to build in more statistical certainty remains an aspiration. (See sites mentioned below and Clifton Quarry in particular as an example.) A critical review of existing radiocarbon dates and a targeted programme of redating key Grooved Ware assemblages to a high standard (in the manner of the *The Times of Their Lives* project: Whittle 2018) is a future challenge.

In the 1990s, the Woodlands sub-style (Fig. 11.3) was seen as late and potentially developing out of an early Clacton sub-style (Barclay 1999; Garwood 1999). The important assemblage from Radley, Oxfordshire (Barclay and Halpin 1999), increasingly looks problematic. Rather than occurring late in the Grooved Ware sequence, this assemblage may actually turn out to be early. A date around the 30th and 29th centuries cal BC appears plausible based on various new dates (Fig. 11.2) but awaits testing by a programme of radiocarbon dating. This revised estimate would also offer a better fit for the spiral-decorated and lozenge-patterned vessels from pit 3196, given their similarity with other notable objects including the decorated Knowth macehead (Barclay 1999, 20 and illus. 2.7; Cleal 1999) and pottery with lattice and lozenge decoration from Pool, Orkney (MacSween *et al.* 2015, 306). A single date (SUERC-88600; 4314±29 BP; 3011–2887 cal BC at 95.4% confidence or, when modelled, *3001–2884 cal BC 95.4% probability* or *2923–2894 cal BC at 68.3% probability*) on pig bone from a Woodlands-associated pit deposit at Halls Close, Drayton, appears to support this (Reynish and Barclay forthcoming). This pit contained vessels with horizontal and oblique raised cordons (converging as a widely spaced lattice and either impressed or plain), knots and rim pellets. One unusual sherd had an applied cordon forming a curvilinear motif, possibly but not certainly part of a double spiral similar to the Radley example but here executed in relief. Other recent sites with Woodlands sub-style pottery include a small number of pits from Siddington Road, Cirencester (McSloy forthcoming), a site that has also produced a shale bead (cf. Yarnton below).

Beyond the Upper Thames Valley in the counties of Worcestershire and Warwickshire are two notable Grooved Ware sites that lend support to an earlier chronology for these sub-styles. Pit 2024 at Clifton Quarry (Worcestershire) contained a set of vessels with Clacton sub-style affinities, although it is noted that Woodlands and Durrington Walls sub-style traits also occur (Edwards 2018). This pit was also unusual in that it contained barley as well as a collection of six stone and flint axeheads (Mann and Jackson 2018). Excavations in the Arrow Valley revealed a pit containing Woodlands sub-style vessels (Gibson 1999, 29–31) along with two polished stone axeheads (Ixer and Bradley 1999, 29; Palmer 1999, 22).

The dates for a group of Clacton sub-style-associated pit deposits at Church Farm, Thame, are surprisingly and consistently early, falling within the late 4th millennium cal BC (Taylor 2012, 191) or, more likely, the 30th century cal BC (Fig. 11.2: modelled as *First dig Church Fm* at *3026–2926 95.4% probability* or *2972–2925 cal BC 68.3% probability*). Representing one of the earliest Grooved Ware pit sites in southern England, it would certainly benefit from further dates to test or refine what could be one of the first appearances of Grooved Ware outside Scotland. This would also fall well within the final use of Peterborough Ware (Fengate Ware in particular). An unusual Clacton sub-style vessel

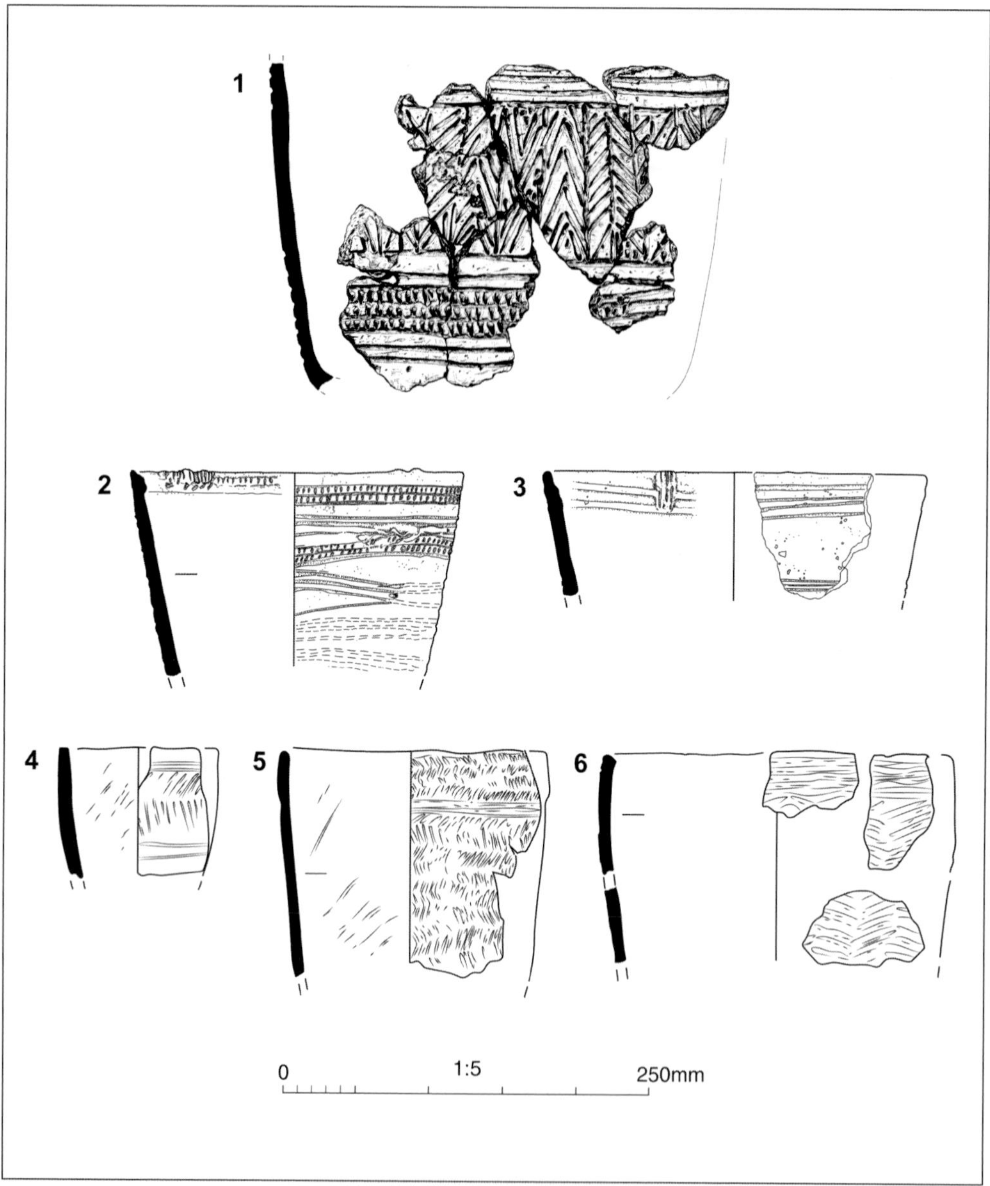

Figure 11.3. Selected Clacton and Woodlands sub-style vessels: 1. Church Farm; 2–3. Halls Close; 4–5. Southam Road, Banbury; 6. Eton Rowing Course (© Thames Valley Archaeological Services, Cotswolds Archaeology, Wessex Archaeology and Oxford Archaeology).

has a broad central band, perhaps equating to a third of the vessel's surface, that was divided by vertical bands containing opposing oblique lines and chevrons. As Raymond (2012, 172 and fig. 10.1) notes, these vertical panels are reminiscent of the Durrington Walls sub-style. However, it can equally be noted that nested zig-zag lines as a motif can be traced back to settlement sites in Orkney. The three Thame pits that produced the radiocarbon dates were part of a wider scatter of between five and eight pits within an area totalling half a hectare. This may have been part of a more extensive pit scatter. Three of the pits, which were spaced 50–60 m apart, have single radiocarbon dates (KIA-42469–71: 4372±39 BP, 4408±35 BP and 4390±42 BP), perhaps suggesting that pit digging here was short-lived.

Only small quantities of Grooved Ware were recovered from a handful of pits at Eton Rowing Lake (Allen *et al.* 2013), alongside small quantities of sherds from preserved occupation deposits. Most significant was a group of at least 11 Clacton sub-style vessels from two pits in Area 16 (Barclay 2013, 398–401 and fig. 8.6, 14–24). Two consistent radiocarbon dates (OxA-13597 and 14090) indicate that the pits were dug at some point during the 29th and/or 28th century cal BC (Fig. 11.2; Allen *et al.* 2013, 398). Very similar in character and date is the pottery from Southam Road, Banbury, in north Oxfordshire (Wakeham and Wells forthcoming), whilst the aforementioned Clacton sub-style pottery from Church Farm, Thame (Taylor 2012), shares many characteristics with the assemblages from these two sites.

The currency of the Clacton sub-style is long, occupying the first quarter of the 3rd millennium cal BC. There is some stylistic overlap between the Woodlands and Clacton sub-styles (summarised for the region by Barclay 1999), although we are less clear about their related temporal development; perhaps the two stylistic strands were simply conflated at times by the potters.

The appearance of Grooved Ware in southern England and, in particular, parts of the Upper and Middle Thames, seemingly in the 30th century cal BC, was sudden. Church Farm seems, at face value, to be precociously early. Whether the Clacton sub-style emerged before the Woodlands sub-style, albeit within a much shorter timeframe (a few generations), also awaits further study although it seems increasingly likely that both were current by or around 2900 cal BC. The duration of any overlap with the Peterborough Ware tradition also warrants further examination, especially in the Thames Valley (e.g. at Yarnton).

LATE NEOLITHIC MONUMENTS AND BURIALS

Stone circles are rare within the Thames Valley, being limited to just two unambiguous examples and a few possible sites, although the Avebury complex sits on the very periphery of the Thames Valley catchment and the Wessex Chalklands to the south. The King's Men (Rollright) Stones, located in the Cotswolds, finds *comparanda* in north-west England while the Devil's Quoits, Stanton Harcourt, on the Upper Thames Gravels, bears similarities to the two stone circles within the great Avebury circle. Also within the Upper Thames are a group of six poorly dated large henge monuments. As with much of the current evidence, their temporal relationship with Grooved Ware remains uncertain. Smaller henges and related monuments again occur in the Upper Thames Valley and have a couple of good Grooved Ware associations.

A small double-entrance henge at Corporation Farm, Abingdon, produced two fragmentary Clacton sub-style bowls, cattle crania fragments and an antler pick (Shand *et al.* 2003, 34 and fig. 3.7), and a hengiform ring-ditch at Radley containing placed deposits of red deer antlers and articulated cattle limbs produced a fragmentary plain bowl of Durrington Walls sub-style (Barclay and Halpin 1999, 35–42 and figs 4.1–4.4). Radiocarbon dates (BM-2712–13: 3860±80 BP and 3950±80 BP: 2568–2048 cal BC and 2842–2200 cal BC at 95.4% confidence) place this depositional event at the end of the local Grooved Ware sequence. As stated above, the site of Radley would benefit from a further critical dating programme to test the reliability of the original dating. A further monument, at Heathrow, produced a probably placed deposit of Grooved Ware (as discussed below).

In the Lower Thames henges are fewer and mostly smaller. The henge with post-circle and central occupation deposit at Tye Field, Lawford, Essex (Shennan *et al.* 1985 and see below and Chapter 10) produced a large assemblage of Grooved Ware (705 sherds, 104 illustrated vessel fragments), mostly of the Durrington Walls sub-style (Smith 1985).

A small number of inhumation burials and cremation cemeteries associated with various forms of ring-ditch include the complex at Dorchester-on-Thames and more recently published examples from Imperial College Sports Ground on the Heathrow terrace (Powell *et al.* 2015). The cemeteries in particular appear to both pre-date and run in parallel with the adoption and use of Grooved Ware and undoubtedly form part of the wider social narrative.

DURRINGTON WALLS: SIMILAR BUT DIFFERENT

That the Durrington Walls sub-style (Fig. 11.4) appeared later than those of Clacton or Woodlands is generally accepted (Copper *et al.* 2021), although its origins are less clear. One possibility is that it emerged out of the Clacton sub-style and late Peterborough Ware by the end of the first quarter of the 3rd millennium, though this requires detailed and critical scrutiny of available context groups and sequences (cf. Chaffey and Barclay 2013, 216). Within the Thames Valley, there is still the need to bolster the number of radiocarbon dates for this sub-style, perhaps including the direct dating of vessels with encrusted food residues and/or absorbed lipids (e.g. from the Tye Field henge; Smith 1985, 174). The large assemblage from Yarnton (Fig. 11.5) would certainly offer the opportunity to explore the spatial development of pit sites with multiple pit assemblages, as discussed below.

The relatively large assemblage from the Tye Field henge mostly fits within the Durrington Walls repertoire (Smith 1985). However, as Smith notes, impressed vessels, including those decorated using cord (mostly whipped), dominate the assemblage. The use of impressed cord instead of grooves is something that occurs in other areas of the Middle Thames but is not so common in the Upper Thames Valley and absent from Yarnton. In many cases the use of cord simply replaces the motifs and patterns that were executed by incision or grooving. However, some vessels are decorated with repeated 'maggot' impressions not dissimilar to those seen on Peterborough Ware. In the lower Thames Valley – an area with a different history in terms of the scale of Peterborough Ware activity and its earlier monumental traditions – a regional variant of the Durrington Walls sub-style may have developed.

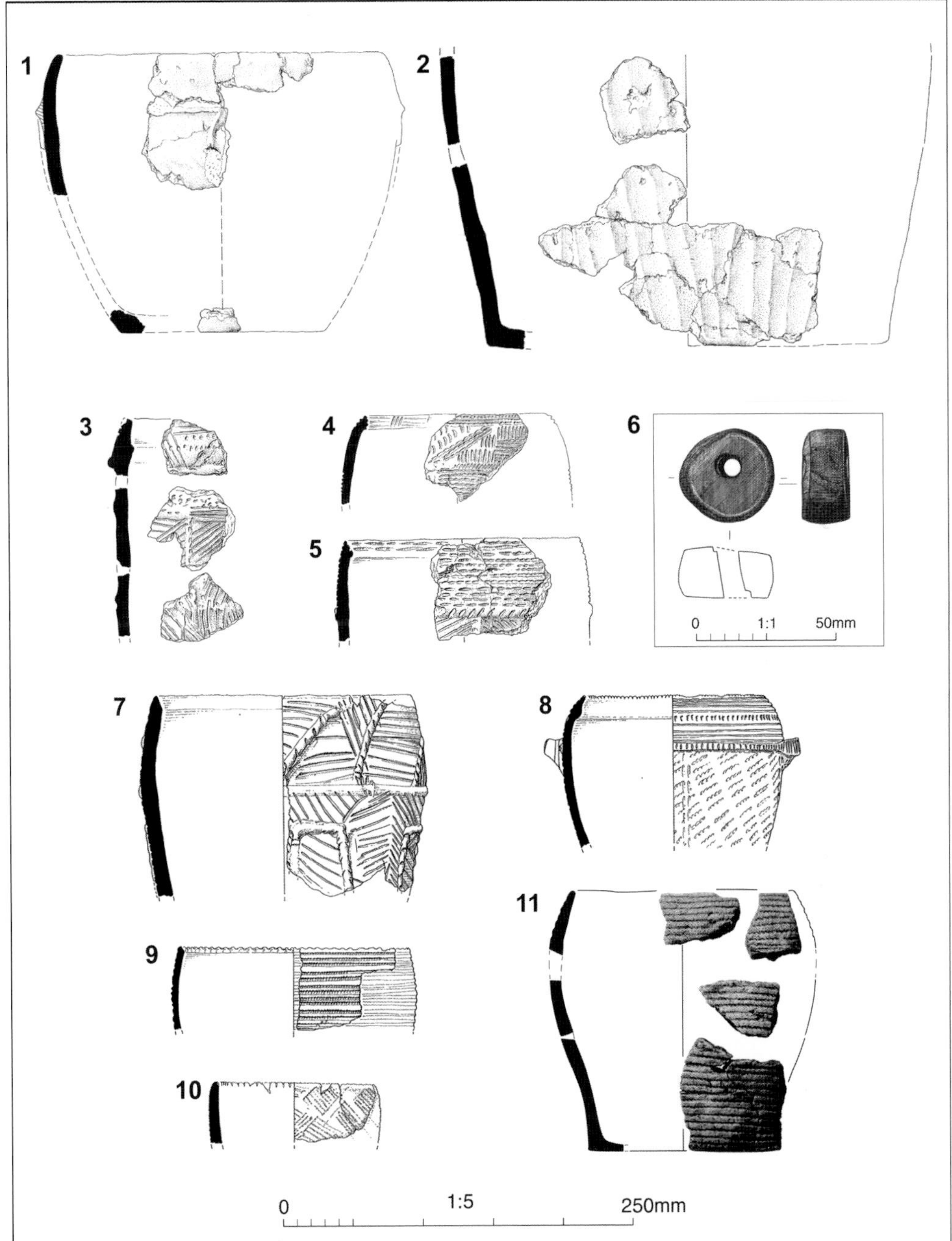

Figure 11.4. Selected Durrington Walls sub-style vessels and shale bead: 1, 2 & 4–6 Yarnton; 7–10. Horton; 11. Slade Farm; 3. Clacton vessel with Durrington Walls traits (© Oxford Archaeology and Wessex Archaeology).

Figure 11.5. Yarnton potscape, Site 7. Pit scatter and structures of Early and Late Neolithic date (© Oxford Archaeology).

Other notable assemblages include those from Kingsmead Quarry, Horton, and Betchworth in the Middle Thames (discussed below); a pit group found on the Childrey Warren pipeline in the Vale of the White Horse (Guarino and Barclay 2023); and five pits at Bourton-on-the-Water in the Cotswolds, where up to 11 vessels were recovered, including a sherd with spiral or circular motif, as well as more typical cordoned vessels (information from SLR Consulting).

One unusual vessel from a site at Slade Farm, Wallingford, bore all-over-cord impressions (Alex Davies, pers. comm.; Davies forthcoming). Its use to decorate all the surface is unusual: normally this type of decoration – a rare feature – is limited to the rim zone. A radiocarbon result puts the date of this vessel before the introduction of Beaker pottery. The pot is a reminder of the similarity that can occur between some Durrington Walls vessels and Beaker pottery, especially in the use of impressed cord, comb stamps and fine grog-tempered fabrics as well as the oxidised firing. Bone temper is also shared by the two traditions. Despite any physical similarities, there is nonetheless a possible discontinuity in the currencies. This topic is something that needs critical review as it could signal an awareness of pottery styles beyond Britain, in particular Corded Ware, whose design influenced the development of All-Over-Cord Beakers.

GROOVED WARE USE IN THE MIDDLE THAMES VALLEY

At the time of the 1990s review, Grooved Ware was relatively rare in the Middle Thames Valley (Barclay 1999; Jon Cotton, pers. comm.). However, with the advent of developer-funded archaeology and the greater use of area excavation, this has presented opportunities to examine areas of the landscape previously subjected just to small-scale watching briefs and rescue archaeology. In particular, the lower Colne Valley and adjacent stretches of the River Thames have produced considerable new evidence for the Late Neolithic, whilst the evidence uncovered for the Early and Middle Neolithic is arguably even more extensive (Lamdin-Whymark 2008; Framework Archaeology 2010; Chaffey *et al.* 2012; Chaffey and Barclay 2013; Powell *et al.* 2015; Cotton *et al.* 2017; Ellie Brook, pers. comm.).

Nearly 15 years ago, Lamdin-Whymark (2008) was only able to list seven Grooved Ware pits from this region. Publication of the West London Gravels project (MOLA (Museum of London Archaeology)) and Kingsmead Quarry, Horton (Wessex Archaeology), will add considerably to the known corpus of sites. Horton, a kilometre-long gravel quarry, has produced an assemblage of Durrington Walls sub-style pottery from six of 15 pits spread over an area of a hectare, as well as a rare inhumation burial. One pit produced a very large assemblage of charred fruits as well as a collected or curated Peterborough Ware bowl, a burnt discoidal edge-polished flint knife, a hammerstone made from crystalline quartz and sherds from a Durrington Walls sub-style jar (Chaffey and Barclay 2013, 216). A relatively isolated pit found outside a ring-ditch of uncertain date contained most of an unusual, lugged vessel and a complete clay ball (Ellie Brook, pers. comm.) (Fig. 11.6). Purposefully made clay balls are quite rare but are found with Durrington Walls sub-style Grooved Ware. A decorated example is known from Kent (Garwood 2011, fig. 3.34) and a plain example, similar to the one from Horton, was found near Salisbury (information from Cotswold Archaeology). These objects may be related to the small chalk balls that are also known to occur in the Late Neolithic (Garrow and Wilkin 2022, fig. 1.48).

The character of the Grooved Ware from Kingsmead Quarry is similar in its range of forms to that from Yarnton (described below), although plain vessels are notably absent. As with other assemblages from the Middle Thames it includes the use of impressed cord, either twisted or, more rarely, whipped, the latter used to make repeated 'maggots'. The use of cord has also been recorded in various assemblages from the Heathrow terraces on the eastern side of the Colne Valley, including the substantial one from Holloway Lane (Jon Cotton, pers. comm.; Leivers 2010). In contrast to the highly decorated assemblage from Kingsmead Quarry is the large pit assemblage (550 sherds, 5.8 kg) of mostly plain, cordoned Durrington Walls sub-style Grooved Ware from Franks' Pit, Betchworth (Surrey), south of the Thames (Williams 2017). This relatively large assemblage (comprising at least 38 vessels) would not be out of place at the great henges and palisaded sites of Wiltshire, as Cotton *et al.* note (2017). Similar pottery was also recovered at Heathrow Terminal 5. Although described as 'Woodlands'

Figure 11.6. Horton vessel and clay ball.

(Framework Archaeology 2010, 41 and figs 2.6, 9 and 10), this fits comfortably within the Durrington Walls sub-style. One vessel that stands out in the overall assemblage is a Clacton sub-style tub or jar (Framework Archaeology 2010, fig. 2.6, 12). Nearly all this pottery is from pits, although a small quantity of Grooved Ware was also found in the lower fills of a ditch of a small enclosure of uncertain form, but possibly related to a henge. Overall, Grooved Ware was recovered over an area extending almost a kilometre east from the line of the Stanwell cursus/bank barrow (Framework Archaeology 2010, fig. 2.56). Given the severe truncation of pits and ditches by later activity, it could be that the extant remains are the last relics of an intensive use of the landscape during the mid-3rd millennium cal BC. Unfortunately, there are no associated radiocarbon dates for these features, although the near-dominance of the Durrington Walls sub-style probably indicates activity in the 27th to 25th centuries cal BC.

THE PITSCAPE, THE UBIQUITOUS GROOVED WARE SITE TYPE

The Late Neolithic landscapes away from monuments are harder to define and even harder to detect and reveal by standard methods of archaeological evaluation. An off-site approach to prehistoric archaeology was, however, successfully employed at Yarnton (Hey *et al.* 2016). Where developer-led archaeology strategies switch from small percentage trench evaluation to whole-area excavation, our knowledge of Late Neolithic landscapes increases, as demonstrated at Yarnton, Perry Oaks/Terminal 5, Kingsmead Quarry and Radley (mentioned above). This approach can also reveal areas where no, or very little, Late Neolithic archaeology is encountered. In the case of the Heathrow terraces, the large-scale excavations at Imperial College and RMC Land to the north of Heathrow produced 76 Peterborough Ware pits spread over an area of nearly a kilometre, along with contemporary cremation cemeteries within two ring-ditches but very little Grooved Ware-associated activity (Powell *et al.* 2015). The intensity of pit digging found on these two sites is not replicated in the Late Neolithic of the Middle Thames Valley.

Most Grooved Ware sites on the gravel terraces are defined by pits or, more rarely, burials, structures, monuments, occupation deposits, deposits within natural features and surface/redeposited material. Pits occur singly, as pairs or as small clusters of both, along with occasional postholes. Refitting material within paired pits suggests a degree of contemporaneity. Many people have suggested that pits relate to temporary occupation; the absence of structures is often explained as due to their being lightly built, akin to modern day yurts. The contents of the pits tend to include often token amounts of used and broken material, along with fire residues and occasional pieces of daub. Occasionally whole objects, some quite finely made, and unusual objects occur. Ceramic assemblages often present a range or set of vessels from small cups to large jars. Sometimes, highly decorated vessel fragments occur. Objects appear deliberately placed or more randomly discarded within pits. The spacing between pits could suggest that groups were deliberately setting up at a regular distance from each other, or that later visits took place at a distance from a previous occupation. Pits were rarely dug in the same location. Of note are the differences in vessels' decorative motifs between spatially distanced individual pits/pit groups within any one site. If larger pit scatters were the outcome of larger gatherings, then groups were choosing to deposit either undecorated vessels, or else differently decorated vessels. With Durrington Walls sub-style assemblages, it is notable how much variation in decorative technique occurs, with nearly every type of tool and stamp being represented (Wainwright and Longworth 1971). This variation is echoed to some extent at some of the great henges and palisaded enclosure sites. At the larger Grooved Ware sites (e.g. Durrington Walls and Mount Pleasant) a degree of spatial patterning has been observed by Julian Thomas and Colin Richards (Thomas 1996; Richards and Thomas 1984) – although whether this represents differences over time, or in the way pottery was used within a site, is hard to say.

YARNTON: A GROOVED WARE LANDSCAPE

One of the largest known non-monumental Late Neolithic landscapes within the Thames Valley was recovered in a gravel quarry at Yarnton near Oxford (Fig. 11.5; Hey *et al.* 2016). The excavators took an off-site approach to the predicted archaeology, based on a series of survey techniques including trench evaluations. Area excavation on the first gravel terrace near the former course of the River Thames revealed 45 Late Neolithic pits and a possible post-built structure. Pits were found in eight excavation areas over a distance of more than a kilometre (Hey *et al.* 2016, fig. 2.9).

At the time of the excavation, mostly undertaken in the 1990s, radiocarbon dating lacked the precision of current standards, whilst the application of Bayesian modelling was only in its infancy. Nonetheless the project archive has future research potential for radiocarbon dating, not least for testing a typochronology for the development of the various Grooved Ware sub-styles and their relationship with earlier Peterborough Ware and later Beaker.

Twenty-three of the 45 pits associated with Grooved Ware at Yarnton came from Site 7, an area of 2.4 ha. The individual pits were spread out at intervals of 40–50 m; a few were much closer, and one was more distant. Most pits occurred singly but a few were paired or grouped in small clusters. The spatial extent of this scatter, whatever its temporal aspect, almost certainly extended beyond the artificial limits of Site 7. The extent of such pit scatters can vary from tens to hundreds of metres.

The Grooved Ware from Yarnton (1948 sherds, 6.7 kg) can nearly all be assigned to the Durrington Walls sub-style with the exception of two pits that produced pottery with Clacton affinities, whilst pottery in the Woodlands sub-style is absent despite the proximity to Cassington, where pits containing this sub-style had been found (see Barclay 1999). Overall, the Durrington Walls sub-style pottery is close in character to that found throughout the Upper Thames and especially around the Oxford area (Barclay 1999). It also reflects the range of vessels found at the site of Durrington Walls itself (Wainwright and Longworth 1971). The total pit assemblage includes mostly straight-sided or slightly ovoid jar forms that range from small cup-sized vessels to large jars. A few shallower bowls are present too. Some of the selected pit groups almost appear to contain a 'set' of vessels – from small cups to substantial jars and occasional bowls. That these sets were more than just coincidental is reinforced by a near-absence of decoration or the occurrence of similarly decorated vessels. Like the pottery from Durrington Walls, the vessels display different choices in the extent to which they were decorated. Some are completely devoid of any surface elaboration, including moulded or applied cordons; some have cordons but no – or limited – impressed or incised decoration; some have all-over decoration and/or cordons; and some have elaborate motifs/all-over decoration and, more rarely, internal decoration. It is difficult to understand the behaviour that created the deposit other than to state a degree of deliberate choice. As has been noted before and by many authors, there is a preference to collect rims and body sherds rather than bases, although at Yarnton there is the occasional pit group that contains a relatively large number of bases. Only a very small proportion of an individual vessel was ever collected for deposition, often just token amounts. In short, only a small minority of Grooved Ware survived and made it into the archaeological record.

The pits scattered across Site 7 could mark short-stay seasonal occupations. One was found within the interior of what would have been the site of a substantial Early Neolithic structure, possibly a hall or house (Hey *et al.* 2016). It seems unlikely that this structure, already at least a thousand years old, would have remained as more than a low mound or platform or would have retained any meaning for those that visited. Yet found within this pit was a shale bead or pendant: a rare occurrence in a Grooved Ware context (Sheridan 2016, 121). At Yarnton, Grooved Ware pit-digging followed on from a similar intensity of Middle Neolithic pit-digging, almost as if a similar pattern of activity was being played out, centuries apart. Pits with Clacton sub-style Grooved Ware were infrequent compared with a much higher concentration of pits associated with Durrington Walls sub-style pottery. In contrast, early Beaker activity was limited to a few isolated pits and a notable flat grave (Hey *et al.* 2016).

DISCUSSION

This review has highlighted the significant evidence that has come to light since the last substantive overview of Grooved Ware in the Upper Thames Valley. Like many of the contributors, I recognise the need to re-evaluate the current typochronology and develop a new system of nomenclature that takes into account a greater degree of complexity and variability, and that acknowledges the Orcadian origin of the tradition overall. Any new system needs to capture regional variation as well as the distribution of similar forms and motifs. Whether the current radiocarbon calibration curve permits any close temporal division seems doubtful, but an attempt to produce a possible typochronology should be made. Future research could try to address some key questions in order to:

- Establish and better radiocarbon date the potentially early Grooved Ware assemblages from the Thames Valley, including the important pit groups from Radley;
- establish the currency of the earliest sub-styles;
- typologically compare those assemblages of 30th century date with those that potentially belong in the 29th and 28th centuries;
- establish the end date for the early styles;
- examine possible stylistic drift either along the Thames Valley into Wessex and from the Midlands/Wales;
- establish where and when the Durrington Walls sub-style emerged; how, and in what directions it spread, and whether there is any regional variation in the character of this sub-style between the Lower, Middle and Upper Thames; and
- establish whether Grooved Ware had mostly disappeared by the time early Beaker pottery appeared, probably in the 24th century cal BC.

ACKNOWLEDGEMENTS

The following have allowed me access to material, provided information and shared ideas: Pippa Bradley, Ellie Brook, Jon Cotton, Alex Davies, Gareth Chaffey, Steve Ford, Paul Garwood, Gill Hey, Ed McSloy, Tom Wells and Gail Wakeham. Particular thanks go to Alex Gibson, who first inspired my interest in pottery as a Leicester undergraduate, and Ros Cleal who encouraged my early years as a specialist. Illustrations in this chapter were kindly produced by Helena Munoz-Mojado of Cotswold Archaeology.

REFERENCES

Allen, T., Barclay, A., Cromarty, A-M., Anderson-Whymark, H., Parker, A., Robinson, M. and Jones, J. 2013. *Opening the wood, making the land. The archaeology of a Middle Thames landscape. Mesolithic, Neolithic and Early Bronze Age. The Eton Rowing Course Project and the Maidenhead, Windsor and Eton Flood Alleviation Scheme.* Oxford: Oxford Archaeology.

Barclay, A.J. 1999. Grooved Ware from the Upper Thames Region. In R. Cleal and A. MacSween 1999, 9–22.

Barclay, A. and Halpin, C. 1999. *Excavations at Barrow Hills, Radley, Oxfordshire. Volume I: the Neolithic and Bronze Age monument complex.* Oxford: Oxford Archaeological Unit.

Bradley, R. 2007. *The prehistory of Britain and Ireland.* Cambridge: Cambridge University Press.

Chaffey, G. and Barclay, A. 2013. The MTV generations: remixing the past in prehistory – or forgetting to change old habits. In A.M. Chadwick and C.D. Gibson (eds), *Memory, myth and long-term landscape inhabitation*, 208–25. Oxford: Oxbow Books.

Chaffey, C. and Brook, E. with Pelling, R., Barclay, A., Bradley, P. and Marshall, P. 2012. Domesticity in the Neolithic: excavations at Kingsmead Quarry, Horton, Berkshire. In H. Anderson-Whymark and J. Thomas (eds), *Regional perspectives on Neolithic pit deposition: beyond the mundane,* 200–15. Oxford: Neolithic Studies Group Seminar Papers 12.

Cleal, R. 1999. Introduction: the what, where, when and why of Grooved Ware. In R. Cleal and A. MacSween (eds) 1999, 1–8.

Cleal, R. and MacSween, A. (eds) 1999. *Grooved Ware in Britain and Ireland.* Oxford: Oxbow Books.

Copper, M., Hamilton, D. and Gibson, A. 2021. Tracing the lines: Scottish Grooved Ware trajectories beyond Orkney, *Proceedings of the Society of Antiquaries of Scotland* 150, 81–117.

Cotton, J., Doherty, A. and Rayner, L. 2017. The prehistoric pottery. In D. Williams 2017, 102–17.

Davies, A. forthcoming. Prehistoric pottery. In A. Davies, C. Champness, G. Thacker and L. Webley, *Slade End Farm and Winterbrook. Prehistoric landscapes around Wallingford, South Oxfordshire.* Oxford: Oxford Archaeology.

Edwards, E. 2018. Late Neolithic and Beaker pottery. In A. Mann and R. Jackson 2018, 76–82.

Framework Archaeology. 2010. *Landscape evolution in the Middle Thames Valley. Heathrow Terminal 5 excavations: Volume 2.* Salisbury and Oxford: Framework Archaeology.

Garrow, D. and Wilkin, N. 2022. *The world of Stonehenge.* London: The British Museum.

Garwood, P. 1999. Grooved Ware in southern Britain. Chronology and interpretation. In R. Cleal and A. MacSween 1999, 145–76.

Garwood, P. 2011. Early prehistory. In P. Booth, T. Champion, S. Foreman, P. Garwood, H. Glass, J. Munby and A. Reynolds, *On track. The archaeology of High Speed 1 Section 1 in Oxford*, 37–150. Oxford and Salisbury: Oxford Wessex Archaeology.

Gibson, A 1999. Neolithic pottery. In S.C. Palmer 1999, 29–31.

Greaney, S., Hazell, R., Barclay, A., Bronk Ramsay, C., Dunbar, E., Hajdas, I. Reimer, P., Pollard, J., Sharples, N. and Marshall, P. 2020. Tempo of a mega henge: a new chronology for Mount Pleasant, Dorchester, Dorset. *Proceedings of the Prehistoric Society* 86, 199–236.

Guarino, P. and Barclay, A.J. 2023. *In the shadow of Segsbury. The archaeology of the H380 Childrey Warren Water Pipeline, 2018–2020.* Cirencester: Cotswold Archaeology.

Hey, G., Bell, C., Dennis, C. and Robinson, R. 2016. *Yarnton. Neolithic and Bronze Age settlement and landscape.* Oxford: Oxford Archaeology.

Ixer, R.A. and Bradley, P. 1999. Polished stone axes, Neolithic. In S.C. Palmer 1999, 27–9.

Lamdin-Whymark, H. 2008. *The residue of ritualised ation: Neolithic deposition practices in the Middle Thames Valley.* Oxford: British Archaeological Report 466.

Leivers, M. 2010. Grooved Ware 3000–2000 BC. In Framework Archaeology 2010, 40–2.

McSloy, E.R. forthcoming. Prehistoric pottery. In S. Sworn, J. Hart and C. Randall, Neolithic, Iron Age and Anglo-Saxon settlement above the River Churn Valley: archaeological investigations at Siddington Road, Cirencester, 2015–16. *Transactions of the Bristol and Gloucestershire Archaeological Society.*

MacSween, A., Hunter, J., Sheridan, J.A., Bond, J., Bronk Ramsey, C., Reimer, P. Bayliss, A., Griffiths, S. and Whittle, A. 2015. Refining the chronology of the Neolithic settlement at Pool, Sanday, Orkney: implications for the emergence and development of Grooved Ware. *Proceedings of the Prehistoric Society* 81, 283–310.

Mann, A. and Jackson, R. 2018. *Clifton Quarry, Worcestershire. Pits, posts and cereals: archaeological investigations 2006–2009.* Oxford: Oxbow Books.

Palmer, S.C. 1999. Archaeological excavations in the Arrow Valley, Warwickshire. *Transactions of the Birmingham and Warwickshire Archaeological Society* 103.

Piggott, S. 1936. Grooved Ware. In S.H. Warren, S. Piggott, J.G.D. Clark, M. Burkitt, H. Godwin and M.E. Godwin, Archaeology of the submerged land-surface of the Essex coast, 186–201. *Proceedings of the Prehistoric Society* 2, 191–201.

Piggott, S. 1954. *The Neolithic cultures of the British Isles.* Cambridge: Cambridge University Press.

Powell, A., Barclay, A.J., Mepham, L. and Stevens, C.J. 2015. *Imperial College sports ground and RMC Land, Harlington. The development of prehistoric and later communities in the Colne Valley and on the Heathrow Terrace.* Salisbury: Wessex Archaeology Report 33.

Raymond, F. 2012. Prehistoric pottery. In R. Taylor 2012, 169–83.

Reynish, S. and Barclay, A.J. forthcoming. Prehistoric and later activity at Halls Close, Drayton. *Oxoniensia.*

Richards, C. and Thomas, J. 1984. Ritual activity and structured deposition in Later Neolithic Wessex. In R. Bradley and J. Gardiner (eds), *Neolithic studies. A review of some current research*, 189–218. Oxford: British Archaeological Report 33.

Shand, P., Henderson, E., Henderson, R. and Barclay, A. 2003. Corporation Farm, Wilsham Road, Abingdon: a summary of the Neolithic and Bronze Age excavations, 1971–4. In A. Barclay, G. Lambrick, J. Moore and M. Robinson, *Lines in the landscape. Cursus monuments in the Upper Thames Valle*, 31–40. Oxford: Oxford Archaeology.

Shennan, S.J., Healy, F. and Smith, I.F. 1985. The excavation of a ring-ditch at Tye Field, Lawford, Essex. *Archaeological Journal* 142, 150–215.

Sheridan, J.A. 2016. Shale bead/pendant. In Hey *et al.* 2016, 120–1.

Smith, I.F. 1985. The pottery. In Shennan *et al.* 1985, 165–77.

Taylor, R. 2012. Excavations of Late Neolithic pits, an Early Bronze-Age ring ditch and an Early Iron-Age pit alignment at Church Farm, Thame. *Oxoniensia* 77, 153–98.

Thomas, J. 1996. *Time, culture and identity: an interpretive archaeology.* London: Routledge.

Wainwright, G.J. and Longworth, I.H. 1971. The Rinyo-Clacton Culture reconsidered. In G.J. Wainwright and I.H. Longworth, *Durrington Walls: excavations 1966–1968*, 235–306. London: Society of Antiquaries.

Wakeham, G. and Wells, T. forthcoming. Neolithic occupation, a Later Bronze-Age enclosure and other remains, east of Southam Road, Banbury. *Oxoniensia.*

Whittle, A. 2018. *The times of their lives: hunting history in the archaeology of Neolithic Europe.* Oxford: Oxbow Books.

Williams, D. 2017. Excavation of a prehistoric and Romano-British site at Betchworth, 1995–96. *Surrey Archaeological Collections* 100, 71–141.

Chapter 12

Recent Grooved Ware discoveries from Bulford and other sites in southern Wiltshire

Elina Brook

In the comprehensive Grooved Ware gazetteers published by Longworth (Wainwright and Longworth 1971) and Longworth and Cleal (1999), the large assemblages in Wiltshire are dominated by those associated with monument complexes such as Durrington Walls (Wainwright and Longworth 1971), Woodhenge (Cunnington 1929), Marden (Longworth 1971) and the West Kennet Palisaded Enclosures (Whittle 1997; Hamilton and Whittle 1999). Other, smaller assemblages derive from isolated or small clusters of pits or occur as residual finds from within barrow mounds. On the whole, this pattern has not changed since these lists were compiled, and so the discovery of over 1300 sherds of Grooved Ware from 38 Late Neolithic pits at Bulford, 3 km to the north-east of Amesbury in south Wiltshire (Fig. 12.1), is significant. The importance of the site is further emphasised by the fact that almost 98% of the collection belongs to the Woodlands sub-style which has, until recent years, been relatively poorly represented in the distribution map for the area, particularly in comparison to the more commonly occurring Durrington Walls sub-style within the county.

The Woodlands sub-style of Grooved Ware takes its name from an assemblage of pottery recovered from four pits found in the back garden of a bungalow (named Woodlands) on the outskirts of Amesbury, less than 300 m south of Woodhenge (Fig. 12.1). The pits, excavated in the 1940s, contained abundant animal bones, antler tines, pottery, bone pins/awls, worked flints including an axehead, a Group VII stone axehead fragment, and pieces of marine shell (Stone and Young 1948; Stone 1949). The ornately decorated pottery, some of 'wafer-like thinness' and characterised by plain and decorated cordons and pellets of clay on the bodies or rims, was identified as being related to the wider tradition of Grooved Ware, including that from Woodhenge, but closer parallels were to be found elsewhere in Britain including, more significantly, Orkney (Stone and Young 1948; Stone 1949). More than 70 years on from these discoveries, the distribution of this sub-style of Grooved Ware is known to extend across Britain and the links to the far north have been emphasised through several detailed scientific dating programmes (e.g. MacSween *et al.* 2015; Copper *et al.* 2021).

Following a brief summary of the nature and context of the Late Neolithic discoveries at Bulford, the Woodlands pottery assemblage will be described. The opportunity is then taken to review other discoveries of Grooved Ware from the area with a focus on those belonging to the Woodlands sub-style.

BULFORD IN CONTEXT

Archaeological works by Wessex Archaeology on behalf of Defence Infrastructure Organisation ahead of development to accommodate additional service personnel and their families based on and around Salisbury Plain took place at several existing military bases as part of the Army Basing Programme (ABP) (Leivers 2021). The various projects found evidence of activity dating from the Early Neolithic to the 20th century AD. Key prehistoric finds from across the scheme include a previously unknown Early Neolithic causewayed enclosure at Larkhill, Early Neolithic pits and burial remains at both Larkhill and Bulford, Late Neolithic pit digging activity (also at Larkhill and Bulford) and the construction of a pair of Late Neolithic henges at Bulford that were subsequently encircled by two continuous ring-ditches in the Early Bronze Age. Other Bronze Age activity across the ABP sites includes Beaker graves and post-pit alignments as well as Middle Bronze Age cremation cemeteries and ditched enclosures (Leivers 2021; Leivers *et al.* forthcoming).

An area of approximately 13.4 ha was excavated at Bulford, astride the chalk ridge on the southern edge of the Nine Mile River Valley and roughly 1 km to the east of where it meets the River Avon. The ridge falls sharply to the north (from *c.* 99 m OD) but slopes more gently into coombes on the eastern, southern and western sides.

The earliest archaeological features found at Bulford are of Early Neolithic date and include the grave of a male on the crest of the ridge (Fig. 12.2). In addition, 12 pits containing varying quantities of Early Neolithic Plain Bowl pottery, stone tools, animal bone and hazelnut shells were found, occurring as pairs, groups or discrete examples dispersed across the site. Following this activity there appears to have been a considerable hiatus in the use of the site until the very beginning of the 3rd millennium cal BC, at which point activity intensified.

Fifty pits at Bulford have been phased to the Late Neolithic (Fig. 12.2), with several of these confidently dated to the 30th century cal BC. Forty-eight form a dispersed band, predominantly extending eastwards from the summit of the ridge; a further two pits were positioned on a spur to the south-west. Within this distribution pairs of pits have been identified, with three pairs including one deeper and one shallower pit. Most pits are subcircular in plan, roughly 1 m in diameter and with a maximum depth of 0.7 m. Profiles vary, with rounded to irregular sides (Fig. 12.2, b–c) depending on the nature of the chalk into which they were dug. Given the absence of naturally weathered chalk rubble within the lower deposits, it is likely that the process of infilling happened relatively quickly.

Some primary fills contained well-defined concentrations of artefacts, whilst others contained ashy deposits rich in charcoal. In the deeper pits, where the stratigraphy is better preserved, these initial deposits were sealed beneath deliberate backfills of chalk rubble which probably derived from their initial digging. Many of the pits may have been only partially backfilled and then abandoned after a single episode of use, but there is also some evidence to suggest that a small number were revisited (Leivers *et al.* forthcoming).

Finds from the pits commonly include Woodlands sub-style Grooved Ware pottery, animal bone from both domestic and wild species, worked flint comprising knapping debris and retouched tools, and varying quantities of charcoal. More unusual finds include unworked spherical flint nodules, carved chalk items, axeheads or axehead fragments in both flint and stone, and an edge-polished discoidal knife, as well as antler and other

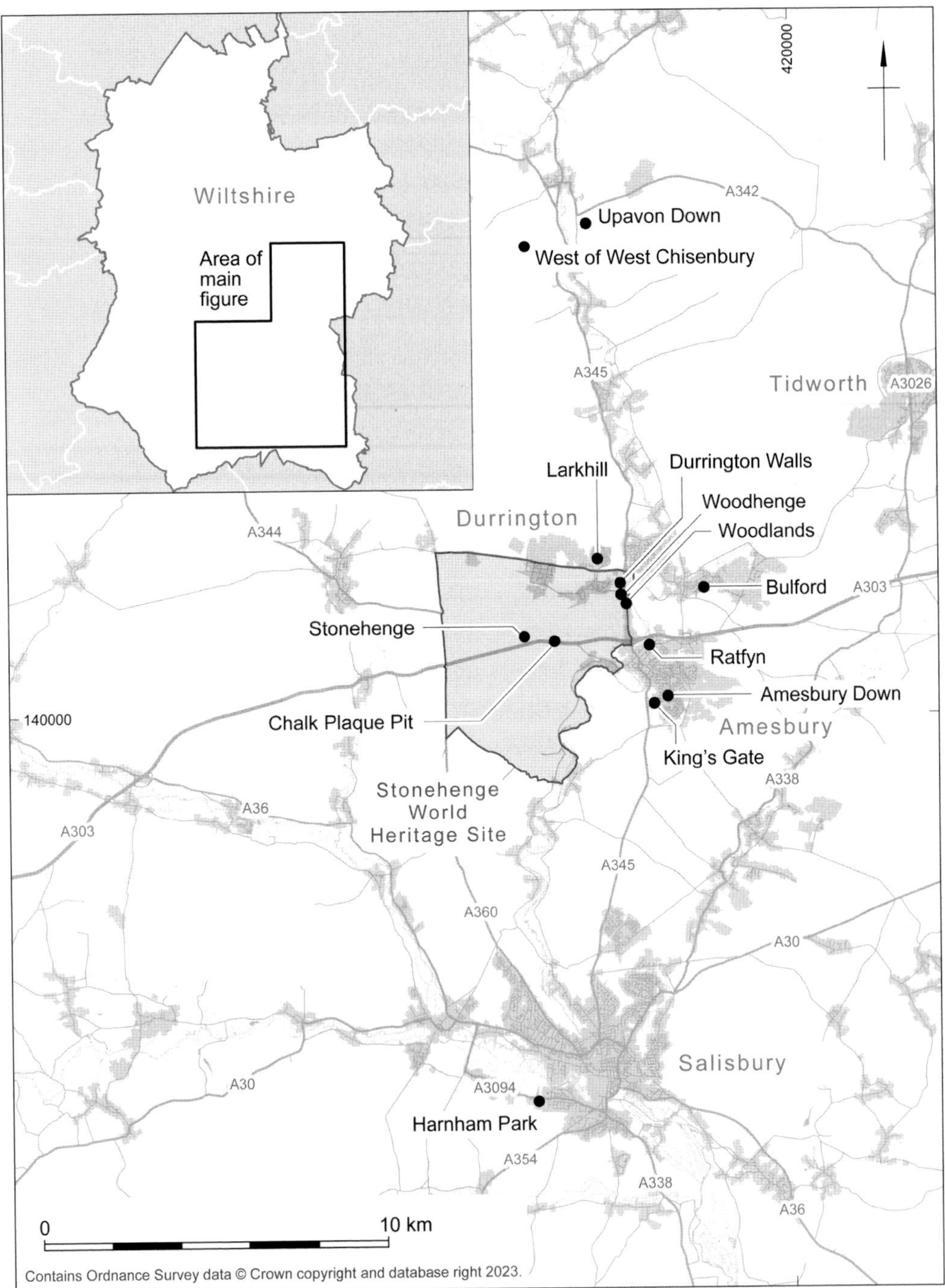

Figure 12.1. Location plan with key sites mentioned in text.

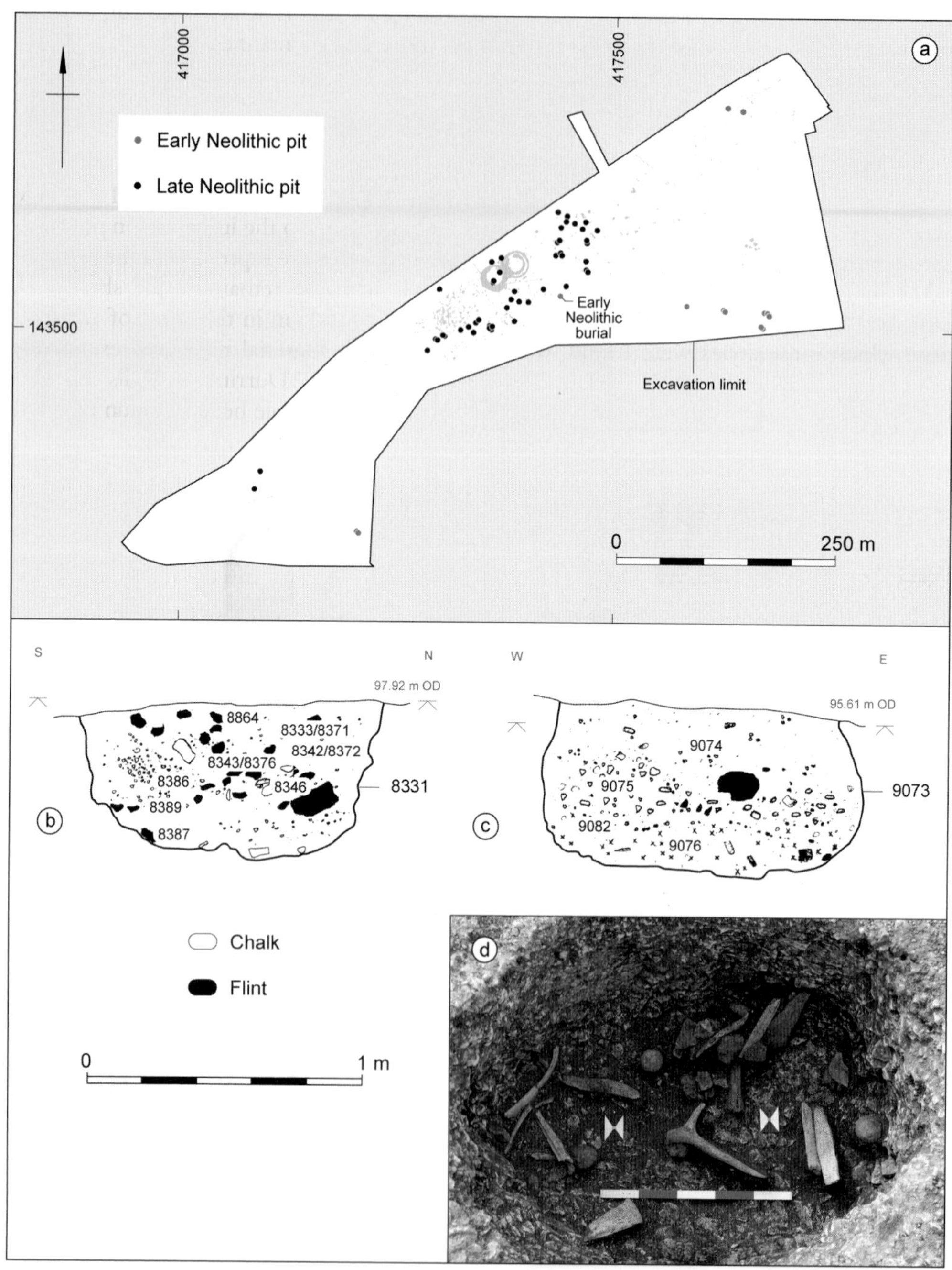

Figure 12.2. Early and Late Neolithic pits (and other features) at Bulford, Wiltshire.

worked bone items (Fig. 12.2, d). In many cases, the scatter of such material throughout the fills indicates refuse disposal resulting from a range of domestic activities but, in other instances, the artefacts have been placed in a far more careful manner.

THE BULFORD GROOVED WARE

The Grooved Ware assemblage (Fig. 12.3) comprises 1340 sherds, weighing 4911 g. At the time of writing, full analysis has not yet been undertaken and so the information provided here is based on the detailed assessment data. Two sub-styles are represented, the majority (1313 sherds) belonging to the Woodlands sub-style with the remainder (27 sherds) of probable Durrington Walls sub-style. There is a clear distinction in the types of deposits from which these styles were found, with the Woodlands material recovered exclusively from the backfills of 38 of the 50 Late Neolithic pits, while the Durrington Walls sub-style sherds predominantly came from the ditch fills of the later double henge monument (Fig. 12.2). This discussion focuses on the Woodlands material.

Figure 12.3. Woodlands sub-style Grooved Ware from Bulford: a) pottery laid out for recording; b) 'herringbone' motif; c) coarseware vessel.

Although detailed fabric analysis has not yet been undertaken, it is clear that a range of fabric types is represented, the most common of which contain crushed shell inclusions or a combination of shell and chalk. Smaller quantities of grog-, chalk- and quartz sand-tempered wares are also present. Some, but not all, of the clay matrices contain common black/brown grains (possibly glauconite), indicating that multiple clay sources were utilised in the manufacture of these vessels. Preliminary thin-section analysis undertaken on two sherds by Rob Ixer has identified that they are probably of local manufacture, with the addition of freshwater or marine bivalve shell (Wessex Archaeology 2020). All these components have previously been identified in other Grooved Ware assemblages of various sub-styles from the area (e.g. Wainwright and Longworth 1971; Cleal *et al.* 1994; Cleal 1995). A further, more detailed programme of thin-section analysis will shortly be undertaken and will, we hope, clarify this picture.

Preliminary assessment has identified 35 rim fragments, although at this stage it is unclear how many individual vessels are represented. Rims can be rounded, flat-topped, internally bevelled, or upright and slightly expanded. Bases, where present, are flat, and where sufficient profiles survive, vessel walls appear to flare outwards slightly, suggesting that some may have had squat, tub-shaped forms typical for the sub-style (e.g. Stone 1949, fig. 1, a).

Decoration is very common (Figs 12.3–5). Techniques are numerous and occur in multiple combinations on individual vessels. They include the use of applied strips and cordons, tooled impressions, incised lines made with sharp implements or grooved lines made by using blunter tools creating wider channels in the clay. Vessels can be decorated on their rims and exteriors. Some pots may have been decorated from rim to base, whilst others are decorated only around their upper parts.

One particularly distinctive form of decoration is the application of short strips of clay, sometimes grooved or with short transverse lines, over the tops of rims (e.g. Figs 12.3, b, 12.4, b, 12.5, a). The inner surfaces of rims can also be decorated, with horizontal cordons, grooved lines or other tooled line motifs, as well as one instance of possible twisted cord impressions. External decoration includes cordons, often arranged in converging lines

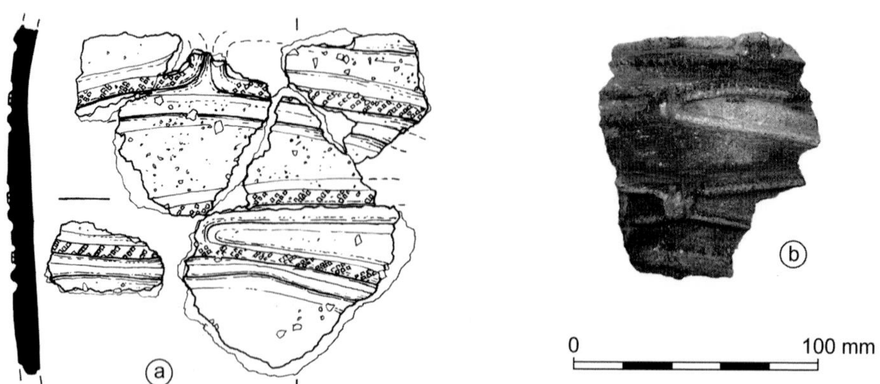

Figure 12.4. Woodlands sub-style Grooved Ware from a) Upavon Down and b) Bulford.

(Fig. 12.4, b). These cordons are made of thin, applied strips, or else are pinched or raised from the surface body of the clay. Some are decorated with transverse tooled impressions. In other instances, pairs of grooved lines have been drawn in the clay and the strip in between has been indented from alternate sides to create a false relief, wavy line motif (Fig. 12.5, a) or, in another variation, a herringbone-like motif (Fig. 12.3, b). A further decorative technique is the addition of clay pellets, or 'knots', placed at the junctions of converging lines, or between parallel lines (Fig. 12.5, a). These pellets, as with the cordons or rim strips, can be either plain or decorated. In one fineware example, the pellets are horizontally perforated. Less typical motifs include a ring of fine tooled lines radiating from an inner circle and four dots around a central larger dot; the effect of both of these is to create a rosette-like motif (Fig. 12.5, b–c). Decoration is not just limited to the finer elements of the assemblage. Similar principles, including the use of applied strips over the rim tops and wavy line motifs on the body of vessels, are used on thick-walled coarsewares (Fig. 12.3, c) as well as on fineware vessels. Overall, a range of small to medium and large

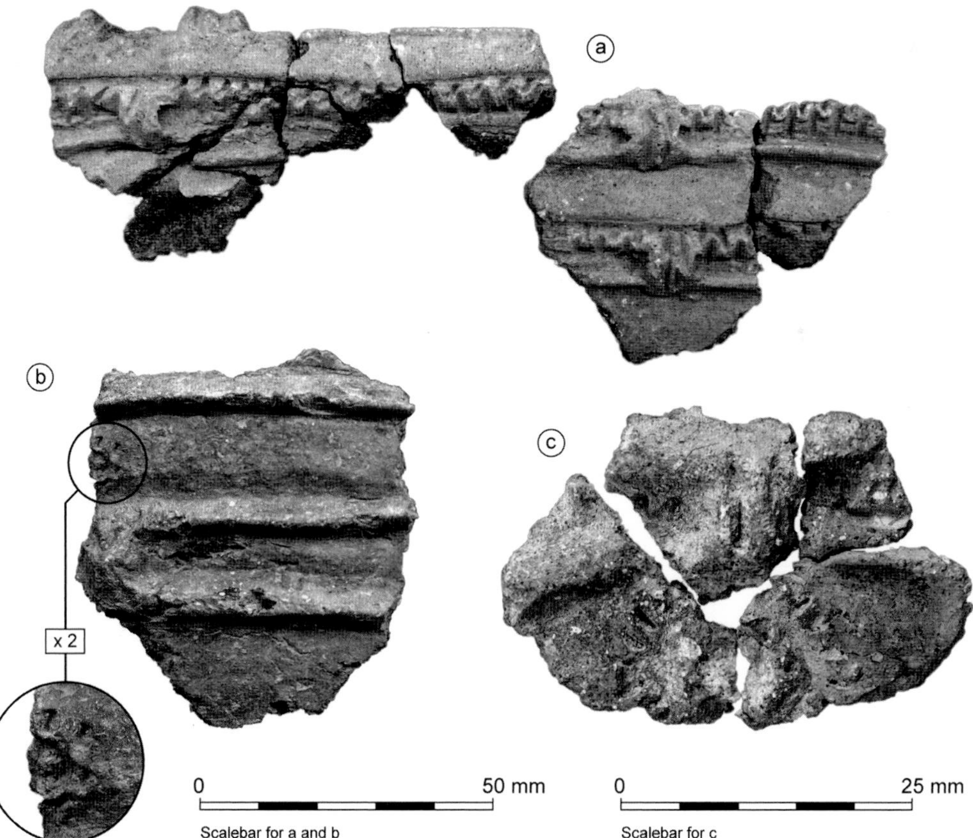

Figure 12.5. Decorated Woodlands sub-style pottery from Bulford: a) fineware vessel; b–c) rosette motifs

vessels is present and it is hoped that forthcoming organic residue analysis will shed further light on the possible uses for some of these vessels.

OTHER GROOVED WARE FROM SOUTH WILTSHIRE

In addition to the large assemblages from Durrington Walls (Wainwright and Longworth 1971) and Woodhenge (Cunnington 1929), other published assemblages of Grooved Ware from sites in and around the Salisbury and Amesbury area include those from the Chalk Plaque Pit (Harding 1988), Ratfyn (Stone 1935), King Barrow Ridge (Richards 1990; Brook forthcoming a) and other sites within the *Stonehenge Environs Project* (Richards 1990), Former MOD Headquarters, Durrington (Leivers 2018a), and the *Stonehenge Riverside Project* (Parker Pearson *et al.* 2020; 2022). Overall, the Durrington Walls sub-style is by far the most common and the Clacton sub-style the least well-represented. The following section reviews more recent discoveries of Grooved Ware that contain a Woodlands sub-style component.

Harnham Park, Salisbury

Approximately 15 km south-west of Bulford, on the southern outskirts of Salisbury, Wessex Archaeology carried out archaeological excavations ahead of housing development at Harnham Park (Fig. 12.1). Activity dating from the Middle Neolithic to the later prehistoric periods was identified (Wessex Archaeology 2022). Three pits contained deposits of Late Neolithic material, including Woodlands sub-style pottery comparable to that found at Bulford, animal bone, worked flint, two worked bone awls, an almost complete valve from a scallop shell and charred plant remains. Sherds of Woodlands sub-style Grooved Ware in a relatively coarse, shell-tempered fabric came from two of these pits. The exterior of some sherds is decorated with combinations of grooved lines and multiple applied fine cordons (some converging) with pellets of clay placed at their junctions. Some cordons are decorated with additional, fine, transverse incised lines. One base angle sherd is decorated with diagonal grooved lines on the exterior wall. The decorative elements on these sherds are extremely similar to some within the Bulford Woodlands assemblage.

Salisbury Plain

During excavations in advance of the construction of new military tracks across parts of the Salisbury Plain Defence Training Estate, Late Neolithic pits and other features were found in Areas 2 (west of West Chisenbury) and 3 (Upavon Down) (Fig. 12.1; Powell *et al.* 2018). Two pits within Area 2 contained a total of 232 sherds of Grooved Ware, whilst a further 184 sherds were recovered from features in Area 3 (Powell *et al.* 2018, table 3). These sherds are present in a range of flint-, grog-, sand- and shell-tempered fabrics (Leivers 2018b, table 6). All three of the Grooved Ware sub-styles are represented. The largest group comprises almost 1 kg of pottery from Pit 9003 in Area 3, the majority deriving from the walls of a large, shell-tempered Woodlands sub-style vessel (Leivers 2018b, fig. 26, 10; Fig. 12.4, a). The exterior is decorated with converging cordons but rather than applied pellets at the junction, as seen on vessels from Bulford and Woodlands (Stone 1949, fig. 1, a), the ends of the cordons turn back on themselves. The alternate use of both plain and transversely decorated cordons on this vessel is also very similar to that seen on one pot from Bulford (Fig. 12.4, b). Pit 9003 also contained a rim fragment from a Clacton sub-style vessel and fragments from a third, shell-tempered vessel of uncertain style (Leivers 2018b, fig. 26, 11–12). Both vessels are decorated with horizontal and diagonal grooved/tooled lines which, in the former case, are infilled with impressed dots and, in the latter, lie above tooled line chevrons. The decorative elements on the vessel published in Leivers (2018b, fig. 26, 12) are in fact closely comparable to those seen on a Clacton sub-style vessel from the Chalk Plaque Pit (Harding 1988, fig. 3, b), and as such could also probably be assigned to that sub-style. In addition to moderate quantities of worked flint, burnt flint and animal bone, small quantities of stone, a worked bone point and a scallop shell were also found within the pit. The remaining Grooved Ware from Areas 2 and 3 can be assigned, with varying degrees of confidence, to the Durrington Walls sub-style and comprises small groups including pieces decorated with cordons, finger-nail impressions and grooves forming chevron motifs (Leivers 2018b, 123).

Amesbury Down and King's Gate

An extended programme of archaeological work carried out by Wessex Archaeology between 1993 and 2015 on an area of chalk downland, Amesbury Down, south-east of Amesbury (Fig. 12.1), revealed extensive evidence for activity dating from the Neolithic through to the Romano-British period (Fitzpatrick 2011; Powell and Barclay forthcoming). Further features of Neolithic, Bronze Age and Iron Age date were also identified at the adjacent King's Gate Development (Powell and Higbee forthcoming).

Late Neolithic activity consists of a post-circle, a post alignment and 42 pits distributed across the site in four broad groups. As at Bulford, the pits are roughly circular, between 0.6 m and 1 m in diameter, with an average depth of 0.3 m. The majority of finds are distributed throughout the fills with little evidence, apart from a few exceptions, for more formalised or special deposits. The range of finds recovered is comparable to those from other sites discussed here, predominantly comprising worked flint, burnt flint, pottery, stone and animal bone including antler picks, as well as worked bone items such as points, gouges and awls. Less common artefacts include fragments of Cornish Greenstone axeheads and nodules of iron pyrites.

The Grooved Ware assemblage comprises 697 sherds (3888 g) from excavations at Amesbury Down (Leivers forthcoming) and 81 sherds (186 g) from King's Gate (Brook forthcoming b). The greater proportion of this material came from pits, with only four small, abraded sherds recovered from features forming the post-circle; no pottery came from the post-alignment. Grog-tempered fabrics, in varying combinations with flint and sand inclusions, are predominant, with smaller quantities of shell- and flint-tempered wares also present. A small number of vessels are attributable to the Woodlands sub-style. One is described as a Woodlands/Durrington Walls hybrid but the majority of the Grooved Ware belongs to the Durrington Walls sub-style (Leivers forthcoming).

Within the Woodlands component, rims are decorated with cabling, incised lines and plastic decoration. Decoration on the exterior of vessels includes incised lines and bands of corrugation formed by adding strips of clay to the surface. The exterior of the Woodlands/Durrington Walls hybrid vessel has multiple bands of converging lines, some curving back on themselves as seen on the Woodlands vessel from Area 3 on Salisbury Plain (as described above), but in this case the motifs are incised rather than applied. Several sherds from a further pit are decorated with incised lines and whipped cord impressions. The latter technique is unusual within the Woodlands sub-style. The Durrington Walls sub-style vessels are far more typical of the tradition, with the use of vertical cordons or incised/tooled lines to create 'panels' infilled with triangles or diagonal lines being characteristic, as is the use of twisted cord and stabbed impressions (Leivers forthcoming).

COMMON THEMES: LOCAL AND MORE DISTANT

Geographically, the closest parallels to the Bulford material are the vessels from the site of Woodlands itself, which lies only 2 km to the south-west. In particular, the use of applied strips to the rim, the wavy line motifs, the use of plain and/or decorated cordons, converging lines and knots are obvious characteristics of both assemblages. One vessel from Woodlands also has a perforated lug attached (Stone 1949, fig. 1, c), comparable to a fineware example from Bulford (Fig. 12.5, a). Given how close these two sites are, it is not unreasonable to suggest that the vessels could even be the work of the same potter or group of potters.

Other components of the finds assemblages, notably the presence of microdenticulates and chisel arrowheads along with worked bone awls and marine shell fragments, appear to be characteristic of the local Woodlands Grooved Ware 'package'. Combinations of these materials all feature in the groups from Woodlands itself (Stone and Young 1948; Stone 1949), Harnham Park (Wessex Archaeology 2022), Amesbury Down (Powell and Barclay forthcoming) and Upavon Down on Salisbury Plain (Powell *et al.* 2018), as well as Bulford (Wessex Archaeology 2020). It has been observed that the flint assemblages associated with Woodlands sub-style ceramics on Amesbury Down and Salisbury Plain can, but do not always, contain very large quantities of finished tools and knapping debris, whilst those with Durrington Walls sub-style pottery were mostly smaller in size and contained higher proportions of waste (Leivers 2018b, 119; Harding and Leivers forthcoming). The marine shells, including scallop, common mussel and oyster, may represent food waste but could have had a secondary use as a tempering agent in pottery manufacture. The latter was confirmed in the analysis of sherds from Woodlands that identified crushed marine oyster shell as a component (Cleal *et al.* 1994, 446). Given the large size (130 × 110 mm) and near-completeness of the Harnham Park scallop shell, it is unlikely that this was accidentally lost and more probable that it was carefully selected for deposition in the pit. It is also worth pointing out that many of these items, whether of flint, bone or shell, could also be used in decorating the Woodlands pottery itself, as the edge of a scallop shell pushed on to a surface could make a very crisp, slightly curved impression comparable to (and easily mistaken for) that of a fingernail.

Parallels for the Bulford Woodlands pottery can also be found from much further afield. Assemblages from sites such as Flamborough, East Riding of Yorkshire (Manby

1974, e.g. fig. 30, 1), and Old Yeavering, Northumberland (Manby 1999), share many of the characteristics outlined above, including the decoration of coarseware jar rims such as those on a vessel from Sawdon Moor, North Yorkshire (Manby 1999, fig. 6.3.5).

Further to the north, the notable assemblage from Balfarg Riding School, Fife (above, Fig. 4.2; Henshall 1993), contains vessels with uncanny similarities to those from Bulford, so much so that the descriptions by Henshall formed a tick-list and useful aid for describing much of the Bulford material. The relevant features include lugs/pellets on the rims and other internal rim decoration as well as the use of cordons, false-relief wavy line motifs, slanted or converging lines, incised designs including chevrons, and stabbed impressions. In particular, the decorative scheme on vessel P54 (Henshall 1993, 97, illus. 28) is an extremely close parallel to one fineware vessel from Bulford (Fig. 12.5, a).

A comparable range of decorative techniques and motifs can also be seen within the assemblage from Barnhouse, Orkney (above, Figs 2.2 and 2.4; Jones 2005; Richards *et al.* 2016). There, as at Bulford and Sawdon Moor, strips of clay decorate the rims of large, coarseware vessels (e.g. Richards 2005, 55, fig. 3.38). In addition to the comparable list of elements noted above from Balfarg Riding School, Fife, some vessels from Barnhouse are decorated with stabbed impressions arranged in a rosette motif which can fill areas between cordons or other bands of decoration (Jones 2005; Richards *et al.* 2016, fig. 4, 4261). This is a less commonly found parallel for at least two vessels from Bulford (Fig. 12.5, b–c).

DATING

A total of 18 radiocarbon dates have been obtained on samples of animal bone, antler and charred plant remains from 12 Late Neolithic pits at Bulford (Wessex Archaeology 2020, table 26). Fourteen of these fall consistently within the 30th century cal BC and, when modelled, suggest that the pits may have been dug over a relatively short period of time, no longer than 46 years (at 68% probability). At Harnham Park, five samples were taken for radiocarbon dating from the Late Neolithic pits and, with the exception of one Middle Bronze Age date on an intrusive cereal grain, span the 30th to 29th centuries cal BC (Inés Lopez-Doriga, pers. comm.), directly comparable to those from Bulford. Future modelling of this group will, it is hoped, refine this contemporaneity more closely. These dates indicate that the Late Neolithic activity at both Bulford and Harnham Park, at which the Grooved Ware is exclusively of the Woodlands sub-style, was broadly contemporary and the earliest in the sequence in relation to the other Grooved Ware sites from south Wiltshire discussed in this paper. The author is also aware of a collection of '62 sherds of an elaborate Woodlands style Grooved Ware vessel' recovered from a pit at Porton Down, 7 km to the south-east of Bulford, referenced by Roberts and Marshall (2019, 13, tables 1 and 3) in their review of Neolithic pit digging in Wiltshire. These sherds are associated with a comparable early Late Neolithic date (i.e. the end of the 4th–early 3rd millennium cal BC) to those from Bulford and Harnham Park. However, at the time of writing, access to the unpublished grey literature report has not been possible and this site has not been included in the above discussions.

The two radiocarbon dates from Pit 9003 in Area 3 at Upavon Down, which contained both Woodlands and Clacton sub-style vessels, fall at the end of the 30th through to the start of the 29th century cal BC. This would appear to be towards the end of the Woodlands sequence at Bulford but indicates a relatively early start for the presence of the Clacton sub-style in the area. The dates are also comparable to that from the Chalk Plaque Pit (Garwood 1999, 152; Barclay 2018, 173, table 25). The dates associated with the Durrington Walls sub-style pottery from Areas 2 and 3 on Salisbury Plain span the 29th–25th centuries cal BC, and although this is thought to include multiple phases of activity there appears to be a focus around the 26th–25th centuries cal BC (Barclay 2018, 175), which is consistent with the later use of Grooved Ware in the area.

Radiocarbon dates were obtained from 14 pits phased to the Late Neolithic at Amesbury Down. The range of dates indicate that pit digging started in the later 28th or early 27th century cal BC and ended during the later 26th century cal BC (Powell and Barclay forthcoming). Unfortunately, these did not include samples from the pits containing the more unusual Woodlands/Durrington Walls hybrid vessel or the sherds with corded decoration that is atypical of the Woodlands tradition. Despite this, however, it is possible that the Amesbury Down dates indicate a fairly lengthy currency for the Woodlands sub-style in the area, as well as enhancing the list of fairly consistent dates for the Durrington Walls sub-style. It is not uncommon for Grooved Ware assemblages to contain features of more than one sub-style, but these more typically include those of Woodlands/Clacton (e.g. Chalk Plaque pit; Upavon Down) or Clacton/Durrington Walls (e.g. Wainwright and Longworth 1971; Cleal 1993) sub-style combinations, although an extreme example from further afield at Wyke Down Henge 2 on Cranborne Chase, Dorset, has elements of all three sub-styles on a single vessel (Cleal 2007, 314, fig. A4.14, P41). This highlights the rather complex picture involved in unravelling the chronological sequences relating to the Grooved Ware tradition.

Modelling of the Orcadian radiocarbon dates suggests that the Grooved Ware from Barnhouse dates to between the 32nd and 31st, or 31st and 29th centuries cal BC (Richards *et al.* 2016, 219), with comparable dates suggested for the start of Grooved Ware use at Pool on Sanday (MacSween *et al.* 2015, 302). Elsewhere in Scotland, carbonised residue on a Grooved Ware sherd from a pit at Balfarg Riding School, Fife, has provided a date of *3090–2909 cal BC* (*95.4% probability*; Copper *et al.* 2018, 223), whilst a further vessel found within Structure 2 from this site has associated dates in the 31st to 28th centuries cal BC (Barclay and Russell-White 1993). The range of dates within the 30th century cal BC from the Woodlands pits at Bulford sits comfortably within this pattern and gives further support to the suggestion of a very rapid spread southwards of the adoption of Grooved Ware from an Orcadian origin.

Returning to a more local scale, the dates of the Woodlands-related activity at Bulford coincide with the construction of the Stage 1 ditch at Stonehenge, thought to have been dug in the period *2995–2900 cal BC* (*at 95% probability*; Marshall *et al.* 2020, 544–6). Located at a distance of just over 5 km to the south-west, it is difficult to envisage that the people undertaking the pit digging at Bulford would not have been aware of, and may even have participated in, this undertaking.

CONCLUSION: WOODLANDS IN PERSPECTIVE

The Woodlands sub-style Grooved Ware pottery manufactured during the early part of the Late Neolithic in the areas surrounding Salisbury and Amesbury shares many affinities with ceramics in the north of England and Scotland. The evidence outlined here indicates that this sub-style is the earliest within the Grooved Ware ceramic tradition in the Salisbury area and is characterised by a range of thin-walled, finely decorated vessels as well as thick-walled coarsewares that are commonly deposited with a range of other, sometimes specific, artefact types in pits. The nature of this activity appears to be, on the whole, domestic and precedes the more ceremonial/monumental activity characterised by the construction of the Bulford double henges by at least 300 years (Leivers 2021).

The Bulford collection is one of the largest Woodlands sub-style assemblages discovered in southern Britain and provides a unique opportunity to study this component of the Grooved Ware tradition in greater detail. It is also important to help widen our understanding of the long-distance connections taking place across Britain and Ireland in the Late Neolithic and ties in with the evidence for long-distance movement of ideas, objects and practices. As the *Tracing the Lines* project (Copper *et al.* 2021) has confirmed the early spread of Grooved Ware in Scotland beyond its probable place of invention in Orkney, the dates of the Bulford assemblage emphasise this point and provide important evidence for the adoption of this earlier style of Grooved Ware in southern Britain, which happened rapidly in the very early parts of the 3rd millennium cal BC.

ACKNOWLEDGEMENTS

Thanks to Phil Harding and Matt Leivers for information regarding site background and stratigraphic sequences at Bulford, Alistair Barclay for help with the initial identification of the pottery, and Alison Sheridan and Ros Cleal who viewed the assemblage for comments. The figures were prepared by Rob Goller. The Army Basing Programme was commissioned by Aspire Defence, Lovell Partnerships and WYG on behalf of Defence Infrastructure Organisation. Work at Amesbury Down and King's Gate was funded by Bloor Homes, Persimmon Homes (South Coast) Ltd and QinetiQ Ltd and that at Harnham Park by Bellway Homes Ltd.

REFERENCES

Barclay, A.J. 2018. Radiocarbon dating. In A.B. Powell *et al.* 2018, 171–9.

Barclay, G.J. and Russell-White, C.J. 1993. Excavations in the ceremonial complex of the fourth to second millennium BC at Balfarg/Balbirnie, Glenrothes, Fife. *Proceedings of the Society of Antiquaries of Scotland* 123, 43–210.

Brook, E. forthcoming a. Prehistoric pottery. In M. Leivers and A. Valdez-Tullett, *The archaeology of the Stonehenge Visitor Centre.* Salisbury: Wessex Archaeology.

Brook, E. forthcoming b. Pottery. In A.B. Powell and L. Higbee forthcoming.

Cleal, R.M.J. 1993. Pottery and fired clay. In R. Bradley, P. Chowne, R.M.J. Cleal, F. Healy and I. Kinnes, *Excavations on Redgate Hill, Hunstanton, Norfolk, and at Tattershall Thorpe, Lincolnshire*, 40–60. Gressenhall: East Anglian Archaeology 57.

Cleal, R.M.J. 1995. Pottery fabrics in Wessex in the fourth to second millennia BC. In I. Kinnes and G. Varndell (eds), *'Unbaked urns of rudely shape': essays on British and Irish pottery for Ian Longworth*, 185–94. Oxford: Oxbow Books.

Cleal, R. 2007. Pottery of Wyke Down 2 henge. In C. French, H. Lewis, M.J. Allen, M. Green, R. Scaife and J. Gardiner, *Prehistoric landscape development and human impact in the upper Allen valley, Cranborne Chase, Dorset*, 313–19. Cambridge: McDonald Institute for Archaeological Research.

Cleal, R. and MacSween, A. (eds) 1999. *Grooved Ware in Britain and Ireland.* Oxford: Oxbow Books.

Cleal, R.M.J., Cooper, J. and Williams, D. 1994. Shells and sherds: identification of inclusions in Grooved Ware, with associated radiocarbon dates, from Amesbury, Wiltshire. *Proceedings of the Prehistoric Society* 60, 445–8.

Copper, M., Hamilton, D. and Gibson, A. 2021. Tracing the lines: Scottish Grooved Ware trajectories beyond Orkney. *Proceedings of the Society of Antiquaries of Scotland* 150, 81–117. https://doi.org/10.9750/PSAS.150.1307.

Copper, M., Sheridan, J.A., Gibson, A., Tripney, B., Hamilton, D. and Cook, G. 2018. Radiocarbon dates for Grooved Ware pottery from mainland Scotland arising from the project Tracing the Lines: Uncovering Grooved Ware Trajectories in Neolithic Scotland. *Discovery and Excavation in Scotland* 19, 222–5.

Cunnington, M.E. 1929. *Woodhenge. A description of the site as revealed by the excavations carried out there by Mr and Mrs BH Cunnington, 1926–7–8. Also Four Circles and an Earthwork Enclosure south of Woodhenge.* Devizes: Simpson.

Fitzpatrick, A.P. 2011. *The Amesbury Archer and the Boscombe Bowmen. Bell beaker burials at Boscombe Down, Amesbury, Wiltshire.* Salisbury: Wessex Archaeology Report 27.

Garwood, P. 1999. Grooved Ware in southern Britain: chronology and interpretation. In R. Cleal and A. MacSween (eds) 1999, 145–76.

Hamilton, M. and Whittle, A. 1999. Grooved Ware of the Avebury Area: styles, context and meanings. In R. Cleal and A. MacSween (eds) 1999, 36–47.

Harding, P. 1988. The Chalk Plaque Pit, Amesbury. *Proceedings of the Prehistoric Society* 54, 320–7.

Harding, P. and Leivers, M. forthcoming. Worked flint. In A.B. Powell and A.J. Barclay forthcoming.

Henshall, A.S. 1993. The Grooved Ware: vessels P41–82. In G.J. Barclay and C.J. Russell-White 1993, 94–108.

Jones, A. 2005. The Grooved Ware from Barnhouse. In C. Richards 2005, 261–82.

Leivers, M. 2018a. Early prehistoric pottery. In S. Thompson and A.B. Powell, *Along prehistoric lines: Neolithic, Iron Age and Romano-British activity at the former MOD Headquarters, Durrington, Wiltshire*, 59–62. Salisbury: Wessex Archaeology.

Leivers, M. 2018b. Pottery. In A.B. Powell *et al.* 2018, 120–7.

Leivers, M. 2021. The Army Basing Programme, Stonehenge and the emergence of the sacred landscape of Wessex. *Internet Archaeology* 56, https://doi.org/10.11141/ia.56.2.

Leivers, M. forthcoming. Neolithic and Bronze Age pottery. In A.B. Powell and A.J. Barclay forthcoming.

Leivers, M., Harding, P. and Valdez-Tullett, A. forthcoming. *Excavations on Defence Sites, Volume 4: Mainly Neolithic and Bronze Age.* Salisbury: Wessex Archaeology.

Longworth, I. 1971. The pottery. In G.W. Wainwright, J.G. Evans and I. Longworth, The Excavation of a Late Neolithic Enclosure at Marden, Wiltshire, 197–215. *Antiquaries Journal* 51, 177–239.

Longworth, I. and Cleal, R. 1999. Grooved Ware Gazetteer. In R. Cleal and A. MacSween (eds) 1999, 177–206.

MacSween, A., Hunter, J., Sheridan, J.A., Bond, J., Bronk Ramsey, C., Reimer, P., Bayliss, A., Griffiths, S. and Whittle, A. 2015. Refining the chronology of the Neolithic settlement at Pool, Sanday,

Orkney: implications for the emergence and development of Grooved Ware. *Proceedings of the Prehistoric Society* 81, 283–310.

Manby, T.G. 1974. *Grooved Ware sites in Yorkshire and the north of England.* Oxford: British Archaeological Report 9.

Manby, T. G. 1999. Grooved Ware sites in Yorkshire and northern England: 1974–1994. In R. Cleal and A. MacSween (eds) 1999, 57–75.

Marshall, P. D., Bronk Ramsey, C., Cook, G. and Parker Pearson, M. 2020. Radiocarbon dating of Stonehenge. In M. Parker Pearson *et al.* 2020, 527–46.

Parker Pearson, M., Pollard, J., Richards, C., Thomas, J., Tilley, C. and Welham, K. 2020. *Stonehenge for the ancestors. Part 1: landscape and monuments.* Leiden: Sidestone Press.

Parker Pearson, M., Pollard, J., Richards, C., Thomas, J., Tilley, C. and Welham, K. 2022. *Stonehenge for the ancestors. Part 2: synthesis.* Leiden: Sidestone Press.

Powell, A.B. and Barclay, A.J. forthcoming. *Between and beyond the monuments: prehistoric activity on the downlands south-east of Amesbury.* Salisbury: Wessex Archaeology.

Powell, A.B. and Higbee, L. forthcoming. *Prehistoric burial, settlement and deposition on the King's Gate Development, Amesbury Down, Wiltshire.* Salisbury: Wessex Archaeology.

Powell, A.B., Beach, S. and Leivers, M. 2018. Prehistoric deposition, burial and settlement on Salisbury Plain: archaeological investigations along the new military tracks, 2009−2012. *Wiltshire Archaeological and Natural History Magazine* 111, 84−193.

Richards, C. 2005. *Dwelling among the monuments: the Neolithic village of Barnhouse, Maeshowe passage grave and surrounding monuments at Stenness, Orkney.* Cambridge: McDonald Institute for Archaeological Research.

Richards, C., Jones, A.M., MacSween, A., Sheridan, J.A., Dunbar, E., Reimer, P., Bayliss, A., Griffiths, S. and Whittle, A. 2016. Settlement duration and materiality: formal chronological models for the development of Barnhouse, a Grooved Ware settlement in Orkney. *Proceedings of the Prehistoric Society* 82, 193–225.

Richards, J.C. 1990. *The Stonehenge Environs Project.* London: Historic Monuments and Buildings Commission.

Roberts, D. and Marshall, P. 2019. *Pit digging and lifeways in Neolithic Wiltshire.* Portsmouth: Historic England, Research Report Series 34-2019.

Stone, J.F.S. 1935. Some discoveries at Ratfyn, Amesbury and their bearing on the date of Woodhenge. *Wiltshire Archaeological and Natural History Magazine* 47, 55–67.

Stone, J.F.S. 1949. Some Grooved Ware pottery from the Woodhenge area. *Proceedings of the Prehistoric Society* 15, 122–7.

Stone, J.F.S. and Young, W.E.V. 1948. Two pits of Grooved Ware date near Woodhenge, Wiltshire. *Wiltshire Archaeological and Natural History Magazine* 52, 287–304.

Wainwright, G.J. and Longworth, I.H. 1971. *Durrington Walls: excavations 1966–1968.* London: Society of Antiquaries.

Wessex Archaeology 2020. *Bulford Service Family Accommodation, Bulford, Wiltshire. Post-excavation Assessment.* Salisbury: Wessex Archaeology, unpublished client report ref. 200770.01.

Wessex Archaeology 2022. *Harnham Park, Netherhampton Road, Salisbury, Wiltshire. Post-excavation assessment and updated project design.* Salisbury: Wessex Archaeology, unpublished client report ref. 227641.04.

Whittle, A. 1997. *Sacred mound, holy rings. Silbury Hill and the West Kennet palisade enclosures: a Later Neolithic complex in north Wiltshire.* Oxford: Oxbow Books.

Chapter 13

Grooved Ware in south-east England: social geographies, chronology and interpretation

Paul Garwood

In the last 25 years, the number of sites with Grooved Ware finds in south-east England[1] has nearly tripled and the scale of the overall assemblage in the region has increased five-fold, yet just as striking is the absence of Grooved Ware from many parts of the region and from most of the extensive excavations conducted by commercial fieldwork organisations. It is also apparent that the occurrence of Grooved Ware is marked by very uneven scales of deposition: most of the total assemblage has been recovered from just five sites. This raises a range of questions concerning the character of Grooved Ware-using communities in the region and the particular social and temporal contexts of Grooved Ware use.

This paper presents, for the first time, a regional review of the geographical and chronological presence/absence of Grooved Ware ceramics, and the kinds of social practices and modes of inhabitation evident at 'Grooved Ware sites' in relation to wider interpretations of social change in south-east England during the 3rd millennium cal BC. This is based on a comprehensive audit of published and grey literature sources, Historic Environment Records and online archives available to the end of 2022, and on queries sent to curatorial archaeologists and archaeological companies who kindly provided substantial additional material such as hitherto unavailable interim excavation reports.

GROOVED WARE IN SOUTH-EAST ENGLAND IN SPACE AND TIME

The Late Neolithic in south-east England

Grooved Ware assemblages and the range of contexts these have been recovered from account for most of what is known of the Late Neolithic in south-east England.[2] The monument categories typically used to characterise this period elsewhere in Britain are almost entirely missing from the region. 'Classic' henges, 'hengiform' ring-ditches and pit circles, and timber and stone circles, are notable for their near or complete absence; there is only one well dated enclosure that may be identified as a henge (Ringlemere, Kent; Parfitt and Needham 2020), while other possible sites are uncertainly dated (e.g. The Meads, Sittingbourne, Kent; Wilson 2015) or uninvestigated (e.g. Bredgar, Kent; NMR 21050-33). Claims made for 'henges' elsewhere, for example on the Sussex Downs (Russell 1997; cf. Garwood 2003, 56–7) and the Isle of Thanet (Moody 2008, 72–6) are not supported by radiocarbon dates or Late Neolithic material in early depositional contexts. The Lord of the Manor I site, Thanet, for example (Moody 2008; Longworth and Cleal 1999, gz. 186), is a multi-phase Early Bronze Age 'cemetery barrow' with a few weathered Grooved Ware sherds redeposited in the fill of the middle ditch.

Other evidence for Late Neolithic activity is sparse, restricted to a few radiocarbon-dated deposits in diverse, geographically scattered contexts (11 dates from eight sites). Most relate to spreads of lithic artefacts, wood-working traces and possible middens in wetland/river-edge settings (e.g. on the Bexhill–Hastings Link Road and at Ebbsfleet: Champness *et al.* unpublished client report; Stafford *et al.* 2020, 379–8). This contrasts starkly with the scale of archaeological records resulting from decades of extensive commercial fieldwork. There is, for example, almost no evidence for Grooved Ware or significant Late Neolithic activity on large sites such as Thanet Earth, Kent (Rady 2019), Peacehaven, East Sussex (Hart 2015), along the Chichester Growth Scheme main sewer route on the West Sussex coastal plain (Sheehan, unpublished client report), or Wey Manor Farm in Surrey (Hayman *et al.* 2015).

Although lithic assemblages are often described as Late Neolithic on typological and technological grounds, their dating is usually imprecise and larger-scale mapping of finds distributions provides us with palimpsests of 'inhabitation' only at very broad temporal scales (e.g. Gardiner 2008). There has also been little chronological consistency in the use of the term 'Late Neolithic'. It often seems a synonym for 'later Neolithic', encompassing material spanning the late 4th and most of the 3rd millennium cal BC. Even distinctive artefact types such as discoidal knives and transverse arrowheads escape precise chronological definition (Gardiner 2008, 239; Cleal 2012). Lithic artefacts thus provide no reliable basis in themselves for defining the chronologies and temporalities of Late Neolithic social life.

Contextualising Grooved Ware in this context is beset with uncertainties and contradictions. Whilst pottery deposition is generally small-scale and dispersed in space and time, this does not necessarily point to sparse Late Neolithic inhabitation, which may have been widely aceramic. At the same time, however, the limited evidence for durable architecture, both ceremonial and 'domestic', may suggest small populations and relatively 'mobile' settlement (Whittle 1997). In this light, our understanding of the Late Neolithic in south-east England still depends mostly on interpretations of Grooved Ware ceramics and the contexts in which these have been found.

Assemblage scale and distribution

In 1999, the total Grooved Ware assemblage in south-east England (Longworth and Cleal 1999, 185, 189, 196) amounted to about 800 sherds from 24 sites (including Thames foreshore finds and the partly reported Betchworth assemblage). In the last 25 years, the scale of this assemblage has increased substantially and now amounts to at least 4200 sherds, weighing over 25 kg, from 68 sites. Yet this material is unevenly and, for the most part, thinly distributed across the region, usually occurring in tiny assemblages ranging from one to 25 sherds. Only 12 sites have produced more than 30 sherds, and over 75% of the total assemblage derives from just five sites: White Horse Stone (475 sherds; Garwood 2011) and Ringlemere in Kent (2044 sherds; Gibson 2020); Betchworth, Surrey

(470 sherds; Williams 2017); and North Bersted (182 sherds; Taylor *et al.* 2014) and Tye Lane, Walberton, in West Sussex (over 150 sherds; Vieira 2021).

The geographical distribution of Grooved Ware finds in south-east England is shown in Figure 13.1. It is difficult to judge how representative the mapping of this material is of the presence of Grooved Ware across the region or how this evidence relates to Late Neolithic landscape inhabitation. The presence/absence of Grooved Ware partly reflects variation in the relative frequencies and scales of fieldwork in different areas. Most of the sites to the south of the North Downs in central Kent, for example, were found along the High Speed 1 rail route (Garwood 2011). The clusters of Grooved Ware finds in Thanet and east Kent, north-west Surrey and on the West Sussex coastal plain similarly occur in areas that have been subject to relatively more extensive and concentrated urban development and/or infrastructure projects. Other areas, in contrast, have seen little recent development, which might help to account for the rarity of Grooved Ware on the North and South Downs and central parts of the Weald. The potential presence of Late Neolithic sites deeply buried in riverine and estuarine sediments and peats remains largely untested everywhere.

Even so, there are some reasons to be confident that known distributions of findspots and relative scales of Grooved Ware deposition are not entirely artefacts of uneven archaeological recording. Monuments on the Sussex chalklands, for example, have for centuries been favourite targets of antiquarian and research excavations, yet Grooved Ware is almost entirely absent. More widely, thousands of developer-funded investigations throughout south-east England, hundreds of which have involved extensive evaluation trenching and/or extensive 'strip, map and sample' excavations of large tracts of land, have effectively demonstrated that Grooved Ware deposition was rare or absent from these areas altogether. These excavations have, in combination, sampled the full range of geological and geomorphological variation across the region, in some areas intensively, such as the coastal plains of Kent and Sussex and their chalkland margins.

On this basis, it is possible to make the following interpretative observations:

1. Grooved Ware finds are thinly and unevenly scattered across south-east England, occurring mainly in lower-lying rather than upland settings, and are almost entirely absent from the central Weald between the South Downs escarpment and the northern Greensand ridge in Surrey and Kent.
2. Taking account of both findspots and assemblage scales, Grooved Ware deposition appears most concentrated in four areas: (i) the Middle Thames Valley in Surrey, and possibly its tributaries; (ii) the lower Medway Valley and its tributaries just to the south of the North Downs; (iii) east Kent and Thanet; (iv) the West Sussex coastal plain.
3. Although the sample size is small, there may be some spatial patterning in the distribution of Grooved Ware styles. Clacton sub-style pottery, and sherds with Woodlands 'features', are most common in the northern part of the region along the Thames and north Kent coast corridor, including the lower Medway and Stour valleys and Thanet. In contrast, Durrington Walls sub-style pottery is more widely distributed, and predominates across the central and southern parts of the region, which might relate to coastal and downland connections with south Wessex.

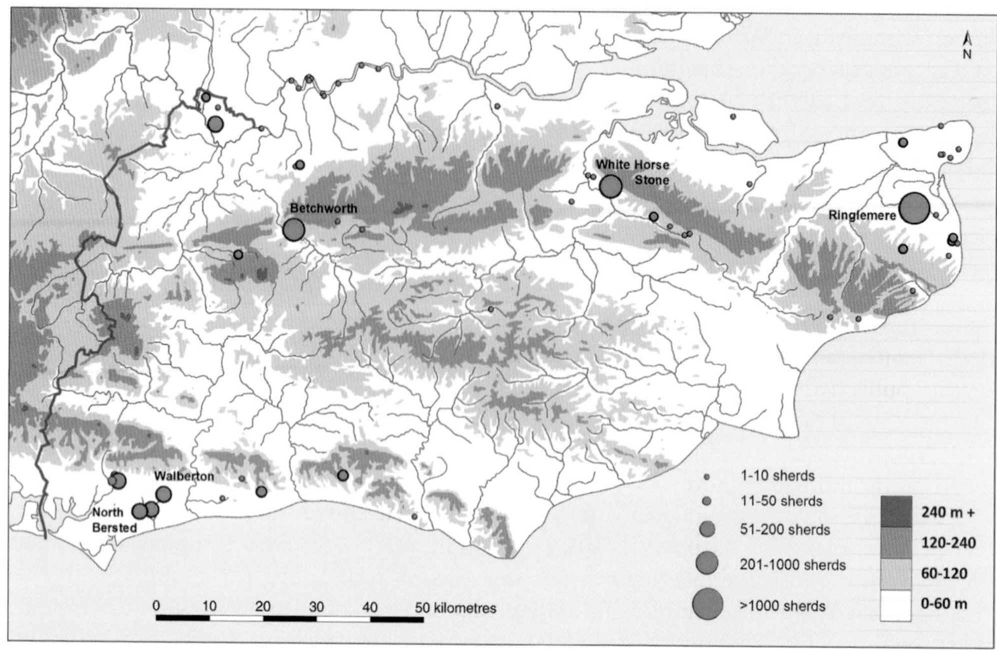

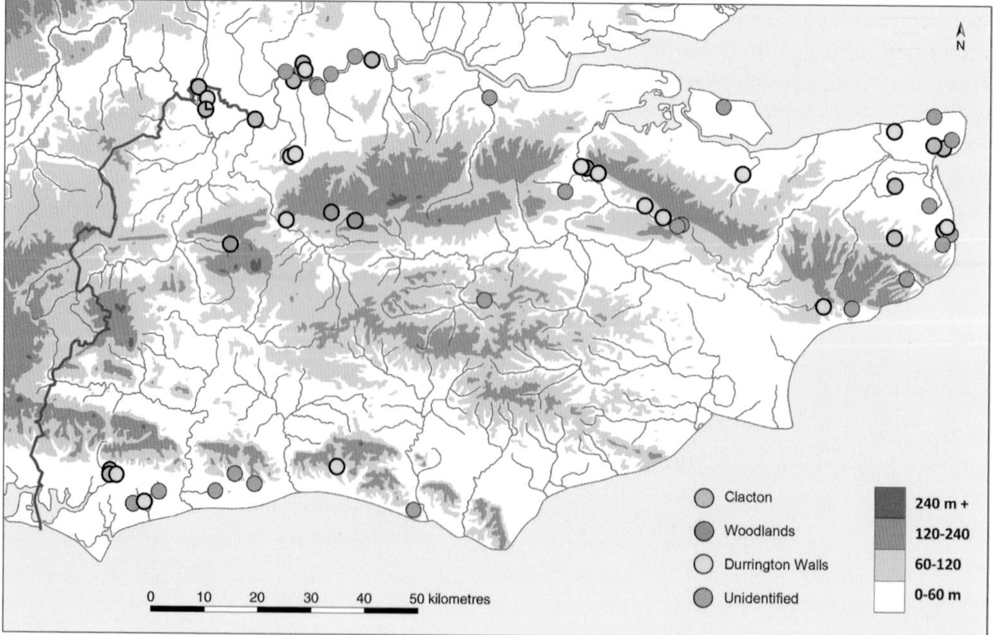

Figure 13.1. Distribution of Grooved Ware finds in south-east England. Upper: assemblage size categories. Lower: Grooved Ware sub-styles.

It is inevitable that future discoveries will lead to substantial modification of the detail of Grooved Ware distributions; just two or three large assemblages could greatly alter perceptions of relative dispersion and concentration across the region. It seems less likely, however, that the overall picture of Grooved Ware distribution in south-east England will change radically unless (or until) there are major new discoveries in river valleys and estuarine/coastal settings.

CHRONOLOGY

At the time the radiocarbon chronology for southern British Grooved Ware was first reviewed (Garwood 1999), there were only two radiocarbon dates from south-east England, neither published when that paper was written (from St Richards and Cross Road, Mill Hill, Deal, Kent; Parfitt 1998). These have since increased in number to 28 determinations from 24 features (Table 13.1; Fig. 13.2), 13 of which derive from short-life sample materials in direct association with pottery (charred residues on sherds, charred apples and hazelnuts, and twig charcoal). The remainder derive from wood charcoal (potentially subject to 'old wood' effects) and disarticulated animal bones (both charcoal and bone samples potentially residual and/or redeposited).

Understanding of Grooved Ware chronology has developed significantly in the last 25 years. In particular, it is now clear that the later 3rd millennium cal BC radiocarbon dates reported for Woodlands sub-style pottery in the 1990s were misleading, either because they were erroneous (due to sample quality; Alistair Barclay, pers. comm.) or because pottery redeposition was underestimated. The Clacton–Woodlands sequence that these dates suggested at the time (Garwood 1999) no longer applies. Woodlands ceramics excavated recently at Bulford, near Stonehenge, for example, are firmly dated to the 30th century cal BC (Leivers 2020, 113–14) and thus contemporary with early Clacton material.[3] Although no definite Woodlands sub-style assemblages have yet been recorded in south-east England, sherds with Woodlands 'features' along the Thames and in north Kent could well date to an early stage of Grooved Ware use.

At present, radiocarbon age ranges for Grooved Ware deposition in south-east England fall almost entirely within the period 2900–2500 cal BC. There is little to indicate any chronological variation between Clacton and Durrington Walls sub-styles. These are broadly contemporaneous, though the latter perhaps starts later and persists longer. A notable feature of the overall chronological distribution of the dates available is temporal clustering: nearly 60% (17) of all uncalibrated determinations fall in the 4200–4100 BP timeframe, and 80% (24) between 4200 and 4030 BP (*c.* 2870–2580 cal BC, and *c.* 2870–2500 cal BC, respectively). Although the corpus of Grooved Ware-associated dates is small, and calibration of dates in the first half of the 3rd millennium cal BC usually results in wider age ranges than their uncalibrated counterparts, current evidence suggests a relatively narrow timeframe for Grooved Ware deposition, probably no more than *c.* 350–400 years. This is far shorter than previous analysis of the wider southern British evidence suggested (*c.* 800 years, 2900–2100 cal BC; Garwood 1999).

At the earlier end of the timescale, there is no strong evidence for Grooved Ware in the region much before 2900 cal BC. Excluding the early date on oak charcoal (probably heartwood) from Ringlemere (Table 13.1), only two age ranges extend into the 30th century cal BC and in both cases their probability distributions suggest that the true ages of the samples are unlikely to fall before *c.* 2930 cal BC. One of these derives from a cattle skull found with other animal bones dated to the period 2895–2630 cal BC (White Horse Stone Hollow 5072; it is likely the cattle skull was curated or redeposited). The other early date, from charred residue on a Grooved Ware sherd (sub-style unidentified) recovered from a pit at Hengrove, Surrey, suggests deposition of this material in the decades around 2900 cal BC. This may point to relatively early Grooved Ware-associated activity along the Surrey section of the Middle Thames Valley in comparison with other parts of the region.

In this light, the threshold for the start of Grooved Ware deposition in south-east England probably lies at the beginning of the 29th century cal BC. This observation applies to both northern and south-western parts of the region: the introduction of Grooved Ware appears to have happened concurrently across widely separated areas. This has significant implications for understanding the transmission and adoption of Grooved Ware and associated practices across south-east England in the early 3rd millennium cal BC, and how these relate to the demise of Peterborough Ware and other Middle Neolithic cultural repertoires (discussed below).

At the other end of the chronological distribution of Grooved Ware-associated dates, only three age ranges extend later than 2500 cal BC. It is doubtful whether these provide reliable evidence for Grooved Ware use into the 25th century cal BC. In two cases (Betchworth Pit 220; Cross Road Pit F41), the dates have large standard deviations (at ±70 and ±60 years respectively), which considerably widen their calibrated age ranges. At Betchworth, the three most reliable dates (Table 13.1), one from each pit, all on charred residues adhering to pottery sherds, span the period 2880–2300 cal BC, yet the close spatial arrangement of the pit group and similar deposits in each feature suggest a single, short-duration occupation episode (Williams 2017, 133). In this light, although the true age of this activity is uncertain (since the data are open to alternative interpretative calculations), the age ranges at 68.2% probability all overlap in the period 2625–2490 cal BC, and none extends later than 2455 cal BC. It is therefore unlikely that the Betchworth depositional events took place later than the early 25th century cal BC.

In the case of the latest Grooved Ware-associated date from the region (2570–2300 cal BC: Cocks Farm, Abinger, pit 2573; Emma Corke 2019, pers. comm.), the short-life twiggy charcoal sample is unlikely to have been disturbed yet the pottery was heavily weathered, possibly due to exposure on the surface or in the topsoil for some time before (re-)deposition. If so, the pottery could date to the 26th century cal BC. Conversely, if it is assumed that the radiocarbon sample and Grooved Ware were deposited simultaneously, and sherd weathering took place *in situ*, this event probably took place in the 25th century cal BC. Whether a 26th or 25th century cal BC threshold is preferred for the 'end' of Grooved Ware in south-east England, the implications for understanding the Late Neolithic-Chalcolithic 'transition' are considerable (discussed below).

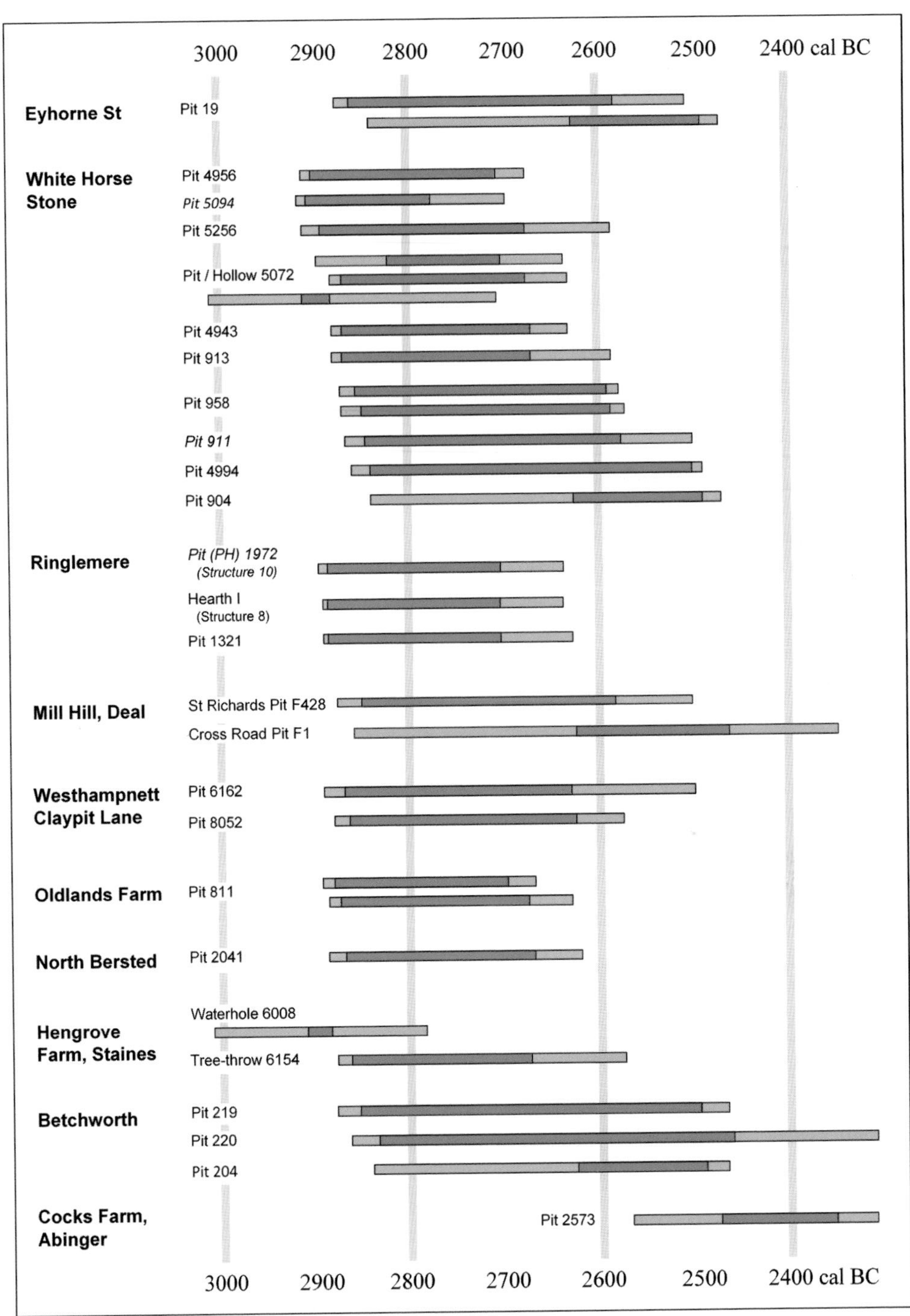

Figure 13.2. Age ranges of radiocarbon dates associated with Grooved Ware pottery in south-east England (see Table 13.1 for sources, and sample and context details).

PLACING GROOVED WARE: AGENCY, ARCHITECTURE AND LANDSCAPE

Places and spaces for Grooved Ware deposition

Contexts of Grooved Ware deposition in south-east England are diverse, yet for the most part the scales of ceramic assemblages recovered from sites of all kinds are small. There are just a few larger deposits (>100 sherds in total) among the pit groups and pit scatters at White Horse Stone, Betchworth, North Bersted and Walberton and, exceptionally, in the buried soil, pits, postholes, enclosure ditch and mound at Ringlemere.

Sixty-one pits containing Grooved Ware pottery have been excavated in south-east England (excluding the dense concentration of features at Ringlemere, discussed separately below), 22 of which were part of ten distinct 'pit groups' (including five at White Horse Stone, Kent; Garwood 2011, table 4.2). A few small assemblages have been found in other sub-surface features (a gully, four tree-throws, and a hollow), and in buried soils at Ospringe (Reid 2012) and the Lydden Valley in Kent (Halliwell and Parfitt 1985), the spatial and depositional contexts of which are uncertain. Even less is known about findspots along the Thames (just 12 sherds from ten locations; Longworth and Cleal 1999; Williams 2017, table 18). Only at three sites is there any association between Grooved Ware deposits and built structures: two round houses at White Horse Stone, one (19140) replaced by the other (5297, associated with a pit group) (Garwood 2011, 109–13); two small pits with stakehole settings at Walberton, West Sussex (reported briefly in Vieira 2020); and structures at Ringlemere that were probably used for ceremonial purposes (Parfitt and Needham 2020).

In addition to identifying the kinds of sites where Grooved Ware assemblages have been found, it is possible to make some observations about places from which they are largely absent. Sites of earlier activity in the Late Neolithic landscape lack evidence for Grooved Ware almost entirely: the total assemblage recovered from the 12 excavated Early Neolithic causewayed enclosures in the region amounts to a few sherds from just two sites (Kingsborough Farm 1, Chalk Hill). There are no recorded Grooved Ware finds at any excavated Early Neolithic mortuary monument (12 sites), nor at possible Middle Neolithic cursus monuments and long enclosures. Ancient places appear to have held no specific interest for those who used Grooved Ware.

A similar point can be made with respect to later activity at Grooved Ware sites. There is little evidence for reuse or 'referencing' of these places in the centuries after they were abandoned. Most telling, only seven of the several hundred excavated Chalcolithic and Bronze Age round barrow and ring-ditch sites in the region have produced Grooved Ware finds, in nearly all cases small assemblages of weathered residual material present in soils disturbed during monument construction. The exception may be Ringlemere, though the zone of Beaker-associated activity is peripheral to the main concentration of Late Neolithic structures and deposits, the visibility of which after 500 years of erosion and soil formation was probably minimal.

Grooved Ware pits and pit groups

Discussion of 'Grooved Ware pits' inevitably evokes themes of 'structured deposition', 'ritual' and symbolic communication (Richards and Thomas 1984; Thomas 1999, 64–74). The expectation that Grooved Ware deposition in general *must* have been intentionally 'meaningful' (in ways that both 'authors' and 'readers' could explicate) has become a pervasive if generic and sometimes imprecise aspect of site interpretation (e.g. ideas of 'structured' and 'special'/'placed' deposition are often conflated). This assumption is dubious; reappraisals of the purposes of pits and depositional and taphonomic processes on Late Neolithic settlement sites (e.g. Harding 2006; Garwood 2011, 107–9), and the idea of structured deposition itself (Garrow 2012), invite more critical evaluations of Grooved Ware in pit contexts.

The evidence from south-east England suggests that Grooved Ware pit deposition was rarely overtly 'symbolic'. There are no definite examples of formally organised, 'placed' deposits of pottery either on pit bases or added during infilling sequences. If rules of symbolic expression were being followed, these did not require a syntax of spatial organisation, association or ordering of materials at moments of deposition. Moreover, very few pits contain objects that may have had 'special' meanings because of their unusual character, and these are unique in each case: e.g. two Cornish stone axehead fragments in Pit 1969, Margetts Pit, Burham (Wessex Archaeology 2010), a bone scoop in Lower Mill Farm pit 22, Stanwell (Jones and Ayers 2004) and a decorated spherical clay object in Eyhorne Street pit 19 (Garwood 2011, 99–101).

Although there are convincing identifications of deliberate 'dumps' of material, for example in pit 6162 at Claypit Lane, Westhampnett (Chadwick 2006), and pits at White Horse Stone (Garwood 2011, 101–9), there is no reason to assume these were perceived as 'messaging', nor do they conform to recognisable, rule-bound modes of depositional process repeated from one event to another. Instead, pit-infilling actions used varied combinations of materials such as pit upcast, burnt refuse, food waste and flint-working debris. These deposits rarely comprise entire pit fills and there is no pattern of depositional ordering. They occur in layers preceding, sealing and interspersed with sediments derived from erosion and soil formation processes.

The most striking pattern in the evidence is spatial clustering of pits in groups of two to four (Fig. 13.3), most notably at Eyhorne Street and White Horse Stone (Garwood 2011, 99–109), Betchworth (Williams 2017) and Claypit Lane, Westhampnett (Chadwick 2006). Analysis of the extensive and detailed White Horse Stone evidence suggests that such pit groups were used for everyday activities, located within and/or just outside houses (Garwood 2011, 109–14). In this case, the linear arrangement of five pit groups and other features parallel to and just upslope from the valley base indicates a high degree of temporal contiguity whether they represent a continuously occupied multi-dwelling settlement or successive inhabitation episodes (Garwood 2011, 114–18). Elsewhere, single pits, sometimes dispersed across large site areas (e.g. at Westhampnett Area 4, and Oldlands Farm, West Sussex: Fitzpatrick *et al.* 2008; Margetts 2019), exhibit the same range of morphological characteristics, fills, artefacts and other materials as those found among pit groups, and appear to have been used for the same range of purposes.

The overall impression, based on the evidence of Grooved Ware pits and associated features, is that Late Neolithic settlement in south-east England was dispersed, involved little investment in durable architecture and mainly comprised short-lived occupation episodes. It is also notable that *all* the Grooved Ware pits in the region containing charred cereal grains were found either at White Horse Stone (four) or at Ringlemere (seven). These are the only sites in the region with evidence for sustained, spatially concentrated activity,

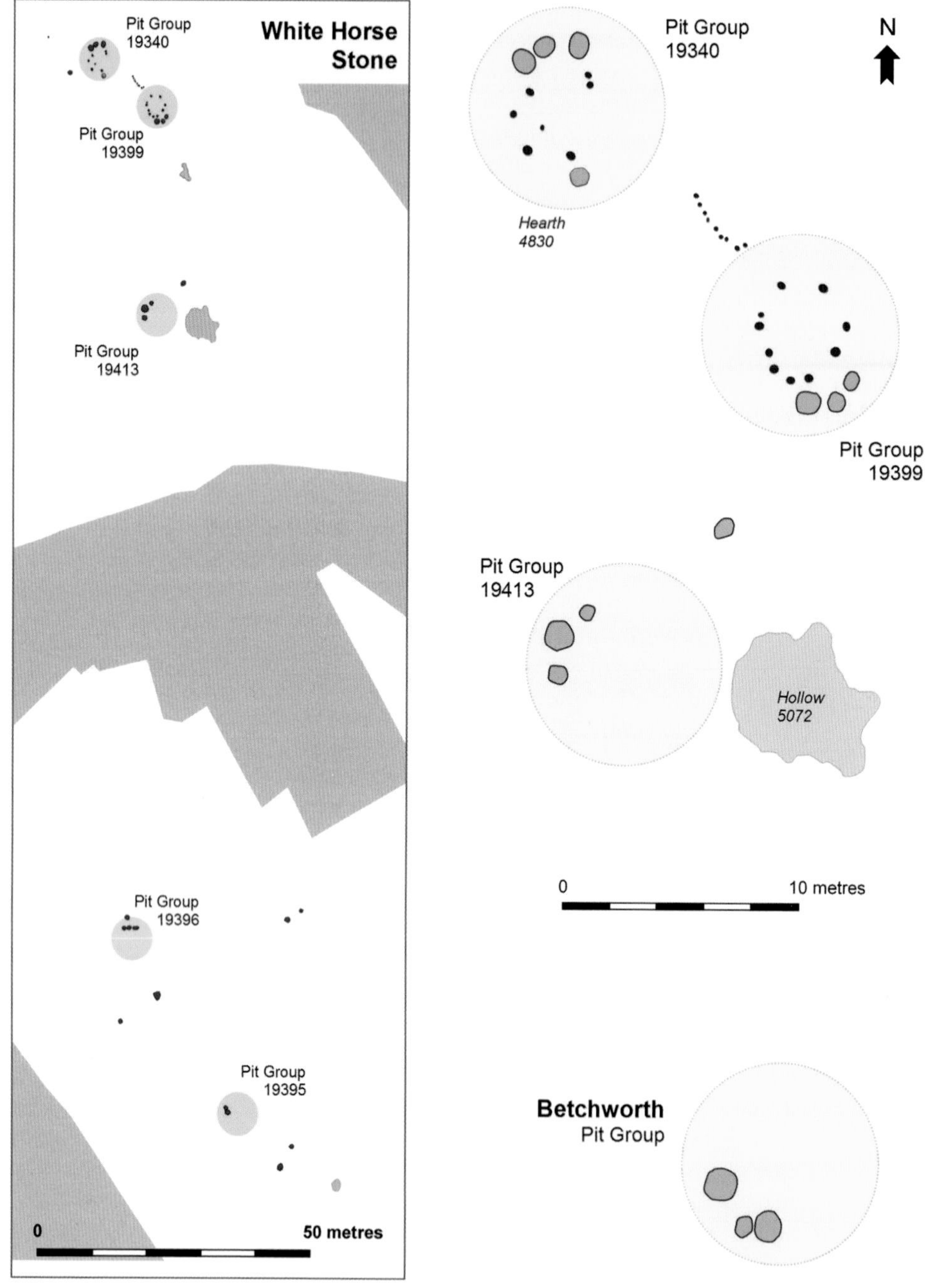

Figure 13.3. Grooved Ware pit groups in south-east England. Left: the White Horse Stone Grooved Ware settlement (after Garwood 2011, figs 3.36, 3.37); right: pit groups at White Horse Stone (19340, 19399, 19413; see Garwood 2011, fig. 3.41) and Betchworth (Williams 2017, fig. 8).

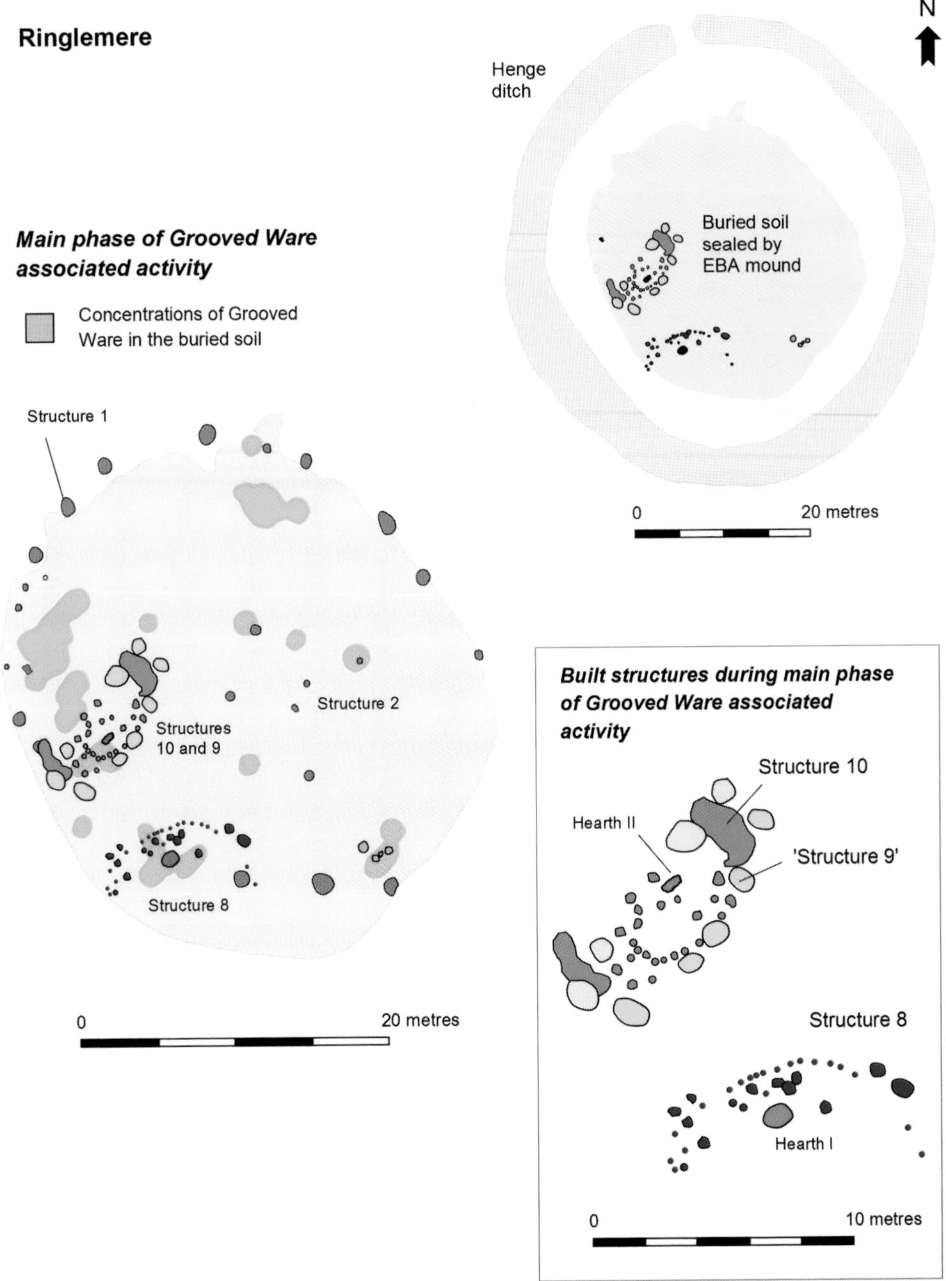

Figure 13.4. Ringlemere. Top right: spatial relationships of the principal Grooved Ware-associated structures, later henge enclosure, and the Early Bronze Age mound-buried soil; left: built structures and pottery concentrations in the buried soil dating to the main phase of Grooved Ware-associated activity (within site phases 2b–c, c. *2850–2650 cal BC); bottom right: details of Structures 8, 9 and 10 (principal sources: Parfitt and Needham 2020, figs 2.4, 2.10, 2.31, 2.36, 2.37).*

which may indicate a connection between arable farming and longer-lived places in the Late Neolithic landscape. In all other respects, the subsistence record is dominated by wild plant foods (fruits, hazelnuts), and domestic animals (cattle, sheep/goat, and some pig).

Ringlemere

The Late Neolithic features and material deposits at Ringlemere are exceptional in south-east England in terms of their complexity, scale and preservation (Parfitt and Needham 2020). The site comprises a multi-phase series of timber structures amidst a concentration of pits, postholes and hearths, all within the area of a single-entranced ditched enclosure interpreted as a type I 'henge'. The enclosure interior was covered by a large Early Bronze Age mound that sealed earlier features (mostly Late Neolithic but also Beaker-associated, including probable graves) and accumulations of cultural material in the buried soil. The Late Neolithic/Chalcolithic/Early Bronze Age site narrative (phases 2–4) is divided into eight sub-phases (Parfitt and Needham 2020, 270–86, table 6.1), Grooved Ware deposition occurring mostly during phases 2b/c. The ceramic finds, comprehensively analysed by Alex Gibson (2020), account for nearly half of the entire regional Grooved Ware assemblage.

There is not enough space here to review the evidence in detail, but several issues are significant for interpreting the Grooved Ware deposits. A major difficulty for understanding the 3rd millennium cal BC site sequence is the dearth of radiocarbon dates (just five, three on wood charcoal), all potentially subject to sample redeposition given the longevity of activity and repeated recutting of soils and fills. Phasing depends on a few stratigraphic relationships, artefact associations, and reasoning based on identifications and potential co-associations of possible architectural features. Consequently, temporal relationships among the Grooved Ware-associated features, the interval between Grooved Ware and Beaker phases and the chronologies of these in relation to enclosure and mound construction, are uncertain.

The earliest of the Late Neolithic structures, the phase 2a 'timber horseshoe setting' (Structure 1), comprises a circuit of pits rather than postholes – they are mostly shallow, ovate, with concave bases, and lack postpipes – though they may mark earlier post settings (F2110 and F2021 may be remnants of these). It is also likely that Structure 1 largely pre-dates Grooved Ware-associated activity; nearly all of the small pottery assemblage was recovered from just two adjacent pits (F1208, F1216) probably (re)cut at a later stage in the site sequence.

Interpretation of Grooved Ware deposition at Ringlemere poses significant challenges. The palimpsest of material in the buried soil (665 sherds) resulted from multiple depositional episodes of unknown duration and sequence, concentrated in and around the areas of Structures 8 and 10 (Fig. 13.4), though finds distributions do not coincide with their physical limits and may pre- or post-date them. These structures are assumed to have had some ceremonial purpose though there is nothing that precludes possible 'settlement' functions. Structure 10, consisting of sub-circular post settings around a hearth, within a rectilinear array of pits and possible posts, has no direct parallels; it is notable, however, that all the charred cereal grains in Late Neolithic contexts came from Structure 10 and features nearby. Structure 8, consisting of an arc of postholes (perhaps part of a screen or compound), with a hearth and numerous pits, bears comparison with structures at both ceremonial and settlement sites elsewhere in southern Britain.

There is no sign of any pattern of formal Grooved Ware deposition. A few possible instances of sherd 'placement' are noted (e.g. in Pit F1321) but other explanations are equally likely. The contextual evidence instead suggests that most Grooved Ware was originally present in surface spreads and heaps that, in some instances, were redeposited when features were backfilled or infilled naturally. It is striking that most of the pottery in pre-mound features (608 sherds) derives from just 13 pits (406 sherds; 67%), some of it deposited in dumps of material towards the end (or after) the phase of Grooved Ware-associated activity, possibly for site clearance/levelling purposes. In this light, the phase of active Grooved Ware use may well have been short, conceivably just a few decades within the period *c.* 2850–2650 cal BC.

Finally, the chronology and form of the 'henge', and its relationship to Grooved Ware use, are far from certain. The internal structures have varied orientations unrelated to the enclosure axis defined by the northern entrance, and only tiny assemblages of Grooved Ware and lithic artefacts were found in the lower/middle ditch fills: just 60 sherds and 726 flint pieces (*c.* 1.5% of site totals). Far larger quantities might be expected if activity involving these materials was contemporary with ditch sedimentation, especially given the proximity of Late Neolithic finds concentrations in the buried soil (Parfitt and Needham 2020, figs 2.4–2.8, 6.4, 6.5). There is no evidence for a barrier impeding spreads of debris, and little to support the idea that fills of a putative early enclosure ditch (phase 2c) were removed by later 'recuts' in phases 3a/b and/or 4a; the suggestion of a pre-phase 2d ditch relies on one line of interpretative inference (Parfitt and Needham 2020, 282–3). It is more likely that the phase of Grooved Ware deposition pre-dates enclosure construction, and that any henge-staged ceremonies were performed long after active use of Grooved Ware ceased.

BEGINNINGS AND ENDINGS

Recent interpretations of cultural change in Britain in the 3rd millennium cal BC have foregrounded themes of identity, 'origins', migration, colonisation and population replacement. These are prominent in discussions of the 'Beaker phenomenon' (Parker Pearson *et al.* 2019, 435–59) and thus the end of the Late Neolithic, including – sooner or later – the cultural repertoires bound up with henges and Grooved Ware. There is also some discussion of the Middle Neolithic–Late Neolithic 'transition' in similar terms, especially with respect to cultural identities and mobilities in the late 4th/early 3rd millennia cal BC (e.g. Thomas 2010; Parker Pearson *et al.* 2021, 100, fig. 10). Yet the beginnings and endings of the 'Grooved Ware phenomenon' remain opaque at local and regional scales, with no clear sense of what really happened 'on the ground'. This review of Grooved Ware in south-east England may, however, clarify some of the cultural, geographical and chronological parameters of social change in the periods *c.* 3000–2800 and 2600–2400 cal BC.

In contrast with the more widespread and frequent presence of Peterborough Ware and other evidence for Middle Neolithic activity in south-east England, Grooved Ware finds are unevenly distributed (Fig. 13.5) and vary greatly in scale. Although most of the areas where Grooved Ware is most common were also foci for earlier monument building (which may relate to favoured settlement zones and long-term demographic processes that sustained relative population densities), there is little to indicate any 'cultural continuity'.

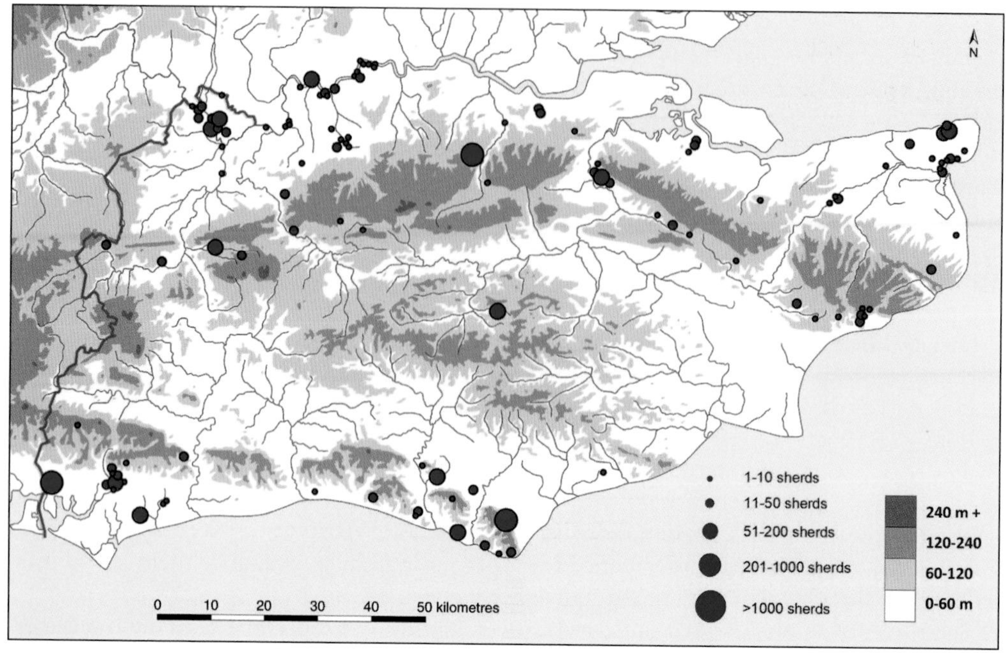

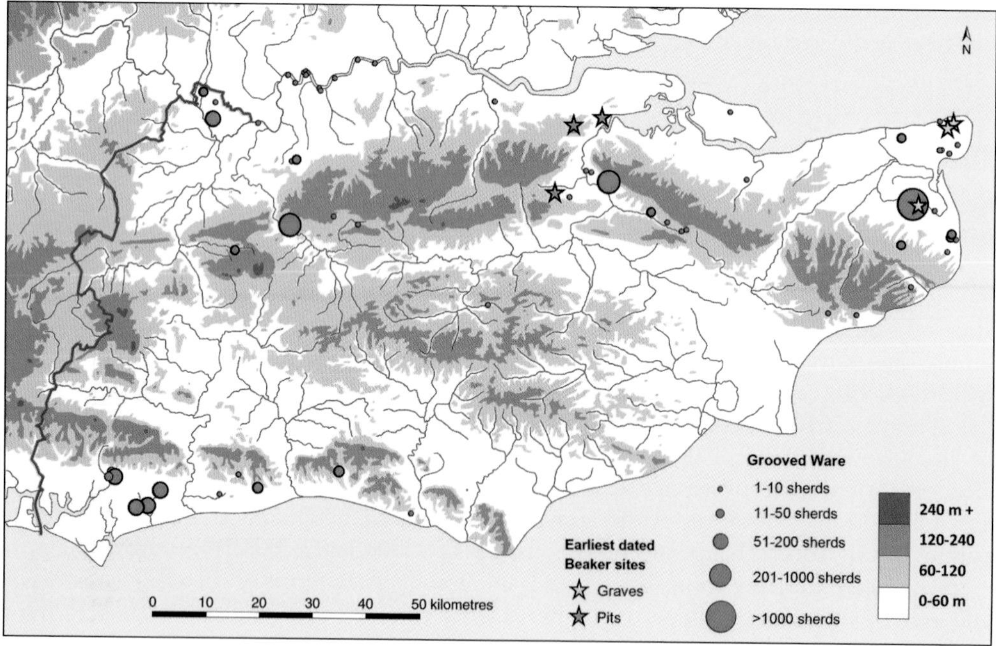

*Figure 13.5. Comparison of Peterborough Ware and Grooved Ware finds distributions in south-east England. Upper: Peterborough Ware (*c. *3400–2900 cal BC); lower: Grooved Ware (*c. *2900–2500 cal BC), with locations of earliest dated Beaker pottery in the region (after* c. *2450 cal BC).*

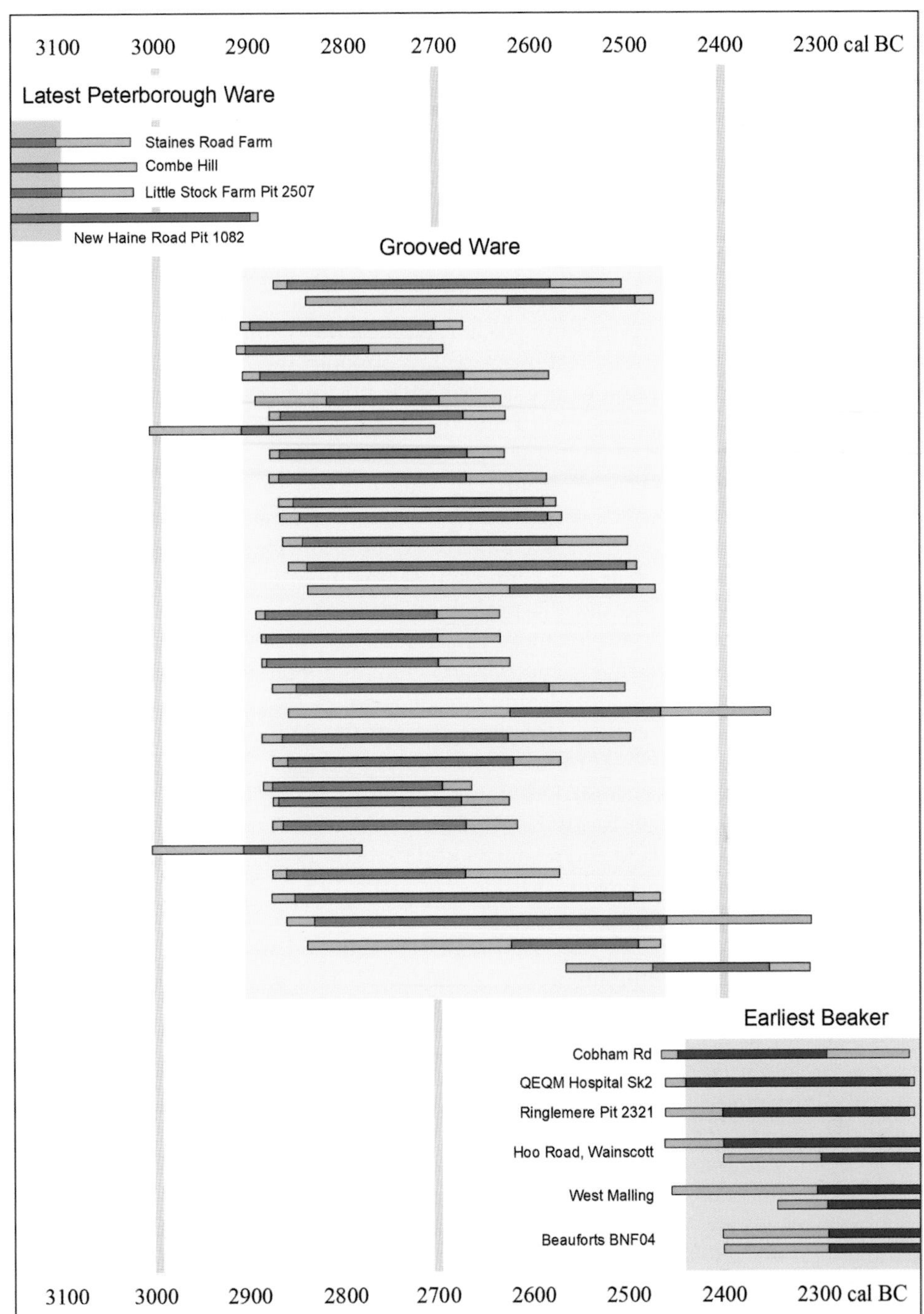

Figure 13.6. Comparison of radiocarbon age ranges for latest Peterborough Ware, Grooved Ware, and earliest Beaker pottery in south-east England.

Indeed, the rapid transmission and take-up of Grooved Ware in widely separated areas within a few generations in the 29th–28th centuries cal BC, and subsequent geographical concentration of Grooved Ware-using communities, may support an intrusive ethnocultural dimension to Grooved Ware 'settlement' (cf. Thomas 2010).

The sense of cultural disconnection and transformation across the Middle–Late Neolithic transition, including avoidance of the vestiges of (alien) cultural pasts, at least with respect to selecting places for inhabitation, ceremonial arenas and depositional acts, is further reinforced by the chronological separation of Peterborough Ware and Grooved Ware. There is almost no overlap in the currencies of these ceramic styles in south-east England even at the limits of age ranges at 95.4% probability (Fig. 13.6). This 'hiatus', if real, may mark some level of population decline, political fragmentation and/or dislocations of social organisation and communal memory. It is possible, therefore, that the landscapes that Grooved Ware users came to occupy (whether this involved movements of people or not), were already largely emptied of the meanings that Peterborough Ware and long abandoned earlier Neolithic monuments may once have had.

The end of Grooved Ware in south-east England is less sharply defined than its beginnings, though just as stark in terms of social and cultural discontinuity. The latest dated Grooved Ware and earliest dated Beaker depositional events in the region (Fig. 13.6) could conceivably overlap by a century. It seems more likely, however, considering sample sources and contexts, and the probability distributions of the dates concerned, that these events were a century or more apart. Whether or not there is a temporal gap in the currencies of Grooved Ware and Beaker ceramics, it seems clear that the frequency of Grooved Ware deposits, if not already rare by the mid-26th century cal BC, declined swiftly thereafter, and had entirely disappeared from the cultural landscape by the time Beaker pottery was widely present in the 24th century cal BC.

It has become widely accepted that the Grooved Ware/Late Neolithic–Beaker/Chalcolithic transition in south-east England involved colonisation by intrusive 'Beaker settlers', appropriations of land and resources and perhaps 'population replacement', albeit of uncertain magnitude and rapidity (Olalde *et al.* 2018, 193–4; Parker Pearson *et al.* 2019, 454–9). It is also possible, however, as the observations above suggest, that Grooved Ware-associated places and practices had been widely abandoned by indigenous populations long before Beaker-using communities were established. This may help account for radical discontinuities evident in site histories and material culture in the region, and the extent to which old 'dead places' in the Chalcolithic landscapes of the 24th–23rd centuries cal BC were rarely reused. From both native and settler perspectives, these may have been irrelevant or dangerous remnants of a past world that lacked positive cultural and political resonance for living social groups.

How such a cultural fissure could have developed may at first sight seem obscure, but one answer might lie in the way very large-scale social structures and political economies were organised in Late Neolithic Britain. Fragile subsistence regimes in the early–mid-3rd millennium cal BC, affected by cool, wet climatic conditions resulting in low crop yields and weak productivity more generally (Stevens and Fuller 2015, 867, fig. 4), may cumulatively have weakened Late Neolithic social resilience and prosperity. Yet communal construction projects and ceremonial centres in Wessex increased vastly in scale during this timeframe, with evidence for extensive networks of social mobilisation and commitment across much of Britain (Madgwick *et al.* 2019; Parker Pearson *et al.* 2021). These may not, however, be contradictory but complementary conditions for explaining regional variation and social change in the period 2600–2400 cal BC.

The asymmetric social costs of political centralisation, collective investment in grandiose architecture, ceremonies and consumption events, and centripetal flows of material and moral resources (and people) from the 'peripheries' of the henge/Grooved Ware *ecumene*, may have been severe. From this perspective, the idea that Late Neolithic ceremonial centres – and Grooved Ware – were media of unification, inclusion and communality (Madgwick *et al.* 2019; Parker Pearson *et al.* 2021), is perhaps an unintended projection of the (authoritarian) ideologies and (fundamentalist?) mythologies of those who inspired monument building and choreographed the ceremonial lives of the faithful. Social realities and lived experiences for those subject to the demands of the Late Neolithic political economy may have been very different. In regions such as south-east England, the effects on communities that acceded or were compelled to be net contributors while vulnerable to fine subsistence margins, may have been impoverishment and destabilisation. In this scenario, it would not be surprising if the endings of Grooved Ware, and everything this pottery represented, encompassed social fragmentation, disillusion, rejection and rebellion.

NOTES

1 South-east England, for present purposes, comprises the counties of West Sussex, East Sussex, Kent, Surrey, and the London boroughs south of the Thames formerly part of the historic counties of Kent and Surrey.
2 The Late Neolithic is defined here chronologically as 2900–2450 cal BC.
3 Calibrated dates cited are at their 95.4% probability range unless otherwise stated.

REFERENCES

Barclay, A., Fitzpatrick, A.P., Hayden, C. and Stafford, E. 2006. *The Prehistoric Landscape at White Horse Stone, Boxley, Kent.* Oxford: Oxford Wessex Archaeology Joint Venture. https://doi.org/10.5284/1008829 (accessed 08/08/2023).

Booth, P., Champion, T., Foreman, S., Garwood, P., Glass, H., Munby, J. and Reynolds, A. 2011. *On track: the archaeology of High Speed 1, Section 1.* Oxford: Oxford-Wessex Archaeology.

Chadwick, A. 2006. Bronze Age burials and settlement and an Anglo-Saxon settlement at Claypit Lane, Westhampnett, West Sussex. *Sussex Archaeological Collections* 144, 7–50.

Cleal, R. 2012. Missing the point: implications of the appearance and development of transverse arrowheads in southern Britain, with particular reference to *petit tranchet* and chisel types. In A. Jones, J. Pollard, M. Allen and J. Gardiner (eds), *Image, memory and monumentality. Archaeological engagements with the material world: a celebration of the academic achievements of Professor Richard Bradley*, 137–45. Oxford: Prehistoric Society Research Papers 5.

Cleal, R. and MacSween, A. (eds) 1999. *Grooved Ware in Britain and Ireland.* Oxford: Oxbow Books.

Corke, E. 2019. Cocks Farm Abinger 2019: part two. *Surrey Archaeological Society Bulletin* 481, 2–7.

Cotton, J. and Field, D. (eds) 2004. *Towards a New Stone Age: aspects of the Neolithic in south-east England.* York: Council for British Archaeology Research Report 137.

Cramp, K. 2005. *The worked flint from White Horse Stone, Pilgrim's Way, East of Boarley Farm and West of Boarley Farm, Aylesford, Boxley, Kent.* York: Archaeology Data Service: CTRL

Specialist Report Series. https://archaeologydataservice.ac.uk/archives/view/ctrl/downloads.cfm?group=957&CFID=6efcc1cb-a3a8-49f0-8f0e-a8b73a5fa97d&CFTOKEN=0 (accessed 08/08/2023).

Fitzpatrick, A.P., Powell, A. and Allen, M. 2008. *Archaeological excavations on the route of the A27 Westhampnett Bypass, West Sussex, 1992: Volume 1: Late Upper Palaeolithic–Anglo-Saxon*. Salisbury: Wessex Archaeology Report 21.

Gardiner, J. 2008. On the production of discoidal knives and changing patterns of specialist flint procurement in the Neolithic in the South Downs, England. *Analecta Praehistorica Leidensia* 40, 235–46.

Garwood, P. 1999. Grooved Ware in southern Britain: chronology and interpretation. In R. Cleal and A. MacSween (eds) 1999, 145–76.

Garwood, P. 2003. Round barrows and funerary traditions in Late Neolithic and Bronze Age Sussex. In D. Rudling (ed.), *The archaeology of Sussex to AD 2000*, 47–68. King's Lynn: Heritage Marketing.

Garwood, P. 2011. Early prehistory. In P. Booth *et al.* 2011, 37–150.

Garrow, D, 2012. Odd deposits and average practice. A critical history of the concept of structured deposition. *Archaeological Dialogues* 19(2), 85–144.

Gibson, A. 2020. Grooved Ware pottery. In K. Parfitt and S. Needham 2020, 201–35.

Halliwell, G. and Parfitt, K. 1985. The prehistoric land surface in the Lydden valley: an initial report. *Kent Archaeological Review* 82, 39–43.

Harding, J. 2006. Pit digging, occupation and structured deposition on Rudston Wold, eastern Yorkshire. *Oxford Journal of Archaeology* 25(2), 109–26.

Hart, D. 2015. *Around the Ancient Track: archaeological excavations for the Brighton and Hove Waste Water Treatment Works and adjacent housing at Peacehaven, East Sussex*. Norwich: SpoilHeap Publications.

Hayman, G., Jones, P., Marples, N. and Robertson, J. 2015. *Prehistoric, Roman, Saxon and medieval discoveries at Wey Manor Farm, near Weybridge, 1994–2004*. Woking: SpoilHeap Publications.

Jones, P. and Ayres, K. 2004. A bone 'scoop' and Grooved Ware vessel from a pit in the Lower Colne Valley, Surrey. In J. Cotton and D. Field (eds) 2004, 148–53.

Leivers, M. 2020. *Bulford Service Family Accommodation, Bulford, Wiltshire*. Salisbury: Wessex Archaeology, unpublished post-excavation assessment report by for the Ministry of Defence.

Longworth, I. and Cleal, R. 1999. Grooved Ware gazetteer. In R. Cleal and A. MacSween (eds) 1999, 177–206.

Madgwick, R., Lamb, A., Sloane, H., Nederbragt, A., Albarella, U., Parker Pearson, M. and Evans J. 2019. Multi-isotope analysis reveals that feasts in the Stonehenge environs and across Wessex drew people and animals from throughout Britain. *Science Advances* 5: eaau6078.

Margetts, A. 2019. On the verge of Wessex? A prehistoric landscape at Oldlands Farm, Bognor Regis, West Sussex. *Sussex Archaeological Collections* 157, 47–81.

Moody, G. 2008. *The Isle of Thanet: from prehistory to the present day*. Stroud: Tempus.

Olalde, I., Brace, S., Allentoft, M., Armit, I., Kristiansen, K., Rohland, N. *et al.* 2018. The Beaker phenomenon and the genomic transformation of northwest Europe. *Nature* 555, 190–6.

Parfitt, K. 1998. Some radio-carbon dates for prehistoric east Kent. *Archaeologia Cantiana* 118, 376–80.

Parfitt, K. and Needham, S. 2020. *Ceremonial living in the third millennium BC: excavations at Ringlemere Site M1, Kent, 2002–2006*. London: British Museum.

Parker Pearson, M., Jay, M., Montgomery, J., Sheridan, J.A., and Needham, S. 2019. Synthesis, discussion and conclusions. In M. Parker Pearson, J.A. Sheridan, M. Jay, A. Chamberlain, M. Richards and J. Evans (eds), *The Beaker people: isotopes, mobility and diet in prehistoric Britain*, 424–60. Oxford: Prehistoric Society Research Papers 7.

Parker Pearson, M., Pollard, J., Richards, C., Welham, K., Kinnaird, T., Shaw, D. *et al.* 2021. The original Stonehenge? A dismantled stone circle in the Preseli Hills of west Wales. *Antiquity* 95, 85–103.

Poulton, R., Hayman, G. and Marples, N. 2017. *Foragers and farmers: 10,000 years of history at Hengrove Farm, Staines. Excavations between 1997 and 2012*. Norwich: SpoilHeap Publications.

Rady, J. 2019. Early prehistory. In J. Rady and J. Holman, *Beneath the seamark: 6,000 years of an island's history. Archaeological investigations at 'Thanet Earth', Kent 2007–2012; Volume 1: Chronological narrative*, 16–94. Canterbury: Canterbury Archaeological Trust.

Reid, P. 2012. *Understanding Ospringe Project 2008–9 and 2011*. Faversham: Faversham Society Archaeological Research Group.

Richards, C. and Thomas, J. 1984. Ritual activity and structured deposition in Neolithic Wessex. In R. Bradley and J. Gardiner (eds), *Neolithic studies: a review of some recent research*, 189–218. Oxford: British Archaeological Report 133.

Russell, M. 1997. 'Neo-realism': an alternative look at the Neolithic chalkland database of Sussex. In R. Topping (ed.), *Neolithic landscapes*, 69–76. Oxford: Neolithic Studies Group Seminar Papers 2.

Stafford, E., Anderson-Whymark, H. and Hayden, C. 2020. Neolithic and Early Bronze Age. In F. Wenban-Smith, E. Stafford, M. Bates and S.A. Parfitt, *Prehistoric Ebbsfleet: excavations and research in advance of High Speed 1 and South Thameside Development Route 4, 1989–2003*, 349–87. Oxford and Salisbury: Oxford-Wessex Archaeology Monograph 7.

Stevens, C. and Fuller, D. 2015. Alternative strategies to agriculture: the evidence for climatic shocks and cereal declines during the British Neolithic and Bronze Age (a reply to Bishop). *World Archaeology* 47, 856–75.

Taylor, A., Weale, A. and Ford, S. 2014. *Bronze Age, Iron Age and Roman landscapes of the coastal plain, and a Late Iron Age warrior burial at North Bersted, Bognor Regis, West Sussex. Excavations 2007–2010*. Reading: Thames Valley Archaeological Services.

Thomas, J. 1999. *Understanding the Neolithic*. London: Routledge.

Thomas, J. 2010. The return of the Rinyo-Clacton folk? The cultural significance of the Grooved Ware complex in later Neolithic Britain. *Cambridge Archaeological Journal* 20, 1–15.

Vieira, T. 2021. *Archaeological excavations on land east of Tye Lane, Walberton, West Sussex*. London: Archaeology South-East, unpublished post-excavation assessment report by for Linden Homes.

Wessex Archaeology 2010. *Margetts Pit, Margetts Lane, Burham, Kent*. Salisbury: Wessex Archaeology unpublished post-excavation assessment report for Aylesford Newsprint Services Ltd

Whittle, A. 1997. Moving on and moving around: Neolithic settlement mobility. In P. Topping (ed.), *Neolithic landscapes*, 15–22. Oxford: Neolithic Studies Group Seminar Papers 2.

Williams, D. 2017. Excavation of a prehistoric and Romano-British site at Betchworth, 1995–6. *Surrey Archaeological Collections* 100, 71–141.

Wilson, T. 2015. *The Meads, Sittingbourne, Kent: 2012 excavation*. Canterbury: Canterbury Archaeological Trust, unpublished post-excavation assessment report for for Marston's Inns and Taverns.

Table 13.1. Radiocarbon dates associated with Grooved Ware pottery in south-east England.

Site name	*Context*	*Sample*	*Lab no, age BP*	*Cal. BC 2 (95.4%)*	*Cal. BC 1 (68.2%)*	*Associations Notes*	*Reference*
				Surrey			
Betchworth	Pit 204	Charred residue	OxA-7710 4045±40	2845–2465 *(2745–2465 @ 89%)*	2625–2490	131 DW sherds (1118g), 104 lithic artefacts (inc. petit-tranchet deriv. arrowhead, 4 scrapers); 564 g burnt flint; 586 g burnt sandstone	Williams 2017
	Pit 219	Charred residue	OxA-7699 4080±-80	2880–2465	2855–2495	221 DW sherds (3695g), 216 lithic artefacts (incl. 35 scrapers); 164g burnt flint, 16g burnt sandstone	
		Charred residue *Low $\delta^{13}C$ value*	OxA-7698 3840±60 *Aberrant late date?*	2470–2135	2450–2205		
	Pit 220	Charred residue	OxA-7700 4015±70	2865–2305 *(2705–2340 @ 84%)*	2835–2460 *(2635–2460 @ 62%)*	119 DW sherds (1025 g), 57 lithic artefacts (inc. 2 scrapers); 22 g burnt sandstone	
Cocks Farm, Abinger	Pit 2573	Twig charcoal	*No info.* 3940±30	2565–2305 *(2495–2340 @ 83%)*	2475–2350	21 sherds (94 g), 177 flint flakes & chips, burnt & unburnt ironstone, burnt clay ('oven dome' frags, some with wattle impressions)	Corke 2019; Emma Corke, pers. comm.
Hengrove	Waterhole/ pit 6008	Charred residue on GW sherd	Beta-409675 4280±30	3010–2785 *(2930–2870 @ 91%)*	2910–2885	25 sherds (also 21 sherds of Ebbsfleet pottery; pit possibly recut); 618 flint artefacts (several refitting groups), incl. 81 tools (2 transverse arrowheads)	Poulton *et al.* 2017
	Tree-throw-6154	Charred residue on GW sherd	Beta-409676 4130±50	2880–2575	2865–2625	45 DW sherds, incl. 29 grog-tempered sherds prob. GW (Durrington Walls style), 241 flint artefacts (mostly debitage)	

(Continued)

Table 13.1 (Continued)

Site name	*Context*	*Sample*	*Lab no, age BP*	*Cal. BC 2 (95.4%)*	*Cal. BC 1 (68.2%)*	*Associations* *Notes*	*Reference*
				Kent			
Eyhorne Street	Pit 19	Charred residue	NZA-20418 4113±40	2875–2505 *(2875–2570 @ 94%)*	2850–2580	22 DW(/CL?) sherds (181 g), 16 flint artefacts, fired clay frags (24 g), decorated clay object	Booth *et al.* 2011, app.3; Garwood 2011, 99–101
		Charred crab apple	NZA-20417 4044±35	2840–2470 *(2670–2470 @ 92%)*	2625–2490		
White Horse Stone	Pit 4965 (Pit group 19400)	Cattle calcaneum	NZA-22737 4230±35	2910–2675	2900–2705	260 CL sherds (1079g), 114 flint artefacts (mostly debitage but inc. chisel arrowhead), burnt flint, charred plant remains (inc. cereals), charcoal, animal bones (290 g)	Booth *et al.* 2011, app.3; Garwood 2011, table 3.2, with corrections here[1], [2]
	Pit 5256 (Pit group 19400)	Charred hazelnuts	NZA-21491 4196±60	2910–2585 *(2910–2620 @ 94%)*	2890–2675	27 CL sherds (98 g), 190 flint artefacts (mostly debitage), burnt quern frag., charred plant remains, charcoal, animal bones (35 g)	
	Pit 4943 (Pit group 19399)	Charred hazelnuts	NZA-21493 4155±30	2880–2630	2870–2670	10 CL sherds (52 g), 66 flint artefacts (mostly debitage, with 1 chisel arrowhead), burnt stones, charcoal, animal bones (13 g)	
	Pit 4994 (Pit group 19413)	Cattle scapula	NZA-21325 4080±35	2860–2490	2840–2500	45 CL sherds (216 g), 99 flint artefacts (mostly debitage), burnt flint & stones, charcoal, animal bones (3452 g)	
	Pit 5094 (Pit group 19413)	*Red deer antler*	*NZA-22813 4238±35*	*2915–2695*	*2905–2775*	*No GW. Lithic artefacts (mostly debitage), burnt stones, charcoal, animal bones & antler (603 g)*	

(Continued)

Table 13.1. Radiocarbon dates associated with Grooved Ware pottery in south-east England. (Continued)

Site name	*Context*	*Sample*	*Lab no, age BP*	*Cal. BC 2 (95.4%)*	*Cal. BC 1 (68.2%)*	*Associations* *Notes*	*Reference*
	Hollow 5072 (Pit group 19413)	Cattle skull	NZA-22750 4271±35	3010–2705 *2935–2865 @ 82%*	2910–2880	1 CL sherd (12g), 65 flint artefacts (mostly debitage, 6 retouched pieces), burnt stones, charcoal, animal bones (1365g). Incomplete figures: part of the assemblage lost	
		Cattle calcaneum	NZA-22751 4195±35	2895–2635	2885–2700		
		Pig scapula	NZA-22749 4161±30	2880–2630 *(2880–2660 @ 90%)*	2870–2675		
	Pit 958 (Pit group 19396)	Aurochs vertebra	NZA-21327 4120±35	2870–2575 *(2780–2575 @ 69%)*	2855–2585	17 CL sherds (126g), 147 flint artefacts (mostly debitage, but incl. 7 retouched pieces and a chisel arrowhead), charred plant remains (incl. cereals), charcoal, animal bones (391g)	
		Cattle phalanx	NZA-21589 4113±35	2870–2575 *(2780–2575 @ 70%)*	2850–2585		
	Pit 913 (Pit group 19395)	Cattle phalanx	NZA-21508 4153±40	2880–2585 *(2880–2620 @ 94%)*	2870–2670	1 CL sherd (5g), 21 flint artefacts (3 retouched pieces), animal bones (85g), cremated human bone (3g)	
	Pit 911 (Pit group 19395)	*Pig mandible*	*NZA-21282 4097±30*	*2865–2500*	*2845–2575 2675–2575 @ 52%*	*No GW* *50 lithic artefacts (debitage, 9 retouched pieces), charred plant remains, polished ironstone ball, animal bones (459g)*	
	Pit 904	Pig radius	NZA-21324 4046±35	2840–2470 *2670–2470 @ 91%*	2625–2490	17 CL sherds (31 g), 36 flint artefacts (debitage only), burnt flints, charred plant remains, charcoal, animal bones (596 g)	

(Continued)

Table 13.1 (Continued)

Site name	*Context*	*Sample*	*Lab no, age BP*	*Cal. BC 2 (95.4%)*	*Cal. BC 1 (68.2%)*	*Associations Notes*	*Reference*
St Richards, Mill Hill, Deal	Pit F428	Cattle bone	OxA-7441 4105±45	2875–2500	2850–2580	4 DW (?) sherds	Parfitt 1998
Cross Road, Mill Hill, Deal	F41	Sheep/goat bone	OxA-7531 4020±60	2860–2345 *(2700–2400 @ 84%)*	2625–2465	3 CL sherds	Parfitt 1998
Ringlemere	Pit 1983, 2e fill 1982 [Structure 9]	Oak charcoal *Aberrant early date: old wood, &/ or redeposited charcoal?*	OxA-25855 4479±31	3340–3030 *3340–3085 @ 89%*	3330–3400	25 CL sherds (618 g); 9 more sherds (25 g) in 2 of the other pit fills. Fills also contained knapping debris & a chisel arrowhead	Parfitt and Needham 2020
	Post hole 1972 (inner ring of Structure 10 around Hearth III)	*Birch charcoal*	*OxA-25854, 4183±32*	*2890–2635 (2820–2665 @ 71%)*	*2880–2700*	*No GW in F1972. Only 30 sherds were recovered from all the Structure 10 features, but pottery, burnt flint and flint artefacts were densely concentrated on/ in the buried soil within the area of the structure*	
	Hearth I (F1464), fill 1463 [Structure 8]	Burnt bone	OxA-25853 4176±28	2885–2635 *2820–2665 @ 72%*	2880–2700	7 CL sherds (30 g)	

(Continued)

Table 13.1. Radiocarbon dates associated with Grooved Ware pottery in south-east England. (Continued)

Site name	*Context*	*Sample*	*Lab no, age BP*	*Cal. BC 2 (95.4%)*	*Cal. BC 1 (68.2%)*	*Associations Notes*	*Reference*
	Pit 1321, interface of fills 1320/1322	*Sorbius aria* & *Buxus sempervirens* charcoal	Beta-183862 4170±40	2885–2625	2875–2675	40 CL sherds (886g). Fills also contained knapping debris	
			West Sussex				
Claypit Lane, Westhampnett	Pit 8052	Charred apple	NZA-16697 4132±50	2880–2575	2865–2625	36 CL(/WO?) sherds (abraded), 72 flint artefacts (mostly debitage). Charred plant remains (apple, sloe & hazelnut shells only)	Chadwick 2006
	Pit 6162	Hazel charcoal	NZA-16617 4144±65	2890–2500 *(2890–2570 @ 94%)*	2870–2630	34 CL(/WO?) sherds, 160 flint artefacts (mostly debitage, with some refitting)	
Oldlands Farm, Bognor Regis	Pit 811	Sooted residue	SUERC-63860 4167±29	2880–2630 *(2825–2665 @ 71%)*	2875–2680	34 DW sherds, 121 flint artefacts (debitage, with 6 cores; no conjoins); fire-cracked flints, charcoal, fired clay frags, 1 bone frag	Margetts 2019
		Maloideae charcoal	SUERC-63859 4187±24	2890–2670	2880–2700		
North Bersted, Bognor Regis	Pit 2041	Alder charcoal	UBA-22757 4163±41	2890–2620 (@ 95%)	2875–2670	7 sherds, 5 flint artefacts, 29 pieces of burnt flint	Taylor *et al.* 2014

1. The numbers of flint artefacts noted in Garwood 2011, table 3.2 (derived from the final integrated site report, Barclay *et al.* 2006), have been corrected here using the site flint report instead (Cramp 2005). The latter seems to be a more reliable source, as the integrated site report omits full analyses of the Late Neolithic flint assemblages, and there appear to be counting errors in the draft report on which it is based.
2. Two dates without direct Grooved Ware associations are included; these derive from pits (5094, 911) in close-set pit groups with other Grooved Ware-associated dates (see Garwood 2011, table 3.2, figs 3.36, 3.37).

Dates are calibrated using OxCal v4.4.4, the calibrated age range limits rounded out to 5 years (cal. BC). Grooved Ware sub-styles (where identified): WO – Woodlands; CL – Clacton; DW – Durrington Walls. Fully italicised rows are used for samples not directly associated with Grooved Ware but recovered from Late Neolithic features close to Grooved Ware pits. The entries in grey are not shown in Fig. 13.2; these are aberrant (too early or too late).

Chapter 14

Grooved Ware in the south-west peninsula

Andy M. Jones and Henrietta Quinnell

The south-west peninsula is usually overlooked in relation to Grooved Ware. This is perhaps unsurprising given that, when the seminal Cleal and MacSween (1999) volume was published, there were just four recorded sites in Cornwall and only one in Devon and, of these, only one site at Davidstow Moor was associated with a radiocarbon determination. It is also noticeable that virtually all the assemblages comprised scrappy sherds which were mostly not ascribable to sub-style, and most were stray finds recovered during the excavation of monuments such as Bronze Age round barrows, cairns, megalithic chamber tombs or caves (for example, Patchett 1950; Rosenfield 1964; Thomas and Wailes 1967; Buckley 1972). Only one assemblage, from Probus, was from a pit (Jones and Nowakowski 1997), and this was then a new discovery which only just made it into the volume.

The volume was published during a watershed period between small-scale investigations and major developer-funded projects which have almost entirely changed our understanding of Grooved Ware and its use in Devon and Cornwall. Two things have, however, remained unchanged. The first is the presence of small quantities of Grooved Ware in very much older Early Neolithic chamber tombs in west Cornwall. Excavation of the chambers at Zennor Quoit and Carwynnen Quoit have both produced burnt bone dating to the Middle to Late Neolithic period and small quantities of Grooved Ware. These are the only chamber tombs to have their chambers excavated under modern conditions, so the association is unlikely to be coincidental, even though the Zennor Quoit date of 3345–3022 cal BC (see Table 14.2) would be very early for Grooved Ware (Kytmannow 2008; Nowakowski and Gossip forthcoming).

Secondly, the Isles of Scilly remain devoid of Grooved Ware, despite modern excavations on the islands. Excavations at Old Quay, St Martin's, have produced the only significant Neolithic assemblage; here certain styles relating to South-Western Bowl pottery had associated dates *c.* 3300–2900 cal BC (Garrow and Sturt 2017). There is then a long gap until Early Bronze Age biconical vessels, which are decorated in styles not found on the mainland (O'Neil 1952; Sawyer 2015). The islands appear to have had their own preferred styles of pottery, with some preference for insular ceramic forms which can show elements of conservatism. Activity on the islands in the 3rd millennium cal BC is apparent in the number of scattered, chance finds of perforated axeheads, adzeheads and maceheads in its museum. Illustrations have been chosen to cover the range of vessels; they do not reflect the frequency of Durrington Walls sub-style vessels with cordons which are the most common: see Tregurra Valley (Taylor 2022, especially fig. 4.4).

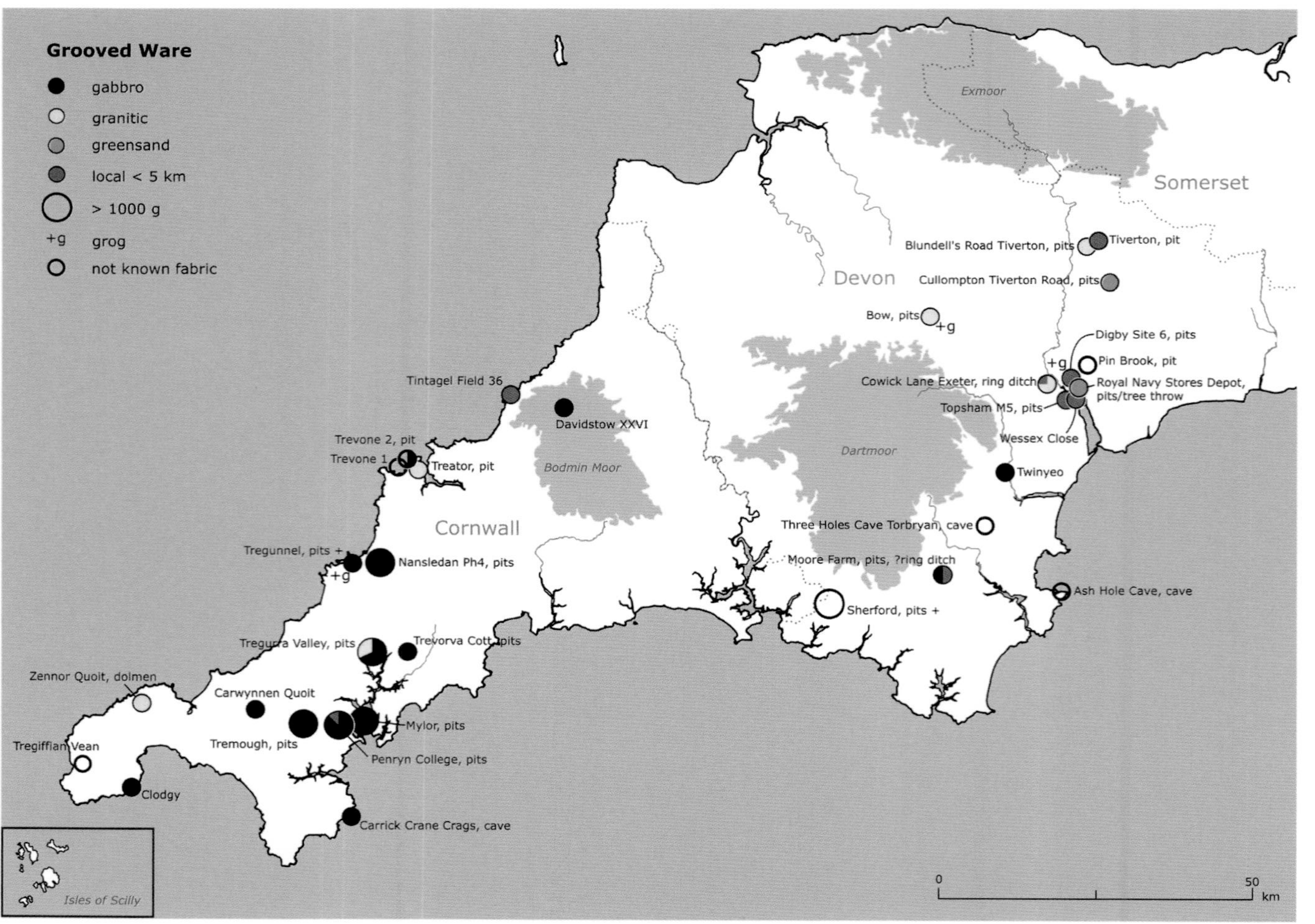

Figure 14.1 Map of sites with Grooved Ware in Devon and Cornwall.

GROOVED WARE STUDIES: DEVELOPMENTS AFTER 2000

The last two decades have seen a major change in knowledge of Grooved Ware, its chronology and the contexts in which it is found. At the time of writing, 18 sites have been recorded in Cornwall and 15 in Devon (Fig. 14.1, Tables 14.1–2) and the authors are aware of further sites awaiting assessment. All three of the sub-styles discussed in the Cleal and MacSween volume – Woodlands, Clacton and Durrington Walls – are found in the region. The Woodlands sub-style is still uncommon, with two findspots in Devon and two in Cornwall. The Clacton sub-style is fairly common but the Durrington Walls sub-style is the most frequent in both counties. (The authors acknowledge the limitations of the terminology used: see further discussion in Chapters 1, 2, 15 and 16, this volume.)

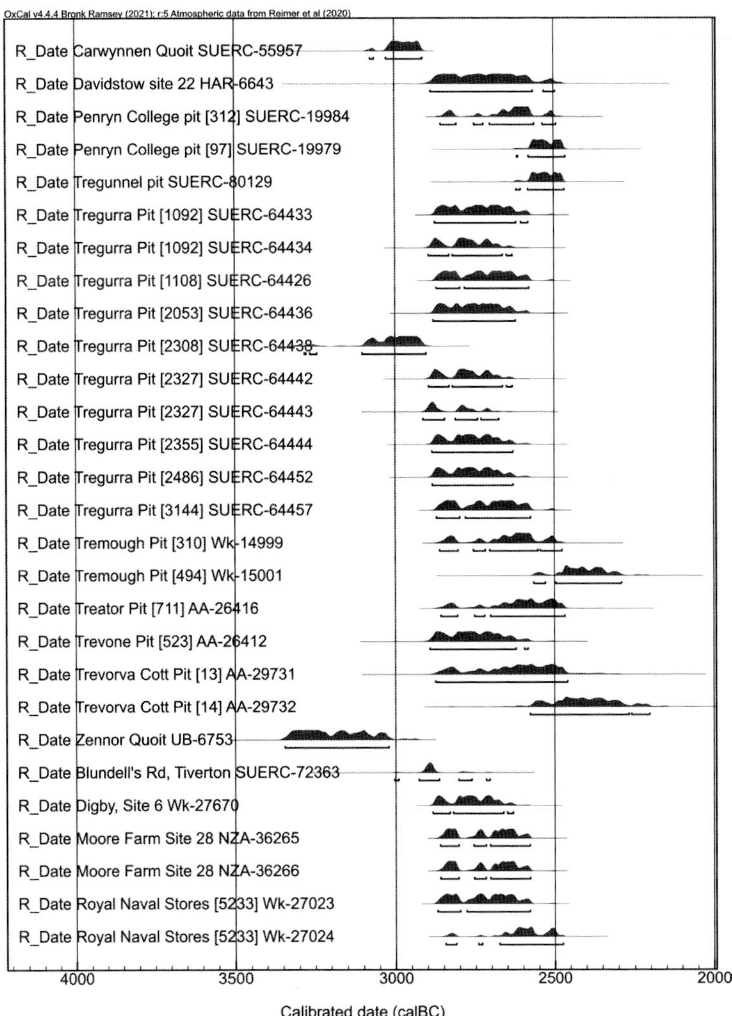

Figure 14.2. Radiocarbon determinations from Devon and Cornwall.

The chronology of Grooved Ware has also been greatly improved with 14 sites now having a total of 28 associated radiocarbon determinations, with the majority falling between *c.* 2900 and 2500 cal BC (Fig. 14.2 and Tables 14.1–2). As might be expected (following Copper *et al.* 2021), the earliest dates are associated with the Woodlands sub-style finds at Tregurra in Cornwall and Blundell's Road in Devon (Rainbird and Quinnell 2018; Taylor 2022). Two earlier determinations falling in the period 3350–2900 cal BC were also obtained from burnt bone from the Carwynnen and Zennor Quoit chamber tombs (Kytmannow 2008; Nowakowski and Gossip forthcoming). In both cases, however, the bone may pre-date the insertion of the Grooved Ware pottery.

In addition to an increasing number of sites and a better understanding of chronology, there is now a much clearer knowledge of the contexts for Grooved Ware which significantly changes the pattern of findspots recorded in 1999 (Cleal and MacSween 1999). Rather than a strong association with monuments or caves, the majority of finds in the south-west peninsula occur in pits (Garrow 2012), which can be single, paired or in small groups (Fig. 14.1). This distribution pattern is largely a reflection of developer-funded projects and one or more pits containing Grooved Ware can be expected to be uncovered on a fairly regular basis during larger-scale excavation projects.

The remainder of this paper will consider the most significant, securely dated finds by county before discussing the relationship between monuments and Grooved Ware. First, however, a brief comment on fabrics will be offered.

FABRICS AND SOURCING IN THE SOUTH-WEST

Vessels are generally well made and oxidised but fabrics do not appear to have inclusions which were designed to be seen and few have obvious tempering of the potting clay. There is some limited use of grog. Figure 14.1 presents current data on sourcing. In Cornwall, gabbroic fabrics are predominant, even more so than in the Early Neolithic (Quinnell and Taylor 2016, fig. 3.1); here Peterborough Ware is little known and gabbroic fabrics form <1% of the only assemblage of that pottery tradition that has been fully published, Tregurra Valley (Taylor 2022, table 4.3). In Devon, only two sites have gabbroic fabrics, Twinyeo (Farnell 2015, 225–6) and Moore Farm (Mudd and Joyce 2014, 48–50). Here, no Peterborough ceramics have yet been identified as containing gabbroic inclusions although small quantities occur in many Early Neolithic assemblages. In both counties granitic fabrics occur occasionally, sometimes, as at Treator (Jones and Quinnell 2014, 108–12), some distance from its source. In east Devon, there is a little evidence for Greensand fabrics but so far only within 20 km of the likely source. The use of 'local' fabrics – defined as being <5 km or less from the findspot – is common, especially in the Exeter area.

GROOVED WARE IN DEVON

The Devon finds are listed in Table 14.1. The earliest site in Devon is found at Blundell's Road, where three shallow pits and a tree-throw were uncovered; a fourth pit, with a later Neolithic date, containing flints but no pottery also formed part of the group (Rainbird and Quinnell 2018). The two smallest pits contained sherds of Grooved Ware, of which

Table 14.1. Grooved Ware from Devon. Key to sub-styles: DW – Durrington Walls; W – Woodland; C – Clacton.

Findspot	Context	No. sherds, (wt, g)	Sub-style	Fabric	Date: Cal BC (95.4% probability)	Date: Lab no.	Date: BP	Date: Dated material	Reference	Fig. no.	Report by HQ?
Ash Hole Cave, Brixham	cave	10+							Unpub; Brixham Museum		ID by HQ
Blundell's Road, Tiverton	pits	71 (475)	W	granitic	Pit [6003]: 2927–2761	SUERC-72363	4268±32	hazelnut shell, *Corylus avellana*	Rainbird and Quinnell 2018, 66–8, fig. 14		Y
Bow	pit	57 (277)	DW	granitic with grog					Poole 2003		
Cowick Lane, Exeter	ring ditch	4 (23)	DW	granitic 75%, local 25%					Caine and Valentin 2011, 102–3, fig. 7		Y
Cullompton, Tiverton Road	pit	28 (172)	DW	Upper Greensand derived					Morris and Rohan 2014		
Digby Site 6, Exeter	pit	9 (108)	C?	local with grog	Pit [984]: 2885–2633	Wk-27670	4174±30	hazelnut shell, *Corylus avellana*	Quinnell and Farnell 2016, 123, fig. 44	14.3, P6.1	Y
Moore Farm, Harberton	pits and ring ditch?	171 (560)	DW	gabbroic 27%, local 73%	Pit [18.12.018]: 2863–2580	NZA-36265	4120±20	hazelnut shell, *Corylus avellana*	Mudd and Joyce 2014, 23–4, 48–51, figs 2.34, 2.35	14.3, P12a	
					Pit [18.12.054]: 2861–2579	NZA-36266	4117±20	hazelnut shell, *Corylus avellana*			

(Continued)

Table 14.1. Grooved Ware from Devon. Key to sub-styles: DW – Durrington Walls; W – Woodland; C – Clacton. (Continued)

Findspot	*Context*	*No. sherds, (wt, g)*	*Sub-style*	*Fabric*	*Date*				*Reference*	*Fig. no.*	*Report by HQ?*
					Cal BC (95.4% probability)	*Lab no.*	*BP*	*Dated material*			
Pin Brook, Exeter	pit	1 (66)		local					Garland 2019, 115, fig. 8		Y
Royal Naval Stores Depot, Exeter	pit/tree throw	26 (116)	C	Upper Greensand derived	Pit/tree throw [5324]: 2871–2580	Wk-27023	4129±30	wood charcoal, *Ulex/Cytisus*	Pearce *et al.* 2011, 37–8, fig. 12	14.3	Y
					2846–2475	Wk-27024	4060±30	wood charcoal, *Ulex/Cytisus*			
Sherford New Town	pits +	large assem-blage	Inc. some W						Wells 2020		
Tiverton	pit	12 (47)							Farnell 2018		Y
Three Holes Cave, Torbryan	cave	1	C						Rosenfield 1964, pl. 1b		
Topsham, M5	pit	2		local					Jarvis and Maxfield 1975, 249–51, fig. 16		
Twin Yeo	pit	116 (693)		gabbroic					Farnell 2015, 226		Y
Wessex Close, Topsham	residual	2 (13)		local					Farnell and Rainbird 2018		Y

Key to sub-styles: DW – Durrington Walls; W – Woodland; C – Clacton.

only one piece was diagnostic, belonging to the Woodlands sub-style. The assemblage was relatively small, comprising 71 small sherds, and was associated with flints and fragments of hazelnut shells which frequently occur in Grooved Ware pits across south-west England. The pit with the Woodlands sherd also contained a greenstone axehead, but in all other regards the assemblage, context and scale are very typical of the region. This can be seen at other Grooved Ware sites including the Royal Naval Stores Depot, Exeter (Fig. 14.3), where nine sherds were recovered from two vessels of Clacton sub-style in an amorphous pit/tree-throw [5234] with flints and hazelnut shells (Pearce *et al.* 2011), and at Pin Brook, Exeter, a single unattributable sherd of Grooved Ware was recovered from a shallow pit, which also contained hazelnut shells (Garland 2019). At Digby, Exeter (Fig. 14.3), seven sherds from two vessels came from pit [682] and were published as Clacton sub-style

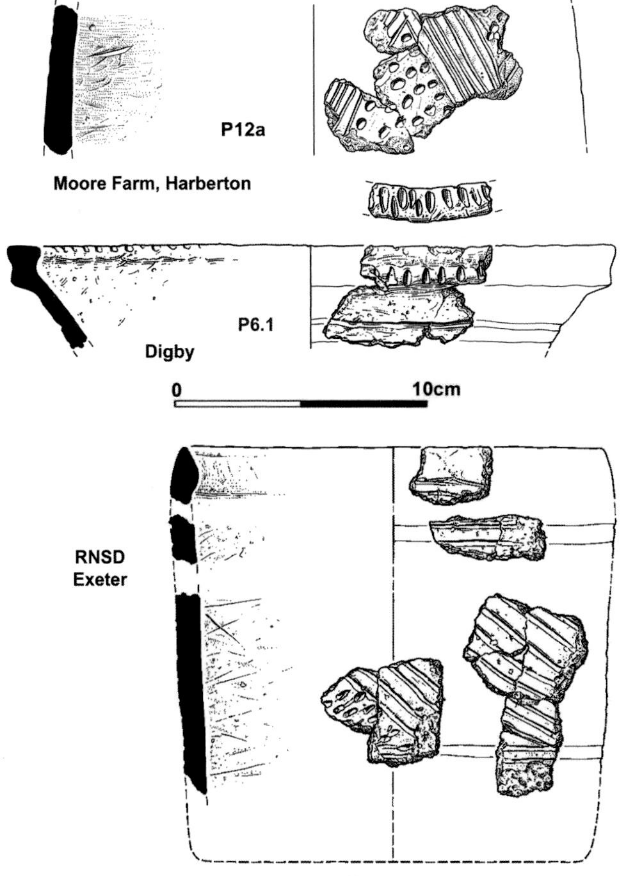

Figure 14.3. Grooved Ware from Devon. Moore Farm, Harberton P12a (after Mudd and Joyce 2014, fig. 2.34; © Cotswold Archaeology); Digby P6.1, Exeter, suggested Grooved Ware (after Quinnell and Farnell 2016, fig. 44; © Devon Archaeological Society) and RNSD, Exeter (after Pearce et al. *2011, fig. 12; © Devon Archaeological Society).*

Grooved Ware; a further 25 small sherds from a second intercutting pit [984] could not be assigned (Quinnell and Farnell 2016). The identification of this material is now considered questionable as the interpretation as Grooved Ware was influenced by the 3rd millennium cal BC date. Alison Sheridan (pers. comm.) suggests this material has closer affinities with some Fengate material.

In general, assemblages from Devon are small and comprise parts of vessels not apparently deposited with formality but accompanied by charred hazelnut shells and flints. This suggests that material from domestic middens or residues from cooking events were gathered together for burial. The lack of apparent formality of deposition does not mean entirely casual discard but rather that there was a ritualisation of the disposal of material generated by domestic activity (Bradley 2005; Thomas 2012). It is also noticeable that to date there are no associations with monuments such as henges (as discussed below).

One of the exceptions to this pattern is the site at Moore Farm, Harberton, where three pits and an adjacent ditch produced 171 sherds from nine vessels in the Durrington Walls sub-style (Mudd and Joyce 2014, 48–51). The interpretation of the ditch is uncertain, possibly a large ring-ditch. The majority of the sherds came from pit [18.12.018] (Fig. 14.3). The size and number of vessels comprising the assemblage are unusual in a Devon context. The presence of charcoal and hazelnut shell fragments are, however, very typical, as is the main context of a small pit group. The difference lies in the number of vessels present, which might suggest that the deposition here involved the memorialisation of a larger-scale event than the majority of others currently known in Devon.

GROOVED WARE IN CORNWALL

The Cornish finds are listed in Table 14.2. Two sites are associated with the earliest Woodlands sub-style in Cornwall. A recent discovery at Nansledan, Newquay (Quinnell 2019), comprised two pits, one of which held sherds from two vessels and a second from one vessel. Altogether, 133 sherds, mostly sizable, were present, making this the largest Woodlands assemblage in the south-west. The site is currently undated but the second site, Tregurra Valley, has an associated radiocarbon determination.

The Tregurra Valley site on the east side of Truro comprised 14 pits, which contained a minimum of 22 vessels (Taylor 2022). A further pit [2502] was identified with an unusual vessel whose published attribution as Grooved Ware (Taylor 2022, 113–14, fig. 4.3, P16) has been questioned on the grounds of the vessel's trunconic shape, which places it far closer to the Fengate style of Peterborough Ware than to Grooved Ware vessel forms (Alison Sheridan, pers. comm.). The associated radiocarbon determination of 3360–3020 cal BC (SUERC-64454; 4480±37 BP; Taylor 2022, 24) might support Sheridan's view but the standard of potting and the fabric are consistent with the Grooved Ware from other pits; sherds from a further five pots from pit [2502] (not illustrated in Taylor 2022) have been regarded as Grooved Ware (Taylor 2022, 114–15) and include some with narrow cordons. The question of the possible influence of Grooved Ware design on Fengate Ware pottery requires further investigation. The pits were located in the eastern half of a large, stripped area, with some being found singly and others in pairs or small groups. All three sub-styles were identified on the Tregurra Valley site, reflecting deposition over several centuries and revealing continuing contacts with other parts of Britain. The earliest radiocarbon determination for pottery of indubitable Grooved Ware type, 3280–2900 cal BC (at 95% probability or 3076–2923 cal BC at 68%; SUERC-64438; 4386±37 BP), was associated with a Woodlands sub-style vessel which had been deposited in pit [2308] (Fig. 14.4). Unlike subsequent depositional events, the vessel was nearly complete, placed upright into the pit cut. Accompanying artefacts comprised 24 flints, some of which were burnt/heat-treated and others fresh, including an arrowhead-shaped piece, blades and scrapers.

The majority of vessels were of the Clacton sub-style (Taylor 2022) and the next securely dated pits, [2355] and [2486], produced near-identical radiocarbon determinations (Table 14.2). Both contained sherds from Clacton sub-style vessels and large quantities of

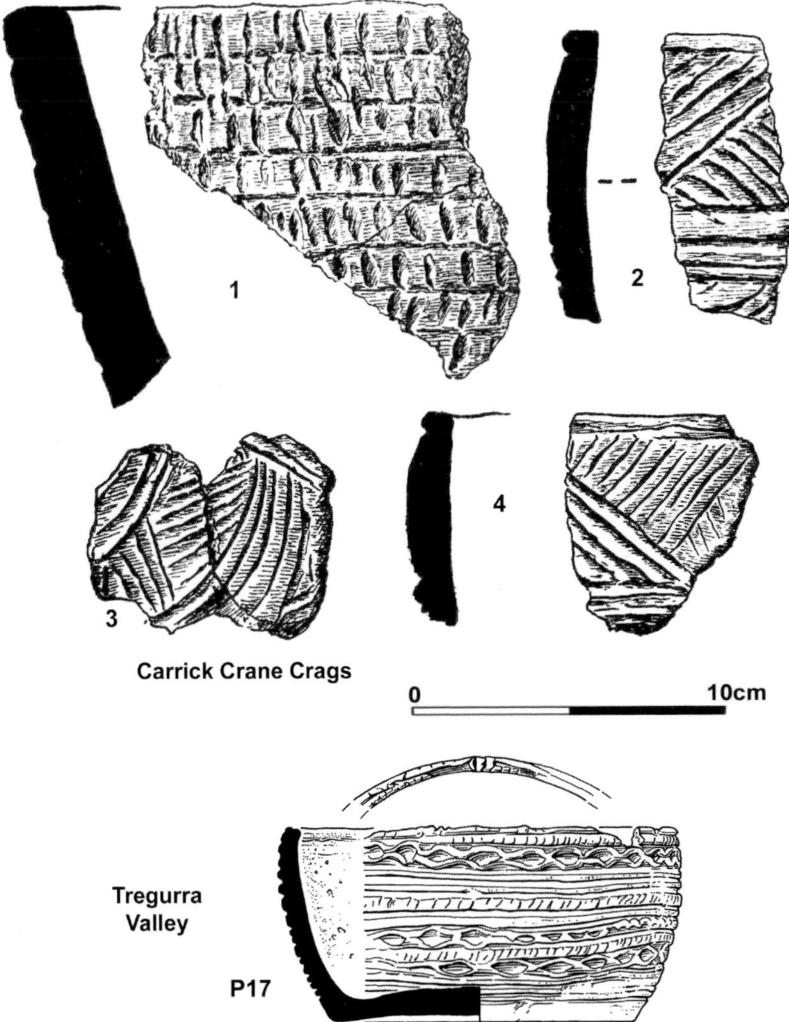

Figure 14.4. Grooved Ware from Carrick Crane Crags cave (after Patchett 1950, fig. 1, nos 1–4 © A. ApSimon archive lodged with English Heritage) and Tregurra Valley P17 (after Taylor 2022, fig. 4.3).

Table 14.2. Grooved Ware from Cornwall. Key to sub-styles: DW – Durrington Walls; W – Woodland; C – Clacton.

Findspot	*Context*	*No. sherds, (wt, g)*	*Sub-style*	*Fabric*	*Date*				*Reference*	*Fig. no.*	*Report by HQ?*
					Cal BC (95.4% probability)	*Lab no.*	*BP*	*Dated material*			
Carrick Crane Crags	cave	4	DW	gabbroic					Patchett 1950, 45, fig. 1	14.4, 1–4	
Carwynnen Quoit	chamber tomb	6		gabbroic	3076–2913	SUERC-55957	4371±19	burnt bone frag.	Nowakowski and Gossip forthcoming		Y
Clodgy Moor, West Penwith	field-walking	200+, small							Jones *et al.* 2013, 15–18, illus. 7		Y
Davidstow barrow XXVI	old land surface below barrow	3	DW?	gabbroic	Pit 6: 2889–2496	HAR-6643	4130±70	wood charcoal, *Corylus, Calluna, Quercus,* Leguminosae & *Salix/ Populus* sapwood	Christie 1988, 121–2, fig. 71		
Mylor, Yacht Club	pits	139 (1388)	DW	gabbroic					Rainbird 2016		Y

(Continued)

Table 14.2 (Continued)

Findspot	*Context*	*No. sherds, (wt, g)*	*Sub-style*	*Fabric*	*Date*				*Reference*	*Fig. no.*	*Report by HQ?*
					Cal BC (95.4% probability)	*Lab no.*	*BP*	*Dated material*			
Penryn College, Falmouth	pits	181 (1430)	DW	gabbroic 88%, local 12%	Pit [312]: 2857–2496	SUERC-19984	4080±30	wood charcoal, *Corylus avellana*	Gossip and Jones 2017, 13–17, fig. 9	14.6, P1	
					Pit [97]: 2580–2468	SUERC-19979	4005±30	wood charcoal, *Corylus avellana*			
					Pits [97] & [312]: 2577–2468	SUERC-19980	4000±30	charred residue on sherd			
Tintagel Field 36	unstrat.	1 (9)		local					Jones and Quinnell 2014, 56		
Tregiffian Vean, St Just-in-Penwith	large 'cist' or megalithic structure measuring *c.* 3.7 × 4.5 m	1							Patchett 1944, 26, A6	14.6	
Tregunnel, Newquay	pits	107 (931)	DW	gabbroic, most with grog	Posthole [6229]: 2620–2467	SUERC-80129	4014±29	wood charcoal, *Corylus avellana*	Brindle forthcoming		Y
Tregurra Valley	pits	275 (4449)	W, C, DW	gabbroic 68%, granitic 32%	Pit [2308]: 3263–2907	SUERC-64438	4386±37	wood charcoal, *Corylus avellana*	Taylor 2022	14.4, P17	Y
					Pit [2355]: 2887–2632	SUERC-64444	4173±37	roundwood charcoal, *Corylus avellana*			

(Continued)

Table 14.2. Grooved Ware from Cornwall. Key to sub-styles: DW – Durrington Walls; W – Woodland; C – Clacton.(Continued)

Findspot	Context	No. sherds, (wt, g)	Sub-style	Fabric	Date				Reference	Fig. no.	Report by HQ?
					Cal BC (95.4% probability)	Lab no.	BP	Dated material			
Tregurra Valley					Pit [2486]: 2886–2631	SUERC-64452	4171±37	roundwood charcoal, Maloideae			
					Pit [1092]: 2895–2639 & 2876–2589	SUERC-64434	4193±37	roundwood charcoal, *Corylus avellana*			
					Pit [2327]: 2896–2633 & 2913–2675	SUERC-64433	4141±37	hazelnut shell			
						SUERC-64442	4193±37	hazelnut shell			
						SUERC-64443	4231±37	roundwood charcoal, *Corylus avellana*			
					Pit [3144]: 2872–2576	SUERC-64457	4121±37	hazelnut shell			
					Pit [2053]: 2881–2623	SUERC-64436	4155±37	roundwood charcoal, *Prunus* cf. *spinosa*			
					Pit [1108]: 2872–2580	SUERC-64426	4130±37	wood charcoal, *Prunus* cf. *spinosa*			

(Continued)

Table 14.2 (Continued)

Findspot	*Context*	*No. sherds, (wt, g)*	*Sub-style*	*Fabric*	*Date*				*Reference*	*Fig. no.*	*Report by HQ?*
					Cal BC (95.4% probability)	*Lab no.*	*BP*	*Dated material*			
Tremough, Penryn	pits	173 (1933)	DW, a little C	gabbroic 95%, local 5%	Pit [331]: 2861–2489	Wk-14999	4079±39	wood charcoal, *Corylus avellana*	Gossip and Jones 2007, 51–7, figs 23–5	14.6, PP4, PP10	Y
					Pit [494]: 2565–2292	Wk-15001	3928±40	wood charcoal, *Corylus avellana*			
Trevone 1, Harlyn Bay	soil beneath cairn	sherds from 1 pot	DW						Buckley 1972, 14–15, fig. 5	14.5	
Treator, Harlyn Bay	pits	9 (32)		granitic	Pit [711]: 2859–2471	AA-26416	4055±50	wood charcoal, *Corylus avellana*	Jones and Quinnell 2014, 109		
Trevone 2, Harlyn Bay	pit	46 (546)	DW, C	gabbroic 29%, local 71%	Pit [523]: 2893–2620	AA-2641	4175±50	wood charcoal, *Crataegus*	Jones and Quinnell 2014, 109–12, figs 95–6	14.5	
Trevorva Cott, Probus	pits	60	DW, C	gabbroic	Pit [13]: 2872–2465	AA-29731	4055±70	wood charcoal, *Corylus avellana*	Jones and Nowakowski 1997		
					Pit [14]: 2579–2204	AA-29732	3930±65	wood charcoal, *Corylus avellana* & *Crataegus*			
Zennor Quoit, West Penwith	portal dolmen	3		granitic	3345–3022	UB-6753	4471±38	human bone, calcined	Patchett 1944, 2–23, fig. 2; Kytmannow 2008		

[1] where it is described as Beaker; illustration by A. ApSimon, English Heritage archive
Key to sub-styles: DW – Durrington Walls; W – Woodland; C – Clacton.

flint, mostly knapping debris. Although not paired, they were found on the same part of the site, with the radiocarbon determinations suggesting broad contemporaneity. The flint assemblages in these pits are unlike any other on the site, with a ritualised clearing away of knapping debris after tools had been produced.

Pit [1092] also contained sherds of vessels of the Clacton and Durrington Walls sub-styles but the accompanying finds suggest an episode of more structured activity as the pit also contained three examples of mobiliary art incised on to slates. Two are incised with simple lines but the third, a disc, is unparalleled in the south-west. The disc is incised with a chequerboard design on one side and infilled lozenges on the other. The patterns on the disc have clear resemblances to motifs found in Orkney in association with Late Neolithic settlements (Card and Thomas 2012; Thomas 2019) and with those found on chalk plaques from Wessex (Harding 1988; Jones and Díaz-Guardamino 2019; Davis *et al.* 2021). As with the Grooved Ware, this confirms that the south-west was in contact with other parts of Britain.

Pit [1092] was adjacent to pit [1108], which produced near-identical radiocarbon determinations (Table 14.2). This is of interest as sherds of one of the two Durrington Walls vessels present in Pit [1108] were also found in pit [1092]. The dating and the pottery suggest that both pits were open at the same time, although the contents of [1092] were far richer; the deposits in both pits appear to have been structured, with sherds of pottery carefully placed on the bottom of the pit cuts (Taylor 2022, 35).

A similar pattern is found at Tremough, near Penryn, where eight shallow pits produced sherds from around 21 vessels, mostly of Durrington Walls and some of Clacton sub-styles (Gossip and Jones 2007). As at Tregurra Valley, the pits were found singly and in pairs, and radiocarbon dating suggests that they had been dug over an extended period of time. Analysis of the pottery revealed contrasting patterns of deposition and the treatment of vessels. Pits [331] and [494] both contained sherds from Durrington Walls vessels. In both cases the sherds were abraded, but in pit [331] the sherds were large, with some conjoining, whereas those in [494] were small. By contrast with both pits, pit [300] contained sherds from several vessels, which were freshly broken and contained conjoining sherds. The three pits therefore contained assemblages which had been treated differently.

The same pattern can be seen on sites with single and paired pits. At Harlyn Bay, pit [523] contained sherds representing most of an unusual Durrington Walls vessel (Jones and Quinnell 2014). The sherds were fresh, conjoining and had been stacked up. Clearly, care had been taken with the deposition of the vessel, which is likely to have been buried shortly after breakage. At Trevorva Cott, Probus, two pits were uncovered that contained a mixture of sherds of the Clacton and Durrington Walls sub-styles, along with flints (Jones and Nowakowski 1997). It could be argued that the deposit here had been structured but for a different reason. The edges of the Trevorva Cott sherds had been deliberately smoothed, which implied that, like other forms of artefact such as beads (for example, Woodward and Hunter 2015), they had been modified and curated prior to burial.

By contrast, there was no apparent attempt to order sherds in the pits at Treator, Harlyn Bay (Trevone) (Fig. 14.5) or Penryn College (Jones and Quinnell 2014; Gossip and Jones 2017; Fig. 14.6), where pottery seems to have entered pits in an unstructured way with other material including charcoal and hazelnut shells. These sherds were probably associated with domestic occupation and deposited as part of a routine practice.

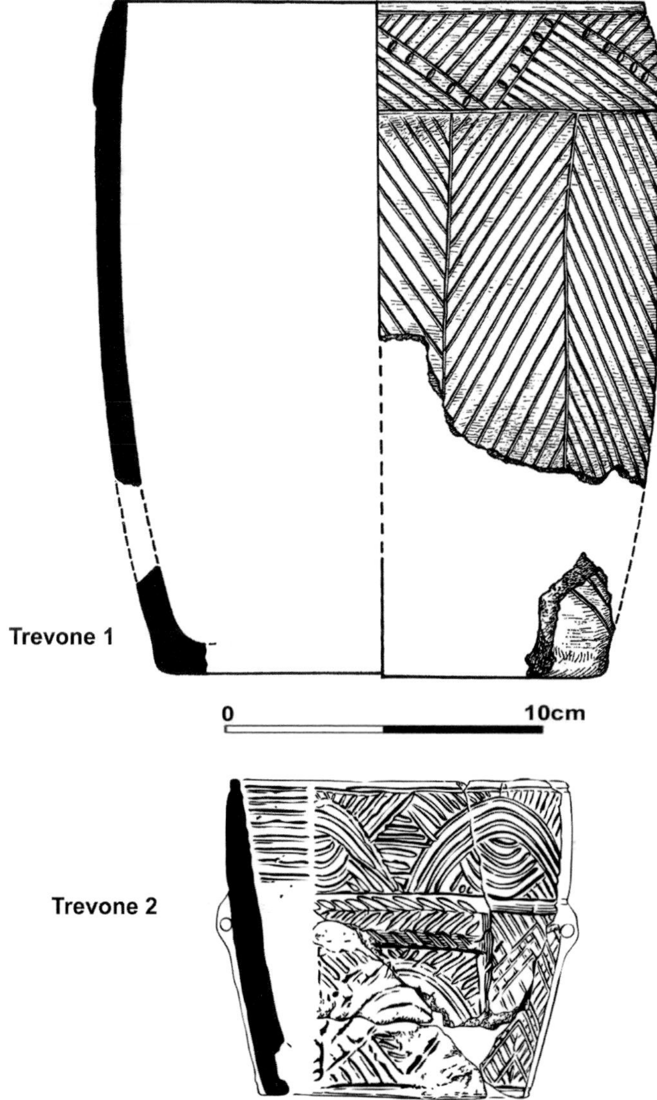

Figure 14.5. Grooved Ware from Harlyn Bay. Trevone 1 (after Buckley 1972, fig. 5; © David Buckley); Trevone 2 (after Jones and Quinnell 2014, fig. 94; © Cornwall Archaeological Unit).

At Clodgy Moor, 256 abraded sherds of Grooved Ware were found during a fieldwalking project on a multi-period, extensive lithic scatter site dating from the Mesolithic through to the Late Neolithic (Jones *et al.* 2013). The lithic scatter was also associated with Group I axehead roughouts and the site is interpreted as a place of axehead making and exchange. The Grooved Ware is likely to have been ploughed out of buried features, such as pits, and probably represents a tiny proportion of the overall assemblage. As such it constitutes

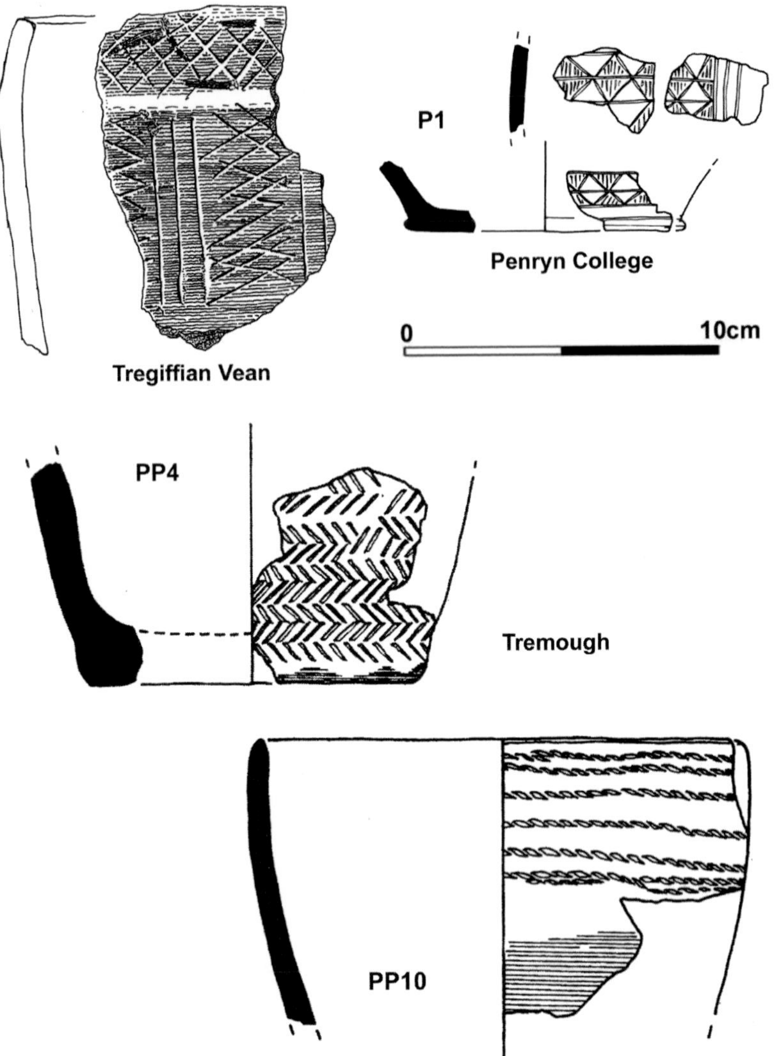

Figure 14.6. Grooved Ware from West Cornwall. Tregiffian Vean, St Just-in-Penwith (Patchett 1944: illustration by A. ApSimon, previously unpublished); Penryn College P1 (Gossip and Jones 2017, fig. 9; © Cornwall Archaeological Unit); Tremough PP4 and 10 (after Gossip and Jones 2007, figs 23–4; © Cornwall Archaeological Unit).

a very significant communal site, perhaps on at least the scale of Tregurra Valley. In common with Tregurra Valley and Tremough, and in contrast with Orkney, the Boyne Valley or Wessex (Eogan and Roche 1997; Schulting *et al.* 2010; Carlin 2017; Leivers 2021; Parker Pearson *et al.* 2022, 93), the larger Grooved Ware assemblages are not associated with monuments, despite ceremonial monuments being present in the wider vicinity (for example, Jones 2016).

GROOVED WARE AND MONUMENTS IN THE SOUTH-WEST

The lack of monumental associations is of interest. Small quantities of Grooved Ware have been found in association with Early Neolithic chamber tombs (as noted above) in west Cornwall, which at the time of deposition were centuries old and likely to have been regarded as ancient monuments; they may have been considered as supernatural or liminal places. Caves may have been considered as having some of the same attributes; Grooved Ware is known from three of these. Carrick Crane Crags on the Lizard produced the first Grooved Ware recognised in Cornwall (Patchett 1950) with Three Holes Cave the first in Devon (Rosenfield 1964). The third, an assemblage from Ash Hole, Brixham, remains unpublished.

Given the evidence for contacts during the Neolithic, it is inconceivable that Late Neolithic communities were unaware of broadly contemporary monument forms found to the east and north of the south-west peninsula. The number of monuments of definite and possible Late Neolithic date in the south-west peninsula is, however, low, and largely comprises a scattering of small henges, timber rings/pit circles and a propped stone monument (Griffith 1985; Griffith and Quinnell 1999; Jones and Goskar 2017; Clark and Foreman forthcoming). Some stone circles may also date to this period, although none is associated with Neolithic radiocarbon dates or artefacts. Furthermore, excavation of some of these monuments reveals that communities seem to have excluded Grooved Ware from them. For example, excavations of the henges at the Stripple Stones and Castilly only produced a few flints and no ceramics, although the scale of excavations at the latter site was small (Gray 1908; Thomas 1962; Preston-Jones *et al.* 2017). Similarly, the post-rings/pit circles at Royalton in Cornwall and Headon Down in Devon were both devoid of artefacts (Dyer and Quinnell 2013; Clark and Foreman forthcoming). Grooved Ware was, so far uniquely for this type of context, recovered from the Early Bronze Age round barrow at Davidstow, barrow XXVI (Christie 1988). Beneath the barrow was a post-ring, pits and an old land surface. A Late Neolithic date was obtained on charcoal from one of the pits and three sherds of Grooved Ware were found on the old land surface. However, the sherds could pre-date the post-ring and may therefore not be directly associated with monument. There are two sites, Moore Farm (Mudd and Joyce 2014) and Cowick Lane, Exeter (Caine and Valentin 2011), where Grooved Ware sherds could possibly be meaningfully associated with ring-ditches, the latter more likely than the former.

Finally, charcoal from a platform beneath a propped stone associated with rock art at Hendraburnick (Jones and Goskar 2017) was radiocarbon dated to the Late Neolithic and produced Late Neolithic flints and a broken perforated greenstone macehead, as well as finds of Early Bronze Age date. Ceramics were, however, entirely absent, which may suggest deliberate exclusion from the monument.

GROOVED WARE IN THE SOUTH-WEST: SOCIALISING THE LANDSCAPE

From the preceding review, it is clear that Grooved Ware was used in the south-west from *c.* 3000 cal BC down to around 2500 cal BC and that small groups of pits predominate as the main context for deposition. The questions therefore arise as to why pits were the preferred mode of deposition and what role Grooved Ware played in the south-west peninsula.

In the south-west, pits containing pottery, charcoal and lithics are known from the beginning of the Neolithic (for example, Leverett and Quinnell 2010; Jones *et al.* 2015; Taylor 2022; Brindle forthcoming) and Grooved Ware pits in the south-west can be interpreted as a continuation of these practices. The intervening Middle Neolithic sees an association of Peterborough Ware pottery in pits, most notably at Tregurra Valley. The majority of Grooved Ware found in pits across the south-west must have derived from domestic activity, presumably involving the preparation and consumption of food, and commensality and contact between community members. There is certainly widespread evidence for the formal sharing of food since at least the beginning of the Neolithic and the anthropological literature draws attention to its significance in cementing social relations and marking significant events (for example, Clarke 2001; Wayland Barber 2013, 313–15). Many Grooved Ware vessels are of a suitable size for liquids and foods in quantities appropriate for communal occasions and residue analyses have revealed traces of both, with recent studies highlighting their use as cooking vessels (for example, Mukherjee and Evershed 2016; McLaren 2022; see also Chapter 7, this volume).

No comparable residue analysis has yet been carried out on Grooved Ware assemblages from Devon or Cornwall, but it is possible to envisage how Grooved Ware was deposited across the landscape. Palaeoenvironmental studies suggest that large parts of the south-west were still covered by woodland in the later Neolithic period (Wilkinson and Straker 2008) and much of the landscape may have consisted of cleared areas linked by woodland pathways. Interconnectivity and movement over long distances are indicated by isotopic work on animal bones from Late Neolithic henge monuments in Wessex which indicate the movement of pigs and cattle across southern Britain, including animals from the south-west peninsula (Viner *et al.* 2010; Madgwick *et al.* 2019). Such connections may have facilitated the spread of ceramic styles and an awareness of monuments and social organisation found elsewhere.

It is possible that clearings along these routes were marked by pits which, as Fontijn (1996) has argued with regard to urnfields, acted to socialise the landscape through certain community practices. Likewise, David Silverman (2019, 26–7), has noted that the native American Wampanoag Indians of the eastern seaboard marked clearings/stopping places with pits containing domestic refuse as a mnemonic which reminded people of past events. Sites such as the Royal Naval Stores Depot may therefore represent one-off events whereas others, such as Tregurra Valley, may indicate sequential events.

As we have seen, despite the evidence for contacts, not all aspects of activities associated with Grooved Ware use were accepted by later Neolithic communities in the south-west and we need to move beyond nationwide 'big picture' narratives towards more nuanced understandings of social organisation at regional and local levels (cf. Gerritsen 2003; Barclay and Brophy 2021). This is particularly important given the fascination that archaeology as a discipline has lavished on the monumental (Graeber and Wengrow 2021).

In particular, monumentality was largely rejected by communities in the south-west. Those monuments which were built were small and, crucially for this paper, excluded Grooved Ware. The rejection of certain practices by neighbouring communities is well-known; for example, Lévi-Strauss (1955, 457) noted that the Tupi-Kawahib of Brazil found the consumption of tobacco revolting despite its widespread use by surrounding communities. Likewise, Graeber and Wengrow (2021, 164–209) note that, in north-west

California, the Yurok people eschewed the potlatching and large-scale feasting of their more northerly Pacific Coast neighbours in favour of an ascetic lifestyle. The authors employ the term *schismogenesis*, whereby communities define themselves by having marked differences from their neighbours (Graeber and Wengrow 2021, 164–209).

Seen in this light, Grooved Ware-using communities in the south-west, although familiar with large-scale monuments found in Wessex and, presumably, associated practices, redefined them according to localised identities. Monuments such as henges could be built but they were used by smaller groups and were not associated with on-site, large-scale feasting. Instead, larger gatherings and exchanges may have taken place in open spaces such as at Clodgy Moor where axeheads may have been exchanged and feasts served from Grooved Ware vessels.

ACKNOWLEDGEMENTS

We thank George Scott for the map, Figure 14.1, and Michael Griffith-Jones for preparing Figures 14.2–5. Holders of copyright acknowledged in Tables 14.1 and 14.2 are thanked for giving permission for reproduction.

REFERENCES

Barclay, G.J. and Brophy, K. 2021. A veritable chauvinism of prehistory: nationalist prehistories and the 'British' late Neolithic mythos. *Archaeological Journal* 178, 330–60.

Bradley, R. 2005. *Ritual and domestic life in prehistoric Europe.* London: Routledge.

Brindle, T. forthcoming. A multi-period prehistoric landscape and Roman burial at Tregunnel Hill, Newquay: excavations in 2012. *Cornish Archaeology.*

Buckley, D.G. 1972. The excavation of two slate cairns at Trevone, Padstow, 1972. *Cornish Archaeology* 11, 9–18.

Caine, C. and Valentin, J. 2011. Part of a prehistoric ring ditch and two post-Roman corn drying ovens on land at Oaklands, Cowick Lane, Exeter. *Proceedings of the Devon Archaeological Society* 69, 95–112.

Card, N. and Thomas, A. 2012. Painting a picture of Neolithic Orkney: decorated stonework from the Ness of Brodgar. In A. Cochrane and A. Jones (eds), *Visualising the Neolithic: abstraction, figuration, performance, representation*, 111–24. Oxford: Oxbow Books.

Carlin, N. 2017. Getting into the groove: exploring the relationship between Grooved Ware and developed passage tombs in Ireland *c.* 3000–2700 cal BC. *Proceedings of the Prehistoric Society* 83, 155–88.

Christie, P. 1988. A barrow cemetery on Davidstow Moor, Cornwall: wartime excavations by C.K. Croft Andrew. *Cornish Archaeology* 27, 27–169.

Clark, P. and Foreman, S. forthcoming. The archaeology of the A30 Bodmin to Indian Queens road scheme. *Cornish Archaeology.*

Clarke, M.J. 2001. Akha feasting: and ethnoarchaeological perspective. In M. Dietler and B. Hayden (eds), *Feasts: archaeological and ethnographic perspectives on food, politics, and power*, 144–67. Washington DC: Smithsonian Institute Press.

Cleal, R. and MacSween, A. (eds) 1999. *Grooved Ware in Britain and Ireland.* Oxford: Oxbow Books.

Copper, M., Hamilton, D. and Gibson, A. 2021. Tracing the lines: Scottish Grooved Ware trajectories beyond Orkney. *Proceedings of the Society of Antiquaries of Scotland* 150, 81–117.

Davis, B., Harding, P. and Leivers, M. 2021. Reflectance Transformation Imaging (RTI) investigation of engraved chalk plaques from the Stonehenge region. *Proceedings of the Prehistoric Society* 87, 133–60.

Dyer, M. and Quinnell, H. 2013. Excavation of a group of Early Bronze Age monuments on Headon Down, Sparkwell. *Proceedings of the Devon Archaeological Society* 71, 55–80.

Eogan, G. and Roche, H. 1997. *Excavations at Knowth*, Vol. 2. Dublin: Royal Irish Academy.

Farnell, A. 2015. Multi-period settlement, burial, industry and agriculture: archaeological excavations 2007–2012 at Twinyeo Quarry, Chudleigh Knighton. *Proceedings of the Devon Archaeological Society* 73, 185–278.

Farnell, A. 2018. *Land off the A361, Tiverton, Devon.* Exeter: ACArchaeology, unpublished client report no. ACD1579/2/1.

Farnell, A. and Rainbird, P. 2018. *Land north of Wessex Close, Topsham, near Exeter, Devon.* Exeter: ACArchaeology, unpublished client report no. ACD1360/3/1.

Fontijn, D. 1996. Socializing landscape: second thoughts about the cultural biography of urnfields. *Archaeological Dialogues* 3, 77–87.

Garland, N. 2019. Prehistoric settlement and burial, early medieval crop processing and a possible early medieval cemetery along the Clyst Valley: investigations south of the Pin Brook, Broadclyst, near Exeter, 2015–2016. *Proceedings of the Devon Archaeological Society* 77, 103–45.

Garrow, D. 2012. Concluding discussion: pits and perspective. In H. Anderson-Whymark and J. Thomas (eds), *Regional perspectives on Neolithic pit deposition*, 216–25. Oxford: Oxbow Books.

Garrow, D. and Sturt, F. 2017. *Neolithic stepping stones: excavation and survey within the western seaways of Britain.* Oxford: Oxbow Books.

Gerritsen, F.A. 2003. *Local identities: landscape and community in the late prehistoric Meuse-Demer-Scheldt region.* Amsterdam: Amsterdam University Press.

Gossip, J. and Jones, A.M. 2007. *Archaeological investigations of a later prehistoric and a Romano-British landscape at Tremough, Penryn, Cornwall.* Oxford: British Archaeological Report 443.

Gossip, J. and Jones A.M. 2017. Later Neolithic pits and an Iron Age and Romano-British settlement at Penryn College. *Cornish Archaeology* 56, 1–44.

Graeber, D. and Wengrow, D. 2021. *The dawn of everything: a new history of humanity.* London: Allen Lane.

Gray, H. St G. 1908. On the stone circles of East Cornwall. *Archaeologia* 61, 1–60.

Griffith, F.M. 1985. Some newly discovered ritual monuments in mid Devon. *Proceedings of the Prehistoric Society* 51, 310–15.

Griffith, F.M. and Quinnell, H. 1999. Barrows and ceremonial sites in the Neolithic and earlier Bronze Age. In R. Kain and W. Ravenhill (eds), *Historical atlas of southwest Britain,* 55–61. Exeter: University of Exeter Press.

Harding, P. 1988. The Chalk Plaque Pit, Amesbury. *Proceedings of the Prehistoric Society* 54, 320–7.

Jarvis, K. and Maxfield, V. 1975. The excavation of a first century Roman farmstead and a Late Neolithic settlement, Topsham, Devon. *Proceedings of the Devon Archaeology Society* 33, 17–40.

Jones, A. and Díaz-Guardamino, M. 2019. *Making a mark: image and process in Neolithic Britain and Ireland.* Oxford: Oxbow Books.

Jones, A.M. 2016. Early landscape and ceremony. In P. Herring, N. Johnson, A.M. Jones, J.A. Nowakowski, A. Sharpe and A. Young, *Archaeology and landscape at the Land's End, Cornwall,* 112–37. Truro: Cornwall Council.

Jones, A.M and Goskar, T. 2017. Hendraburnick 'Quoit': recording and dating rock art in the west of Britain. *Time and Mind* 10, 272–92.

Jones, A.M. and Nowakowski, J.A. 1997. *Archaeological investigations along the Probus Bypass, Cornwall 1995.* Truro: Cornwall Council.

Jones, A.M. and Quinnell, H. 2014. *Lines of investigation along the north Cornwall coast.* Oxford: British Archaeological Report 594.

Jones, A.M., Gossip, J. and Quinnell, H. 2015. *Settlement and metalworking in the Middle Bronze Age and beyond: new evidence from Tremough, Cornwall.* Leiden: Sidestone Press.

Jones, A.M., Lawson-Jones, A., Quinnell, H. and Tyacke, A. 2013. Landscapes of stone: contextualising greenstone working and lithics from Clodgy Moor, West Penwith, Cornwall. *Archaeological Journal* 170, 2–29.

Kytmannow, T. 2008. *Portal tombs in the landscape: the chronology, morphology and landscape setting of the portal tombs of Ireland, Wales and Cornwall.* Oxford: British Archaeological Report 455.

Leivers, M. 2021. The Army Basing Programme, Stonehenge and the emergence of the sacred landscape of Wessex. *Internet Archaeology* 56. https://doi.org/10.11141/ia.56.2

Leverett, M. and Quinnell, H. 2010. An Early Neolithic assemblage from Waylands, Tiverton. *Proceedings of the Devon Archaeology Society* 68, 1–20.

Lévi-Strauss, C. 1955. *Tristes tropiques.* London: Picador.

Madgwick, R., Lamb, A.L., Sloane, H., Nederbragt, A.J, Albarella, U., Parker Pearson, M. and Evans, J.A. 2019. Multi-isotope analysis reveals that feasts in the Stonehenge environs and across Wessex drew people and animals from throughout Britain. *Science Advances* 5(3). eaau6078. doi: 10.1126/sciadv.aau6078.

McLaren, D. 2022. Expanding current understanding of the function, style and chronology of Grooved Ware from the A9 Dualling. *Proceedings of the Society of Antiquaries of Scotland* 151, 31–73.

Morris, B. and Rohan, N. 2014. *Tiverton Road, Cullompton, Devon. Results of a desk-based assessment and archaeological evaluation.* South Molton: South West Archaeology Ltd. doi.org/10.5284/1035618.

Mudd, A. and Joyce, S. 2014. *The archaeology of the South-west Reinforcement Gas Pipeline, Devon: investigations in 2005–7.* Cirencester: Cotswold Archaeology.

Mukherjee, A. and Evershed, R.P. 2016. Organic residue analysis of the Early Neolithic and Grooved Ware pottery from Stonehall, Crossiecrown and Wideford Hill. In C. Richards and R. Jones (eds), *The development of Neolithic house societies in Orkney: investigations in the Bay of Firth, mainland, Orkney (1994–2014)*, 393–6. Oxford: Windgather Press.

Nowakowski, J.A. and Gossip, J. forthcoming. Regaining a lost cromlech: the investigation and restoration of Carwynnen Quoit, Camborne, Cornwall, 2009–2014. *Cornish Archaeology.*

O'Neil, B.H. St J. 1952. The excavation of Knackyboy Cairn, St Martins, Isles of Scilly. *Antiquaries Journal* 32, 221–34.

Parker Pearson, M., Pollard, J., Richards, C., Thomas, J., Tilley, C. and Welham, K. 2022. *Stonehenge for the ancestors: Part 2.* Leiden: Sidestone Press.

Patchett, F.M. 1944. Cornish Bronze Age pottery. *Archaeological Journal* 101, 1–49.

Patchett, F.M. 1950. Cornish Bronze Age pottery: part II. *Archaeological Journal* 107, 44–65.

Poole, C. 2003. *Planning Report on an archaeological watching brief of Bow, Devon.* Bath: Bath Archaeological Trust, unpublished client report.

Pearce, P., Steinmetzer, M. and Quinnell, H. 2011. An Early Neolithic pit alignment, Grooved Ware and Bronze Age field boundaries at the former Royal Navy Stores Depot, Old Rydon Lane, Exeter. *Proceedings of the Devon Archaeological Society* 69, 23–51.

Preston-Jones, A., Attwell, D.C., Gossip, J., Kirkham, G. and Smith, R.P. 2017. Survey, restoration and repair at the Stripple Stones circle-henge, Blisland, Cornwall. *Cornish Archaeology* 56, 225–36.

Quinnell, H. 2019. *AC22018. Nansledan Phase 4. Finds assessment for ACArchaeology, Exeter.* Exeter: ACArchaeology, unpublished client report.

Quinnell, H. and Farnell, A. 2016: Prehistoric sites in the Digby area of Exeter. *Proceedings of the Devon Archaeological Society* 74, 65–170.

Quinnell, H. and Taylor, R. 2016. Revealing complexity: the sourcing of Early Neolithic ceramics in South-West Britain. In E. Sibbeson, B. Jervis and S. Coxon (eds), *Insight from innovation. New light on archaeological ceramics. Papers for David Peacock*, 42–56. Southampton: Highfield Press.

Rainbird, P. 2016. *Land east of Penarrow Road, Mylor Churchtown, Cornwall (NGR SW 8180 3466): results of archaeological investigations.* Exeter: AC archaeology, unpublished client report no. ACD332/1/0.

Rainbird, P. and Quinnell, H. 2018. Three Late Neolithic pits at Blundell's Road, Tiverton, Devon. *Proceedings of the Devon Archaeological Society* 76, 29–56.

Rosenfeld, A. 1964. Excavations in the Torbryan Caves, Devonshire. II. Three Holes Cave. *Transactions of the Devon Archaeological Exploration Society* 22, 3–20.

Sawyer, K. 2015. *Isles of the dead? The setting and function of the Bronze Age chambered cairns and cists of the Isles of Scilly.* Oxford: Archaeopress.

Schulting, R., Sheridan, J.A., Crozier, R. and Murphy, E. 2010. Revisiting Quanterness: new AMS dates and stable isotope data from an Orcadian tomb. *Proceedings of the Society of Antiquaries of Scotland* 140, 1–50.

Silverman, D.J. 2019. *This land is their land: the Wampanoag Indians, Plymouth Colony, and the troubled history of Thanksgiving.* New York: Bloomsbury.

Taylor, S.R. 2022. *Down the bright stream: the prehistory of Woodcock Corner and the Tregurra Valley.* Oxford: Archaeopress.

Thomas, A. 2019. Image and process in an architectural context: decorated stonework from the Ness of Brodgar, Orkney. In A. Jones and M. Díaz-Guardamino (eds) 2019, 143–63.

Thomas, A.C. and Wailes, B. 1967. Sperris Quoit: the excavation of a new Penwith chamber tomb. *Cornish Archaeology* 6, 9–23.

Thomas, C. 1962. The Society's 1962 excavations: interim report. *Cornish Archaeology* 2, 23–8.

Thomas, J. 2012. Introduction: beyond the mundane. In H. Anderson-Whymark and J. Thomas (eds), *Regional perspectives on Neolithic pit deposition: beyond the mundane,* 1–12. Oxford: Neolithic Studies Group Seminar Paper 12.

Viner, S., Evans, J., Albarella, U. and Parker Pearson, M. 2010. Cattle mobility in prehistoric Britain: Sr isotope analysis of cattle teeth from Durrington Walls (Wiltshire, UK). *Journal of Archaeological Science* 37, 2812–20.

Wayland Barber, E. 2013. *The dancing goddesses: folklore, archaeology, and the origins of European dance.* New York: W.W. Norton & Company.

Wells, T. 2020. *Sherford New Community – Phase 1:1, Plymouth, Devon (2017–2019 works). Post-excavation assessment.* Salisbury: Wessex Archaeology, unpublished client report no. 107560.21.

Wilkinson, K. and Straker, V. 2008. Neolithic and Early Bronze Age environments in South-west England. In C. Webster (ed.), *The archaeology of south-west England. South-west Archaeological Research Frameworks: resource assessment and research agenda*, 63–74. Taunton: Somerset County Council.

Woodward, A. and Hunter, J. 2015. *Ritual in Early Bronze Age grave goods: an examination of ritual and dress equipment from Chalcolithic and Early Bronze Age graves in Britain.* Oxford: Oxbow Books.

Chapter 15

Comments on Grooved Ware from a bemused sceptic: questions of classification and terminology, dating and interpretation

David Clarke

Most of us encounter Grooved Ware only in specialist contributions to excavation reports. These contributions are usually the work of individuals drawn from the priesthood of pottery experts. Their practices are rooted in those akin to connoisseurship in art history. By that I mean that they are principally concerned with attributions of style and the identification of parallels for individual sherds. Their framework, insofar as Grooved Ware is concerned, remains the sub-styles set out by Longworth 50 years ago, themselves a reworking of groups first identified by Smith. Here I briefly sketch out some issues relating to Grooved Ware that should, I think, concern all students of the British Neolithic.

THE PROBLEM OF THE SUB-STYLES

Longworth's approach, a variant of the procedure he had previously used to distinguish so-called Primary Series Collared Urns, depended upon the identification of a limited number of core traits that characterised each sub-style. The number of these traits for each sub-style varied from six to eight. Sub-style recognition required only the presence of a single trait (Wainwright and Longworth 1971, 236–43). This methodology throws up several problems. Perhaps the most important of these is that it enables only the attribution of individual sherds to a particular sub-style rather than a meaningful and inclusive description of assemblages. And even that is complicated by the defining traits not all having equal value. For instance, among the 5861 Grooved Ware sherds found in the 1966–68 excavations at Durrington Walls, five of the traits defining the Durrington Walls sub-style occur on less than 10% of the total assemblage. The specific rim forms amount to 9% of the recovered rims and the same percentage is recorded for rims with internal incised decoration. Whipped cord is found only on one sherd and twisted cord appears on only 2.5% of the decorated sherds, while spirals/concentric circles occur on only four vessels, with two others perhaps showing this form of decoration. This leaves only three traits that are relatively common at Durrington Walls and, expanding to other Grooved Ware sites, only one – vertical plain or decorated cordons dividing the body surface into panels – that makes a near-universal appearance among pottery groups identified as belonging to the Durrington Walls sub-style (Wainwright and Longworth 1971, 59–71). The consequence of this is that most sherds from Durrington Walls are not demonstrably made in the Durrington Walls sub-style.

More generally, the limited number of traits defining any sub-style leads to high levels of variation in assemblages that are all claimed as members of the same sub-style. (See Smith's characterisation of six Durrington Walls assemblages in her discussion of the pottery from Lawford, Essex: Shennan *et al.* 1985, 176, table 2.) And similarly, pottery from single-site assemblages shows traits of more than one sub-style. Thomas (1999, 116) estimates that a quarter of Grooved Ware assemblages from southern Britain contain elements of more than one sub-style. In extreme cases single pots appear to be simultaneously representative of three different sub-styles (Clarke 1976, 12, fig. 5.12). While the latter cases might encourage belief in the unity of Grooved Ware, it does nothing to support the integrity or value of the four sub-styles identified by Longworth within the overall tradition (namely Clacton, Woodlands, Durrington Walls and Rinyo). Those sub-styles are neither geographically separate nor, as Garwood showed (1999), chronologically distinct. In their formulation, Longworth offered no discussion of what, beyond variation in motif and rim form, these sub-styles might reflect. Nor have more recent considerations engaged with this central issue.

According to MacSween (1995, 41), Longworth posed three key questions at the Neolithic Studies Group meeting looking at Grooved Ware in 1994. These questions were: 'Have we got the number and definition of sub-styles correct?', 'Do the sub-styles all belong to a single unitary tradition?', and 'Do the sub-styles mask chronological variation?'. In the same article, MacSween sought to engage with some of these issues by offering an alternative way of interpreting Grooved Ware from Scotland based largely on the methods of decoration, the range of motifs and the position of the decoration on the vessels, although it was still structured by the same presence/absence approach favoured by Longworth. This is nevertheless the only serious attempt to propose an alternative classification method for Grooved Ware and in her wise commentary she drew attention to '[t]he problems of easily splitting … assemblages into coherent sub-styles'. As noted above this has been a continuing issue since the first outline of Longworth's sub-styles. Some have struggled to deal with it through the adoption of adapted definitions of individual sub-styles. For example, Cleal (1991, 136) identified a sherd (P26) from the Fir Tree Field pits at Down Farm, Cranborne Chase, as Clacton style even though 'it does not possess any of the six diagnostic features listed by Longworth' because 'its tub-like form, and the decoration arranged in horizontal zones, are strongly reminiscent of that style'. More recently, Barclay (2017, 17), commenting on a Northamptonshire assemblage of over 200 sherds said: 'This style [Durrington Walls] of Grooved Ware can include entirely plain vessels (without cordons), cordoned vessels with limited decoration but in which grooving is absent, and vessels with grooved or incised decoration'. This approach only provides some semblance of unity for the individual assemblage in question. Yet building inclusive definitions for individual assemblages offers no path to a more precise definition of the individual sub-styles.

By the time the publication of the 1994 meeting appeared (Cleal and MacSween 1999), Longworth's questions had been conveniently forgotten with one of the editors assuring us in her introductory piece that although '[t]he reality or otherwise of the four sub-styles defined in 1971 is given some consideration here … on the whole they have stood the test of time well' (Cleal 1999, 1). Neither claim, I would suggest, had much accuracy. Perhaps the most important contribution to these issues was Garwood's suggestion that the Woodlands sub-style may be a later version of the Clacton sub-style with 'the two styles constituting a single ceramic sequence within the Grooved Ware tradition' (1999, 157). But Thomas felt that the Woodlands sub-style might be 'quite distinct from other Grooved Ware and used for different purposes' (1999, 120). At much the same time, Pryor *et al.* (1998, 213) had noted that the finds from Etton, Cambridgeshire, seem to represent a fusion of Durrington Walls and Woodland sub-styles, perhaps to be explained as a regional style. Suggestions of regional styles have surfaced from time to time, but they are largely rooted in considerations of single assemblages (e.g. Hamilton and Whittle 1999; McLaren 2022). Others looking at wider canvases have not found the identification of such styles to be at all straightforward (e.g. MacSween 1995; 2018; Sheridan 2016, 204–6).

When Longworth proposed his sub-styles, he did so in the then universally shared belief that Grooved Ware originated in southern England, there being no obvious antecedents on the adjacent Continent, and that it subsequently spread northwards. On this wider matter our thinking is now wholly reversed but it has caused little reconsideration of the validity of the original style structure. The only example I am aware of is MacSween's perceptive suggestion (2018, 64) that 'it is possible that the Rinyo sub-style was a local development from an earlier incised Grooved Ware'. This suggestion receives considerable support from recalling that the identification of the Rinyo style in 1971 relied essentially on just the Skara Brae and Rinyo assemblages, where the vast bulk of the pottery was recovered from the latest contexts on both sites. Moreover, MacSween's suggestion could be equally applicable to the other three styles, in which case we have been discussing Grooved Ware without recognising or defining the earliest forms. Yet demonstrably early forms will probably provide us with our best opportunities for understanding the initial spread of Grooved Ware, both in terms of its geographical extent and its timescale.

Despite the current substantial corpus of Grooved Ware, greatly enhanced from the time of Longworth's original list, no comprehensive evaluation of the validity of the sub-styles nor, if their value is confirmed, more rigorous definitions of these styles has occurred. Instead, quite the opposite has happened. Some have sought to invest individual styles with functional differences through vague and unsubstantiated suggestions that served only to legitimate the present range of sub-styles (Thomas 1999, 114–16). The present sub-styles 'work' because they are so loosely characterised as to avoid any serious challenge to their meaning or legitimacy. So, what do we think the real world meaning is of styles that are not geographically or chronologically separate and, in some instances, not even exclusively found in single site assemblages? Our current Grooved Ware pottery reports seem all too often to be typological studies with no purpose other than the bolstering of expertise.

ACKNOWLEDGING THE IMPLICATIONS OF CURATED FRAGMENTS

In an important paper, Woodward (2002) set out strong arguments for the presence of heirlooms and relics (used in a non-religious sense) in the British Early Bronze Age. One of the examples she used as a case study was the occurrence of apparently curated fragments of Beakers, ideas prompted by her work on the pottery from the Lockington gold hoard (Woodward 2000). She subsequently offered a tighter definition of the term 'heirloom' with diagnostic criteria that relies heavily on observed wear found on the object (Woodward and Hunter 2014, 472–3). While wear is clearly an important means of recognising heirlooms, it cannot be the sole measure for distinguishing such pieces. Woodward's heavy dependence on wear patterns involves assumptions about past behaviour for which we have no confirmatory evidence. Wear does not certainly provide a very helpful approach to recognising curated pottery sherds.

A comparable case to that outlined by Woodward for some Beakers can, I think, be made for a significant number of Grooved Ware sherds. After all, it has long been recognised that 'Grooved Ware is the first major ceramic style, in southern Britain at least, to carry complex decoration, in contrast to the simple decorative schemes of Mortlake and Ebbsfleet Wares, which are extensions of the limited repertoire of the Bowl tradition' and that '[s]uch complexity of decoration seems to imply a high degree of symbolic content' (Healy *et al.* 1993, 76). Following wider opinion, Woodward herself described Grooved Ware as 'a ritual category of containers' (1995, 196). Grooved Ware is, then, widely seen as a type of pottery that could well provide heirlooms or relics.

Additionally, there are some aspects of Grooved Ware that might reasonably be seen as supporting this view. The most obvious of these is the presence of pairs of drilled holes on Grooved Ware pots intended to repair, and thereby extend the life of, damaged vessels. Cleal (1988, 140), in drawing attention to this situation, noted that 'holes drilled after firing occurred more frequently on Grooved Ware vessels than on those of the Peterborough or Beaker traditions'; repairs of Grooved Ware were some four times more common. She suggested several straightforward factors that might lie behind such repairs without suggesting that the creation of heirlooms was one of them, although she did observe that 'Grooved Ware seems to be the first ceramic tradition to carry a significant symbolic content' (1988, 142). More recent commentators have seen these repairs as reflecting the importance of the history of such pots (Bradley 2002, 57) and as efforts to preserve them as heirlooms (Caple 2010, 308).

A less straightforward contribution to this discussion comes from the tempering of Grooved Ware. Cleal, in a study of pottery fabrics from Wessex, found that grog was 'an unpopular inclusion until the appearance of Grooved Ware' (1995, 192), a view supported by Darvill's study (2004) in areas to the north and west. The use of grog, essentially the reworking of earlier pots, can be seen as enhancing the importance of the newly created pot by the inclusion of fragments from earlier, historically important pots. In such cases, the use of grog strengthens the likelihood that the pot will eventually merit becoming an heirloom. Interestingly, Cleal (1995, 192) links this use of grog in Grooved Ware with the greater number of drilled repair holes. More speculatively, the use of marine shell to temper Grooved Ware may show that some pots were consciously created to embody aspects of the past and promote its continuing importance in the future. Shell appears to be even more common than grog as an inclusion in Grooved Ware, a preference 'irrespective of local sources of marine shell, shell-bearing clays, or rock with fossil shell' (Cleal *et al.* 1994, 445). Several sites in Wiltshire, such as Chalk Plaque Pit, Woodlands and Ratfyn, have produced pottery tempered with marine shell even though these sites are *c.* 50 km from the nearest coast (Cleal *et al.* 1994, 446–7). Could this widespread use of shell be reaffirming an awareness of the sea-bound islands of Orkney, the apparent origin centre of Grooved Ware? Perhaps some support for these suggestions is provided by the situation in Orkney. Here shell is not the key tempering agent for Grooved Ware and grog is absent. These origin communities have other means of reflecting their past.

Woodward's work on Beakers was somewhat restricted, but certainly not invalidated, by the large number of occasions when the excavation reports failed to describe the presence of fragments rather than whole pots in burials. This is fortunately not the case with regard to Grooved Ware. Even among the largest assemblages, those with more than 5000 sherds, the number of pots where sufficient sherds exist to establish conclusively their complete profile is in single figures. This does not correspond with our quotidian experience where breakage of a pot results in us collecting the fragments and disposing of them together in a single act and place. Although post-depositional factors will offer a partial explanation, they cannot wholly account for the observed absence of single pot concentrations. And this situation is, of course, mirrored by pottery assemblages from a wide range of contexts throughout later prehistory.

Certainly, evidence for the single deposition of a broken vessel is extremely rare in the larger Grooved Ware assemblages and virtually absent from the smaller collections that make up most of the recorded discoveries. But Grooved Ware is found in pits more often than any other style of Neolithic pottery – for southern Britain, see Thomas (1999, 69, fig. 4.4) – and pits are by far the largest number of contexts from which Grooved Ware has been recovered while stray finds are remarkably rare – for southern Britain see Thomas (1999, 112, fig. 5.11). Thomas has undertaken a wide-ranging review of these early pits (1999, 64–74). From this he concluded (Thomas 1999, 68) that 'Neolithic and Early Bronze Age pits are unsuitable both in size and shape for the storage of foodstuffs. They seem to have been dug and backfilled within a relatively short space of time, with a matrix of material that shows evidence of burning but containing artefacts which have rarely been burnt'.

The rapid digging and filling, together with the small number of recorded layers in individual pits, make it seem reasonable to regard them as examples of a closed context. Woodward considered such contexts essential to allow the recognition of the absence of complete objects as a reflection of 'social action' (Woodward and Hunter 2014, 473). Many of these pits show clear signs of the formal and deliberate deposit of artefacts, food remains and unworked stone. At the very least those with large sherds of Grooved Ware must be possible heirlooms or relics. This is probably an unnecessarily minimalist view. Of course, recognising which are curated pieces and which are the result of contemporary breakage is not at all straightforward. But the presence of curated pieces is clearly visible in the material recovered from some pits. A fine example is provided by Pit 01 at King's Stanley, Gloucestershire (Evans 2010). The pit, with maximum dimensions of 3.8 × 1.8 × 0.8 m, had a sharp profile with no indication that it had been open for any significant period of time. Its fill was a fine reddish-brown clay with many limestone fragments, together with pieces of sandstone, mudstone, chalk and haematite. The colour of the fill was unique on the site. At the base of the pit were sherds from up to five Grooved Ware vessels, two of which were from large pots. These sherds were smaller and more abraded than those of two heavily decorated Mortlake bowls sitting in the centre of the pit above the

Grooved Ware. A substantial part of one of these bowls was present but the second bowl was represented by only a few sherds. Other finds included an incised limestone plaque, a perforated sandstone fragment and a possible cylindrical bead. The flint assemblage of 376 pieces was largely flakes and blades but the only recognisable tools were Mesolithic microliths and burins. A radiocarbon date, 2470–2200 cal BC (OxA 15346: 3856±33 BP), was obtained from a charred hazelnut shell below the Mortlake sherds. It seems clear that both the Grooved Ware and the Mortlake sherds from 'a tradition of pot-making that had ceased at least 400 years before its deposition here' (Ray and Thomas 2018, 313) were old and deliberately selected for inclusion in the pit contents. The same may be true for the Mesolithic flint tools, as Anne Teather (2018) has shown that several dates, significantly earlier than the Neolithic, have been obtained from apparently curated objects securely stratified in Neolithic deposits.

If we can accept, then, that we have evidence for the occurrence of curated pieces in closed contexts, we must face up to the consequences for our chronologies. Woodward (2002, 1046–7), in her discussion of heirlooms and relics, provided only a cursory review of this issue because she was confident that such items can be readily recognised. I am much less sure that we have identified appropriate criteria for distinguishing curated pieces. Instead, we regard their presence in closed contexts as sufficiently rare as to be inconsequential for our mainstream interpretations. Yet their existence, and particularly the very real prospect that they are common finds, effectively remove the value of 'association' as a chronological tool. The materials in the King's Stanley pit came together in any meaningful way as a group only when they were deposited in that pit. The radiocarbon date can only relate to the charred hazelnut shell and even then, we have no way of determining how old it was when it arrived in the pit. A quick glance at Garwood's list of dates for southern Grooved Ware (1999, 164–76) will show how dependent we are on dates from associated organic material, often from pits similar to that at King's Stanley. Nor has the situation changed much since that list was compiled. On many occasions, we have no evidence that the taphonomic paths of the pottery and the organic material have been at all coincident before arriving in the context from they are both recovered. This should lead us to question what value the date has relative to the pottery. It certainly offers no realistic guide to the date of the pottery's manufacture or indeed much of its use. Even dates from organic residues adhering to Grooved Ware only give us an undefined moment in what may have been a very long series of lives. We need to define, if we can, what aspect of these pots with potentially multiple lives our dates refer to.

IS THERE A GROOVED WARE COMPLEX?

A few years ago, Thomas (2010) raised the possibility that British archaeology might witness 'the return of the Rinyo-Clacton folk'. After due consideration he deemed their second coming to be ill advised. His main purpose, while raising this spectre, was to reconcile the ideas around Grooved Ware as 'a special-purpose assemblage, connected with inter-regional contacts between socially pre-eminent groups' with its appearance in apparently everyday contexts. His solution centred on imagery emanating from the house and household. More significantly, he developed his ideas within the framework of a single, unified Grooved Ware complex. The concept of a 'Grooved Ware complex' is now fully embedded in the literature. I want to suggest that thinking in terms of a single Grooved Ware complex, geographically spread from Orkney to southern England and temporally present through more than eight centuries by current reckoning, is mistaken. To think in terms of a single complex is to create expectations of similarity and constancy of practice that are unlikely in real life and cannot be readily found in the archaeological record.

Perhaps because it takes place in Orkney, we have failed to acknowledge the nature of the transformation that the creation of Grooved Ware as a pottery style appears to represent. First and foremost, it is a complete break with earlier potting traditions used for perhaps half a millennium even though it does not seem to signal the end of those earlier styles. If, as seems generally accepted, making pots was a female craft in prehistory, what does this wholesale change in both form and decoration imply about gender roles and relationships in late 4th millennium Orkney? It is not just that the appearance of these new pots is a complete change, radical though that is. Round bases, as Barley notes (1994, 33), spread heat evenly in cooking. In the absence of tables and hard surfaces, round bases set in depressions in the ground or placed on rings have the advantage that the pot can be positioned at any angle suitable for the user. The introduction of Grooved Ware's flat bases may, therefore, have required appreciable changes in culinary and other practices in both a commonplace and a ritual sense.

Nor, critically, is this new pottery form the only change. New stone and particularly bone types are integral parts of the Orcadian Grooved Ware assemblages. These assemblages, apart from the variable survival of bone, are remarkably consistent at every site and contain a range of distinctive types. It has long been clear from the assemblage recovered at Knap of Howar (Ritchie 1983, 75–83), and more recently in the case of the stone tools from the Bay of Firth sites (Clarke 2016), that the characteristic stone and bone types found with round-based pottery forms are not, in most instances, the same as those associated with Grooved Ware. The latter, then, seem best explained as part of the same transformational processes that saw the creation of Grooved Ware. This is not, of course, to suggest that these events need be strictly contemporary, only that they are part of the same wider social change. Yet these distinctive stone and bone types are absent from areas to the south. This point was first made by D.L. Clarke (1970, 269) but it has subsequently been consistently ignored. Indeed, Wainwright and Longworth went so far as to make the wholly mistaken claim that '[t]he associated artefacts [in Grooved Ware assemblages] include flint, bone and stone types, none of which occurs exclusively with any of the ceramic sub-styles' (1971, 266). They doubtless felt justified in making this statement because they had noted that the stone types at Skara Brae and Rinyo and the bone types at Skara Brae were 'unique', both groups the result of 'the environmental conditions prevailing in the region of these settlements', a dubious appeal to environmental determinism (Wainwright and Longworth 1971, 262–3). Now that Orkney is viewed as the epicentre of emerging Grooved Ware traditions, their absence from other areas cannot be explained by invoking these supposed environmental reasons, particularly for the bone tools and ornaments. These are often manufactured from the bones of domesticated animals, so the appeal to environmental conditions seems even less credible. At Skara Brae, for example, there are thousands of beads made predominantly from the bones and teeth of cattle and sheep/goat. The manufacture of these cannot be seen as environmentally determined and yet comparable beads are effectively absent from Grooved Ware contexts stretching from mainland Scotland to southern England. This absence of most stone and bone object types raises important questions about the expansion of Grooved Ware from its Orcadian homeland.

It might be thought that this claim of stone and bone types exclusive to Grooved Ware communities in Orkney is significantly weakened by the presence among the assemblages of those Orcadian communities of three types found elsewhere in Britain: carved stone balls, stone maceheads and bone skewer pins. These types can, of course, be readily interpreted in two distinct ways. They might be regarded as types that developed amongst the Grooved Ware communities in Orkney but equally, they could be types that developed elsewhere among groups different from the Orcadian Grooved Ware communities. The argument in either case is not conclusive but what evidence we have points to their being Orcadian adoptions of types developed elsewhere. There is no reason to suppose that a single place of origin applies to all three types even though only in Orkney are they found in settlement contexts.

Unlike in the rest of Britain, Grooved Ware in Orkney is associated with a series of substantial stone settlements, most notably those excavated at Skara Brae (Childe 1931), Rinyo (Childe and Grant 1939; 1947), Barnhouse (Richards 2005), Links of Noltland (Moore and Wilson 2011) and Pool (Hunter 2007). All these settlements have the same characteristic house type. These houses are not perhaps as standardised as we thought when Skara Brae and Rinyo were the only known sites but, nevertheless, a single arrangement seems to constitute the basis of the layout of all houses. At Skara Brae we see modifications to this form in the second phase of Grooved Ware occupation but these still retain the overall design integrity of the layout of the earlier houses. Features of these houses are also seen in the buildings at the Ness of Brodgar, but their overall size and form suggest that they differ in function from the houses of the settlement sites (Card *et al.* 2020). Equally, some of the settlement sites have buildings of a size and form that suggest they were not houses. Structures 2 and 8 at Barnhouse (Richards 2005, 129–94) and the Grobust structure at Links of Noltland (Clarke and Sharples 1985, 67–8, fig. 4.5; Moore and Wilson 2013) are indicative of the forms involved. But crucially, like the bone and stone tools, these houses represent a comparable break with past practices through major differences in plan and layout from earlier and contemporary houses in Orkney that are not associated with Grooved Ware. The contrast is best demonstrated at Knap of Howar, Papa Westray (Ritchie 1983) but is equally present in the less well-preserved structures in the Bay of Firth area of Mainland (Richards and Jones 2016).

Houses were an essential part of Thomas's discussion of the Grooved Ware complex. And key to his discussion is the claimed similarity between houses found at Durrington Walls and those at Skara Brae. The comparability of the structures at these two sites is rather difficult to evaluate, as they have not yet been published in sufficient detail to confirm the claim. The excavators have seen close similarities with both Phase 1 and Phase 2 structures at Skara Brae (Parker Pearson 2007, 140; Thomas 2010, 5; Parker Pearson *et al.* 2013, 169). An important element is that the similarities are not just based on the overall plans of the buildings' walls but on the presence of wooden furniture equivalent to that seen in stone at Skara Brae (Parker Pearson *et al.* 2013, 169). Yet the phase 1 and 2 structures at Skara Brae do not provide comparisons that are as interchangeable as is assumed here. The Phase 1 houses are, as far as we can tell, free-standing structures closely comparable to those excavated at other Orcadian sites. The Phase 2 structures are, apart from House 7, built against one another so that some walls are common to two structures. Access to all of them is via narrow, low passages. Consequently, these might as reasonably be regarded as rooms in a single structure as the remains of individual houses. This is especially so towards the end of the settlement when they have been rendered semi-subterranean by the surrounding midden. Moreover, these Phase 2 structures are at present found only at Skara Brae. Understanding what any similarities between the Durrington Walls and Skara Brae structures might mean is further complicated by the disparities in date between the two sites that Thomas (2010, 5) noted. It may be these differences in date that account for the pits dug in the floors of the Durrington houses 'as part of the abandonment process' (Ray and Thomas 2018, 183, 253), a feature not seen in the Orcadian houses. Nor indeed are pits otherwise a feature of Grooved Ware contexts in Orkney in contrast to most of mainland Britain.

In addition to the houses at Durrington Walls, Thomas claims that other houses are comparable to those at Skara Brae based on a diagram showing the similarities and differences of early and late houses at Skara Brae (2010, 5, fig. 3). This diagram is a modified version of one originally published by me (Clarke 1976, 11). It was originally designed to draw attention to the internal modifications introduced in the Phase 2 structures. It was not intended to show the external walls of the houses because for Phase 1 houses we did not have, nor have we subsequently recovered, sufficient evidence to show the external wall line and the original diagram carefully avoided doing so. Redrawing of this diagram by others has led to the Phase 1 houses acquiring an external wall and a rather circular overall shape, neither of which is present in the archaeological record. It is this unwarranted external wall that enabled Thomas mistakenly to compare houses at Wyke Down, Dorset (French *et al.* 2007, 86–8), Trelystan, Powys (Britnell 1982) and Upper Ninepence, Powys (Gibson 1999, 29–47) with the early houses at Skara Brae.

A comparable difference to that found in the overall range of house types in Neolithic Orkney is also seen in the chamber tombs. The Maeshowe passage tombs are associated with Grooved Ware whereas the Orkney-Cromarty tombs contain round-based pottery. The architectural links between these groups of houses and tombs in Orkney have long been acknowledged (Hodder 1982, 218–28). The Maeshowe tombs are usually considered to have been inspired by contacts with the Boyne valley in Ireland (Sheridan 2004, 16–17), although current radiocarbon dates place Orcadian passage graves among the earliest from Britain and Ireland (Bayliss *et al.* 2017, 1184), and perhaps earlier than the emergence of Grooved Ware.

What really matters in the context of a unified Grooved Ware complex is that the wholesale transformation associated with Grooved Ware in Orkney finds no parallels elsewhere in Britain. Neither the house type, except perhaps for the rather late houses at Durrington Walls, nor Maeshowe tombs are found outside of Orkney, not even in adjacent areas of mainland Scotland such as Caithness, where the geology that enabled the building of Orkney-Cromarty tombs like those in Orkney would certainly have allowed the construction of comparable Maeshowe tombs. Equally, the most distinctive bone and stone artefact types, so plentiful in Orkney, are absent from the rest of Britain. Only the pottery shapes and decoration are widespread. None of this suggests that a unified Grooved Ware complex is a helpful way to engage with the problems sketched out in this essay.

ACKNOWLEDGEMENTS

I would like to thank Ann MacSween and Alison Sheridan for information and discussion, without in any way committing them to supporting any of my statements.

REFERENCES

Barclay, A. 2017. The Grooved Ware pottery. In M. Cuthbert and B. Zeepvat, Late Neolithic pits and an Early Bronze Age cremation cemetery at Middleton Chase, Banbury Lane, Middleton Cheney, 15–17. *Northamptonshire Archaeology* 39, 11–36.

Barley, N. 1994. *Smashing pots: feats of clay from Africa.* London: British Museum Press.

Bayliss, A., Marshall, P., Richards, C. and Whittle, A. 2017. Islands of history: the late Neolithic timescape of Orkney. *Antiquity* 91, 1171–88.

Bradley, R. 2002. *The past in prehistoric societies.* London: Routledge.

Britnell, W. 1982. The excavation of two round barrows at Trelystan, Powys. *Proceedings of the Prehistoric Society* 48, 133–201.

Caple, C. 2010. Ancestor artefacts – ancestor materials. *Oxford Journal of Archaeology* 29, 305–18.

Card, N., Edmonds, M. and Mitchell, A. 2020. *The Ness of Brodgar: as it stands.* Kirkwall: The Orcadian.

Childe, V.G. 1931. *Skara Brae: a Pictish village in Orkney.* London: Kegan Paul, Trench, Trubner.

Childe, V.G. and Grant, W.G. 1939. A Stone Age settlement at the Braes of Rinyo, Rousay. Orkney (first report. *Proceedings of the Society of Antiquaries of Scotland* 73 (1938–39), 6–31.

Childe, V.G. and Grant, W.G. 1947. A Stone Age settlement at the Braes of Rinyo, Rousay, Orkney (second report). *Proceedings of the Society of Antiquaries of Scotland* 81 (1946–47), 16–42.

Clarke, A. 2016. The coarse stone from Neolithic sites around the Bay of Firth: Stonehall, Wideford Hill, Crossiecrown, Knowes of Trotty and Brae of Smerquoy. In C. Richards and R. Jones (eds) 2016, 445–72.

Clarke, D.L. 1970. *Beaker pottery of Great Britain and Ireland.* Cambridge: Cambridge University Press.

Clarke, D.V. 1976. *The Neolithic village at Skara Brae, Orkney, 1972–73 excavations: an interim report.* Edinburgh: HMSO.

Clarke, D.V. and Sharples, N. 1985. Settlements and subsistence in the third millennium BC. In C. Renfrew (ed.), *The prehistory of Orkney*, 54–82. Edinburgh: Edinburgh University Press.

Cleal, R. 1988. The occurrence of drilled holes in later Neolithic pottery. *Oxford Journal of Archaeology* 7, 139–45.

Cleal, R. 1991. Cranborne Chase – the earliest pottery. In J. Barrett, R. Bradley and M. Hall (eds), *Papers on the prehistoric archaeology of Cranborne Chase*, 134–200. Oxford: Oxbow Books.

Cleal, R. 1995. Pottery fabrics in Wessex in the fourth to second millennia BC. In I. Kinnes and G. Varndell (eds) 1995, 185–94.

Cleal, R. 1999. Introduction: the what, where and why of Grooved Ware. In R. Cleal and A. MacSween (eds) 1999, 1–8.

Cleal, R. and MacSween, A. (eds) 1999. *Grooved Ware in Britain and Ireland.* Oxford: Oxbow Books.

Cleal, R., Cooper, J. and Williams, D. 1994. Shells and sherds: identification of inclusions in Grooved Ware, with associated radiocarbon dates, from Amesbury, Wiltshire. *Proceedings of the Prehistoric Society* 60, 445–8.

Darvill, T. 2004. Soft-rock and organic tempering in British Neolithic pottery. In R. Cleal and J. Pollard (eds), *Monuments and material culture. Papers in honour of an Avebury archaeologist: Isobel Smith*, 193–206. East Knoyle: Hobnob Press.

Evans, D. 2010. Two Neolithic pits at King's Stanley, Gloucestershire. *Transactions of the Bristol and Gloucestershire Archaeological Society* 128, 29–54.

French, C., Lewis, H., Allen, M.J., Green, M., Scaife, R. and Gardiner, J. 2007. *Prehistoric landscape development and human impact in the upper Allen valley, Cranborne Chase, Dorset.* Cambridge: McDonald Institute for Archaeological Research.

Garwood, P. 1999. Grooved Ware in southern Britain: chronology and interpretation. In R. Cleal and A. MacSween (eds) 1999, 145–76.

Gibson, A. 1999. *The Walton Basin Project: excavation and survey in a prehistoric landscape 1993–7.* York: Council for British Archaeology Research Report 118.

Hamilton, M. and Whittle, A. 1999. Grooved Ware of the Avebury area: styles, contexts and meanings. In R. Cleal and A. MacSween (eds) 1999, 36–47.

Healy, F., Cleal, R. and Kinnes, I. 1993. Synthesis and discussion. In R. Bradley, P. Chowne, R. Cleal, F. Healy and I. Kinnes, *Excavations on Redgate Hill, Hunstanton, Norfolk, and at Tattershall Thorpe, Lincolnshire*, 70–7. Gressenhall and Sleaford: East Anglian Archaeology 57.

Hodder, I. 1982. *Symbols in action: ethnoarchaeological studies of material culture.* Cambridge: Cambridge University Press.

Hunter, J. 2007. *Investigations in Sanday, Orkney. Vol. 1: excavations at Pool, Sanday. A multi-period settlement from Neolithic to Late Norse times.* Kirkwall: The Orcadian.

Kinnes, I. and Varndell, G. (eds) 1995. *'Unbaked urns of rudely shape': essays on British and Irish pottery for Ian Longworth.* Oxford: Oxbow Books.

MacSween, A. 1995. Grooved Ware from Scotland: aspects of decoration. In I. Kinnes and G. Varndell (eds) 1995, 41–8.

MacSween, A. 2018. Regional and local identities in the later Neolithic of Scotland as reflected in the ceramic record. In L. Campbell, D. Wright and N.A. Hall (eds), *Roots of nationhood: the archaeology and history of Scotland*, 55–73. Oxford: Archaeopress.

McLaren, D. 2022. Expanding current understanding of the function, style and chronology of Grooved Ware from the A9 Dualling: Luncarty to Pass of Birnam. *Proceedings of the Society of Antiquaries of Scotland* 151, 31–73.

Moore, H. and Wilson, G. 2011. *Shifting sands. Links of Noltland, Westray: interim report on Neolithic and Bronze Age excavations, 2007–09.* Edinburgh: Historic Scotland.

Moore, H. and Wilson, G. 2013. Sands of time: domestic rituals at the Links of Noltland. *Current Archaeology* 275, 12–19.

Parker Pearson, M. 2007. The Stonehenge Riverside Project: excavations in the east entrance of Durrington Walls. In M. Larsson and M. Parker Pearson (eds), *From Stonehenge to the Baltic: living with cultural diversity in the third millennium BC*, 125–44. Oxford: British Archaeological Report S1692.

Parker Pearson, M., Marshall, P., Pollard, J., Richards, C., Thomas, J. and Welham, K. 2013. Stonehenge. In H. Fokkens and A. Harding (eds), *The Oxford Handbook of the European Bronze Age*, 159–78. Oxford: Oxford University Press.

Pryor, F. with Cleal, R. and Kinnes, I. 1998. Discussion of Neolithic and Early Bronze Age pottery. In F. Pryor, *Etton: excavation at a Neolithic causewayed enclosure near Maxey, Cambridgeshire, 1982–7*, 209–13. London: English Heritage.

Ray, K. and Thomas, J. 2018. *Neolithic Britain: the transformation of social worlds.* Oxford: Oxford University Press.

Richards, C. 2005. *Dwelling among the monuments: the Neolithic village of Barnhouse, Maeshowe passage grave and surrounding monuments at Stenness, Orkney*. Cambridge: McDonald Institute for Archaeological Research.

Richards, C. and Jones, R. (eds) 2016. *The development of Neolithic house societies in Orkney: investigations in the Bay of Firth, Mainland, Orkney (1994–2014)*. Oxford: Windgather Press.

Ritchie, A. 1983. Excavation of a Neolithic farmstead at Knap of Howar, Papa Westray, Orkney. *Proceedings of the Society of Antiquaries of Scotland* 113, 40–121.

Shennan, S.J., Healy, F. and Smith, I.F. 1985. The excavation of a ring-ditch at Tye Field, Lawford, Essex. *Archaeological Journal* 142, 150–215.

Sheridan, J.A. 2004. Neolithic connections along and across the Irish Sea. In V. Cummings and C. Fowler (eds), *The Neolithic of the Irish Sea: materiality and traditions of practice*, 9–21. Oxford: Oxbow Books.

Sheridan, J.A. 2016. Scottish Neolithic pottery in 2016: the big picture and some details of narrative. In F. Hunter and J.A. Sheridan (eds), *Ancient lives: object, people and place in early Scotland. Essays for David V Clarke on his 70th birthday*, 189–212. Leiden: Sidestone Press.

Teather, A. 2018. Revealing a prehistoric past: evidence for the deliberate construction of a historic narrative in the British Neolithic, *Journal of Social Archaeology* 18, 193–211.

Thomas, J. 1999. *Understanding the Neolithic*. London: Routledge.

Thomas, J. 2010. The return of the Rinyo-Clacton folk? The cultural significance of the Grooved Ware complex in Later Neolithic Britain. *Cambridge Archaeological Journal* 20, 1–15.

Wainwright, G.J. and Longworth, I.H. 1971. *Durrington Walls: excavations 1966–1968*. London: Society of Antiquaries.

Woodward, A. 1995. Vessel size and social identity in the Bronze Age of southern Britain. In I. Kinnes and G. Varndell (eds) 1995, 195–202.

Woodward, A. 2000. The prehistoric pottery. In G. Hughes, *The Lockington gold hoard: an Early Bronze Age barrow cemetery at Lockington, Leicestershire*, 48–61. Oxford: Oxbow Books.

Woodward, A. 2002. Beads and Beakers: heirlooms and relics in the British Early Bronze Age. *Antiquity* 76, 1040–7.

Woodward, A. and Hunter, J. 2014. *Ritual in Early Bronze Age grave goods: an examination of ritual and dress equipment from Chalcolithic and Early Bronze Age graves in England*. Oxford: Oxbow Books.

Chapter 16

Grooved Ware in Britain and Ireland, 2023: retrospect and prospect

Alison Sheridan

The contributions to this volume have demonstrated just how far our understanding of Grooved Ware in Britain and Ireland has moved on in the 24 years since Ros Cleal and Ann MacSween published their *Grooved Ware in Britain and Ireland* volume in 1999. Thanks largely to developer-funded excavations, the number of findspots has increased to such an extent that it was deemed impossible to attempt a comprehensive gazetteer for this volume (although individual chapters provide a sense of this step-change in the size of our evidential base), and the geographical distribution of Grooved Ware pottery has expanded, with Wales (Lynch, Chapter 6) and the south-west peninsula of England (Jones and Quinnell, Chapter 14) now having increasing numbers of finds from formerly 'blank' areas, for instance.

There has also been an impressive rise in the number of radiocarbon dates pertaining to Grooved Ware, due partly to developer-funded archaeology, and partly to targeted radiocarbon dating programmes – namely Alasdair Whittle and Alex Bayliss's European Research Council-funded *The Times of Their Lives* project, which has injected some 150 new dates into the set of Orcadian Grooved Ware dates (Bayliss *et al.* 2017; Sheridan *et al.* in prep.); Mike Copper's Historic Environment Scotland-funded *Tracing the Lines* project, focusing on dating Scottish Grooved Ware south of Orkney, which added 28 new dates to the Scottish 'pot' (Copper *et al.* 2021; https://scarf.scot/national/scarf-neolithic-panel-report/neolithic-case-studies/tracing-the-lines-uncovering-grooved-ware-trajectories-in-neolithic-scotland/tracing-the-lines-grooved-ware-catalogue/, accessed 29/05/23); and Seren Griffiths' AHRC-funded *Project TIME* (Griffiths *et al.* 2023), which promises to produce over 180 Grooved Ware-associated dates for Britain and Ireland (Seren Griffiths, pers. comm.). Moreover, advances in radiocarbon dating (Casanova *et al.* 2020) have meant that it is possible to obtain accurate radiocarbon dates from absorbed lipids in pottery (as demonstrated, for example, by Olet *et al.*, Chapter 7). This means that, along with dates obtained from encrusted organic residues on pot interiors, there is an increasing body of dates directly pertaining to vessels themselves. This should help to address the issues of residuality or long-term curation as flagged up by David Clarke (Chapter 15). The increase in dates also means that issues of overlap in the currency of different ceramic traditions – namely Fengate Ware and other pottery that had been in use prior to the appearance of

Grooved Ware, and Beaker at the other end of the timeframe – can be explored (e.g. by Cleal and Pollard, Chapter 10).

Advances in scientific analysis, specifically in the identification of absorbed lipids in pottery, have also provided a new dimension to our understanding of how Grooved Ware was used – and how its use may have varied in different parts of its distribution area, with many more pots in southern England showing the presence of porcine lipids than in northern Britain (Olet *et al.*, Chapter 7). Meanwhile, Nick Card's long-running research excavation at the Ness of Brodgar on Orkney Mainland has provided invaluable information on the massive assemblage of Grooved Ware from this key site and is helping to transform our understanding of the context of Grooved Ware use in Orkney and of the nature of Orcadian society at that time (Card *et al.* 2020).

The in-depth examination of Grooved Ware in its broader social and ideological context of use, i.e. as part of a broader (but geographically variable) set of novelties and changes in the centuries around 3000 cal BC, and as an enduring but changing ceramic tradition used by interconnected communities, is also helping us to conceptualise the role and meaning of this distinctive pottery style (as shown, for example, in Cleal and Pollard's contribution, Chapter 10). Identification of a range of evidence for long-distance connections plays into broader (and contested) narratives of how society operated during the late 4th and the first half of the 3rd millennia cal BC (e.g. Thomas 2010; Parker Pearson 2012; 2020; Barclay and Brophy 2020).

It is clear, however, that several major issues remain to be resolved in the study of Grooved Ware, not least the issue of nomenclature and classification, as David Clarke's trenchant critique makes clear (Chapter 15). When the Orcadian origins of this ceramic tradition now appear unassailable (Sheridan, Chapter 2; Copper, Chapter 4, *contra* speculation by Alasdair Whittle about possible Continental connections in Chapter 1), it seems absurd that a findspot in Wiltshire (Woodlands) is still widely used as the type-site for the earliest kind of Grooved Ware. Moreover, despite it having been acknowledged as long ago as 1994 – when the Neolithic Studies Group's Grooved Ware conference that led to the 1999 volume took place – that there were serious issues involved with the use of Ian Longworth's model of Grooved Ware sub-styles, this model continues, problematically, in widespread use.

This contribution sets out to summarise our current state of knowledge, clarify the outstanding issues and suggest ways in which we may address those issues.

GROOVED WARE: THE PICTURE IN 2023

The dramatic increase in Grooved Ware findspots and relevant dates allows us to state that this ceramic tradition was in use, at various times in its currency, over large parts of Britain and Ireland (but by no means everywhere), and that it appeared probably during the 32nd century cal BC and endured until the third quarter of the 3rd millennium cal BC (although the evidence for its latest use remains to be checked and clarified). Its geographical reach extended to the Isle of Man – a much-overlooked island, where the presence of Grooved Ware has been known since before Cleal and MacSween's volume was published in 1999 (Burrow 1997) – but, interestingly, not as far north as Shetland, despite claims to the contrary and despite the fact that the inhabitants of that archipelago will have been aware of developments in Orkney (Sheridan 2014a). The massive contrast in the size of Grooved Ware assemblages between Orkney and elsewhere remains, despite the substantial growth of the Durrington Walls assemblage from the 5861 sherds reported upon by Longworth (1971) thanks to further excavations by Mike Parker Pearson (Parker Pearson *et al.* 2011). It has been estimated that the Ness of Brodgar sherd tally currently stands at over 100,000, for example (Anne Mitchell, pers. comm.), and tens of thousands of sherds have been found at Links of Noltland (according to the excavators' Facebook posts), awaiting post-excavation work. Such figures contrast starkly with the pattern of finds from elsewhere, where often only a small number of pots are present.

As argued in Chapter 2, it appears (at least to this author) that, regarding the appearance of this type of pottery, we are dealing with that rarest of phenomena, the deliberate invention of a ceramic tradition. Within the context of the social dynamics of late 4th millennium Orkney, we can view its invention as part of a strategy, by certain ambitious and prosperous farmers on mainland Orkney, to create a new world order, featuring themselves in a position of power. The flat-based dishes, jars and tubs of the earliest Orcadian Grooved Ware stand in stark contrast to the round- and slightly pointed, saggy-based vessel shapes that had hitherto been in use (and continued to be used, in some cases) on the archipelago; and the designs, with their references to motifs on Irish passage tomb art that may well have been deemed sacred, constitute an adoption and adaptation of the iconography in use in the Boyne Valley in eastern Ireland. Its inventors were well travelled, having joined other 'pilgrims' from elsewhere in sailing to the Boyne Valley to participate in the midwinter ceremonies and to acquire esoteric knowledge; in building Maeshowe passage tomb they were recreating the massive passage tomb of Newgrange. They were also innovative and, within a northern British context at least, it could be argued that they invented a new type of monument for their seasonal ceremonies, the stone (and probably also timber) circle, surrounded at the Stones of Stenness by a ditch and bank. We know, from radiocarbon dating of deposits from the ditch and central hearth at the Stones of Stenness, that this monument was constructed within the *3030–2895 cal BC (95.4% probability)* timeframe (Bayliss *et al.* 2017). News of these impressive new monuments and the ceremonies carried out at them will have travelled far, along existing and emerging networks of contacts. Over time the area around the Lochs of Stenness and Harray on the Orkney mainland became a 'magnet' for 'pilgrims' in its own right – hence the development of the Ness of Brodgar as a place where far-travelled, privileged visitors could be accommodated, feasting and sharing their stories with the local elite.

It was this emergence of the heart of Mainland Orkney as a ceremonial centre to which people from far and wide came – possibly even eclipsing the Boyne Valley as a centre for 'pilgrimage' – that accounts for the astonishingly extensive and rapid spread of Orcadian-style Grooved Ware. Vessels that could go unnoticed among Orcadian assemblages dating to within the *c.* 3200/3100–2900/2800 cal BC bracket have been found as far away as County Cork in south-west Ireland (Grogan and Roche, Chapter 8), Tregurra Valley in Cornwall (Jones and Quinnell, Chapter 14), the area around the first-phase monument at Stonehenge in Wessex (Brook, Chapter 12) and Ringlemere in Kent (Garwood,

Chapter 13). Curiosity and a desire to participate and emulate, rather than climate change or a supposed switch to a more mobile lifestyle (as mentioned in Chapter 1), satisfactorily explain this rapid and extensive adoption of Grooved Ware outside Orkney. Indeed, as regards the palaeoenvironmental record, there is no evidence for any significant climatic downturn in Orkney during the late 4th millennium cal BC, such as would have occasioned any kind of exodus. Indeed, modelling of the changing landscape of Neolithic Orkney by Bunting *et al.* (2022) has instead highlighted an intensification of agricultural (and especially pastoral) activity during the late 4th millennium, which accords with other evidence – including for the deliberate interbreeding, probably off-island across the Pentland Firth, of domesticated cattle and aurochsen to maximise beef yield (Card *et al.* 2020, 269) – suggesting that ambitious farmers were able to build up impressive agricultural surpluses at that time, and thereby to 'fuel' their monument building, feasting and other self-aggrandising practices.

It was not just the design of pottery that was adopted far away; down the west and east sides of Scotland, and arguably further afield, one sees the construction of timber and stone circles associated with Grooved Ware (as, for example, at Calanais on Lewis in the Outer Hebrides, Machrie Moor on Arran, Balfarg henge in Fife and Balbirnie stone circle, Fife). This implies an adoption of the beliefs and practices associated with such monuments, in particular those marking the period around midwinter solstice. Even though timber circles have not been discovered in Orkney, the association of Orcadian-style Grooved Ware with a timber circle at Machrie Moor (Haggarty 1991; Copper *et al.* 2021; Copper this volume) suggests that it is only a matter of time before one is found in Orkney. The use of ovoid, pestle-shaped and cushion maceheads, which were popular both as weapons for inflicting fatal blows and as weapons of social exclusion, and which are known to have been manufactured at the Ness of Brodgar (Card *et al.* 2020), also spread elsewhere, including the western passage tomb under the main mound at Knowth in the Boyne Valley, and even at the first-phase monument at Stonehenge (Garrow and Wilkin 2022, fig. 1.47). At Knowth, miniature versions of the carved stone balls in use in Orkney have been found and miniature macehead pendants are known from several Irish passage tombs (Sheridan 2014b). Orcadian designs, including the distinctive horned spiral, turn up elsewhere, for instance pecked into a rock surface at Achnabreck, near the southern end of Kilmartin Glen in western Scotland; on a stone in the Temple Wood South stone circle, in Kilmartin Glen (Sheridan 2021); and on the famous Maesmor-type macehead found in the western passage tomb under the main mound at Knowth (Garrow and Wilkin 2022, fig. 2.35). Moreover, the Orcadian 'eyebrow' motif, as seen on a figurine found at Links of Noltland and pecked on the wall of a chamber tomb at Holm of Papa Westray South, occurs along with other Orcadian designs on the chalk 'drums' found at Folkton, North Yorkshire and Burton Agnes, East Yorkshire (Longworth 1999; Garrow and Wilkin 2022, figs 2.39, 2.41). A growing number of other stone objects decorated with designs of the kind found incised into structural and other stones in Orkney (Thomas 2016) have been found at considerable distances from Orkney, including the eastern passage tomb at Knowth, Ronaldsway; on the Isle of Man (Fig. 16.1); Woodcock Corner in the Tregurra Valley in Cornwall; and King's Barrow Ridge near Stonehenge (Garrow and Wilkin 2022, figs 2.16, 2.40). Those known to the author are listed in Table 16.1. These could have acted as mnemonics, reminding long-distance travellers of the designs they had seen in Orkney.

Figure 16.1. Schist plaque decorated with incised chevrons and lozenges, echoing Orcadian designs, from Ronaldsway, Isle of Man (photo: National Museums Scotland).

Table 16.1. Stone plaques and fragments with designs reminiscent (to varying degrees) of Orcadian designs from the Ness of Brodgar and Skara Brae.

Findspot	*Reference*
Upper Largie, Argyll and Bute	Ellis 2021(where they are described as 'worked slate'); Sheridan unpublished report
Knowth, east tomb under main mound	Eogan and Shee Twohig 2022, fig. 4.19
Ronaldsway, Isle of Man	Burrow 1999, fig. 5
Glencrutchery, Isle of Man	Burrow 1999, fig. 5
Ballavarry, Isle of Man	Burrow 1999, fig. 5
Graig Lwyd, Penmaenmawr, Group VII rock axehead quarry site, Conwy	Warren 1922
Rothley Lodge Farm, Leicestershire	Clay and Hunt 2016, figs 15–17
Over, Cambridgeshire	Evans *et al.* this volume, fig. 9.9.2
Chalk Plaque Pit, King Barrow Ridge (Stonehenge Bottom), Amesbury, Wiltshire	Harding 1988, 322–5; Garrow and Wilkin 2022, fig. 2.40
Butterfield Down, Boscombe, Wiltshire	Fitzpatrick 2005
King's Stanley, Gloucestershire	Evans 2006; 2010
Woodcock Corner, Tregurra Valley, Cornwall	Thomas 2022, figs 5.1–3

For additional possible examples, see Thomas (2022, 131).

As pointed out by Cleal and Pollard with regard to a later period of Grooved Ware use (Chapter 10), we need to accept long-distance travel and connectivity as a norm – and as a strategy for enhancing and underlining power – for a certain part of Late Neolithic society in Britain and Ireland. A complex pattern of connectivity, not exclusively linking to Orkney, could account for the presence of fragments of axehead of Group VII rock (augite granophyre from the Graig Lwyd quarry site, Penmaenmawr, north-west Wales – the findspot of an incised plaque, Table 16.1) in a pit with Orcadian-style Grooved Ware at Woodlands, Wiltshire (Brook, Chapter 12) and with Grooved Ware in West Kennet Avenue Hole 1, Wiltshire

(Longworth 1971, 261; see that publication for further examples of far-travelled axeheads). It might also account for the presence of enigmatic, small, smooth stone or ceramic balls, smaller than the stone examples known from Orkney, that have been found with Orcadian-style Grooved Ware at Bulford, Wiltshire (Garrow and Wilkin 2022, fig. 1.48), with Grooved Ware at Durranhill, Carlisle (Botfield and Hey, Chapter 5), and with the Burton Agnes chalk 'drum'. A pair of such balls, of fired clay, was found suggestively placed either side of a stone rubber in a pit at Rothley Lodge Farm, Leicestershire; in a nearby pit was an engraved sandstone plaque (Botfield and Hey, Chapter 5). It would be worth investigating isotopically whether the scallop shells found along with Orcadian-style Grooved Ware at Harnham Park, Wiltshire, and on the Salisbury Plain Defence Training Estate, Wiltshire (Brook, Chapter 12), might have been brought all the way from Orkney (and see Longworth 1971, 265 for other examples of marine shells from inland Grooved Ware findspots). Moreover, as Clarke has pointed out (Chapter 15), the marine shell used as a tempering agent in inland Wessex Grooved Ware assemblages such as at Woodlands could have been a reminder of the maritime journeys undertaken by the users of this early, Orcadian-style pottery in southern England.

Following the rapid and widespread adoption of Orcadian-style Grooved Ware, divergent trajectories of change can be traced in this ceramic tradition: in Orkney itself, localised novelties such as painted pots emerged (at the Ness of Brodgar: Sheridan, Chapter 2; see MacSween and Clarke, Chapter 3, on developments in Skara Brae pottery), while in Ireland, there appears to have been a shift to a much plainer repertoire, with minimal decoration (Grogan and Roche, Chapter 8) and in Wales, a distinctive variant incorporating elements of Fengate Ware seems to have emerged in and around Anglesey (Lynch, Chapter 6). The heavily decorated pottery found in East Anglia (e.g. at Clacton) may constitute another of these regionally-specific variants (Evans and Pollard, Chapter 9). In some areas, such as the Isle of Man and the Outer Hebrides, there seems to have been very little use of Grooved Ware (with Ronaldsway type pottery being the predominant Late Neolithic ceramic tradition on Man: Burrow 1999).

It remains unclear where the distinctive variant of Grooved Ware usually labelled 'Durrington Walls sub-style', with its skeuomorphism of wickerwork basketry, first emerged, but its extensive distribution, from Cornwall in the south (Jones and Quinnell, Chapter 14) to Inverness in the north (Copper, Chapter 4), indicates a renewed phase of widespread design sharing during the second quarter of the 3rd millennium, accompanied by much other evidence for long-distance movement of ideas, materials and artefacts (Cleal and Pollard, Chapter 10; see also Copper, Chapter 4, on Scottish examples dating to the first quarter of the 3rd millennium). As for the demise of the use of Grooved Ware and its apparent replacement by Beaker pottery, this is explored in some detail by Cleal and Pollard (Chapter 10) and also touched upon by Copper (Chapter 4), but much detail remains to be filled in.

OUTSTANDING ISSUES AND HOW THEY MIGHT BE ADDRESSED

Characterisation, classification, terminology

A major issue that hinders our understanding of the nature and dynamics of the Grooved Ware ceramic tradition remains the use of the outdated and frankly misleading Longworth model of 'Clacton', 'Woodlands' and 'Durrington Walls' sub-styles; his fourth, 'Rinyo', tends not to be used. Many of the problems have been discussed by Clarke in Chapter 15, and others (such as the chronological overlap of the 'Woodlands' and 'Clacton' sub-styles) were aired in the 1999 Cleal and MacSween volume (e.g. Garwood 1999). In addition to those, there can be a degree of subjectivity in the attribution of pottery to a specific sub-style, particularly as far as the 'Woodlands' and 'Clacton' labels are concerned; moreover, as noted above, these southern English 'type-site' labels obscure the fact that we are dealing with the adoption and adaptation of a ceramic tradition that originated in Orkney. Hard-pressed ceramic specialists need to have some vocabulary for characterising the pottery they are describing but, in this author's opinion at least, the Longworth scheme has long outlived its usefulness.

So, how are we to characterise Grooved Ware, in all its longevity and variability? Copper, in his consideration of the organic evolution of the tradition in Scotland south of Orkney (Chapter 2), has helpfully proposed descriptors featuring references to trajectories, and the current author would like to propose the use of the term 'Orcadian-style Grooved Ware' to encompass much of what is currently labelled as 'Woodlands' and 'Clacton' pottery. However, in order to arrive at a more helpful vocabulary of description than the one we currently have, what is needed is a comprehensive and fully-illustrated database of Grooved Ware in Britain and Ireland, complete with all the associated dating evidence. This would enable people to judge what kind of pots in the Grooved Ware tradition were in use when and where, and to map trajectories of change over time and place. The focus of comparison should not be on individual motifs or decorative schemes, but on the repertoires of vessel form, size, design and manufacturing techniques in use at any one time. *À propos* manufacturing techniques, we might usefully take a leaf out of our French colleagues' *chaîne opératoire* approach (e.g. Pioffet and Ard 2017) to assess the extent to which practices and traditions may have been shared, or may have changed or diverged; regionally shared practice might account for the distinctive soft, yellow fabric noted in some Welsh Grooved Ware (Lynch, Chapter 6), for example. And rather than seeking to define specific, discrete 'styles' or 'sub-styles', ceramic specialists could usefully consult the voluminous ethnoarchaeological literature on how and why ceramic traditions evolve and change (e.g. Gosselain and Livingstone Smith 2013) and consider alternative terminology to characterise the somewhat fluid and organic way in which Grooved Ware tradition evolved.

Achieving this encyclopaedic database of British and Irish Grooved Ware would, however, be a gargantuan task, not helped by the difficulties of accessing primary information. As noted in Chapter 2, key assemblages in Orkney remain unpublished (although the definitive Skara Brae monograph should appear within the next two years) and in Ireland, some of the grey literature, constituting the only record of Grooved Ware, is not available online – although the uploading of reports to the Digital Repository of Ireland (https://www.dri.ie) proceeds apace and is a welcome development. In many cases, however, 'grey literature' reports do not present the final results of specialist reporting, and even with the final publication of an excavation (e.g. Armalughey, Co. Tyrone: Carlin 2016), there is a disturbing trend for pottery illustrations to be minimal, almost certainly as a result of budgetary considerations. This issue is by no means limited to Ireland, which is why the editors of this volume felt it important to include numerous pottery illustrations here (especially for Wales: Lynch, Chapter 6). The first moves have been made towards a more systematic recording of Grooved Ware with Copper's database of Grooved Ware in Scotland south of Orkney, referred to above, and with Griffiths' *Project TIME*, whose aims include a comprehensive review of radiocarbon dates pertaining to Grooved Ware in Britain and Ireland. The regional reviews presented in this volume, together with previous syntheses (e.g. Cleal and MacSween 1999), help to lay the foundations for a definitive British and Irish database, and a collation of all the information and illustrations already available in publications and grey literature is an achievable task. Designing and achieving the comprehensive database are perhaps things to which members of the Neolithic Studies Group could turn their efforts, and it is to be hoped that research funding could be channelled towards its realisation.

Relationship to other ceramic traditions

The other issues pertaining to Grooved Ware include the questions of what pottery, or other kind of container, was in use during the Late Neolithic in those areas where Grooved Ware was not used; and how the Grooved Ware ceramic tradition articulated with the other ceramic traditions that preceded, succeeded, and in some cases overlapped with its currency. Answering the first question will largely be a matter of chance and of radiocarbon dating, although a synthesis of all pottery currently known to have been in use in Britain and Ireland between *c.* 3100 cal BC and *c.* 2300 cal BC, including Ronaldsway Ware, would be a useful first step. Answering the second will require targeted programmes of dating – although Beaker pottery is already well covered thanks to the *Beaker People Project* (Parker Pearson *et al.* 2019) and the key issue here pertains instead to the latest use of Grooved Ware, a topic discussed in several chapters here (Chapters 2, 4 and 10). Regarding the preceding and concurrent ceramic traditions, it is indeed ironic that when the organisers of the symposium whose proceedings are published here notified the honorand, Alex Gibson, of its topic he exclaimed 'But can't you do one on Impressed Wares instead?' A critical review of the dating of the Middle to Late Neolithic pottery variously known as 'Peterborough Ware' (with its Ebbsfleet, Mortlake and Fengate variants) and as 'Impressed Wares' (and its Irish congeners) is long overdue and, as Sheridan's review of Scottish Neolithic pottery pointed out (2016), the existing terminology does not do justice to the variety of pottery in use. Meanwhile, the intriguing association between Grooved Ware and a Mortlake bowl in a pit at King's Stanley, Gloucestershire (Evans 2010), reported on by Alex Gibson, reminds us of the issues involved in interpreting depositional patterns. While David Clarke (Chapter 15) proposes that this appears to be the case of depositing an ancient pot alongside one in more recent use, Gibson (2010, 41) has argued that the two traditions could have been in contemporary use after all.

Changing perspectives, and different ways of 'putting it all together'

There can be no doubt that, with successive generational shifts and a diminution in the number of ceramic specialists, approaches to Grooved Ware (and to material culture in general) have been changing, and continue to change. While a move away from predominantly typological considerations and a focus on improving chronology so that stories at the generational scale can start to be written are welcome developments, it is incumbent on those who espouse 'the New Materialism' (Griffiths *et al.* 2023) to ensure that the material culture in question is well understood – and this is where the creation of a comprehensive, accessible database will prove to be an essential resource. There most certainly is a continuing need for ceramic specialists and, with the ageing profile of the current 'priesthood' (as Clarke uncharitably calls them, Chapter 15), there is scope for younger researchers to develop their expertise and for trans-generational skill-sharing to take place.

Another fairly recent development has been the so-called 'ontological turn' (Harris and Cipolla 2017; Harris 2021) whereby agency, and the capacity to affect the world, are not restricted to people but are extended to objects and things. Such a perspective is not new, however; it has been used to great effect (albeit not dressed in the cloak of a fashionable theoretical movement) by Pierre Pétrequin in his work on the Neolithic axeheads of jadeitite and other Alpine rock that circulated widely across Europe (e.g. Pétrequin *et al.* 2012). Here, a persuasive argument that these objects may well have been regarded, and treated, as powerful, living, divine entities has been meticulously built up using multiple sources of data. As currently applied to Grooved Ware, however, one might reasonably question the heuristic value of this approach, especially since so many of the statements made by its proponents are assertions that cannot be verified by reference to firm evidence. For example, Harris (2021, 73) hints at materials as being 'vibrant and active players in the histories of Neolithic Britain' and asserts that 'Grooved Ware pottery bound people, animals and places together' (2021, 107) but he does not elaborate as to precisely how the pottery was vibrant and an active player, nor how it achieved this binding. It is a moot point (and one not made by Harris) whether the motifs on Grooved Ware that were copied or inspired by the sacred designs on Irish passage tombs were regarded as conferring any supernatural power to the pots themselves (or to their contents or users); while this is an interesting idea and may have been the case, it would be hard to prove or disprove such a claim. Such vessels were indeed used in ceremonies as well as for more mundane purposes and they would have been an effective way of spreading awareness of the iconographic motifs that adorned their surfaces, especially when used in communal feasting. Some could theoretically have contained substances (e.g. alcoholic drink) that altered consciousness – and in this regard, the description by Evans *et al.* (Chapter 9) of the 'shaman's pit' at Over, Cambridgeshire, complete with its Grooved Ware and traces of belladonna, a highly toxic hallucinogenic substance, gives support to the idea that ceremonies could involve attempts to commune with otherworldly powers through the use of consciousness-altering substances. (It should be noted here, however, that a much-publicised claim for the presence of henbane, another hallucinogenic substance, on a Grooved Ware pot from Balfarg Riding School (Moffat 1993) has been thoroughly disproved by the re-analysis of the organic residue in question (Long *et al.* 1999).) Other claims for the use of Grooved Ware to produce and serve ale (Dineley 2004) require verification; the lipid analysis so far undertaken (as discussed in Chapter 7) does not support this claim, and specialised lipid analysis directed towards the identification of cereal traces is yet to be undertaken on Grooved Ware.

Finally, as regards the aforementioned 'big picture' narratives (and the associated heated debates) that have sprung up around Grooved Ware and the broader developments in Britain and Ireland over the first half of the 3rd millennium, many unresolved issues remain. Not least of these is the question of a claimed isolation of Britain from the Continent at the time when Grooved Ware was in use, which ignores the evidence, from Atlantic rock art, suggesting interactions along the Atlantic façade over this timeframe (Valdez-Tullett 2019; Bradley 2022). The intriguing question of the relationship (or rather, disjunction) between Grooved Ware and Atlantic rock art is one to be pursued elsewhere, not here; as noted by Botfield and Hey (Chapter 5), the geographical proximity (4 m) of a find of Grooved Ware and a panel of Atlantic rock art on Fylingdales Moor does not demonstrate any association or even contemporaneity between the two.

In constructing new narratives that situate Grooved Ware use within the wider world of Late Neolithic Britain and Ireland, we should focus on building plausible narratives at various scales, from the local to the supra-regional; it is hoped that the contributions to this volume have gone at least some of the way to achieving that.

CONCLUSIONS

The year 2036 will see the centenary of the term 'Grooved Ware', a term coined by a young Stuart Piggott, who produced the first gazetteer of this type of pottery (Piggott 1936). If the pace of discoveries between now and then matches what we have witnessed over the past quarter century or so, we may expect the density and geographical extent of Grooved Ware finds to be even greater than they are today. Whether researchers will be able to integrate new discoveries into the compendious database proposed above remains to be seen, but it is hoped that the various issues that currently stand in our way of understanding fully this ceramic tradition and its meaning will at least have been addressed, if not resolved. With all the developments that are currently underway, we should be able to create rich and nuanced narratives of this fascinating type of pottery.

ACKNOWLEDGEMENTS

My co-editors are thanked for their constructive suggestions on this text.

REFERENCES

Barclay, G.J. and Brophy, K. 2020. A veritable chauvinism of prehistory: nationalist prehistories and the 'British' late Neolithic mythos. *Archaeological Journal* 178(2), 1–31.

Bayliss, A., Marshall, P., Richards, C. and Whittle, A. 2017. Islands of history: the Late Neolithic timescape of Orkney. *Antiquity* 91, 1171–88.

Bradley, R.J. 2022. *A comparative study of rock art in later prehistoric Europe.* Cambridge: Cambridge University Press.

Bunting, M.J., Farrell, M., Dunbar, E., Reimer, P., Bayliss, A., Marshall, P. and Whittle, A. 2022. Landscapes for Neolithic people in Mainland, Orkney. *Journal of World Prehistory* 35, 87–107.

Burrow, S.P. 1997. *The Neolithic culture of the Isle of Man: a study of the sites and pottery.* Oxford: British Archaeological Report 263.

Burrow, S.P. 1999. The Ronaldsway pottery of the Isle of Man: a study of production, decoration, and use. *Proceedings of the Prehistoric Society* 65, 125–43.

Card, N., Edmonds, M. and Mitchell, A. (eds) 2020. *The Ness of Brodgar: as it stands.* Kirkwall: The Orcadian.

Carlin, N. 2016. Discussion of the timber circle at Armalughey (Sites 18 and 20). In C. Dunlop and J. Barkley, *Road to the west. A road to the past, Volume 2*, 194–210. Belfast: Northern Archaeological Consultancy Ltd.

Casanova, E., Knowles, T.D.J., Bayliss, A., Dunne, J. Baránski, M.Z., Denaire, A. *et al.* 2020. Accurate compound-specific ^{14}C dating of archaeological pottery vessels. *Nature* 580, 506–10.

Clay, P. and Hunt, L. 2016. Late Neolithic art and symbolism at Rothley Lodge Farm, Leicester Road, Rothley (SK 592 140). *Transactions of the Leicestershire Archaeological and Historical Society* 90, 13–66.

Cleal, R. and MacSween, A. (eds) 1999. *Grooved Ware in Britain and Ireland.* Oxford: Oxbow Books.

Copper, M., Hamilton, D. and Gibson, A. 2021. Tracing the lines: Scottish Grooved Ware trajectories beyond Orkney. *Proceedings of the Society of Antiquaries of Scotland* 150, 81–117.

Dineley, M. 2004. *Barley, malt and ale in the Neolithic.* Oxford: British Archaeological Report S1213.

Ellis, C. 2021. Upper Largie Quarry extension – phase 3. *Discovery and Excavation in Scotland* 22, 41.

Eogan, G. and Shee Twohig, E. 2022. *The megalithic art of the passage tombs at Knowth, County Meath.* Dublin: Royal Irish Academy.

Evans, D, 2006. An engraved Neolithic plaque and associated finds from King's Stanley, Gloucestershire. *PAST* 52, 3–4.

Evans, D. 2010. Two Neolithic pits at King's Stanley, Gloucestershire. *Transactions of the Bristol and Gloucestershire Archaeological Society* 128, 29–54.

Fitzpatrick, A. 2005. A sacred circle on Boscombe Down. *Current Archaeology* 195, 106–7.

Garrow, D. and Wilkin, N. 2022. *The world of Stonehenge.* London: The British Museum.

Garwood, P. 1999. Grooved Ware in southern Britain: chronology and interpretation. In R. Cleal and A. MacSween (eds) 1999, 145–76.

Gibson, A. 2010. The pottery. In D. Evans 2010, 35–41.

Gosselain, O. and Livingstone Smith, A. 2013. A century of ceramic studies in Africa. In P. Mitchell and P.J. Lane (eds), *The Oxford handbook of African archaeology,* 177–88. Oxford: Oxford University Press.

Griffiths, S., Carlin, N., Edwards, B., Overton, N., Johnston, P. and Thomas, J. 2023. Events, narrative and data: why new chronologies or ethically Bayesian approaches should change how we write archaeology. *Journal of Social Archaeology*, Online First, doi.org/10.1177/14690532311153499 [accessed 30/05/23].

Haggarty, A. 1991. Machrie Moor, Arran: recent excavations at two stone circles. *Proceedings of the Society of Antiquaries of Scotland* 121, 51–94.

Harding, P. 1988. The Chalk Plaque Pit, Amesbury. *Proceedings of the Prehistoric Society* 54, 320–7.

Harris, O.J.T. 2021. *Assembling past worlds: materials, bodies and architecture in Neolithic Britain.* Abingdon: Routledge.

Harris, O.J.T. and Cipolla, C.N. 2017. *Archaeological theory in the new millennium: introducing current perspectives.* Abingdon: Routledge.

Long, D.J., Milburn, P., Bunting, M.J., Tipping, R. and Holden, T. 1999. Black henbane (*Hyoscyamus niger* L.) in the Scottish Neolithic: a re-evaluation of palynological findings from Grooved Ware Pottery at Balfarg Riding School and Henge, Fife. *Journal of Archaeological Science* 26(1), 45–52.

Longworth, I. 1971. The Neolithic pottery. In G.J. Wainwright and I.H. Longworth, *Durrington Walls: excavations 1966–1968*, 48–155. London: Society of Antiquaries.

Longworth, I. 1999. The Folkton Drums unpicked. In R. Cleal and A. MacSween (eds) 1999, 83–8.

Moffat, B. 1993. An assessment of the residues on the Grooved Ware. In G. Barclay and C. Russell-White, Excavations in the ceremonial complex of the fourth to second millennium bc at Balfarg/Balbirnie, Glenrothes, Fife, 108–10. *Proceedings of the Society of Antiquaries of Scotland* 123, 43–210.

Parker Pearson, M. 2012. *Stonehenge: exploring the greatest Stone Age mystery*. London: Simon and Schuster.

Parker Pearson, M. 2020. Orkney: the view from Salisbury Plain. In N. Card *et al.* (eds) 2020, 312–9.

Parker Pearson, M., Sheridan, J.A., Jay, M., Chamberlain, A., Richards, M.P. and Evans, J. (eds) 2019. *The Beaker People: isotopes, mobility and diet in prehistoric Britain*. Oxford: Prehistoric Society Research Papers 7.

Parker Pearson, M., Pollard, J., Richards, C., Thomas, J., Welham, K., Albarella, U., Chan, B., Marshall, P. and Viner, S. 2011. Feeding Stonehenge: feasting in Late Neolithic Britain. In G. Aranda Jiménez, S. Montón-Subías and M. Sánchez-Romero (eds), *Guess who's coming to dinner: commensality rituals in the prehistoric societies of Europe and the Near East*, 73–90. Oxford: Oxbow Books.

Pétrequin P., Cassen, S., Errera, M., Klassen, L. and Sheridan, J.A. (eds) 2012. *JADE. Grandes haches alpines du Néolithique européen. Ve et IVe millénaires av. J.-C.* Besançon and Gray: Presses Universitaires de Franche-Comté and Centre de Recherche Archéologique de la Vallée de l'Ain.

Piggott, S. 1936. Grooved Ware. In S.H. Warren, S. Piggott, J.G.D. Clark, M. Burkitt, H. Godwin and M.E. Godwin, Archaeology of the submerged land-surface of the Essex coast, 186–201. *Proceedings of the Prehistoric Society* 2, 191–201.

Pioffet, H. and Ard, V. 2017. From sherds to potters: the contribution of techno-morphological approaches to understanding the British Neolithic. *Archeologické rozhledy* 69, 281–306.

Sheridan, J.A. 2014a. Shetland, from the appearance of a 'Neolithic' way of life to *c* 1500 BC: a view from the 'mainland'. In H.C. Gulløv and D. Mahler (eds), *Northern worlds – landscapes, interactions and dynamics*, 67–92. Copenhagen: Nationalmuseet.

Sheridan, J.A. 2014b. Little and large: the miniature 'carved stone ball' beads from the eastern tomb at Knowth, Ireland, and their broader significance. In R.-M. Arbogast and A. Greffier-Richard (eds), *Entre archéologie et écologie, une préhistoire de tous les milieux. Mélanges offerts à Pierre Pétrequin*, 303–14. Besançon: Presses Universitaires de Franche-Comté.

Sheridan, J.A. 2016. Scottish Neolithic pottery in 2016: the big picture and some details of the narrative. In F.J. Hunter and J.A. Sheridan (eds), *Ancient lives. Object, people and place in early Scotland. Essays for David V Clarke on his 70th birthday*, 189–212. Leiden: Sidestone.

Sheridan, J.A. 2021. Marking time in prehistoric Scotland: the social and ideological significance of astronomical alignments. In H. Meller, A. Reichenberger and R. Risch (eds), *Zeit ist Macht. Wer macht Zeit? (Time is power. who makes time?)*, 89–106. Halle: Landesmuseum für Vorgeschichte.

Thomas, A. 2016. *Art and archaeology in Neolithic Orkney: process, temporality and context*. Oxford: Archaeopress.

Thomas, A. 2022. Mobiliary art. In S.R. Taylor, *Down the bright stream: the prehistory of Woodcock Corner and the Tregurra Valley, Cornwall*, 127–38. Oxford: Archaeopress.

Thomas, J. 2010. The return of the Rinyo-Clacton folk? The cultural significance of the Grooved Ware complex in later Neolithic Britain. *Cambridge Archaeological Journal* 20, 1–15.

Valdez-Tullett, J. 2019. *Design and connectivity: the case of Atlantic rock art*. Oxford: British Archaeological Report S2932.

Warren, S.H. 1922. The Neolithic stone axes of Graig Lwyd, Penmaenmawr. *Archaeologia Cambrensis* 77(1), 1–32.